Management for Professionals

The Springer series Management for Professionals comprises high-level business and management books for executives, MBA students, and practice-oriented business researchers. The topics span all themes of relevance for businesses and the business ecosystem. The authors are experienced business professionals and renowned professors who combine scientific backgrounds, best practices, and entrepreneurial vision to provide powerful insights into how to achieve business excellence.

Jianlin Zhang · Kezhen Ying ·
Kanliang Wang · Zhigang Fan · Ziyi Zhao
Editors

Innovation of Digital Economy

Cases from China

西安交通大学出版社
XI'AN JIAOTONG UNIVERSITY PRESS

Springer

Editors
Jianlin Zhang
Alibaba Business School
Hangzhou Normal University
Hangzhou, China

Kezhen Ying
Information Institute, Zhejiang University of Finance & Economics Dongfang College
Haining, China

Kanliang Wang
Renmin Business School
Renmin University of China
Beijing, China

Zhigang Fan
Alibaba Business School
Hangzhou Normal University
Hangzhou, China

Ziyi Zhao
Alibaba Business School
Hangzhou Normal University
Hangzhou, China

ISSN 2192-8096 ISSN 2192-810X (electronic)
Management for Professionals
ISBN 978-981-99-1740-2 ISBN 978-981-99-1741-9 (eBook)
https://doi.org/10.1007/978-981-99-1741-9

Jointly published with Xi'an Jiaotong University Press
The print edition is not for sale in China (Mainland). Customers from China (Mainland) please order the print book from: Xi'an Jiaotong University Press.

This Springer imprint is published by the registered company Springer Nature Singapore Pte Ltd.
The registered company address is: 152 Beach Road, #21-01/04 Gateway East, Singapore 189721, Singapore

Review Committee

Director: Liu Jun
Members: Chen Jin, Qin Zheng, Sun Baowen, Liu Lanjuan, He Shengyu, Qi Li, Peng Lifang, Zhang Runtong, Hua Ying, Zhang Ronggang, Yezheng Liu, Xiong Li, Shuai Qinghong, Li Wenli, Cao Jie, Ye Qiongwei, Kanliang Wang, Pan Yong, Wei Mingxia, Guo Weidong, Hu Tao, Li Minqiang, Yu Baoqin, Yao Weixin, Yulin Zhang, Chen Xi, Sun Ximing, Yin Jianwei, Qu Chunhua, Sun Jianhong, Zuo Min, Chen Axing, Zhang Liyi, Ni Ming, Xie Kang, Zhou Zhongbao, Wang Lifang, Zhang Shuqin, Yang Xingkai, Li Ming.

Foreword

The fast development of digital economy and the continuous integration of modern business have given rise to the new mode, idea, and path of enterprise development, e-commerce and digital economy have become the key industries of the global economy in new development era with the largest scale, the fastest growth speed, the widest coverage, and the most active innovation and entrepreneurship. New phenomena in the domestic e-commerce industry still continue to emerge, the domestic industry has become the pioneer of digital economy development. For the practical circle, new phenomena and industry modes force enterprises to consider the orientation and the importance of digitalization and the approaches to reconstruct value creation and value acquisition. Carrying out the teaching and research of e-commerce and digital economy in colleges and universities, finding out the theoretical logic behind the front edge, echoing and implementing the overall deployment of the Ministry of Education for new humanities and social sciences (HSS), promoting the development of e-commerce majors, and cultivating a new generation of e-commerce and digital economy talent are of great importance.

In order to further enhance the discipline competitiveness of e-commerce and strengthen the quality of talent cultivation, targeting at the demand of building a digital economic power and industrial transformation and upgrading, the Center for E-commerce and Digital Economy Cases in Higher Education launched "The First Collection Activity of Excellent Cases of E-commerce and Digital Economy for Colleges and Universities" around the country, aiming to promote the growth of new business and advance the comprehensive literacy of e-commerce and digital economy talent under the guidance of the Nationwide E-commerce Teaching Steering Committee of Schools and Universities of the Ministry of Education.

E-commerce theories can draw inspiration from innovative enterprise cases, containing the application of artificial intelligence and big data in the operation and marketing of enterprises, the exploration of the network consumer behavior theory, and the innovative researches of business models and management mechanisms of e-commerce enterprises. These theories are considered to be of far-reaching significance for enterprises in deepening their reforms and improving self-competitiveness in the digital economy. The theories from China embrace the opportunities to expand them to the overseas market, helping global enterprises to respond to the challenges of business change and strategic focus, thus advancing the upgrading of theories and practices by taking this book as a carrier.

Enterprise cases on the basis of practices meet the requirements and orientation of cultivating e-commerce and digital economy talent. New positions and the demand for intelligent talent keep emerging, the shortage of high-level innovative talent has become an increasingly prominent issue under the background of digital economy advancing the accelerated growth of e-commerce. Case teaching has the dual functions of imparting professional knowledge and improving practical training and expertise. Case collection in this book will conduct standardized sorting of knowledge and skills related to transferring them into good teaching resources to carry out professional training of knowledge and practice, thus meeting the development needs of e-commerce and digital economy.

Focusing on the key areas and issues in the development of e-commerce and digital economy, *Innovation of Digital Economy: Cases from China* provides a new platform for refining local characteristics and broadening theoretical research horizons, and also contributes to the cultivation of the next generation of digital economy talent and the exploration of close cooperation between universities and enterprises.

July 2022

Liu Jun
Director of E-commerce Teaching Steering
Committee of Universities and Colleges
Ministry of Education
China

Preface

The revolution of digital technology has fundamentally changed the operation mode of human society. The economic development environment of the digital economy is characterized by dynamic changes, high degree of uncertainty, complexity and ambiguity, and data information is listed as a key production factor in this era. Facing the surging wave of digital economy, global enterprises are facing the opportunities and challenges brought by digitalization. Effectively obtain, arrange, and use data information is a necessary mean for enterprises to gain insight into the external environment. Reduce uncertainty and complexity, obtain necessary complementary resources, and then enhance the core competitiveness of enterprises through digital transformation are key issues for enterprise development.

In the past 5 years, China's digital economy has developed rapidly. It has built the world's largest 5G network and becomes the largest digital economy in the world. The digital economy is in the second place in the world and represents fertile ground for highly active digital innovation and entrepreneurship. Under the guidance of the innovation-driven development strategy, Chinese enterprises are actively exploring new business forms, methods, and models that integrate real industries and digital technologies.

In this context, this book compiles representative examples of enterprises to demonstrate the best practices and lessons learned by Chinese enterprises in seeking innovation development in the digital economy era. Around the international new trend in the digital economic development, themes of the cases include digital marketing, Industrial Internet of Things, cross-border e-commerce, and digital transformation of traditional enterprises, depicting how the vertical industry leaders, unicorn companies, and regional benchmark enterprises explore new ways of development and growth combined with the digital technologies. The best practices of the case enterprises will provide valuable first-hand guidance to practitioners in the global digital economy; meanwhile, each case is written in a structured and academic manner, which can provide field cases for research and teaching in e-commerce and digital economy-related disciplines.

The book has three characteristics: first, the selected cases focus on the emerging new phenomena in the field of digital economy, covering the new knowledge of digital economy and e-commerce, which can match the academic courses of e-commerce and other majors in colleges and universities; second, all cases are developed based on primary data, introducing and analyzing the management practices of representative enterprises, which are original and innovative; third, the book provides complete supporting materials. The cases are attached with teaching notes, videos, and relevant supplementary materials, which will help to promote teaching, research, and learning.

This book is a compilation of the case results of the "First Collection Activity of Excellent Cases" of the Center for E-commerce and Digital Economy Cases in Higher Education under the guidance of the Teaching Guiding Committee of E-commerce Majors of the Ministry of Education. My thanks go to the Teaching Guiding Committee of E-commerce Majors of the Ministry of Education, all the case authors and case review experts, the Case Construction Guiding Committee of the Case Center, the Case Construction Working Committee, and the Beijing Bodao Qiancheng Information Technology Co., Ltd. for their guidance and contributions to this round of case collection and the construction of the Case Center.

July 2022

Jianlin Zhang
Director of the Higher Education Case Center for
E-commerce and Digital Economy
Xixi National Wetland Park
Hangzhou, China

Contents

Contributors

Bin Chen, Kecheng Chen, Yanxi Chen, Xusen Cheng, Xiaohui Dai, Xuanshun Zhai, Wenting Ding, Xiaolin Ding, Wenqi Duan, Zhigang Fan, Yunxia Feng, Han Gao, Shuai Gao, Jiarong Guo, Yawen He, Yufan Hou, He Hu, Jiaxian Huang, Wenze Huang, Xiaoxin Huang, Yuanchun Jiang, Chunfeng Jiao, Yu Jin, Guichao Jin, Yanlin Jin, Hengyang Kong, Jiawei Li, Lanying Li, Peiqiang Li, Wenhua Li, Yongfa Li, Zhan Li, Hanmi Lin, Shiting Lin, Jingxian Liu, Pingfeng Liu, Yezheng Liu, Junfeng Lu, Yanjun Lu, Guxian Miao, Zhijing Niu, Xiaofeng Shang, Lan Shen, Juping Shou, Chenqing Su, Lu Sun, Huijing Sun, Jianshan Sun, Xiaoxia Sun, Juan Tang, Minjun Teng, Ying Wang, Yu Wang, Junping Wang, Kanliang Wang, Runbo Wang, Wenxing Wang, Yizhen Wang, Jingwen Xiong, Rui Xu, Ying Yan, Junxin Yan, Yulu Yan, Bo Yang, Xueyan Yang, Jiahui Ye, Hongfu Yu, Zhifang Yu, Jie Zhang, Li Zhang, Huiqin Zhang, Jiahui Zhang, Yulin Zhang, Yueli Zhang, Guohao Zhang, Jiaorong Zhao, Ziyi Zhao, Hao Zheng, Shaoqing Zheng, Xiutian Zheng, Ziyi Zheng, Yong Zhou, Chuanbo Zhu.

About the Authors

Professor Jianlin Zhang is the Executive Dean of Alibaba Business School, Hangzhou Normal University. His main research directions are e-commerce, business intelligence, data mining, and information management technology. He is a member of the Teaching Steering Committee of E-commerce Majors in Higher Education Institutions, Ministry of Education of China; member of Expert Committee of Mobile Commerce, China E-Commerce Association; and member of China Cloud Computing and SAAS Service Expert Committee. He is the Secretary-General of the Teaching Steering Committee of E-commerce Logistics Majors in Higher Education Institutions in Zhejiang Province; Director of the Education Special Committee of the Electronic Commerce Promotion Association, Zhejiang Province; Head of electronic commerce key majors in Zhejiang Province; and the Director of the Hangzhou Electronic Commerce Expert Advisory Committee.

Dr. Kezhen Ying is an Associate Professor and Associate Dean of the Information Institute, Dongfang College, Zhejiang University of Finance and Economics. Her main research area is e-commerce. At present, she is in charge of a number of teaching projects, including the provincial first-class specialty construction of e-commerce, the construction of provincial first-class courses of Web Front-end Technology, etc.

Dr. Kanliang Wang is a Professor and Doctoral Supervisor at Department of Management Science and Engineering of Renmin Business School, Renmin University of China. His research areas are Management Information Systems and E-commerce, Information Technology and Decision-making Behavior. He was selected into "New Century Excellent Personnel Training Program" of Ministry of Education, China. He has presided over a number of scientific research projects including key project, general project, and youth project of the National Natural Science Foundation, and his research has been published on Management Science, MIS Quarterly, Decision Support Systems, Information & Management, and other academic journals. He is a member of The E-commerce Specialty Teaching Steering Committee of Higher Education Institutions, Ministry of Education, Vice

Chairman and Secretary-General of the Fourth Committee of Chinese Branch of International Information Systems Association (CNAIS), member of the Chinese Society of Systems Engineering, etc.

Dr. Zhigang Fan is graduated from School of Management, Zhejiang University, with a Ph.D. in management, who is currently the Vice Dean and Associate Professor of Alibaba Business School, Hangzhou Normal University. He is also the Deputy Director Secretary of Teaching Steering Committee of E-commerce Majors in Higher Education Institutions, Ministry of Education of China, and the Vice President of Digital Economy Research Institute of Hangzhou Normal University. His research is mainly engaged in fields of government and enterprise strategic innovation, Internet economics, etc., and he has presided over and participated in nearly ten high-level scientific research projects such as the National Social Science Foundation, the National Natural Science Foundation's major international cooperation projects, the National Natural Science Foundation's Youth Project, and the Humanities and Social Sciences Fund of the Ministry of Education. He has published more than 30 academic papers in Worldwide significant journals.

Dr. Ziyi Zhao is an Assistant Professor and Master Supervisor at Department of Digital Economy and Management of Alibaba Business School, Hangzhou Normal University. Her research interest is the innovation strategy of latecomer enterprises. She has participated in and presided over a number of scientific research projects, and published more than 10 academic papers at international journals and conferences. She has developed a series of cases focusing on the growth and transformation strategy of digital platforms and Industrial Internet of Things, two of which have been awarded Zhejiang Excellent Postgraduate Teaching Cases.

Zuo Zhang is an Associate Professor, Founder, and a member of the Board of Directors of Alibaba Business School, Hangzhou Normal University. He has been engaged in Internet business research and innovation and entrepreneurship education for many years. His research directions are higher education reform, e-commerce and digital economy business model, and entrepreneurship in digital economy. He has presided over many provincial and municipal e-commerce development plans and e-commerce industrial park projects, and served as the judge and mentor of many national entrepreneurship competitions such as China Youth "Internet +" Innovation and Entrepreneurship Competition, National College Students "Innovation, Creativity, Entrepreneurship" competition, and National College Students "Challenge Cup".

Jian Duan is currently the Chairman and General Manager of Beijing Bodao Information Technology Co., Ltd. Since 1999, he has started research on the e-commerce industry. In 2001, he led the entrepreneurial team to develop an experimental teaching system for e-commerce majors. He has undertaken the Science and Technology Planning Project of Xi'an City. He also participated in the writing of the textbook "E-commerce Experimental Systems", which has won the

2014 National E-Commerce Vocational Education Teaching Achievement Special Award issued by the National E -Commerce Vocational Education Teaching Steering Committee, and the first prize of the National Teaching Achievement Award of the Ministry of Education in September 2014.

Dr. Gongbu Gao is an Associate Professor and Master Supervisor of Business School of Yangzhou University. His research interests are e-commerce and information resource management. In recent years, he has presided over more than 50 national and 863 sub-projects, World Bank consulting projects, Education reform projects of the Ministry of Education, and Education reform projects of Jiangsu Province, and published more than 30 papers. He has won more than 40 teaching and research awards such as Outstanding cases of industry-school cooperative education of the Ministry of Education, the first prize of Beijing Teaching Achievement Award, and the Award of Excellent Undergraduate Teaching of Yangzhou University. Eight textbooks and works, including Introduction to E-commerce and Case Analysis of E-commerce, have been published. He is the Executive Director of the E-commerce Research Center of Yangzhou University, an expert in the compilation of the National E-commerce Development Plan for the 14th Five-Year Plan, a specially invited expert of the China International E-commerce Center of the Ministry of Commerce, the Executive director and deputy Secretary-General and rotating President of the National E-commerce Digital Education Development Alliance, and the Chief Expert of the Entrepreneurship Guidance Expert Group of Jiangsu Province.

Rooted in Medical Skills, Came Out of Benevolent Hearts: The User Growth Strategy of DingXiang Doctor Platform

Ziyi Zhao, Zhijing Niu, and Yulu Yan

1 Introduction

"Now, let's welcome Mr. Li, the founder of the leading company of Internet Medical Care, DingXiangYuan (DXY), and Dingxiang Doctor!" Accompanied by the moderator's loud voice, Li Tiantian, dressed in a crimson purple suit, appeared on the stage in vigorous steps. Li attended the "Digital Medical 2020" Development Forum and gave a speech on the topic of Internet medical care and platform development.

Internet medical care comes from the cross-border integration of the concept of "Internet+" and the medical field. With the buoyant growth of science and technology, the deep application of medical big data and the continuous upgrading of information means, the integration of Internet and traditional medical industry is deepening. Internet medical care enterprises harness information technologies such as 5G, big data, cloud computing and Internet of Things to digitize traditional medical resources and provide medical services through digital platforms.

There has been more than a decade since the birth of Internet medical care. These years have witnessed the ups and downs of the rapid development under the strategic layout of "Internet+" and the policy of "mass entrepreneurship and innovation", and the rock bottom caused by poor regulation and technical restrictions. The sudden hit of the COVID-19 pandemic swept the world in 2020. When medical staff was struggling in the front line, Internet Medical Care, known as the "second battlefield", also played its part to fight against the pandemic, providing services such as dispelling rumors and science popularizing, online consultation, medical e-commerce and statistical analysis of data. These have played a positive

Z. Zhao (✉) · Z. Niu · Y. Yan
Alibaba Business School, Hangzhou Normal University, Room 508, Shuyuan 1, Hangzhou Normal University Cangqian Campus, Hangzhou, Zhejiang Province, China

J. Zhang et al. (eds.), *Innovation of Digital Economy*, Management for Professionals,
https://doi.org/10.1007/978-981-99-1741-9_1

role in avoiding the crowd gathering, relieving people's panic and balancing medical resources. With "Healthy China 2030" becoming a national strategy and China comprehensively entering into the "post-pandemic era" of regular pandemic prevention and control, people's awareness of health management has obviously been improved, and the demands for health products and services have increased dramatically. The value and advantages of this industry that cannot be ignored have gradually showed up in the fight against the COVID-19 pandemic. The Internet medical care industry, which has been silent for a long time, has finally ushered in its own highlight moment after the COVID-19 pandemic.

At present, there are several giants working on Internet medical care platforms, such as Chunyu Doctor, Ping An Good Doctor, Ali Health and Dingxiang Doctor. The positioning of and products and services provided by these platforms are overlapping yet different, and they have played different roles in fighting against the COVID-19 pandemic. Baidu cooperated with many medical experts to write entries of novel coronavirus, provided relevant search data, and launched an intelligent self-testing tool for COVID-19. Ping An Good Doctor, WeDoctor, Dingxiang Doctor, and haodf.com have launched free online consultation channels. At the early stage of the outbreak of the COVID-19 pandemic, Dingxiang Doctor launched the "Pandemic Map" (i.e., "Real-time Dynamic of COVID-19") to provide statistical analysis of data, and integrated online free clinic, expert rumor dispelling, authoritative science popularization and other functions. With 2 billion page views in less than one month, it became the top new media health platform in China.

Why can Dingxiang Doctor stand out from all Internet medical care giants and rocket to the top? Dingxiang Doctor, a brand of DingXiangYuan (DXY), specializes in health consultation and popular science information services for the general public at C-terminal, and its success cannot leave the support of DingXiangYuan (DXY).

The success of Dingxiang Doctor has aroused great repercussions in the industry. At this "Digital Medical 2020" forum, the guests praised Dingxiang Doctor and expressed their desire to learn from Li Tiantian. They wondered how DingXiangYuan (DXY) survived the influence and hit of the crisis and realized the growth of Dingxiang Doctor. Hearing the question, with a microphone in his hand, Li looked at the audience, and his thoughts were brought back to 2014.

2 From Targeting a Niche Market to Creating Value for the Public

DXY was founded in 2000. Due to the inaccessibility to relevant medical literature, Li Tiantian, a medical student, set up the website of DXY to provide literature retrieval services for medical students. Based on this literature retrieval service, Li started "DXY Forum", which serves as a platform and space of professional communication for users in the medical field. The forum sections gradually increased in number and covered all medical disciplines, bringing together many medical students and occupational physicians. In 2005, Li went to Hangzhou and formed an entrepreneurial team with Zhang Jin and Zhou Shuzhong. They incorporated Hangzhou Lianke Meixun Biological Medicine Technology Co., Ltd. and continuously expand the "territory" of Internet medical care. After that, in 2007, "DX Talent Online" was introduced to build bridges between hospitals, biomedical industry and fresh medical graduates. In 2008, the information platform "Biomart" for scientific research institutions and instrument manufacturing enterprises was launched; and in 2011, DXY released "Drug Assistant", a tool to provide authoritative drug information inquiry for doctors. In 2012, Dingxiang Doctor was officially launched, which inherits the advantages of medication data and convenient interaction of "Drug Assistant" and has functions such as targeted medicine prescribing, medication safety warning, family medical kit, medicine/health food information inquiry and nearby pharmacies searching. In September 2014, the WeChat official account of Dingxiang Doctor was officially put into operation. By December 2021, the number of followers has exceeded 10 million, ranking first in the monthly list of the new health category.

With the development of Internet medical care industry and the expansion of the company, DXY needs to explore new business segments to realize the vision of long-term sustainable development. In 2014, Li Tiantian received Series-C financing from Tencent, and how to manifest the value of Internet medical care became one of his important issues. The day in 2005 when his son was born occurred to him. "My son was born prematurely with respiratory distress syndrome, and he was taken to ICU ward at birth and rescued for 15 consecutive days……" (Li, 2017). Li was heartbroken outside the ward, and this experience helped him understand the role of "patient". He thought: "how does DXY ignite patients' hope, and serve patients and the mass medical market?

2.1 The Arrival of "Imperial Doctor"

Tian Jishun is a well-known doctor from Women's Hospital School of Medicine Zhejiang University. Before Zhihu was open for registration, Tian was invited to provide quality answers on questions frequently. By the time the registration was available, he had accumulated thousands of followers on Zhihu. Chu Yang, a former orthopedist, served as the director of medical communication in DXY later. In 2014, Chu invited Tian to a podcast program "The arrival of Imperial Doctor" on Zhihu in order to provide the audience with medical knowledge from the doctors' point of view. The view counts of "Imperial Doctors are coming" was quite amazing, and followers who like them called them "Imperial Doctor Tian" and "Imperial Doctor Chu" respectively.

Chu's successful attempt in the new media such as Zhihu made Li Tiantian realize the needs of the huge mass consumer group. With the rising awareness of health, the public is eager to learn medical knowledge. This is not an area that can be covered by "folk science" such as health preservation or traditional medicine communication. Li held a meeting with two online celebrity "imperial doctors" and two other founders from the traditional medicine field of DingXiangYuan (DXY).

At this meeting, Li's opinion on the mass consumer business was questioned by others. After all, in the past, DXY aimed to meet various needs of doctors, and never involved ordinary users. **How can DingXiangYuan (DXY), not well-known among ordinary users, get close to mass market users and provide valuable contents that meet their needs?** Even Chu was skeptical about that: "when doctors take off their gowns and communicate with patients, how can we guarantee the authority of communication contents? And how to build a trust relationship with our consumers?" (Chu, 2021) Moreover, there are unknown risks because of no perfected example of Internet medical care business model for mass consumers. What kind of strategies does DXY need to take to stand out from the complicated markets of C-terminal Internet medical care?

2.2 The Potential Energy of Professionalism

Li Tiantian and Chu Yang decided to start with creating a WeChat official account. The number of WeChat official accounts at that year has reached 5 million, but the accounts related to the healthcare field still kept booming. In terms of the number of subscribers, views, reposts and comments, head WeChat official accounts in the healthcare field were quite different from the popular official accounts in other categories. In September 2014, the WeChat official account of Dingxiang Doctor went into operation officially, to which Chu was appointed to be fully responsible for the management and operation. As the first C-terminal product of DXY, the success or failure of Dingxiang Doctor was related to future C-terminal businesses of DXY. The strategy of it has become "D+C Dual-core Drive", in which, "D" refers to doctor, and "C" refers to consumer.

To enhance the authoritativeness of Dingxiang Doctor, "cooperating with doctors" was deemed as the core advantage by Chu Yang, because 70% of professional doctors around the country can be covered by DXY. Therefore, "Dingxiang Doctor has never been a person, but so many behind-the-scenes doctors in China." (Chriss, 2020) DXY's advantage of originating from professional doctors was called as "professional potential energy" by Chu, which can create professional influence and native inspiration for the health-related contents of Dingxiang Doctor.

On the one hand, by building a professional content production team with medical and communication background, contracting with a number of doctors and inviting science popularization authors in the medical area, Dingxiang Doctor has developed a peer review system similar to the paper contribution. As soon as the contribution is received, the system will submit it to "peer review committee" for examination, and check whether there are any nonstandard and unscientific contents in accordance with FABE principle (feature, advantage, benefit and evidence) to ensure the accuracy and professionalism of contents. After confirming that there are no faults, the contents will be released, and there is a "gatekeeper" at the end of each post.

On the other hand, Dingxiang Doctor insists on imparting professional knowledge with user-friendly and plain expressions. Most popular science articles in the medical field are obscure, which has become a wall between doctors and the public. However, Chu Yang found the key to solve this problem, i.e. choosing "dispelling rumors" as the first topic selection. At that time, health-oriented WeChat official accounts were still in rebellious period, and complex contents always made people puzzled and could not distinguish between true and false. In combination with different scenarios, Dingxiang Doctor uses comics and cases aptly to dispel rumors and help readers understand, thus making articles more simple and understandable and widely disseminated.

Driven by professional influence and native inspiration, the WeChat official account of Dingxiang Doctor gained a sudden popularity. As of April 2015, Dingxiang Doctor, which was established for only 5 months, has become the main official account in the field of healthcare with 2 million subscribers.

2.3 The Escalation of Products

In the development of Dingxiang Doctor, the innovation of products not only enhance the user growth of the platform, but also continuously creates a variety of new value points.

With the increasing growth of users of the official account of Dingxiang Doctor, many followers began to ask questions about the prevention of infectious diseases and the treatment of common cold. Li Tiantian has sensitively recognized their demands, and he thought that a new product should be developed to solve the questions asked by followers of "Dingxiang Doctor". Later, this idea evolved into a new product, "Ask the Doctor". "Ask the Doctor" is an online consultation product launched by Dingxiang Doctor for followers. Followers with the demand for consultation can immediately meet doctors from Grade A Class 3 hospitals in China face to face with only CNY10. By creating professional and friendly online consultation products, "Ask the Doctor" provides professional and personalized medical services for users of Dingxiang Doctor, helping it to upgrade to a higher value dimension.

After receiving the "positive feedback" from "Ask the Doctor" that it has operated smoothly and achieved profits, Li Tiantian turned his attention to the "immobile" offline scenarios. He found that there was a lack of a sound clinic system in China, and the professionalism of grass-root clinics has been questioned because of no professional department structure. Clinics are usually regarded as "prescription institutions" by many people, therefore, even if patients catch a cold, they will register in a Grade A Class 3 hospital. Li believes that offline clinics are a "blue ocean market". Relying on mature online consultation experience and professional brand essence of Dingxiang Doctor, more users can enjoy professional medical services and better medical experience by establishing clinics with general-practice medical system, so that people are willing to come to clinics for the medical treatment and physical examination. DXClinics carried out pilot projects in Hangzhou and Fuzhou first, attracting many patients who came

Table 1 List of series of products of Dingxiang Doctor

Name	Characteristics
WeChat official account of Dingxiang Doctor	Popularizing health-related contents to the public
Ask the Doctor	Providing professional and friendly online mobile consultation
DXClinics	Creating the offline consultation community with a general-practice medical system
Dingxiang Mama	Science popularization of mother and infant-related contents and pregnancy services

Source Sorted by authors

here for the brand. The goal of Li is to promote this offline general-practice consultation system across the country, so that it can cover more areas and provide services for more people. From online consultation to offline clinics, Dingxiang Doctor has smoothed the development and promotion of new products based on the experience and reputation of existing products, and achieved omnichannel and whole-area coverage on its consultation services.

Li Tiantian also noticed that maternal product users have strong demands and potentials for the scientific parenting knowledge. Therefore, he decided to work deeply in this market segment and launched "Dingxiang Mama" to better meet the needs of this group. However, facing the rapid speed of user iteration, short life cycle of consumption and high demands of users' emotional value, how does Dingxiang Doctor deal with these new challenges? Li discussed with obstetrician, Dr. Tian Jishun. On the one hand, Dingxiang Doctor should continuously popularize authoritative content on the basis of its rich medical resources, and on the other hand, it can cooperate with famous maternal and infant brands, focus on digging vertical areas of the market and effectively reach a new generation of young parents, thus stimulating their emotional resonance to accumulate more followers. The success of Dingxiang Mama provides experience for Dingxiang Doctor to explore more market segments and launch products serving specific groups (see Table 1).

3 From Market Segment to Creating Value with Consumers

3.1 Segmentation

The prosperous development of WeChat official accounts requires that efforts shall be made to classify users into different categories and solve the demands of segmented populations. Chu Yang often receives user feedbacks claiming that they want to deepen their knowledge on certain diseases, which are far from the contents and subjects of Dingxiang Doctor. At the same time, the mommies and daddies-to-be in the company also gave feedback to Chu that whether maternal and child-related contents could be posted, some colleagues wanting to lose weight desired to know how to eat more healthily and what kinds of living habits can make them have a healthy life. With the emergence of such demands, Chu began to have an idea of creating other accounts. He planned to register special official accounts of corresponding diseases for science popularizing and disease prevention, so as to meet the specific needs of users. He also initiated an idea to register official accounts to share contents about healthy eating and living habits. Under the same standards of Dingxiang Doctor, the contents uploaded on these official accounts are tagged with the identification of Dingxiang Doctor. As a result, official accounts about gout, hypertension, diabetes, hyperthyroidism and mental illness, Dingxiang Shitang, and Health Headlines were registered. All of these are praised by users and boost the rapid quantity increase of users of Dingxiang Doctor.

A matrix of WeChat official accounts has been formally established, with Dingxiang Doctor as the main body and including Dingxiang Mama and a number of official accounts about diseases, health and lifestyle. These accounts are subject to the same professional endorsement and complete review mechanism and edited in a warm, friendly and reliable writing style, just as Dingxiang Doctor does. But they deliver different contents precisely for different target groups. The aggregation effect of WeChat official accounts matrix has played an important role in shaping the brand awareness. The Dingxiang-series WeChat official accounts quickly occupies the top ten among health-related accounts, and the brand gains fame as an Internet medical care knowledge platform (see Fig. 1).

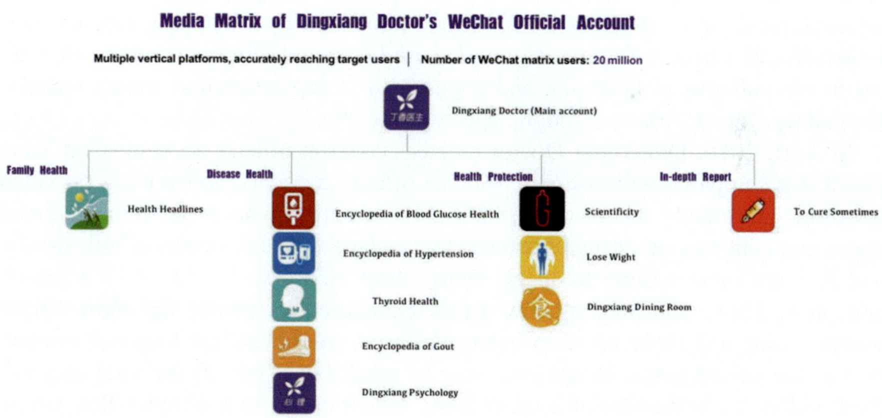

Fig. 1 Media matrix of Dingxiang Doctor's WeChat official account. *Source* Official website of DingXiangYuan (DXY)

3.2 Breaking Through

In 2017, the number of users of Dingxiang Doctor's WeChat official account suffered dismal growth. The user traffic is the key to the profit growth of Dingxiang Doctor. Though it comes to the top in the "inner matrix", it is still a "hidden champion" in vertical field. Dingxiang Doctor still has to break through the wall urgently. Chu Yang believes that high frequency in forwarding refers to the times that an article is forwarded; and high following refers to the user retention from sharing. Articles that cannot assist in building the brand awareness or retain users make little sense even if they are characterized by good contents. **So how to improve the brand awareness of "Dingxiang" from the perspective of users, and how to "break through" and attract more users?**

Chu Yang and his team focused on other public traffic platforms other than WeChat, such as Tiktok, Zhihu and Weibo, and developed a new media pattern of "external matrix". There are a smaller quantity of accounts in the external matrix, but they are in better quality, with "Dingxiang Doctor" and "Dingxiang Mama" as the main. Social media platform, Weibo, question-and-answer platform, Zhihu, and short video platform, Tiktok, occupy the main positions of the new media.

Returning to Weibo in 2017, Dingxiang Doctor captures the public opinions and takes measures quickly within 1 to 2 h, striving to respond with high-quality contents and obtaining the wave of traffic dividend at the first time. "The reason to choose Weibo mainly depends on trends of the rising traffic and social topics on it, and Dingxiang Doctor has advantages of high-quality contents." (How Does the New Media Matrix of Millions …, 2019) In addition to focusing on public opinions, Dingxiang Doctor makes topics actively relying on conflicts caused by information asymmetry. In 2018, an article published by Dingxiang Doctor, *Ten-billion Health Product Empire of Quanjian, and Haunted Chinese Families*, directly led to the collapse of Quanjian and triggered a strong resonance among readers. Dingxiang Doctor "broke through" successfully.

In April 2018, Dingxiang Doctor created a Tiktok official account. Chu Yang found that compared with users of WeChat official accounts, active users on video platforms are mostly the young in their early twenties, who prefer unconstrained styles and contents, other than speeches by teachers who are serious or talk slowly, and they are more willing to accept funny short videos with a lot of information and plots. Thus, Chu and his new media team tried to control the short videos within 2 min, and those on short video platforms were even less than one minute. Just as the saying goes, "A sparrow may be small but it has all the vital organs." Each video is a reflection of a short story, which caters to hot topics that young people are interested in. For example, it talked about if it was healthy to "make tea with goji berry and keep it warm in a thermos" as the lyrics of *Calorie*. Under the relaxing and humorous interpretation of popular doctor Tian Jishun, the videos produced by Dingxiang Doctor were launched one after another. By the end of 2018, Dingxiang Doctor had 6 million followers and more than 700 million views on Tiktok.

Table 2 New media "External Matrix" of Dingxiang Doctor

Attribute	Social communication	Question and answer	Videos	Videos	Media	Portal websites
Principal platforms	Weibo	Zhihu	Bilibili	Tiktok	TOPBuzz	Baidu, Sohu, Netease, etc
Target groups (the number of followers)	Dingxiang Doctor (5.804 million)	Dingxiang Doctor (3.13 million)	Dingxiang Doctor (813,000)	Dingxiang Doctor (7.71 million)	Dingxiang Doctor (2.035 million) Dingxiang Shitang (10,000) Dingxiang Health (115,000)	Dingxiang Doctor Dingxiang Shitang
	Dingxiang Mama (114,000)	Dingxiang Mama (206,000)		Dingxiang Mama (673,000)	Dingxiang Mama (151,000) Weight Loss (52,000)	Dingxiang Mama Weight Loss

Source Sorted by the authors in December 2021

With the rapid growth of followers on the new media platforms, Dingxiang Doctor teams increased the frequency of internal meetings to make content and operation teams of different platforms can access the publishment, traffic information and existing problems of others. Therefore, high standardized contents can be quickly reused on other platforms.

By the end of December 2021, the total number of followers of the new media "external matrix" of Dingxiang Doctor exceeded 20 million, being the "top" in the field of Internet healthcare field (see Table 2).

3.3 Co-creation

How does Dingxiang Doctor connect a series of "breaking-through" products and millions of loyal users **through the resource integration to achieve the multiple growth of the number of platform users and value?**

Chu Yang realized that the users of Dingxiang Doctor were relatively isolated from each other on different platforms, and there was no information exchange between them, which led to their strong platform dependence. "Taking a family of three people as an example. They all follow accounts of Dingxiang Doctor, but the father may follow the WeChat official account, the mother may be a follower of Weibo and Zhihu, and the son may be a loyal user of Tiktok." Chu thought that the user growth "fission" could be realized with existing resources if users on different platforms could be connected.

Dingxiang Doctor made new attempts to achieve the user flow on different platforms. In June 2018, Dingxiang Doctor released a video on Tiktok, "Correcting 'arched shoulder' with 10 s", and also posted the text version on its official account. Followers noticed that QR code of its Tiktok was attached to the end of the article. And, the top comment on Tiktok was accompanied by a link to the article on the official account. From the backend data, Chu Yang was pleasantly surprised to find that the article published on WeChat official account and the video on Tiktok all received far more readings and likes than usual. After reviewing and analyzing, he found that, in addition to the selection of topic in line with users' concerns about health issues, the action of "user attraction" played an important role. Some new users replied on Tiktok that they gained information from the official account. Users from different platforms were connected for the first time. Chu also released articles to respond some concerned questions about health issues on Zhihu, enabling users from different platforms to have a deeper understanding and communicate with each other. "A family of three people finally subscribes to the same channel." Users gradually get rid of their dependence on the original platform. If the WeChat official account of Dingxiang Doctor doesn't update on time today, they will turn to Tiktok to watch short videos uploaded and then participate in the discussion in Zhihu.

In addition, in the development process of accounts of Dingxiang Doctor, Chu Yang has always put users first and tried to create contents that conform to the users' value. "Altruism is self-interest," Chu firmly believes this. He posted the slogan "Earning more money is to serve more users" at the entrance of the company to indoctrinate his employees. Among the numerous users of Dingxiang Doctor, people with medical backgrounds and engaging in the healthcare account for a certain proportion. They are active in different platforms and can write wonderful comments on message boards to spark discussions. Chu defines them as "core users" and actively invites them to take part in the content creation. By doing so, their articles can be more in line with users' preferences, thus making these articles more popular among users, and the number of users will naturally increase steadily. With the development of e-commerce platforms and the trend of "selling goods", Dingxiang Doctor also engaged in such trend. Different from other platforms, Dingxiang Doctor invites some users to be "co-experience officers", who can use the goods first for free. The "product experience reports" from these officers will be published on the official account, becoming "advertisements without the natures of traditional advertisements". This "product promotion mechanism" is based on users' experience and it has achieved "win–win-win" results for consumers, platforms and manufacturers.

4 Value Expansion: Platform Empowerment

4.1 Nurturing New Opportunities in Crisis: Dingxiang Doctor's Responses to the COVID-19 Pandemic

At the beginning of 2020, the sudden outbreak of the COVID-19 pandemic affected the normal life of every Chinese, and "home quarantine" disrupted people's pace of life. During that special period, people suddenly had more time to spend, and those people who didn't care about health care before began to pay attention to this field, especially the real-time information related to the COVID-19 pandemic. Knowledge popularization of COVID-19, the processes of self-prevention and control, and channels to purchase standard and affordable medical supplies, all such information have become hot topics for each account on the Internet. Just as the saying goes, "misfortune may be a blessing in disguise". For Li Tiantian and Dingxiang Doctor's team, this is an opportunity more than a challenge.

How did Li Tiantian cope with it? First of all, Li believed that among all information, the real-time information about COVID-19 cases is undoubtedly the content that users care about most. Authoritative and timely information could provide the public with the changes of the COVID-19 pandemic quickly. Dingxiang Doctor's team quickly summoned all its members, and it took only one day to officially launch the pandemic map in the early morning of January 21, 2020, which was quicker than its peers and major media. At the same time, it was launched in internal and external media matrix and mobile applications, integrating the information about the COVID-19 pandemic into a "Real-time Dynamic Link of COVID-19 in China". The pandemic map was created by combing and summarizing to the case data released by the National Health Commission of the People's Republic of China, the Chinese Center for Disease Control and Prevention and the medical and health institutions in most provincial administrative regions of China, and was then visually presented to users in the form of the map of China. With the spread of the COVID-19 pandemic worldwide, Dingxiang Doctor quickly switched from the map of China to a global pandemic map, thus making its audience expand to global users. As of March 16, 2021, the pandemic map products launched by Dingxiang Doctor have accumulated more than 4.5 billion page views, which has played an important role in transmitting information about the COVID-19 pandemic. This public product made Dingxiang Doctor enjoy a great first-mover advantage. According to the real-time demands, they optimized such diversified presentation forms as the original contents, total number of COVID-19 cases, itemized statistics of data tables and national trend chart. In addition, they added new interactive modes with the help of resource advantages of professional doctors and online consultation products. Dingxiang Doctor's channel influence and reputation were improved rapidly in a short time due to the traffic growth brought by the huge number of visitors. According to statistics, since the launch of the "Pandemic Map", the download ranking of Dingxiang Doctor has been significantly improved, and the average daily active users have increased from 21,800 to 79,500.

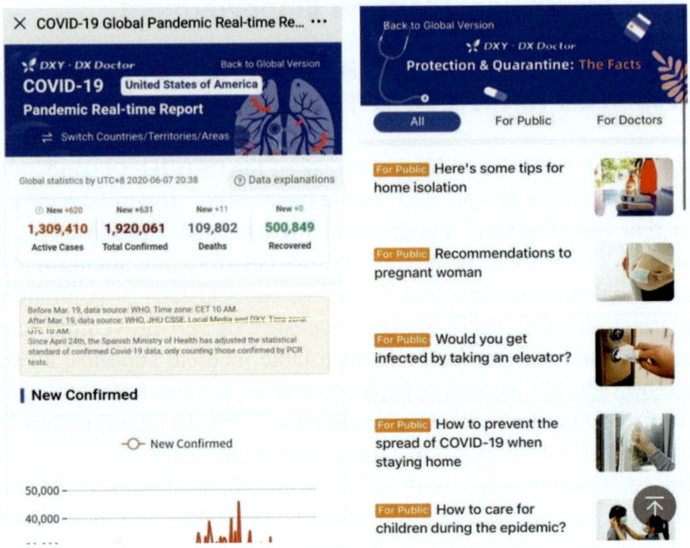

Fig. 2 "Pandemic Map" of dingxiang doctor. *Source* Official Account of Dingxiang Doctor

Secondly, Dingxiang Doctor's internal and external matrix produced and published articles and videos about COVID-19 and how to prevent it, which were endorsed by national infectious disease epidemiologists, in order to stabilize people's anxiety and uneasiness at the first time. In 2020, the update frequency of Dingxiang Doctor on each platform became faster, the internal and external matrix have published over 3,600 image-texts with a pageviews of more than 4 billion. Accordingly, the main official account and the life-type official account promoted in 2020, Dingxiang Life Research Institute, of Dingxiang Doctor, both gained millions of new followers during the COVID-19 pandemic. The COVID-19 pandemic made more people realize the importance of health, and learn knowledge of healthy living through the Internet. Such group of people becomes new followers of Dingxiang Doctor. Therefore, Dingxiang Doctor did not suffer the negative impact of this crisis, but also maintained a high-speed user growth. It "made breakthroughs" successfully and became the leading accounts in the comprehensive ranking of major platforms (see Fig. 2).

4.2 Breaking New Ground in Changes: Platform Empowerment and Innovation in the Value Chain

The COVID-19 pandemic made the physical market suffer a lot. Many enterprises lost their main offline sales channels, but it also brought new opportunities to the e-commerce market. Li Tiantian tried to tap into new business opportunities. Can Dingxiang Doctor, which has 50 million mass consumers and 2.1 million doctor users in the whole network, **build a healthy e-commerce market with its platform endowment, and form a new value connection between enterprises and consumers?** Under the research and development of the team, Dingxiangjia went online. With the theme of "Health Marketing, Dingxiang Creation", Dingxiangjia helps enterprises match target customers on the platform, and enables consumers to quickly seek the products they need by fully exploiting the product value of enterprises and accurately depicting user portraits on the platform. Li also introduced the scientific audit mechanism into Dingxiangjia. All products are checked by Dingxiang's scientific audit team before going online, and then recommended to the homepage of users through accurate algorithms. By the end of 2020, Dingxiangjia has accumulated more than 1.5 million service paying users, covering health scenarios such as maternal and infant, skin care, oral cavity, rhinitis, sleep, home and food nutrition.

In addition to helping companies of health consumer goods develop their value and connect customers, Dingxiang Doctor also empowers biomedical companies. Many pharmaceutical companies face the problem of accumulating profound R&D experience, but relatively backward marketing level. "Enterprises that seriously do research and development can't make money, while unreliable enterprises can earn much." Based on Dingxiang Doctor's content marketing experience for many years, platform resources of Dingxiang's new media matrix and the value of Dingxiang Doctor's IP assets, Li Tiantian set up a Dingxiang digital marketing platform to provide professional marketing solutions for pharmaceutical enterprises and help enterprises build brand reputation at both ends of doctors and patients by taking "B-D-C link as the key link to improve the digital marketing efficiency of pharmaceutical enterprises" and focusing on both doctor education and popularization of science for the public. Li believed that the core strengths of Dingxiang Doctor's digital marketing lie in five major aspects, i.e. accurate insight, professional credibility, brand driver, content influence and native inspiration. He also planned a blueprint for the future of digital marketing: "Our goal is simple, that is, we want to build an industrial ecosystem together with everyone, and make this ecosystem more benign and healthy. With such a mission in mind, we have come together with more and more professional forces, and at the same time, DXY has truly given 'half of its life' to its partners."

In the context of the COVID-19 pandemic, medical institutions and physician groups have come into the spotlight and received a lot of attention. Currently, 80% of medical institutions in China suffer from a lack of digital capabilities and poor brand operation. Li Tiantian wanted to remain true to the original aspiration with platform resources of Dingxiang Doctor, so as to help medical institutions provide brand operation solutions in the digital era and promote the positive development of brands in China's medical industry. Hospital hub was born, providing a complete of digital operation solutions for medical institutions. It is divided into three main steps. The first step is to plan and operate the whole hospital brand by sorting out the competitive advantages of the hospital side (H-terminal) customers, clearly planning the whole communication process of hospital brands, and enhancing the brand influence of hospitals. The second step is to dock and integrate with

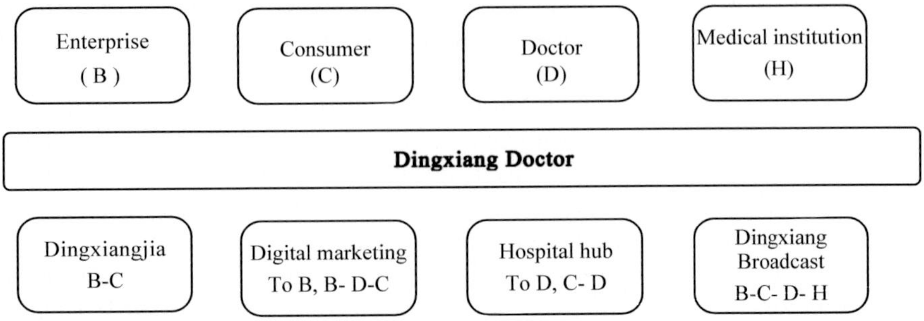

Fig. 3 Business display of Dingxiang Doctor. *Source* Sorted by the authors of the case

the industry and platform resources owned by Dingxiang Doctor, and export the Dingxiang Doctor system to the H-terminal. The third step is to promote brands on Dingxiang Doctor. By the end of 2021, the cooperative medical institutions of hospital hub reached more than 20, and more and more patients from platforms are visiting these hospitals.

The live broadcast is the most popular emerging media form in the post-pandemic era. The characteristics of instant interactivity, strong socialization, subject diversity and interestingness lead to its rapid user growth. Dingxiang Broadcast is a live broadcast interaction platform for doctors under DingXiangYuan (DXY), which effectively integrates the user channels and data resources of Dingxiang Doctor, and relies on Dingxiang Doctor's brand advantages to realize the online live broadcast of doctors' lectures, departmental meetings, patient education, recruitment seminars and multi-disciplinary expert consultations for hospitals, medical institutions and enterprises across the country during the COVID-19 pandemic, becoming an "online academic service station" for medical professionals. According to statistics, more than 180,000 viewers study and attend the conference during this period with Broadcast. In the next step, Dingxiang Broadcast will also develop new products to serve B-terminal and C-terminal customers, connect different value subjects, and create Dingxiang Broadcast network ecology (see Fig. 3).

5 Epilogue

The achievements of Dingxiang Doctor have made Li Tiantian be filled with emotion, "now, many people may not know what DXY is doing, but they have definitely heard of or used Dingxiang Doctor. "In terms of content, business and booster fighting against the pandemic, Dingxiang Doctor has achieved outstanding results. "With the vision of 'more health, better life', Dingxiang Doctor will continue to be a leader in China's Internet medical care business and help more people have a healthy lifestyle." At the end of Li's speech, there was ceaseless applause.

Back to the company, Li Tiantian did not feel relaxed, instead, some recent news made him lose in thought. The quality of Dingxiang Doctor's contents has declined and his marketing practices have been doubted. For example, in mid-2021, Dingxiang Life Research Institute published an original article, *You may buy "fake" whole-wheat bread! 7 Kinds of Bread Brand Recommendation after Picking from 50 Brands*. In the article, Dingxiang Life Research Institute ranked Tianyuanzhuyi whole-wheat bread as the first on the recommendation list. However, this kind of whole-wheat bread was then pointed out by Shanghai Consumer Council for false labeling of ingredients and misrepresentation (News, 2021). Facing the question of "selling goods", Dingxiang Doctor chose not to speak or respond at this time. In October 2021, Dingxiang Doctor's assertion that "drinking sugar-free carbonated beverages will not damage teeth" sparked controversy again, and it apologized on Weibo that night. "101 dispelling rumors" of Dingxiang Doctor in its early stage were constantly rehashed by netizens to "dispel rumors again", leading to questions such as "consumption guidance behind the science". It seems that there is still a long way to go for Dingxiang Doctor to balance professionalism and commercialization. In addition, the development of business chains of Dingxiang Doctor is uneven, and how to achieve balanced and sustainable development of the platform by integrating resources and sharing internal experience is still an urgent problem to be solved.

References

Chriss. (2020, August). Half of Life to Partners, DingXiangYuan (DXY) Building a New Ecology of Pharmaceutical Digital Together with the Industry. *Tencent News*. https://new.qq.com/rain/a/20200803a0s97w00.

Chu, Y. (2021, March). Ice President of DingXiangYuan (DXY): Dilemma and Breakthrough from an Official Account to a Healthy Lifestyle Brand, *36 Krypton*. https://36kr.com/p/1156150471591297.

How Does the New Media Matrix of Millions of Followers of Dingxiang Doctor Formed? (2019, August). Everyone Is a Product Manager. http://www.woshipm.com/evaluating/2656744.html.

Li, T. T. (2017, March). From DingXiangYuan (DXY) To Dingxiang Doctor. *DingXiangYuan (DXY)*. http://6d.dxy.cn/article/517941.

Tencent News. (2021, September). No Response after Reporting of Bad Goods Quality. Is the Recommendation of Dingxiang Doctor Certainly Good? https://new.qq.com/omn/20210908/20210908A0BYZC00.html.

Sootoo Network: Technology-Driven Business Model Change of New Media Enterprises

Xusen Cheng, Bo Yang, and Kanliang Wang

1 Introduction

Founded in 2009, Sootoo Network is a leading "new media ecological operator" in China. Its main businesses include three business segments, i.e. "new media products and services, content marketing services, and new media marketing platform business". It has an industry-leading capability of new media product ecosystem service. Micromedia Alliance has become one of the largest WeChat WeMedia Alliances in China, covering dozens of industries such as the Internet, cute pets, yoga, automobile, entertainment, education, and games. Operating more than 100 WeChat official accounts and covering hundreds of millions of mobile users, Micromedia Alliance is one of the professional WeMedia Alliances with the largest number of followers and widest industries in China.

This article takes the new media service provider, Sootoo Network, as the research object, and makes an in-depth process analysis of its business change process, industry background and problems faced by enterprises in their development. Our findings provide certain theoretical guidance and suggestions for China's new media service enterprises in the process of future growth.

X. Cheng · B. Yang
School of Information, Renmin University of China, Beijing, China

K. Wang (✉)
Renmin Business School, Renmin University of China, Beijing, China

J. Zhang et al. (eds.), *Innovation of Digital Economy*, Management for Professionals,
https://doi.org/10.1007/978-981-99-1741-9_2

2 Development and Current Situation of the Company

Founded in 2009, Sootoo Network is a leading new media ecological operator in China. Its main businesses include three business segments, i.e. new media products and services, content marketing services, and new media marketing platform business. It has an industry-leading capability of new media product ecosystem service.

2.1 Born Unique: Vertical Media Era (2009–2012)

The foundation of Sootoo Network was exactly the dusk of the era of Web 1.0. Fan Feng, the founder, believed that sootoo.com should be positioned as China's Internet social media, while the existing system of Web 2.0 could not audit and supervise the information released by users. What Sootoo wanted to create was not only a platform for information sharing but also a function of comprehensive supervision of the content produced by users. It was also hoped that this platform would possess Internet social functions. In other words, registered users could comment on it, and establish a two-way communication connection.

Thus, sootoo.com was established at the beginning of the foundation of Sootoo Network. But at the time of setting up sootoo.com, there was almost no vertical media in China that specialized in reporting the Internet industry. Therefore, sootoo.com became the first media to focus on Internet industry reports, and gradually grew into the largest industry website and the position of public opinion and social communication in China's Internet industry, which was known as the "Catcher of China Internet". Over 4,000 enterprises registered on it a year after its launch.

2.2 Riding the Wind: Social Media Era of Tencent (2012–2016)

After 2004, the new generation of social media represented by Facebook, Twitter, YouTube, MySpace, Weibo, and WeChat began to emerge and grow rapidly. Fan Feng, with his keen sense, laid out opportunities that many media people did not realize. He dared to be the first, accumulating the strength for the subsequent development in this period. In the very beginning, Sootoo Network tried to use Weibo to broaden its marketing business, but the results were not satisfactory. Because Sootoo Network didn't build its own KOL (Key Opinion Leader) group in advance, it had few resources. Most of the resources were purchased from KOLs and Internet celebrities, though it could combine its marketing with Weibo.

Having learned lessons from marketing on Weibo, Sootoo Network seized the advantages of WeChat official accounts. As soon as the WeChat official account was launched, Sootoo Network took the lead in registering and reserving many official accounts and laid out the WeChat in advance. This rush registration made Sootoo a major source of future traffic. Later, Sootoo Network established "Q

Media Alliance" based on QQ official account, and laid out its own Q Media Alliance according to the favorites of post-00 s, covering fashion, ACGN, black technology, and others, and capturing the younger generation of users compared with WeChat.

2.3 Breaking Through the Block: Diversified New Media Era (2016–2019)

The development of short videos entered a vigorous stage with the rapid development and promotion of information technology. Short video platforms have gradually become the main channel for users to obtain Internet information due to the popularity of short videos. From the end of 2015 to 2016, the remark that the dividend period of WeChat had passed began to show signs. Fan Feng also noticed and thought about such a remark. To prevent the situation of "lagging and being vulnerable to attacks", Sootoo Network had settled in several content platforms with its deep accumulation of media resources, jumping out of the single ecology of Tencent.

Based on the experience of operating WeChat official accounts, Sootoo Network settled many WeChat official account editors on Toutiao, UC (Dayu), yidianzixun.com, and other platforms, and set up relevant accounts. Sootoo also launched the arrangement on short video platforms such as Tiktok, Kwai, and Vigo Video to create a new IP based on short videos and get attention with the traffic of video platforms. Furthermore, Sootoo combined short videos with enterprise services. On New Year's Day of 2017, Sootoo Network made a short video more characterized by public welfare and social responsibility for Legend Holdings, with the view count of two or three hundred thousand and good results. Furthermore, Sootoo also made some targeted strategies on such audio platforms as Dragonfly FM, Himalaya, and live broadcast platforms including INKE and Huajiao. In 2017, Sootoo set up Sootoo Film, Sootoo Education, and Answer Idea successively, and actively laid out other industries related to the new media.

2.4 Self-innovation: New Marketing + New Consumption (2019—Present)

On January 20, 2019, the annual conference of Sootoo Network was held at its headquarters in Beijing, representing the end of the first decade of Sootoo and the beginning of a new one. In the past decade, Sootoo noticed the disruptive business model reconstruction of the industry from the iteration of user demands, timely discovered and quickly grasped the core driving force of enterprise reform in the new media era, and realized the magnificent transformation from the vertical social media to the brand ecological operator. In the field of new marketing business, Sootoo Network currently embraces four brands, i.e. Netwayer, Answer Idea, Sootoo Entertainment, and Sootoo Health, as well as three new consumption IPs, i.e. "Daily Yoga", "Here comes the cat" and "Human Resource Management". At present, the independent operating company of "Here comes the cat" and "Daily Yoga" has been established, and the internal incubation has been realized.

During this period, Sootoo went through four stages of transformation, and now, headquartered in Beijing. It has opened branches or offices in Zhengzhou, Shenzhen, Shanghai, Guangzhou, and Hangzhou. Sootoo Network and its subsidiary "Netwayer" have been assessed as national high-tech enterprises consecutively for many years. Today, Sootoo Network is defined as a "mobile creative workshop", becoming a full ecological service provider of intelligent marketing and new consumption in China. It is mainly committed to providing intelligent marketing solutions based on big data for enterprise customers, as well as providing content and life services based on new technology platforms for the majority of mobile internet users. Its three major segments, Sootoo New Marketing, Sootoo New Media, and New Marketing Joint Research Center, corporate with each other and support mutually to create the "business circle" of Sootoo's intensive cultivation and promote the brand to enter the fast lane.

3 Industry Background

3.1 Vertical Media—Text Contents

The foundation of Sootoo was exactly the dusk of the era of Web 1.0. The rise of Blogs, the application of RSS technology, and the widespread popularity of P2P technology, HTML5, NodeJS, SNS, etc., make Web 2.0 characterized by decentralization, openness, and sharing a new trend of the times. Network users are entitled to reproduce. Information and services are jointly developed by platforms and reproducers. As a result, the benefits are also owned by them. One of the objects directly impacted by Web 2.0 is the network media in the era of Web 1.0. Based on the technology and ideology of Web 2.0, the most prominent feature is the emergence of UGC (user-produced content) network media platforms. The public includes the receiver and producer of information. In China back then, Renren.com and Kaixin001.com were established successively, which opened the curtain of China's social networks. A wide range of products appeared successively in different shapes and all kinds are in bloom. At this point in time, vertical social networks are mostly combined with games, e-commerce, career recruitment, etc. In this period, user-generated content was still mainly in texts.

3.2 Social Media is Coming—Image-Text Contents

In September 2011, at Baidu World Conference, Li Yanhong listed the recommendation engine, cloud computing, and search engine as important strategic planning and development direction of the Internet in the future. Personalized recommendation and "personalized concepts" gradually become the concern of many industries.

Meanwhile, the concept of big data also attracts many entrepreneurs' attention with the discussion of foreign scholars. Many people may not completely comprehend the concepts of big data and personalized recommendation, but they have already made a unanimous judgment about the significance of all kinds of data resources in the future, that is, data will be an essential asset in the future and all kinds of data battles should be prepared in advance. The media industry inherently has a large variety of data. However, due to the degree of hardship and short-term benefits, such complex data is rarely accumulated by operators. Sootoo, with a keen sense, laid out opportunities that many media people did not realize. It dared to be the first, thereby accumulating the strength for the subsequent development in this period.

3.3 "Blowout" of Multi-media—Video Content

The evolution and maturity of technology always drive the continuous change of the medium, and the rapid increase in the number of smartphone users. The high prevalence of 4G communication technology and wireless network make short video enter a blooming stage of expansion. According to the 43rd *Statistical Report on Internet Development in China* issued in December 2018, the scale of short video users in China has stood at 648 million, with a usage rate of 78.2%. Meanwhile, the AI technology has already penetrated all segments of short videos and is applied in different stages such as video production, transmission, consumption, etc. AR camera pose estimation, intelligent video coding, intelligent dark light enhancement, human posture estimation, and other technologies give users more pleasure in video making, and also contribute to video distribution and accurate recommendations. Short video platforms have gradually become the main channel for users to obtain Internet information due to the popularity of short videos. The concept of "private traffic" has increasingly become popular in the Internet industry. Since many Internet companies have realized the incremental ceiling and the exhaustion of traffic dividends, it has been a consensus of all companies to explore more values from old users. Customers, the most valuable asset, have been given the attention it deserves. At that time, the remark that the dividend period of WeChat had passed began to show signs.

3.4 Digital Technology to Drive the New Consumption—Live Broadcast Content

The interference and management of the enterprise ecosystem by big data intelligent technology will lead to a new era of comprehensive quantitative operation, in which the entire ecology relies on the organic collaboration of each ecological partner to accomplish all tasks. The dual-wheel engine of "technological innovation plus business model innovation" will guide all departments and personnel of companies to establish a new situation of collaborative innovation, enabling enterprises to realize high-quality development and growth. The major new media platforms seek for "live broadcast plus" model and establish a diversified content ecosystem. With the growth of new media, the traditional e-commerce market has reached saturation point. "Live broadcast plus e-commerce" has significantly enhanced the user experience with its real-time and interactive advantages, and KOL "selling goods" mode has raised the business conversion rate, which brings enormous business dividends to the industry and becomes a new growth driver for the live broadcast industry. Additionally, the scale of users in cities below the third tier is huge, and users have more disposable time and more potential to realize, which becomes a sinking market for the live broadcast industry in the future.

4 Problems and Solutions

4.1 Increased Difficulty in Maintaining User Stickiness

With the growth of the new media, the Internet has stepped from the increment era to the stock era. There have been some bad phenomena, such as the gradual fading of the demographic dividend, the gradual slowing down of the growth rate of the user scale, the increasingly prominent "Matthew effect" of the media industry, and more intense competition in the stock market.. For Sootoo Network, the accumulation of followers (or consumers) in the early stage is easy to realize. However, once bring focused or segmented later, there will be a thin follower base of the same preference, type, and region, which also leads to increased difficulty in maintaining the consumer stickiness later. For consumers, whether they consume goods, information or time, these can be considered as consuming products or services. Consumers have requirements for increasingly high quality, coupled with the increased difficulty of innovation and the reduction of the traffic dividend period, which has led to a continued increase in users' loss and the difficulty of sustained realization.

Fan Feng said that *the market is the most important boss of our company*. Therefore, he adheres to the concept of "user demands first" and attempts to create a super "IP". Taking "Moe Factory ", a cute pet official account on the verge of "death", as an example, Sootoo refined its operation from customer demands, shifted its attention to the increasingly active cat fanatics and the post-90 s "empty-nest youths" and "cataholic" who work alone, and transformed "Moe Factory" into an official account of "cat-oriented and mainly for the fans of cats (including cloud cataholic)" to realize traffic monetization through advertising, soft articles, reward, e-commerce and paid contents. Afterward, Sootoo successfully created such super "IPs" as "Daily Yoga" and "Human Resource Management" with a similar model. Sootoo's new consumption model puts consumers at the core, aims at meeting consumers' demands, reconstructs the relationship between consumers and businesses, and completes the overall full-factor upgrade of the industry.

4.2 High Employment Costs

At present, the new media is mainly operated manually. With the current climbing labor price in China and the emergence of new hot content, the cost of manual operation has been a serious shackle limiting the development of the WeMedia industry. Meanwhile, human productivity is impacted by factors such as emotion, and the work effect is unstable. The liquidity of human resources will also have an obvious influence on the stability and quality of media platforms. Sootoo Network runs 55 major accounts, requiring 37 professional editors with extensive experience in text writing. These editors can only meet the standards required after a long time of training. This manual editing has at least two distinct limitations. Firstly, the labor cost is extremely high. In the last few years, with the development of Chinese national economy, the economic level of the Chinese has improved obviously. This is reflected in the sharp increase in labor costs for employers. As a result, high labor costs have become a sore point in the new media industry. Secondly, there is a large staff mobility. The main consumers of new media are young people in the new era. Consequently, the new media industry is also mainly occupied by young people. However, young employees are typically featured by less experience and a high job-hopping rate. Media editors, particularly for specific topics, require a long period of study and training to adapt to the job. These trained editors will also become the targets of competition from new media enterprises. This creates a vicious competition that all new media enterprises want to directly poach editors trained by others rather than taking their own time and energy to cultivating them.

With the development of computer technology, especially the advancement of natural language processing technology, the introduction of AI technology into the media industry has become a topic with high practical application value. On the introduction of AI technology, the leadership of Sootoo Network is very decisive and forward-looking. He took the initiative to cooperate with the School of Information, Renmin University of China to conduct relevant research and experiments. So far, the information system based on AI technology has become an important assistant for the development of Sootoo Network. In order to solve the problem of manual operation of Sootoo Network, School of Information, Renmin University of China studies the deep learning algorithm which combines data and knowledge according to the characteristics of new media data. Based on the new algorithm, an automatic content selection and push system and an automatic response system are developed for new media platforms.

4.3 How to Advance the Business Transformation Smoothly and Steadily

The products, services, and processes provided by enterprises are changing with the development and application of modern information technologies and communication means such as big data, cloud computing, artificial intelligence, and blockchain technology. Consequently, new business models are being created and channels such as enterprise resource planning, customer relationship management, and supply chain management are being transformed. The new technology is setting off a tide, in which all walks of life will either stand on the crest of the tide or die under the waves. Working behind closed doors will gradually be replaced by more open and inclusive innovation approaches.

In the past decade, Sootoo noticed the disruptive business model reconstruction of the industry from the iteration of user demands, timely discovered and quickly grasped the core driving force of enterprise reform in the new media era, and realized the magnificent transformation from the vertical social media to the brand ecological operator. In the following digital era, Sootoo must seize the opportunity given by big data and artificial intelligence to build its own traffic pipeline, and make the traffic pool the source of wealth through accumulation and operation. To this end, Sootoo and Renmin Business School jointly set up the "New Marketing Joint Research Center". Based on the school research and cutting-edge practice, the "New Marketing Joint Research Center" conducts in-depth visits to benchmark enterprises in the industry. It keeps tracking, developing, and promoting more effective marketing experiences and models, revealing new marketing codes and "Rubik's cube" rules in an all-round way, which makes itself a smart platform for new marketing of enterprises.

5 Epilogue

First of all, in the era of rapid development of new media, to give full play to the traffic dividend, only through continuous explorations and trials and errors by multiple business units, summarizing and sharing practical experience in trial and error processes, and constantly updating their own products and services can they maximize the discovery of effective practices and promote them internally as soon as possible. At the same time, attention shall be paid to peers, broadening the breadth of vision and summarizing the experience of peers to avoid unnecessary risks. Secondly, breaking the shackles of manual operation and realizing the automation of the new media industry have become important measures to solve the above maladies. The automatic content selection and push system of the new media can solve the bottleneck of manual editing, liberate productivity and improve the profitability of companies. With the development of computer and AI technology, especially the progress of natural language processing technology, AI technology can enter the media industry. Hence, an important direction to solve the current manual operation problem for Sootoo Network is to study the deep learning algorithm that combines data and knowledge according to the characteristics of new media data, and develop an automatic content selection and push system and an automatic response system for new media platform based on the new algorithm. More importantly, new media has become a "severely afflicted area" of Internet chaos since 2018, as well as the focus of relevant departments' supervision and governance. In the previous critical reports of *Focus Interview*, six major problems in the field of new media were pointed out, namely “vulgar pornography, click-bait, rumors, gangsterdom PR, click farming and pseudo original”. As for Sootoo, then, how to maintain independence and judgment in this dilemma remains to be considered.

"Cloud Matching Promotes Trade Investment": The Breeding Road of Jutong Talent Network

Wenqi Duan, Xiaohui Dai, Wenting Ding, and Zhifang Yu

1 Introduction

Professor Duan Wenqi, as a middle-aged and young discipline leader in colleges and universities in Zhejiang Province, has been engaged in college and university education for many years, and at the same time has devoted himself to the research of platform enterprise management for a long time, and has achieved important results. Apart from academic research and teaching activities, Professor Duan often applies theory into practice, and revises theory in practice, and exchanges and studies with international students, local governments and enterprises, thus realizing a virtuous circle between theory and practice.

Since the outbreak of the COVID-19 pandemic, Professor Duan has been paying close attention to the dynamics of foreign trade enterprises. His attention has been drawn to a report on the current situation of foreign trade enterprises under the impact of the epidemic. General Manager A of a foreign trade enterprise once said that with less knowledge about overseas markets than domestic markets, he/she couldn't obtain first-hand data such as market information and economic intelligence. What's more, the high cost of transnational research makes the development of foreign trade business uncertain, and the outbreak of the COVID-19 pandemic further aggravates these problems. On the other hand, by 2020, the number of international students in China has reached nearly 500,000, according to the data of the Ministry of Education of China. And they were also affected by the COVID-19 pandemic, unable to return to school or participate in offline teaching activities normally, and wanted to do something valuable and meaningful

W. Duan (✉)
Business School, Taizhou University, Taizhou, China

X. Dai · W. Ding · Z. Yu
School of Economics and Management, Zhejiang Normal University, Jinhua, China

J. Zhang et al. (eds.), *Innovation of Digital Economy*, Management for Professionals,
https://doi.org/10.1007/978-981-99-1741-9_3

to enrich themselves, but they didn't know what to do. Professor Duan began to think about whether foreign trade enterprises can obtain target market information as soon as possible, solve the dilemma of localized talent and save transnational business costs through cooperation between enterprises and students. In practice, the international students could also exercise their own abilities, accumulate work experience and enrich their experience of studying abroad.

However, how to realize the cooperation between the two is a difficult problem, and various digital platforms emerged during the COVID-19 pandemic suddenly enlightened Professor Duan. "DingTalk" and "Tencent Classroom" have set up cloud classrooms for millions of students to keep learning outside the schools. Freshhema and other food delivery services, as well as take-out services such as Meituan and Eleme, have put up the dining table for ordinary people during the COVID-19 pandemic (Chen, 2020). Professor Duan has made up an idea in his heart. How about we can using digital technology to build a platform to realize the cloud connection between foreign trade enterprises and international students, so that the two sides can be matched and then their coordinated development can be achieved? He immediately searched for information for this idea, and found that there were few platforms for interaction and cooperation between foreign trade enterprises and international students in China. This situation strengthened his determination to build such a platform. Thus, the story of Jutong Talent Network ("Jutong" for short below) kicked off…

2 Gather Strength and Draw a Blueprint Together

Professor Duan sorted out his thoughts by the window, then went back to his desk and began to list the plans for building the platform. He began to plan to set up a team at the end of January of 2020. After thinking, some members-to-be emerged in his mind. By sharing and communicating with them, the project gathered people with specialties in computer software, enterprise operation and platform management. The initial team was composed of professors, graduate students and personnel from enterprises.

After the team was set up, he organized the first meeting for team members. During the waiting, everyone began to communicate and discuss, seeming to be very interested in this idea. During the formal meeting, Professor Duan said, "In recent years, with the slowdown of the world economic growth and the rise of the trade protectionism, and the continuous spread of the COVID-19 pandemic in the world in 2020, China's foreign trade frictions continued. The development of foreign trade enterprises has also been facing great difficulties. Though the epidemic has seriously hindered the development of foreign trade enterprises, the rapid development of digital economy and digital trade has provided a new opportunity to solve their problems. I think that based on digital technologies, we can build a bilateral service platform for international students and foreign trade enterprises to start businesses together. Foreign trade enterprises can take advantage of those international students' superiority that they are more familiar with the markets in their motherlands to carry out foreign-related business and promote overseas investment; meanwhile, international students can exercise their abilities and accumulate employment experience with the help of the resources and platforms of foreign trade enterprises. I believe that this is an interesting and meaningful exploration."

Manager Yi mentioned, "Indeed this idea does not only conform to the background of the COVID-19 pandemic, but also meet the needs of the development of the time, and can achieve multi-win results. It can not only help government departments to solve the problems of foreign trade and foreign trade enterprise supporting, but also provide new ideas for the education, training and enrollment of international students in colleges and universities, which is greatly beneficial to foreign trade enterprises and international students at home and abroad. However, we need to further analyze and explore the implementation environment to ensure the feasibility and reliability of the platform." "Yes, we need to know clearly the environment we are facing, the resources and advantages we have, and what we can do, so as to make the implementation of our platform more directional." He echoed.

Then Professor Duan added, "What you said really needs us to think about deeply. What's more, as a business ecosystem, the platform needs to consider its relationship with the external environment. As for the input of external environment to the platform: firstly, sufficient knowledge reserves for the construction and operation of the platform ecosystem has been provided by the operation and management of the platform and the improvement of cross-border e-commerce knowledge system; secondly, with the development of digital technology and Internet technology, it is more convenient to obtain market, industry and technical information. Furthermore, the servers built by the platform are continuously upgraded and optimized, and the related human resources are sufficient, which provides relatively complete material conditions for the operation of the platform. In addition, a good social and policy environment for the operation of foreign trade platforms has been provided by the government's support and attention to foreign trade enterprises. As for the output of the platform to the external environment, the platform provides new ideas for the coordinated development of foreign trade enterprises and international students, and provides targeted products and services for bilateral users. For instance, foreign trade enterprises can publish tasks on the platform to obtain international students' resources, and can obtain overseas information and market analysis reports. Most importantly, we can make use of our special skills and do some meaningful things to overcome the COVID-19 pandemic together with foreign trade enterprises and international students."

Hearing this, Xiao Liu said excitedly, "We have many advantages. Whether for platform building, foreign trade enterprises, data analysis, or platform operation, we all have professional personnel. And our school has the African Research Institute, which is a key institute cultivated by the Ministry of Education, and international students from various countries. Besides, we have social networks between universities and international students. They can all be our resources!" And Xiao Dai added, "In that case, based on the background of the COVID-19 pandemic, we can conduct a demand investigation on our foreign trade enterprise users and international student users to listen to their voices. In this way, we can develop a demand service matrix according to the user demand list, and extract the core services and derivative services of the platform. Through such an investigation, we can not only understand the users' demands, but also understand their feedback on the platform concept." Others nodded in agreement. As the discussion deepened, everyone became more determined about platform building, and the discussion continued…

3 Digital Empowerment and Bridging

3.1 Planning Investigations to Dig Deeply into User Demands

At the beginning of April 2020, according to the discussion in the previous meeting, everyone knew that if you want to define the content of the platform, you must understand the needs of core users and stakeholders. The platform is an ecosystem, and every component related to it should be taken seriously. Therefore, Professor Duan planned to carry out investigation activities for foreign trade enterprises and international students, the core service subjects of the platform, to truly understand the user demand. Xiao Dai and Xiao Liu were respectively responsible for the two investigation activities.

First of all, Manager Yi and Xiao Dai were responsible for carrying out the national foreign trade investigation on the COVID-19 pandemic prevention and overcoming difficulties in the context of the epidemic. This activity took foreign trade enterprises in hundreds of prefecture level cities nationwide as samples and postgraduate students of Zhejiang Normal University as the main body to form an investigation team. The investigation was carried out in the form of questionnaires and interviews to collect, analyze and sort out first-hand data in a timely and effective manner to understand the real business difficulties of foreign trade enterprises, Actively reflect the existing problems to the government and relevant departments, and provide relevant decision-making consulting reports to help solve the difficulties and pain points of enterprise development, use big data to help enterprises better "survive and develop", and provide diversified, personalized and professional solutions for foreign trade enterprises. Under the guidance of the expert team which includes Professor Duan, Secretary Zheng and President Sun of the university, and with the efforts of more than two hundred graduates and undergraduates, 2023 questionnaires were collected, 197 business interviews and 16 interviews with relevant government departments were carried out during the investigation of foreign trade enterprises. Through this investigation activity, the team has grasped first-hand information about the needs of foreign trade enterprises, and through communication and feedback with relevant government departments, it has supplemented the demands of foreign trade enterprises from multiple perspectives, so that the user demands were more clearly positioned.

Next, Professor Duan led the team to conduct questionnaire surveys and interviews with the international students of Zhejiang Normal University. The purpose of this investigation is to understand the trend of international students coming to China, investigate and explore the important role played by this group in stabilizing foreign trade and foreign capital in China and its motherlands, so as to help foreign trade enterprises better "survive and develop" with the help of the students. In this activity, the postgraduate students and the international students team led by Xiao Liu conducted a month-long online investigation, and nearly 456 questionnaires were collected in the end. Under the guidance of Professor Duan, they also communicated with 6 teachers of international student affairs management in Zhejiang Normal University. Through questionnaires and interviews with international students, we learned that international students are eager to enter China's foreign trade enterprises for internship and employment. And through communication with the management personnel of international students in colleges and universities, we learned about the needs of colleges and universities and updated our understanding of the needs of international students from them.

After the two investigations, Professor Duan and his team have more clearly identified the needs of core users, and further verified the practical significance of Jutong in helping foreign trade and international students' education. Then, Professor Duan emphasized that the platform is a business ecosystem composed of core users and stakeholders, and it would be biased to only understand the user demands on both sides. Therefore, he asked Xiao Dai to carefully sort out the investigation results, and the user demands related to the platform with the help of the Internet, literature and other relevant materials. See Table 1 for details.

Table 1 List of user demands related to the platform

Members demands	Foreign trade enterprises	International students in China	Relevant government departments	China's colleges and universities	Third-party service providers
Demand 1	Knowing product status, competitor dynamics and other trade information	Seeking opportunities for one to practice professional knowledge	Timely understanding of our country's foreign trade situation, monitoring the market	Improving education quality for international students in China	Seeking cooperation opportunities
Demand 2	Learning the culture, language and trade policies of the trading countries	Seeking opportunities to play one's own advantages and improve their comprehensive abilities	Knowing the status quo of foreign trade enterprises and providing timely help	Exploring new channels of teaching practice for international students	Broadening cooperation channels

(continued)

Table 1 (continued)

Members demands	Foreign trade enterprises	International students in China	Relevant government departments	China's colleges and universities	Third-party service providers
Demand 3	Finding local talent in the target market as soon as possible	Accumulating work experience in preparation for employment	Promoting Sino-foreign economic and trade cooperation and development	Enhancing the enrollment quality and scale	Opportunities for publicity and promotion
Demand 4	Seeking new thoughts on reducing the cost of international research and ensuring the quality of business	Making use of leisure time to earn certain labor expenses	Seeking multi-channel methods and ideas to manage foreign economic and trade affairs	Publicizing educational achievements of the university and enhancing its influence	Digging for resources that benefit themselves
Demand 5	Seeking for partners	Attracting investment for the motherland and promoting the cooperation between enterprises of the two countries	Promoting the coordinated development of other aspects of China while developing foreign trade	Strengthening the multi-party cooperation among the school, government and enterprises	Seeking innovation or learning operation of enterprises

It is found that foreign trade enterprises and international students do have urgent demands to be met, and the solution of the core demands of foreign trade enterprises and international students can bring positive chain reaction to the whole ecosystem through the above analysis. For example, when foreign trade enterprises solve the dilemma of lack of localized talent with the help of international students, international students also obtained the practice platform and opportunities. Universities and colleges can also solve the teaching practice problems of international students in this way, and improve the education quality of international students to a certain extent, and increase the popularity of Chinese universities and colleges. The sound development of foreign trade enterprises can reduce the concern of government departments for enterprises, and also provide new ideas for their management work. Finally, it can help third-party service providers find new cooperation opportunities and provide new thinking for their transformation or development of new cooperation channels.

3.2 Extract Demands and Design Service Architecture

At the beginning of June, the demands of relevant stakeholders on the platform were collected, and Professor Duan began to think about how to refine the core services and derivative services to design the service architecture. He mentioned that users have a "wait-and-see" attitude towards platforms due to conversion inertia and switching costs, and are reluctant to waste time and resources working on an uncertain platform. In this case, the platform provides services that can help users overcome the resistance to using the platform. Therefore, Professor Duan led the team to conduct an in-depth analysis of the list of user demands, aiming to translate the user demands into specific services of the platform. Based on the service architecture construction theory, Professor Duan led the team to construct the demand-service matrix table of Jutong, as shown in Table 2.

The results in the table show that: some services can meet the demands of foreign trade enterprises and international students; and some can only satisfy one side with demands. We define the services that solve the core pain points of bilateral users as core services, which are also the most competitive services of the platform (Duan et al. 2016). We preliminarily determine that the matching between people and enterprises is the most important service of the platform. On the one hand, foreign trade enterprises are in urgent demand of localized talent, while international students are in urgent demand of foreign trade enterprises. On the other hand, as long as bilateral matching is established, other demands can be effectively solved through bilateral negotiation and platform auxiliary services through comprehensive analysis. These auxiliary services include information recommendation, data information of foreign trade products, business partner information, hot spots and excellent case sharing.

Professor Duan then reminded us that we need to test whether the above services can meet the demands of users, that is, the matching degree between the services of Jutong and the user demands. In addition, since the demand of bilateral users changes dynamically with market environment and time, we need to timely feedback to both of them to update the information. After the inspection, Professor Duan also optimized the service architecture of Jutong from two dimensions of user demand and business model, and finally the service architecture of Jutong was basically determined.

3.3 Innovation and Design of Business Model

In September, Professor Duan began to think about how to implement the above services and build an effective business model to achieve value creation, value delivery and value capture. Analyzing cases of domestic Internet platform and combining the characteristics of Jutong and theoretical research results, Professor Duan proposed a business model for Jutong based on bilateral markets.

Table 2 Demand-service matrix of Jutong

Demands services	Foreign trade enterprises							International students						
	Enterprise promotion and publicity	News in foreign trade	Related product data	Market consultation report	Overseas missions release	Overseas talent recommendation	Cooperation intention release	Personal information confidentiality	Chinese enterprise information and enterprise recommendation	Practice opportunities	Work experience	Money subsidies	Accumulation of entrepreneurial resources	Attracting investment for one's motherland
Grasping the industry trends, paying attention to the development of foreign trade, and getting the latest information		√							√				√	
Organizing customs product database			√											
Designing templates for task release and undertaking, and constantly optimizing the accurate matching algorithm					√	√			√	√	√	√	√	
User information collection, confidentiality, enterprise authentication and other security work						√		√	√					

(continued)

Table 2 (continued)

Demands services	Foreign trade enterprises							International students						
	Enterprise promotion and publicity	News in foreign trade	Related product data	Market consultation report	Overseas missions release	Overseas talent recommendation	Cooperation intention release	Personal information confidentiality	Chinese enterprise information and enterprise recommendation	Practice opportunities	Work experience	Money subsidies	Accumulation of entrepreneurial resources	Attracting investment for one's motherland
Actively communicating with foreign trade enterprises and students to introduce users						√			√					
Experts and professors studying and formulating intelligent analysis reports				√										
Case sharing of enterprises or international students	√								√					√

(continued)

Table 2 (continued)

Demands services	Foreign trade enterprises							International students						
	Enterprise promotion and publicity	News in foreign trade	Related product data	Market consultation report	Overseas missions release	Overseas talent recommendation	Cooperation intention release	Personal information confidentiality	Chinese enterprise information and enterprise recommendation	Practice opportunities	Work experience	Money subsidies	Accumulation of entrepreneurial resources	Attracting investment for one's motherland
Training for international students and enterprise advices				√		√					√			
Human-enterprise communication and two-way evaluation mechanism					√					√	√			
Problem feedback and suggestion collection	√	√	√	√	√	√	√	√	√	√	√	√	√	√
Collating national and corporate data and developing business partner information							√		√				√	√

(1) Customer interface. Based on the different roles played by each user in the platform ecosystem, the platform customers were divided into members such as platform leaders (Jutong enterprises), platform key users (international students and foreign trade enterprises), backbone users (third-party service providers and partners, universities, personnel training institutions), and supporting users (government departments). These members created value for others while realizing their own value creation and value capture.
(2) Channels. Jutong introduced foreign trade enterprises mainly through offline research, promotional activities and China-Africa economic and trade conferences. Through network recruitment and campus recruitment, all-round coverage of various talent resources online and offline can be achieved. Under the influence of the COVID-19 pandemic and the general trend of cloud recruitment, Jutong launched the "Cloud Talent Selection" model, which aimed to break the geographical and spatial restrictions, save recruitment costs for foreign trade enterprises and achieve the goal of effective orientation. Specifically, it included "Cloud Lecture", "Cloud Mutual Selection" and "Cloud Interview".
(3) Key activities. Based on the scale of users and technical advantages, Jutong has established a complete service system. For foreign trade enterprise users, the platform first provided market analysis reports, business partner intelligence, etc. to help foreign trade enterprises gain an insight into the market situation. Second, it offered task release. Foreign trade enterprises can post overseas tasks such as market research, marketing planning, online consignment sale, and connection matching on the platform. For international student users, the platform firstly provided them with functions such as career personality test and interview training to help international students make career planning. Secondly, it provided undertaking tasks, and foreign students can choose whether to undertake tasks according to their own abilities and task types. In order to achieve accurate matching of both users and save the cost of screening and matching, the platform adopts the model of "mobile big data matching + direct recruitment". Matching international students according to the portraits required by foreign trade enterprises with them and allowing direct online communication between them, so that both sides can quickly judge the degree of job matching.
(4) Core resources. It mainly includes blockchain and big data matching technologies. The platform utilized the features of distributed storage, decentralization, tamper-proof, openness and transparency, and verifiability of the blockchain, combining with attribute-based encryption as a data access control strategy, to propose a scheme for identity information sharing and authentication. Specifically, by establishing cooperation with universities at home and abroad, the universities uploaded the real file resumes of talent to the platform and use the blockchain and strong encryption to create an authentication infrastructure that can control the complete achievement record and improve the credibility of bilateral user information. Big data matching technology helped the

platform identify the demand matching degree between international students and foreign trade enterprises, build user portraits and make accurate recommendations.

(5) Source of income. The main income came from business partner information, market analysis reports, and membership income. Other operating income included advertising income and income from vocational training for international students. The platform was still in the growing stage with meager profits.
(6) Cost structure. It included platform construction and maintenance costs, operation costs and promotion costs. In order to increase awareness, the platform has spent a lot of money to hold various marketing activities and planned to put marketing advertisements in various platforms to expand the scale of bilateral users and increase the market share
(7) Value proposition. Precisely recommending localized international talent to foreign trade enterprises in China, and vice versa, to achieve the synergistic development of enterprises and talent through the precise matching of both sides.
(8) Core partners. It already has two partners. Hangzhou Tuxiang Technology Co., Ltd. offered talent and information resources for the platform; and Hangzhou Xinzhishuo Big Data Technology Co., Ltd. offered technical support for the platform.
(9) Customer relationship. The platform has established a community for gathering international students for convenient management. Besides, it would send some policies and practice opportunities related to international students in the community, and help them find suitable enterprises for employment or internship. In order to achieve the mutual benefit of bilateral user exchanges, the platform would hold online seminars from time to time and invite foreign trade enterprises and international students to participate, so as to realize the "cloud" communication between them.

4 Begin with Steady Operating

It was March 2021 when the platform was built successfully and passed the function test. Professor Duan immediately thought about how to operate the platform and attract users to use it, so that they can verify the value of the platform and optimize its functions according to users' experience. He thought that every step of the platform building should be linked, so that they can be continuously improved during further building and use. Inspired by this, the word "user stickiness" occurred to him. By focusing on user stickiness in platform operation, users' dependence on the platform could be promoted on the one hand, and the matching degree between user demands and platform services could be measured again in the process of designing operation strategies (Pan, 2020). Based on the characteristics of users and the comparative analysis of the cost and profit of users' investment in

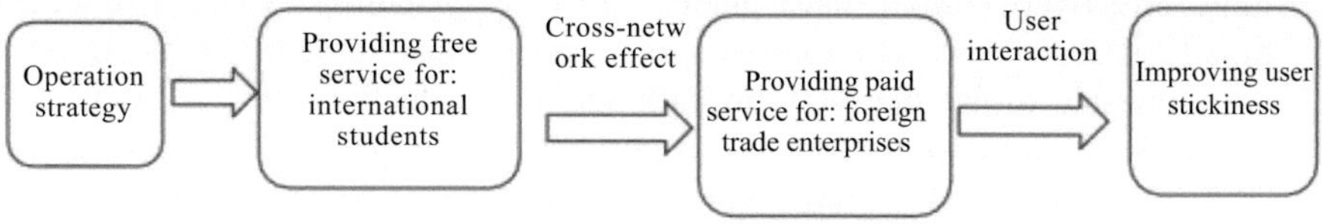

Fig. 1 Jutong's flow chart to improve user stickiness

using the platform, we provided international students with free services, so that their costs for conversion and trial and error were relatively lower than foreign trade enterprises who paid for the services. Therefore, when finishing the platform building and content design, we first introduced international students to use the platform, and followed by foreign trade enterprises. Finally, through the interaction between users of the platform, user activity and loyalty were constantly improved, so as to realize the promotion and communication of the platform among users' social networks (Li & Cao, 2020). Figure 1 is the flow chart of Jutong's process of improving user stickiness. Based on the analysis above, we implemented the platform operation strategy mainly from three aspects: content design, activity planning and user interaction.

(1) Content design. First of all, the content should meet user demands and reading habits. The users will use it only when the content we provide meet their demands, such as information that enables foreign trade enterprises to learn the latest foreign trade market trends, and that enables international students to access enterprise information and undertake tasks for practice. Next, the language and layout should conform to the user's reading habits. Based on the different language habits of enterprises and international students, we designed the language switching function between Chinese and English on the platform for their convenience. Furthermore, the content design should also be differentiated. If the content provided remains the same, users may lose interest in viewing it. Therefore, different from the traditional service platform for foreign trade or international students, Jutong is committed to the collaboration between the two groups of users and provides a new idea for foreign trade development. Finally, content design should keep pace with the times. In order to increase users' interest, the platform will not only collect relevant information for users, but also report current affairs and hot spots from time to time, or share excellent cases to help users acquire knowledge and experience.
(2) Activity planning. Regarding activity planning, Professor Duan mentioned that in order to really activate users, in addition to enabling them to access valuable information and interact effectively with the platform or other users, activities could be planned for them to get involved in the operation of the platform, including user opinion collection and feedback, user exchange meetings and investigations. In order to introduce and activate international students

more effectively, Jutong have planned an activity named "Voice of International Students", which recruited some international student volunteers who are interested to use the platform, talk about their feelings after using it, and put forward suggestions for what are dissatisfying or needed to be optimized. And we would make timely improvement according to the actual situation, and express our gratitude to those who made suggestions. In addition, we also look for international students from different countries who are interested in Jutong to record promotional videos for Jutong in their mother tongue, which play a good feedback role in the promotion and publicity towards international students.

(3) User interaction. As a bridge, the platform is committed to realizing the coordinated development of the two groups of users. Therefore, in addition to the platform's own content design and related activities, the platform has also taken measures to promote the interaction between the two groups of users. Through the positive interaction between users, the platform improved the satisfaction of users, increased the user's return rate, and increased the visibility and reputation of the platform. Specific operational strategies include: sorting out the information of foreign trade enterprises to enable international students to have a clearer understanding of foreign trade enterprises; specially designing accurate matching algorithm and matching keywords to minimize the possibility of users' reading useless information, so that they could quickly obtain the information that best matches their demands, and the accurate matching between foreign trade enterprises and international students could be realized; and establishing a community of international students to gather them, selecting and training spokespersons, so as to promote the communication between international students and users. The team improved the interaction quality by improving the effective interaction between users and provided supporting services, thus continuously enhancing the user stickiness and advancing the promotion of the platform.

5 In Full Bloom, the Future Can Be Expected

After more than one year's joint efforts, Jutong has entered a stage with steady progress with Professor Duan leading the design and planning. At present, Jutong has accumulated more than six hundred international students and a group of student spokespersons. The student group dominated by postgraduates actively participated in the investigation activities of foreign trade enterprises and international students during the COVID-19 pandemic under the guidance of various professors, applied what they learned to solve practical problems in the market, actively gave feedback on the current situation and demands of foreign trade enterprises, made suggestions for enterprises and the government, published corresponding media reports, and broadened the channels for the dissemination of new ideas of Jutong.

Jutong's idea of "non-contact foreign trade development" has also been recognized by some local governments and users.

Besides, in terms of building the platform, the service functions planned at the beginning of the platform were basically realized, and passed the internal tests of team members and the sampling tests of international students and enterprises. But in this stage, the stage management still has the problems of insufficient understanding of the feedback of the market and user demand, inadequate design of the platform and internal service mechanism, lack of user stickiness, unassured user quality, insufficient optimization and promotion of the platform, and slowed user growth. Therefore, the platform considered to solve these problems from the following aspects.

First of all, always pay attention to user demands, meet their expectations, and on this basis, carry out product or service improvement and innovation. Secondly, pay attention to the quality of both users of international students and enterprises, formulate relevant codes of conduct and guidelines to restrain the behaviors them, ensuring the quality of cooperation and reducing dishonest behaviors. Thirdly, use the tide effect and positive feedback mechanism, and adopt forms of advertising promotion or low price subsidy to attract users to join, use and actively share the platform. All in all, the platform should continuously consider the evaluation and positioning in the process of future development and make timely adjustments to itself to cope with the changing internal and external environment.

Currently, Jutong is just a beginner and has a long way to go in the future. But with the experience of platform building previously, everyone has strengthened their belief to continue to promote the development of Jutong. Although the team may encounter greater challenges and difficulties afterwards, we believe that as long as we are down-to-earth and free from arrogance and impetuosity, carry out the features and concepts of the platform ecosystem into the whole process of platform building, and always adhere to the principles of common building and sharing, and win–win cooperation, Jutong will definitely continue to bloom. We will continue to devote ourselves to the collaborative development of foreign trade enterprises and international students, assist in China's foreign trade, and shoulder the responsibilities of a "lamplighter" in exploring the road of human-enterprise collaborative development platform.

Case Appendix

Appendix 1 WeChat QR Code of the Platform

For more information about the platform and products, please scan the QR code with WeChat (see Fig. 2).

Fig. 2 QR code of Jutong WeChat official account

References

Chen, S. (2020). Research on online teaching platform tool and its application effect in epidemic period. *China Video Education, 5*, 44–52.

Duan, W. Q. & Xuan, X. (2016). *Research on dynamic modeling, competitive strategy and management method of platform ecosystem from the perspective of network*. China Social Sciences Press.

Li, S. Q., & Cao, J. (2020). *Design and management of modern E-commerce platform*. Higher Education Press.

Pan, D. (2020). *E-commerce operation management-strategy, method and management*. Posts & Telecom Press.

Crossing the Gap: Kang Nai Xin Reconstructed the Closed Loop of Its Business Model

Yongfa Li, Hengyang Kong, Yufan Hou, and Yanlin Jin

1 Introduction

At the end of November of 2021, the network-wide "Double Eleven Shopping Carnival" came to an end. The total network-wide sales were CNY965.1 billion, indicating an increase of CNY105.1 billion compared to CNY860 billion in 2020, and a year-on-year increase of 12.2%, according to the data on www.huaon.com. Tmall had 290,000 merchants participating in the event, of which 65% were small and medium-sized merchants, merchants from industrial belt and of new brands. Jiangsu Kang Nai Xin Advertising Co., Ltd. ("Kang Nai Xin" for short below), an advertising agency located in Bioscikin Innovation Community in Nanjing, was also one of them this year.

Kang Nai Xin, a media agency (that is, an advertising agency) established in 1998, has represented nearly 100 brands and cooperated with more than 30 TV stations. In 2018, it founded the wine brand "RAYEN", and then in 2020, it officially opened a C shop, which is an independent market store, on Taobao marketplace, entering the e-commerce track. Within one year, it successively opened online stores on Suning, Tmall, JD.COM and other platforms. The business model of Kang Nai Xin once built a closed extendable loop between value creation and value capture, but how to cross the gap between them at present?

Y. Li (✉) · H. Kong · Y. Hou
School of Business Administration, Anhui University of Finance and Economics, Bengbu, China

Y. Jin
Nanjing Sanshiji Culture Media Co., Ltd., Nanjing, China

J. Zhang et al. (eds.), *Innovation of Digital Economy*, Management for Professionals,
https://doi.org/10.1007/978-981-99-1741-9_4

2 Background

2.1 Background of Enterprise and Founder

With a registered capital of CNY2 million, Kang Nai Xin was founded by Ma Jiayi, who once served as the Deputy Director of Jiangsu Broadcasting Corporation and the Director of the Advertising and Information Center, a standing member of the Television Committee of China Advertising Association, the Vice President of Jiangsu Advertising Association and the Vice President of Nanjing Advertising Association. After his retirement, he set up Kang Nai Xin Advertising Co., Ltd., thus starting his road of business in his fifties. Ma Jiayi was mainly responsible for competitive publicity and advertising management when he was in the Jiangsu Broadcasting Corporation. As a retired TV practitioner, he had both professional skills and resources, and undoubtedly strong competitiveness, attracting many young people with ideals and ambitions. Kang Nai Xin has been adhering to the concept of "Faith, Knowledge, Diligence and Truth-seeking", serving customers wholeheartedly and thus making remarkable achievements since its establishment in 1998. The annual sales of Kang Nai Xin keeps climbing to new heights. It has gradually established stable strategic cooperative relations with many powerful media, and its cooperative customers cover many mainstream industry fields such as daily chemicals, food, medicine and wine industries. It has grown from a single media purchasing company to a comprehensive media group, with media strategy and purchasing as its core, comprehensively carrying out various businesses such as case agency, media strategy, media purchasing, market monitoring and evaluation, and crisis PR service. Kang Nai Xin began to explore the secondary industry in 2015, and successively tried to step into industries such as jewelry, wine and Chinese spirits (as shown in Fig. 1).

Fig. 1 Maj or events of Kang Nai Xin

2.2 Industry and Market Background

Various provincial TV stations started their satellite channels in the 1990s. At that time, TV content was unitary and information was blocked. People were eager to know the wonderful outside world. In this regard, the satellite channels broadened people's horizons, and were well received by them. Simultaneously, they stimulated the development of the whole TV industry chain.

After Deng Xiaoping's speech on his southern tour in 1992, the advertising demands of various enterprises increased greatly, which triggered the great increase of the advertising scale of the media. By the end of the 1990s, the annual advertising revenue of TV and newspapers reached CNY10 billion. The media companies started to explore more diversified business models besides advertising, triggering the tide of industrialization. TV stations at all levels began to exert their strength. Thus, the number of programs and channels increased rapidly. Cable network and satellite, as the two new transmission modes, officially stepped onto the historical stage, and the coverage and influence of TV are getting bigger, which makes the advertising effect amazing and the advertising revenue increase rapidly. The television advertising revenue in China reached CNY1 billion in 1991, surpassing that of newspaper advertising for the first time, and exceeded CNY10 billion in 1997, reaching CNY11.44 billion. TV advertising resources were extremely scarce during this period. In 1994, CCTV first launched a prime-time advertising bidding, which was well received by advertisers, such as Kong Fu Yan, Qin Chi and other Chinese spirits production enterprises. The advertising revenue through broadcasting exceeded CNY1 billion in 1997. The advertising revenue through newspapers also exceeded CNY10 billion in 1998. Some evening newspapers and metropolis newspapers rose, such as West China City Daily and Xinmin Evening News, and they became popular newspapers. The media advertising business has formed a scale during this period, and advertising has gradually become the main source of media's revenue.

At the beginning of the twenty-first century, the development of digital technology further promoted the transition from analog to digits in radio and television, and promoted the newspaper industry to enter the digital transformation in an all-round way. With the popularization of the Internet, a brand-new media form, the functions that media can provide were becoming more and more diverse. In the second decade of the twenty-first century, media technologies began to develop in the direction of intelligence and integration. New formats such as OTT, cloud services and cross-screen interaction appeared. Big data and artificial intelligence (AI) began to widely affect all aspects of the media, subverting the old media form, content production mode and media business mode.

3 Good Start and Excellent Development

Kang Nai Xin was positioned as a full case company at the beginning of its establishment. The so-called full case company referred to the whole process from planning to launching and to making plans, and finally making the image of enterprises appear on TV. When an enterprise owner has demand, Kang Nai Xin will first do market surveys on consumer groups and TV programs or advertising time, with the purpose of clearly informing it of the best sales channels, consumer groups and the coincidence between channels and groups. Then, based on the analysis of the survey results, it will design the plan and deliver it to the enterprise owner. If the plan meets the needs of and is recognized by the enterprise owner, the image of the enterprise will be further presented on TV.

At that time, as TV stations were mostly charged by local publicity departments, advertising resources were relatively monopolized. Enterprises could not put advertisements without certain channels or connections, and they needed advertising agencies with channels to build the connection. On the other hand, all major TV stations started to find their own sections and develop into subdivided fields, such as Hunan Satellite TV, which takes entertainment, youth and whole country" as its positioning, and Anhui TV, which features "TV series go global". Therefore, to match the positioning of enterprise products with TV channel programs has become a skilled task, which requires certain professionalism. Whether an advertising agency has good channel and whether it's professional is the basis for judging its competitiveness.

Ma Jiayi has received professional training in the media field, with abundant professional knowledge and resources, which are conditions that some other companies do not have. He also stressed that details determine success or failure, and his strict control of details brought the rapid growth of a group of salespeople in Kang Nai Xin. With professional people doing professional work, he has brought Kang Nai Xin to the forefront of the industry in a short time.

The development of Kang Nai Xin is accompanied by the development of the TV advertising industry. Competition for TV advertising peaked between 2010 and 2012, when bidding replaced quotation and became the mainstream form of advertising recruitment. In 2010, Jiangsu Satellite TV released a new novel and wonderful dating show named *You Are the One*, which has gained great attention since its stunning appearance, and won a good reputation while creating a new high in ratings. Therefore, advertising positions of the program has become a hot spot in the eyes of many enterprises. The top bidder[1] was a customer of Kang Nai Xin with a price of more than CNY15 million for one quarter. This helped Kang Nai Xin gain fame in a short period. But as Kang Nai Xin reached its prime, the crisis had quietly approached.

[1] It refers to the bidder with the highest price. At that time, the top bidder of the advertisement bidding could have its advertisement play first.

4 Crisis

After 2014, although the number of advertising customers has not decreased, the budget for TV advertising has declined. In the same year, China shipped nearly 450 million smartphones, and the number of netizens in China reached 632 million. According to the report of iiMedia in the same period, China's online advertising revenue exceeded 150 billion in 2014, indicating a year-on-year increase of 40%. With the popularity of smartphones, We Media such as Weibo and WeChat official account have occupied users' time and obviously attracted audiences from TV stations. With the TV audiences left continuously, the TV stations lost the advantages of advertising. However, the advertising price of TV stations remained very high. Therefore, high price and few users drove advertisers to throw their budgets at new media advertisements.

The rise of the Internet caused a decline in the market share of the traditional media. Although Kang Nai Xin has a large number of customers, it didn't escape the division of customers by the Internet. Since traditional media is divided up, why didn't it switch to new media? However, this is not easy for Kang Nai Xin.

As a new industry, the operation of the Internet is different from traditional media. Although traditional media is no stranger to the Internet, it is different from the new media in operation techniques. Failure to keep up with the trend of the times, that is, to catch up with the Internet platform, led to the loss of some customers of Kang Nai Xin. Some enterprises once intended to advertise on new media platforms through Kang Nai Xin, but the lack of talent in this field has become a inescapable problem for Kang Nai Xin. Both traditional media and new media need a large-scale professional team to provide technical support. At this time, with more of its talent being good at the operation and service of traditional media, Kang Nai Xin had limited talent and energy to operate new media.

Facing the weakness in new media and the loss in traditional media, Kang Nai Xin walked into a dilemma.

5 Exploration of a Secondary Industry

5.1 Exploration in High-End Jewelry Customization

Facing the challenges from new media, Kang Nai Xin has not continued to transform in the advertising industry. Ma Jiayi thought that advertising is much too prone to the environment and it is not as stable as the traditional entity industry. Kang Nai Xin's customers were advertisers, who were literally the Party As. Most of them belonged to entity economy, which was more stable than the virtual economy. Seeing the advantages of the entity industry, and based on customers with relatively high spending power accumulated in recent years, Kang Nai Xin intended to make money by its own resources. In 2015, Kang Nai Xin started its first attempt in the entity economy.

Considering that its customer base is relatively high-end and jewelry as a luxury has a high profit margin, Kang Nai Xin focused on the jewelry industry at first. The regularized design and product packaging of ordinary brand jewelry have become increasingly mature, and the style is fixed and conservative and cannot reflect individuality. Kang Nai Xin realized that with people's higher material and spiritual demands, people need to find jewelry suitable for themselves, and that's why Kang Nai Xin Fine Jewelry Customization Center "Meihou" came into being.

Although it has rich experience in operating advertising agencies, the real industry is different from advertising after all. Kang Nai Xin's first attempt has seen problems in personnel, sales and management. In addition, as the accumulated foundation of advertising business at that time still had a much higher revenue than the jewelry business, its focus was still mainly placed on the traditional business. Therefore, Kang Nai Xin did not keep on trying, but decisively chose to close up shops. It began to summarize experience while focusing on traditional business, and pay close attention to market information and look for new opportunities.

5.2 Aiming at Wine

After the failure of "Meihou", Kang Nai Xin has realized that it should get fully prepared before making any decision, and should base itself on lots of investigations and market analysis to make clear the key information, such as cost, investment and output ratio.

With the rapid development of China's economy, the resident consumption has been upgraded and the purchasing power has been significantly enhanced. In 2017, Kang Nai Xin noticed that, in terms of diet consumption, more and more consumers began to learn about the importance of health and alcohol consumption was turned to light and nutritious alcoholic drink. As a product in line with this trend, wine would inevitably achieve the a development. In terms of wine, Kang Nai Xin has conducted comprehensive study, learning that most customers believe that there is no good or bad wine apart from the price. Most consumers didn't know what a winery is and what a distillery is. Most of them even didn't know which country and which winery produced the most delicious wine.

In 2018, with the rise of short videos, the new media industry continued to bring a new wave of impact to the advertising industry, causing a sharp decline of TV advertising volume. Therefore, Kang Nai Xin had to find a new economic support point and develop new businesses. Kang Nai Xin attended the Food & Drinks Fair in 2018, and met many foreign friends, getting a brief introduction to some common sense about wine. In June 2018, in order to further investigate the prospects of wine industry, Ma Jiayi led the team with wine specialists to Spanish and Hessian of Germany, carrying out field survey in five wineries including Freixenet and Diehl Blees. In addition, Ma Jiayi put forward the principle of "quality, specialty and scale".

In November 2019, Ma Jiayi came to the second China International Import Expo to find a breakthrough point, and he obtained a clear understanding that the alcoholic beverage industry has a large sales volume, and wine, as a fast moving consuming good, has a good market prospect in China. Besides, considering that the General Manager of the Product Department had professional knowledge in brewing, Kang Nai Xin decided to further explore the wine business.

5.3 Synchronous Operation Offline and Online

After the comparative study on the whole alcohol market, it was found that offline channels were limited, and many businesses have occupied most of the domestic market, therefore, Kang Nai Xin considered operating online and offline at the same time. In order to expand online channels, Kang Nai Xin has registered a brand for its wine—RAYEN, with a brand value of "Let RAYEN take you to enjoy good wine", that is, it is necessary to walk into the hearts of customers to break the cognition already overflowing in their hearts, and it is hoped that its product could arouse the resonance among customers after tasting, thus improving customer stickiness.

After determining the new sales model, the offline channel was guaranteed by high-quality products and professionalism, and with the special wine culture of Kang Nai Xin, the cooperation with distributors was growing steadily. Considering that this was a brand new practice, Kang Nai Xin has set up a young online operation team and a New Retail Department. In order to empower the new department, a group of young talent was transferred to the New Retail Department by Kang Nai Xin.

In July 2018, Kang Nai Xin reached a cooperation intention with Suning.com. As a dealership, Kang Nai Xin supplied goods to Suning.com, who was responsible for the subsequent operations. In 2019, Kang Nai Xin officially started the self-operated path of e-commerce of alcoholic products.

5.3.1 From Taobao C Shop to Worldwide Store

In October 2019, Kang Nai Xin registered a C shop on Taobao. Only after getting a real understanding of Taobao shop, Kang Nai Xin found that e-commerce was more about "selling pictures", which was in essence decorating[2] the online shop, including shop signs, main pictures and details pictures. Beautiful and appropriate online shop decoration can bring aesthetic feelings to customers, increasing the staying time of buyers in online shops to improve page views. In order to better operate the online shop and learn the marketing concept, Li Rui, the head of the New Retail Department, signed up for relevant courses and learned the relevant

[2] The essence of online store decoration is web page design, which is the design and layout of online store pages through computers. Online shop decoration belongs to the category of visual marketing, making the shop look rich in content and beautiful through the reasonable use of colors, layout, images and characters. It aims to bring more real visual impact to consumers, so as to attract the attention of potential consumers and stimulate their desire to buy, thus achieving the effect of winning the market.

knowledge of wine from professionals. Li Rui said, "I didn't want to miss any customer who might make a deal with us when starting operation. And we have tried our best to meet their requirements, even when we encountered cautious customers who want to taste wine first." Negative reviews not only affected the favorite rate, but also affected the conversion rate, score, reputation, search ranking and advertising, thus affecting the sales volume. Therefore, during the opening stage, Kang Nai Xin needed to accumulate a lot of favorable reviews with product pictures to increase online store reputation.

With a store, the next step is to promote the product and attract customers. Relying on years of experience and resources as an advertising agency, which were made advantages of in the e-commerce operation, RAYEN entered the live broadcasting room of a famous star named Hu Haiquan and was sold as an emerging wine merchant in the column "The Real One".[3] With the celebrity effect and the intuitive nature of the live broadcast, Da Yan got a breakthrough in the sales of a wine called "Kabukatuo", accumulating a lot of favorable reviews and buyer shows, which also brought a number of potential customers to the brand. And the link of this wine slowly grew up.

Taobao C shops form a network retailer circle, which is a C2C personal online trading platform. With the advantages of small cost and easy operation, it is very suitable for newcomers. But the problem is that good and bad merchants are mixed up, the traffic is insufficient with low conversion rate. To achieve greater traffic, RAYEN must enter the high-end circle.

Taobao Global Shopping is Taobao's first discount website for fine products from abroad and Hong Kong, Macau and Taiwan of China, which gathers numerous Taobao merchants to truly meet the needs of members "to buy global fine products without leaving home". Only products that are purchased in Hong Kong, Macau, Taiwan of China and abroad can be applied for listing in Global Shopping. Since all of RAYEN's wines were imported and have quarantine certificates with complete procedures and qualifications, the operation team upgraded the store into a Global Shopping store after six months.

5.3.2 Settle in Tmall

Tmall, a comprehensive shopping site that sells well-known offline brands, is a B2C online trading platform. For a brand that wants greater traffic, Tmall is definitely a better choice.

On April 19, 2021, RAYEN met a new opportunity when Tmall lowered the threshold for opening a store and would pilot the "Tmall trial operation period" for the first time. Merchants applying for Tmall stores will have their qualifications simplified, and will become official Tmall stores after passing a seven-month

[3] "The Real One" is a star reality show. The program uses the concept of "the friend circle of stars" to invite the host's friends to participate in a private wine club. In the atmosphere set off by games and wine, the stars would tell unknown stories and show their actual selves.

trial operation capability test. Simplifying the written qualification audit, and taking the actual operation capability of merchants as a standard for them to open Tmall stores lower the threshold for merchants to open stores. After Kang Nai Xin submitted its company and brand qualifications as well as media resources and passed the audit, its Tmall store "RAYEN Wines Flagship Store" officially started its operation.

As stores in Tmall are brand stores, compared to Taobao, the customers are more high-end, the competition between merchants is more intense, and the customer needs are more diversified. Consumers shopping for a product in one store may purchase another product along with it. In order to drive sales of other products, RAYEN's operation team chose to open up the market by presenting main promoting wines on the details pages of hot-sale wines and giving away samples. Using sample gifts to empower sales can both increase the added value of the main products and the possibility of customer orders, and attract traffic and new customers for other products.

Kang Nai Xin once received such a real feedback from customers: when I got home from work I was physically and mentally exhausted and didn't want to cook, then I opened a bottle of "Moscato", and instantly found the feeling of being in love. Such a case made Kang Nai Xin realize that the operation of Tmall requires high requirements for copywriting, shaping of consumption scenarios, and construction of the customer group and profile. If a brand does not have any romance tone or story, there is no way to attract people or to move people, and consumers will not be interested, and then will not be willing to buy.

In addition to the requirements of copywriting and positioning, the team's ability to present also faced a great challenge. For an online store, whether it can attract consumers to click on the product link depends on whether the main picture or video is attractive enough. At first, Kang Nai Xin didn't have a professional shooting team, let alone a scriptwriter, so they had to explore slowly.

However, with the explosive development of live broadcast on short video platforms such as Tiktok and Kwai, a lot of Tmall customers were divided up, and Kang Nai Xin could not escape the impact and had no choice but to find another platform.

5.3.3 Move to JD.COM

Kang Nai Xin also had cooperation with some private domain platforms. A purchasing director from TuNiu suggested Kang Nai Xin to focus on JD.COM, which coincided with Ma Jiayi's strategic layout. According to statistics, the beverage sold on JD.COM accounts for more than 50% of China's entire online beverage sales,[4] making it the largest beverage retail platform in China. In 2021, the cumulative sales volume of Chinese spirits on JD.COM in the 618 Shopping Festival exceeded 5 million bottles. The major brands that have been maintaining a close relationship with JD.COM have not only collaborated more closely with it

[4] https://data.iimedia.cn/page-category.jsp?nodeid=44276767.

in terms of big data analysis and channel expansion, but also cooperated with it deeply in areas such as comprehensively deepening and customized product in the 618 Shopping Festival. Deepening the C2M reverse customization also achieved excellent results, with the cumulative sales of beer exceeding 300,000 cases, 20 times that of the same period in 2020; and more than 1 million bottles of exclusive customized wine products were sold at the same time. JD.COM has become the No.1 e-commerce platform for selling wines.

Considering that at the beginning of operating the Taobao C shop, the traffic was insufficient due to the inferior store qualifications, the operation team of the New Retail Department intended to supply the products directly to the beverage department of JD.COM and open its own self-operation store. JD's self-operation is to sell JD.COM's own products on the platform, the store owners, customer service personnel, logistics and warehouses are all arranged by JD.COM. And the suppliers of goods are invited by JD.COM, or they can apply to be suppliers by themselves. The products of JD's self-operation may come directly from the brand manufacturers or the dealers. Therefore, it is actually not like ordinary e-commerce business, but more like supplying products to offline supermarkets. Because JD.COM is a brand itself and has its own brand influence, settle in JD's self-operation made it more easily to obtain consumer recognition. At the same time, the sales of the products will be operated by the team of JD.COM without paying high operation and management fees. In addition, one can also exempt from the usage fee of the platform and participate in its activities for free, which will help improve the exposure rate of the store and gain more traffic.

However, the application for JD's self-operation is not a smooth sailing. Stores of JD's self-operation, regardless of traffic or operation, is on a ceiling level in the JD platform, with only more than 50 stores across the country, so the competition is quite fierce. Due to the lack of awareness of the brand and the operation team, RAYEN's first application was rejected. However, the more frustrated RAYEN was, the braver it was. After adjusting its strategies, it integrated off-site resources and major TV stations' promotion resources and presented the follow-up marketing plans to the direct purchasing department of JD's self-operation. Finally, Kang Nai Xin gained access to the JD's self-operation. On August 21, 2021, RAYEN officially started to operate in JD.COM and its products entered the warehouses.

5.4 Marketing Upgrade

At present, RAYEN has been stationed in the four major integrated e-commerce platforms in China, and the reputation and favorable rate are both satisfactory. However, being on a platform does not mean that you can definitely obtain good sales. As a brand that delayed in entering the market, how did RAYEN find its market? Online, there are JD.COM and Tmall stores, and offline, there are group buying and distribution. In order to distinguish different scenarios and positioning,

RAYEN's operation team made a careful distinction between wines. For different scenarios and needs, it found products in diversified production areas, and introduced them into China after finding products with cost performance.

In the autumn of 2021, RAYEN launched its non-alcoholic series, including non-alcoholic dry red wine, sparkling wine, dry white wine and even grape juice. Non-alcoholic wine is a perfect combination of the mellow flavor of dry red and the tasty and refreshing nature of sweet wine, which not only retains the nutrients in the grapes, but also has a more memorable taste. Alcohol-free wine is made from wild and artificially cultivated amur grapes or hybrid grapes, and goes through special processes such as fermentation, cellaring, aging and impurity removal. The alcohol content does not exceed 1%, and the 8 amino acids and resveratrol contained in it are several times higher than those in ordinary wines, which have extremely high nutritional and healthy effects. It's not the wine in the traditional sense, but it's great for scenarios where you have to drink but still need to drive, or for consumers who are afraid of forgetting themselves after drinking. For consumers, once they get used to this targeted scenario-based segmentation, they will become loyal customers of RAYEN.

Kang Nai Xin, which comes from a media background, is well aware of the importance of cultural heritage for an industry, and its culture runs through the whole process of the brand building for RAYEN, both online and offline. Chinese wine culture is very weak compared to other countries, as it has history but no culture. The marketing of it is in the primary stage, i.e., the stage of learning and accepting the wine culture of European and American countris. Most consumers know about wine through advertisements in films and TV shows and the Internet. However, there is still a lack of in-depth wine culture education. As a result, most consumers are still in the stage of "drinking indiscriminately". "Without culture, wine is just a kind of expensive drink". Seizing the pain point of the lack of wine culture in the Chinese market, RAYEN was also committed to making more people aware of the wine culture while selling its products.

In the current environment of new retail, online channels were indispensable for RAYEN. RAYEN had a high goal for its positioning and future development. In this case, Kang Nai Xin invested a lot of money to acquire hardware and software. For example, in order to cater to online sales and live broadcast for goods, it established its own live broadcasting room and configured specialized equipment, relying on which 4 to 5 scenes of the live broadcast can be done at the same time, and hired professional planners and software engineers.

6 Crossing the Gap

Kang Nai Xin started in the advertising media industry, and its business model achieved a virtuous circle of value creation and value capture. However, changes in the external environment forced it to explore the second growth curve. From Suning to Taobao C shop, and then to Tmall and JD.COM, RAYEN, a brand of imported wines, has been continuing to expand its influence, with its sales volume rising steadily, and online marketing publicity improving. As far as Kang Nai Xin is concerned, due to the resources and experience accumulated by its primary industry, the promotion of its secondary industry could be smooth and handy. For the platform resources of Tmall and JD.COM, Kang Nai Xin naturally made the best use of everything. But for off-site product promotion, including but not limited to Tiktok, Xiaohongshu and even micro-videos, although the elements were different in those platforms, the new media elements were all connected subtly with the traditional media that Kang Nai Xin is good at. Therefore, the secondary industry of Kang Nai Xin has made remarkable achievements in just four years.

Up to now, Kang Nai Xin has officially become a commercial group integrating media and e-commerce. The media agency projects of Kang Nai Xin covered media strategy, media planning, media purchase, market research, brand management, crisis public relations and other fields. After the Internet and the wine industry were established, its traditional media industry and the wine industry formed a complementary relationship. The wine industry could develop with the help of traditional media, which can in turn be an entity support and backup force. The traditional media and wine industry of Kang Nai Xin are now in a development trend. The two businesses belong to two operation systems, and more detailed planning will be carried out in the future.

On March 14, 2021, Kang Nai Xin and Shanghai Guijiu Co., Ltd. held a signing ceremony for strategic cooperation in Ziwei Hall, Zixi Building, Nanjing Dongjiao State Guesthouse, officially entering the Chinese spirits market. On September 30, 2021, Kang Nai Xin held a video conference with the Terramagna Group of Spain. The two parties conducted in-depth research and exchanges of the current market environment, product production, sales platform, market promotion and other issues. From advertising to jewelry, and to wine, and then to Chinese spirits, is it possible for Kang Nai Xin to reconstruct a stable, scalable and self-reinforcing business model closed-loop for value creation and value capture?

Reference

IIMEDIA. (2020). Development status and retail data of new retail market for liquor products in China. IIMEDIA Think Tank. https://data.iimedia.cn/page-category.jsp?nodeid=44276767.

Codoon: The Gamification Experience as the Cornerstone of Consumer Loyalty

Yawen He, Huiqin Zhang, and Yu Wang

1 Introduction

At 6:30 am on November 14, 2021, a Sunday, in a residential area in Chengdu, Zhou Jingwei, who worked at a bank, turned off the alarm clock on his mobile phone, got up to wash up, changed into his sportswear, and got prepared to participate in the long-awaited "Double Gold Competition" (IAAF Gold Label Road Race Events, CAA Gold Label Road Race)—Chongqing Marathon 2021. At 7:30 am, he came to the park where he carried out routine exercise, opened the Codoon APP in white and green placed on the homepage, connected sports headphones, and opened his electronic race bag. Then he joined a wonderful online marathon together with 261,042 contestants from all over the world and heard the host's energetic and passionate cheering. The offline Chongqing Marathon 2021 has been postponed for many times due to the COVID-19 pandemic. On December 7 (Beijing Time), it is announced finally to cancel the competition. Due to impacts of the COVID-19 pandemic, on March 31, 2020, with the issuance of the *Notice of General Administration of Sports of China on Temporarily Not Resuming Marathon and Other Sports Events* to reduce the risks brought by the flow and gathering of people for pandemic prevention and control, it was uncertain whether to resume crowd gathering activities such as marathon, and road running industry may encounter a recession. As a popular "Internet+ sports" brand, Codoon led the industry to create the online marathon activity as early as in 2014. As the COVID-19 pandemic persists, more road race lovers choose to participate in online events with unlimited time, space and distance. Some marathon events are also held online. In 2021, a total of 284 events (online + offline) were held by Codoon, with a total of 41,792,537 participants. The total distance of running in the whole year reached

Y. He (✉) · H. Zhang · Y. Wang
College of Management Science, Chengdu University of Technology, Chengdu, China

J. Zhang et al. (eds.), *Innovation of Digital Economy*, Management for Professionals,
https://doi.org/10.1007/978-981-99-1741-9_5

748,443,665 km, which could circle the earth 58,674 times. In this far-reaching crisis unseen in a century due to the COVID-19 pandemic, huge opportunities presented a frenzy of virtual marathon events.

On the day when Chongqing Marathon was announced to be cancelled, a meeting for investors was in full swing and order in the meeting room of the headquarters of Codoon in Chengdu. Ma Wei, the head of Codoon Events Division, is professionally and enthusiastically introducing the vigorous development of online sports event with big data information after the COVID-19 pandemic to investors. As the first sports social software in China, Codoon possesses more than 200 million users, meeting tens of millions of sports demands from 210 countries and regions around the world every day, holding more than 1,000 online and offline events, with more than 300,000 sports groups all over the country. In December 2021, Codoon completed a new round of strategic financing, gathering overall USD20 million. It is reported that this round of financing was led by Solomon JFZ (Asia) Holdings Limited, and Codoon would start a round D financing, with a planned amount of USD520 million. Previously, Codoon has completed six rounds of financing, with a cumulative amount exceeding USD120 million (Sports Social Platform "Codoon" Completed Strategic Financing …, 2021).

Looking at his team members introducing business information in an orderly manner, Shen Bo, the founder and CEO of Codoon, couldn't help recalling some important fragments of the past 12 years' development from 2010 to 2021. As time went by, in the first year of Codoon, the first generation of fitness tracker was released; in 2012, the Codoon Sports APP was released; in 2014, the first online marathon was held by Codoon; in 2015, a sport social platform was created; in 2018, Codoon turned to fitness courses; and in 2019, Codoon began its running coach service. After piecing together these important business decisions, a complete development process of Codoon is clearly presented in front of us, from "hardcore ability" to "soft power", from an efficient and practical "tool" to "experience" bearing feeling value, from product quality to user experience first. Codoon's emphasis on user experience may explain why the company can enhance diverse values of products, stickiness and loyalty of users, and ensure innovation development in the field of sports APP.

2 Development and Current Situation of the Company

2.1 Development Process of Codoon

Chengdu Codoon Information Technology Co., Ltd. was established in 2010, and the brand of Codoon came out. Sports tracking service has been provided since the online sports exploration period of the company. The company advocates that technologies should be people-oriented, and has obtained more than 20 patents at present. Since its establishment, Codoon has been tirelessly pursuing innovation in technology, products and services, and providing users with simple, fast and reliable Internet pan-sports services through powerful sports data, AI and other technical approaches.

(1) Initial exploration stage with product-centered philosophy from 2009 to 2012

Key words at this stage are starting with hardware, leading technology and software exploration.

At the end of 2009, the concept of "wearable devices" was rarely heard at home and abroad, while Codoon was one of the earliest Internet companies involved in such devices in China. As there were only a few early entrants of the same kind, Codoon, as a rare target, won tens of millions of CNY from the angel wheel of Shanda Group in early 2011. Since then, Codoon began to focus on hardware, invested a lot in research and development, obtained a number of patents, and won the title of "Dark Horse Enterprise" in that year. In 2012, the hardware product line of Codoon was improved one after another, and the "Codoon Sports+" APP was officially released and launched. Codoon began to transform and moved towards the road of "software + hardware".

(2) Exploration and development stage of user demand orientation from 2013 to 2016

Key words at this stage are user demand, sports social interact, user experience.

In 2014, "Codoon Sports+" was officially renamed "Codoon"; "Codoon ROM" was released and further improvement was achieved on open source hardware and platform operation, entering a new era of "sports social + open source hardware"; then, the concept of "online marathon" was firstly launched, and cooperation was conducted with the sponsor of Beijing Marathon—Adidas to launch the first online marathon; In 2015, Codoon successfully held more than 30 online marathons, becoming the world's largest provider for online marathons and online cycling services, and developed offline or online events of its self-owned IP successively such as Running Girl, Entrepreneurship Race, City Micro Marathon, Marathon Season and City Leading Runner. In 2016, Codoon entered the era featured by "national sports ecosystem", which consisted of sports data collection and management mode, and combined video live broadcast, graphic interaction and information transmission to create a high-value sports social content platform. Codoon has had more cross-border cooperation with partners of all parties, opened the interface of sports data platform, and continuously improved the solutions such as mobile payment and intelligent hardware access. Through all-round services of activities like online marathon, bicycle race and self-owned IP events, the sports users' experience will be continuously improved. This has forged a key node for the later construction of the ecosystem of the Codoon Sports, and also laid a data foundation for the follow-up stage of high-speed development.

(3) Rapid development stage with technology empowerment from 2017 to 2019

The rapid development of Codoon at this stage was based on the empowerment of new technologies relying on users' big data.

At the beginning of 2017, Codoon announced its intelligent sports strategy. Specifically, it increased its investment in new technologies such as AI, and laid out new retail offline, and built a consumer brand. From "Exercise with Codoon" to "All the intelligent exercises are in Codoon", Codoon combined sports equipment and training courses with AI technology, and launched out a series of products such as Codoon intelligent running shoes that can guide in real time the users to exercise scientifically through AI technology, thus reducing injuries and maintaining safer and more efficient exercise for users. What's more, based on the V-COACH virtual coaching service pioneered by Codoon and the live broadcast course of CODOONLIVE, online real-life private education has been realized. In 2018, Codoon has built a new platform of "data + service", and has created a virtual AI coach and improved the sports business ecosystem through independent research and development of implanted intelligent engines and chips, and collected dozens of industry-leading sports data dimensions and rich sources with the rapid growth of intelligent interactive technology and efficient application of multi-dimensional big data and humanized adjustment of training courses, as well as the all-round coverage of the mobile Internet, taking sports big data as a solid foundation at the same time. In 2019, Codoon subverted tradition and broke down industry barriers. Through big data of sports of over 100 million people and AI technology, it made sports "countable and checkable" (see Table 1).

(4) Stage of turning crisis into "opportunity" under the influence of COVID-19 from 2020 to now

In this stage, Codoon can be described as dancing gorgeous waltz on the edge of a cliff called "COVID-19 pandemic". In 2020, as the spread of the COVID-19 pandemic in China, Codoon has searched for opportunities in the crisis as an enterprise with a strong sense of social responsibility for ten years, and made full use of the advantages of the Internet platform, actively responded to national policies and calls, and quickly opened up and improved the product functions of home sports, created rich courses suitable for home sports training, such as live broadcasts and videos, actively developed fitness equipment suitable for home sports, and helped hundreds of millions of users to enhance their immunity, improved their physical fitness, jointly resisting the epidemic through sports. Owing to the efforts of such a series of anti-pandemic measures, Codoon has won many prizes such as the "Most Worthy of Investment Value Award in 2020" of the 9th China Finance Summit, the "Sichuan Sports Industry Demonstration Unit in 2020", and the title of "2020 Unicorn Enterprise Brand to be of Cover News".

Affected by the COVID-19 pandemic, marathon and other crowd gathering activities could not be held regularly in order to reduce the risk in pandemic prevention and control caused by the flow and gathering of people. At present, marathon events in China have basically stopped, and consumption driven by marathon has almost stagnated. As the leading brand of "Internet+ Sports", in

Table 1 Development process of Codoon

Year	Milestone
2010	Chengdu Codoon Information Technology Co., Ltd. was formally established. The Codoon brand was born, and fitness tracker products and Codoon network platform were launched
2011	Codoon won the first favor of investors with grand angel investment of CNY22 million from Shanda, and successfully applied for more than 20 national hardware patents. Its high-quality products were exported overseas
2012	The hardware product line of Codoon has been gradually improved. The "Codoon Sports+" APP has been officially released, which means it embarks on the road of "software + hardware"
2013	The first smart wearable sports devices in China, "Codoon Bracelet S" and "Codoon Bracelet 2", were officially released
2014	The "Codoon Sports" was officially renamed as "Codoon"; "Codoon ROM" was released and further improvement was achieved on open source hardware and platform operation, entering a new era of "sports social + open source hardware"; then, the concept of "online marathon" was firstly launched, and cooperation was conducted with the sponsor of Beijing Marathon—Adidas to launch the first online marathon
2015	Codoon published the *White Paper on Running in China in 2014*, and built a social platform for national sports, put forward the concept of "Running together at Codoon", and successfully held more than 30 online marathons
2016	Codoon's overseas version was officially renamed Runtopia, with more than 1 million users; it pioneered the "Sports Carnival" in the vertical subdivision of Internet sports, and the sales volume obtained explosive growth; there are hundreds of thousands of Codoon "sports groups", covering more than tens of millions of sports population. Nearly 100 thousand offline activities have been launched; and it has created a sports ecological platform/tool specially for the enterprise-level market—"Enterprise Codoon"
2017	The number of Codoon's users exceeded 90 million Codoon released the intelligent sports strategy, increased investment in new technologies like AI, laid out new retail offline, and built a consumer brand, upgrading the slogan from "Exercise with Codoon" to "All the intelligent exercises are in Codoon". It combined sports equipment and training courses with AI technology, and then developed and launched the Codoon series products
2018	The number of Codoon's users has exceeded 150 million; combining sports equipments and training courses with AI technology, Codoon has developed and launched more intelligent series products and Codon V-coach; it upgraded the strategy with "Fitness 3.0, Alive", officially stepped into the fitness field, and launched the first intelligent live broadcast course CODOONLIVE in China to realize online huamn private education
2019	The number of Codoon's users has exceeded 180 million; Codoon App has introduced the online running coach and added the function of running guidance to let the users clearly understand the status of their each running; Sports Watch X3 and Running Elf, two new sports hardware, were released, which can greatly improve the efficiency of greenway operation and commercial greenway intelligent sports system

(continued)

Table 1 (continued)

Year	Milestone
2020	Codoon's first live broadcast competition in voice has attracted 10,000 people to sign up. Facing the growing demand for sports and fitness in the post-pandemic era, Codoon promoted the model innovation of online marathon into model 2.0 and created a healthier and more perfect online sports experience for its users
2021	The "New Journey Red Marathon Series" launched by sports.news.cn along with Codoon was officially launched; Codoon introduced the FITMORE intelligent fitness mirror and officially entered the track of family fitness

the face of the growing demand for sports and fitness in the post-pandemic era, Codoon focuses on promoting the model innovation of online marathon 2.0, making online events more and more similar to offline marathon in terms of experience and competition, driving the phenomenal trend of virtual online events, and creating a healthier and more perfect online sports experience for users. It is expected to accelerate the online and offline integrated development of sports, and promote the national fitness program to usher in a new outbreak.

2.2 Development Status of Codoon

As China's first GPS sports + social APP, Codoon has evolved from a simple running-assisting tool to a one-stop intelligent sports and healthy life platform with accurate sports records, diversified events, crosstown activities, a community of experts, a complete range of sports equipment and professional training courses, becoming the advocate and pioneer of intelligent sports in China and the most influential intelligent sports social platform. By 2021, Codoon has possessed more than 200 million users, meeting tens of millions of sports demands from 210 countries and regions around the world every day, holding more than 1,000 online and offline events, with more than 300,000 sports groups all over the country. Through cloud computing, AI technology and a team of sports R&D experts, Codoon has provided customized intelligent services and high-quality sports equipment to over 400 million sports enthusiasts nationwide. In its ten years of existence, the company has focused on providing sports solutions for sports population, and has derived new businesses such as Codoon (Enterprise Version), Healthy Meals, intelligent hardware, and an overseas version of the App, covering all aspects of consumers' "food, clothing, and exercise". The Codoon APP itself focuses on the domestic online sports market, building the platform around user demand as a breaker of sports dilemma through intelligent hardware, content operations, event operations, e-commerce, and other segments.

(1) Introduction of product matrix

As China's first GPS sports social APP, Codoon combines multiple attributes such as sports, social interaction and personalized services, and has gradually launched intelligent hardware, overseas version, Codoon Health and Enterprise Codoon in its more than 10 years of development.

The APP uses GPS positioning principle and unique "Codoon algorithm" to accurately record sports data and deliver sports knowledge, sports events, sports equipment preferences, personalized training services and other content to meet user demands in all aspects. In addition to the most basic sports function, Codoon boldly explores the sports social field, with sports venues, social activities as the carriers, through online and offline resources channel, builds the rich network, links sports enthusiasts, and fully excavates social factors in sports, to create an unique sports community. Taking running shoes, healthy food and fitness equipment as examples, to enrich the user experience, Codoon Health spans across multiple fields such as diet, clothing, equipment and devices, and is committed to developing new products that are healthier and more practical. As one of the most representative designs of the APP, the bluetooth heart rate sports earphone, sports bracelet and other sports equipment equipped with a variety of intelligent hardware are popular among users. With the help of intelligent hardware, users can easily access more professional sports support and services, effectively expanding the intelligent sports scenarios. To enter the overseas market and class B market, Codoon launched an overseas version of its APP named Runtopia and an enterprise sports eco-platform "Enterprise Codoon" in 2016. Runtopia is dedicated to providing overseas users with advanced coaching functions such as tracking exercise data, customizing training plans, and weight loss and fitness guidance; and Enterprise Codoon, on the other hand, focuses on providing sports and health business for B2B enterprises and API-based data service business to encourage employees to participate in individual challenges, team activities, fun sports lists, and other segments to develop active and healthy exercise habits (Introduction of Codoon, n.d.) (see Figs. 1, 2 and 3).

(2) User profile of Codoon APP

As of June 2019, the number of Codoon APP users has exceeded 180 million, among which the average daily active users are 1.7507 million and the average monthly active users are 9.6768 million. Among the large number of active users, the majority of middle-and high-income people in their golden age maintains a daily opening frequency of 2.75 times per capita. According to the data of Qianfan.tech, male users account for 56.40%, and female users account for 43.60%, with the gender ratio closing to 3:2, and almost all users love night running and

Fig. 1 Codoon product matrix

Fig. 2 Core product features of Codoon APP

Fig. 3 Introduction of other core businesses of Codoon

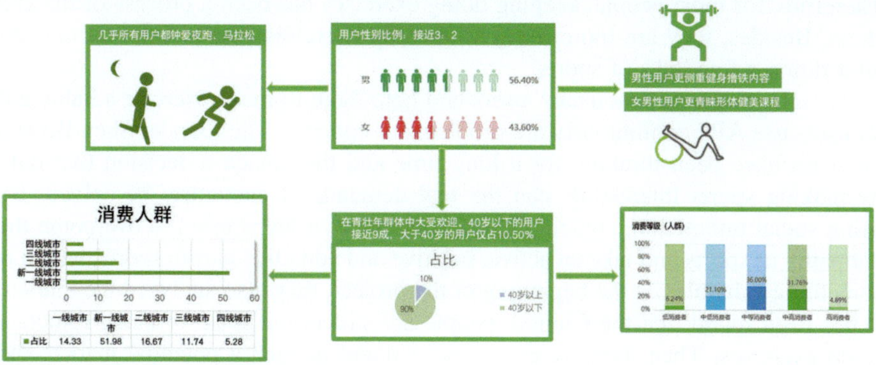

Fig. 4 User profile of Codoon APP

marathon. Among them, male users also focus on fitness content, while female users prefer bodybuilding courses. In terms of age, the APP is very popular among young and middle-aged people. Nearly 90% of users are under 40 years old, and only 10.50% are over 40 years old. From the perspective of consumer groups, over 70% of users are from middle-and high-income groups and most of them come from first-and second-tier cities. Medium consumers accounted for 36.00%, medium and high consumers accounted for 31.76%, and high consumers accounted for 4.89%. Users from new first-tier and first-tier cities accounted for 66.31%, and users from second-tier cities accounted for 16.67%, accounting for 82.98% in total (Codoon Sports, n.d.) (see Fig. 4).

2.3 Creating the Ultimate Experience for Consumers Based on Gamification

It can be clearly found that the number of users, user stickiness, daily/monthly active users and consumer loyalty of the APP maintain at a high level. On the one hand, richness of Codoon's products can meet different demands of users, who can find various products related to sports in Codoon; and on the other hand, the starting point of Codoon is the demands of customers, making great efforts to optimize consumer experience, thus increasing the user stickiness. Throughout all the products and services of Codoon, the incentive mechanism based on sport habits of big data and the virtual online real-time competition in 2020 fully exploit this feature.

(1) Motivation mechanism of users' sports behavior based on gamification

For the public, all kinds of sports have thresholds, even running which is the most simple form without any equipment. For the human nature, though we always need to maintain the idea of keeping healthy, the nature of human actually is laziness.

Therefore, for most people, keeping doing exercises has been a process of fits and starts. Besides, they are more likely to give up exercises due to different reasons after doing a few days of sports.

Therefore, how to "motivate" users and help them to make exercise a habit and let users use APP continuously are problems of concern. The founder Shen Bo and his team have been thinking for a long time and then made a decision that only by making sports interesting, can the real demands of customers be solved. By using social interaction, content and entertainment, it helps users to overcome the antipathy of sports and take an active, positive and addictive part in sports, which is something valuable. At the beginning of the project, they also analyzed the market. It has been found that the Chinese people are still in the stage of being reluctant to do exercises. Then, how to arouse the demand in such a potential market and help people do exercise more scientifically, safely and effectively? To this end, Shen Bo's team refined 4 keywords: fragment, entertainment, socialization and intelligence. Whether cultivating the sports of users through entertainment and gamification or transforming into the social platform of the national movement in 2015, or later launching the intelligent sports strategy to increase the investment to new technologies like AI and enter the competition of home intelligent fitness, these 4 keywords have been running through the whole development course of Codoon.

① Way to develop sports habits of Codoon's users

To cultivate sports habits of users, Codoon often uses the following three ways:

(1) Target plan (set the training goal + training method + schedule)
(2) Honor system (medal, completion certificate + prize)
(3) Interesting exercise process (playlists/voice coach/podcast access).

The following elements are used by Codoon to develop the motivation system: grade system, activities, LBS social interaction and achievement medals.

② Motivation system based on gamification

Grade and points system: It is similar to that of the game mechanism. Users can obtain a certain grade on the basis of 30-day average amount of exercise, and then they can find someone with the same grade for competition. As for card coins, there are three methods to obtain card coins, including doing exercises with assisting devices, using Codoon Sports and winning in competition. However, failure in the competition would lead to corresponding loss of card coins. Besides, card coins also can be exchanged for gifts and used to take part in the lottery draw.

Achievements: medals, rankings, records, prizes (see Fig. 5).

Fig. 5 Motivation system based on gamification

③ Motivation system based on social intercourse

Running group/LBS social interaction: Find people and groups nearby through "Nearby" in the interests circle to participate in sports together.

Offline running groups of communities: Led by the head of the group, the offline running groups carry out training twice a week, which has become very popular. At present, there are over 300,000 running groups across the country.

(2) Virtual online events based on sense of immediacy
① Background and development of online events

On March 31, 2020, with the issuance of the *Notice of General Administration of Sports of China on Temporarily Not Resuming Marathon and Other Sports Events* to reduce the risks brought by the flow and gathering of people for pandemic prevention and control, it was uncertain whether to resume crowd gathering activities such as marathon, and marathon events are inevitably suspended. For companies which have businesses related to road running events, the COVID-19 pandemic is a heavy blow, which has affected several aspects such as event operation, commercial development and business development. How to survive such a cold winter? It has become an inevitable problem for every practitioner. Affected by the COVID-19 pandemic, in the road running markets with severe damage, Codoon has found its own rhythm in challenges. It makes efforts to develop online events with no time, space and distance limits, moving offline tracks to the cloud, thus turning a crisis into opportunities, which can be seemed as dancing waltz on the edge of the cliff.

As the creator of online races, Codoon pioneered the concept of online marathons in October 2014, and launched the first online virtual marathon in partnership with Adidas, the sponsor of Beijing Marathon. In 2015, it successfully held more than 30 online marathons and became the world's largest online marathon and online cycling event provider. Besides, it successively developed its self-owned IP offline/online events such as Running Girl, Entrepreneurship Race, City Micro Marathon, Marathon Season and City Leading Runner. In the following years of development, it combined its own technical and data advantages to dig deep into user behavior data. And combining the characteristics of offline races, in August 2020, with the influence of the COVID-19 pandemic, Codoon's first real-time online race in live broadcast attracted 10,000 registrations. Faced with the growing demand for sports and fitness in the post-pandemic era, it promoted the model innovation of online marathon 2.0 to create healthier and more complete online sports experience for users. It not only launched the "New Journey Red Marathon Series" in conjunction with sports.news.cn, but also created the first online marathon expo, leading the scientific exercise craze during the COVID-19 pandemic prevention and control period and setting off an online event frenzy. In 2021, a total of 284 events (online + offline) were held by Codoon, with a total of 41,792,537 participants. The total distance of running in the whole year reached 748,443,665 km (*Codoon Events Annual White Paper of 2021* Was Released …, 2021).

② Creating the ultimate experience by launching Codoon online real-time race with a sense of immediacy and competition

199 online races were held in 2021, with an average of 210,012 participants and an average finish rate of 78.13% for each online race. According to Codoon big data, 1 out of every 5.7 Codoon users have experienced an online race; and one runner of Codoon participates in 7.91 online races a year on average, and the frequency of participation climbs year by year. From the above data, it can be seen that Codoon's online events are loved and recognized by users. Online races can break the limitations of time and space, allowing runners to have the sense of participation in the race whenever and wherever possible, which is a form with obvious advantages under the regular pandemic prevention and control. Codoon's online marathon 2.0—the real-time voice online race, built on the data and technology foundation and by constantly updating and iterating, gives runners a sense of participation that will be increasingly similar to the offline real-time experience.

If the marathon site is too far away from you, or running alone is boring and unsafe, you can participate in the Codoon real-time online marathon, equipped with new AI technology and real-time live broadcast, with an immersive marathon experience, breaking through time and space limitations, allowing you to run and compete with tens of thousands of people at any time (see Fig. 6).

Fig. 6 Variable online event IP

3 Industry Background

3.1 Industry Macro-environment

(1) The release of national policy dividends promotes the rapid progress of the sports and fitness industry

Vigorous development of the sports industry is a national strategy, the sports industry will enjoy the continued release of policy dividends. About 20+ policy provisions have been released since 2014, the sports industry planning is becoming clearer, and the supporting space is huge. It includes a number of directions, such as competitive sports, popular sports, ice-snow sports and Winter Olympics, outdoor sports and sports tourism. For Codoon's most important business, running, a series of policies advocate optimizing the industrial layout, further promoting sports consumption, encouraging running competitions and expanding the consumption space. In order to enhance the public running service consumption, the policies advocate optimizing the consumption environment, strengthening financial guarantee, improving the sports consumption policy system, strengthening the protection of sports consumption rights and interests, and encouraging the development of running service and running event service (see Fig. 7).

(2) Economic development stimulates high-quality demand, and sports and fitness sector is face consumption upgrade

The contradiction between the people's ever-growing demands for a better life and unbalanced and insufficient development is the main contradiction in China at the moment. China's GDP per capita in 2020 was USD11,300, much higher

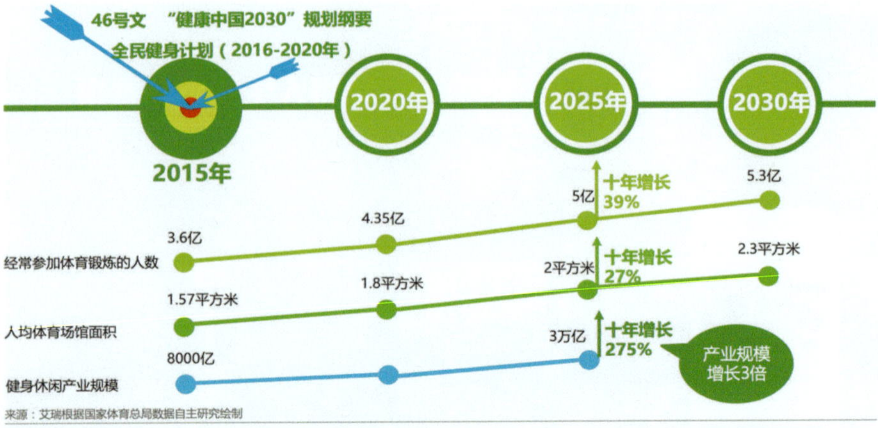

Fig. 7 Development goals of China's sports and fitness industry from 2016 to 2030

than the economic level of the U.S. sports industry during the "blowout" period. The added value of the sports industry accounted for 0.8% of the GDP, a low percentage but with a significant increase. According to the correlation between the level of GDP per capita and sports, running becomes popular when the GDP per capita exceeds USD6,000, and the participants of cycling and skiing will start to increase when it exceeds USD8,000. It can be predicted that with the growth of GDP per capita, there will be deeper development of diving, outdoor activities and rock climbing in the next stage. With economic development, improved living standards and increased health awareness among the general public, consumers' demand for quality fitness resources and high-quality fitness services has gradually come to the fore; the traditional sports and fitness industry has developed in a relatively crude manner and has a limited level of technology, making it difficult to detect and meet the new demands of users.

(3) Favorable socio-cultural environment and gradual formation of values for a healthy lifestyle

With the industrialization, urbanization, population aging and changes of ecological environment and lifestyle, chronic diseases have become the main cause of death and disease burden of the urban population. Facing health problems, participating in sports and developing a healthier lifestyle are important to prevent chronic diseases and improve physical and mental health. Advocated by the idea of the national fitness program, people spent more time and money in sports. The number of potential sports consumers will reach its peak within ten years, and the scale of users sees great potential to expand. For Internet sports enterprises, according to *The 44th China Statistical Report on Internet Development* released by China Internet Network Information Center (CNNIC), the number of mobile Internet users in China has reached 846 million in June 2019, with 411 million of them aged 20–39 (CNNIC Released *The 44th China Statistical Report on Internet Development*, 2019). As the products and services of Internet+ popular sports proliferated and upgraded rapidly, the popular sports population began to form new sports ecosystem and living habits. The users and popular sports products and services led each other to change, speeding up the upgrade of industrial chain and opening up a broader market.

In addition, the COVID-19 pandemic has become a catalytic factor to promote the development of sports and fitness industry. The public started to pay attention to personal health and the awareness of sports and fitness was awakened, and the values of healthy lifestyle have gradually formed. As the COVID-19 pandemic situation has made people realize the importance of health again, people changed their health concepts and fitness habits and devoted themselves to sports and fitness. The increasing public attention to health gradually made sports a new fashion and changed people's lifestyle, and fitness emerged as a new healthy way of socializing.

(4) With empowerment from AI, big data, and Internet of Things, the sports and fitness industry ushered in a new era

With the development of artificial intelligence (AI), big data and Internet of Things, the sports and fitness industry is more and more closely related to AI technology. New technologies such as big data, mobile internet, high-definition live broadcast and intelligent devices have been widely used in the sports industry, and the main changes focus on scenes, products and user experiences. At present, AI technology has been applied in intelligent sports and fitness industry to different degrees. As to the intelligent fitness hardware, AI is able to correct the posture by technologies like motion recognition, and it can provide personalized suggestions for fitness courses by analyzing the sports performance of users. The Internet of Things can comprehensively improve the experience of intelligent fitness for users by combining chips, sensors and computing platforms at the basic level with computer vision, speech recognition and machine learning at the technical level.

The new trend brought by these new technologies in the industry has offered three advantages: (1) the fitness efficiency of users was improved; (2) the management and capturing of fitness data was optimized; and (3) the interactive experience of fitness was enhanced. As an advocate and pioneer of intelligent sports and the most influential social platform of intelligent sports, Codoon advocated people-oriented technology from its birth, and has won more than 20 patents. Since its establishment, Codoon has been tirelessly pursuing innovation in technology, products and services. Through powerful sports data, AI and other technical means, Codoon has continuously developed new products and improved the quality of service to meet the diverse needs of consumers for fitness. Since 2017, Codoon has planned an intelligent sports strategy, which increased investment in AI and other new technologies, laid out offline new retail and built consumer brands. As its slogan transformed from "Exercise with Codoon" to "All the intelligent exercises are in Codoon", it combined sports equipment and training courses with AI technology, developed and launched a series of products such as intelligent running shoes, which can evaluate and score users' physical conditions according to sports big data analysis. The equipment monitors the relevant data in real time and provides safe and scientific voice guidance as the users are running. In 2018, Codoon strategically upgraded "Fitness 3.0, Alive" and officially entered the field of fitness. At the same time, CODOONLIVE, the first intelligent live broadcast course in China, has been launched. It created an online gym with innovative and intelligent gameplay, and realized online real-life private education. In 2021, as FITMORE was grandly introduced as an important new brand of family intelligent sports and fitness, and FITMORE intelligent fitness mirror was launched, Codoon formally entered the market of family fitness. Science and technology empowerment has always kept Codoon at the forefront of combining application of science and technology, and the integration of intelligent technology has developed in depth, constantly refining fitness sports scenarios, better meeting the diverse sports needs of consumers, enhancing consumers' experience and continuously creating value for consumers. What's more, technical barriers were formed, which equipped Codoon with advantages in industry competition (see Table 2).

3.2 Industry Development Status

(1) China's Internet popular sports service industry

With the influence of positive factors such as policy advocacy, the formation of the social fashion of fitness, the rising demand for popular sports and the upgrading of lifestyle, popular sports industry has ushered in huge market opportunities. At the same time, driven by the Internet technology dividend, the Internet sports population rises rapidly. According to the survey conducted by Qianfan.tech, the number of monthly active users of online sports and health APPs exceeded 71 million in July 2019, with walking step counting, running and fitness APPs accounting for the majority of online traffic. However, although the level of sports consumption of Chinese sports population is increasing year by year, from the perspective of structure, it is more concentrated on the consumption of sports goods, and service payment is still in the cultivation period.

As the products and services of Internet+ popular sports proliferated and upgraded rapidly, the popular sports population began to form new sports ecosystem and living habits. The users and popular sports products and services led each other to change, speeding up the upgrade of industrial chain and opening up a broader market.

Focusing on the main battlefield of Codoon—the running sports service track, the running sports industry in China is encouraged by the national policy, the national fitness program boom, the increase of sports population and other favorable factors, and the overall scale of the industry is developing well. By the end of 2019, the scale of the running-related industry will reach CNY360 billion, and

Table 2 Relevant policies of sports and fitness in China

Year	Policy	Content
October 2016	Planning outline for "Health China 2030"	The government has designated sports as an industry for national happiness, and made national sports and fitness a top-level national strategy. By 2030, 530 million people will regularly take part in physical exercise, and the total scale of the health service industry will reach CNY16 trillion
March 2017	National fitness program (2016–2020)	National fitness program will be taken as a strong support for building a healthy China and a national name card for building a moderately well-off society in an all-round way
March 2018	Government work report	Efforts should be intensified to promote the development of intelligent sports and broaden the penetration of intelligent life
August 2018	Annual report on development of sport for all in China	Build intelligent construction service platform and fitness equipment
January 2019	Action plan for further promoting sports consumption	Make greater efforts to promote the sustainable development of fitness programs
July 2019	Healthy China action (2019–2030)	By 2022 and 2030, the proportion of people who regularly take part in physical exercise (exercise 3 times a week or more with 30 min or more for each time and the intensity of medium or above) will be 37% or more and 40% or more respectively
September 2019	Outline for building a leading sports nation	Sports will become a landmark cause for the great rejuvenation of the Chinese nation, and a number of internationally competitive well-known sports enterprises and independent sports brands will be built. By 2035, more than 45% of the people will take part in physical exercise regularly, and the per capita space of sports venues will reach 2.5 square meters. By 2050, China will become a great modern socialist country of sports

(continued)

Table 2 (continued)

Year	Policy	Content
November 2020	The proposal for the 14th five-year plan (2021–2025) and the vision 2035	Basically achieve the vision goal of socialist modernization by 2035. Build a great country of sports, improve the quality of the people, and highlight the soft power of culture; improve the quality and diversification of services, including sports
August 2021	National fitness program (2021–2025)	Promote the digital transformation of the sports industry, encourage sports enterprises to "go to the cloud and use data to enpower the intelligence", and promote the data to empower the coordinated transformation of the whole industrial chain. Provide intelligent fitness services for all, promote online and smart sports events, and support emerging sports such as smart fitness, cloud events and virtual sports

Source Sort out by the authors

by 2020, it will exceed CNY400 billion. In the subdivision field, the mature running shoes and clothing market will maintain stable development, accounting for the majority; with the increase of new device types and the improvement of device functions, the market share of smart devices will further increase; as the proportion of core runners (runners who exercise more than 3 times a week with a moderate exercise intensity) expands, runners' demand for sports services increases, and large enterprises' demand for cultural construction of running teams develops steadily, the scale of running services market will continue to increase. The operating revenue of running events, which consists of registration fees, tickets and sponsorship income, will maintain a steady growth, and there is a large space for further exploration of running events and competitive tourism driven by them. Compared to other sports type, the industry chain of running sports is relatively perfect, and the running APPs form stable service modes. Since January 2018, the user scale of running online services has grown by 19%, with changes and fluctuation occuring, and the scale tends to be stable, heralding that the running online service enterprises in the aspect of user scale expansion are entering into a relatively stable period, and the services need to be further optimized to ensure user stickiness (see Fig. 8).

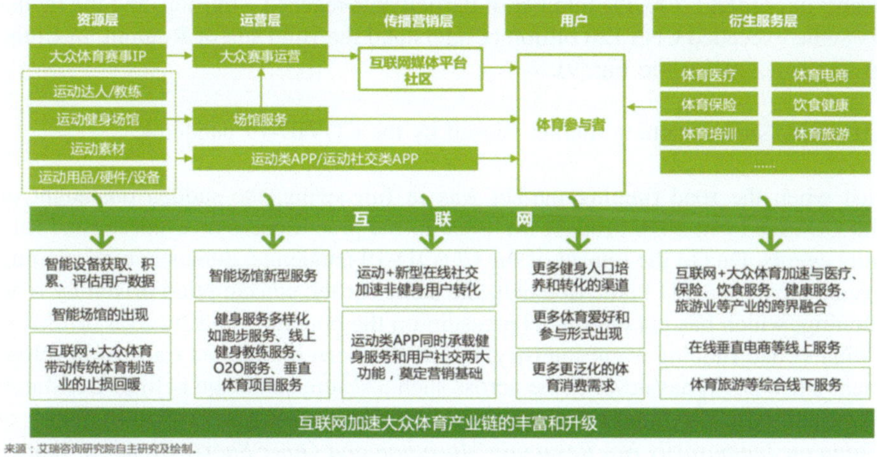

Fig. 8 Industry Chain of Internet+ popular sports service

(2) Road running services in China

Road running events include cross-country races, marathon races and all kinds of leisure running races.

From the perspective of operating revenue, the operating revenue of road running events increases steadily, and non-scale events increases at a high rate. Running events in our country can be divided into scale and non-scale events according to the scale of running events. The operating revenue of running events consists of registration fees, tickets and sponsorship income. With the growth of the number of running events and the scale of participating population, the overall market scale of running events will maintain a steady growth.

From the perspective of subdivision categories, the development of large-scale running events is relatively mature, the population size of a single race is limited, the match between the race volume and the level and number of sponsored brands is stable, and the growth rate of direct revenue will slow down year by year. By 2019, the operating revenue of large-scale events has reached CNY3.9 billion. Non-scale events are more distinctive, and the development has just started. The market saturation is low and the future development will still maintain a high growth rate. By 2019, the operating revenue of non-scale events will reach CNY1.49 billion.

In terms of the scale of participants, the growing momentum of running scale events and the number of participants maintains excellent, with a promising future. According to the data of Chinese Athletics Association in 2019, China's scale events exceeded 1,700, the number of participants reached 7 million, and the industry scale exceeded CNY120 billion (Understand the Big Data of Running in China in 2019 …, 2019) (see Fig. 9).

(3) China's road running market paused by the COVID-19 pandemic

Just when the road running market was in full swing, the sudden onslaught of the COVID-19 in 2020 brought the issue to the practitioners of Chinese road running events. Due to the impact of the COVID-19 pandemic, domestic road running events have basically come to a halt, the same for the consumption driven by road running, which has put enormous pressure on the operation and survival of SMEs. China's road running event industry, which has been on the fast track of development since 2014, has never come across such a severe challenge before. On March 31, 2020, with the issuance of the *Notice of General Administration of Sports of China on Temporarily Not Resuming Marathon and Other Sports Events* to reduce the risks brought by the flow and gathering of people for pandemic prevention and control, it was uncertain whether to resume crowd gathering activities such as marathon (General Administration of Sport of China … 2020). The suspension of events has inevitably led to a shrinkage in operating revenue. The losses incurred by relevant companies as a result of the COVID-19 pandemic were obviously significant. The PIC of Jiangsu Sports Marketing Co., Ltd. Said that "the losses of the company is expected to reach half of our full-year revenue" (China Athletics

来源：企业访谈，艾瑞咨询研究院自主研究及绘制。

Fig. 9 Definition and classification of road running-related events in China

Association: Encouraging the Safely … 2020). For companies which have businesses related to road running events, the COVID-19 pandemic is a heavy blow, which has affected several aspects such as event operation, commercial development and business development. How to survive such a cold winter? It has become an inevitable problem for every practitioner, and also a dilemma they want to break.

4 Confronting Problems

As a veteran person of the Internet+ sports industry, Shen Bo clearly understands that as competition in the industry becomes increasingly feverish, Codoon, as a segmented vertical APP, currently has nearly 200 million registrations and an average of 9.6768 million active monthly users. The huge volume of data behind the app is the efforts made by Codoon in the face of changing market conditions over the years. However, with the gradual disappearance of the mobile Internet demographic dividend, the industry competition has become more focused on the stock market, and the battle for demographic dividend has become a battle for user stickiness. The revenue that can be generated by acquiring new customers is very limited, and it also means that it is more difficult and expensive for Codoon to acquire new customers. It can be said that maintaining one loyal customer is better than developing 10 new customers. How to develop more valuable products and services from the existing pool of users, to boost the spending potential of existing users, and to tap the value of customers in all aspects is an important issue for Codoon to consider.

In December 2021, after the annual year-end debriefing meeting, CEO Shen Bo brought together the PICs of the three divisions of the company primarily responsible for the operating revenue, the Advertising Business Division, the E-commerce Business Division and the Events Division, to discuss the work plan for the new year around this issue.

4.1 Advertising Revenue is the King: Dig Deeper into Data Assets to Enhance Accurate Matching

"The essence of the Internet is to occupy users and to maintain their high frequency of using, and the profits would naturally come!" Jiesen, the head of the Advertising Business Division, which is one of the pillars of Codoon's revenue, took the lead and said, "As long as we build on our existing user base and combine hard tactics with soft, our business customers will recognize the value of ads placement as long as we continue to have high traffic and be highly active. All the mainstream sports APPs are currently using this approach, and with the traffic of millions of people, naturally they will not let go of collecting advertising fees. And for commercial advertisers, there are two questions to ponder when choosing a delivery channel: the first is the efficiency of advertising delivery; and the second is the product design, that is, whether the user can notice the advertisement when using. Through the powerful big data system, Codoon refines its algorithms and systems to improve the comprehensiveness and accuracy of user data, to tap the value of massive data, to do a good job in accurate matching, and to better serve the corporate advertisers with the smallest investment for maximum benefit, which is not only in line with the classic rules of the business world, but is also the main mode of operating revenue for sports APP companies in China at present. I believe that the Advertising Business Division can do even better for the company."

4.2 Focusing on E-commerce Business: Using Technological Empowerment and Abundant Products to Meet Diversified Needs

Yaqi, from the E-commerce Business Division, has her own insights into the future. "As a mainstream APP in the vertical field of sports, we have gathered many sports enthusiasts at present. When users' sports habits are cultivated, equipment needs will naturally arise. If a sports APP is approved by users, it is easier for them to accept sports products recommended by it along with its own teaching courses and information content. Then the track of E-commerce became one feasible to develop. This is also the strategy adopted by our company at present. Self-built shopping malls are a more common source of profit than advertising according to the data I have. In terms of commodity types, clothing equipment, smart accessories, hardware facilities and nutritional supplements are the most common ones. Now the largest part of the national consumption expenditure on fitness is in shoes and clothing accessories, accounting for more than 70% of the total expenditure on sports consumption. It can be seen that sports APP manages for as many profit opportunities as possible by encouraging people to spend on shoes and clothing accessories through e-commerce. There is no big problem with this stategy. We have such a huge user base at present, and as long as we well solve the supply chain problems, and continue to maintain our technological advantages of science and technology orientation and build a brand commodity matrix, and develop products in various forms and rich contents to meet the needs of different users, we can attract users, enhance their willingness to buy and dig deep into their value."

"Moreover, Codoon's intelligent hardware and wearable devices have been laid out for nearly 10 years. We have accumulated a lot of technology patents and supply chain resources, from our professional shoes and clothing, professional sports watches, smart bracelets and heart rate belts, to FITMORE, an intelligent fitness mirror for a brand-new subdivision track that conforms to the home fitness scenario extended from the regular pandemic prevention and control in 2021. Codoon's early technology-oriented thinking and technology accumulation provided us with competitive advantages (Codoon Released New Family Intelligent Sports … 2021).

We have full advantages in product and supply chain. Thus, we should develop harder the ability of sales in the coming year. We have adopted marketing promotion methods like e-commerce live broadcast and dealership business cooperation. As long as the market of this part is opened, I believe that in the future, the e-commerce division will give full play to the existing advantages of our company and set a new high for the company's revenue."

4.3 Dig Deep into the Value of the Sports Events, Enhance the Delivered Value Form the Users' Experience, and Focus on the Stock Market

Ma Wei, the PIC of the Events Division, believed that value-added services should be the key point in digging deep into the value of existing users in the future. She said gently, "The competition in the stock market is becoming fierce with the gradual disappearance of the demographic dividend. The dispute in demographic dividend has evolved into the dispute of users' online time and user stickiness in the online sports health industry where Codoon located. Thus, how to enhance users' online experience, create value for customers to the maximum extent, meet their diverse needs and enhance customers' loyalty is the foundation of all businesses."

"Due to the COVID-19 pandemic, there have been a great success in online sports events, which have become one of the important sources of our revenue. We have deeply combed the user's sports behavior data, and combined them with the characteristics of offline events. Then in August 2020, the first online competition in voice live broadcast was held, which maximized the charm of offline events through online display and met the growing demand for sports and fitness in the post-pandemic era to the largest extent. Codoon promoted the model innovation of online marathon 2.0, creating healthier and more perfect online sports experience for users. In 2021, a total of 199 online competitions were held, with an average of 210,012 participants in each online competition, and the average completion rate of each online competition reached 78.13%. Online virtual events play a huge role in cultivating users' exercise habits, improving user stickiness and customer loyalty, and company revenue."

Ma Wei talked about another point next, "In the recent 2 years, we also wanted to make efforts in the development of event IP to contribute to the enhancement of Chinese cultural confidence. From our Chinese dynasty running series to the cultural relics running series in cooperation with major museums, and then to the 'New Journey Red Marathon Series' launched by Codoon and sports.news.cn, they all showed our national pride and feelings. Codoon Sports has always been an enterprise with social responsibility, as well as national pride. Meanwhile, our cooperative relationship between the official marathon organizations and us was always difficult to establish before the COVID-19 pandemic. After all, they have the brand appeal of being official Gold Label Road Race holders. But due to the pandemic, offline events stopped. And we have established good cooperation with many official events and government agencies at home and abroad via online sports events. Codoon was officially authorized to hold 28 online events in 2021, including international Gold Label Road Races like Boston Marathon and Xiamen Marathon, attracting millions of runners to participate. These resource advantages can be maintained, and they are also important resources for attracting professional road running users. Through the online sports events as a carrier, we can integrate advantageous resources in media communication, brand assets platform technologies and other aspects, deeply construct the event service system including popular online races, team custom races, and running team training camps."

"On the other hand, under the combined effect of many favorable factors, running is a sport with great potential for development, and is also the project with the low participation threshold and the widest population base in the category of popular sports. Its development is the result of multiple factors such as national policies and major social events. From the support of many policies to the self-discipline habit of a large number of elite entrepreneurs, the label of 'self-discipline, health and elite' was brought to running, and it has been widely popularized among the public. Further, the popular running has started to upgrade to events and activities. The direct or indirect economic benefits brought by the events are worth digging deeper, especially the value of the events such as derived tourism revenue, cultural and creative product revenue and event medical and financial revenue. Due to the impact of the COVID-19 pandemic, the revenue of event tourism, which once constituted the largest part of the revenue of the Events Division, was almost zero in the past two years, but I believe that when the pandemic is under control, the demand side will definitely usher in a retaliatory rebound, so we should advance the layout, and prepare for the deployment of the incoming 'spring'."

For Codoon, starting from the needs of its core users, improving the user experience and cultivating their exercise habits and willingness to pay are all things that have to be done solidly step by step. Among the numerous value-added services, Codoon's business of road running events will be an important revenue generator in the future.

5 Epilogue

After the meeting, Shen Bo sat alone in his office and fell into thinking. From the point of view of industry characteristics, the current mainstream sports APPs are providing functions with few barriers, and the industry homogeneity characteristics are highlighted. As there are too many similar products, it is impossible to charge the users. Many sports APP enterprises rely on advertising implantation for their profitability, but while Codoon has the advantage of a large user base, there is also the risk of damaging the user experience.

The development of e-commerce business has high investment costs, and there are cost factors such as inventory. As Codoon has never tried live broadcast, whether it can open the sales road is still uncertain…

Events Division this year has a really excellent performance, but other sports APPs have been involved in this field, the future competition will certainly be fierce. Offline events-related tourism and registration and other extended business will bring in revenue when the COVID-19 pandemic comes to an end. But no one knows when the day will come…

So what kind of future layout should Codoon have? Or should it start thinking about a new business, and what will it be? Shen Bo and his team still need to continue to explore these questions…

Case Appendix

Appendix 1 Honors of Codoon

Source www.codoon.com

Appendix 2 Diagram of Codoon's Product Function Structure

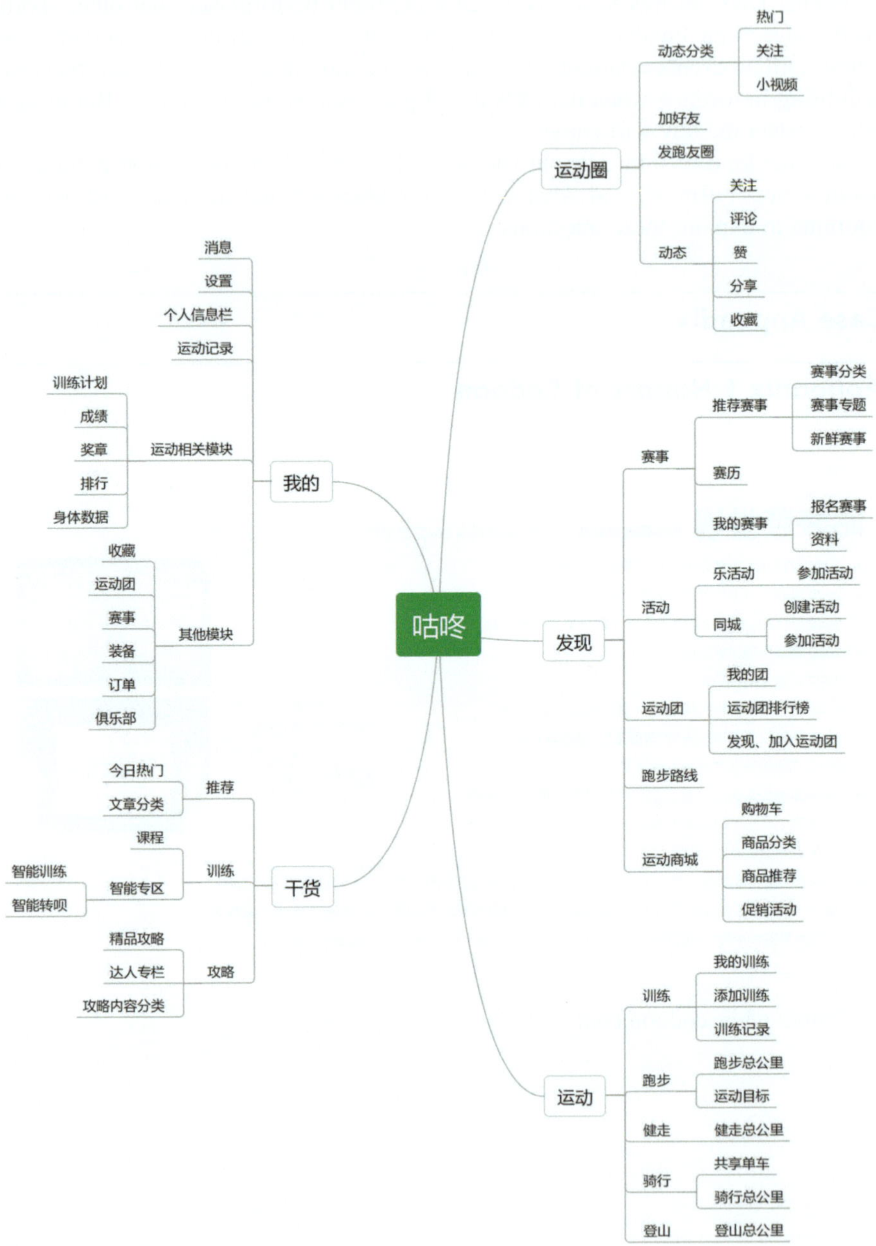

References

China Athletics Association: Encouraging the Safely and Orderly Resumption of Races, and the Industry Maintains an Overall Positive Trend. (2020, April). Xinhuanet. Retrieved from http://sports.xinhuanet.com/c/2020-03/24/c_1125761270.html.

CNNIC Released *The 44th China Statistical Report on Internet Development*. (2019, August). *The Paper.* https://m.thepaper.cn/newsDetail_forward_4298618.

Codoon Events Annual White Paper of 2021 Was Released, with 284 Events Held and over 41 Million Participants. (2021, December). *Sports Money.* Retrieved December 13, 2021, from http://www.sportsmoney.cn/article/107320.html.

Codoon Released New Family Intelligent Sports and Fitness Brand FITMORE and Various New Products for the Family Fitness Track in 2021. (2021, May). *Hexun.com.* http://news.hexun.com/2021-05-28/203683685.html.

Codoon Sports. (n.d.). *Qianfan.tech.* Retrieved November 13, 2019, from https://qianfan.analysys.cn.

General Administration of Sport of China: Notice on Temporarily Not Resuming Marathon and Other Sports Events. (2020, April). *Xinhuanet.* http://sports.xinhuanet.com/c/2020-04/06/c_1125819217.html.

Introduction of Codoon. (n.d.). *Codoon Sports.* Retrieved January 31, 2022, from https://www.codoon.com/h5/codoon-welcome/about.html?pm_vt=164990944949691&pm_r=cpm_https%3A%2F%2Fwww.codoon.com%2Fh5%2Fcodoon-welcome%2Fequip.html_url.

Sports Social Platform "Codoon" Completed Strategic Financing and Will Open a Round D Financing. (n.d.). *CNMO.* Retrieved December 13, 2021, from https://new.qq.com/omn/20211213/20211213A046J200.html.

Understand the Big Data of Running in China in 2019: 5 Marathons Were Held on Average A Day. (2020, May). *The Paper.* https://www.thepaper.cn/newsDetail_forward_7108272.

ZongTeng Group: Fighting Against the COVID-19 Pandemic, and Being the Hero in Harm's Way of Cross-Border E-commerce Logistics

Ying Wang and Shuying You

1 Introduction

As the "Belt and Road Initiative" has taken effect, the scale of cross-border e-commerce transactions have continued to expand. According to statistics from customs and other departments: in 2019, the import and export volume of China's cross-border e-commerce retail reached CNY186.21 billion, five times higher than that in 2015, with an average annual growth rate of 49.5%. There were nearly 155 million cross-border online shopping users. The process of high-quality development of China's foreign trade driven by the cross-border e-commerce driving is accelerating. In the *Report on the Work of the Government 2020*, it is pointed out: "We will accelerate the growth of cross-border e-commerce and other new forms of business, and enhance our international shipping capacity." As of April 8, 2020, there were already 105 comprehensive pilot zones for cross-border e-commerce, and the scale of cross-border e-commerce market would be further expanded. In 2020, the import and export transaction volume reached CNY280 billion, and the number of cross-border online shopping users is expected to reach 235 million. At the same time, overseas pilot zones such as eWTP and Africa E-commerce Alliance are being rolled out worldwide. The cross-border e-commerce is accelerating the globalization of supply chains, and the international trade is also going digital.

In early 2020, the COVID-19 pandemic hit all walks of society and disrupted the operation rhythm of the entire cross-border e-commerce industry. At the beginning of the COVID-19 pandemic, enterprises had to stop work and production. Subsequently, the international demand shrank and foreign trade orders decreased. As a result, enterprises' cash flow pressure increased. Because of the logistical

Y. Wang (✉) · S. You
International Digital Economy College, Minjiang University, Fuzhou, China

J. Zhang et al. (eds.), *Innovation of Digital Economy*, Management for Professionals,
https://doi.org/10.1007/978-981-99-1741-9_6

disruptions and increased transportation costs, the global supply chains suffered from shock. All of these are serious challenges for enterprises in the cross-border e-commerce industry. In Q1 2020, after the outbreak of the COVID-19 pandemic at home and abroad, the product demand on cross-border e-commerce platforms declined, and it was difficult to make transactions. In January and February, China's import and export, export, and import (in CNY) fell by 9.6%, 15.9% and 2.4% respectively. According to iiMedia Research, the cross-border e-commerce market is expected to see a slight decline in 2020, with the transaction scale reaching CNY10.3 trillion. Most cross-border e-commerce merchants had the problems of out of stock in February, orders "cut" in March, a spike in demand for some categories of products in April and May, and excessive inventory in June. Merchants had mood swings in the first half of the year, and they said that "the industry uncertainties encountered in these six months are more than those in six years since the start-up."

However, there is a cross-border e-commerce enterprise that is growing against the trend. On April 17, 2020, CCTV-2 *On Time Finance* reported that ZongTeng Group, as a representative of cross-border e-commerce logistics (Figs. 1 and 2), had taken numerous effective measures to guarantee the normal operation and maintain the stable development of the industry in the face of multiple challenges brought by the COVID-19 pandemic.

What kind of cross-border e-commerce enterprise is ZongTeng Group and what tests did it go through after the outbreak of the COVID-19 pandemic? How did it

Fig. 1 *We are the World*, international anti-pandemic documentary of ZongTeng group in 2020

Fig. 2 CCTV, BBC and other related reports

make quick and accurate emergency decisions in the face of the uncertainty caused by the crisis? What measures did it take to break through the difficulties and stand out from many cross-border e-commerce enterprises?

2 Company Background

ZongTeng Group, founded in Fuzhou, China in 2007, currently is headquartered in Shenzhen. ZongTeng Group was one of the earliest companies to carry out the cross-border e-commerce in China. Initially, it was a big buyer of cross-border e-commerce business. But later, after transformation, it turned to focus on **basic logistics service providers**. It has service brands such as "Goodcang", "YunExpress" and "Goten", providing one-stop service of international logistics including overseas warehouse, special line logistics and distribution. In 2019, ZongTeng Group, positioned itself as a "Global cross-border e-commerce infrastructure service provider", focuses on value-added services such as e-commerce overseas warehousing and distribution, small-package special line logistics, first-haul transportation services and supply chain finance, and provides cross-border e-commerce enterprises with efficient, convenient, and cost-effective integrated logistics services. ZongTeng Group has built a cross-border e-commerce logistics service network covering the United States, Europe, Japan, Australia and other countries and regions. It has nearly 20 overseas warehousing and transit hubs, covering a total area of over 400,000 square meters, and the daily handling capacity can be more than 600,000 orders. There are more than 2,000 employees, including over 1,000 overseas employees, with branches in seven major developed countries and Fuzhou, Wuhan, Chengdu and other places around the world. Being the recommended logistics service provider for third-party e-commerce platforms such as Amazon, WISH, JOOM, and AliExpress, its service customers cover top cross-border e-commerce enterprises and brands in China. Since the outbreak of the COVID-19 pandemic, ZongTeng Group has overcome multiple obstacles and taken a number of measures to ensure smooth logistics. During this period, it actively carried anti-pandemic materials for the international community and achieved a rapid growth.

3 Measures of ZongTeng Group During the COVID-19 Pandemic

3.1 Early Development Stage During the COVID-19 Pandemic (Late January to Mid-February 2020)

3.1.1 Sudden Outbreak of the COVID-19 Pandemic

The COVID-19 pandemic broke out in Wuhan, China. At this time, the COVID-19 pandemic situation in China was so severe that China took unprecedentedly strict measures to reduce the movement of people and exposure by 80% in a short period. Many factories and enterprises faced problems of shutdown, production suspension and difficulties in resuming work.

At this stage, ZongTeng Group mainly paid attention to two things, i.e. purchasing anti-pandemic materials from abroad and transporting them to China, and speeding up the resumption of work and production to ensure the smooth logistics for donated materials. However, due to the weakness of the disaster relief and emergency response system, the rules related to the import and donation of anti-pandemic materials in China are updated constantly, and there are great uncertainties each day. Therefore, it is necessary to deal with a series of problems arising from the changes of rules. In addition, the personal safety of employees is the most important concern for companies. Li Cong, the vice president of ZongTeng Group, said: "In fact, at that time, the most basic problem was to risk one's life when going out to work. The safety of life was probably the biggest concern."

At this moment, what initiatives have ZongTeng Group taken to protect itself, its supply chain and its customers, and what core competencies related to supply chain security have been developed to defuse the crisis?

3.1.2 Flexible Organization and Quick Decision-Making

In this situation, the executives of the ZongTeng Group held an urgent meeting to share information, exchange discussions, and make quick reactions and decisions. Wang Zuan, CEO of ZongTeng Group, said that "we had an emergency meeting every day at 3 pm from the Lunar New Year's Day. The senior management attended the meetings to discuss and plan to make in-depth predictions and forward-looking researches". Branches of ZongTeng Group worked together closely to **set up temporary emergency response teams** to carry out the organization restructuring in light of the changes in the external environment caused by the crisis and new tasks, and often had cross-department cooperation, so that the boundaries among departments were diluted and the organization was more flexible. On the first day, the emergency team consisted of 3–5 members; on the second day, there were 9–10 members; and on the third day, there were about 30 members. With the passage of time, thousands of employees around the world joined the team. They united and worked together across time and space barriers to restore the normal operation of companies.

While many people were celebrating the Spring Festival with families, ZongTeng Group started working on the procurement of anti-pandemic materials for the Chinese government. Li Cong said, "we keep an eye on everyone and the overall situation instead of only our own business. In this process, we gained firsthand experience of the changes of the COVID-19 pandemic situation, and realized the time points of the peak demands for anti-pandemic materials, rushing to purchase because of panic, plummet of demands for anti-pandemic materials, etc." Based on the experience acquiring in the pandemic prevention, ZongTeng Group can be prepared in advance for the outbreak of the COVID-19 pandemic worldwide.

3.1.3 Taking Strict Measures in the Pandemic Prevention and Control and Providing Security

At that moment, the most urgent task was to resume work as soon as possible and to ensure the personal safety of employees who returned to work. ZongTeng Group took **strict pandemic prevention and control measures** (Fig. 3). The management of "Goodcang" listed ten measures (Appendix 1) to popularize and strengthen employees' understanding of pandemic prevention and control. Actions were also taken to strictly monitor employees' health conditions, apply remote office software, and adopt flexible work systems to resume work orderly. The warehouses of Goodcang are located all over the world, and most of overseas employees are foreigners, who have different cultural backgrounds. Towards overseas employees, ZongTeng Group has made many pandemic-related advertising campaigns to arouse their awareness of pandemic prevention and control. In many enterprises, employees were laid off during the COVID-19 pandemic, however, ZongTeng Group recruited new employees due to the shortage of manpower in overseas warehouses. In addition to the salary increase, ZongTeng Group made efforts to reduce the risk of infection, such as "providing accommodation for employees nearby", which could retain existing employees and attract new ones. It was the rapid response of ZongTeng Group in the face of the COVID-19 pandemic that encouraged employees to return to work instantly.

The pandemic prevention and control measures protected the safety of life of employees, pacify their minds, and encouraged them to work together and play an active part in the work. On February 10, the subsidiaries of ZongTeng Group, including Goodcang, YunExpress, Goten, KUABEI Supply Chain Service System and WORLDTECH all resumed operation officially.

Fig. 3 Positive response of employees both at home and abroad to the pandemic prevention and control. *Source* ZongTeng group

3.2 Situation Deterioration of the COVID-19 Pandemic (Mid-to-Late February to Mid-March)

3.2.1 Virus Spread and Deepening Crisis

After mid-February, the COVID-19 pandemic spread in outbreaks all around the world, and both domestic and overseas were in an extraordinary response phase. When the situation in China was improved, many factories were preparing to resume work and production, but there was still a long way to go before the resumption of normal production and life. Because of the global spread of the COVID-19 pandemic, there were frequent changes in the transport and logistics policies of countries (Appendix 2) and the pressure of international express made cross-border e-commerce enterprises face with challenges of waiting and overloading, significantly reducing the logistics timelines and increasing the costs.

First, there was a significant reduction in flights to and from national airlines, especially to China, Japan, South Korea, the United States, Italy and others, resulting in a decline in the overall international airline capacity. As of March 27, according to the incomplete statistics of CARNOC.com (Appendices 3 and 4), 77 airlines suspend all international services (including 63 airlines that suspend completely), 14 airports stop the operation, 7 airports shut down part of terminals and 9 airports close towers. About half of global airline cargo transportation depends on the belly holds of passenger planes. When the vast majority of international passenger flights are suspended, it means that the "airline capacity is cut by at least half".

Second, the logistics efficiency was reduced. Under the influence of the COVID-19 pandemic, in the processes of the domestic goods export, international transit and import of destination countries, repeated quarantine and disinfection were required. The measures of control, inspection and quarantine were stricter, and the time for customs clearance increased. Countries with severe situation may even temporarily close border crossings.

Third, with the decline of logistics capacity, operation costs of enterprises rose, and logistics costs also increased significantly. The outbreak of the COVID-19 pandemic has seen the surge of logistics costs (Fig. 4).

The COVID-19 pandemic situation in China was gradually controlled and the resumption of cross-border e-commerce export and import businesses were carried out in order. But for ZongTeng Group, it also faced the following challenges: serious problems in the long-distance transportation and terminal distribution of the foreign cross-border e-commerce export, work and production suspension in American local distribution companies, such as UPS, USPS and Fedex, resulting in the overstock, delivery efficiency decrease, and surge in the amount of returns. The entire cross-border e-commerce market was in a state of turmoil.

At that time, ZongTeng Group was under the pressure of cargo routes due to the declining airline capacity and the drastic price fluctuations in the cargo market. **It had to decide "whether to increase the number of chartered flights earlier than previous years and whether the revenue from chartered flights could be higher than the cost when the COVID-19 pandemic situation was still going worse and**

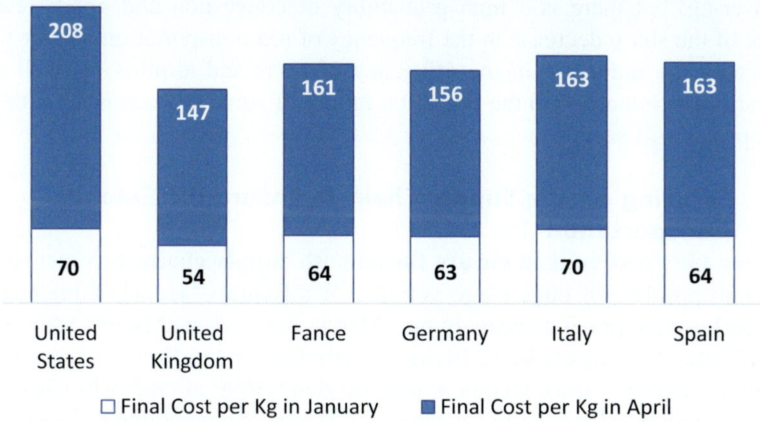

Fig. 4 Postage comparison of YT after the outbreak of the COVID-19 pandemic. *Source* Data compilation of YT

the cost of chartered flights had already increased significantly"? To predict market demands and capacity supply trends more accurately, it was necessary for the Group to grasp the development trend of the COVID-19 pandemic in advance based on the data mining technology.

3.2.2 Data Analysis and Trend Prediction

First, ZongTeng Group **analyzed the data related to the COVID-19 pandemic**. It believed that the data analysis "shall be deep into the essence, rather than becoming a mere formality." The analysis was based on the data of confirmed COVID-19 cases in four days. The prediction would be made by analyzing the growth rate of each set of data, and the sliding averages. At the same time, ZongTeng Group, taking advantage of the research report released by Imperial College London on March 16 (Appendix 5) and authoritative foreign data websites, collected data on the COVID-19 pandemic in various countries regularly and actively, and analyzed and compared the number of hospital beds and ICU beds, the capacity of nucleic acid testing, the strength of social or government control and the degree of aging (which is closely related to the mortality rate) and other indicator factors in each country through the data mining technology. It made predictions on the COVID-19 pandemic situation in European and the United States and other regions by taking into account the actual situation in each country, such as demographic factors, medical resource allocation, authoritative overseas prediction data and differences in policy measures, and formulated corresponding response plans. This initiative, based on the analysis of data related to the COVID-19 pandemic, provided a necessary basis for making quick and accurate market judgments and business decisions.

Li Cong said, "we have made predictions on air and sea transport logistics, and concluded that freight prices may surge. We can see that the export trade is recovering, but there is a high probability of congestion and goods retention because of the sharp decrease in the frequency of sea transportation and air flights. Added with the reduction in the efficiency of ports and airports, as well as the information asymmetry and the operation failure of some links, it is definitely that freight prices will soar."

3.2.3 Focusing on the Supply Chain to Ensure the Smooth Transportation

ZongTeng Group **strived to ensure the smooth supply chain**. In order to solve the current problem of huge cargo volume, "YunExpress" launched the chartered flights earlier than previous years in mid-March. Six chartered flights were booked in March, and there would be 12 flights directly from Hong Kong to European and the United States in April, among which the B747-800F aircraft was used for the European services with a cargo capacity of 120 tons. Although the freight cost was much higher, about 2–3 times higher than that before the outbreak of the COVID-19 pandemic, the revenue growth of ZongTeng Group was beyond expectation because the cargo volume was also growing.

The advantages of chartered flights were fully reflected, which could make up for the deficiencies of other logistics modes in terms of positions, timeliness and certainty, allowing overseas buyers to truly enjoy the convenience of air logistics and effectively boosting the overall confidence of the foreign trade industry. "Yun-Express" opened several chartered flights from Hong Kong, China to Los Angeles, Maastricht, Liège, etc. 3–4 chartered flights would be arranged per week to ensure a sufficient capacity. According to an announcement from Hong Kong's largest airline, Cathay Pacific, on April, 28, there would be fewer flights maintained in May and June 2020, and the passenger network capacity would be cut to 3% in May. The situation of nearly "0" flight departing from Hong Kong would be continued. After analyzing the situation of the COVID-19 pandemic and changes in the market supply and demand, in May, the chartered flight plan of "YunExpress" was upgraded in further, and several direct air lines were arranged from Hong Kong to European and the United States. There were a total of more than 40 flights with the capacity of over 2,000 tons, and 4–5 flights were planned per week to fully meet the demands of customers.

"Goodcang" also activated the backup fulfillment to ensure the smooth operation of overseas warehousing, and exerted its anti-risk capacity in the United States, the United Kingdom, the Czech Republic, France and other countries (Fig. 5) to openly and transparently discuss with customers about the COVID-19 pandemic situation and prevention and control measures, so as to ensure the timely delivery of parcels, the smooth operation of the foreign trade industry chain and supply chain, and help cross-border merchants to overcome the difficulties.

In order to help merchants fight against the COVID-19 pandemic scientifically, understand changes in overseas markets and prepare goods reasonably, "Goten" releases the *Forecast Report on Foreign Pandemic Trends* every two weeks. In February, anti-pandemic materials in seven categories were urgently launched and they were ready to support major European and the United States with a severe

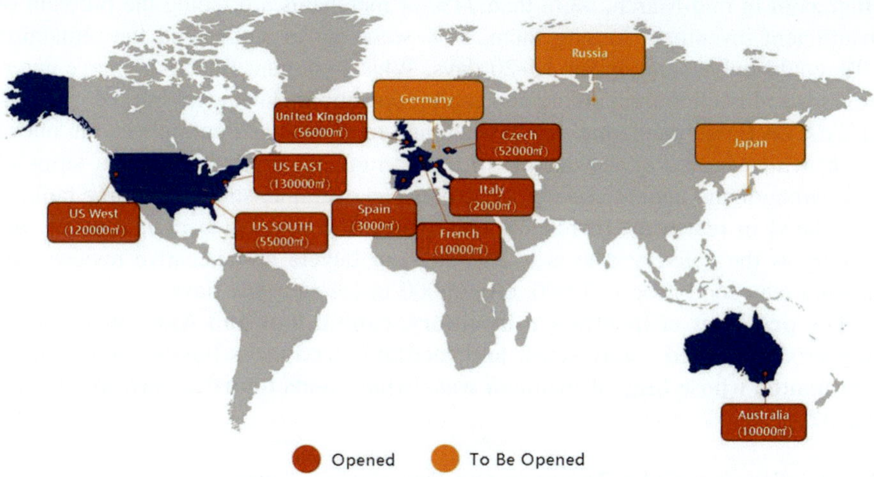

Fig. 5 Operation of overseas warehouses of ZongTeng group (as of March 31, 2020). *Source* ZongTeng group

situation. According to the changing consumer demands, the area of anti-pandemic materials for home quarantine was introduced in advance in March, with new categories of auto-parts and well-known brand products. It was expected that the best-sellers would be prepared in mid-May. Moreover, product prices would be monitored strictly to ensure no price increase during the COVID-19.

3.3 Global Spread of the COVID-19 Pandemic (Mid-to-Late March to Early May)

3.3.1 Global Spread and New Crises

With the global spread of the COVID-19 pandemic, the situation abroad deteriorated rapidly. According to the real-time statistics of WHO, as of 18:00, March 18, Central European Time (1:00 March 19, Beijing Time), there were 207,860 confirmed COVID-19 cases in the world from 166 countries and regions. As of 10:00 a.m., May 27, Central European Time (17:00, May 27, Beijing Time), there were 5,488,825 confirmed COVID-19 cases in the world from 255 countries and regions, with a death toll of 349,095. New crises were coming with the emergence of the latest COVID-19 pandemic situation.

The trade restrictions worldwide were escalating and operation rules for cross-border e-commerce platforms were also changing frequently as the COVID-19 pandemic situation becoming worse, for example, the restrict sales of masks and hand sanitizers in Amazon, and non-necessities and medical supplies in FBA. It could be inferred that the review procedures of medical products on platforms would be stricter and there would be higher thresholds. The review ports for some products may be completely closed. According to a survey conducted by

Hugo.com in mid-March, more than 77% of merchants are facing the problem of insufficient inventory. Among them, 51% were out of stock, and the remaining 49% could only maintain for 10–20 days. What important for e-commerce enterprises is to maintain the ranking and capital operation. However, with the outbreak of the COVID-19 pandemic, many small and medium-sized enterprises ran out of stock, which leaded to the decline of online ranking, a great burden in terms of both strength and capital. Taking Amazon as an example, since the online ranking is updated in real time, merchants may spend 3–6 months to rank top 100, but as long as the delivery date is over 3 days, or buyers give negative reviews, the ranking may soon drop to 1,000, even 5,000 in the next few days.

The problems of insufficient inventory, capital flow and Amazon's restriction crisis haunted many small and medium-sized cross-border e-commerce merchants, whose biggest problem was "what goods to order, how much, and when?".

3.3.2 Staying Calm Towards the Restriction Crisis

"There is a buzzword in the industry that the selection of products accounts for 70% while the marketing accounts for 30%." In the difficult times of the industry, merchants shall pay more attention to select products, finding the feedbacks of buyers' comments, sales volume and quickly adjusting the product structure. Before Amazon released the banned category, ZongTeng Group had predicted based on the data in advance, **giving priority to the product selection**, avoiding restricted products and preparing best-sellers. Li Cong said, "the earlier to find opportunities before the market, the more chance to win. Do not wait for others to tell you, otherwise, it will definitely miss the opportunity." The market information showed that the prediction was valuable, and the data verified later have already existed, which could only offer a reference. High profits are always ready for those who can predict the upcoming risks correctly.

By using data analysis tools to actively gain experience against the COVID-19 pandemic in China, summarize the general development law, predict the situations and category demands abroad in combination with user portraits, ZongTeng Group gave priority to purchase goods that could meet market demands and were relatively scarce. Li Cong also mentioned that "the most important thing is that we have arranged in these aspects when most of our competitors have not been ready." According to the data provided by Tmall Global, from March to April, the sales of different categories on the cross-border e-commerce platforms were entirely different. On the one hand, orders of outdoor gardening products decreased by about 40% year-on-year; and on the other hand, the sales of indoor products increased rapidly. The sales volume of indoor sports equipment, including table tennis grid, football table and chess, demonstrated a year-on-year increase of 230%; and that of musical instruments, such as ukulele (a four-string plucked instrument) and harmonica, increased by 74% year-on-year. According to merchants,[2] the orders of dog food and treadmills increased three or four times year-on-year, and those of jigsaw puzzles increased about 10 times year-on-year. "The market has been on fire from April to May. The order volume of toys and household products is twice as high as the peak in previous years."

3.3.3 Holding Hands to Fight Against the COVID-19 Pandemic and Making Joint Effort with the Brand Matrix

The sub-brands of ZongTeng Group gave full play to their own advantages, and the brand matrix makes joint efforts to provide better service for customers and maintain the stability of the industry.

First, the freight price increasing and the suspension of the delivery of parcel post made it difficult for small and medium-sized merchants to sustain their existing modes. Therefore, "Goten" launched the substitute delivery for one piece in overseas warehouses, and direct delivery in overseas warehouses for non-general goods and large-sized products, so as to ensure that merchants had goods to sell. "Goten" **not only broadened the sales channels for small and medium-sized merchants, but also promoted the sales capacity, helping them to increase the stocking scale without adding any burden**. Li Cong said, "enterprises can buy our products on "Goten" without paying in advance. Instead, they can settle the payment after the products are sold out, so as to get rid of the financial pressure". During this period, "Goten" has helped some enterprises increase the sales volume by 328% with its own advantages.

Second, in order to help more merchants solve the problem of expensive logistics costs, "Goodcang" decided to drop the fulfillment of Fastway in Australia by 13% and add TOLL (Priority) TOLL (Standard) services from April 4 to ensure that overseas warehouses could operate normally. Wang Zuan said: "as a leading enterprise in the industry, it is our responsibility to guard the safety of the industry, especially a stable logistics environment." During the COVID-19 pandemic, "Goodcang" undertook the due obligations as a leading enterprise of cross-border logistics and warehousing. All employees stuck to their posts, overcame difficulties, and made efforts to ensure the smooth operation of warehouses. They also communicated with customers actively and provided timely solutions.

ZongTeng Group made the market forecast analysis and deployment in advance to help merchants tide over hard times. On April 8, dozens of business magnates in the cross-border industry, including Rondaful, Zehui Group and Yibai Network, were invited to attend an online discussion to **talk about the developing trend and countermeasures in the era of the COVID-19 pandemic**. At the meeting, according to the comparative analysis of the number of ICU beds, the capacity of nucleic acid testing, social control and mortality rate in major countries suffering from the COVID-19 pandemic, Li Cong concluded that developed countries tended to have fewer ICU beds instead. According to the recent data of confirmed COVID-19 cases in European countries, the lockdown measures implemented in Italy, Spain and other European countries a few weeks ago took effect, and the growth curve has tended to be flattened. It was expected to ease in late April, and the overall economy would gradually return to normal with the resumption of work in May. The recovery in the United States may be delayed for a month. In mid-to-late May, there would be a clear situation. Italy and Spain, the countries hardest hit by the COVID-19 pandemic in Europe, had seen a turning point after taking measures, and were expected to resume work in May. These predictions on the COVID-19 pandemic situation provided merchants of cross-border e-commerce with market information and evidence for decision-making on operations and stocking up, boosting their confidence for business.

The sales director of "Goodcang", Chen Kaibin, suggested that, due to the implementation of home quarantine abroad, the consumption peak of home life as the main category may appear in April to May. Merchants can replenish by sea and make specific analysis and decision based on their own situation. From May, with the gradual easing of the COVID-19 pandemic situation worldwide, and according to the analysis, it was highly likely that Europe would emerge from the COVID-19 pandemic earlier than the United States. It was suggested that merchants on platforms could prepare as early as possible for operation and stock up, and seize the market opportunities in Europe in May, especially exploiting the potential of home furnishing consumption.

4 Outlook of ZongTeng Group in the Post-Pandemic Era

4.1 Enhancing Capitalization Barriers

At present, the self-purchase of infrastructure equipment occupies a low proportion in the cross-border e-commerce industry, such as airplanes and aviation fulfillment distribution. With the few resources, most enterprises rely on the integration of external resources. In order to improve the overall control ability of the supply chain, it is necessary to increase capitalization investment and raise the proportion of self-purchase and self-operation.

4.2 Improving the Construction of G2G Network

In the post-pandemic era, the competitiveness of cross-border e-commerce enterprises, the concentration of the whole cross-border e-commerce industry, and the capacity of cross-border e-commerce market have to be improved in accordance with the principle of survival of the fittest. It requires the faster and more stable supply chain support and response. Therefore, ZongTeng Group should speed up the global network layout of G2G (Global To Global).

4.3 Enhancing the Ability to Withstand Supply Chain Risks

In the post-pandemic era, when new cross-border e-commerce brands transform overseas, the upstream supply chain should control the overall situation and enhance the risk resistance ability of the supply chain. There shall be no cultural differences in the sales links at the end of the supply chain. Attention shall be paid to grasp overseas culture and changing trends, focus on Tiktok and other channels, and try to exert the influence of brands on consumers in the cultural respect.

In conclusion, in the post-pandemic era, China has gradually recovered and resumed work and production orderly. The situation abroad has also eased, but it has left us with a long-term thinking. Li Cong said, "black swan events will happen sooner or later. Only a long-termist who can withstand the test every time and make quick and accurate decisions in the face of 'uncertainty' will win as the 'leftovers'." Reviewing the development course of cross-border e-commerce enterprises in China, those with advantages will always stand out after crisis, and they explore in the crisis, gain profit in risks and seize opportunities.

Case Appendix

Appendix 1 List of Quarantine Measures for "Goodcang"

Measures	Specific analysis
Health status report	One week before the resumption of work, the company began to deploy in all aspects and required employees to carry out the "daily health report" to ensure the physical health of all employees and respond to problems in time
Questionnaire	With the increasing number of people returning to work, the company issued a questionnaire entitled *Fight against the COVID-19 Pandemic Together, and Return to Work in Good Health Status* to ensure the life safety of employees returning to work and reduce risks
Online assessment	Before returning to work, the company issued the online course and examination of *Knowledge on the Prevention and Control of the COVID-19 Pandemic*, requiring employees to study and pass the examination with 100 points
Office management	The heads of first-level departments were required to strictly control the resumption of work, and divided the employees into three parts for management, i.e. on-site office, telecommuting at home and unable to telecommute, to overcome difficulties together
Strengthening the prevention and control	The company strengthened the prevention and control before resumption of work, and explained and investigated the situation of employees returning to work to ensure the enforceability
Telecommuting guidance	The company issued the *Telecommuting Guidebook for Employees* and *Notice on the Use and Specification of Telecommuting*. The telecommuting personnel were managed by the network management team of the technology department, and the work process and the company's management process were clarified to ensure the normal operation

Measures	Specific analysis
Standardized administration	The company established a WeChat group for telecommuting personnel, clarified the work discipline, and required all employees to sign-in before and after the noon break besides the daily attendance. It strived to create the same working state as usual with the strict management
Comprehensive disinfection	The company carried out strict disinfection measures on office foyers, corridors, conference rooms, elevators, staircases, toilets and other public parts, and controlled the public facilities that may be exposed comprehensively. The disinfection would be carried out twice a day to ensure a safe working environment for on-site employees
Distribution of masks	The company set up a mask distribution area at the gate, and distributed two masks per person every day. There were special dustbins for masks at the entrance of fire elevators on each floor, and the company would centrally dispose and disinfect these dustbins regularly
Dining requirements	Employees were encouraged to bring their own meals, and delivery men were prohibited from entering office buildings. In the grocery store in the company, there were convenience foods for employees to purchase with QR code payment

Source ZongTeng group

Appendix 2 List of Logistics Modes and Policy Changes of Each Country under the COVID-19 Pandemic

Country/Region	Logistics mode	Policy change
North America	Air passenger transport (mainly affecting the cargo transportation of belly holds of passenger planes)	Suspension of round-trip flights of China until the end of March or April
Europe		Suspension of most round-trip flights until the end of March and until mid-April for British Airways
Asia/Middle East/Africa		Suspension for some airlines until the end of March, and no specific date for some others
Australia/New Zealand		Suspension of round-trip flights of China until the end of March for Australia and New Zealand's airlines

Country/Region	Logistics mode	Policy change
China		According to civil aviation, since February, more than 50% of domestic flights have been canceled daily
Australia	Sea transportation	Quarantine of 14 days for ships from Chinese mainland from February 1, and another 14 days in case of any crew members were sick during this period
Philippines		Cancelling the right of ships passing through ports in countries affected by the COVID-19 pandemic to directly access to berths
Vietnam		Quarantine of 14 days for ships from countries with a high incidence of COVID-19, such as China, at a specific location
Malaysia		Quarantine of all ships from China until the completion of local inspections
United States and Singapore		Strengthening the quarantine for passengers, crew, and vessels visiting Chinese mainland within 14 days
Kuwait		Prohibiting all ships (except oil ships) from Chinese mainland, Hong Kong, Iraq, South Korea, Italy, Thailand, Singapore, Japan and other countries and regions from February 25
Brazil		Filling out the "Maritime Health Declaration"
Italy	Postal service	Suspension of the receipt, acceptance and delivery of parcels and express mail in some areas of China

Source Statistics of marketplus

Appendix 3 Suspension of Global Flights (as of March 27, 2020)

Emirates Airlines	100%	Avianca Airlines	100%	Lufthansa	95%
Cebu Pacific Air	100%	Blue Air	100%	Thai Airways International	90%
HongKong Express	100%	Cape Verde Airlines	100%	Air Finland	90%
Philippine Airlines	100%	Cayman Airlines	100%	Fiji Airways	90%
Starlux Airlines	100%	Comair Aviation	100%	Air France-KLM	90%
Jetstar Asia Airways	100%	Copa Airlines	100%	Scandinavian Airlines	90%
Thai Lion Air	100%	Czech Airlines	100%	EasyJet Airline	90%
Iraqi Airways	100%	EgyptAir	100%	TAP Portugal	90%
Royal Jordanian Airlin	100%	IndiGo	100%	Norwegian Airlines	85%
Kuwait Airways	100%	Kkulula Aviation	100%	EL AL Israel Airlines	85%
Porter Airlines	100%	La Compagnie	100%	Korean Air	85%
Austrian Airlines	100%	Luxair	100%	American Airline s	80%
LOT Polish Airlines	100%	Middle East Airlines	100%	Virgin Atlantic	80%
Brussels Airlines	100%	Montenegro Airlines	100%	Alitalia	75%
Jat Airway	100%	Qazaq Air	100%	IAG	75%
Air Ukraine	100%	Royal Air Maroc	100%	WestJet	75%
Jet2	100%	RwandAir	100%	QatarAirways	75%
Air Malta	100%	South African Express Airways	100%	Alaska Airlines	70%
Lauda Aviation	100%	SpiceJet Airlines	100%	Delta Air Lines	70%
Air Uganda	100%	Sunwing Airlines	100%	GOL Airlines	70%
Air Greenland	100%	Transavia	100%	LATAM aviation	70%
Etihad Airways	100%	Vistara Airlines	100%	United Airlines	60%
Air Antwerp	100%	Ryanair	100%	FlyArystan	60%
Air India	100%	Dubai Aerospace	100%	Air New Zealand	60%
Air India Express	100%	Air Arabia	100%	Malaysia Airlines	50%
Air Madagascar	100%	Kenya Airways	100%	Loganair	50%
Air Moldova	100%	AirBaltic	100%	Azul Airlines	50%
Air Transat	100%	Israir	100%	JetBlue Airways	40%
Philippines AirAsia	100%	South African Airways	100%	Hawaiian Airlines	40%
AirAsia India	100%	Air Astana	100%	Allegiant Air	35%
Air Zimbabwi	100%	Singapore Airlines	96%	Icelandair	35%
Israel Airlines	100%	SilkAir	96%	Spirit Airlines	25%
Arkia Israeli Airlines	100%	Cathay Pacific Airways	96%		

Source CARNOC.com

Appendix 4 Global Airport Closure (as of March 27, 2020)

Stop the operation	Shut down part of terminals	Closed tower
Dubai International Airport	JFK Airport	Chicago Midway Airport
Dubai World Central International Airport	Heathrow Airport	Las Vegas McCarran International Airport
Aeroport de Paris Bouvais-Tille	Manchester Airport	JFK Airport
Paris Orly Airport	Almeria Airport	Indianapolis International Airport
London City Airport	Charles de Gaulle Airport	Newcastle Williamtown Airport
Khujand Airport	Fiumicino Airport	LaGuardia Airport
Dushanbe Airport	Boryspil International Airport	Long Island MacArthur Airport
Nadi International Airport		Republic Airport (FRG)
V.C. Bird International Airport		Greater Peoria Airport
Sana'a International Airport		
Rome Ciampino Airport		
Beirut-Rafic Hariri International Airport		
Brussels South Charleroi Airport		
Salajevo International Airport		

Source http://www.CARNOC.com

Appendix 5 Research Report Released by Imperial College London

Discovery	Analysis	Basic strategy and impact
The highest death toll can be 510,000	The detailed figures of death toll in the United Kingdom under different measures were predicted through modelling If the government does not take any action on COVID-19, 81% of its population will be infected, which will cause 510,000 deaths; if the government insists on limited control measures, such as home quarantine of symptomatic patients, the number would be halved to 260,000; and if the strictest measures were taken, such as closing schools, banning gatherings, and enforcing home quarantines, the death toll would fall to less than 20,000 in two years since the outbreak	According to Imperial College London, there are two basic strategies that countries are currently using for the prevention of the COVID-19 pandemic: (1) Mitigation, which focuses on slowing the spread of the virus. It may not stop the spread, but it can effectively reduce the peak demands for medical care because of the outbreak of the COVID-19 pandemic and safeguard the lives of those with severe symptoms. This is the strategy currently adopted in the United Kingdom (2) Suppression, which aims at completely reversing the growth trend of the COVID-19 pandemic through strong intervention, and reduce the number of confirmed cases to a very low level and remain. This is the strategy currently adopted in China. Both strategies have their advantages and disadvantages. For the mitigation strategy, the threshold is relatively low, and the government can reduce the medical demands at the peak of the COVID-19 pandemic by 2/3 and halve the number of deaths through measures such as home quarantine of suspected cases and "social distancing" of the elderly and the less immune population But taking the measure could still result in hundreds of thousands of deaths, and health systems (especially the intensive care units) would still end up being overwhelmed For suppression measures, the government needs to take the measure of "social distancing" towards the entire population of the country, quarantine confirmed cases and their family members, and close schools. Such strong interventions can be effective in reducing the number of confirmed cases in the short term, although they may put a huge pressure on the health system Adopting this measure requires the government to maintain "strong intervention" until the vaccine is in use, which can take as long as 18 months or more. It is difficult for many countries Therefore, the study concluded that the best approach is to adopt an adaptive control policy, that is, to implement flexible control measures depending on the number of ICU beds in the United Kingdom
Peak of mortality after 3 months	If nothing is done, the peak of mortality in the United Kingdom could come in 3 months, almost around mid-June	
Inevitable pressure on NHS	In case of no control measures taken, there will be no ICU beds left in the United Kingdom by the second week of April, and during the peak period, the demand for ICU will be about 30 times than the current volume of ICU beds available in the United Kingdom	
Only easing pressure on NHS by closing schools	Research shows that closing schools does not necessarily ease pressure on NHS. If no measures are taken, the peak of demand for ICU will be around April, and taking measures can only delay the onset, and the number of ICU beds in demand will be the same as that without any measures. If schools are closed, although it will effectively curb the spread of the COVID-19 pandemic in the short term and keep the demand for ICU below the number that the nation can afford, a similar peak will still occur in the future after restrictions are lifted But if schools are not closed, while there will be a short-term surge in the demand for ICU, which will exceed the hospital capacity, the rebound will be relatively subdued after October when restrictions are lifted	

Discovery	Analysis	Basic strategy and impact
Vaccine R&D, the only "exit mechanism"	However, with stricter measures in place, society as a whole also needs an "exit mechanism", that is, people choose when to end the control measures and go back to normal life Otherwise, once the restrictions are lifted, the virus is likely to make a comeback For this "exit mechanism," the report states that vaccination is "the only feasible exit mechanism" To avoid another rebound in virus transmission, these policies must be maintained until a large stockpile of vaccine is available, which will likely take 18 months or more In other words, according to the current plan, the British people need to maintain a "social distancing" life for up to 18 months	
Limited effectiveness of single non-pharmacological interventions (e.g., home quarantine)	In the report, the researchers evaluated the effectiveness of a number of current public health interventions, also known as non-pharmaceutical interventions (NPIs). These measures are primarily designed to reduce the rate of population exposure and thus slow the spread of the virus And this study concludes that the effectiveness of any single non-pharmaceutical intervention is very limited, and that a combination of interventions is needed to have a substantial impact on virus transmission	

Source Impact of non-pharmaceutical interventions (NPIs) to reduce COVID19 mortality and healthcare demand, a research report released by Imperial College London

Appendix 6 Growth Rate of Confirmed COVID-19 Cases per Million Population by Country from April 5 to 9

Country	Speed increase	New infections per million		Country	Speed increase	New infections per million	
		4.9–4.5	4.1–4.5			4.9–4.5	4.1–4.5
Indonesia	66%	1.1	0.7	Italy	5%	61.2	58
Chile	52%	28.8	19.0	Austria	3%	35.1	34
Malaysia	48%	8.0	5.4	Pakistan	0%	1.8	1.8
UK	46%	71.5	49	Denmark	0%	54.7	55
Baxi	46%	7.3	5.0	United States	−2%	91.7	93.6
Thailand	40%	1.4	1.0	Japan	−11%	2.3	2.6
Mexico	37%	2.6	1.9	Germany	−13%	49.9	58
Turkey	32%	48.7	36.8	Spain	−19%	116.0	143
India	32%	0.6	0.4	France	−33%	82.4	124
South Africa	28%	1.3	1.0	Iran	−40%	19.4	32.5
Argentina	24%	2.6	2.1	South Korea	−44%	0.9	1.7
Sweden	23%	56.8	46				
Australia	16%	8.3	7.2				

Source Forecast Report on Foreign Pandemic Trends of ZongTeng group

Appendix 7 Confirmed COVID-19 Cases per Million Population from April 5 to 9

Countries pending on the left have seen a rise in the number of cases confirmed while countries taking off in contrary, are having landings.

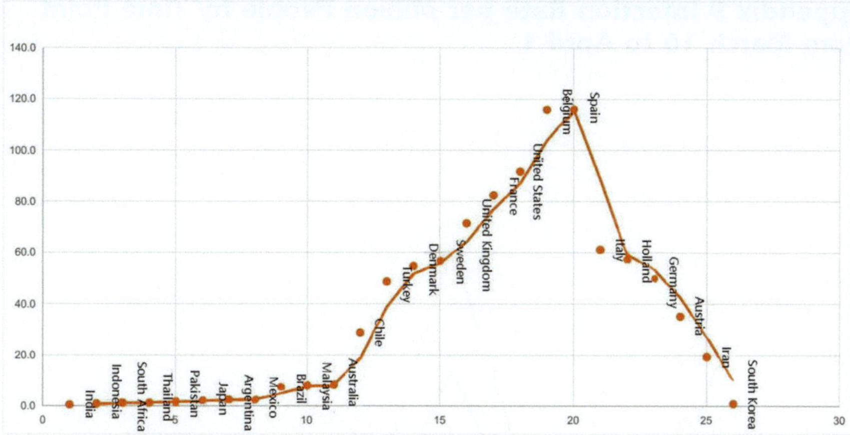

Source Forecast Report on Foreign Pandemic Trends of ZongTeng group

Appendix 8 Confirmed COVID-19 Cases per Million Population from April 1 to 5

The United States: all states are expected to go over the roller-coaster hill one after another within the next 3 weeks.

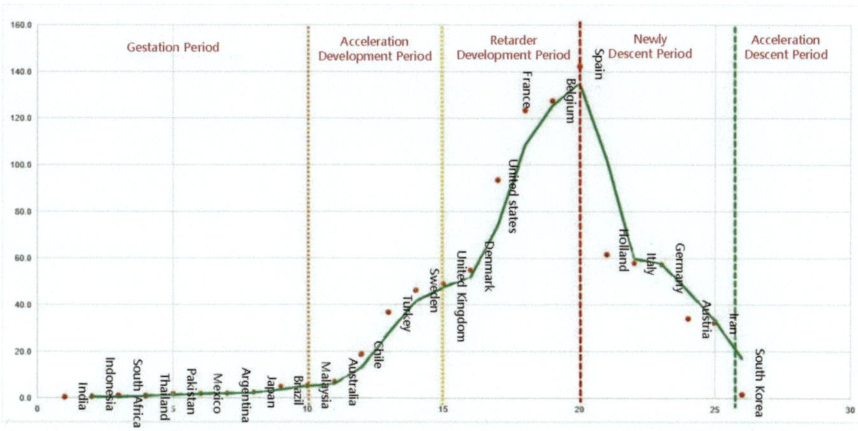

Source Forecast Report on Foreign Pandemic Trends of ZongTeng group

Appendix 9 Infection Rate per Million People by Time Point from March 16 to April 1

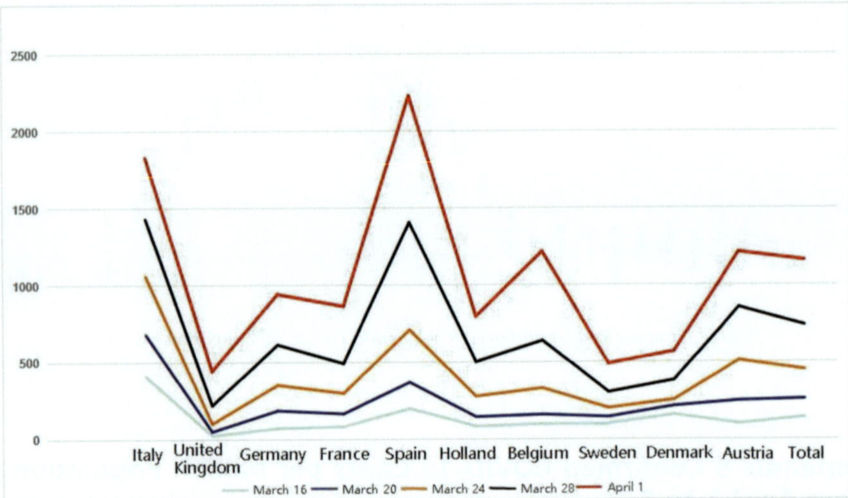

Source Forecast Report on Foreign Pandemic Trends of ZongTeng group

Digital Marketing Transformation of Down Clothing Brand Under "New Retail+Live Broadcast"

Guxian Miao

1 Introduction

The national production of down clothing was 196 million units from January to December 2019, with the market sales of CNY106.8 billion. At present, the penetration rate of down clothing in China is less than 10%, where the rigid demands drive the growth of the industry scale. In addition, the living standard of residents has improved rapidly, which will drive the further expansion of the market scale of down clothing industry in China. The demand for fashion is becoming increasingly strong, and the traffic marketing will break the "ceiling" of the industry. With the in-depth application of digital technologies such as Internet, big data and cloud computing, as well as the rise of live broadcast and short video marketing, textile and apparel e-commerce have undergone great changes. The industry presents the online and offline integration. The "social+content+e-commerce" model has become a breakthrough, and the market has sunk to third and fourth tier cities and digital transformation. Textile and apparel have become the largest category of e-commerce live broadcast, which can effectively alleviate the pain point of online shopping through multi-dimensional display and strong interaction of live broadcast. In line with the report of AliResearch, the overall penetration rate of the live broadcast on Taobao in 2020 is twice that of the same period in 2019, and the number of products purchased by users through live broadcast has increased by 190% year on year, becoming the mainstream of new commerce. The essence of digital transformation and upgrading is to comprehensively digitize the industrial chain by using digital technology driven by end consumer demand. The digital marketing is the first step of enterprise digital transformation. Through the precipitation analysis of numerous sales data, it can guide the business links such as

G. Miao (✉)
Fanli Business School, Shaoxing Vocational and Technical College, Shaoxing, China

J. Zhang et al. (eds.), *Innovation of Digital Economy*, Management for Professionals,
https://doi.org/10.1007/978-981-99-1741-9_7

enterprise R&D and production. How to promote the digital marketing transformation and upgrading of down clothing enterprises under the trend of new retail and e-commerce live broadcast?

2 Development Status of the Company and E-Commerce

Zhejiang Baisihan Down Co., Ltd., founded in 1998, is engaged in down acquisition and sales (Fig. 1). In 2006, Baisihan was officially established. The concept of "professional down bedding and original goose down fashion" was introduced by Baisihan, which entered the domestic market as the self-owned brand. In 2008, Baisihan vigorously promoted its e-commerce business, incorporating non-traditional channels such as e-commerce into the company's long-term development strategy. In 2016, Baisihan officially launched the professional down platform plan, putting forward the central after-sales service system, and bringing out the concept of "10-year warranty", which marked a new era for Chinese down industry. In March 2017, Baisihan was officially listed on NEEQ, opening up a brilliant chapter at a new starting point. In 2018, the first "Down Life House" flagship store was opened in Nantong, and in October of the same year, the brand shop in Lijiang, Yunnan Province was opened, marking Baisihan's official entry into the terminal market, which created a new model of home texture display, different from the traditional ones. The company is currently building a new production line of fine down with 1,000 tons per annum and the first professional tourist experience factory in Chinese industry, which will deeply integrate the innovations of the Internet and enhance the innovation and productivity of the real economy.

The company has begun to have brand effects. Since its establishment, it has initially formed a certain brand effect in the down home textile industry by relying on the industrial advantages in the region and its own advanced quality control methods, combined with Internet e-commerce sales. Great significance was attached to the company by various e-commerce platforms, some of which focus on supporting the company's brand to become the leading one in the down home textile industry. The company has won many awards on e-commerce platforms, becoming the first benchmark brand in the online down home textile industry and leading the sales of down products in the "Double Eleven" event for many years.

Fig. 1 Brand of Baisihan

Fig. 2 E-commerce sales channels of Baisihan

The company has long-term and stable cooperation with many e-commerce platforms. After years of development and accumulation, the company has formed a large-scale sales network, and currently has close cooperation with all major e-commerce platforms, such as Tmall, JD.COM, Taobao, Vipshop, Pinduoduo and Tiktok Shop (Fig. 2). The above-mentioned e-commerce platforms are all mainstream e-commerce platforms with a high number of visitors and strong influence, which can expand the publicity effect for the company, recommend potential customers and provide services such as industry data analysis to ensure the continuous growth of the company's operation scale.

On the new retail business expansion, in 2020, relying on years of Internet operation experience, through the use of fan big data, combined with offline experience, and online transaction business model, Baisihan followed the "experience to enhance the popularity and then to promote sales" market development policy, and focused on: "tourism factory tour and experience entertainment tour" industrial development pattern to build down culture, tourism experience boutique line overall idea, create two experience theme tourism, carry out the construction of five special sections, and build mobile sales mini program. The company will enhance its interactive experience; and comprehensively promote the brand of Baisihan and enhance its industrial scale and efficiency. The project effectively responds to the market development trend and the times, providing new opportunities for the company's future business development, thus ensuring the company's continued profitability.

2.1 Market Positioning of Down Clothing and Home Textile

The company specializes in the production and sale of down bedding and clothing, and has been focusing on the development of its main business since its establishment. Relying on the favorable conditions of being located in the light textile city of Keqiao District, Shaoxing City, and using the Internet e-commerce sales model, the company is actively expanding its clothing and down home textile categories, and insists on high quality and is committed to improving the quality of the company's products. The company implements quality control into every production step to ensure that the products sold meet national and industry standards and customer requirements. After years of business development, the company has formed an integrated production management system from the purchase of down raw materials, production and processing, and e-commerce sales, and has accumulated a number of stable quality customers.

2.2 Digital Technology Empowers the Enterprise Development

Embracing external empowerment: Baisihan has taken the initiative to embrace external empowerment in the hope of gaining professional escort while developing autonomously. Platforms and specialist service providers who have access to data and technology become key enablers of brands' digital practices.

Countermeasures: the company will continue to cultivate quality, strictly control the quality of raw materials and the process, and combine with the emerging self-media consumption channels, using the newly built down products sightseeing factory in 2019, from the online and offline two-pronged approach to improve brand awareness and increase sales to improve the core competitiveness of the brand (Fig. 3).

Reintroducing the shop value: the argument that e-commerce is impacting the entities has been broken, and the advantage of shops reaching consumers directly makes them the basic carrier for brands to build their digital scenarios.

Fig. 3 Offline experience factory

Online and offline integration: with the continuous transformation of digitalization, the depth and breadth of the online and offline integration of brands have been strengthened. The effect of $1 + 1 > 2$ is increasingly significant.

Layout of social e-commerce: the traffic value and incremental value of social e-commerce have been verified, and the WeChat platform, with the most well-polished products and the largest social traffic, is about to become the new high ground of the retail battlefield.

3 Industry Background

3.1 Macro Market

Shaoxing is the most complete and competitive textile industry cluster in the world, and has become the "Fashion Textile Capital", the "Global Hosiery Capital" and the "International Tie City", where global textile indices are published, product standards are set and fashion creativity is led.

Data show that in 2015, 2016 and 2017, the national production of down clothing was 336, 333, 286 million pieces respectively, and 196 million pieces from January to December in 2018. The declining trend of down clothing production was due to the closure of some small factories led by tightening environmental protection policies. According to China National Garment Association, the scale of down clothing market in China was about CNY106.8 billion in 2018, up more than 10% compared with the previous year. In recent years, due to the huge clothing consumption market in China and the gradual expansion of the market, foreign clothing brands have entered China one after another (Fig. 4).

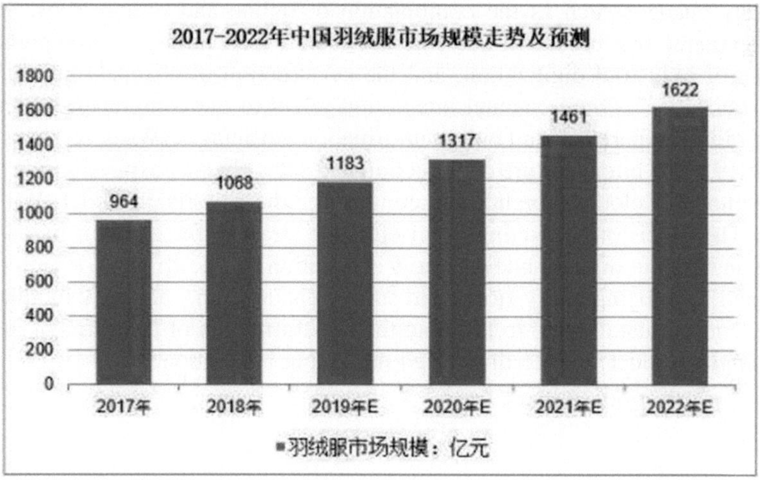

Fig. 4 Scale of down clothing market in China

3.2 Micro Market

The age group analysis of popular women's down clothing of Chinese brands shows that the online selling mainly demarcates the age positioning of women's down clothing by 5 years with the ranges of 18–24, 24–29, 30–34 and 35–39.

In the age group demarcation related to the best-selling women's down clothing of the brand, the main range of 25–29 years old accounts for 65%, the following range of 18–24 years old accounts for 24%, and the ranges of 30–34 and 35–39 years old account for only 5% and 6% respectively. It can be inferred that the online sales of women's down clothing of Chinese brands mainly focus on consumers aged 18–29.

In 2019, the top 10 brands accounted for 29.78%, with more competitive brands and high market concentration. The top 3 brands in October were Bosideng, Misun and Yaloo, accounting for 7.53%, 5.93% and 4.31% respectively. As for the sales of top 10 brands of thickened down clothing this month, the market share pf these three brands far exceeded others.

4 Problems in the Development of Enterprises

4.1 New Retail Era for the Garment Industry

"New retail" is a new industry mode in which enterprises use digital technology to realize the omni-channel transformation of products from design, production to sales, and integrate marketing based on consumer big data (Zhao & Xu, 2017). The new relationship of "people, goods and markets" is reconstructed by online and offline sales and modern logistics. The core of "new retail" is to improve the user experience (Xiao & Liang, 2020). At present, in the garment industry, there are many changes such as the combination of online and offline sales, the rise of e-commerce live broadcast and Internet celebrity economy, the comprehensive upgrade of industrial digitization, and the construction of channels in "third and fourth tier cities". Omni-channel integration refers to the comprehensive integration of offline experience and online information advantages (Wang & Shen, 2019; Zhu, 2019). The brand culture construction and sales channel expansion are important methods of clothing brand marketing under the new retail model (Wu et al., 2020). The precision marketing is an effective strategy for garment brands. The online and offline organic integration is a direction of "new retail", which can be explained as utilizing entity stores and supply chain offline, and new mobile technology and big data online to promote the transformation of the garment industry from single product sales to diversified marketing interaction.

4.2 Rise of E-Commerce Live Broadcast of Clothing Brands

As a popular marketing mode, the live broadcast marketing makes full use of the online interaction and communication between live-streamers and users to achieve sales targets. The emerging live broadcast platforms tend to develop with diversification and differentiation, which provides a solid foundation for the development of new retail. Due to its advantages of active interaction and participation, the sense of reality scene, free and extensive contents and forms, e-commerce live broadcast has been an important opportunity for the development of garment brands. For marketing strategies under e-commerce live broadcast, efforts shall be intensified to three live broadcast elements of traffic, content and form, complete the upgrading and innovation of e-commerce live broadcast, and satisfy customers' needs for personalized service and consumption upgrading. The similarity of communication style between live-streamers and customers during the live broadcast will also affect the purchase intention. The strategies of garment e-commerce marketing in the era of live broadcast shall be updated continuously (Niu & Shen, 2020). New modes of brand marketing must be original, high-quality, professional and unique. The product innovation allows consumers and enterprises to interact and cooperate with each other in the design, development, production and consumption of products or services.

4.3 Digital Marketing Transformation and Upgrading in the Industry

Clothing products are characterized with no standard, diversification in aesthetics and changing trends. Consumers in the era of mobile Internet become more independent and pursue diversity. Therefore, for brands, it is necessary to improve their understanding of consumers through the digital innovation. The essence of clothing retail digitalization is a comprehensive digital upgrading of the industrial chain with big data and new technologies and consumers as the main driven, and finally realizes the improvement of efficiency and experience through the online and offline integration. The digital marketing is the first step of enterprise digital transformation. Through the precipitation analysis of numerous sales data, it can guide the business links such as enterprise R&D and production. Marketing channels are extremely important in the digital transformation of brands, which requires the online and offline omni-channel layout. The precision marketing on new media platforms, and the creation of digital scene experience are the most effective marketing strategies (Li, 2017). The full-process digital interaction between enterprises and customers is available with CRM system. Through delving deep into data and statistical analysis, the sales process can be continuously adjusted and optimized. Several significant evaluation indicators in the digital transformation, including the product service innovation rate, customer value proposition, and data capitalization, can be reached with the layout of digital channels, generation of customer data value, precision marketing, and SCRM social relationship management (Wu, 2020; Ren & Zheng, 2019).

5 Digital Marketing Strategy of Down Clothing Brand Under "New Retail+Live Broadcast"

5.1 Building Online and Offline Omni-Channel Marketing Centered on Consumers

With the trend of consumption upgrading, online and offline channels are integrated. Digital marketing channels shall be reconstructed focusing on "people, goods and markets" to achieve the omni-channel marketing. A closed loop of consumer service experience can be built at the terminal sales channel through online and offline synchronizations as it directly relates to consumers (Hong, 2018). Focus shall be put on creating a digital channel with both social e-commerce and traditional e-commerce as methods of traffic attraction, and offline physical stores as the carrier of experience service. Figure 2 shows the digital marketing channels of down clothing. Value of stores: in the circumstance of the new retail, stores are the primary carrier of digital channels of brands to solve problems of online shopping. Facing the difficulties of traffic decline and high cost on promotion, traditional e-commerce channels are actively expanding the traffic and content of e-commerce live broadcast. Layout of social e-commerce: attracting followers from the private traffic to traditional e-commerce, including the content promotion and word-of-mouth marketing on Tiktok, Kwai, WeChat official account, Xiaohongshu, e-commerce live broadcast and others, the traffic value of social e-commerce has been verified.

5.2 Precision Marketing Relying on the Big Data Analysis

The essential difference between the new retail and traditional retail is that for online stores, the most important thing is building relationships with consumers rather than selling products. More accurately, it refers to building the physique database of Chinese based on services and data and constructing the consumer experience system that can satisfy the needs of habits and preferences of consumers. To carry out the precision marketing based on the big data analysis, it requires to send advertisements as per the situation of customers, reinforce the precision of market positioning and improve the degree of personalized service (Li, 2017). The precision marketing based on the big data analysis is presented as Fig. 5. The first stage, data collection, includes the obtaining of user identity and data of product, marketing and channel. In the second stage, data analysis, the collected data are entered into the big data target marketing model, and analyzed with the big data mining technology to fetch such effective information as customer behavior characteristics, including the basic attributes of consumers,

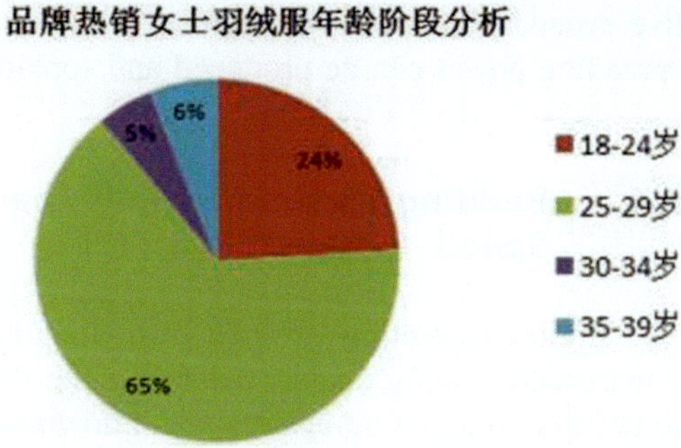

Fig. 5 Precision clothing marketing relying on the big data analysis

product preferences, purchasing power, promotion interests, consumer behaviors and social interests. In the third stage of implementing marketing strategies, the intelligent precision marketing in accordance with multi-position labels will be achieved. Based on the big data analysis and driving, the core marketing capability of down clothing brands will be built. The data in the sales process can be precipitated and used, and two aspects of business thinking, i.e. management insight (data present), and instructions sent to other business systems after the algorithm calculation, can be formed.

5.3 Content Innovation Marketing with E-Commerce Live Broadcast

There is the phenomenon of content homogeneity in the live broadcasting with the further development, causing the aesthetic fatigue and income decrease. The scenario is a core competitiveness, which requires merchants to figure out more and better ways to display products than platform e-commerce and traditional offline channels. For the content innovation, the retention time of viewers is very important in the live broadcast industry. Therefore, more interesting contents are needed to keep viewers in live broadcast rooms. New consumption scenes are constructed through live broadcast to make the path from content to consumption smoother. New way of existence of brand marketing requires original, high-quality, professional and unique live broadcast contents, including: cooperation of Internet celebrities and stars in the aspect of functional requirements; and emotionally touching and brand stories in the aspect of emotional needs. The novelty of live broadcast has become the focus of users' attention. How to tell their own brand stories and establish their own brand personality are the key to the development of clothing e-commerce brands. The live broadcast content are shifting from UGC user production to PGC professional production. Content producers can quickly reflect the needs of users or consumers and give timely responses and adjustments, which greatly reduces the time for brands to understand user demand compared with other methods. As live broadcast platforms are characterized by high interaction, consumers and live-streamers interact and participate in the creation of live broadcast contents. Therefore, a large number of Internet memes with great spreading power can be produced and spread rapidly.

5.4 Building Flexible Supply Chains According to the Response Speed

The digital marketing extends from intelligent manufacturing to upstream and downstream supply chains, achieving the data-driven operation, putting the customer first, integrating upstream and downstream supply chains, data-oriented and end-to-end operation, and horizontal integration of orders, planning and whole logistics process. Consumers have a stronger personalized demand for products, and they are more inclined to replace delayed gratification with instant gratification. Based on the support of digital technologies such as mobile and Internet of Things, it provides new and convenient products and personalized services for consumers. Therefore, from the live broadcast, ordering, production, logistics and door-to-door delivery, it is necessary to solve the pain points of consumers' selection of goods in a one-stop shop, and produce products that meet enough consumers' expectations in the shortest time. Because of this, e-commerce platforms are also making changes. They all start to target upstream factories to quickly launch and ship products cooperated with platforms. The advantages of C2M (reverse customization) e-commerce mode dominated by the consumer market are gradually emerging. It is to build a digital flexible supply chain of value chain (end-to-end integration) to transform traditional supply chain into intelligent, efficient and connected digital supply chain, including design, manufacturing, channel, sales and other business links. The data collection and analysis are carried out with the digital technology, the supply chain data integration is conducted with the value chain analysis, and the intelligent decision-making and control are realized with digital modules acting on business processes.

5.5 Product and Service Innovation Based on Terminal Consumption Demands

Clothing brand merchants need to make use of digital marketing transformation and constantly excavate and create demands to realize the continuous communication and effective transformation. New products and services for customers shall be developed through continuous digital marketing cycles. The consumer connection effect under the live broadcast includes multiple links such as consumers and brands, consumers and consumers, and consumers and opinion leaders. The publicity in the early stage of live broadcasting, the realization of live broadcasting, and the tracking service of products in the later stage are inseparable from the real-time interaction and sharing between brands and consumers on the live broadcast platforms. Multi-link connections enable users to participate deeply in the product development process and stimulate their enthusiasm to engage in the development of new products. According to their own brand characteristics, clothing e-commerce brands timely reflect the needs of consumers and launch joint personalized customization through the interaction with consumers. High participation and interaction can shorten the distance between consumers and brands, improve the user experience, strengthen the cognition towards brands, and ultimately help to increase the brand loyalty of consumers.

6 Epilogue

Down clothing brands need to accelerate the digital transformation and upgrading through new retail and e-commerce live broadcast in the post-pandemic era. The digital marketing is the first step of enterprise digital transformation. Through the precipitation analysis of numerous sales data, it can guide the business links such as enterprise R&D and production. Efforts shall be intensified to build online and offline omni-channel marketing with consumers as the center, reconstruct "people, goods and markets", and create closed-loop consumer service experience. Based on big data analysis, precision marketing is realized to strengthen the precision of market positioning and improve the degree of personalized service. The content innovation marketing shall be carried out through the e-commerce live broadcast to create new consumption scenes and make paths from content to consumption smoother. The brand merchants shall build flexible supply chains according to the response speed, achieving the data-driven operation, putting the customer first, and integrating upstream and downstream supply chains. Product and service innovation shall be conducted based on terminal consumption demand to realize continuous communication and effective transformation. The development of down clothing brands and the digital transformation and upgrading of enterprises will be promoted by the combination of new retail, e-commerce live broadcast and digital economy. On such basis, enterprises will develop towards a personalized, customized and intelligent "new retail" enterprise driven by data.

References

Hong, C. (2018). Research on marketing strategy of live shopping guide based on customer loyalty. *Business Economy, 11*, 90–91.

Li, J. (2017). Research on network marketing strategy based on big data precision marketing. *Business Economic Research, 2017*(06).

Niu, S., & Shen, L. (2020). Strategic analysis of marketing channels of clothing brand under digital transformation. *Wool Textile Journal, 48*(4).

Ren, L., & Zheng, H. B. (2019). Drive and evolution of the new retail design for silk brands under the omni channel. *China Textile Leader, 2019*(11).

Shao, P., & Liang, J. (2020). Research on omnichannel integration model of clothing brands in new retail era. Fangzhi Xuebao. *Journal of Textile Research, 41*, 150–157.

Wang, R. R., & Shen, L. (2019). Analysis on marketing strategy of new fashion brand under retail. *Wool Textile Journal, 47*(4).

Wu, Y. F. (2020). Study on upgrading path of decentralized transmitted model in chinese fashion brands-taking live broadcast as an example. *China Textile Leader, 2020*(07).
Wu, N., Ning, C. H., & Gong, X. X. (2020). Research on the mechanism of the role of communication style similarity on purchase intention in live marketing. *Foreign Economy and Management, 42*, 81–95.
Zhao, S. M., & Xu, X. (2017). The meaning pattern and development path of 'new retail.' *China Business and Market, 31*(5), 12–20.
Zhu, Z. Y. (2019). Research on retail omni-channel marketing strategy under OTO model. *Modern Marketing, 2019*(04).

Value Co-creation of Community E-commerce Platform: How Does Bilibili Balance Between Content and Commercialization?

Lu Sun, Jiahui Zhang, and Juping Shou

1 Introduction

The rise of social computing tools, such as Web2.0, and the emergence of Facebook, Twitter, WeChat, Weibo and other various online media have witnessed an era of social commerce (Efraim et al., 2018). As a new form of social commerce, a community e-commerce platform can not only be used for social interconnection, but also conform to forms of expression of the community, such as emphasizing social relationships derived from interests, with more attention on the content, interaction and sharing than those of social e-commerce. Therefore, community e-commerce is neither a subversion of social e-commerce nor a simple extension of it. For community e-commerce platforms, on the one hand, high-quality content should be continuously provided when facing high input costs; on the other hand, commercialization should be realized without affecting user experience. This is the common problem encountered by community e-commerce in the development process. How to balance between ensuring the quality of community content and realizing commercialization? For example, "Meilishuo", a community e-commerce platform in the vertical field focusing on women's fashion sharing in the past few years, was once the largest community-based media in women's fashion in China. After the introduction of e-commerce to realize commercialization, the community function of the platform was seriously weakened, and the platform merged with

This case was funded by the following projects: Regional Program of National Natural Science Foundation of China (71,962,013); Humanities and Social Sciences Research Project of Ministry of Education (19YJC630146); Hangzhou Normal University Scientific Research Start-up Fund Project (RWSK20201025); Hangzhou Philosophy and Social Sciences Planning (Z21JC100); Zhejiang Provincial Basic Public Benefit-oriented Research Plan Project (LY22G02005).

L. Sun (✉) · J. Zhang · J. Shou
Alibaba Business School, Hangzhou Normal University, Hangzhou, China

J. Zhang et al. (eds.), *Innovation of Digital Economy*, Management for Professionals,
https://doi.org/10.1007/978-981-99-1741-9_8

its typical imitator http://www.Mogu.com in 2016 and transformed into a type of shelf-based e-commerce. The root cause lies in the fact that in the process of commercialization, enterprises have not found solutions on how to keep a dynamic balance between content and commercialization, growth and user experience, and have not figured out the process of value creation between enterprises and other participants.

Founded in 2009, Bilibili is now the most active cultural community for young people. The growth path of Bilibili is shown in Fig. 1. In March 2018, Bilibili (NASDAQ: BILI) was successfully listed on NASDAQ in the United States. In March 2021, it was listed for the second time in Hong Kong (Hong Kong Stock: BiliBili-SW09626). In just three years, the market value of Bilibili has nearly quadrupled. According to its Q3 financial report of 2021, monthly active users of Bilibili reached 267 million, and the average daily usage time reached a record high of 88 min. Healthy user growth and enlarged community ecosystem help realize the commercialization of Bilibili (Bilibili, 2021). At the same time, it faces an unavoidable problem: heavy losses! Why can Bilibili achieve high-speed user growth and gain recognition from the capital market under the condition of continuous loss? In the face of continuous loss, how does Bilibili alleviate the anxiety to achieve a balance between content and commercialization? Has Bilibili found a way to break the balance between content and commercialization?

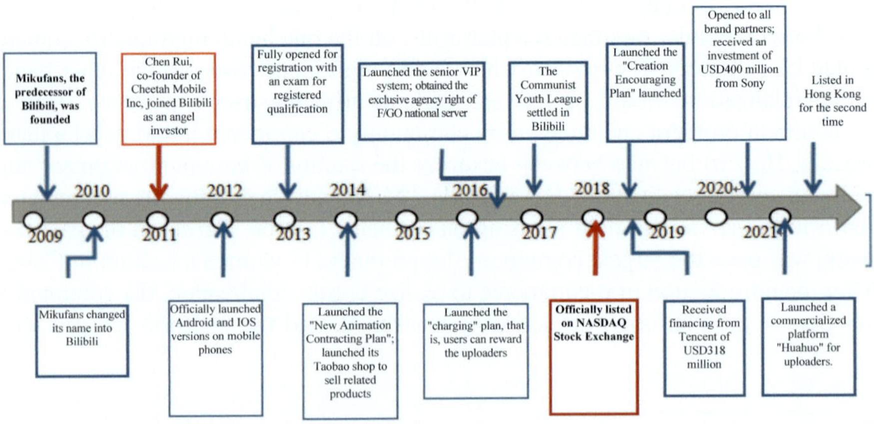

Fig. 1 Development course and key events of Bilibili

2 Small Website

One day in 2009, an official member user of AcFun[1] named "⑨bishi" (Xu Yi) left the website. On June 26, 2009, he set up another bullet screen video website, Mikufans, and began to attract new users. This is the predecessor of Bilibili, which was renamed in January 2010. Initially, Bilibili was designed as a bullet screen website to provide users with ACG (Animation, Comic and Game) contents, supporting instant bullet screen comments. Videos usually came from new animations broadcasted by Nippon Television Network, NICONICO and YouTube, and also included domestic animation works and re-creation contents produced by animation lovers. Followers affectionately called it "Small Website".

2.1 Standby Website—A More Stable Sharing Website for Bullet Screen Videos

In the early days, Xu Yi founded Mikufans, also called the Standby Website of Acfun and the predecessor of Bilibili, because the website server of Acfun was unstable and caused poor user experience. The original version of Bilibili was very simple, with only basic comment function, bullet screen sending, video watching and submission. With a quite lukewarm popularity, it only acted as a small community website with a stable and good community atmosphere for ACG culture lovers. Users mainly came through the recommendation of ACG lovers and some users from AcFun. The user number accumulated slowly, but the platform owned high attractiveness and the community atmosphere was harmonious. At the beginning, Bilibili users basically held the ideal of building a home for ACG, and came to Bilibili completely because of pure love for ACG, not for the benefit. Most of them were severe ACG culture lovers. At that time, Bilibili was a quite small community that did not even get registered, and the website did not make any profit. Obviously, at that time, Bilibili was positioned as a bullet screen website for ACG, providing a better and more stable video sharing community for ACG lovers.

2.2 Value Co-creation Activities in the Beginning Stage

(1) Social interaction

Bilibili is a community sharing platform for ACG lovers, and its value co-creation activities are mainly manifested in creating cultural atmosphere and social interaction for the purpose of attracting users' attention. Bilibili is very good at using

[1] AcFun was established in June 2007, whose name is short for Anime Comic Fun. It is the first bullet screen video website in Chinese mainland and was wholly acquired by Kwai in 2018.

content interaction to create a good community atmosphere. For example, in February 2010, it organized 40 uploaders to produce the first Spring Festival greeting video (later developed into the New Year Carnival), which attracted many netizens to watch and gathered quite a lot of popularity. Through the effort of uploaders,[2] videos and movies based on ACG elements in the external networks were carried onto Bilibili to quickly attract ordinary users with similar hobbies and needs to watch, and enhance user stickiness and community identity; at the same time, based on the founder team's fanatical love for ACG culture, after the establishment of the platform, Bilibili witnessed stable update and optimization, continuously reduced its deficiencies, to improve user experience, sharing functions and social interaction.

(2) Content interaction

When most users adapt to the community atmosphere, they will actively share their re-creations[3] or ideas related to ACG culture, which is called UGC (User Original Content). As users share their re-creations and ideas in the online community, the interaction is extended from social level to content level. As the original content gradually replaced reposted video to dominate the platform, the content structure has been continuously improved. With the continuous growth of users and videos, the platform and users promote each other, and the community atmosphere is getting strong. Bilibili and users are accumulating energy to achieve value creation, thus forming a benign cycle of mutual benefit.

(3) Functional interaction

When Bilibili was still a niche community, it already had the basic characteristics of value creation: interactivity, that is, the interaction between uploaders and users. Although the website is simple, the main functions of the website, such as comments, voting and bullet screen, connect the uploaders and users to have real-time conversations. All lines in the bullet screen have equal weight. This is a unique interactive mechanism of Bilibili, and it was rare on other Internet platforms at that time. The comments of both VIP users and ordinary users have equal chance to be exposed on the bullet screen and seen by everyone. It is a truly flat and completely decentralized interactive mechanism.

[2] Uploader is a network buzzword. It mainly refers to the person who uploads videos in Bilibili. Uploaders are mainly divided into two categories: the carriers who mainly repost videos of other uploaders to Bilibili with marking of information and sources; and the original creators who participate in the production of videos themselves, and will check the "self-made" option when uploading.

[3] Re-creation is a work that users re-edit, re-dub and re-produce based on other videos, which is the characteristic content of Bilibili, such as the auto-tune remix-themed content, and the series of "3-min to know a movie".

3 Develop from Nothing

In 2011, Chen Rui, co-founder of Cheetah Mobile Inc, joined Bilibili as an angel investor. In 2014, he officially entered Bilibili and became chairman and CEO. In 2018, he successfully led Bilibili to the capital market. When Chen Rui just joined Bilibili, it was a small club driven entirely by ideals and hobbies, with almost no corporate governance system. As a senior and successful professional manager, and a big fan of animation, Chen has, step by step, achieved the corporatization operation of Bilibili from scratch. In fact, Bilibili started its commercial exploration as it accepted the first angel investment. In this process, it has transformed from a niche community available in PC terminal to an enterprise-operated community e-commerce platform.

3.1 Put Users First

Bilibili originated from a niche ACG website, and community is the most typical feature of it. It is Bilibili's initial intention to create a friendly, inclusive community for ACG fans. Connecting uploaders and users and continuously creating value for users is bilibili's value proposition. Just as Chen Rui said, "As long as you can continue to create value for users, then you will be able to find the commercial value of yourself. Over-emphasis on user growth and commercialization can easily weaken the core culture of the community and lead to the loss of users." With the development of the corporation, Bilibili began to make attempts of commercialization in games, advertisements, live broadcasts, offline activities and e-commerce. What follows is the problem of balancing content and commercialization. For example, in 2016, a pre-roll was added to an animation series in Bilibili, and soon panicked the community, as users worried that the platform would be "polluted" by commerce (Wenku, 2012). Chen finally made a promise that "never add pre-rolls to authorized dramas". Although this practice made Bilibili lose its main revenue source as a video platform, it provided users with better experience. Later, when Bilibili introduced the senior VIP system, users worried that the platform would be more and more inclined to members who are willing to pay in the future and betrayed its original intention (Wenku, 2012). For this, Bilibili took priority of the opinions of users and made appropriate adjustments. Bilibili once closed the entrance to register for senior VIP. In the face of problems that may arise at any time in development, Bilibili always adheres to its own value proposition, that is, provide quality content and immersive interactive experience for more users of Z+generation.[4]

[4] Z+generation generally refers to Chinese people born from 1985 to 2009.

3.2 Value Co-creation Activities

(1) Social interaction

First of all, Bilibili is a community with users of high loyalty, high activity and great interaction. The platform itself represents social interaction. In 2011, Bilibili launched its first New Year Carnival, with a total of 210 uploaders participated in its preparation. Since then, the New Year Carnival began to hold on a yearly basis. Secondly, since Chen Rui officially joined Bilibili as chairman in November 2014, in addition to online community activities, Bilibili began to actively carry out offline activities featuring typical ACG, animation exhibitions and large-scale festivals, and it cooperated with many platforms in bullet screen. Since 2014, the large-scale offline concerts "Bilibili Macro Link" (BML) have been held in Chengdu, Guangzhou, Xi'an, Beijing, Shanghai and other cities. In 2015, Bilibili introduced "Meng Festival" and "Bilibili community Carnival", and the first popularity competition of the animated characters kicked off. In 2016, Bilibili introduced the function of "charging", that is, rewarding the uploaders. Since January, the Bilibili train from the activity of "Bilibili Love with You" has come to subways and bus stops in more than ten cities across the country with Canton Tower in Guangzhou as the last station; on December 3, Bilibili reserved 70 Wanda Cinemas in 49 cities across the country and invited its users from all over the country to watch the phenomenal Japanese animated film *Your Name* for free, and more than 110,000 movie tickets were taken by Bilibili users in one hour and four minutes.

By connecting uploaders and ordinary users in reality, Bilibili built stronger ties between them and strengthened the community atmosphere. With the help of the high reputation accumulated by the community and members for many years, diversified consumption and entertainment scenes were created to meet the offline emotional experience and contact needs of users. At the same time, the head uploaders had more opportunities to talk and communicate with users in offline activities, which helped them realize self-worth and gain a great sense of satisfaction, thus ensuring the continuous output of high-quality content for the community.

(2) Content interaction

The video content of Bilibili in this stage is centered on Professional User Generated Video (PUGV), which is a kind of high-quality video made by users and professionally planned and produced. For Bilibili, whether the community culture, community atmosphere and user experience can unite the core users depends on the uploaders to continuously produce high-quality content on the platform, which is the fundamental guarantee to maintain the community culture of Bilibili and retain the core users. Therefore, high quality video (PUGV) created by uploaders is the top priority of Bilibili's contents, which constitutes content interaction. In addition, Bilibili cooperated with other content producers to produce a lot of high-quality content, such as *Masters in the Forbidden City*, a big movie co-produced by Bilibili, which was released nationwide in December 2016. In the same year, the documentary channel CCTV9 entered Bilibili and live broadcast the documentary *Force of Nature* live on Bilibili.

(3) Functional interaction

At this stage, the interface design and functional Settings of Bilibili APP and web page tend to be personalized, with special emphasis on functional interaction with users. In addition, the underlying logic of the content distribution and personalized recommendation mechanism of Bilibili is to realize the efficient connection between content and users, so as to meet the personalized needs of different users and improve the using experience. The platform itself also constitutes a functional interaction. Just as Chen Rui said, "The recommendation system of Bilibili determines whether the content is worthy of recommendation based on the data of "likes, coins and collections". The main data source of the recommendation system is the positive feedback of users, including "likes, coins and collections", positive bullet screen and comment content." Bilibili has set up quite a few interactive functions, such as following, subscribing, playing, commenting, sending bullet screen, likes, coins, collecting and forwarding, allowing users to interact with content. For the platform, using these data can realize content tagging and user tagging. In order to gather core users and form community culture, Bilibili has formulated very strict rules. For example, the platform has an extremely sensitive screening mechanism for bullet screen content. Bilibili has set the highest membership entry threshold among Internet products in China to screen high-quality users (Wenku, 2012). In order to ensure that the community atmosphere is inclusive enough, Bilibili would deliberately guide the comment section, with almost no negative comments. Chen Rui said, "Creators need no troll, but the audience who love him/her."

(4) Commercial interaction

With the growing community base and increasing user demand, the commercial value of Bilibili, as the largest fashion culture and entertainment community for young people in China, quickly attracted major advertisers. But in fact, it has always seen users as the top priority, and has been relatively restrained in the commercial aspect, such as that it would not add pre-rolls in the original animation series. Before and after the listing in 2018, the advertising business, senior VIP, live broadcasting and other value-added services of Bilibili have just started, and its commercial interaction is mainly manifested in the ACG games. 2016 witnessed the first explosion of ACG games in China. In September of the same year, the national server of *Fate/Grand Order* (F/GO), of which Bilibili was the agent, went online and quickly became a vertical ACG blockbuster. Meanwhile, spontaneous re-creations by followers introduced a large amount of traffic. During this period, a strong ecological closed-loop of "ACG community+ACG IP games" was gradually formed. Then, Bilibili also obtained the agency of domestic ACG game *Azur Lane*, and also achieved good results. For other businesses, in 2017, Bilibili developed e-commerce businesses in the form of "member purchasing", and the e-commerce businesses were significantly different from traditional e-commerce businesses like those on Taobao and JD.COM, and it is also different from community e-commerce represented by Xiaohongshu. The core of the e-commerce business is still about anime derivatives (including games, related products, e-commerce, VIP members, and offline concerts). As the platform with the best knowledge of ACG, Bilibili has gathered a large number of hardcore followers and a large number of loyal user groups, who have huge potential demand for ACG derivatives. At present, its businesses of selling related products and acting as ticket agent for performances have formed a large scale, forming its unique e-commerce sales mode. In order to meet the more diversified purchasing needs of more users, Bilibili is actively expanding the cooperation with third-party brand merchants and guiding them to settle in the platform and establish brand numbers. After being audited and certified, the BGC (Brand Generated Content) related to its own brand can be released in the platform. A bullet screen or message with a purchase link can be added to the video to directly attract audience to the store, completing one-stop closed-loop sales at Bilibili and further promoting commercial interaction.

4 Breaking Through

In 2018, Bilibili went public in the United States. Three years later, it went public again in Hong Kong, which ushered in another climax of its commercialization. From 2020, Bilibili has been opening its ecosystem to all brand partners to build brands with high-quality merchants, and launched the Huahuo business cooperation platform to guide MCN (Multi-Channel Network) organizations[5] to settle in. Evolved from the initial small ACG subculture community to a comprehensive video community which covers a wide range of content categories and diversified video consumption scenarios, from a bullet screen video sharing website loved by young ACG culture fans to a culture community and video platform gathering Chinese young generation, there is no doubt that Bilibili is no longer a "Small Website". It has strived to grow into a spiritual paradise of contemporary Chinese young people.

[5] MCN institutions originate from the overseas mature economic operation mode of online celebrities. An example is companies that help contracted celebrities continuously output and realize. They combine the PGC (Professional Content Production) contents, with the strong support of capital, ensure the continuous output of content, and finally complete the stable realization of business.

4.1 All the Videos You're Interested in are on Bilibili

At present, Bilibili is the community with the highest concentration of Chinese young people and has extraordinary good traffic. At Bilibili, users and uploaders are growing at a high rate, and user retention rate is consistently above 80%. According to the Q3 financial report of 2021, the user interaction level reached an all-time high, and key metrics such as active users, paying users, and overall pay rate are also growing rapidly, with user stickiness and engagement increasing even further, once again achieving high-quality growth. Bilibili has a clear value proposition, which is to build a community with a strong sense of belonging, vitality and health, to establish an emotional connection for users with cultural pursuits, high-quality content and talented creators, to create a spiritual paradise for the Z+generation, and to enrich the daily working life of young people in China. Just as Chen Rui said, "We will be a company that deserves the respect of users and stands the test of time. I hope that ten or twenty years from now, people will still remember that there is a place where we can share hobbies, joy and emotions together."

4.2 Value Co-creation Activities in the Rapid Growth Stage

(1) Social interaction

At present, Bilibili has become a young people's cultural community with 15 content divisions and more than 7000 cultural circles (Dong, 2018). "Community priority" is the development strategy of Bilibili, and maintaining the core atmosphere and user experience has always been the top priority of it. As Chen Rui said in a public speech, "Bilibili is very special. The company can only partly represent it. It is like a community, where Bilibili is the property management company and the users are the house owners." Bilibili officially launched the "Creation Encouraging Plan" in 2018, which provides a comprehensive assessment of the self-made manuscripts created by uploaders and proposes a support plan with corresponding revenue, further optimizing the community atmosphere.

(2) Content interaction

Content creation is the essence of Bilibili, and content-based interaction is rooted in it. According to the Q3 financial report of 2021, 93% of Bilibili's view counts comes from PUGV contents created by uploaders, with the average monthly number of active uploaders reaching 2.7 million and the monthly average video contribution volume exceeding 10 million. In addition, Bilibili has a number of OGC (Occupationally Generated Video) productions. The Bilibili community has formed a multi-layered and multi-dimensional content ecosystem by continuously introducing high quality animation series and maintaining the unique attribute of ACG, while investing in and producing many high quality movies, documentaries, variety shows and other OGC contents by signing with uploaders, obtaining agent rights of events and copyrights of films and dramas, and producing self-made variety shows, etc. From niche ACG subculture gradually to popular culture, Bilibili continues to make breakthroughs through content interaction and co-creates value. In 2019, Bilibili launched a New Year's Eve Party on the occasion of its tenth anniversary, which was praised by the *People's Daily* and the Communist Youth League. The number of people online in the live broadcast at that same time exceeded 80 million, the total view counts exceeded 43 million, and the total number of bullet screen reached 1.3 million. "This is the party that goes deeply into young people's hearts."[6] In 2020, from the "rear wave"[7] to "into the sea", and[8] then to "happy reunion",[9] Bilibili has evoked the collective memory of the post-80s, post-90s and post-00s again and again. In fact, social interaction and content interaction are complementary to each other. The good atmosphere of the community largely comes from the quality content, and the power of the community in turn drives the improvement of the content quality. Because "we have always believed that it is very difficult to judge the quality of content. After experimenting with a lot of data, we found that positive feedback from users can best filter out good content for the platform over time (Chen, 2021)".

(3) Functional interaction

To achieve a positive interaction between users, quality content, uploaders and brands, and to establish an emotional bond, Bilibili has carefully designed many functional interactions, such as the most iconic bullet screen, to enhance user participation and improve user experience. The unique formal membership assessment system ensures that users who enter the platform to make comments are screened high quality users, enhancing the user's sense of belonging to the community and ensuring the core community atmosphere. Besides supporting users, in order to create a beautiful community with a strong sense of belonging, Bilibili pays more attention to the health of the community than the scale. It will continue to support the development of uploaders in terms of traffic support, creation encouragements, creation tools, training system, submission process, etc., to promote the generation of diversified quality contents on the platform.

---

[6] Li Ting, Shi Dan. u17's "Wandering": From Shanda, Alpha to Bilibili, the Commercialization of IP in China Is Difficult to Get through. *Business Management Review*. http://www.bmronline.com.cn/index.php?m=content&c=index&a=show&catid=9&id=6315

[7] "Rear wave" is a manifesto film dedicated to the young generation by Bilibili in conjunction with CCTV News, *Guangming Daily*, *China Youth Daily*, *Global Times*, *Beijing News*, and http://www.Guancha.com.

[8] "Into the Sea" is an MV released by Bilibili in conjunction with singer Mao Buyi, dedicated to young people who are about to graduate or have already graduated.

[9] "Happy Reunion" is a specially made promotional video for the 11th anniversary of Bilibili, which means that all the videos you're interested in are in Bilibili.

(4) Commercial interaction

During the rapid development stage, Bilibili has promoted the commercialization and upgrade through games, live broadcast, content payment, advertising and e-commerce, which constitute the commercial interaction of Bilibili. In 2018, Bilibili launched the "Reward Program" in cooperation with Alibaba to support the e-commerce function in opening stores by uploaders. Specifically, uploaders can add links for products in their videos or add advertisements of their recommended products below the videos. In 2020, Bilibili upgraded its reward program to further improve the e-commerce ecosystem of the platform. It was also in 2020 that Bilibili launched the Huahuo business cooperation platform and began to recruit MCN cooperation platforms, launching the "Z+Plan" and clearly proposing the value proposition of its commercialization, which is "to provide fertile land for brands to build a trusting partnership with users". In 2021, Bilibili integrated high-quality marketing resources and established a new generation of video marketing platform—http://www.e.bililibi.com, as its official marketing website. Despite the fact that content and commercialization is difficult to balance for community e-commerce, Bilibili still relies on the guidance by a good community atmosphere and careful selection of topics and ideas for commercialized videos by high-quality uploaders, insists on high-quality requirements for video content, and requires that "brands should be like uploaders, use the language of young people to communicate and interact, produce high-quality content to gain favorable impression, and build trusting relationships with long-term operation" (Chen, 2021), creating a good community atmosphere for business which gains positive feedback from users.

5 Epilogue

In the past few years, many changes have taken place in Bilibili. For instance, the number of users, especially young ones, is increasing, so is the number of uploaders. It is still the platform with the highest concentration of young Internet users in China. The content quality of uploaders' creations is getting higher with greater influence. Many excellent videos of some uploaders have become hot topics and have been forwarded and reported by mainstream media such as *People's Daily*, Xinhua News Agency and CCTV News for more than 22,000 times.[10] However, we can see that Bilibili is still in huge losses today. Is the commercialization sustainable? When could Bilibili make a profit? Questions like these kept emerging one after another, and Bilibili is repeatedly questioned. With the sharp increase of users, the commercialized feature of the community platform, and the pressure of making breakthroughs, the originally clean and harmonious "community" is

[10] Excerpted and summarized from Chen Rui's speech at Bilibili's 12th anniversary celebration.

now used by some unscrupulous merchants from time to time, full of soft advertisements, false information and even prohibited content. For instance, in 2020, relevant departments have arranged talks with Bilibili for more than 10 times, with administrative penalties for 6 times and being reported for more than 500 times. There are many problems and difficulties. For a community e-commerce platform, high-quality content and commercialization seemed to be irreconcilable contradictions.

Bilibili blocked the easiest road from the very beginning, which is different from the profit model of traditional community e-commerce of relying on advertising. In its process of development, it constantly sought for solutions and was exploring a new road, that is, to maintain the harmonious atmosphere of the community and the high stickiness of users with high-quality content, build scenarios based on high stickiness, and lay out diversified industries, to realize value creation, and break through the difficulty of commercial realization. For Bilibili, this is actually a long and complicated journey. It's easier said than done. Though Bilibili users' high loyalty and stickiness have great realization potential, there are still too many uncertainties in its business model. However, the endgame of Bilibili has not yet arrived, and the future can still be expected.

References

Baidu Wenku. (2012). Half of the young people in China are using bilibili. What did CEO Chen Rui do right? https://baijiahao.baidu.com/s?id=1710976789688046349&wfr=spider&for=pc. Retrieved 2 Jan 2022.

Bilibili. (2021). Bilibili released its Q3 financial report of 2021, with revenue of CNY5.21 Billion, Net Loss of CNY1.6 billion, Stock Price Plunged by 17.17% to USD67.12. Bilibili. https://www.bilibili.com/read/cv14083317?from=search&spm_id_from=333.337.0.0. Retrieved 31 Dec 2021.

Chen, N. X. (2021). Chen Rui of Bilibili: Pursuing community priority over scale priority. Changjiang Times. https://new.qq.com/omn/20210705/20210705A058NV00.html. Retrieved 2 Jan 2022.

Dong, D. J. (2018). Flying with two wings of PUGV and OGV, Bilibili has made breakthroughs after its 10th anniversary. TechNode. https://cn.technode.com/post/newsnow/allbebil/. Retrieved 2 Jan 2022.

Efraim, T., & Judy, S., & Li, X. L. (2018). Trans. Zhu Zhen et al. *Social commerce: Marketing, technology and management*. China Machine Press.

Shanghai APCOM: The Transformation of Traditional Foreign Trade Factories to Cross-Border E-commerce from 0 to 100 Million

Shuai Gao and Wenxing Wang

1 Introduction

"I am a foreign trader born in the 1960s. I started my factory in 2005, and cross-border e-commerce in 2018. In 2021, I got overseas orders with an amount of CNY100 million through cross-border e-commerce." In January 2022, Xu Jingqian, general manager of Shanghai APCOM Compressor Machine Co., Ltd., introduced himself at the beginning of the sharing meeting held in Alibaba Binjiang Park. The presented guests were all shocked at this. The seemingly unrelated words "1960s", "factory" and "cross-border e-commerce" made everyone curious about the experience of the company.

Shanghai APCOM Compressor Machine Co., Ltd. (APCOM for short below) is a typical manufacturing factory in China. Founded in 2005, it's a high-tech enterprise engaging in the R&D, manufacturing and sales of air compressors. It

This case was supported by fund program: The project titled "Study on the Paths and Countermeasures of Live Broadcast E-commerce Empowering High-quality Development of 26 Counties in Mountainous Areas of Zhejiang" of Zhejiang Federation of Humanities and Social Sciences Circles (2022N107); the project titled "Current Situation and Countermeasures of Cross-border E-commerce Development of SMEs in Hangzhou" of China (Hangzhou) Cross-border E-commerce Comprehensive Pilot Area in 2022; and the project titled "Research on the Teaching Mode of Cross-border E-commerce Practice Courses Based on Big Data" of cross-border e-commerce major construction of Zhejiang Gongshang University Hangzhou College of Commerce (PX-2721314).

S. Gao (✉)
School of Economics and Law, Zhejiang Gongshang University Hangzhou College of Commerce, Hangzhou, China

W. Wang
Shenwan Hongyuan Financing Services Co., Ltd., Hong Kong, China

J. Zhang et al. (eds.), *Innovation of Digital Economy*, Management for Professionals,
https://doi.org/10.1007/978-981-99-1741-9_9

has two main product lines, including oil-free scroll air compressor and permanent-magnet VF screw air compressor. With both national and overseas sales service networks, its goal is to become a world-class small air compressor manufacturer.

Xu Jingqian (Mr. Xu for short below) saw everyone's doubts, and said, "At the very beginning, we were a traditional foreign trade factory. Four years ago, we tried the cross-border e-commerce. In the early 2020, during the COVID-19 pandemic, we experienced doubts, attempts, failures and adjustments when we had a complete online transformation. We received 60 million orders in 2020, which was a huge leap brought to us by cross-border e-commerce!" Staring at the audience, Mr. Xu's thoughts went back to 2017…

2 Industry Background

Mr. Xu founded APCOM in Yiwu City, Zhejiang Province in 2005, which belongs to the air compressor industry. Air compressor is a kind of air pressure generator. It converts low-pressure gas into high-pressure gas by compression, through which mechanical energy of the prime mover (usually electric motor) can be converted into gas pressure energy. Air compressors are widely used in equipment manufacturing, automobile, metallurgy, electric power, electronics, medical treatment, textile and other industrial fields. Air compressors belong to strategic emerging industries such as "7.1.1 High-efficiency and Energy-saving General Equipment Manufacturing", in accordance with the *Classification of Strategic Emerging Industries (2018), Green Industry Guidance Catalogue (2019 Edition)* issued by the National Development and Reform Commission and *National Recommended Catalogue of Industrial Energy-saving Technology and Equipment (2019)* issued by the Ministry of Industry and Information Technology.

Mr. Xu has been engaged in the air compressor industry for more than ten years. Thus, he knew this industry like the back of his hand. He first introduced the current situation of the industry at home and abroad.

2.1 The Domestic Market is Growing, but the Growth Rate is Slowing Down

He said, "Our industry is relatively conventional. Although the domestic market scale is increasing year by year, the growth rate is relatively slow." The revenue scale of China's air compressor industry in 2016 was CNY49.165 billion according to the data of Huajing Industrial Research Institute, and the industry showed an upward trend from 2016 to 2018, with a compound growth rate of only about 3%. The sales volume in 2020 reached CNY58.336 billion. Considering the increasingly strict policies related to energy conservation and environmental protection in China, the demand for energy conservation transformation in the industry will continue to increase, and the market size is expected to reach CNY60.554 billion in 2021 (Fig. 1).

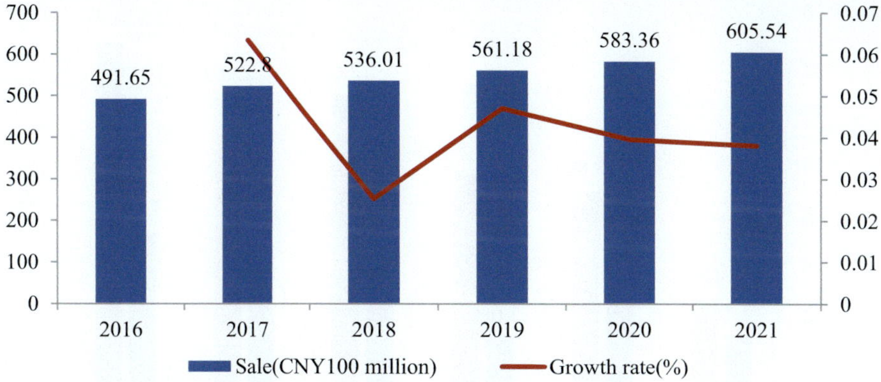

Fig. 1 Sales and growth rate of China's air compressor industry from 2016 to 2021 (Unit: CNY100 million). *Source* Huajing industry research institute

2.2 Large Export Scale with Low Added Value

Mr. Xu has long set his sights on a broader overseas market like other domestic manufacturers. China is a big importer and exporter of air compressors. At present, the added value of export products is relatively low. The import and export value of domestic air compressors increased from 2015 to 2020, among which the import value of air compressors reached USD720 million and the export value was USD1.47 billion in 2020 according to the data of China Customs. Although the trade surplus of domestic air compressors showed an increasing trend, China's exports mainly low-end products. The average unit price of imported air compressors in China was USD1,112.61/set in 2019, which was nearly 10 times of the export unit price. The export average unit price was far less than the import average unit price (Fig. 2).

2.3 Global Industry Competition Pattern

At present, the high-end compressor market is mainly occupied by overseas enterprises such as Atlas from Sweden, Ingersoll Rand from Ireland, Gardner Denver from the USA and Sullair from Japan. The low-end market also sees a fierce competition. Developed countries have great advantages in high-end fields because of their long-term development and leading technical level. In China's low-end market, most enterprises do not have the capacity to design and produce, and still stay in the stage of purchasing mainframe for assembly production, which shows problems of single product structure, low added value of technologies and serious homogenization of products. APCOM is in the second echelon of the industry. It can independently develop products with some imported parts, and it has 25

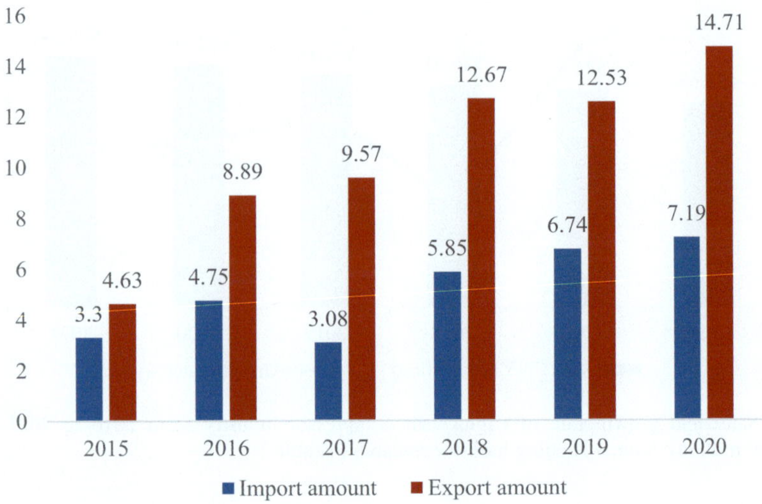

Fig. 2 Import and export amount of China's air compressors from 2015 to 2020 (Unit: USD100 million). *Source* Huajing industry research institute

patents, 1 provincial research institute and 1 provincial famous brand. Thus, it has certain industry competitiveness (Fig. 3).

With the favorable national policies and the strengthening of domestic enterprises, domestic air compressors are also facing opportunities in the international market, so Mr. Xu thinks highly of the overseas market.

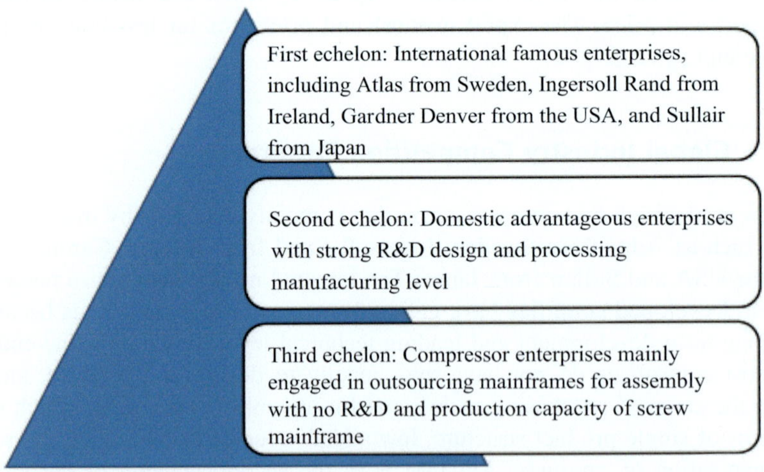

Fig. 3 Global air compressor industry competition pattern. *Source* Data compilation of www.huaon.com

Firstly, the domestic air compressors industry is growing, and the gap between the domestic level and international advanced level is shrinking. With the continuous improvement of the overall level of China's industry, and the strengthening of comprehensive strength, China's air compressor industry will continue to develop rapidly and continue to approach or even surpass the international advanced level.

Secondly, the "Belt and Road" brings development opportunities and expands the market for China's industrial exports, which will assist in the further development of China's industrial sector and increase the demand for air compressors, bringing opportunities for the air compressor industry to Southeast Asian, Central Asian, Northeast Asian and African markets.

3 Open Up Cross-Border E-commerce

Before 2017, the company's sales focus has been on offline channels. Mr. Xu led the team to exhibit in the Hannover Messe in Germany every year in person, and with excellent quality, high cost performance and perfect after-sales service, each time they gained some success. In 2016, with the efforts of all the staff in the company, the turnover of APCOM exceeded CNY200 million.

Two events at the beginning of 2017 caused Mr. Xu to be alerted. One is that although the visitor flow at that year's exhibition is similar to that of previous years, the number of orders has decreased, which makes him a little puzzled. The other is that a customer delayed the order after negotiation, and the customer manager found that the customer cooperated with another supplier through the cross-border B2B platform. The customer said that through the cross-border e-commerce platform, he/she can know more manufacturers and products, which gained him/her more choices. In addition, he/she was more comfortable with large transactions guaranteed by the platform. Although the deal was finally reached after the company's efforts, the idea of trying cross-border e-commerce took root in Mr. Xu's mind.

One day in 2017, Mr. Xu called the Foreign Trade Department and said, "We all know that many of our peers have started to use Alibaba International Station to develop customers, but we still mainly rely on old customers to repurchase and exhibitions, which was limited. And after the exhibition, we also have some free time. How about we have a try?".

Immediately, Mr. Gao replied, "Mr. Xu, we are already in the middle and upper stream of the industry, the main APCOM screw air compressor is in a relatively moderate competition, and the old customer orders are stable, why do we need to catch up with the fashion of e-commerce?" Mr. Gao is an old employee who followed Mr. Xu since the early years, and has accumulated a lot of customer resources, so he was not that willing to develop new channels.

And Liu echoed, "Yes, Mr. Xu, it's not as simple as buying bargains on Taobao, as the unit price of our air compressors is tens of thousands to hundreds of thousands of CNY. An order is easy to exceed a million, so why would foreign customers believe us when they can only rely on online communication without seeing and touching our products!" Liu was also doubtful about whether online shopping was suitable for valuable products.

Xiao Li added, "In recent years, e-commerce is really developing fast, and my wife also often buys cosmetics and milk powder from abroad through online shopping. But we do not have experience in e-commerce, and do not know how to carry it out." Xiao Li was a young man who has just graduated for two years and was willing to try new things, but he was not confident enough due to the lack of experience in cross-border e-commerce.

Finally, Manager Wu, head of the Foreign Trade Department, pointed out that "cross-border e-commerce is indeed a new idea. Since offline channels currently have a downward trend, we can take cross-border e-commerce as a supplement to the existing channels. I think that we can recruit people with cross-border e-commerce experience to do it, but I'm afraid it's not easy to find such people in Yiwu."

After listening to everyone's opinions, Mr. Xu felt the difficulties. But he believed that cross-border e-commerce will be as popular as domestic e-commerce, and if they want to seize the first opportunity, they must lay out in advance and take the initiative to embrace new things. In the end, Mr. Xu settled in the Alibaba International Station against all the odds in 2017.

4 Facing a Failure

Although the store was opened up on the Alibaba International Station, there were also many obstacles to overcome. Mr. Xu soon encountered the first obstacle, the HR said that it was difficult to recruit mature and professional e-commerce operation staff.

In 2017, cross-border e-commerce was still an innovation, which has high requirements on the comprehensive ability of operation personnel, including skilled foreign language ability and cross-cultural communication ability, professional knowledge of the company's products, as well as the skills and experience of e-commerce operation. At that time, only a small number of universities in Zhejiang Province opened majors and courses of cross-border e-commerce, and it was difficult for the company to recruit graduates with the matched majors, let alone middle and senior operation talent who could help build the entire online business of the company.

What Mr. Xu did not expect was that he managed to recruit e-commerce operators, but in less than a year, four employees have come and gone. Mr. Xu found a resigned employee to ask about the reasons. It turned out that the company focused on offline channels, and its resources were inclined to offline channels, with little attention paid on online channels. The employees felt that the cross-border e-commerce was regarded as something dispensable. Besides, other business staff still followed the previous practices and had no awareness of e-commerce, so it is difficult for to communicate and cooperate with them. The cooperation of copywriting, art design, shooting, editing and so on was in need to decorate the online store and release the products, but the company could not provide these supporting work, and the employee could not do it alone. After listening to the complaints, Mr. Xu always felt that it was not that easy to run cross-border e-commerce well.

When the 2017 financial report was delivered to him, he was quite shocked by the company's input and output in cross-border e-commerce throughout the year. "We have invested CNY570,000 with no reward at all", Mr. Xu commented on the situation of the company's cross-border e-commerce business in the first year.

5 Going into Battle in Person

Shocked by the results, Mr. Xu wondered: is it wrong to try cross-border e-commerce? In the dead of night, he often thought about it. Is cross-border e-commerce not suitable for the air compressor industry? Maybe not, as there are also peers who are doing a good job. Did the company invest enough in cross-border e-commerce? Yes, CNY570,000 was not a small number. And if the failure of cross-border e-commerce is due to the failure to find the right operating talent, who can take the responsibility? Should we give up or keep going?

Mr. Xu thought about trying it himself, but he was over 50 years old, and he was not sure whether he could master the novel knowledge of cross-border e-commerce. He recalled the past ten years of entrepreneurship, and found that the company was developing through continuous learning. Mr. Xu has a technical background. After leading the technical team to develop products, in order to solve the problem of product sales, he, with an unyielding strength, learned foreign languages, foreign trade knowledge and sales skills, and led the company to develop from a manual workshop to a brand in the upper stream of the industry. As the bell rang at 12 o'clock, Mr. Xu made up his mind to operate cross-border e-commerce himself.

Since 2018, Mr. Xu has been studying hard in his spare time. He started from the most basic office software as he did not even know how to use the computer, and how to create Excel tables at that time, and even typing was a problem. To understand e-commerce operation, he studied platform rules, background reports and software tools. In order to better promote their products, he even obtained a live broadcast certificate, made use of We Media marketing, and became an "influencer" of the industry.

"It was a painful process to learn e-commerce operations from learning typing. But we should grasp the trend, and learn what we need to learn. The learning process has opened my horizon again", Mr. Xu said at the sharing meeting. Under the leadership of Mr. Xu, his store on Alibaba International Station gradually improved, began to receive some inquiries and orders, and he opened two new stores.

6 Braving Winds and Waves

At the beginning of 2020, the COVID-19 pandemic caused many Chinese enterprises to halt the production. In March, APCOM was greatly affected by the COVID-19 pandemic. Sales staff could not go abroad, and foreign customers could not come in. Orders suddenly decreased, factories were shut down, and the overall plan was disrupted. This period of time is the most anxious time since Mr. Xu started the business, and he often stared blankly at the machines in the empty factory.

At this time, the experience learned in cross-border e-commerce operation came in handy. Mr. Xu decided to make a comprehensive transformation to the online business. He first recruited his college school mate, a senior executive at a listed company in Zhejiang, to serve as the vice president of the company, and took over the daily operation management of the company to stabilize the domestic market. On the other hand, he personally led the e-commerce team to make a big move. By the end of April, the domestic COVID-19 pandemic was basically under control and production resumed. At the same time, the pandemic began to break out abroad, and a large number of foreign orders poured into China online. Mr. Xu carefully operated the cross-border B2B platform, and invested more than CNY100,000 to upgrade the 3 ordinary stores to verified suppliers. In addition to displaying the performance parameters of products, the stores also use videos and VR exhibition halls to show the overall strength and manufacturing details of the factory in an all-round way, so that foreign customers can feel like visiting the site as if they were there personally. An Ethiopian buyer could not come to the factory for inspection due to the COVID-19 pandemic, but finally chose the products of Mr. Xu's company through online comparison, with a transaction of USD100,000. The customer later told Mr. Xu, "I chose you because you looks like a source supplier, instead of a 'two-way merchant'". From April to the end of the year, the store had hundreds of inquiries each month, bringing in orders with an amount of about CNY60 million. In 2021, Xu led his team to make further efforts, the amount of online orders exceeded CNY100 million, and the company's overall revenue reached CNY350 million.

Finally, Mr. Xu shared his three "magic weapons" of operating on the Alibaba International Station, which are product, traffic and team.

First, the products should be made into superior products and best-sellers. APCOM has been deeply engaged in the industry for many years, with many trademarks and patents, and is confident about their products. "You have to take the trouble to let customers see their desired products". To beginning with, on-site and off-site tools should be made full use of for digital product selection to accurately select products suitable for online sales. Then, the selected products should be packaged with optimized titles and filtered keywords, and accompanied by quality videos and copywriting. At present, the number of superior products accounts for 46% of the 713 products in the company's platform. Mr. Xu concluded, "The more superior products, the better we can push up our merchant power, thus gaining more exposure on the platform and boosting conversion rates."

Second, traffic should be paid the greatest attention to in an e-commerce platform. Mr. Xu divided the traffic into scene traffic, paid traffic and private traffic, and said that merchants need to pay attention to and develop each type of traffic to attract traffic for their stores and products. "B-terminal live broadcast, short videos, 3D exhibition halls and other scenarios emerging this year are all high-conversion tools", said Mr. Xu. In addition, by actively participating in platform events and purchasing festivals, you can get a lot of low-cost traffic.

Third, the training of the e-commerce team should be paid attention to. The key for the company to go further is still to rely on the team. In half a year, Mr. Xu's e-commerce team increased from 2 to 12 people, and is still absorbing more talent. On the one hand, Mr. Xu passed on his experience in e-commerce operation to his team without reservation; on the other hand, he asked external executives to develop detailed job descriptions, product knowledge manuals, systematic workflow, detailed training materials and a clear reward and punishment system to build a system of "recruitment, training, retention and promotion".

Mr. Xu's sincere, simple, passionate and fruitful sharing triggered many times of applause on the spot, and the audience reflected that they benefited a lot.

7 Epilogue

In the process of learning by doing, Mr. Xu became more and more confident in the new journey of digital foreign trade. In 2020, he signed up for the 2020 Digital Zhejiang Merchant Talent Race, and competed with young people as an entrepreneur over 50. From the audition, regional competitions to the top 6 of the finals, he won the title of "Digital Operating Talent", and became a contracted instructor of Alibaba International Station. He humbly said that he participated in the competition in order to work side by side with young people, learn from them and try to transform from an old foreign trader to a digital trade trendsetter. After the sharing meeting, Mr. Xu hurried back to the company. The street lights illuminated the way forward. His pace has never stopped in the journey of cross-border e-commerce transformation.

Lin Qingxuan: The Way to Survive in the Dark

Juan Tang, Jingxian Liu, Yanxi Chen, and Rui Xu

1 Introduction

At the beginning of New Year 2020, Sun Laichun, the founder of Lin Qingxuan, optimistically predicted that this year would be a key year for Lin Qingxuan to show its brand advantages. Unexpectedly, Wuhan was locked down on January 22 due to the COVID-19 pandemic only after Sun Laichun had a dinner with his colleagues in Wuhan on January 18. The darkness of the night has been already around the corner…

2 Making a Prompt Decision When the COVID-19 Pandemic Hits the World: Dying to Survive

The sudden outbreak of the COVID-19 pandemic made the company's performance worse and worse. The Golden Week around the Chinese New Year, which is usually the busiest time of the year, witnessed the close of half of the shops this year, with the overall performance down by 90%. The company just had about CNY60 million on its books to support for at most two months, meaning that Lin Qingxuan was only 62 days away from "death" at most…

For 10 whole days, from January 22 to January 31, Sun Laichun experienced a dark moment, both physically and spiritually. In the early hours of January 31, Sun Laichun, who was on the verge of collapse, wrote a 10,000-character article to his staff, *A Letter from the Darkest Hours* (see Fig. 1), and without much thought, released it immediately afterwards. This was because he believed that if Lin Qingxuan wanted to save itself, it must first give its staff confidence.

J. Tang (✉) · J. Liu · Y. Chen · R. Xu
School of Management, Nanjing University of Posts and Telecommunications, Nanjing, China

J. Zhang et al. (eds.), *Innovation of Digital Economy*, Management for Professionals,
https://doi.org/10.1007/978-981-99-1741-9_10

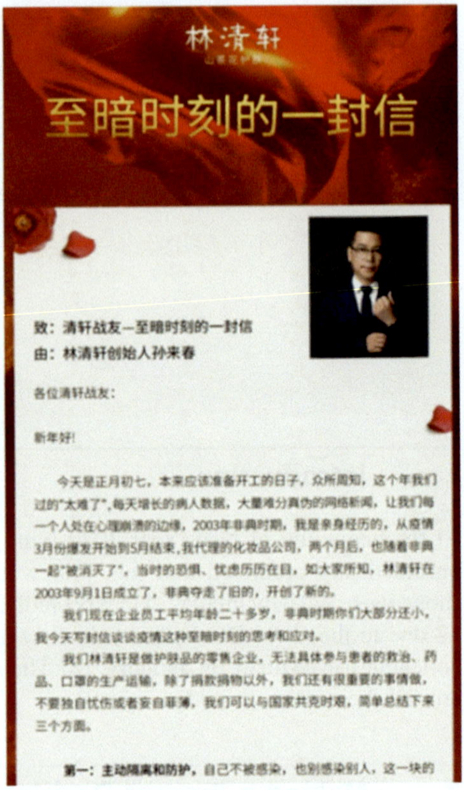

林清轩

至暗时刻的一封信

致：清轩战友—至暗时刻的一封信
由：林清轩创始人孙来春

各位清轩战友：

新年好!

今天是正月初七，本来应该准备开工的日子，众所周知，这个年我们过的"太难了"，每天增长的病人数据，大量难分真伪的网络新闻，让我们每一个人处在心理崩溃的边缘，2003年非典时期，我是亲身经历的，从疫情3月份爆发开始到5月结束，我代理的化妆品公司，两个月后，也随着非典一起"被消灭了"，当时的恐惧、忧虑历历在目，如大家所知，林清轩在2003年9月1日成立了，非典夺走了旧的，开创了新的。

我们现在企业员工平均年龄二十多岁，非典时期你们大部分还小，我今天写封信谈谈疫情这种至暗时刻的思考和应对。

我们林清轩是做护肤品的零售企业，无法具体参与患者的救治、药品、口罩的生产运输，除了捐款捐物以外，我们还有很重要的事情做，不要独自忧伤或者妄自菲薄，我们可以与国家共克时艰，简单总结下来三个方面。

第一：主动隔离和防护，自己不被感染，也别感染别人，这一块的

Fig. 1 Screenshots of *A Letter from the Darkest Hours*. *Source* Sun Laichun, https://www.sohu.com/a/371911421_374080

As soon as the letter was released, it immediately went viral on the Internet and the entrepreneurial community "shocked"…

3 Seizing the Opportunity to Develop Online: Actively Carrying Out the Network Marketing

On the morning of February 1, Sun Laichun woke up to the message that CEO of Dingtalk, Chen Hang was willing to open a video conference for Lin Qingxuan so that its entire staff could resume work online. Lin Qingxuan immediately went through Weimob smart retail solution and started the cloud shopping.

On February 7, more than 400 employees of Lin Qingxuan and Sun Laichun received the training on live broadcast. As soon as the training was finished, the staff started their live broadcast "debut" with mobile phones in their homes, shops and dormitories.

Sun Laichun himself did not expect that a few days later, more than 2,000 employees of Lin Qingxuan adopted the telework, and 1,600 service assistants, who have never been on camera, became webcast anchors. Everything has been steadily moving forward…

Sun believed that the brand power of enterprises should be well protected both online and offline. Soon, with his keen insight, he quickly adjusted his marketing strategies to promote the concept of "repairing face skin problems due to mask wearing at home". In this way, consumers would first think of the repairing effects of Camellia Oil, thus enhancing the brand power!

4 Regaining Confidence from a Desperate Situation: Initial Success in the Sales Performance

On February 14, Valentine's Day, Sun Laichun himself and one hundred super service assistants held a public live broadcast entitled "214 Wuhan, My Lover" (see Fig. 2). For every bottle of Camellia Oil sold, Lin Qingxuan would donate a bottle of the same oil to the front line of the pandemic battle in Wuhan. This is the first live broadcast of Sun Laichun, which was watched by more than 60,000 people, with sales of nearly CNY400,000 in two hours. Such a caring initiative on the special day of Valentine's Day was even more touching.

Half a month later, the sales performance rebounded across the board, up 45% on the same period last year. At this point, Sun Laichun said categorically that Lin Qingxuan could basically save itself, and if the status quo could be maintained by March, Lin Qingxuan would survive definitely. He also commented that if the company didn't conduct digital layouts in advance on Alibaba and other large platforms, such offline store-led entity brands as Lin Qingxuan would really face the destruction, let alone the growth of performance.

Fig. 2 Poster of Sun Laichun's live broadcast debut on February 14. *Source* Live broadcast debut of Sun Laichun, the founder of Lin Qingxuan (2020-02-18). http://www.xfrb.com.cn/article/stjj-ssxw/09583987446423.html

5 Epilogue

Lin Qingxuan survives temporarily, but the COVID-19 pandemic will end eventually. For Lin Qingxuan, not only will it face the upcoming challenges of the online and offline integration and digital full-chain operations, but also more unknown challenges. Will it be able to successfully overcome, or even survive again? Let's wait and see what will happen…

Can Digital Agriculture Realize the Sustainable Development of Rural E-commerce?

Xueyan Yang, Yueli Zhang, and Lanying Li

1 Introduction

Digital agriculture involves many new technologies such as computer technology, network technology, GIS, GPS, remote sensing technology, sensors, automation technology, agricultural drones, big data, artificial intelligence (AI), 5G mobile technology, cloud computing and blockchain and other new technologies, which have integrated usage during the past several years. And combined with geography, ecology, pedology and plant physiology, digital agriculture began to collect and process all kinds of data information in the whole process of agricultural production, environment, sales and management, and carry out digital management such as agricultural environment visualization, growth process simulation, sales and management informationization, to achieve the reasonable utilization of agricultural resources, reduce agricultural costs, improve the ecosystem and the quality of agricultural products and finally enhance the competitiveness of agricultural products. Since 2018, the Central Committee of CPC and the State Council have successively released a series of documents on rural revitalization and digital village. In 2019, Ministry of Agriculture and Rural Affairs issued *Digital Agriculture and Rural Development Plan (2019–2025)*.

2 Digital Development Process of the Nut Industry in L County

L County of Zhejiang Province (now a district in Hangzhou City; hereinafter referred to as "L County" uniformly) is a remarkable tourist city in China known

X. Yang (✉) · Y. Zhang · L. Li
College of Economics and Management, Zhejiang A&F University, Hangzhou, China

J. Zhang et al. (eds.), *Innovation of Digital Economy*, Management for Professionals,
https://doi.org/10.1007/978-981-99-1741-9_11

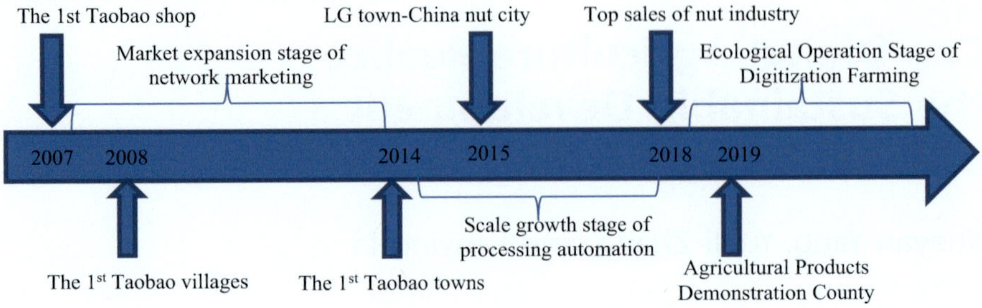

Fig. 1 Digital development process of the nut industry in L County

for its excellent ecological environment and 5A-level national scenic spots. Rural e-commerce in L County started rather early with a typical bottom-up development model, from BN Village of the first batch of Taobao Villages recognized by Alibaba to the first batch of Taobao Towns.

Data collected by O&O Consulting in 2019 suggested that, nut snacks from L County ranked the 10th in the online sales of popular agricultural products made from different counties, with its products accounting for 0.59% of the online retail sales of agricultural products around the country. However, the total online retail sales of the nut industry in L County far exceed the above-mentioned number, as a proportion of products of many well-known online retailers for agricultural products, such as Three Squirrels, Be & Cheery, Bestore, LYFEN, ChaCha, are produced in L County, and the sales of these brands are among the top 10 or even the top 5 in the list. In 2020, the total online retail sales in L County stood at CNY9.39 billion, with 3,150 active online retail stores of various types. For example, there existed 250 Tmall stores in L County, with active stores accounting for 92.6%. Among the active Tmall online stores, there were 220 flagship stores, 16 franchised stores and 14 exclusive stores respectively, with flagship stores accounting for 88.0% of the total. The total number of active online retail stores ranked the 47th in Zhejiang, of which 63.5% of retail sales derives from food and health care industry.

The digital development process of the nut industry in L County has experienced three stages as suggested in Fig. 1.

2.1 Market Expansion Stage of Network Marketing (2007–2014)

In 2007, the first Taobao shop was established in BN Village, L County, focusing on the selling of pecans, a well-known specialty in L County. In less than a year thereafter, farmers established online shops on Taobao one after another, and in 2008 BN Village was selected as one of the first batch of Taobao villages in China. By the end of 2014, supported by platform dividends and first-mover advantages, there were 56 online stores in the village, with 2 stores with a sales of over CNY10 million, 4 with a sales of over CNY20 million, and 2 settled in Tmall. In 2014, sales of Taobao shops in BN Village reached CNY200 million, with more than CNY1 million obtained on the day of "Double 11" alone, among them, the annual pecan sales accounted for about 63% of the total. For example, the sales of "Wenwen" Taobao shop exceeded CNY20 million. The demonstration effect of BN Village radiated and spilled over into the whole L County, among which QLF Town became one of the first six Taobao towns in China in 2014, with four Taobao villages in the town, and a total of CNY420 million online sales.

Network marketing was the first step of digitalization of the nut industry in L County. Its effectiveness drove the gradual improvement of government, association and third-party services. The government has introduced various policies in finance, land and human resources in a timely manner, and contacted planting experts, various third-party service providers and scientific research institutions for farmers and enterprises. The association helps farmers solve practical difficulties through various initiatives, such as financing the construction of roads for villages located above 600 m above sea level, coordinating service costs with logistics companies, and various third-party service providers have landed in rural and mountainous areas of L County.

2.2 Scale Growth Stage of Processing Automation (2014–2018)

The success of network marketing has improved the sales of pecans, and meanwhile, categories of nuts sold began to enrich, expanding from pecans to hickories, Brazilian pine nuts, etc. Most of these nuts are processed locally in L County, which has promoted the local processing industry, especially LG Town and QLF Town located in the westernmost part of L County. The two towns own a long history of pecan frying and processing. Initially mostly were done in family workshops, and then manual processing with semi-automatic processing equipment was introduced. After 2014, as the business volume has witnessed rapid progress, a great many of processing enterprises began to utilize fully automated processing equipment. At present, there exist over 230 processing enterprises above designated size, among which more than 70 are located in LG Town and more than 130 in QLF Town. YL, GL, YK, HZB and TY are all processing enterprises above designated size, promoting the county to become a major nut processing area in China. In Town LG, a China Nut City was established, gathering small and medium-sized processing enterprises together, meanwhile providing equipment and functions in trade, warehousing and automated logistics to achieve digitalization of processing and manufacturing.

The automation of processing and manufacturing in turn further promoted the scale growth of the nut industry. By 2018, over 1,100 e-commerce shops of agricultural products had been operating in L County, among which there were 2 enterprises have a total sales of more than CNY100 million, 15 have a total sales of more than CNY20 million, and 38 have a total sales of more than CNY5 million. In the whole district, online sales of the nut industry has achieved CNY5.5

billion, of which the e-commerce of agricultural products in L County featured by nuts has exceeded CNY2 billion; The pecan planting scale also expanded, to reach 640,000 mu. In 2018, the pecan yield was 13,600 tons, with a primary industry production value of CNY820 million, the whole industry chain output value of 3.73 billion yuan; L County has also become the main processing place of nut industry. More than ten well-known nut brands such as Three Squirrels began to choose L County for nut product processing. In 2019, L County was successively awarded the titles of one of the first batch of "Marketing Model Demonstration Unit of Internet + Economic Forest Product (Pecan)", "China's Top 100 E-commerce Development County", "Provincial E-commerce Demonstration County", "Top 10 Innovation Sample of Zhejiang E-commercialization", and "National E-commerce Demonstration Area of Agricultural Products".

2.3 Ecological Operation Stage of Digitization of Farming (2019–)

After 2018, rising prices of agricultural inputs and labor, and increased sales channels such as WeChat and self-media brought about fiercer market competition, resulting in a significant reduction in the comparative efficiency of the pecan marketing industry and a significant decrease in the planting and processing input–output ratio, from 25% in 2000 to less than 5% in 2018. On the other hand, production and processing had an impact on the local environment. The excessive fine management of pecan planting led to pecan forest ecosystem degradation and frequent ecological disasters.

It has become an urgent requirement for the industry development to improve the industry and brand premium of pecans and to do a good job in the quality control and ecological safety supervision of the planting and production links. To this end, the local government, with the financial support of the province, invested tens of millions of CNY. Subsidized by the farm machinery station, tracks for 6 digital empowerment demonstration bases of pecans were laid, and subsidized by the government, UAV prevention and control of diseases and pests were carried out by third parties. The cloud platform for the whole pecan industry chain named "Digital Brain" was built. By 2021, it has been connected with 6 pecan digital empowerment demonstration bases, 160 pecan processing enterprises and 4,870 pecan online merchants, and connected with departments of agriculture and forestry, meteorology, land and market regulatory to implement whole-process supervision. It currently uses blockchain technology to generate a digital certificate of land assets that integrates the base pecan area, tree condition, pests and diseases, and yield, which is used to guide green production and provide a reliable assessment reference for credit and loan traceability.

The above development history shows that the digitalization of the pecan industry in L County first began with the networking and e-commerce application of the tertiary sector, and the low threshold and rapid economic returns of e-commerce stimulated the rapid spread of pecan online sales, leading to the automation process of the local nut frying industry. The large-scale processing prompted the local roasted snacks enterprises to gradually eliminate the original all-manual or semi-manual nut frying process, and gradually begin digital transformation. On the one hand, the rapid development of the secondary industry and tertiary industry drove the local economy, but affected the local ecological environment. Therefore, the digital transformation of the production and breeding links of the primary industry and ecological environmental supervision was imminent.

3 Sustainable Effect of Nut Industry in L County

The nut industry of L County is a good example of the scale of e-commerce development of agricultural products leading to industrial clustering. According to the 2020 China Taobao Village Research Report by AliResearch, 5,425 Taobao villages and 1,756 Taobao towns in China obtained CNY1 trillion in transactions on the Taobao in 2020. Industrial cluster may have a two-sided impact on local rural development, and the case analyses its positive and negative impacts in three dimensions: economy, ecology and society.

3.1 Impact from the Perspective of Economic Production

Positive impact—scale expansion of the nut e-commerce industry. A dozen Taobao villages in L County formed a nut e-commerce industry cluster with pecan online sales as the core. In the 2018 China Fruit Regional Public Brand Evaluation, the brand value of pecans from L County was CNY2.495 billion, ranked the top again. Online sales of nuts were increasingly rich. In addition to pecans, there are melon seeds, pistachios, hickories, almonds, macadamia nuts, Brazil pine nuts, etc. And apart from pecans, other nut raw materials were imported from Guangdong, Guangxi, Hong Kong, South Africa, Vietnam, etc. The scale of the industry continued to increase, occupying a third of the national market for nuts. Nut processing in L County was mainly done in the LG town, which had a relatively long history of pecan frying and processing, initially in family workshops. Today, L County has more than 250 nut processing enterprises, including more than 70 in LG town, more than 130 in QLF town, with an output value of more than CNY20 billion. And there are more than 30 enterprises above the designated scale, such as YL, JL, YK, HZB and TY, all with an annual output value of more than CNY100 million. In addition to automation and digital transformation of their manufacturing processes, these enterprises are also actively participating in the digital marketing segment. Table 1 shows the top processing enterprises in terms of output and their digital marketing.

Positive impact—cultivating local leading enterprises in e-commerce sales. There are three kinds of e-commerce enterprises that reinvigorate the sales of

Table 1 Nut processing enterprises and E-commerce relationship in L County

Enterprise	Enterprise automation transformation	Development of enterprise digital marketing
YL	Invested more than CNY13 million; semi-automatic processing equipment, and self-provided refrigeration room; main business is macadamia nuts processing; raw materials come from Australia and South Africa	Three Squirrels' first-generation supplier, an OEM, offering no less than 15 tons of products a day
JL	Net assets of CNY31.8 million, with semi-automated processing equipment; a leading enterprise, a famous brand enterprise and a famous trademark of Hangzhou; focuses on the processing of pecans (kernel), hickories (kernel), almonds, etc.; the offline sales of independent brand account for 50%	supplier for Three Squirrels, ChaCha, Bestore and LYFEN; OEM of small package snacks (such as almonds)
HZB	Fully-automated and mechanized production line (the most advanced roasted snacks production line in China); the only enterprise with a degree of automation reaching 90%;	90% of the pecans are processed for LYFEN

nuts for L County. The first is Taobao shops operated by Taobao villages in L County, most of which are C shop. On the one hand, they started early, which helped them accumulate large customer base and high reputation; and on the other hand, due to their low operation costs, they have occupied a leading position in the e-commerce field of nuts. For example, the shop named "Qiqi Xiaoge" was started in 2009, and now it has become a four-crown shop, with an annual sales exceeding CNY5 million. With promotion mainly relying on old customers and WeChat, it has become a typical entrepreneurship of "unique and excellent" (a concept proposed by Taobao, which refers to a small shop with its own characteristics). The second is e-commerce operation agencies, such as LZY, CL, XNG, GDF and DS, who expand sales channels on platforms including Tmall and JD.COM, thus becoming the local leading enterprises of nut e-commerce. There are 10 enterprises with an annual online sales over CNY100 million, 100 enterprises with an annual online sales over CNY10 million, and 1000 enterprises with an annual online sales over CNY1 million. The third is enterprises integrating processing and e-commerce sales, which not only provide sources for e-commerce, but also develop their own brands for online sales. For example, "SWTY" registered on Tmall in 2013, and in the first year, its sales have reached CNY6,000,000.

Negative impact—serious and vicious competition among enterprises within industry. Among more than a dozen of Taobao villages in L County, most of the Taobao shops are still small in scale, and most are family-run ones. Though "unique and excellent", due to severe product homogeneity, the price competition dominates, which easily result in vicious competition and lemon effect. The small scale of most enterprises also leads to varying quality of products: although nuts are different from fresh fruits and vegetables, they also need a refrigeration room and cold chain transportation system. Taking pecans as an example, they are picked every year after the White Dew, and ate within a few months after processing is the best. Therefore, in order to ensure its freshness and taste, it is better to store the original nuts in the refrigeration room; non-local products such as hickories also need the cold chain system during the transportation from overseas source areas and storage. However, due to the small scale of most enterprises and the lack of a sound cold chain system, quality of products is easy to be affected.

Negative impact—the possibility of deteriorating into "the place of origin and processing". Although some enterprises have expanded with the help of the industrial aggregation effect, most enterprises are still restricted by scale: the human resources featured by family-run stores and the physical space featured by mixed commerce with residence results in insufficient localized brand building due to the need of relocation when the stores are expanding. Even local leading nuts e-commerce enterprises, such as LZY, CL, XNG, GDF, and DS, also put their processing and delivery links in L County, while their brands, channels and operations are in cities like Shanghai. However, though processing enterprises above designated size maintain a close relationship with e-commerce, most of them provide products to non-local online nuts retail brands (such as ChaCha, Three Squirrels, LYFEN, COFCO, Be & Cheery and Bestore) as OEMs.

3.2 Impact from the Perspective of Environmental Ecology

Positive impact—improving traffic and environment in mountainous areas. Most of the Taobao villages in L County are located in mountainous areas, among which MX Village is located on a mountain at an altitude of 500 m. The reason why MX Village can be a Taobao village identified by Alibaba was originated from that a young man, who is disabled but have a strong will, tried to start operating Taobao shop to sell pecans and teas in the village at the very beginning. Due to the lack of transportation, even postmen could not come to the village every day at that time. However, as more and more villagers opened Taobao shops, logistics companies began to visit the village every day. After the villagers became prosperous, with the joint efforts of the county and town governments and villagers, the cement-poured winding road was completed in 2012, which closed the distance between the village and cities, and the beautiful environment in mountainous areas also attracted tourists from home and abroad.

Negative impact—environmental pollution led by scale cultivation. Universities and colleges had close cooperation with institutions, which efficiently promoted the application of key technologies such as ecological and standardized operation, underwood planting, soil testing and fertilization, recovery with net, and insect pest control, but in order to enlarge the scale and output, the excessive use of herbicides and fertilizers led to a large number of harmful pests, dry rot and root rot. In

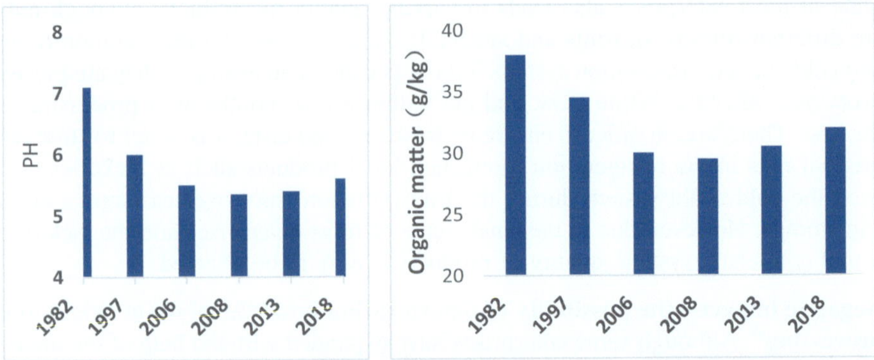

Fig. 2 Changes of soil pH and organic matter contents in pecan forest in L County

addition, coupled with the impact of acid rain, the pecan forest was degrading and even died. From 1982 to 2018, the mean pH of forest soil decreased from 7.1 to 5.5, and the content of soil organic matter also decreased from 38.4 g/kg to 33.7 g/kg, as shown in Fig. 2.

Negative impact—water pollution due to increased waste water from processing. Processing 1 kg of dried pecan seeds will produce 3 kg of pecan peel. Pecan peel is strongly alkaline and non-perishable, so disorderly heap (except part of them would be sold for activated carbon manufacturing) will lead to water pollution. And processing pecans leads to waste water pollution (although the government has centrally arranged sewage treatment, some companies still discharge sewage without permission).

Negative impact—long-term reclamation leading to degradation of pecan forest land. Long-term reclamation also leads to the degradation of woodland soil quality; fine tillage causes bare tree roots and sparse underwood vegetation; biodiversity is destroyed; soil and water loss is serious; and debris flow and landslide accidents increase, resulting in casualties.

3.3 Impact from the Perspective of Social Governance

Positive impact—rural income increase and poverty reduction. The development of rural e-commerce has brought about an increase in rural income. People in QLF Town alone have CNY2.5 billion deposited in the Rural Credit Cooperative. For MX Village, which is located at 500 m above sea level, thanks to the development of e-commerce, logistics and express delivery companies have settled in the village, and special optical fiber and third-party services and other related supporting services were introduced, which not only solved the economic problems of a few disabled and poor families in the village, but also led the whole village to become prosperous. 2020 witnessed a good atmosphere for employment and entrepreneurship of e-commerce, which directly created 8,730 jobs and indirectly mobilized 22,950 jobs.

Positive impact—rural cultural revival. The pecan culture has penetrated into every aspect of people's life in L County, and has also created the unique tough and simple humanistic characteristics of people in L County. The characteristic tourism festival was created, the tourist routes of raw pecans and cultural galleries and pavilions were built, and villages with superior resources were selected to guide the construction of agritainment and courtyard life stations to revitalize the native culture of pecans.

Negative impact—business conflicts bringing about neighborhood conflicts. The small size of the site has limited development, and the village committee has performed special arrangements for some e-commerce families and approved the construction of warehouses near their houses, which has affected the interests of other villagers and caused new inequalities and neighborhood conflicts.

Negative impact—common lack of human resources. The development of rural e-commerce is in urgent need of talent, but the solution to the talent problem can not only rely on enterprises. The reluctance of college graduates to return to rural areas and the difficulty in attracting and retaining talent is caused by multiple factors, such as the lack of development opportunities, poor network infrastructure, inadequate medical services, and inadequate education and culture.

4 Conclusion

The sustainable development of nut e-commerce industry in L County represents an universal problem throughout the country. For example, in Qingyanliu Village of Yiwu, the residential environment was once greatly affected by the mixed land use of residence, commerce, warehousing and logistics, which was finally solved by building the e-commerce industrial park. Some of the Taobao villages whose main products are industrial products do not fit in with the local resource endowment and can not integrate with the local primary industry, thus becoming "OEMs". And the pollution caused by industrial development is more likely to bring the impact and damage to the local ecology which are difficult to repair.

The case of the pecan industry in L County raises the reflection on county e-commerce: how to maintain the balance between regional economic development and local resource endowment in the process of digitalization and achieve sustainable and coordinated development?

Moses: Digital Intelligence Empowers More Than 10,000 Express Outlets to Solve the Last 100 M Delivery Problem

Shuai Gao, Junfeng Lu, Bin Chen, and Shaoqing Zheng

1 Introduction

"Your delivery has arrived at Moses on the first floor of the gymnasium of Zhejiang Gongshang University Hangzhou College of Commerce. Please pick it up as soon as possible with the pick-up code of 18–04-8472. Please call if you have any questions!" Whenever Miss Wu, a student, received such a short message, she knew that the goods she bought online have arrived. Then, Miss Wu walked into the Moses express station, went straight to the 4th layer of shelf No.18, found her parcel, scanned the barcode, and signed for the parcel. It took less than one minute for the whole process.

Miss Wu smiled and said, "Moses provides convenience for people like me who receive packages almost every day. In the past, we provided the express number for the employees who helped us find them one by one manually from the pile. It took a long time to pick up my parcel, especially in peak period. In winter, it would be rather suffering. Now I know the accurate location of my package, and I can find it soon. It's so convenient!".

Behind the convenient experience brought by tens of thousands of express terminal outlets to users, Moses plays a key role. Moses, headquartered in Hangzhou, Zhejiang Province, is a platform that provides terminal public distribution and automatic sorting services for express outlets in third-, fourth-and fifth-tier cities and rural areas. The company mainly focuses on providing SaaS parcel management software to franchised stores, providing users with express collection, e-commerce purchasing agent, shopping guide, goods return, third-party O2O

S. Gao (✉) · J. Lu · B. Chen · S. Zheng
School of Economics and Law, Zhejiang Gongshang University, Hangzhou College of Commerce, Hangzhou, China

J. Zhang et al. (eds.), *Innovation of Digital Economy*, Management for Professionals,
https://doi.org/10.1007/978-981-99-1741-9_12

life service and providing SaaS management software to outlets for mixed sorting, improving personnel efficiency, reducing distribution costs and bringing cost advantages for express outlets. Moses has established service outlets in many provinces in China, providing diversified, personalized and smart services for millions of users, and has become the pioneer and practitioner for the leading terminal logistics model in China.

Despite the busy business of the company, Chen Linghua (Ms. Chen for short below), founder of Moses, often takes time to inspect outlets, listen to the voices of users and think about further improvement. Seeing the flooded users in outlets, Ms. Chen smiled and recalled the rapid progress of the express delivery industry when she first started her business in 2016.

2 Overview of the Last 100 M Delivery Problem of Terminal Outlets of China's Express Delivery Industry

2.1 Status Quo of China's Express Delivery Industry

After 2010, with the help of favorable national policies and increasing penetration rate of e-commerce, the total business volume of China's express delivery industry keeps increasing year by year, with a compound annual growth rate of over 50%. Since 2014, the express delivery industry has been written into the Government Work Report for four years in a row. At the Two Sessions in 2014, the Government Work Report firstly mentioned that "it is necessary to deepen the reform of the circulation system, remove various barriers that hinder the national unified market, reduce circulation costs, and promote the development of logistics and distribution, express delivery industry and online shopping". According to the Government Work Report in 2015, "it is imperative to boost the development of logistics and express delivery to revive the emerging consumption based on Internet featured by online and offline interaction". According to the Government Work Report in 2016, "online and offline coordination and interaction should be promoted to boost the innovation and transformation of Physical business. The logistics and distribution network should be further perfected to promote the healthy development of the express delivery industry".

These favorable policies encouraged Ms. Chen to prepare for the second entrepreneurship in the express delivery industry, and the later development of the industry also confirmed her judgment. According to *Statistical Communique of the People's Republic of China on the 2020 National Economic and Social Development*, the total business volume of China's express delivery stood at 83.36 billion pieces, with a revenue of CNY879.5 billion (Fig. 1).

New retail supported by the Internet and the Internet of Things will develop rapidly. The diversification and socialization of online retail and various consumer needs will bring a new round of increment to the express delivery. It is predicted that the express delivery business will maintain a rapid growth in the next five

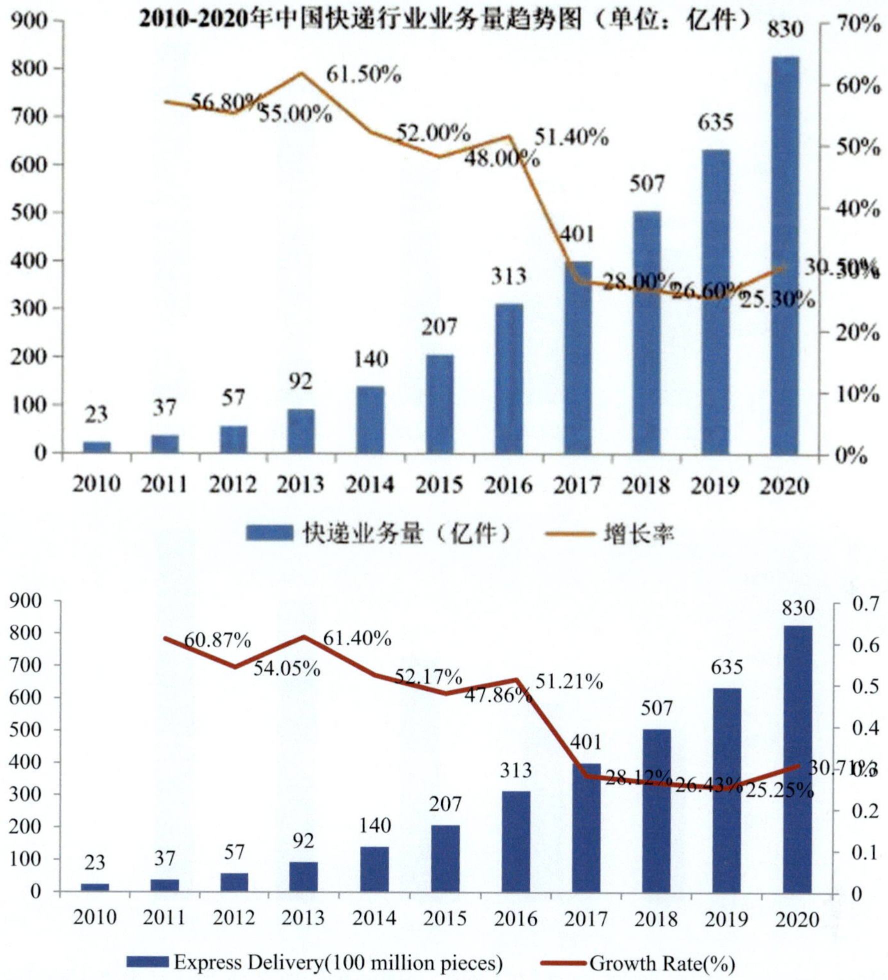

Fig. 1 Trend chart of business volume of China's express industry from 2010 to 2020. *Source* data collected by State Post Bureau

years. By 2025, business volume of the express delivery will reach around 227.6 billion pieces, with a revenue of about CNY1,726.7 billion (Fig. 2).

The surge of the express delivery business boosts rapid progress in express terminal outlets. Third-party terminal stores such as CAINIAO, Fengzhan, Best Store+, YTO Express Station and ZTO Express Supermarket began to emerge. According to the data released by the State Post Bureau in 2019, the number of registered express terminal outlets in China has exceeded 120,000. The massive expansion of China's express outlets has promoted the all-round improvement of the service quality in acceptance, collection, delivery, after-sales and information

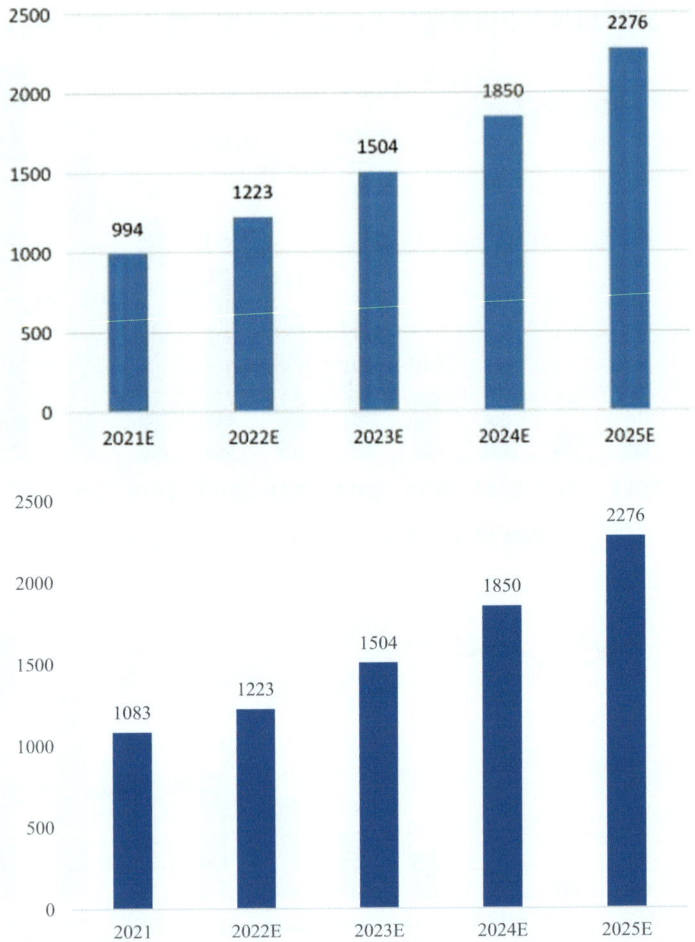

Fig. 2 Forecast chart of business trend of China's express industry from 2021 to 2025 (Unit: 100 Million Pieces). *Source* Collated according to the data of Forward Industry Research Institute

services. There are more than 2,500 express delivery enterprises founded and managed by entrepreneurs born in Tonglu, and most of the founders of express delivery brands such as YTO, STO, ZTO and YUNDA come from the county. Many people in Tonglu are associated with the express delivery industry to a certain level. Ms. Chen is no exception. She is a veteran of China's express delivery industry. She experienced the rise of the express delivery industry and keenly discovered the opportunities brought by the expansion of express terminal outlets.

2.2 The Last 100 M Delivery Problem of Express Terminal Outlets

There is a saying in the express industry that "those who have terminal outlets win". After noticing the opportunities brought by the expansion of express outlets, Ms. Chen set his eyes on the end delivery. The terminal delivery of express is completed by the franchised outlets of express companies. The main revenue of the outlets comes from the delivery fees for incoming and the express sheet fees for departure. The number of express orders directly determines the revenue of a outlet, which can range from hundreds to tens of thousands of items per day. The commission to deliverymen is counted by pieces, the number of which is directly related to their daily income. Nowadays, most residents in urban communities go to work during the day, leaving only the elderly at home, so it is not convenient for them to pick up parcels. Two or even three times of delivery will affect the success rate of delivery and greatly reduce the speed. Therefore, deliverymen started to think about developing convenient pick-up outlets, looking for stores or the property management company in the community to cooperate. The last 100-m delivery problem of express delivery is a bottleneck in the rapid growth of express delivery business, and it is also a problem that express giants, e-commerce giants and independent third-party enterprises have been working to solve. At that time, Ms. Chen investigated the following two modes of terminal outlets.

The first is intelligent express cabinets, such as Hive Box, China Post E Cabinet, JD Smart Locker, Spaster, YourBox, Parcel Cube and so on. At present, intelligent express cabinets can support users to pick up their own parcels 24 h a day, which is safe and convenient, and also saves labor costs to the greatest extent. But at the same time, the cost of material delivery and operation and maintenance are relatively high, and problems such as large parcels, parcel damage and empty cabinets in third—and fourth-tier cities have yet to be solved, giving customers a general sense of experience.

The second is the storage by the property management company or the convenience store as agents. In this way, home delivery is not necessary, which improves the delivery efficiency. The defect is that the signing rate cannot be guaranteed, resulting in more delays and losses, poor customer experience and even complaints, and the express brands may be affected. There is no special parcel management system in the property management company, and maybe some residents get the wrong parcel with the same name, or even steal other's parcels. In this case, the property management company will not compensate, and the deliveryman should be responsible for it. Complains with bring a huge fine to the deliveryman.

In recent years, the number of express orders has soared, but the survival situation of express outlets is not optimistic, trapped in a strange situation of rising revenue and declining profit. Through chatting with the boss of express outlets, Ms. Chen had an in-depth understanding of the current situation and the pain points of express terminal outlets.

2.2.1 Profits Fell Under the Price War

From 2011 to 2020, the average unit price of express delivery industry decreased year by year. In 2020, it dropped to CNY10.55/pcs, and from January to May of 2021, it further dropped to CNY9.90/pcs. In recent years, with the rise of Taobao, Pinduoduo and live broadcast e-commerce, especially at the outbreak of the COVID-19 pandemic in early 2020, some express delivery enterprises have adopted the strategy of competing for volume at low prices and launched a fierce price war. In 2020, the profit per piece of YTO, ZTO, YUNDA and STO were all below CNY0.4. The cost per piece of Best Logistics was greater than the revenue, and the gross profit per piece was CNY −0.01. The price war of express companies was bound to be transmitted to the grass-roots outlets, and the profits of the outlets decreased as the headquarters reduced the distribution fee. In this context, express outlet owners generally were unwilling to invest more in the outlets, such as investing automation equipment which costs hundreds of thousands of CNY (Fig. 3).

2.2.2 Rising Employee Costs and High Turnover Rate

The express delivery industry has the typical characteristics of labor intensive industries. The outlets assign one person per 500 pieces per day. Express outlets have a large demand for personnel, low requirements for cultural quality, and a higher turnover rate than other industries, reaching 70%. In recent years, the direct feeling of deliverymen is that there are "more jobs, but less pay", and terminal outlets are faced with the problem of employee recruitment and retention. In order to retain employees, it is inevitable for outlets to raise the salary of deliverymen, which increases operating costs.

2.2.3 Inadequate Terminal Outlet Management

Franchised outlets are mainly individual or family-run stores. In order to stabilize the operation of the outlets, some employees are also relatives and friends of the outlet owners. Employee training is carried out by the senior employees for the new comers. In addition to the training arranged by the headquarters, the outlets themselves are difficult to provide systematic training and standardized management. In addition, according to the 2019 Report on Development of Youth in China, the average age of express delivery workers is 27.62 years old, and those with a high school education background or below account for 81.02%. The employees of express outlets are relatively young and have a low educational level, which also increases the difficulty of outlet management.

2.2.4 Increasing Demand of Consumers for Service Quality

With the increasing maturity of e-commerce, consumers have higher requirements for service quality. Since September 1, 2016, *The Specification on Logistics Service of Electronic Commerce* promulgated by the Ministry of Commerce has been officially implemented in the country. It goes deep into the e-commerce logistics system, warehousing, transportation, distribution, return and exchange of goods

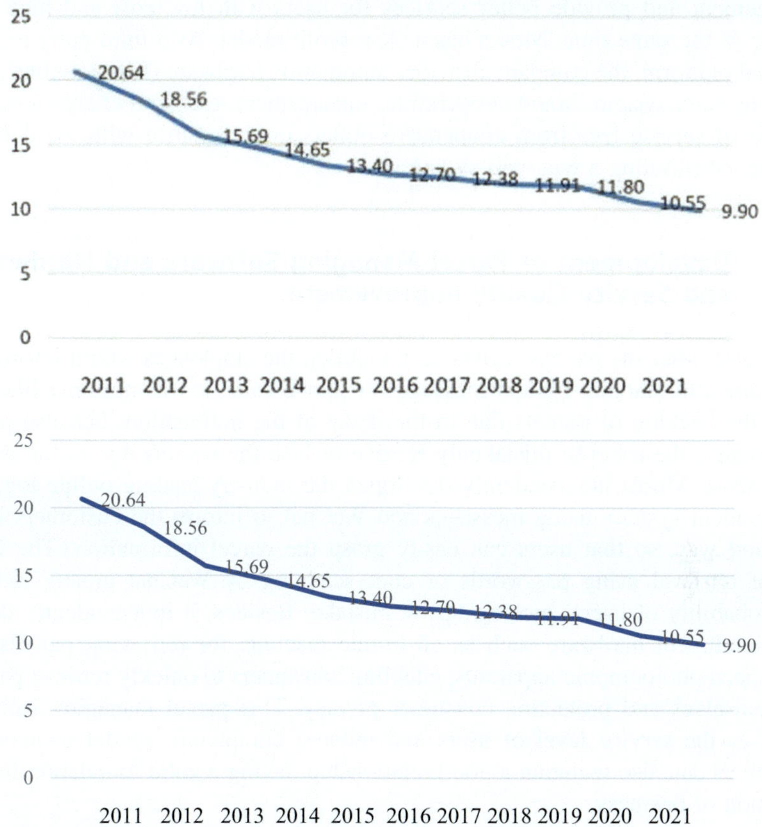

Fig. 3 Trend of average unit price of China's express delivery industry from 2011 To 2021 (Unit: CNY/Pcs). *Source* Collated according to the data on www.huaon.com

and other links. The headquarters of express companies have more and more stringent requirements on the time limit and service quality of the outlets, and the simple and crude strategy of "managing by penalty" has increased the burden of the outlets, which further intensifies the tension between the headquarters and the terminal outlets.

3 Digital Empowerment to Solve Last 100 M Delivery Problem

After understanding the last 100-m delivery problem of the terminal outlets, Ms. Chen, sensing the coming of a digital economy era, offered the "prescription" to solve it, that is, from scale driven to technology driven, empowering third-party terminal outlets by digital technologies such as hardware and software and an innovative sharing mode, to improve the intelligent and digitalized level of outlet management and provide better services for users with low cost and high efficiency. At the same time, Moses has a clear profit model. As a third party express terminal platform, the company provides automation hardware (PDA), online management SaaS system, brand cooperation, management, etc., and charge a certain amount of service fees from cooperative outlets in accordance with the delivery volume, constituting a win–win situation.

3.1 Development of Parcel Managing Software and Hardware and Service Quality Improvement

In the past, after the parcels arrived at the outlet, the employees would inform the users one after another by text messages or phone calls. It was not only likely to cause the backlog of parcels due to the delay of the notification, but also possible to cause the users to mistakenly receive or lose the parcels due to the wrong notification. Moses independently developed the industry-leading online logistics management system, using messages and WeChat to inform the customers in an all-round way, so that users can easily grasp the parcel information. The function of retrieval using passwords or code-scanning by WeChat greatly reduces the probability of users' picking up by mistake. Besides, it independently developed intelligent hardware such as all-in-one machine for retrieving parcels and high-speed photographic apparatus, enabling consumers to quickly retrieve parcels by themselves and protecting consumer privacy. This parcel managing software improves the service level of users and reduces complaints. Outlet owners and consumers can also maintain a good relationship, laying a good foundation for the extension of business.

3.2 Development of Mixed Sorting System to Improve Personnel Efficiency

The personnel configuration of the terminal outlets is usually composed of delivery workers, warehouse operators and management personnel, and large outlets are also equipped with customer service personnel. In the past, the increase in the number of parcels in express outlets could only be solved by increasing the number of employees. Therefore, Moses developed the parcel managing software Moses and training services for terminal outlets. Employees scan the package information into the system, and messages will automatically be sent and WeChat will also remind users of the arrival of their parcels, reducing the delivery frequency and delivery cost, and increasing the efficiency of delivery workers to 5 times than before. Meanwhile, the system automatically distributes parcels for the deliverymen, with a clear arrangement of daily distribution task and delivery situation. Digital background improves the management efficiency of the terminal outlet owners.

3.3 Integrated Centralized Distribution at Terminals to Reduce Distribution Costs

The team of Moses was engaged in express logistics industry before, with rich experience and resources, and has cooperated with more than 30 express company headquarters, such as China Post, SF Express, YTO Express, STO Express, ZTO Express and YUNDA Express. By opening up the express delivery system, business of multiple express delivery companies can be integrated for docking with cooperative outlets, creating economies of scale. For example, if one delivery company sends 100 parcels to a community, the combined delivery volume of various companies may exceed 500. In addition, the headquarters of Moses developed hardware and services such as automation equipment, local warehousing and standardized management to reduce the input costs of terminal outlets and increase profit levels.

3.4 Expanding Value-Added Services for Users to Increase Diversified Revenue

The original revenue source of the outlets was relatively single, that is, the headquarters provided the delivery fees for incoming and the express sheet fees for departure. The online and offline traffic of parcels was not well exploited to generate added value. The COVID-19 pandemic accelerates the rapid development of city-wide life services. In addition to providing parcel collection, Moses also provides value-added services for terminal outlets such as e-commerce shopping, shopping guide, goods return, third-party O2O life services, advertising implantation and resource recycling to expand multiple sources of revenue for terminal outlets (Fig. 4).

4 Future Prospects

Ms. Chen designed a set of methods for Moses, which precisely solves the last 100-m delivery problem of terminal outlets, and the mode of light assets also lays the foundation for its rapid promotion. In order to avoid head-to-head competition with CAINIAO in the East China market, Moses has adopted the market strategy of "encircling cities from rural areas", focusing on third-, fourth- and fifth-tier cities and rural towns. This strategy has proven to be somewhat successful and Moses is now in an overwhelmingly dominant position in North and Central China.

Looking through the 2021 performance reports just delivered, it can be seen that Moses has promoted and established service outlets in twenty provinces, municipalities directly under the Central Government and autonomous regions, including Beijing, Tianjin, Hebei, Liaoning, Jilin, Heilongjiang, Inner Mongolia, Xinjiang, Zhejiang, Shanghai, Hubei, Shandong, Guizhou, Jiangxi, Chongqing, Sichuan and Guangzhou, with 10,000 cooperative terminal outlets, handling millions of orders

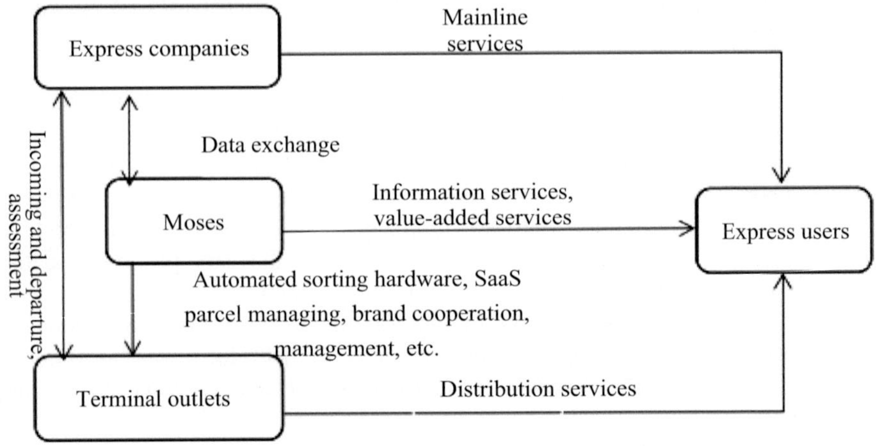

Fig. 4 Business model of moses

per day and serving a user base of nearly ten million people. It has become the head brand of third-party terminal delivery.

Ms. Chen always keeps a sober mind. With express companies like SF Express and third-party platforms like CAINIAO fighting for the terminal outlet market, how to maintain and expand the competitive advantages of the market will be the next stage of the hard battle for Moses. She looks out the window at the bustling street under the neon lights, and is once again lost in deep thought.

Acknowledgements We are grateful to Ms. Chen Linghua and Moses for providing first-hand corporate resources and valuable advice to enrich the content of this case!

YI Group: Three Sectors to Create an Internet Medical Ecosystem

Jie Zhang, Xiaolin Ding, Yanjun Lu, Runbo Wang, and Yizhen Wang

1 Introduction

With the development of "Internet +", various advanced information technologies have led to the rapid development of the digital economy, and at the same time, a new development trend emerged in the medical field which combines with the digital economy—a large number of non-traditional medical enterprises have sprung up. These medical enterprises have deeply integrated mobile Internet technologies with the medical industry, giving full play to the convenience of mobile devices and the efficiency of Internet technologies, providing a broad platform for the expansion of medical products and the extension of medical services.

Under the traditional healthcare system, our medical diagnosis industry face many problems. The uneven distribution of medical and health resources makes some people face the dilemma of "difficult to see a doctor and expensive to buy medicine", and the medical conditions in remote areas are difficult to be guaranteed, and it is also difficult to register for medical treatment in large hospitals. Some industry chaos such as illegal registration has exacerbated the conflict between hospitals and patients. This imbalance between supply and demand of healthcare resources has been accentuated under the outbreak of the COVID-19 pandemic in 2020. With the easy spread of the virus, it is difficult for many patients to ensure their safety to go for offline medical diagnosis. As a result, the "Internet + medical" model has been rapidly promoted in 2020, which gained widespread attention and recognition among the people for its advantages of avoiding people gathering and dispersing pressure on hospitals. The YI Group, which is unique in China's Internet health sector, quickly stands out at this time. In 2010, Yu Gang and

J. Zhang (✉) · X. Ding · Y. Lu · R. Wang · Y. Wang
Capital University of Economics and Business, Beijing, China

J. Zhang et al. (eds.), *Innovation of Digital Economy*, Management for Professionals,
https://doi.org/10.1007/978-981-99-1741-9_13

Liu Junling devoted themselves to fusing Internet technologies and the pharmaceutical industry to create YI Group in order to change the status quo of "difficult to see a doctor and expensive to buy medicine" for Chinese people. It uses innovative Internet technologies and IT to provide online medical treatment, drug purchasing, health management and other services, reducing intermediate links, optimizing the supply chain, increasing the efficiency and transparency of drug circulation, and providing a complete solution as well as affordability and convenience for the Chinese public to access medical treatment and purchase drugs. Currently, YI Group supports its business by three main sectors: "1 drug network" and "1 diagnosis" platforms in B2C mode, and "1 drug city" in B2B mode. Through innovative technologies, the integration and development of B-terminal and C-terminal, online and offline, self-operation and platform, medical care and medicine are fully realized, and a technology-driven medical health platform with the organic integration of online and offline is built, empowering doctors, pharmacies, hospitals, pharmaceutical companies and drug distributors, and promoting the development of health care ecosystem.

2 Birth of "1 Drug Network", and Exploration of Pharmaceutical B2C E-commerce Development

In 2010, the development of China's Internet industry showed a positive trend, all walks of life began to explore the e-commerce service model. At that time, Yu Gang and Liu Junling keenly perceived the arrival of the Internet dividend era, and resolutely chose to resign. Embraced the dream of Internet entrepreneurship, together they created the online supermarket store 1, which was the first in China. Store 1 operates a wide range of products, including food, clothing, cosmetics and pharmaceuticals, and 1 drug network was the first online pharmacy as a pharmaceutical sub-channel of store 1.

Before the establishment of 1 drug network, there was no online pharmacy platform in China, and people had to go to formal hospitals or offline pharmacies to buy drugs, so the channels for buying drugs were very limited, so there was a phenomenon of "difficult to see a doctor and expensive to buy drugs" to be solved. Yu Gang, the vice president of Amazon's global supply chain at that time, went to the United States on a business trip and found that people could not only choose to buy drugs offline, but also choose to buy drugs online and pick them up offline. The expansion of drug purchasing channels provided great convenience for patients and created conditions for pharmaceutical companies to broaden their drug sales channels. That trip to the United States made Yu Gang think of the social background of "difficult to see a doctor and expensive to buy medicine" in China at that time, so he had a bold idea, that is, why can't we start an online pharmacy in China? That's why when Yu Gang and Liu Junling started the store 1, they deliberately created the sub-channel of 1 drug network. In 2012, 1 drug network began to operate independently, and in 2015, store 1 was acquired by Walmart, at which time Yu Gang and Liu Junling made another very important decision. They gave up on store 1 to devote themselves to the operation of 1 drug network, and thus started the exploration of YI Group (1 drug network).

2.1 Online Retail Channel

The initial retail channel of 1 drug network was very single, with the sales channel of drugs being mainly online. Specifically, consumers placed orders online and the platform was responsible for offline delivery. In order to attract C-terminal users and increase user traffic, 1 drug network has cooperated with major well-known pharmaceutical companies, which include Bayer, Pfizer, Johnson and Johnson, Tongrentang, Yunnan Baiyao and other well-known pharmaceutical manufacturers at home and abroad, which has not only ensured the quality of drugs purchased by consumers, but also enhanced the credibility of the platform. At the same time, in order to provide users with a better drug purchasing experience, 1 drug network has carefully designed the platform layout, marketing, logistics and many other aspects. In terms of category management, consumers can clearly see the classification of all drugs when they open the network, which helps them to quickly find the right drug according to their drug purchasing needs; in terms of marketing, the network offers wholesales discounts, and discounts on promotion days, which help to increase user traffic on the platform; and in terms of logistics, the network tracks consumers' orders throughout the entire process, and more than 50% of orders are delivered within 24 h.

2.2 Full-Channel Retail

With the advent of the new retail era, having online network channels and offline physical channels has become a common feature in all industries. YI Group, as a leader in the pharmaceutical e-commerce industry, has also started to increase its drug sales by adding offline channels. Consumers could not only purchase drugs through the e-commerce platform of 1 drug network, but also directly went to the drugstore "Yi Hao Pharmacy" subordinated to the 1 drug network or the cooperative drugstores nationwide to purchase drugs offline. However, there were many problems in the development process of expanding product sales only by increasing channels. For consumers, the inconsistency of online and offline categories, prices and services increased the time cost of making purchasing decisions and reduced the satisfaction of consumers' shopping experience. And there was a problem of channel conflict for pharmaceutical companies. Therefore, in 2017, YI Group started to build an integrated online and offline platform, which can ensure that the online and offline products are of the same style, quality and price and are launched at the same time. When consumers visit 1 drug network through online channels, the system will display the nearest cooperative drugstore to consumers and whether the corresponding products are still in stock in the drugstore.

Under such conditions, consumers can switch between all channels anytime and anywhere and choose their preferred channels for drug purchasing.

2 "1 Diagnosis" Service Was Initiated, and B2H Realized the Integrated Development of "Doctor + Medicine"

In 2016, when many large Internet e-commerce business platforms, such as Alibaba and JD.COM, also found the dividends of medical e-commerce, Ali Health, JD Pharmacy and other medical e-commerce platforms gradually began to appear. Although relying on the advantage of being a pioneer, 1 drug network has become the largest self-operated B2C medical e-commerce platform, the platform location was very simple. Patients can only purchase medicine online on the platform, and then the platform is responsible for offline delivery. Such a simple model soon became uncompetitive as those large Internet medical care e-commerce platforms joined. At that time, Yu Gang quickly realized that the 1 drug network had other missions apart from just being a drug purchasing platform. How to bring a better drug purchasing experience to patients and stand out in such a competitive medical e-commerce market has become an urgent problem for YI Group.

Yu then noticed the mobile health market, which was already taking shape, but still facing many challenges. For example, in the field of mobile health care, doctors are both scarce resources and service subjects. While the medical industry has a long training period of talent, it is unrealistic to increase the number of medical and health personnel in a short time. In addition, some mobile medical enterprises have not established complete patient information files, and user information could not be tracked. Most mobile medical enterprises have only realized front-end consultation, because offline diagnosis and treatment resources were not in place, and they could not effectively undertake back-end treatment. In order to create a better medicine purchasing experience for patients and solve the "pain points" in the mobile medical market at that time, in 2016, YI Group established its own mobile medical platform—"1 diagnosis", which opened the integration mode of "diagnosis + treatment".

The 1 diagnosis mobile medical platform has its own Internet hospitals and offline cooperative hospitals, and thousands of contracted doctors. In order to better integrate the resources of doctors, these contracted doctors include not only full-time doctors, "full-time medical experts of 1 diagnosis", but also part-time doctors in various hospitals. In addition, it covers multiple departments. Users can realize online image-text consultation, telephone consultation and video consultation through the platform or the 1 drug network. Doctors can issue electronic prescriptions according to symptoms, and drugs are delivered by Yi Hao Pharmacy. After receiving the online consultation, patients can also choose to go to YI Group's offline cooperative hospitals for further services. In addition, 1 diagnosis also establishes comprehensive family health records for patients, with the goal of "permanent traceability for you to find historical sources of disease anytime and anywhere". Perfect family records can also provide patients with comprehensive health advice including diet, nutrition, fitness medication, and medical treatment.

With the spread of COVID-19 in 2020, various provinces and cities issued policies asking people to minimize going out and avoid gathering together. In addition, due to the impact of the pandemic, some offline medical institutions have suspended medical services, which has limited the satisfaction of people's demand for daily medical and health services. In this regard, YI Group launched free online consultation to the whole country based on the 1 diagnosis mobile medical platform, and launched the service of "free revalidation of prescription + home delivery of medicine" for patients with chronic diseases. This consultation mode and drug delivery service not only greatly reduced the risk of patients going out for consultation during the COVID-19 pandemic prevention and control period, but also provided time-saving and effective treatment for patients. It provided a guarantee for the health of patients, and also changed the traditional consultation environment and method, bringing great convenience.

The establishment of the 1 diagnosis platform not only provides individual health information files and long-term effective health consultation for every medical and health demander, but also formulates different drug demand analysis and prediction for pharmaceutical suppliers through big data statistics to reduce inventory operating costs. At present, the 1 diagnosis platform promotes the tripartite unification of healthcare service demanders, healthcare product providers and healthcare service institutions, reduces losses and costs through omni-channel integration, and realizes the interdependent foundation for the health ecosystem under the B2C model. At the same time, it meets and optimizes the demands of B-terminal manufacturers and C-terminal users, and truly promotes the integration and upgrading of "doctor + medicine" mode.

3 With the Establishment of "1 Drug City", B2B Business Suddenly Rises

In 2017, the B2C business of YI Group was faced with an increasingly fierce competition environment, and the competition, operation and promotion costs of the pharmaceutical retail e-commerce (B2C) at that time were very high, no matter for opening a store on a third-party platform or operating directly on official website. In this case, the B2C business of YI Group suffered serious losses. However, with the development of B2C business for many years, YI Group has established a good and stable partnership with hundreds of famous pharmaceutical manufacturers and enterprises. The high-quality resource supply side has created new opportunities for YI Group to start its B2B business of pharmaceutical e-commerce. At the same time, for the lack of an integration of upstream high-quality medical resources suppliers and a comprehensive coverage of downstream pharmaceutical retailors, hospitals and clinics, in 2017, YI Group began to operate new business mode named "1 drug city", a B2B pharmaceutical e-commerce platform. 1 drug city aims to provide services for upstream and downstream enterprises of the medicine circulation field, compress intermediate links and save costs, thus increasing the efficiency of supply chain and giving full play to its advantages to be a third-party intermediary platform.

3.1 Cooperation with Upstream Medicine Suppliers

In the B2B business field, YI Group actively expands cooperation with major pharmaceutical manufacturers around the world to ensure the richness of medicine supply categories and to meet the quality demand of medicine supply. As of 2021, it has formed strategic cooperation relationships with 259 pharmaceutical companies, including Eli Lilly, Novartis and other large multinational pharmaceutical enterprises. And the reason why YI Group can attract so many pharmaceutical companies to cooperate with it is that the group helps them to realize omni-channel commercialization of drugs, which makes a great contribution to expanding the sales channel of medicine and promoting their medicine. Yu Gang once mentioned it in an interview, "We can do a lot of work for pharmaceutical companies such as supply chain integration. Besides, some enterprises, such as Ali Health, Ping An Good Doctor and JD Health, all purchase from us since we have the most complete medicine and efficient supply chain. At the same time, we also carry out digital marketing, customer insight and all kinds of patient management for them." Therefore, strengthening the cooperation with pharmaceutical companies can provide assistance for the B2B development of YI Group, and these companies also can achieve greater growth with the help of the empowerment of science and technology from the platform.

3.2 Cooperation with Downstream Drug Retailers

The downstream enterprises of the B2B business supply chain of YI Group contain hospitals, offline retail pharmacies and clinics, among which offline retail pharmacies have been the main coverage objects due to the small limitation on medicine procurement and circulation and the huge quantity. By 2021, YI Group has built a network covering over 280,000 pharmacies across the country, accounting for more than 50% of the total number of pharmacies in China. Wherein, the pharmacy coverage rate in third- to sixth-tier cities has exceeded 63%.

In turn, offline retail pharmacies also can enjoy value created by B2B cooperation. For example, an ordinary retail pharmacy may only have 2,000 to 4,000 kinds of medicine, but 1 drug city can provide nearly 300,000 kinds of medicine for their wholesale purchase. Besides, pharmacies can purchase medicine from the platform at any time, and the products also can be delivered with 24 h, equivalent to that the business scale of the cooperative pharmacies has expanded directly to 300,000 kinds of medicine (Fig. 1).

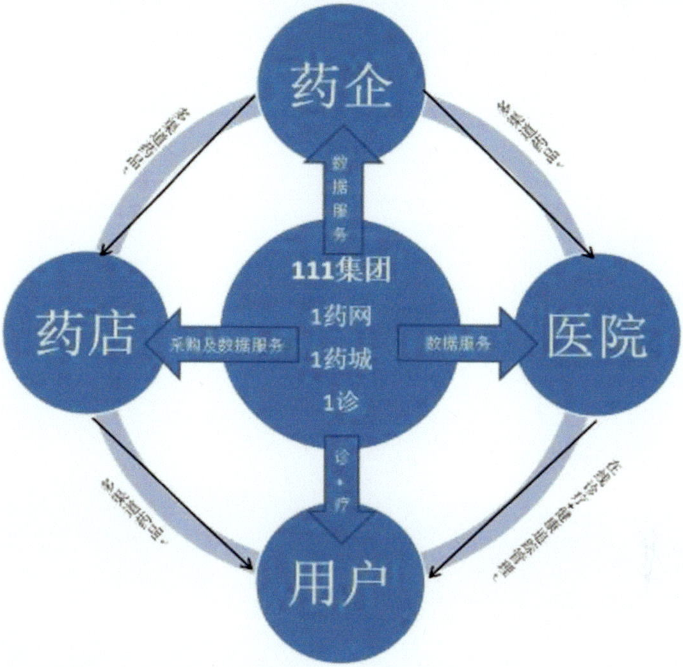

Fig. 1 Internet medical ecosystem of YI group

4 Epilogue

Three business sectors of YI Group connect pharmaceutical companies, pharmacies, hospitals, customers and other drug circulation enterprises, optimize services through empowerment of science and access online and offline retail terminals, thus forming a mutually beneficial coexistence of multiple organizations, including third-party service platform, pharmaceutical companies, pharmacies, hospitals and customers, and forming a health ecosystem of Internet medical care with stable development.

However, the current development of YI Group is also facing many problems. For example, the 1 drug network, which was the earliest platform established by the Group, has been a platform with less sense of existence and serious loss of users in the highly competitive pharmaceutical B2C e-commerce field. Moreover, the profitability of YI Group has been average. Therefore, there are two problems to be solved by YI Group: one is how to increase the B2C-terminal user stickiness to enhance user loyalty, and the other is how to enhance the sustainable profitability and explore an appropriate profit model through big data in the field of medical e-commerce.

The Rapid Rise of Social E-commerce Pinduoduo—An Analysis of Its Business Model

Peiqiang Li and He Hu

1 Introduction

With the popularization and development of mobile Internet, the business environment is showing increasingly complex and dynamic changes. Rapidly innovations are emerging in various industries, enterprises and even employee levels. Barriers in traditional industries are constantly being broken, and business tycoon are being overthrown. The reasons behind these are inseparable from the support of technology, products, services, and business model innovation. Among them, business model innovation has received a lot of attention recently and is being researched by academics and business elites both domestically and internationally. The innovation of business model in terms of value orientation, business structure and profit model not only effectively improves customers' consumption experience, but also quickly occupies the market share. However, the business model is not immutable. In an environment of escalating corporate competition, clinging to the inherent success model will only be overtaken by competitors coming from behind. In the past,scholars focused more on technology and product innovation in the past; however, as technology itself is not profitable, and creative products could not be guaranteed to obtain excessive economic returns. Without the support of business model, it is challenging to attract customers even with excellent products and technologies. With the development of communication technology and Internet, the consumer Internet is closely related to the industrial Internet; moreover, social media and e-commerce platforms are no longer separated from each other. The cross-border interconnection and restructuring of business profit models will become an irresistible trend, and business model innovation is gradually becoming the key for enterprises to gain sustainable competitiveness.

P. Li (✉) · H. Hu
School of Business, Hebei Normal University, Shijiazhuang, China

J. Zhang et al. (eds.), *Innovation of Digital Economy*, Management for Professionals,
https://doi.org/10.1007/978-981-99-1741-9_14

In the era of digital economy, the e-commerce industry is developing rapidly. As a dark horse under the social dividend in the mobile internet era, Pinduoduo went public in the United States only three years after its establishment, and its market value reached trillions only five years after its establishment. Based on this, this paper combs the relevant research on business model innovation by domestic and foreign scholars, and analyzes the development path of Pinduoduo's business model based on relevant theories.

2 Case Background

With a focus on C2M group shopping, Pinduoduo is a mainstream third-party social e-commerce platform for mobile Internet in China. The company was found in September 2015, and it was selected as one of the top 100 brands of China's Brand Development Ceremony in 2019. By the end of 2020, the number of active buyers in Pinduoduo reached CNY788.4 million, making it the largest e-commerce platform for Chinese users. Pinduoduo launched a 'social + e-commerce' shopping mode, encouraging users to purchase products by sharing. By initiating groups with friends, family, and neighbors, users can buy high-quality goods at a lower price. Aiming to gather the strength of more people, Pinduoduo intends to let people buy better things at lower prices, and allow users to experience more benefits and fun. The social concept shaped through communication and sharing has formed a unique and new social e-commerce model in Pinduoduo.

3 Pinduoduo's Business Model Canvas

See Fig. 1.

4 Analysis of Pinduoduo's Business Model

4.1 Analysis of Important Partners and Key Activities Choices in Pinduoduo

4.1.1 Choices of Pinduoduo's Important Partners

Vital partners are the elements on the left side of the business model canvas, which are a group of partners and supplier partners needed to make the business model operate effectively. Cooperative relationships mainly include the following four types: strategic alliance relationship, strategic cooperative relationship, joint venture relationship, and supplier relationship. In the case of Pinduoduo, we focus on the first two relationships of the three dimensions,-government, enterprise, and platform.

Since 2020, the COVID-19 pandemic has had a significant impact on the economic growth of many regions, including tourism, consumption, and agriculture.

<table>
<tr><td rowspan="2">Key Partnerships

Local government
Corporation
Entry merchants
Media platform
WeChat platform</td><td>Key Activities

Platform network
Marketing services</td><td rowspan="2">Value Propositions

Innovation
Low price
Customization
Risk reduction</td><td>Customer Relationships

With entry merchants
With consumers</td><td rowspan="2">Customer Segments

Housewife
Retired elderly people
Wage earner
Student
White collar</td></tr>
<tr><td>Key Resources

Intellectual assets
Human assets</td><td>Channels

Paid traffic
Free traffic</td></tr>
<tr><td colspan="3">Cost Structure

Subsidies and promotion costs, R&D expenses
Management costs</td><td colspan="2">Revenue Streams

Online marketing service revenue, trading revenue
Merchandise revenue</td></tr>
</table>

Fig. 1 Analysis chart of nine elements for pinduoduo business model canvas

In such a case, government departments at all levels have cooperated strategically with Pinduoduo. From Jiangsu, Zhejiang, and Shanghai in coastal areas to Hubei, Sichuan, and Yunnan in inland areas, and also from provincial governments to municipal and county governments, many mayors and county magistrates appeared in e-commerce live broadcasts of Pinduoduo to promote local distinctive industrial products or agricultural by-products. The above phenomenon not only reflects the strong demand of local governments to restore the economy in the late period of the pandemic, but it also reflects the influence of Pinduoduo as a digital economy platform in the entire economy industry chain.

In cooperation with the government as an essential partner helping agriculture, rural areas, and farmers has become a crucial breakthrough point in Pinduoduo. In order to better solve the problem of unsalable agricultural products in remote areas, Pinduoduo responded to the call of the national government and lauched a series of special sales and promotion activities of agricultural products through live broadcast, These activities not only solved the problem of unsalable products, but also brought high-quality and inexpensive products to consumers; thus laying a good brand reputation for Pinduoduo to further open up the market.

In addition to working with the government, Pinduoduo also has deep brand cooperation with enterprises, such as strategic cooperation with Gome Holdings Group. It subscribes its US$200 million convertible bonds. Gome continuously puts its home appliances on Pinduoduo for sale and participates in the Ten Billion Subsidy Plan. Anxun Logistics, a subsidiary of Gome Holdings Group, is mainly responsible for providing consumers with a complete set of service solutions in logistics, warehousing, delivery and after-sales.

In addition to enterprises, there are also key platforms to attract customers for Pinduoduo. These platforms are the most important partner of Pinduoduo in its initial stage and are also known as the WeChat platform of its investor Tencent.

As the first social platform, WeChat's daily active users are from all over the country. Moreover, with the cooperation with Tencent, its social shopping mode can continuously attract customers on WeChat platform. These customers have become the most loyal customer group in the early days of Pinduoduo and the key factor for Pinduoduo's rise to become one of the three giants in e-commerce.

4.1.2 Key Activities of Pinduoduo During Its Development

Key activities should be focused on and done by enterprises, which are generally divided into product manufacturing, platform network, and solutions. In comparison, operation management, such as network service and trading platform software, are all key business components. To provide customers with valuable solutions, it is necessary to improve the management of critical activities. Since Pinduoduo is an e-commerce platform that has not set foot in the field of self-manufacturing products, this research will focus on the key activities under the platform network.

In order to continuously attract a number of customer groups on both sides and attract merchants to settle in, Pinduoduo proposed support policies such as zero cost and zero commission in the early days. On the consumer side, vigorously promote the group shopping model and take customers themselves as the key to attract customers. On the other hand, huge capital costs were invested in launching the program of Ten Billion Subsidies to attract consumers to become its buyers.

In order to meet the low-price demand of price-sensitive people, Pinduoduo quickly obtains customers mainly through two modes, namely group shopping and reverse customization. The price under the group shopping mode is more favorable than self-purchase, and the cost is to let others join the group by forwarding the group. Reverse customization, on the other hand, is the process of feeding platform sales back into the product manufacturing stage, which can not only meet the price advantage of large-scale production but also effectively reduce inventory or even reach zero inventory, forming an advantage in cash flow that other platforms cannot match.

4.2 Analysis on Core Resources and Value Creativity of Pinduoduo

4.2.1 Core Resources Available for the Rise of Pinduoduo

Core resources are the key resource elements necessary for the effective operation of the business model. In addition to people and property, there are intangible knowledge assets, including brands, patents, and technologies. From the balance sheet, Pinduoduo is a typical light-asset enterprise. This paper believes that the core resources of Pinduoduo include human resources and knowledge assets such as brands and patents.

In terms of brand, Pinduoduo has become a household name through social groups and brand variety events. In addition, it is equally important that Pinduoduo also promotes the online sale of agricultural products through live broadcast, which improves the market reputation in e-commerce poverty alleviation, thereby making the brand effect significant.

In terms of patent right (patented technology), Pinduoduo's own patented technology is far behind other e-commerce giants in terms of quantity and quality. However, unlike traditional e-commerce platforms that use centralized AI to serve a single consumer, Pinduoduo uses distributed AI technology to empower the platform effectively. Distributed AI is open to all users and can be supervised by them, so that users can regain the leading power of decision-making, which improves the matching efficiency between consumers and commodities, and creates different consumption scenarios and customized products for different consumers. By developing fake product identification algorithms and building models based on data mining analysis, the breeding of fake products on the platform is effectively restricted, and the brand's public image is indirectly maintained.

Regarding human resources, talent strategy is the source of Pinduoduo's development. The scale of employees is constantly expanding, with more than 50% of the technical engineers always being the backbones. Every year, Pinduoduo attracts e-commerce talent from all over the country through campus recruitment. Numerous young technical talents provide guarantee for algorithm design and technology upgrading. Pinduoduo provides high-quality compensation and welfare for talent retention and incentives, and also provides multi-dimensional care such as platform growth and personal development. The prospectus also published that the equity incentive plan will be used to attract and retain talent as well as constantly strengthen the incentive for core talent.

4.2.2 Pinduoduo's Value Creativity

The value proposition is used to depict a series of products and services that create value for customers in the service market, meeting customers' demands, solving their problems, and delivering values. The difference in the value proposition of different companies determines whether the company can survive and seek long-term development in the market. The value proposition has a series of brief elements such as novel design, performance, brand, price, cost, and risk. In this paper, we will talk about Pinduoduo's value proposition from innovation, price, customization, and risk reduction.

Pinduoduo's innovation is somewhat disruptive, and its origin is Chris Anderson's long tail theory. Christensen's disruption theory also provides a theoretical basis for its development. At the beginning of Pinduoduo's establishment, the e-commerce field formed an unshakable pattern of Alibaba and JD.com, and other giants. However, the head effect exists in the higher maturity platforms. As a result, excessive platform fees and promotion costs cause many merchants to be unprofitable. In other words, most small and medium-sized merchants have no profitable living space. Pinduoduo seized this opportunity and adopted a series of preferential policies like zero commission to attract small and medium-sized merchants to the platform. It started from the long tail businesses and sinking market ignored by giants, which makes Pinduoduo stand out.

The price is the crucial way for Pinduoduo to rise. In the early days, Alibaba's Taobao platform also had incomparable price advantages; however, with the development of the platform and the maturity of the profit model, its algorithm recommendation mechanism is no longer based on low prices. And due to consumption upgrading, most products pursue quality brands rather than cost performance in advance, which really wins the favor of users in first-tier and second-tier cities. However, the low-price demand of sinking markets always exists, even if the performance of the product is generally acceptable. Pinduoduo won a significant victory in the value proposition dimension of price due to the satisfaction of the demand of the sinking market.

However, the risks brought by low prices cannot be ignored, such as the prevalence of counterfeit goods, brand reputation damage, and other risks. In order to avoid the risks affecting its long-term development, Pinduoduo vigorously combats counterfeit products within the platform, such as through the algorithm technology to identify accurate identification of counterfeit goods and illegal business, leaving no space for the fake and inferior products that dare not return without freight. One of the reasons for the low price of Pinduoduo in the early stage is its role of de-stocking. In the small commodity and clothing manufacturing industry with serious overcapacity, a large amount of inventory has become a hidden danger to the cash flow of enterprises. Therefore, dealing with the inventory at a low price is a wise choice for enterprises and a win–win result for businesses and platforms. Furthermore, Pinduoduo develops reverse customization after further expansion. In recent years, the customization scale has been sufficient for production and technical conditions. For example, Pinduoduo adopts support plans such as the new brand plan to preposition consumer demand so as to determine the direction of product development and design, reducing the risk of uncertainty in the production and sales of enterprises.

4.3 Analysis of Pinduoduo's Customer Segmentation and Customer Management

4.3.1 Pinduoduo's Customer Segmentation

Customer segmentation is the different groups of customers or organizations that a company wants to interface with and serve in its business model. Specifically, it refers to the important customers and target groups that we create value for. From the market level, it can be divided into the mass market, multilateral market, niche market, and segmented market. In this paper, we will not differentiate the above market types, but we will focus on customer groups and make a portrait of the people served by Pinduoduo according to different factors such as gender, age, occupation, and region.

From the search index of Pinduoduo, it can be found that the peak of daily activity and trade index is more obvious on weekends, which can be inferred that these customers are free students and salaried people on weekends, in line with the characteristics of Pinduoduo users with high demand for low prices. Moreover, according to the proportion of the population age of three major e-commerce giants, Taobao, JD.com and Pinduoduo, the users in each age group of Taobao and JD.com account for a relatively balanced proportion, but the proportion of Pinduoduo under the age of 25 and over the age of 55 exceeds that of Taobao and JD in the same age group. And its female users account for a high proportion.

According to the above analysis, we can summarize that the main customer groups of Pinduoduo are divided into the following categories: housewives, young people who have not worked long, retired elderly people, students, social group affiliates, and 10 billion RMB subsidy recipients. Compared to students and employees, housewives and retired elderly people have more free time and lower time costs. Therefore, they are willing to spend more time browsing product selections. In addition, they have a stronger social relationship intimacy, and they have the characteristics of private domain sharing and communication, and the price is their key consideration. When two attributes of low price and easy dissemination are combined, Pinduoduo is quietly popular in these two groups.

Students and employees have less leisure time, but their desire to buy is stronger than housewives and retired elderly people. They are not the targets of consumption upgrades and do not pursue product design, packaging, and quality brands too much. The cost performance of products is an important factor determining their purchase. Therefore, with the low price and less exquisite daily necessities and clothing, Pinduoduo has become the first choice for these two groups.

Moreover, Pinduoduo takes multiple measures in customer expansion and makes heavy efforts. In order to win the favor of white-collar workers in first and second-tier cities, Pinduoduo provided tens of billions of subsidies with hard cash. Pinduoduo's target was no longer limited to low-cost consumer goods but mainly subsidized high-end mobile phones such as Apple, high-end appliances such as Dyson, and various high-end clothing brands. The result of burning money was to get a large number of purchasing power to pursue the quality of urban white-collar customers. In product design, for the interface design and pop-up mode that young people don't like, Pinduoduo actively reformed the simple and clear purchase interface on the WeChat applet, which is highly praised.

4.3.2 Customer Relationship Management in Pinduoduo

The customer relationship is a connection established with customers in the operation of the business model to achieve its business goals. Customer relationship has three main drivers: developing new customers, maintaining old customers, and increasing single customer repurchase. In this report, we will analyze the customer relationship of Pinduoduo from two customer dimensions: the resident merchant and the consumer.

The entry merchants and the Pinduoduo platform are partners. Merchants provide the platform with products for trading, and Pinduoduo provides them with traffic for conversion. In order to attract more merchants, Pinduoduo proposed zero cost entry and a series of exposure measures at its early stage, and only a certain deposit was required to open a store on the platform to sell goods. However, with the growth of Pinduoduo, the problem of counterfeit goods was endless. Therefore, Pinduoduo added a series of harsh regulations and corresponding penalties in the merchant entry clause. Many merchants were deducted and fined a huge breach of contract for selling counterfeit. In addition to the new brand support program, Pinduoduo provided a variety of help and protection for qualified small and medium-sized merchants.

Consumers and Pinduoduo have automated service relationships, community relationships, and private relationships. According to big data analysis based on consumers' usual commodity browsing, search and order placement, Pinduoduo infers consumer types and preferences and then continues to push relevant product content based on algorithms, so as to reduce their decision time and improve repurchase rates. Due to the WeChat sharing-based group purchasing, there is essentially a community relationship between acquaintances and groupmates, which needs to be supported by a steady stream of high-quality and inexpensive goods. And the communication between consumers and the customer service of merchants and Pinduoduo is a personal relationship. Both patient answers before sales and considerate service after sales can promote the conscience cycle of customer relations.

4.4 Pinduoduo's Promotion Channel Selection

Channel access refers to the way and channel through which an enterprise reaches its target customers to deliver value propositions. For Pinduoduo, it refers mainly to the promotion channel. The main purpose of promotion is to obtain traffic, and there are inside traffic and outside traffic, like Taobao. For the settled merchants, the promotion channels inside the station include Duoduo Jinbao, Zhitongche, star stores, and marketing activities. The outside traffic includes Wechat Moments, WeChat groups, QQ groups, post-bar, forums, etc. This articles will focus on analyzing the four main types of traffic for Pinduoduo merchants.

Paid traffic, also called paid promotion, accounts for a certain percentage of Pinduoduo's revenue. For example, Zhitongche is not based on the following single volume but based on the number of clicks. This kind of promotion has the disadvantages of high cost and unstable conversion rate. In the long run, it is not as stable as the ranking, so most merchants take both ways into account. In addition, except for paid traffic, there are also some other kinds of traffic as drainage from other platforms, platform activity drainage, and platform-free traffic. Among them, other platforms, such as Yizhibo, Weibo, and other social platforms, most of the activity traffic and natural search traffic are free, and there is a positive correlation between product display rate and traffic.

4.5 Analysis of Pinduoduo's Revenue Sources and Cost Structure

According to the financial statements disclosed by Pinduoduo, the revenue structure has changed with the expansion of its scale. Earlier, Pinduoduo belonged to self-operated e-commerce, with revenue of CNY456 million from merchandise sales in 2016 (i.e. selling agricultural product to buyers); however, it completed the transformation of its platform model in 2017, with online service revenue of CNY1.74 billion and merchandise sales of only CNY3.39 million that year. By the first quarter of 2018, all of Pinduoduo's revenue came from online services, with CNY1.384 billion in revenue for the quarter.

Its online service revenue was mainly comprised of commission income and online marketing services. In the second quarter of 2018, online marketing service revenue was CNY6.467.1 billion, accounting for 88.6% of the total revenue of CNY7.29 billion. In the third quarter of 2020, online marketing service revenue was CNY12.888 billion, accounting for 90.7% of the total revenue of CNY14.2 billion, while transaction service revenue was CNY1.312 billion. Therefore, Pinduoduo relies mainly on online advertising and transaction commissions, and its business model is no different from other e-commerce companies. In the first three quarters of 2020, Pinduoduo's operating revenue was CNY32.944 billion, an increase of CNY13.595 billion, a year-on-year growth of 70.26%; the operating cost was CNY7.753 billion, an increase of CNY3.452 billion, or 80.26% year on year, and the gross operating profit was CNY25.192 billion. Net profit in the first three quarters of 2020 was CNY-5.803 billion, a decrease of CNY587 million year-on-year (Figs. 2 and 3).

In the third quarter of 2020, Pinduoduo's operating expenses were CNY12.241 billion, reaching the peak since 2019, including the management cost was CNY369 million, a year-on-year decrease of CNY67 million or 15.37%; R&D expenses

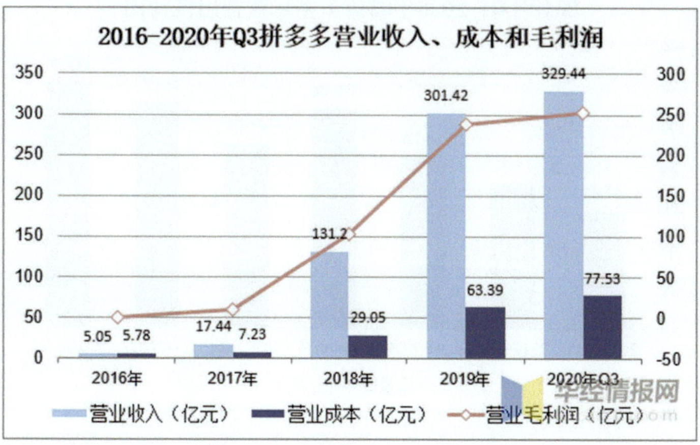

Fig. 2 Pinduoduo's operating revenue, cost and Gross profit in Q3 from 2016 to 2020

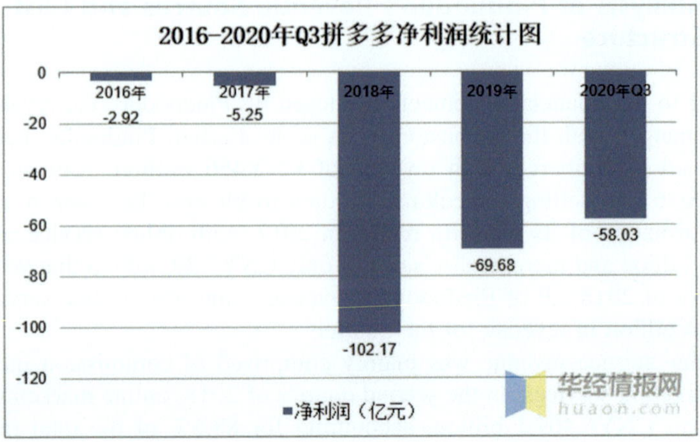

Fig. 3 Pinduoduo's net profit statistical chart in Q3 from 2016 to 2020. (*Data source* financial report of the company, compiled by Huajing Industrial Research Institute)

were CNY1.8 billion, an increase of CNY673 million or 59.72% year-on-year; Subsidy and promotion expenses were CNY10.072 billion, an increase of CNY3.162 billion and 45.76% over the same period of last year (Figs. 4 and 5).

We can see that subsidies and promotion expenses account for a large percentage of Pinduoduo's operating expenses, accounting for 82.28% of total operating expenses in the third quarter of 2020. The CNY10 billion subsidy activities started from 2018. In the past, daily necessities and clothing were cheap, while up to now, big brands are also cheap, which has enhanced Pinduoduo's brand image and market reputation. As a result, although Pinduoduo's operating expenses have

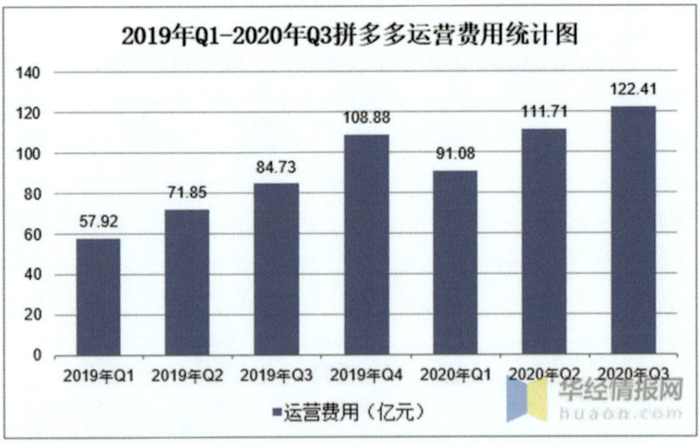

Fig. 4 Pinduoduo's operating expenses statistical chart from Q1 in 2019 to Q3 in 2020

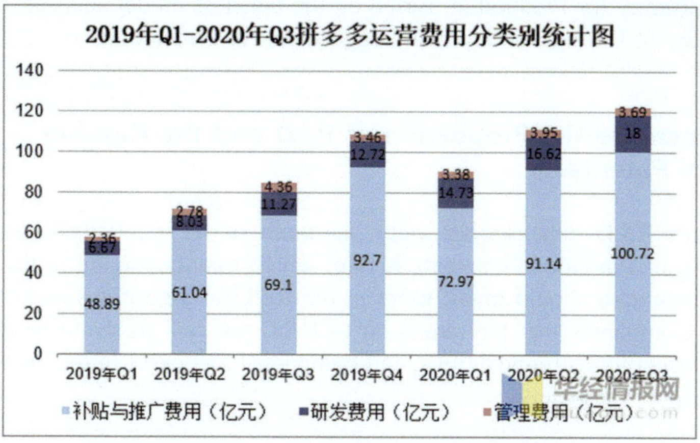

Fig. 5 Pinduoduo's operating expenses classification statistical chart from Q1 in 2019 to Q3 in 2020. (*Data source* financial report of the company, compiled by Huajing Industrial Research Institute)

significantly increased, its market has rapidly expanded. And the subdivided customer market has expanded from the sinking market to the whole market, including first-and second-tier cities, showing a rising trend.

5 Suggestions for the Stable Development of Pinduoduo

Based on the knowledge assets such as brand, algorithm technology, and core resources such as human resources, Pinduoduo has established a large market for housewives, retired people, students, wage earners, white-collar workers, and other groups. By providing a platform and online marketing services to merchants, establishing partnerships with them, providing consumers with low-cost and customized services, and establishing personal relationships, platform relationships, and automated relationships with them, establishing a multi-platform business model in key promotion channels such as paid traffic and free traffic. It creates value by promoting the interaction of different groups, and the value is mainly realized by expanding the number of merchants and users, so as to gradually occupy the market and form the combined effect.

With the 'surround the cities from the countryside' strategy, Pinduoduo has successfully won the sinking market's heart where price-sensitive people are concentrated by the low price. After that, Pinduoduo continued to aggressively attack first-tier and second-tier cities through 'subsidies of 10 billion yuan', enhance brand reputation through advertising and activity sponsorship, and enhance users' goodwill by cracking down on fake and shoddy products. This system has virtually robbed the users of its competitors, such as Ali and JD. Compared with Ali and JD, it is more difficult to obtain traffic, and the low customer acquisition cost is a huge opportunity for Pinduoduo. Based on the business model analysis, this paper proposes the following development suggestions for Pinduoduo:

5.1 Increase the Proportion of R&D and the Number of Patents.

Pinduoduo's R&D expenses are only one-tenth of the publicity expenses, and the number of Pinduoduo's patents is rare, which mainly staying in the interface design. Pinduoduo should invest more in the R&D of algorithms and other technologies. Companies that pay attention to R&D are less likely to be eliminated in future technological innovations, and companies that excel in the invention will win the respect of society.

5.2 Pay More Attention to Talent Development and Employee Growth.

Human resource is the key resource for enterprise survival and development. Training employees can improve their professionalism, and caring employees can improve their loyalty, both of which are indispensable. Unfortunately, in the past six months, Pinduoduo has suffered frequent accidents in terms of labor and employment. News such as squeezing employees to cause sudden death, snooping on employees' privacy, and firing employees have seriously damaged the brand image of Pinduoduo, and therefore lost the opportunity to cooperate with the 2021 Spring Festival Gala.

5.3 Promote Self-operated Business and Reduce Cash Flow Risk

Lower commission income is detrimental to the cash flow of the business, which is particularly evident in the run-up to 2018. With lower revenue elasticity, Pinduoduo can actively explore new growth points as its existing revenue profit model matures. In the past six months, Internet companies such as NetEase, Huawei, and other communication companies have begun to explore technical interventions for the pig industry, and Pinduoduo can also capture new market opportunities based on its own strengths.

5.4 Refine the Value Proposition to Better Serve Users

It continues to crack down on counterfeit sales and inferior products, enrich and optimize product categories, improve the interface design of the Pinduoduo platform, increase practicality and convenience, and reduce set-ups. In addition, it transforms from low-price marketing to content marketing, attracting users' active participation by enhancing storytelling and interactivity. Meanwhile, it reduces users' decision time in the pre-sale experience, improves users' experience and satisfaction in the post-sale experience, and truly serves users with value.

From the Peak to the Mire, How Should the Straggling TuNiu Break Through?

Wenze Huang and Yulin Zhang

1 Introduction

Due to the continuous development of Internet technology, some activities offline have been gradually replaced by trading activities online. Meanwhile, the main goal of the people has changed into the demand for a better life due to the continuous development of the domestic economy. The development has led to the expansion of the scale of tourism. Moreover, the enthusiasm of national tourism consumption is increasing. Such development makes it a new hotspot to provide various tourism products and services based on the Internet, such as plans before travel, hotel information collection, air ticket booking, catering, transportation consumption and scenic spot ticket purchase during travel, and experience sharing and evaluation after travel.

TuNiu (TuNiu Tours/TuNiu Traveling/TuNiu.com) found business opportunities. To meet the needs of various customers, TuNiu strived to survive in the cracks. It sought breakthroughs from the competition with Ctrip and eLong by customizing tourism routes and services to create an exclusive brand and enhance the sense of experience for customers. However, there were many new competitors appearing in the online travel industry because of the development and application of Internet technology. In response to strong industry pressure, TuNiu transformed from "complete tourism" to "tourism + finance" service, which meant that it gradually realized the transformation of the enterprise by combining online travel agency with online financial business. Nevertheless, cracks emerged in the company soon.

This case is sponsored by the National Natural Science Foundation of China (72,071,040) and the National Social Science Fund of China (21&ZD118).

W. Huang (✉) · Y. Zhang
School of Economics and Management, Southeast University, Nanjing, China

J. Zhang et al. (eds.), *Innovation of Digital Economy*, Management for Professionals,
https://doi.org/10.1007/978-981-99-1741-9_15

Its internal senior management was influenced. The founder team left one after another. Therefore, the team gradually lost its cohesion. Meanwhile, the innovation of the enterprise was impacted by the new platform, whose competitiveness had been declining. Its customized tour that TuNiu had always been proud of was imitated. In addition to the impact of the COVID-19 pandemic on offline stores and the tourism industry, there were problems with the capital chain of TuNiu, which made it gradually fall out of the first echelon of domestic online travel enterprises. Its U.S. stock market was facing the risk of delisting. How to save the "middle-aged" TuNiu from the crisis was a difficulty for all the staff of the enterprise.

For TuNiu, it was inevitable to make a transformation to regain its market share and turn losses into profits in the era of digital economy. The enterprise shall make breakthroughs in technology, including big data, cloud computing, the Internet of Things, blockchain, artificial intelligence and other emerging technologies. Furthermore, the enterprise shall complete the change of its quality through "new retail" and "new manufacturing" in its application, which helped them get out of the backward predicament. Therefore, it is possible for TuNiu to gain more investment in the future and open a new chapter for its further development.

2 Development and Current Situation of the Company

TuNiu was founded in Nanjing, Jiangsu Province in October 2006 with the slogan of "make tourism easier". At that time, Ctrip and eLong already accounted for a large proportion of the online travel market in China. There was little possibility to replicate the profit models of these two companies for development. Therefore, TuNiu has broke the inherent thinking of traditional users and service providers since its establishment. The enterprises opened a new chapter by a novel model of precise positioning and online travel route ordering.

During the first half of the year, the enterprise spent a lot of time to build a scenic spot database, which was more comprehensive in China then. Besides, the company creatively launched two products, "roadmap" and "platter". Travelers from all over the country could exchange their tourism experiences with them, which made tourism easier.

Its initial operation mode was middleman. Then, there were many offline travel agencies in China. Each one had its own travel routes. TuNiu integrated and classified these routes. Tourists could check the routes of the major travel agencies by visiting www.tuniu.com and make reservations on its website. TuNiu, as a middleman, would provide free consulting services to give consumers a better user experience. The enterprise earned the price differences between the price paid by consumers to the platform and the contract signed with the agency, as well as the commission regularly fed back by the travel agency after the tourists signed the contract (Liu et al., 2021).

At first, TuNiu had only a little popularity. Yu Dunde and his partners, as its founders, tried their best to improve the popularity of their enterprise. TuNiu was an Internet enterprise. Online bidding has become its main marketing skill. In the next few years, it gained a lot of customers by online bidding.

However, the source of customers from marketing means was not a long-term solution. The enterprise continued to improve its innovation ability. The enterprise won the favor of venture capitalists soon after its establishment with the innovation of new products and technologies (Li, 2018). TuNiu created a series of high-quality products such as "Niuren Special Line" for high-quality group tours in 2009. The line soon became a new star in group tours by its unique product ideas and high-quality services. The experience of tourist has also been improved by its continuous upgrading of products and services, which created a competitive barrier of TuNiu (Wanyu et al., 2018). The Niuren Special Line has served more than 5.5 million tourists by 2021 with customer satisfaction reaching 97%. It had more than 500 lines with more than 99% satisfaction for tourists to choose from.

Therefore, TuNiu won the first round of venture capital for multi—million dollars from Gobi Partners in 2011. The enterprise was awarded the potential growth award of "Most Influential Brand in the Consumer Market in China" and the "Second Runner up of the 11th Top 100 Chinese Enterprises" in 2012. It was awarded the "Online Tourism Industry—Most Influential Brand Award" after a year. It was also awarded the "China's Best Customer Experience Award" in 2014. TuNiu, as a leading leisure travel company in China, was successfully listed on NASDAQ in the United States in May of the same year. It has gradually become a diversified Internet tourism company, including online and offline group following, self-service, self-driving, cruise, scenic spot tickets, corporate tourism, air tickets, hotels and others.

With the help of the rapid growth of the online leisure tourism market in China and the broad support of the users, TuNiu has always ranked first in the online leisure tourism market share in China since the fourth quarter of 2015. TuNiu ranked as the "Top 100 Internet Enterprises in China" and won the award of "Best Online Travel Brand" in 2016, which was the highest honor in the industry. After a long loss period, the enterprise finally turned losses into profits in the third quarter of 2018. As the scale of suppliers continued to expand, more than 16,000 service providers had made cooperation with TuNiu by the end of 2018. Besides, more than 2.2 million kinds of diversified services could be provided for users, including group following, self-service, hotels, air tickets, visas and others. As of the first quarter of 2019, it had provided services to more than 108 million tourists in total. Moreover, it had received more than 6 million user reviews, with a high praise rate of 93%. The "Niuren Special Line" of TuNiu won the honor of "China Service" tourism product innovation case in 2019. The brand image of "high-quality group tour" has gradually become popular since then (Xu, 2016; Huang & Wu, 2019).

The COVID-19 pandemic broke out at the beginning of 2020. The tourism industry got great impact. As a leader in the industry, TuNiu adhered to the principle of customer first and fully protected the rights and interests of them for a long time. At the beginning of the global pandemic, the enterprise provided customers with industry-leading refund services and guarantees at the first time with the industry-leading speed. For customers stuck by the pandemic, TuNiu returned the undamaged part in full in cash. The damaged part was provided with equivalent travel allowance vouchers. During the COVID-19 pandemic, the enterprise suffered a direct loss of more than CNY100 million for customers who unsubscribed. Besides, the refunds paid to customers for suppliers also exceeded CNY100 million. TuNiu suffered huge financial pressure. However, it had established more than 30 domestic and foreign self-operated local agencies, providing travel product bookings for 420 cities by December 2020.

Generally, TuNiu created two products, namely "roadmap" and "platter" in 2006, which made tourism easier with the scenic spot database. In 2009, TuNiu launched its core product "Niuren Special Line", which was a high-quality group tour. Compared with the fixed tour routes of travel agencies, "Niuren Special Line" was improved from various service links of group tours, focusing on the experience and satisfaction of tourists. In 2015, TuNiu comprehensively upgraded the special line 2.0 in transportation, Internet access and guide services, and bound the customer review data to the daily management of guides to ensure that it could provide professional, standardized and meticulous services to tourists. In the same year, the popularity of a series of parent–child programs such as "Dad, Where Are We Going" made a large number of "Internet + parent–child tour" products emerged. In this context, TuNiu launched the product brand "Melon and Fruit Parent–child Tour" in December 2015, which was favored by parents and children. In 2016, TuNiu released new spring products such as the "Happy Tour for Parents". The "Happy Tour for Parents" is another independent product brand created by TuNiu after the "Melon and Fruit Parent–child Tour" for the market segment of travelers. In 2019, the 10th anniversary of the launch of the "Niuren Special Line", the service standard has been upgraded again, upgrading the "Niuren Special Line", promoting the "Niuren Strict Slection", focusing on the head products to continuously improve the customer experience. In addition to continuing to develop the self-operated product "Niuren Special Line" with high customer experience, the "Niuren Strict Slection" products jointly selected by TuNiu and its partners are also welcomed by more and more tourists with high quality. In 2020, the brand of high-quality group tours will be upgraded again to make the one-stop service specialized and precise.

In the service model, the main service in the early stage of TuNiu's creation was to summarize the travel routes of major travel agencies for consumers to choose centrally, and then gradually launched its own high-quality "Niuren Special Line" and a series of other products to promote the quality of group tours. After harvesting financing and gaining a firm foothold while expanding its audience, TuNiu gradually opened up self-drive tours, self-guided tours and other forms of travel as well as diversified services including cruises, scenic tickets, air tickets and hotels, becoming an all-round online travel service company. Later, it launched promotions such as small group tours and special tours, and provided 24 h full-process services in terms of pre-consultation, mid-operation and post-feedback of tourism, making high quality and personalization the label of TuNiu tourism.

In terms of revenue, TuNiu's revenue has continued to grow since 2011, peaking at CNY10.548 billion in 2016. With the increased investment in R&D, TuNiu's

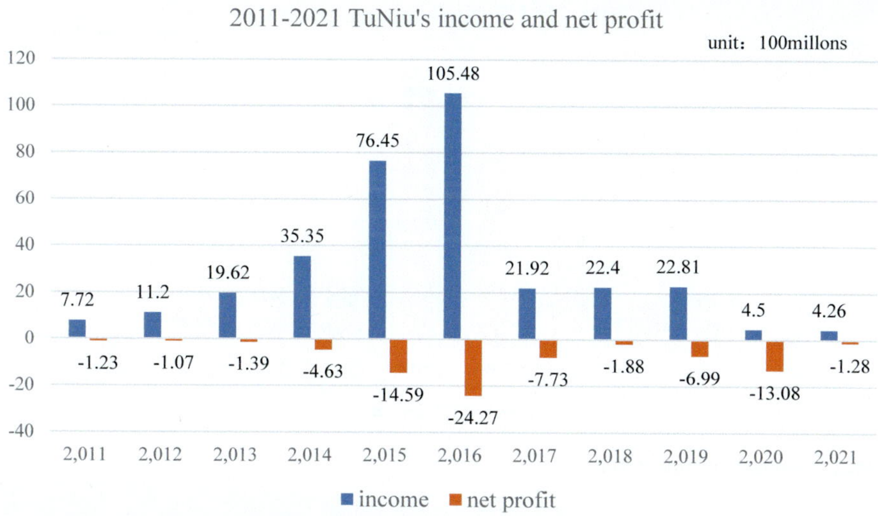

Fig. 1 TuNiu's income and net profit

annual net profit has been increasing negatively, with a loss of CNY2.427 billion in 2016. Affected by the market shock, TuNiu's revenue had a significant drop from 2017–2019, just maintaining around CNY2 billion. The outbreak of COVID-19 in 2020 had a serious impact on tourism. In 2020, TuNiu's annual revenue hit its lowest point with only CNY450 million and a loss of CNY1.308 billion (see Fig. 1). In terms of revenue structure, the main business of TuNiu from 2011–2016 is packaged tours (packaged tours), accounting for more than 95%. After 2017, when TuNiu's revenue was unsatisfactory, it continued to expand other businesses (other), and the proportion of revenue from packaged tours was reduced (as shown in Fig. 2-figure supplement 3).

3 Industry Background

3.1 Macro Environment

The political environment in China is quite favorable for the development of TuNiu. China has always placed the development of tourism in an important position of domestic economic development, and has promulgated many laws, regulations and policy measures to promote structural reforms in tourism, building it into a pillar industry of the national economy. The significance of tourism development is self-evident. Tourism, as an important pillar in the fight against poverty, can drive economic development. It is also a booster for the construction of beautiful China, and gives many Chinese entrepreneurs the opportunity to innovate and start their own businesses. Therefore, accelerating the development of the tourism

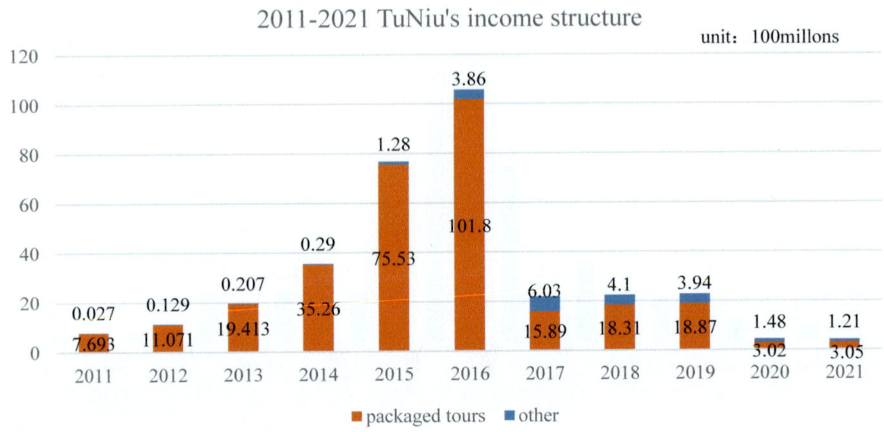

Fig. 2 Income structure of TuNiu

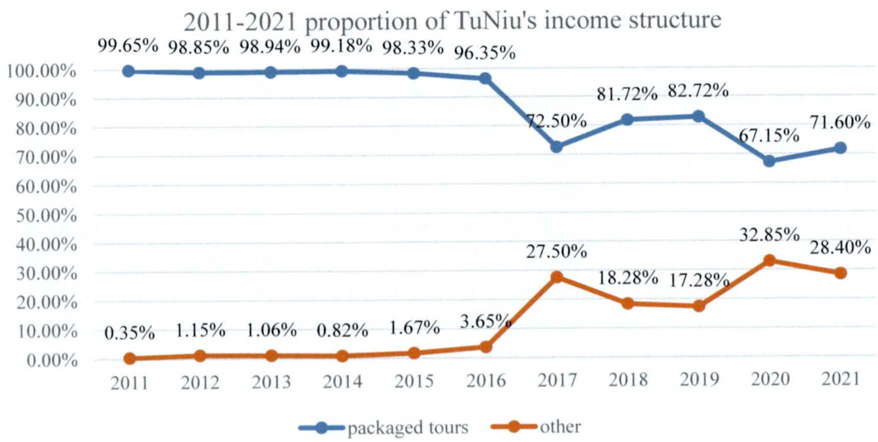

Fig. 3 Proportion of TuNiu's income structure

industry, constantly strengthening the hardware infrastructure of the tourism industry, strengthening market supervision, and promoting the combination of all-area tourism and tourism + Internet can help the national economy to improve quality and increase efficiency.

Our economic environment is also very good. Per capita disposable income has been rising, people's living standards have improved significantly, and the building of a moderately prosperous society has entered a new era. Since the establishment of TuNiu in 2006, now it has experienced the financial crisis and once-in-a-century pandemic. Thanks to Chinese wisdom and Chinese solutions, China has made our economy and society recover quickly. Currently, while the pandemic is still hampering tourism, the increase in per capita disposable income and the effective prevention and control measures for the domestic pandemic have enabled people to spend more on tourism.

The social and cultural environment in China is also moving forward in the direction of favorable tourism. With the development of the domestic economy, the people's education level has also been significantly improved, which has led to a great change in their consumption concept. During traditional holidays, many people prefer traveling to going home for family reunion. Traveling during holidays has become a new industry mode. Based on the tourism report, China's online travel industry has been developing continuously in recent years. Despite the outbreak of COVID-19 pandemic, tourism has pursued progress while ensuring stability since the fourth quarter of 2020. Self-guided traveling is the top priority for most people at present. The age group with the highest proportion of online travel vacation users is 31–35 years old, followed by 25–30 years old. It is foreseeable that the more individual pursuit of the 18–24 age group of the original Internet users, the future will become the main force of online travel.

The constant upgrading of Internet communication technology also provides a solid technical guarantee for the development of tourism. With the abolition of traffic roaming charges and mobile networks becoming more convenient and cheaper, mobile internet users have a more secure and stable network while reducing the cost of traffic usage, providing a good environment for the development of online e-commerce. Relying on this network e-commerce platform, the online travel industry has launched its own products and services for booking hotels, airline tickets, visas and itineraries. Transparent pricing announcements by merchants and a stable source of income for users have provided a strong injection for the tourism industry. More and more tourists are abandoning traditional travel agency orders and choosing to order their travel online. This brings new opportunities for development in the online travel agency, and challenges.

3.2 Internal Environment of the Industry

According to data collated by the Ministry of Culture and Tourism, Fastdata and Smart Research Consulting, the New Crown pandemic has had a serious impact on the tourism industry. 2.88 billion domestic tourist arrivals in 2020, 3.12 billion fewer than in 2019, a decrease of 52.1 per cent year-on-year. With the pandemic effectively under control in China, tourism has been gradually recovering since May 2020, with 265 million domestic tourist arrivals in a single month in December, up 209 million from February, an increase of 373.21% year-on-year. The number of monthly active online travel users has gradually returned to previous levels since the second half of 2020. The monthly active users of online travel in China were 132 million in December 2020, with a recovery rate of 92.1% for monthly active users of online travel compared to December 2019.

China Online Travel Industry Research Report 2021 by Ariadne shows that the number of domestic travelers in China recovered to 57.6%, 65.2%, 77.5% and

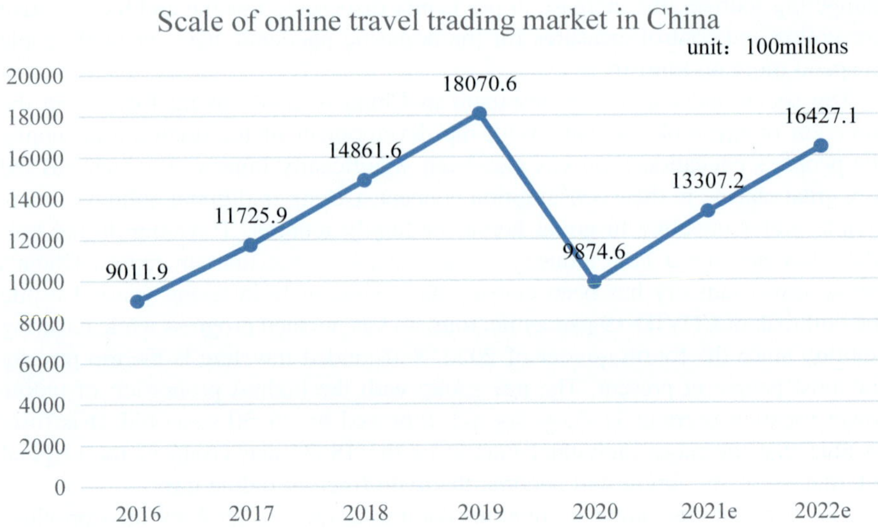

Fig. 4 Scale of online travel trading market in China

79.2% of 2019 from the first quarter to the fourth quarter of 2021, respectively, with the market maintaining an upward trend. Along with the acceleration of the digital transformation of the whole society under the pandemic, the demand side, the field side and the supply side promote each other's development. Demand-side user demand upgrade to promote tourism products and services iteration, field-side content operation to help improve tourism supply and demand chain reach efficiency, supply-side pandemic to promote the supply side gradually began to pay attention to the private domain traffic operation. The transaction size and forecast of China's online travel market in the past five years is shown in Fig. 4, with China's online travel market achieving resilient growth of approximately CNY1.3 trillion in 2021. In 2022, it will basically return to the level before the pandemic.

The tourism industry will continue to be younger, more content-oriented and more digital. The trend of youthful travel users will drive the industry and product transformation, the youthfulness of user attributes and content-based user habits will drive the development of the travel content industry, and digital living habits on the demand side will drive further digital transformation of the travel industry.

Overall, although China's online travel market failed to achieve a rapid recovery in 2021, national travel demand will be gradually released as residents gradually become accustomed to living with the pandemic under environmental factors such as the gradual easing of the pandemic in the country, strong prevention and control efforts, improved control processes, and mass vaccination of the COVID-19 vaccine. At the same time, trends such as the youthfulness of the travel community, the localization of travel consumption and the digitalization of the travel experience are gradually emerging.

In addition, TuNiu is in the online travel agency (OTA) and competition within the industry is fierce for four main reasons.

First, although the development speed of online travel agency (OTA) has slowed down in recent years, there is still much room for development, but the competition in the industry is fierce. This industry is mainly about customer flow and the building of channels, without too much technical difficulty, the technical barriers are relatively low, while the initial investment capital requirements are not very high. These make the OTA industry highly attractive to outsiders, and the profitability of Ctrip and TuNiu has shown outsiders how profitable this industry can be. Some traditional offline store-based travel agencies, such as CYT, travel user-generated content (UGC) platforms and AntBee's Nest Travel, have opened up their internet travel capabilities, which also allow for online travel planning. There are also many single service platforms, such as online accommodation platforms, and online transportation platforms, which also include a tourism element in their platforms, where consumers choose accommodation along with recommended travel routes and tourism resources. Low barriers to entry and high profits make potential competitors in the online travel industry a great threat.

Second, customers have strong ability to choose and bargain. Compared to traditional offline store-based travel companies, online travel enterprises on the internet need to face a strong price comparison problem, where customers can easily compare prices on the internet. There is a wide variety of platforms in the industry and prices vary, giving customers more bargaining power. While online travel customers do not have the ability or the means to influence the pricing of online travel (OTA) companies, they can choose the lowest price among them for similar products, and they can choose a different platform each time, with no switching costs in between. This makes consumers price sensitive and less loyal to tourism products.

Third, alternatives are constantly emerging. Young consumers currently account for a large proportion of the national travel vacation population, and this age group is heavily influenced by the Internet and is more likely to choose online platforms to purchase tourism products. Moreover, travelers in this age group yearn for freedom and are more inclined to travel on their own. Take the example of B&B resource integration platforms such as Airbnb, they provide accommodation far beyond what ordinary and similarly priced hotels can offer nowadays. Large housing areas and creative rooms becoming one of the selling points for travel. These B&Bs will also provide corresponding travel support, such as nearby attractions and food introductions. These make free travel more convenient and make the traditional A to B to C fixed travel itinerary become out of style. These new platforms, and even the travel services provided by platforms such as WeChat, Weibo and Xiaohongshu, can get benefits from the online travel industry.

Fourth, there are many enterprises in the industry, with serious factions and little product differentiation. At present, many enterprises in China's online travel industry are mainly divided into four categories, including Ctrip, HNA, Ali and others. According to the 2016–2020 market evaluation of the domestic OTA, the market share of the domestic OTA is mainly occupied by Ctrip, and TuNiu is only in the second echelon. The core of Ctrip's main business model is the booking of hotels and airline tickets, supplemented by the sale of travel vacations. It has more than 5,000 member hotels, airline ticket booking covering all domestic and international routes, and vacation supermarket covering many domestic and international destinations, in addition to business travel management business. As the industry leader, Ctrip has the most online travel resources. Similar to Ctrip, Tongcheng provides many hotel reservations at home and abroad, airline ticket reservations covering all routes in China, scenic spot ticket reservations, global popular performance ticket reservations, city car rental reservations, and domestic and overseas quality travel vacation reservations are the main services. In addition, it is the first travel booking platform in the industry to provide value-added services such as "compensation in advance" and "bonus for reviews", and as a travel booking platform, it develops quickly in China. Caissa, supported by HNA, has the main business model of air ticket booking and is one of the best outbound travel agencies in terms of reputation. Fliggy Travel is a comprehensive tourism service platform owned by Ali, which fully reaches users in Taobao, Alipay, Amap, DingTalk, Koubei and other scenarios. However, they are different from the traditional OTA production and sales mode, Fliggy Travel still focuses on platform business. Ideally, the toB mode service space of Fliggy Travel is more open: The seller opens a store in the Fliggy Travel, with the operational initiative in as their own digital assets. Qunar.com as the rising star of online travel platform, through the platform of price comparison, to provide consumers with low-cost travel goods, but the final product is not provided by Qunar, it only through the user's click to get profits. It can be seen that the current online travel industry market transactions are mainly in three aspects: transportation, accommodation and vacation, of which transportation and accommodation are the main aspects. However, in online transportation and online accommodation, Ctrip occupies the main share of the market, and the Ctrip system has a high market share and a large competitive advantage. Although TuNiu has been relying on various marketing campaigns to maintain its popularity in the industry, it is also facing many obstacles.

4 Confronting Problems

4.1 Strengths

4.1.1 Enterprise Human Resources Training

In addition to building a special line, TuNiu has also worked on its employee training system. The principles of TuNiu's employee training system are full participation, overall control and hierarchical management. Led by the general principles, TuNiu has a comprehensive internal training course system called "TuNiu's way". The course system is designed according to the objects of training. For example, there is pre-employment induction training for new employees, job qualification training and other business technical training. For example, for new employees, there is pre-employment orientation training, for job qualifications, there is job qualification certification training, other business technology training, management training, management leadership training and so on. The instructors of these courses are not externally hired, but come from internal personnel who know more about the actual needs of enterprises. Each year, through the selection and certification of the company's internal instructors for TuNiu's way, they will prepare the corresponding syllabus, handouts, assessment and evaluation programs according to the needs, so that the training is more effective and more targeted.

In addition, TuNiu has established a job competency model, and the concept of talent production line is a positive PDCA cycle of planning, doing, checking and acting on the job competency model, job competency matching, job competency rate, performance evaluation, performance management, performance improvement, training management and application of results. Through this cycle, the goal of "job competency" is set up among employees, and the shortcomings of employees are found in the actual work. Therefore, through appropriate training or job adjustment, everyone can do their own job and give full play to their strengths. It also enables continuous follow-up and measurement of training effects.

This series of training and assessment methods for people has now become a common method for many companies to evaluate their personnel.

4.1.2 Business Model and Profit Model Selection

The business model of TuNiu is "group tour + self-guided tour", "Internet + call center + physical stores", and three parallel channels, online and offline. According to the market demand, TuNiu will provide different types of tours such as group tours, self-guided tours, theme tours and so on. Through some combinations and bundles, the company can achieve diversification to meet the different needs of different customers. In terms of business model, TuNiu adopts the strategy of combining wholesale and direct procurement, acting as an agent between wholesalers and tourists, and integrating products on its own for direct transactions with customers. In the early days, TuNiu mainly engaged in wholesale activities, with less resources. TuNiu first cooperated with travel agencies to attract customers, and then gradually formed a certain scale. The proportion of direct procurement business gradually increased. Compared to wholesale, direct procurement will save a lot of costs at third-party agents and wholesalers. The profit margin will be higher. For example, in 2017, the domestic group tours of direct procurement accounted for 80%-90%, and the overseas group tours accounted for 20%-30%. Increasing the proportion of direct procurement has always been pursued by TuNiu.

Yan Haifeng, the original co-founder of TuNiu, said, "We did market research on tourism products at that time. In fact, this market is enormous. If you engage in online e-commerce of hotels and airline tickets, there is less opportunity. Due to the great market competitiveness, we as a latecomer to do it again would not be appropriate.“ At the early stage of construction of TuNiu, in the field of online e-commerce for hotels and air tickets, Ctrip and Elong had already created a clear advantage in channels, product resources and other aspects of first-mover, forming a high competitive barrier. TuNiu did not go head-to-head, but choose the road of differentiation (Wen, 2020).

In the profit model, the main revenue of TuNiu comes from the income brought by tourism products and the joint income of other projects. Among them, the revenue of tourism products mainly comes from group tours and self-guided Tours, and the differential profit model is adopted, that is, profits are made through the difference between the price paid by customers to TuNiu and the price paid by TuNiu to suppliers. Another part of the revenue comes from commissions returned by suppliers for the number of people. Moreover, after customers purchase products, TuNiu provides them with coupons, vouchers, member credits and other rewards, and provides incentives for items purchased in advance, which to a certain extent reduces the marketing expenses in the later period.

4.1.3 Establishment of Enterprise Brand and Use of Marketing Strategy

Since the creation of high-quality "Niuren Special Line" in 2009, TuNiu has continuously differentiated its audience and designed more targeted tourism product brands such as "Happy Tour for Parents", "Melon and Fruit Parent–child Tour" and "Aggressive Customized Tour". Yu Dunde, the founder of TuNiu, once said in an interview: "In a large number of industries with high per customer transaction, customer trust in the brand is the key to doing a good job. The packaged tours products of TuNiu are exactly the products of high per customer transaction, which need TuNiu to operate its own products, integrate the industrial chain, and improve users' trust in the brand. Packaged tours product means a longer service chain. Thus, we need to polish every link and get the service right to fully satisfy our customers." (Xu, 2016).

A brand is an intangible asset of an enterprise. The competitive online travel agency (OTA) increasingly needs to foster differentiation. With the development of the domestic economy, people's disposable income has been improved qualitatively, who pay more and more attention to the quality of products instead of their low prices. As a result, the price gap is often not the most important factor for people to consider, and service, brand and innovation capability gradually become the focus of their attention. Over the years, TuNiu has been committed to brand promotion to enhance its brand competitiveness and influence by influencing customers' consumption decisions.

TuNiu strives to build its own high-quality brand in the following three aspects. First, find their own positioning and provide relatively professional services. At the beginning of its establishment, TuNiu avoided the business traveling mode of booking air tickets and hotels and focused on tourism and holiday products. Meanwhile, it has made great efforts on travel agencies' routes, put all the routes on the website for customers to choose from, and provided them with professional guidance and one-stop service, thus being able to open up a road of its own among numerous tourism websites.

Second, standardize the process and provide humanized services. TuNiu has been carrying out standardized operations since its establishment. Specific and detailed specifications and requirements have been formulated in various processes such as reservation, pre-sales, operation, after-sales, customer relationship and customer service standards. From the moment tourists logged on to the website, no matter they communicated with each other in the early stage of their purchase and booking, traveled with the team, or revisit evaluation in the later stage, to a large extent, it helped TuNiu to improve itself. Thus, it could control its own quality problems well and attract customers with high-quality characteristics. From the beginning of cooperation with thousands of travel agencies to only dozens of travel agencies, TuNiu has chosen the best among the best, and only selected the enterprises with good results for further cooperation to achieve specialization and precision. In 2016, TuNiu set up Xiamen Suixiang International Travel Agency Co., Ltd., becoming the first offline self-controlled destination reception agency. It improved the ability of product control by optimizing the supply chain. Through the guide management system, it implements reward and punishment measures to regulate the behavior of guides. In the aspect of after-sales service, after the customers' travel, the customer service staff would timely take the initiative to call back, and ask customers to evaluate their travel experience satisfaction. In the process of telephone return visits, if customers were not satisfied with something, TuNiu would give them small gifts or use other ways to deal with their complaints. The construction of such a user-friendly platform is conducive to understanding customer needs, finding the improvement direction of the route in the evaluation of tourists, and constantly improving the service and consumer loyalty. These measures provided strong support for TuNiu to stand out in competition with brands such as Ctrip.

Third, strengthen technological innovation and pay attention to providing personalized services. The biggest difference between online travel services and traditional tourism is that the former can provide various personalized customized services through two-way communication. TuNiu has a special database management system, that is, a business operation support system (BOSS) that can meet the specific requirements of tourists. The system has a powerful tourism information database function, which can make customers search according to their specific needs and quickly find the information. In 2013, the NG-BOSS system, the upgraded version of the BOSS system, was developed and launched, realizing the automatic docking between the inventory of self-service travel products and the system, making the booking process simpler and faster, and greatly saving the time and labor costs in the business process. These are the advantages of TuNiu highlighted by its continuous efforts in technology.

In terms of marketing means, TuNiu also has many advantages. In the early stage of construction, TuNiu took marketing as its brand mission. It made full use of new media platforms such as blogs, Weibo and WeChat to convey its ideas, products and service information to customers, established good relationships with customers, and then carried out marketing promotion through good word-of-mouth effect. On these Internet platforms, there were specially assigned persons to carry out the daily maintenance of platform accounts. They attracted customers' attention through creative activities such as creative pictures, publishing advertorials and holding prize-giving activities, which paved the way for attracting new customers and maintaining old customers. In the early stage of the construction of TuNiu, it also made full use of Baidu's paid listing, so that TuNiu can get a higher position in Baidu's web search, attracting a large number of potential customers, effectively improving the order volume, sales and brand awareness in a short period of time. For instance, one year after the establishment of TuNiu, although it was not well-known in the industry, it could earn millions by relying on Baidu's listing, and nearly CNY ten million in the second year of its establishment. TuNiu paid attention to taking advantage of typical occasions for brand publicity. TuNiu seized the opportunity at the beginning of the construction of the Nanjing Metro and became the first Internet company in the industry to advertise in the subway.

After the brand has been promoted to a certain scale, TuNiu began to enter the second and third-tier cities through advertisements on CCTV and local satellite TV, started the double spokesperson model of Jay Chou and Lin Zhiying, and became the sponsor of variety shows such as *If You Are the One*, *Super Brain*, *Keep Running*, which imperceptibly instilled the TuNiu brand in customers. After that, TuNiu's advertisements covered places such as elevators, cinemas and building outer walls, forming an all-round and multi-level marketing model. The brand promotion through advertising in *Detective Chinatown* made TuNiu the first online travel enterprise to carry out "tourism + Internet + film". In order to attract more customers, TuNiu also carries out special promotions appropriately, such as "CNY1 to travel" and "CNY1 to travel aboard" activities, which are continuously launched to gain guests' attention with preferential prices, enhance tourists' awareness of the TuNiu brand through high-quality products and services, and gradually build tourists' loyalty and reputation to the brand to expand its influence.

TuNiu is also good at using concise words for brand promotion, and the slogan "Travel by TuNiu" quickly spread all over the country. The "JIA6" special line created by TuNiu, adhering to TuNiu's core values of "simple, shared and excellent", is also very meaningful. Among them, "JIA" means family, vacation, participation, excellence in Chinese, and the number "6" represents TuNiu's commitment to creating excellent quality and service in six aspects, route, policy, mode, quality, service and price. In the context of the Belt and Road initiative, the JIA6 special project created by TuNiu provides consumers with an elegant and warm family atmosphere, which illustrates the core values (Xiao et al., 2019).

4.2 Disadvantages

As competition in the industry intensifies and the tourism market size shrinks significantly in stages due to the pandemic, the development of TuNiu, an emerging Internet company, is facing new challenges.

4.2.1 Insufficient Funds

In 2014, TuNiu made further plans for its future development and strategy, and its spending on brand building and technology research and development more than doubled at least compared to 2013. Under the condition of low industry share, TuNiu has expanded itself through large-scale brand promotion, and also increased its brand awareness and influence. As the economy continues to develop and Internet technology becomes more sophisticated, TuNiu has increased its user conversion rate and brand adhesion with quality customer service by investing heavily in research and development. For TuNiu, these plans to seize market share first and then base on the future through the first-mover advantage of high customer unit price are extremely far-sighted.

However, the successive departure of the two founders in 2018 brought a big blow to them. The third quarter 2018 reported for the first time that TuNiu achieved a net profit of CNY28 million, but previous years of losses made this "profit" more dependent on cutting expenses in exchange. In order to reduce management costs and R&D costs, TuNiu has started continuous layoffs since the end of 2017. For example, in 2018, media reported that TuNiu laid off a number of R&D technicians in order to reduce investment in R&D, while general employees also took pay cuts, as a direct result of which R&D and management costs have been significantly reduced. However, this also means that the TuNiu's product innovation and marketing is weak, the market exposure is insufficient, and easy to lose the consumer's brand impression and brand consumption. The reduction in R&D means a decline in investment in innovation, and this reliance on cost reduction for short-term profitability is very fragile, and in the long run, is a fundamental strategy.

At the same time, the reduction of R&D also reflects the difficulty of capital turnover. As an online travel industry with low technical barriers, foreign forces are constantly pouring in, all of whom want to get a share in this high-profit industry. At the initial stage of TuNiu's construction, it was the time when the international financial crisis broke out. The unfavorable environment made investors unable to invest easily, and it took a lot of money to develop their own product library at the initial stage of construction, which made TuNiu difficult at the beginning of the period. After several years of hard work, TuNiu has found complementary partners, such as the HNA Group's joining in 2015, which has realized the integration of high-quality resources of both parties and promoted the improvement and perfection of their respective products and services. The good times did not last long. Although TuNiu had a brief turnaround in 2018, this was in exchange for a temporary cost reduction, after which it was once again plunged into a debt crisis and the outbreak of the COVID-19 pandemic brought an overall setback to the tourism industry. Today is different from the past, and TuNiu still has a long way to go to really turn losses into profits.

4.2.2 Reconstruction in Internal Organizational

TuNiu also experienced many major personnel changes during its operation. In 2016–2017, three senior executives, including Yan Haifeng, co-founder, president and chief operating officer, and Yang Jiahong, chief financial officer, left the company. Shortly after the senior executives left, it was rumored on the internet that

TuNiu laid off more than 400 people. Later, although the relevant personnel specifically refuted the rumor and mentioned that the layoff ratio below 3% is a normal personnel flow (Yi, 2012). However, the resignation of many senior executives and the layoffs of more technical personnel reveal that there are problems in the company's personnel structure, especially in R&D personnel structure. This reduction in personnel expenses is the simplest and easiest way to improve profitability. According to the standard of the average monthly salary of CNY10,000—15,000 for R&D staff, the monthly labor cost can be reduced by about CNY2-3 million after staff reduction, and the company's financial indicators will be significantly improved in the short term (Qianlong.com, 2017; Jiemian News, 2017). Affected by the impact of the COVID-19, online travel in 2020 is in the recovery of growth, but offline travel and travel industry chain opportunities and space become larger. However, the average annual cost of offline stores is CNY30 million, which is not a small challenge for TuNiu, which has quickly laid out offline stores and has 500 offline stores.

TuNiu's top personnel adjustment seems to be very frequent. In 2020, Chen Shihong, a key executive, stepped down as chief technology officer of TuNiu, and Xin Yi resigned as chief financial officer (CFO) of TuNiu (Wen, 2020). Two executives stepped down within one year, and three chief technology officers left in groups for three consecutive years. The drastic changes in personnel make people worry about the development prospects of TuNiu.

4.2.3 Imitation Risk and Industry Competition

Since 2006, starting from the low-end market, TuNiu has been focusing on outbound and group tours, avoiding the positive competition with Ctrip and Tongcheng, which were engaged in online travel at the time. From the financial indicators, TuNiu's main income is the company's income from packaged tour products and others, while the competitor, Ctrip, has accumulated numerous high-quality users. The addition of HNA Group in 2015 somewhat eased the crisis, and now HNA is also insolvent and declared bankrupt. With the constant changes in the market, Ctrip, which has obvious first-mover advantage, sinks and explores in many vertical fields of tourism, which makes TuNiu's existing efforts vanish. TuNiu, on the other hand, is still wandering in the normal state of letting traditional offline travel agencies surf the Internet to reduce the distance from users.

In addition, Wang Xing, founder of Meituan, once said that the most dangerous opponents are often not those expected. For example, Alibaba Group has been staring at JD.COM all these years, but Pinduoduo stood out in the end, and the number of users exceeded Taobao in one fell swoop. It seems that eLong has been merged by Tongcheng, and there are only a few competitors in the online travel industry, such as Ctrip, Tongcheng and Qunar, but this is not the case. Meituan gradually engaged in business travel and leisure travel. Relying on the huge passenger flow, Meituan quickly gained the advantage of online travel agency by using the mode of "high frequency wins low frequency".

On short video sites, TikTok and Xiaohongshu, there are content sharing of Internet-famous attractions and cities at home and abroad. These Internet-famous attractions are competing with some traditional attractions, and the business expansion of many short videos and social platforms makes some online travel platforms face fiercer competition. These new competitors are taking away users' time and traffic, as well as the business of TuNiu and other online travel agencies. These Internet-famous attractions and cities are actually transforming the online travel industry from a price war of products to an exhibition of product features. Short videos and social platforms rely on traffic to make many customers break away from traditional online travel enterprises such as TuNiu.

In 2020, the annual online travel (OTA) market share shows (Fig. 5) that Ctrip ranks first, followed by Meituan, Qunar.com, and LY.com. TuNiu is no longer a major online travel platform, and its share is less than one-sixth of that of Ctrip and less than one-third of that of Meituan (TechWeb, 2020).

In the current, TuNiu, with a single revenue structure, seems to be abandoned by the capital, and it seems unlikely to enter the field of business travel. The market size of group tours, compared to online travel, is not worth mentioning, and its revenue chain is more complex. TuNiu has a short time of glorious days. The marketing expenses and offline layout spent in this short period of glory do not match with the market size it deserved, even not a distinctive impression on users. The direct operation model adopted by TuNiu's physical stores is different from Ctrip's franchise model. The former is characterized by high requirements for capital. By the end of 2019, the number of self-owned stores of TuNiu was 509. The expanding of offline market will inevitably increase operating costs and further reduce the profits of platforms. TuNiu had to give up part of its market shares because of the lack of capital.

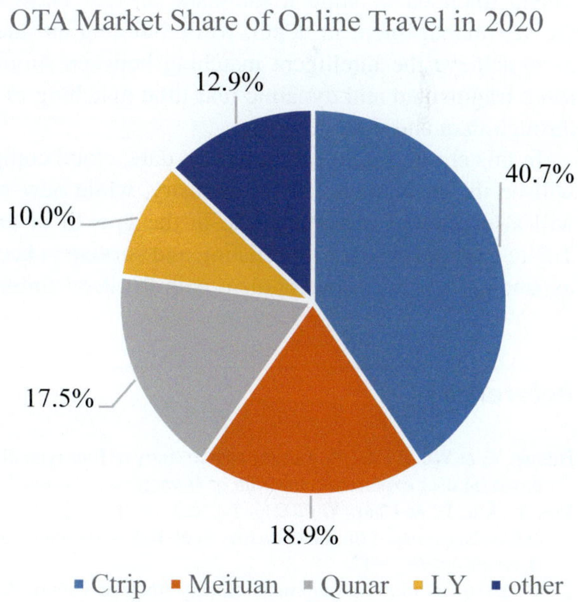

Fig. 5 OTA Market Share of Online Travel in 2020

5 Epilogue

Because of the sudden outbreak of the COVID-19 pandemic, just in 2020, 6,456 travel enterprises cancelled their registration, including 1,670 travel agencies and 46 enterprises related to scenic areas (The Paper, 2021), among which, there is the well-known travel enterprise Baicheng.com. TuNiu has a short time of glorious days. TuNiu has operated at a loss for seven years since its list. And now, the online travel industry shows a situation of tripartite confrontation of Ctrip, Alibaba Fliggy and Meituan. TuNiu is ruled out from the first echelon. The day before TuNiu announced its financial report as a listed company in March 2021, TuNiu made the largest-scale shareholding change in its history. The share of the founder Yu Dunde with a technical background was changed from 28.66% to 80.99%. The existing shareholders have given up, and the "white knight" did not arrive as promised. As the founder of TuNiu, Yu Dunde had to bear all risks and pressure.

The COVID-19 pandemic has spread for more two years. The whole world is still under its severe influence and the travel industry still registers huge losses. The situation abroad is still very severe and there are many uncertainties for the recovery of the outbound travel market. The main service of TuNiu is group tours in China, and some split hotel services, all of which are not the advantages of TuNiu. It is necessary for TuNiu to carry out the reform in order to survive the post-pandemic era.

TuNiu has also tried to make changes. In 2020, TuNiu created its own Tiktok account during the pandemic to earn traffic through Tiktok live broadcast of self-driving tours and selling goods. Far from enough, TuNiu shall have a better idea and raise more money (Chinanews.com, 2020). The founder, Yu Dunde, said that TuNiu intended to build a sales and service network and continued to develop the self-management in depth, while building an intelligent network platform, so as to achieve the intelligent matching between supply and demand and realize a more fragmented and dynamic real-time matching of resource supply and demand through data and deep learning.

In this era of digital economy, big data, cloud computing and Internet of Things will be the mainstream of the industry, while new retail and new manufacturing will also play an important role in the growth of enterprises. The only way for TuNiu to avoid the risk of delisting and survive is keeping pace with the times and expanding a unique development path for itself through continuous reforms.

References

Huang, Y., & Wu, P. (2019). A comparative study of four typical tourism website marketing models based on user experience. *Journal of Huanggang Normal University, 39*(4), 122-126.

Liu, Y., Lai, J., & Chai, Y. (2021). A study on the impact of internet business model on travel enterprises—based on the comparison of TuNiu and uzai.com. *Communication of Finance and Accounting, 18*, 3–12.

Li, C. (2018). Market development strategy study of TuNiu. *Business & Economy, 5*, 64-65.

Personnel Reduction of Technical Team, the On-going Restructuring of TuNiu [EB/OL]. Retrieved February 26, 2017, from https://www.sohu.com/a/212771120_161623

TechWeb. Financial report of TuNiu: Increased investment in branding, and R&D with a big increase in revenue in Q1 [EB/OL]. Retrieved January 9, 2020, from https://tech.huanqiu.com/article/9CaKrnJEWrc

The Paper. TuNiu: Keeping operation after a long term of depression [EB/OL]. Retrieved August 31, 2021, from https://m.thepaper.cn/baijiahao_14287795

Wanyu, J., Chang, L., & Hongzhi, C. (2018). Current development of the online travel industry—taking TuNiu as an example. *China Circulation Economy, 22*, 66–68.

Wen, L. (2020). Three CTOs in three years, the resignation of TuNiu executives [EB/OL]. Retrieved January 9, 2020, from http://www.wenlvpai.com/27388.html

Xie, Y. (2020). Can TuNiu Survive by the In-person Live Broadcast of Boss after 6 Consecutive Years of Losses and Executive Resignation? [EB/OL]. Retrieved April 30, 2020, from https://baijiahao.baidu.com/s?id=1665324076694945125&wfr=spider&for=pc

Xiao, X., Jiang, L., Lu, Y., Song, Y., & Deng, W.: Research on travel route optimization and innovation of TuNiu based on "the belt and road" initiative. *Modern Business Trade Industry, 40*(07), 13-14.

Xu, Z. (2016). Research on brand building strategy of TuNiu. *Industrial & Science Tribune, 15*(23), 130-132.

Yang, H. (2015). TuNiu's transformation to "Tourism + Finance" [EB/OL]. Retrieved October 20, 2015, from http://finance.china.com.cn/roll/20151020/3391736.shtml

Yi, J. (2012). Talent training channel of TuNiu. *Enterprise Management, 10*, 47–49.

Zheng, C. (2017). Sudden personnel reduction of the R&D department of TuNiu for reducing expenditures and earning profits [EB/OL]. Retrieved December 22, 2017, from https://www.jiemian.com/article/1835443.html

The Remarkable Transformation of Cross-Border E-commerce Service Providers Named Cifnews

Zhigang Fan, Huijing Sun, and Xuanshun Zhai

1 Introduction

Since 2020, China's cross-border e-commerce industry has been experiencing ups and downs. Due to the COVID-19 pandemic, cross-border e-commerce has developed rapidly, and most of cross-border e-commerce enterprises have achieved business growth. With a large number of entrepreneurs joined the industry, the competition became fiercer. However, in April 2021, Amazon, a global e-commerce giant, banned a large number of Chinese merchants on the grounds of "manipulating comments of users". This dealt a painful blow to cross-border e-commerce merchants and compelled cross-border players to find new development channels in a market with the fierce competition.

The rise of Shein, Anker and other enterprises represents a new direction for the development of cross-border e-commerce industry. Multi-channel layouts, independent cross-border stores and direct to customer (DTC) brands going abroad have become new choices for Chinese cross-border players. Consequently, a growing number of cross-border e-commerce service providers emerged, and they have actively participated in the cross-border e-commerce industry chain, value chain, transaction chain and supply chains, connecting transaction platforms, manufacturers and other service providers. This has enabled them to provide single or one-stop comprehensive services such as cross-border logistics, cross-border payment, trademark registration, overseas marketing and software as a service (SaaS) product selection. Those providers empowered Chinese enterprises to "go global" in a more diversified way.

Among a number of cross-border e-commerce service providers, Cifnews' performance was particularly remarkable. Since its establishment, Cifnews has

Z. Fan (✉) · H. Sun · X. Zhai
Alibaba Business School, Hangzhou Normal University, Hangzhou, China

J. Zhang et al. (eds.), *Innovation of Digital Economy*, Management for Professionals,
https://doi.org/10.1007/978-981-99-1741-9_16

cooperated with other cross-border e-commerce players to create "content factories", and has gradually built an empowerment platform organization that "broke through the traditional employment relationship". By creating a platform aggregating various resources in the industry, Cifnews built a collaborative network and realized empowerment in the process of deeply linking with other entities through strengthening cross-organization, cross-level and cross-network interactions and cooperation. Due to its pivotal position in the industry, Cifnews owned the ability to provide one-stop full-link services and realized empowerment for cross-border players from multiple dimensions such as resources, costs and capabilities.

Cifnews not only empowered cross-border e-commerce practitioners, but also cultivated a keen sense of the industry.[1] As early as 2018, it began to launch the layout of brands going abroad after acquiring an European consulting company and establishing an independent incubation base. At the Google Partners Summit 2021, held in December 2021, Cifnews stood out from many official first-class agents of Google in China and won the Going Global Impact Award. At the ceremony of the Facebook China Reseller Award, held in May 2020, it won the Best Acquisition Award. When delivering his acceptance speech, Liu Hong, COO of Cifnews said, "Cifnews links the global cross-border e-commerce sales channels, and the production and supply chain of Chinese merchants to assist Chinese brands in starting overseas business in batches" (Cifnews, 2021).

In fact, Cifnews, which has wide influence and recognition in the industry, has only existed for about seven years, but it has evolved from being an original new medium in cross-border e-commerce to being an intelligent service platform for cross-border e-commerce, and it has been transformed into an industrial internet platform for brands going overseas. As a pioneer in the industry, how did Cifnews interconnect upstream and downstream enterprises in the cross-border e-commerce industry chain, empower cross-border e-commerce merchants and realize its own growth? The story began in 2013…

2 Cifnews 1.0: A Cross-Border E-commerce New Medium with Content Empowerment

"Today's cross-border e-commerce is identical to e-commerce when Taobao arose ten years ago". Around 2013, a group of entrepreneurs were keenly aware that the cross-border e-commerce market was fostering an abundance of business prospects. At the same time, traditional foreign trade companies and original equipment manufactures (OEMs) began to pour into cross-border e-commerce. On the predominant cross-border e-commerce sites, product prices were often several times higher than domestic product prices. Products made in China with high cost

[1] According to the survey by Cifnews, 70% of the cross-border e-commerce merchants achieved performance growth in 2020. Wherein, 23% achieved growth of more than 100%.

performance should be a "trump card" for entrepreneurs to enter overseas markets, but the reality was rather different.

Weng Yaoxiong, a financial journalist who had been engaged in foreign trade for a long time, found that there was a huge information gap between domestic and foreign markets when communicating with foreign trade practitioners. Many newcomers did not understand the demand from the foreign e-commerce market, and were confused about how to carry out marketing on cross-border e-commerce platforms and how to provide a positive user experience. Here comes a chance! Weng Yaoxiong resolutely left the newspaper industry and founded Cifnews, initiating content production in his own area of expertise.

2.1 Accumulation of Content Users

At the beginning of establishment, Weng Yaoxiong rarely left the inception of Cifnews, as he translated and disseminated a large amount of knowledge on operation and information on market demand about major overseas markets such as Europe, America and Southeast Asia. These high-quality contents should have been rapidly distributed to cross-border e-commerce practitioners who were severely upset by information asymmetry in domestic and international marketplaces, but unfortunately, the carefully prepared contents have not received wide attention from practitioners.

How can the information be quickly and accurately disseminated? At that point, content distribution channels became his most pressing concern. In the absence of user traffic base, Weng Yaoxiong started from third-party channels and settled in many influential third-party platforms such as Alibaba Foreign Trade Circle and Toutiao (as shown in Table 1), releasing a large number of news reports and operational skills on the international market, traditional foreign trade, cross-border e-commerce and other fields. As he answered issues posed by practitioners in an online forum, he rapidly amassed a following. At the same time, the self-built channels were enhanced. Subdivided sectors were designed to optimize website and enable users to search for information more efficiently. Additionally, the launch of Cifnews APP was accelerated, and its official Weibo and WeChat official account were established.

Through the above two channels, Weng Yaoxiong and his colleagues swiftly disseminated information, and Cifnews was known by more and more cross-border e-commerce insiders, thus becoming famous gradually. In September 2014, Cifnews participated in the annual meeting of "China Cross-border E-commerce Conference" as a cooperative media, and was awarded the "Best Media Award for Cross-border E-commerce in China". This honor has greatly encouraged the Cifnews team and strengthened Weng's will to expand Cifnews and assist more cross-border e-commerce practitioners.

Table 1 Third-party platforms settled in Cifnews from 2013 to 2014

Time	Milestone
May 2013	Cifnews became the moderator of Alibaba Foreign Trade Circle
June 2013	Cifnews became a source of Baidu News
July 2013	Cifnews settled in Sohu News APP
August 2013	Cifnews settled in FOB5 and opened a column
August 2013	Cifnews settled in EasyReader
January 2014	Cifnews settled in Baidu News APP
June 2014	Cifnews settled in Toutiao

2.2 Accelerating the Layout of Content Business

In the following three years, Cifnews accelerated its business structure (refer to Table 2), continued to improve its content quality, and widened the routes through which its content reached merchants.

Both "Cifnews Friends Circle" and "Cifnews Forum" invite experienced industry experts or senior merchants in the field of cross-border e-commerce to share platform operation experience, practical skills and various lessons, thus supplying sufficient "nutrients" for the growing cross-border e-commerce practitioners. However, due to the quick changes occurring in the cross-border e-commerce market, merchants may meet various challenges during actual operation and be unable to resolve them. In response to this pain point, "Orchard" in Cifnews not only had the rule explanation about various platforms, strategy scheme to create popular products and solutions for warehousing logistics, but also invited successful cross-border e-commerce operators and salespeople to settle in Cifnews. Meanwhile, a Q&A section was built to create a circle for real-time interaction and communication, which ensured the prompt resolution of difficulties and timely adjustment of merchants' operation programs.

Table 2 Major new businesses of Cifnews from 2014 to 2017

Time	Business	Form	Positioning
October 2014	Cifnews Friends Circle	Online	Irregular talk shows on WeChat
December 2014	Cifnews Forum	Offline	Offline practical meeting for cross-border e-commerce
November 2015	Cifnews Orchard	Online	Knowledge, experience and talent related to cross-border e-commerce
August 2017	Cifnews Courses	Online/offline	Online learning and training community platform for cross-border e-commerce

Sharing information, imparting experience and interacting in a real time can be achieved through this "small circle" of Cifnews. Therefore, a large group of cross-border e-commerce entrepreneurs learned from each other while working, and shared their acquired entrepreneurial knowledge with the latecomers. With the influx of more and more followers, Weng realized that only by helping merchants establish a complete knowledge system of cross-border e-commerce, can they go further. Therefore, Cifnews launched the online "Cifnews Courses", inviting teachers with senior operation capability and team management experience to act as lecturers, and launching courses such as "Opening Shop on Platform" and "Promotion and Operation" to enhance the comprehensive operation capability of merchants and help them transform from "beginners" to "masters".

2.3 Gaining Multilateral Recognition

The output of a series of high-quality content made Cifnews quickly gain positive reputation among cross-border e-commerce merchants, and attracted both online and offline users. Through establishing cross-border e-commerce practitioner community, Cifnews interacted deeply with merchants, enhanced the understanding of them in the process of answering questions, and found their difficulties and pain points related to the operation, thus updating the website and the APP and optimizing the existing businesses. Facing the problem of "selection of products", the number one problem in the e-commerce community, Cifnews tried to hold the offline "Cifnews Cross-border Ecommerce Exhibition" (CCEE) and the online "Online Product Selection Platform ccee.com" and "Connect Factories and Merchants". During this process, Cifnews played a role of an intermediary agency to achieve bilateral empowerment between factories and merchants.

With over 6,400 participants, the first CCEE was a resounding success. It not only won the favor of merchants and suppliers, but also gained significant support from mainstream cross-border e-commerce platforms and service providers. Through the CCEE, merchants and factories attained multi-dimensional category contact and interaction at a zero distance. Platforms such as AliExpress, Lazada, Zilingo and Paytm shared market information and strategies for platform promotion to merchants, assisting them in figuring out the market demand and export trend. And ccee.com broadened the channels for high-quality products to reach cross-border merchants, allowing factories to advertise through short videos, live broadcasts and other forms. Additionally, merchants can make online inquiries through ccee.com to find the products they want. Since then, CCEE has evolved into an annual large-scale offline event hosted by Cifnews, where more and more high-quality product factories, influential merchants and e-commerce platforms connect, communicate, and cooperate.

By creating "golden cards" in content, forums, courses, product selection and other sectors, Cifnews and many platform participants "based on the extensive sharing of interests, achieve mutual achievements, grow together, and jointly create new value for users" (Luo et al., 2017), gradually constructing an empowering platform organization with cooperation as the central theme, which further promotes the in-depth interaction between Cifnews and users, and fully stimulate the initiative and creativity of platform participants. Cifnews has become the preferred platform for cross-border e-commerce entrepreneurs to learn and communicate, and has further evolved into a major role in connecting various industry resources by capitalizing on the organizational benefits of resource aggregation.

3 Cifnews 2.0: Aggregate Resources to Empower the Whole Industrial Chain of Cross-Border E-commerce

Looking at the growing scale of the CCEE and the growing number of participants, Weng Yaoxiong feels both happy and anxious. The "information gap" can be gradually bridged through various forms of real thing sharing, and the problem of product selection can be solved to some extent through CCEE. However, it is still not easy for merchants to do a good job in cross-border e-commerce. Most merchants struggle with the questions of what kind of platform to join, what are the characteristics of emerging platforms, and where to find locate international service providers? In the face of numerous choices, how to find a better suitable road has become their most concerned problem, and cross-border e-commerce trade platforms, factories and service providers also hoping to partner with more cross-border merchants. How can we connect the requirements of all parties?

It is better to be a platform that can integrate resources in various fields! Weng and his team members hit it off immediately and started gathering superior worldwide industrial chain resources. Based on the accumulated content user traffic and good reputation in the industry, Cifnews soon attracted many upstream and downstream enterprises of cross-border e-commerce industry chain including Pingpong, LianLianPay and DHL to settle in. Cifnews served as a catalyst to encourage better communication and interaction among all parties.

3.1 Launching a Cross-Border E-commerce Intelligent Service Platform

In August 2018, Cifnews 2.0—"Cifnews Cross-border E-commerce Intelligent Service Platform" was officially launched, which transformed Cifnews from simple information matching to service matching. Based on strong vertical industry traffic and big data of user behavior tracks, Cifnews adopted the OGC (Occupationally-generated Content) model to build exclusive content aggregation pages and product details pages for cross-border e-commerce practitioners using the logic of content-flow-product-conversion (retention), through which it created a new service product ecosystem chain, and derived an intelligent service platform, and an intelligent product selection platform (Cifnews, 2018).

The intelligent service platform combines the self-operation service resources and third-party service resources of Cifnews to provide service matching for cross-border e-commerce practitioners; and the intelligent product selection platform helps connect Chinese manufacturers with global small business. In terms of self-operation services, Cifnews integrates the Cifnews Courses, offline training, Cifnews Forum and other businesses to establish a smart education section, while introducing third-party cross-border e-commerce services such as logistics, payment, trademark, software and platform. The product selection part of ccee.com brings together a variety of manufacturers who have "flexible supply" capabilities, enabling them to offer merchants ongoing supply services with MOQ (Minimum Order Quantity) of 10 pieces. And offline CCEE speeds up the process of "going abroad", cooperates with Meorient and other exhibition companies, lays out overseas, and leads exporters in traditional foreign trade and cross-border e-commerce to explore untapped markets.

In this way, under the two-wheel drive of "intelligent service" and "intelligent product selection", the online resource aggregation platform is gradually taking shape, and the service system created by Cifnews is growing. With the establishment of the third group of comprehensive pilot zones for cross-border e-commerce, the industry once again faces new opportunities for development. And Cifnews has also moved into the Xiamen Free Trade Zone, working with the local government to build an offline ecosystem for the enhancement of the value chain for cross-border e-commerce.

3.2 Building a Global Cross-Border E-commerce Center

At the beginning of the establishment of "Cifnews Global Cross-Border E-Commerce Center" ("Cifnews Center" for short below), Weng Yaoxiong hoped to create an offline ecosystem for the improvement of the cross-border e-commerce value chain, and at the same time, to contribute to the plan of brands going abroad in the free trade zone. Therefore, Cifnews Center covers a brand incubation base, a brand service center and a brand marketing center, not only to help companies achieve cross-border e-commerce brand marketing training and incubation based on Shopify and other platform building tools, but also to introduce cross-border e-commerce industry chain-related service providers of brand design, overseas marketing, and e-commerce operation around the world, while providing exhibition halls and live broadcast rooms to support manufacturers to send samples to the Cifnews Center for showing to global small business merchants.

However, with more and more cross-border e-commerce "profit-dividers", some sensitive merchants began to explore other methods and new channels for word-of-mouth marketing and brand development. Therefore, Cifnews integrated and updated the brand marketing center and brand incubation base, and constructed the first cross-border e-commerce independent station incubation base in China. In fact, as early as April 2018, Cifnews fully purchased OBOR, a company that assists European companies with brand operation consulting, and helped dozens of Chinese companies achieve marketing abroad of B2C and B2 tiny B independent stations. After the establishment of the independent station incubation base of Cifnews Center, the operation team of OBOR China became the core of the business, and when combined with the supporting training courses of Cifnews, it assisted merchants with strong brand awareness, high customer order price and good quality in developing cross-border e-commerce independent stations rapidly.

Cifnews Center has also attracted famous enterprises at home and abroad, such as Vcan, Shenzhen Forest Shipping and FW856.COM, and thus a cross-border e-commerce product ecosystem covering platform, logistics, payment, software tools, SNS platform, trademark, VAT and other services was created to provide offline one-stop services and first-hand domestic and international market consultation for the settled merchants, opening up the upper stream and lower stream of cross-border e-commerce and realizing resource sharing.

3.3 Forming a Pool of Resources

In October 2019, Cifnews launched the “Spring Rain Program” on the Cifnews Forum for merchants that need to open businesses on global emerging cross-border e-commerce platforms. It not only provided Cifnews members with a full range of global platforms to open stores and incubation training services, but also cooperated with major platforms, service providers and senior merchants to develop a comprehensive product ecosystem of services to deeply empower them, and help cultivate them (Cifnews, 2019).

With a series of online and offline business integration and deep layout, Cifnews formed a pool of international e-commerce resources. In terms of users, from cross-border e-commerce “beginners” to “gold merchants”, from traditional OEMs to brand manufacturers, and from cross-border e-commerce service providers to major trading platforms, the network effect triggered by the accumulation of multilateral users has laid a solid foundation for its transformation. In terms of business, from focusing on content and information resources at the beginning to aggregating a variety of service resources and providing one-stop services for cross-border e-commerce practitioners, Cifnews has realized its own business optimization and upgrading while linking upstream and downstream resources in the industry chain. Finally, through the intelligent service platform and the Cifnews Center, it connected upstream and downstream enterprises and parallel enterprises, and brought together the global service provider resources of the whole link of cross-border circulation, connecting the various nodes originally scattered in the cross-border e-commerce industry chain, with all parties sharing elements, resources and results, and creating a synergistic network with the goal of a win–win situation. Cifnews has steadily shifted from the main body of resource gathering to the main body of empowerment and service supply.

4 Cifnews 3.0: Building an Ecosystem to Empower the Cross-Border E-commerce Brands for Going Abroad from Every Aspect of the Value Chain

Since 2020, Cifnews has been gaining momentum in development. The number of registered users has exceeded 1.1 million, with a monthly number of UV (Unique Visitor) of more than 3 million and a monthly number of active users of more than 100,000, and the weight in Baidu has rose to 7…But at the same time, Weng Yaoxiong also noted that due to a variety of disadvantages in the restructuring of global trade chain under the COVID-19 pandemic, and the over reliance on cross-border e-commerce trading platform, the potential of independent stations and minor language markets had increased, which had brought unprecedented new opportunities for brands going abroad. Therefore, Cifnews grasped the opportunity and launched Cifnews 3.0—industrial Internet platform for brands going overseas in early 2021, and officially changed its name to Cifnews, gathering a group of cross-border platforms for cross-border merchants, matching demands, providing one-stop refined services, and helping more Chinese brands to go abroad (Weng, 2021).

4.1 Content Ecology, Resource Ecology and Service Ecology

In this stage, Cifnews further optimizes the quality of content, expands the methods of content production and content distribution channels. Following the "observer program" in 2019, the "new observer program" was launched in September 2020, providing more traffic support for observers who insist on producing original content and are recognized by users. By January 2021, Cifnews had more than 2,500 articles with PGC, UGC and OGC, and more than 100 live broadcasts every month. In terms of content distribution channels, it has settled in WeChat, Toutiao, Baidu, Tiktok, etc. to reach users. In order to reduce the entry threshold and learning cost of the emerging platforms, Cifnews official website and APP launched eight sectors including "content, service, newcomer, real thing, learning, information, Q&A, and investment", to provide cross-border merchants with a complete knowledge system.

At the same time, based on an increasing number of Cifnews user portraits, Weng found that merchants have strong common demand such as making good use of tools, data and platform mechanism to improve marketing efficiency and increase profits. Based on this, Cifnews further precipitates the resources of global high-quality service providers, including shop opening, payment, VAT, trademark, logistics, software, product selection, off-site promotion and other service resources to help merchants realize one-stop procurement on Cifnews.

However, in addition to the common needs, different levels of merchants need different services. Therefore, Cifnews 3.0 created a more refined service ecosystem to help merchants with different volumes and business categories find the most matching services. "Take opening an Amazon store as an example, in addition to opening a store, for different merchants, we will provide them with manufacturing+, fashion+, enterprise purchase, VC plan, Amazon store and other different sales plans according to their research and development ability, design ability and supply chain strength" (Leon, 2021). The one-stop and customized service system basically covers the whole life cycle of cross-border e-commerce practitioners, and the service ecosystem of Cifnews is becoming more complete.

4.2 Building the Cifnews Model of Brands Going Abroad

While creating the ecosystem, Cifnews is stepping up the pace of its brands going abroad. At the Cifnews Brands Going Abroad Summit in 2021, which focuses on "positioning", Weng Yaoxiong said, "The current wave of brands going abroad is unstoppable. As an industrial Internet platform for brands going abroad, Cifnews takes the vision of 'letting more Chinese brands appear around the world', and has been supporting Chinese enterprises to go global in the whole industrial chain and in the whole life cycle of enterprise growth." As the top partner of Google, Facebook and other giants, Cifnews jointly launched the one-stop service for independent station/Google/Facebook. Station construction services, advertising services, account opening and tool guidance… all services can be found in Cifnews. Cifnews also cooperates with official platforms such as Shopify to help more Chinese brands better complete their overseas work with big data product selection support and localization operation support.

As a stepping stone for Chinese brands going abroad, Cifnews, on the basis of strategic cooperation with overseas platforms, empowers various brands and merchants to open the market quickly, bypass the overseas agents in the inherent mode, so as to be more competitive and seize the market with overseas counterparts. At present, Cifnews has successfully tested this model in South Korea, and it will soon be replicated in Japan, Southeast Asia, Europe and the world. The platform can not only reduce the cost of going overseas, but also rapidly improve the brand's popularity in overseas markets, and even copy the success for numerous Chinese brands (Internet Times Social League Planet, 2021).

4.3 Growing Together with Many Cross-Border E-commerce Practitioners

From "content factory" to "resource pool" and then to "service ecosystem", Cifnews has implemented the concept of win–win cooperation throughout its entire growth process, helping thousands of small and medium-sized cross-border e-commerce merchants to achieve their own operational goals and collaborative evolution. As a core enterprise in the ecosystem, Cifnews relies on its information resources, digital technology and other advantages. On the one hand, it helps small and medium-sized cross-border e-commerce merchants to improve their ability to obtain and integrate resources. On the other hand, by building a fully empowered ecological atmosphere, it empowers other ecological enterprises relying on Cifnews to continuously obtain competitive advantages.

Cifnews did not expand its scale through traditional approaches such as merger and acquisition, but relied on the derivation and evolution of the core products and services to continuously enhance network externality and expand the coverage of collaborative networks (Li & Hu, 2016). By making greater efforts in the upstream and downstream industrial chain, it promotes the integration and development of the entire industry, and improves the quality and efficiency of cross-border e-commerce. Under the connection of Cifnews, all subjects engage in extensive cross-border cooperation, a complete closed loop and a big ecosystem that encouraged interconnection, sharing and empowerment had been built (Hao & Yin, 2018), thus achieving a win–win situation.

5 Epilogue: Can Cifnews Achieve Its Ambitious Dream?

Reviewing Cifnews' development process, with its links to the upstream and downstream industrial chains, the company has built a collaborative network with itself as the core that empowers cross-border merchants, manufacturers, service providers and cross-border brands from three dimensions: content, resources and services. While promoting the development of all parties, it has completed its remarkable transformation from being a cross-border e-commerce new media focusing on "sharing new things", to being a cross-border e-commerce intelligent service platform focusing on "resource integration", and then to being an industrial Internet platform focusing on "one-stop overseas service" (Fig. 1). Its content empowerment is reflected in its release of information that meets the needs of practitioners through various channels and its capacity to improve the ability of cross-border e-commerce merchants to grasp the industry development trend and bridge the "information gap". Resource empowerment means that Cifnews formed a substantial resource pool in the 2.0 stage, thus improving its ability of the empowered to obtain and use resources from all parties. Service empowerment refers to Cifnews' one-stop service system of Cifnews for platforms, independent stations and brand going abroad, which can help practitioners develop and optimize their business in all directions, thus improving the comprehensive operation capability of the empowered and realizing the value growth.

As an "empowerment subject", through mechanisms such as content co-construction, resource supply, service support, process interaction and benefit sharing, Cifnews supports cross-border e-commerce practitioners who serve as the "empowered objects" to continuously improve their capacity in such regards as information acquisition, learning of experience, decision optimization, grasping of opportunity and business operations, thus helping them improve their individual ability, association ability and cooperation ability required to engage in the cross-border e-commerce industry. At the same time, it breaks down the information barriers and opens the industrial chain to further upgrade and develop the resource

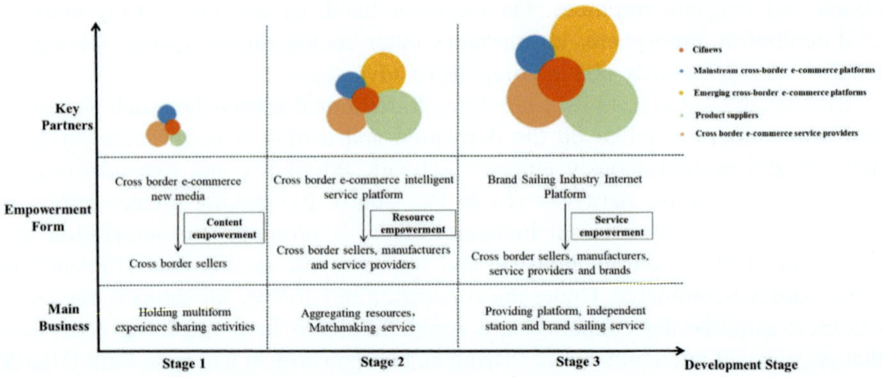

Fig. 1 Evolution of Cifnews

and service ecology based on content ecology, thereby building a unique ecological system. In the process of providing high-quality content and services, Cifnews has continuously attracted users. "The growth of our direct network externality and the collaborative value of users attracts more complementary suppliers to join the ecosystem, thus indirectly strengthening the network externality" (Li & Hu, 2016), and increasing Cifnews's value.

In May 2021, Cifnews obtained an exclusive investment from CITIC. The CEO Weng Yaoxiong said that "the newly raised funds will be mainly invested in three areas. The first is technology development. Cifnews is building middle and large platforms for brands going abroad to help Chinese brands enter new traffic channels. The second is setting up the localized operations and after-sales teams in international markets such as South Korea, Japan, Europe and Latin America. The third is the layout of the national industrial belt. This year, Cifnews will set up offices in several industrial belt cities around the country, and advance the brands that close to the industrial belt going abroad" (36 Kr, 2021).

Although the future is bright, it is evident that Cifnews still confronts numerous development obstacles. The users increment of the paid Cifnews Courses needs to be improved, and at the same time, the views of content distributed through multiple channels remain low. How to maintain the advantage of "the largest traffic portal for cross-border e-commerce"? Facing the competition from other cross-border e-commerce service providers, how to adjust the layout of business? As the cross-border e-commerce ecosystem built by Cifnews expands, how to lead and coordinate with other parties, develop a decentralized empowerment network and improve ecological governance is also a significant issue. Under the situation of pandemic prevention and control, Cifnews has taken many new actions since 2022, such as using WeChat communities to promote online projects docking, providing member services for CEOs and senior executives, and launching new multi-channel marketing platforms. However, with the more pronounced trend of cross-border integration and operation and rapid development of platform economy and service provider economy, Cifnews still has a long way to go.

Appendix 1: Segmentation Industry Mode of Cross-Border E-commerce

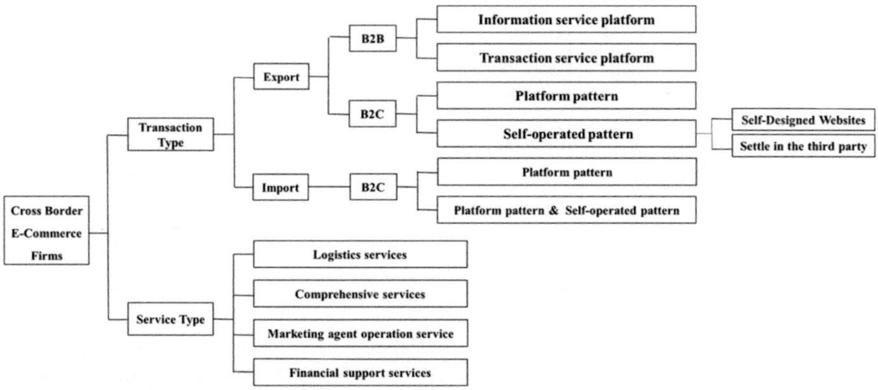

Source Research Report on Market Prospects and Investment Opportunities of China's Cross-border E-commerce Industry by AskCI

Appendix 2: Cross-Border E-commerce Service Providers that Received Financing from January 2020 to June 2021

Established time	Company name	Orientation	Established time	Company name	Orientation
2015	Airwallex	Providing integrated solutions for cross-border payment	2016	Skyee	Cross border payment service provider
2018	AfterShip	SaaS platform for cross border e-commerce	2016	Seller Motor	Enable global e-commerce through AI
2018	Jijia ERP	Providing digital management solutions for cross-border e-commerce	2018	iZhiliu	One stop business solution centered on cross-border e-commerce of Southeast Asian brands

Established time	Company name	Orientation	Established time	Company name	Orientation
2017	LingXing	Cross border e-commerce SaaS service provider	2009	Lianlian Global	Cross border payment service
2010	Mabang ERP	Cross border e-commerce ERP service provider	2014	Meetsocial	International marketing services in overseas markets
2014	Dianxiaomi	Cross-border e-commerce one-stop service platform	2019	E.vat master	European one-stop VAT tax service platform
2020	Easyya	Providing cross-border export e-commerce supply chain services	2019	Qbit	One-stop cross-border fund management platform
2016	Captain BI	Cross border e-commerce SaaS service provider	2017	Shop Lazza	Providing technical services for brand being out
2020	Pongo	Providing international digital marketing services for domestic brands	2020	Joying Box	Cross border e-commerce logistics service provider
2013	Eccang ERP	Cross border e-commerce middle platform service provider	2013	Xiaoman	Seagoing SaaS service provider
2011	Sowow	International brand one-stop agent operation service provider	2013	Panexwd	Cross border e-commerce integrated service provider

Established time	Company name	Orientation	Established time	Company name	Orientation
2020	Tuotuodigital	Cross border e-commerce financial technology platform	2009	Zongteng Group	International logistics service provider
2018	Selmuch	Cross border e-commerce marketing and SaaS service providers	*2014*	*Cifnews*	*Industry internet platform for brand sailing*

Source Cross-border E-Commerce Service Provider Financing Data List in 2020 and China Cross-border E-Commerce Service Provider Financing Data List for the First Half of 2021 from CBEC.100EC.CN; data as of June 2021. The chart was drawn by the author

Appendix 3: Cifnews's Development History and Milestones

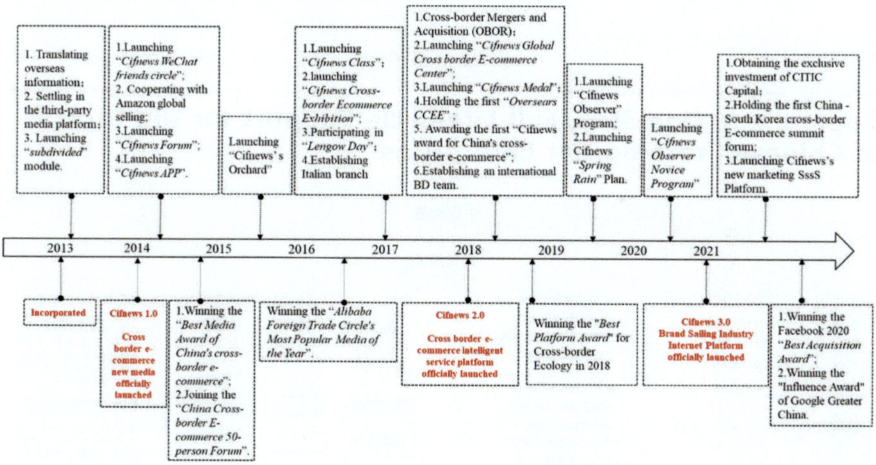

Source Compiled by the author

Appendix 4: Cifnews's Business Process of Brands Going Abroad

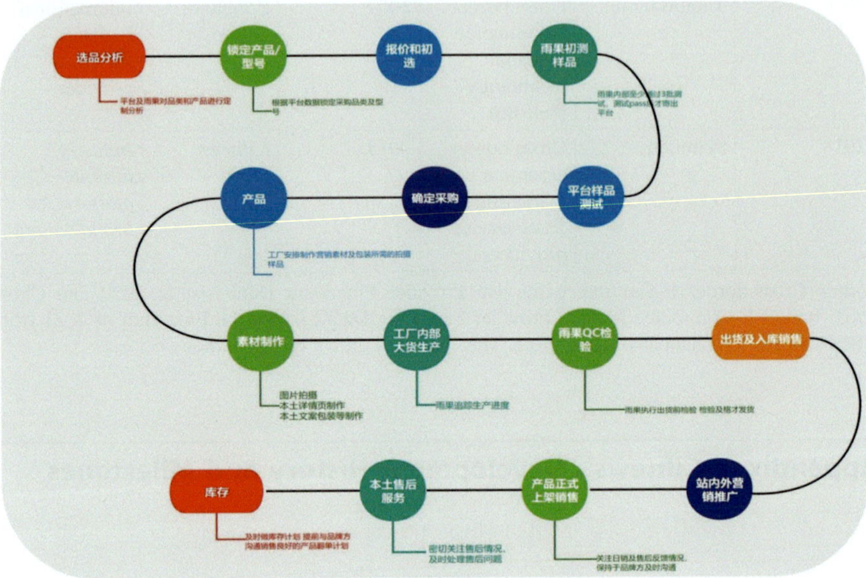

Source Cifnews

Appendix 5: One-Stop, Full Life-Cycle Support for the Growth of Chinese Cross-Border Enterprises

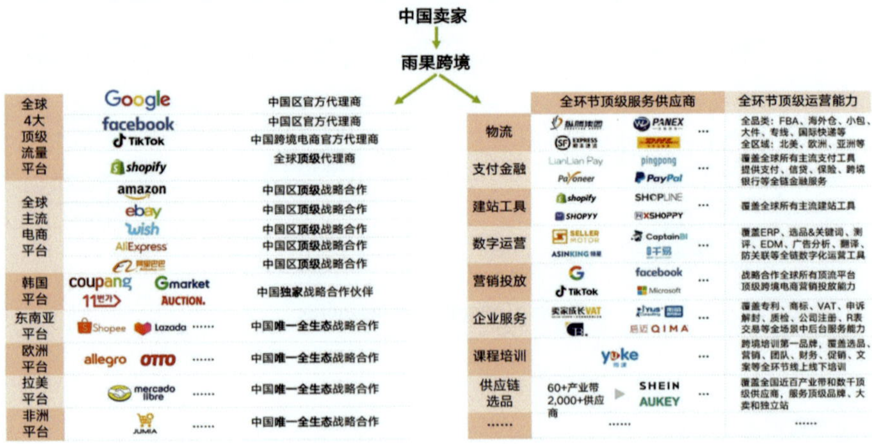

Source Cifnews

References

Cifnews. (2018, August). *Cifnews launched its cross-border e-commerce intelligent service platform to create a new product ecosystem.* Retrieved from https://www.cifnews.com/article/37355.

Cifnews. (2019, October). *Cifnews's first recruiting fair of the "Spring Rain Program" in 2020 is hot, the USD100 billion market in South Korea attracted much attention.* Retrieved from https://www.cifnews.com/article/52064.

Cifnews. (2021, May). *Cifnews wins Facebook 2020 award for new customer development.* Retrieved from https://mp.weixin.qq.com/s/vEHCYw2cmqv3QAmqCZ78gg.

Hao, J., & Yin, M. (2018). Sharing economy: Empowerment, value creation and business model innovation—A case study of ZBJ.COM. *Commercial Research, 05*, 31–40.

Internet Times Social League Planet. (2021, January). *"Cifnews" is arrived with a comprehensively upgrade of the "Industrial Internet Platform for Brands Going Overseas"*. Retrieved from https://mp.weixin.qq.com/s/m7QfStBdj7hFJxXJGT9tYg.

36 Kr. (2021, May 25). *Cifnews completes a new round of financing to reproduce the success of Chinese brands going abroad.* Retrieved from https://36kr.com/p/1233861968138630.

Leon. (2021, January). CTO of Cifnews: Cifnews 3.0 is launched to make more Chinese brands appear in the world! *Cifnews.* Retrieved from https://www.cifnews.com/article/87575.

Li, P., & Hu, H. (2016). Research on the mechanism and path of the transition from companies to platform ecosystem. *Science & Technology Progress and Policy, 33*(10), 1–5.

Luo, Z., Li, X., Song, X., & Li, Y. (2017). Evolution of enterprise organizational structure—Based on the case study of HSTYLE. *China Industrial Economics, 09*, 174–192.

Weng, Y. (2021, January). Weng Yaoxiong, Founder and CEO of Cifnews: Global trade chain reconfigured under the COVID-19 pandemic, and DTC brands going abroad comes across a historic opportunity. *Cifnews.* Retrieved from https://www.cifnews.com/article/87557.

POP Mart: How to Maximize IP Value in the Field of Art Toy?

Xiaoxia Sun, Yu Jin, and Xiaoxin Huang

1 Introduction

In the Internet age, driven by consumption upgrading, "Her Economy" bonus, the rise of Generation Z, and art toy culture, the blind box economy becomes rather popular. Pop Mart took the lead in combining art toys with blind box sales, and became the front runner of "blind box economy" by virtue of its first-mover advantage.

In August 2021, Pop Mart held its first International Art Toy Online Exhibition through the live broadcast of the WeChat channel. In the online exhibition, over 150 fashion toy brands participated, and more than 800 limited products made their debut, with 1.52 million online visits. The average stay time reached 10 min, far exceeding the industry average. The number of online viewers of the three-day live broadcast exceeded 1.3 million, with a cumulative turnover of CNY25.2 million (Sohu.com, 2021).

On the whole, China's blind box and art toy industry is still in the early stage of development. Leading enterprises, such as Pop Mart, can meet consumers' demands accurately and carry out more efficient IP design and marketing planning thanks to its large follower scale. And leading enterprises have stronger bargaining power with suppliers because of their high market share. Therefore, it can be predicted that the market concentration degree of the blind box art toy industry will continue to increase, while the edge of leading enterprises will continue to expand.

Why can Pop Mart win out? The following is an analysis of how Pop Mart makes a profit from the perspective of the most popular business model (Fig. 1). Let's look back to the birth of Pop Mart.

X. Sun (✉) · Y. Jin · X. Huang
School of Finance and Trade, Wenzhou Business College, Wenzhou, China

J. Zhang et al. (eds.), *Innovation of Digital Economy*, Management for Professionals,
https://doi.org/10.1007/978-981-99-1741-9_17

Fig. 1 Analytical perspective of Pop Mart's business model

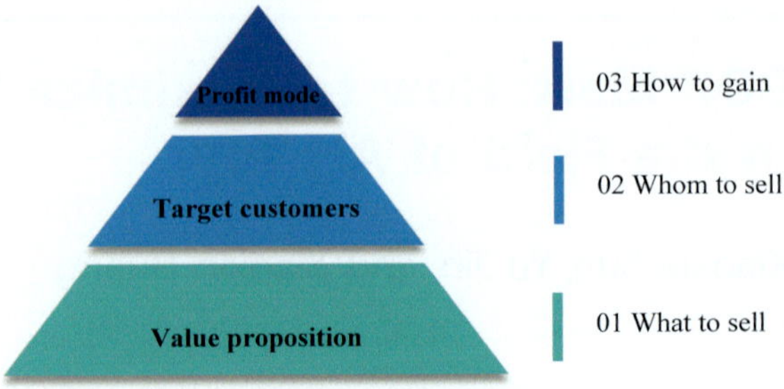

2 From a Lattice Store to an IP Brand Operator

Wang Ning, the founder of Pop Mart, was born in Xinxiang, Henan province in 1987. In 2005, he entered the university and began to study advertising (Zhang & Wang, 2021). In 2008, when Wang Ning was still an university student, he discovered the new retail model of "Lattice Store" with his friends. There are all kinds of creative products in a "Lattice Store", also called a mini creative department store, attracting the attention of young people to stop by. The lattice shop opened by Wang Ning was very successful, but gradually he found that this was an unsustainable model. One reason was the emergence of imitators, with over a dozen lattice stores opened around the campus. And due to the low threshold for opening stores, it was easy to cause a price war, which eventually leads to the dilemma that no one can make a profit.

How to solve the dilemma? Around 2010, in China's retail market, there were rare "creative or trendy goods" on the "supply side". On the basis of the lattice store, Wang Ning wanted to adopt a retail model featured by unified procurement, sound control over quality and gross profit, and rich product categories. To this end, Wang Ning and his team inspected trendy retail places in many cities. They found a company called "Log On" in Hong Kong, where trendy products were successfully displayed and sold like supermarket goods. "Log on" opened many stores in Hong Kong, and the sales volume of its products was quite satisfying. This coincided with the expected retail business model imagined by Wang Ning, and then he founded Pop Mart in Beijing with reference to this model. In November 2010, the first physical store of Pop Mart officially opened in EC Mall, Zhongguancun, Beijing, and Wang Ning's idea for a trendy creative retail platform was materialized (Fig. 2).

However, after the opening of Pop Mart's first physical store, its operation was not smooth and faced many challenges. First of all, in the early stage of Pop Mart's business, in order to save costs, it mainly selected products with its channel advantages in the art toy market. Although such model reduced the cost and risks in the product development, it also presented problems such as difficult product selection, unstable product supply and lack of core competitiveness. Next, as the physical store was opened in a high-end shopping center, competitors would surely change from "lattice stores" to leading brand stores. Although Pop Mart is

Fig. 2 Map of Pop Mart physical stores

designed in a fashionable style, compared with other brand stores in the shopping center, it was still in a lower grade, hence attracting few consumers. Finally, the company lacked excellent talent with retail management experience. At that time, Wang Ning and his team were almost all graduates in their twenties. Although they had the entrepreneurial experience of a "lattice store", they were not very professional in retail operation management, and there was even a time when the store staff resigned en masse due to operational difficulties.

2.1 Survival from a Desperate Situation

At the end of 2011, Pop Mart had to consider business transformation because of the challenges it encountered.

In terms of product selection, in order to enhance the competitiveness of products, it took Wang Ning a year to find all kinds of high-quality products suitable for Pop Mart from all over the country, but the revenue and operational efficiency of stores were still low. After thinking, Wang Ning thought that he could try to package and sell high-quality goods to people who want to open a shop like himself, so he created "Taohuo". However, the website, after the establishment, demanded huge funds for promotion and operation, which required the introduction of venture capital. In 2012, Wang Ning met more than a dozen venture capital institutions, but they all rejected him. Finally, he met Mai Gang, an angel investor, and finally got an investment of CNY2 million. But Mai Gang said that he was not interested in Taohuo, but in Pop Mart, and the money was for Pop Mart.

This "life-saving money" not only saved the first physical store of Pop Mart, but also realized Wang Ning's wish to open another three stores. Enterprises engaged in the retail industry can generally realize that multiple stores or "chain stores" can share costs, and it is difficult for a single store to make profits. Under the support of venture capital, Pop Mart's store survived and continued to expand its scales, and the multi-store model shared the back-office costs, making the profit margin rise.

Wang Ning also met the dividend of the era, in which consumer demand for trendy department stores was increasing. From 2012 to 2015, Pop Mart developed rapidly among the youth, while many institutions invested money one after another. These investment institutions include industrial investors in the retail industry, who helped improve Pop Mart's retail system. In the reviving market and under the support of funds, Pop Mart developed from an entrepreneurial team of several people to a standardized enterprise, and the management of stores became more and more efficient.

2.2 Toy Collection to Become the Success Secret

The market environment was constantly changing. In 2015, in the wave of "new retail + consumption upgrade + supply-side reform", Wang Ning felt the changing trend in the art toy industry, as the sales volume of physical stores and the gross profit of Pop Mart once again declined, and the overall business environment began to deteriorate. What should Pop Mart do next facing the sluggish market environment?

First of all, it should learn by experience and find a new way out in the analysis. Just as Groupon, the leader in group buying, was established when the founder saw that on the soon-to-be-closed "The Point" website for helping petitioners find supporters, the hottest activity was actually created in group buying. When Wang Ning summed up his experience, he said he was inspired by a product. Sonny Angel is a very common category operated by Pop Mart, but since the second half of 2015, it has become rather more popular with its sales soaring. The monthly sales volume increased from several thousand to tens of thousands pieces, and many limited editions were snapped up as soon as they hit the shelf, and some followers even lined up to snap up (Fig. 3).

What's the secret behind the popularity of Sonny Angel? Through the analysis of Sonny Angel (Table 1), Wang Ning discovered a huge market—collectible toys. Collectible toys are usually based on the characters of various well-known cartoons, animations, games and film and television works. Most of these IP (Intelligent Property) originated from overseas and have not yet developed in China. IP can be understood as "an image or brand that has plenty of room for exploitation" when it comes to culture and content industries (Wang, 2021).

In addition, Wang Ning also found that there was an overlap between collectible toys and the ACGN handicraft market, but there were also differences. ACGN handicrafts are products made into the shapes of characters or animals in animation, comics, games and other works, authorized by the original author or copyright owner. The main difference between collectible toys and ACGN handicrafts is that ACGN handicrafts are peripheral products based on the original animation and comics, so the original content is the core, and they should be faithful to the original characters, with limited secondary processing.

Fig. 3 Product drawing of Sonny Angel

Table 1 Analysis of the hot-sale Sonny Angel

Secret of Sony Angel		
Blind box sales	Collection properties	Decompression method
The "blind box marketing" is similar to the merchandising of the raffle game, which can stimulate the users' repurchase rate	Collectible toys are sold to users with high IP loyalty and often a hobby of collection	The "high-pressure" life makes young people seek "excitement" to relieve stress. The excitement of "hidden models" can help consumers to relieve stress

Compared with ACGN handicrafts, there is more room for artistic creation in the IP of collectible toys. For example, the blind box IP does not require a long time to accumulate content, and design different IP series and a variety of IP images can meet the personalized aesthetic needs of the younger generation, as their primary consideration when buying is the toy's appearance. Many young consumers like to collect these toys, which is a way for them to relieve stress.

Wang Ning, who got the success secret, transformed Pop Mart from a simple retail company to a service platform with IP operation and incubation, merchandise development and production, and chain retail as its main business. Pop Mart, as an IP brand operator, has successfully launched a number of explosive IP products, opening up a whole new market, and its brand awareness is constantly rising (Fig. 4).

3 User Group

The core users of Pop Mart are concentrated in "Generation Z" with the greatest consumption force. "Generation Z", also called "Internet Generation", " ACGN

Fig. 4 The development history of Pop Mart. *Source* Company announcement, ebrun.com, CICC Global Institute

Generation", and "digital media natives", generally refers to young people born between 1995 and 2009, who possess a large size of population and huge consumption potential. There are about 260 million "Generation Z" in China, whose expenditure reaches CNY4 trillion, accounting for about 13% of the total household expenditure nationwide (CBN Data, 2020) (Fig. 5).

In addition, 90% of Pop Mart's users earn more than CNY8,000 a month, and the percentage of female users is more than 70%. These users also show stronger loyalty for companionship, and aesthetic and social needs, with a repurchase rate of more than 50% (Fig. 6).

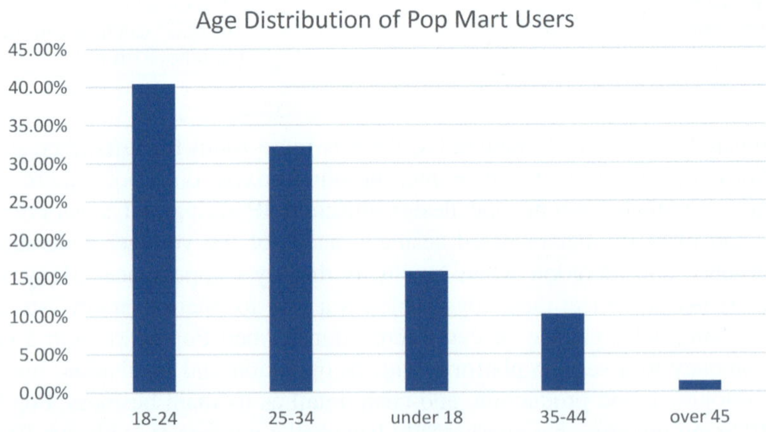

Fig. 5 Age distribution of Pop Mart users. *Source* POP MART User Research Report by Leader in 2021

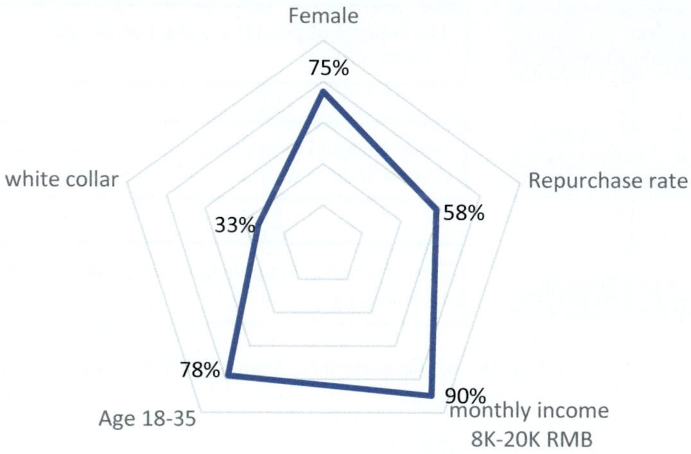

Fig. 6 Pop Mart's user portrait. *Source* POP MART User Research Report by Leader, Sinolink Securities Research Institute

3.1 Consumption Features of "Generation Z"

"Generation Z" likes to follow and create trends. At the same time, they are also "face judgers", advocating that beauty is justice. They are the recommendation generation, seeking personalization, unique but not alone. They have become the main force of fashion consumption, and are also the first choice of promoting trendy goods. Compared with "millennials", "Generation X" and "baby boomers", they have a different consumption attitude (Fig. 7).

The needs of "Generation Z", who have been immersed in the Internet since childhood, can be summarized as "virtual companionship" and "trendy aesthetics". In today's age of material affluence, household disposable income has increased and domestic families are investing more money in the cultivation of Generation Z, which make Generation Z potential consumers. At the same time, they enjoy the convenience of online consumption brought by the mobile Internet, and they

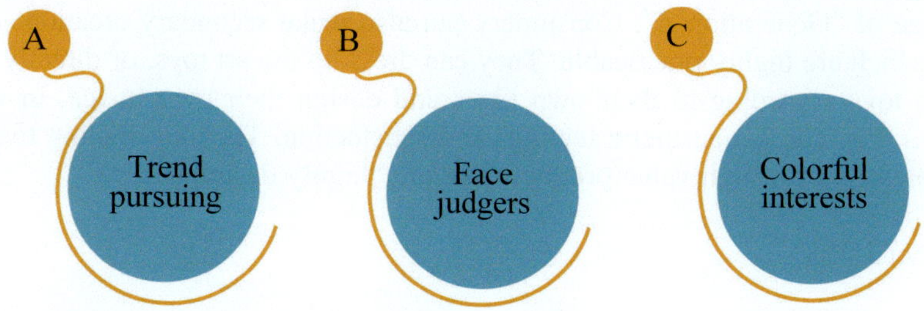

Fig. 7 Consumption attitude of "Generation Z"

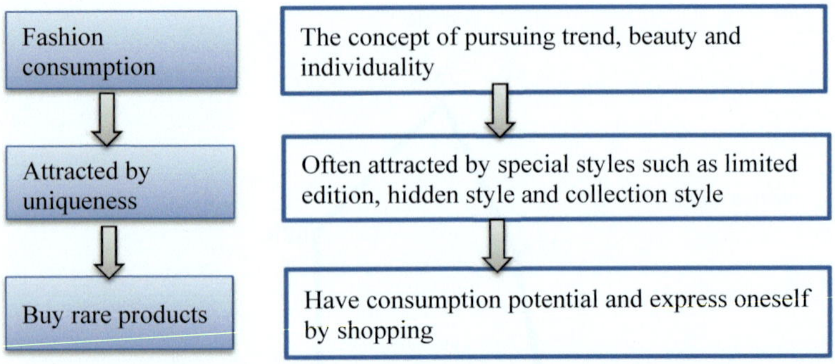

Fig. 8 Consumption characteristics of "Generation Z". *Source* Sinolink Securities Research Institute

are used to communicating and catching up with new trends such as food, games and toys (Fig. 8).

3.2 Pop Mart Meets the Needs of "Generation Z"

As an art toy, Pop Mart mainly meets the needs of "Generation Z" in the following three aspects.

(1) Companionship needs

Art toys are placed and collected in the home as the emotional support and spiritual companionship for "Generation Z", and many consumers will appreciate the art toys to relieve their boredom, loneliness and other negative emotions. Art toys are usually produced based on virtual images, and these toys have come out of the virtual world to become the friends and travel "companions" of "Generation Z".

(2) Aesthetic needs

Art toys are shaped beautifully, and fashionably designed, in line with the pursuit of value of "Generation Z". Consumers can also make secondary creations of art toys, which are highly practicable. They can dress up the art toys, or directly paint on the toys according to their own ideas and design their own image, in which process they can get aesthetic feelings and satisfaction. They are willing to pay a high premium for high value products that are "highly desirable".

(3) Social needs

Among the "Generation Z", an only child in a family often becomes a new user due to the social attributes of the product. Those only children love trendy culture and to follow the trend. The information about art toys released by influencers or friends on social media platforms will stimulate the interests of "Generation Z" in art toys, and then they will buy it and share on social media to achieve self-identification through others' evaluation. And with the hobby of art toys as a link, the dialogue on the virtual space will also extend to offline interaction, making "online friends with the same hobby" become friends in real life.

4 Competitive Barrier: IP Value Maximization

Quality IP resources are the core competitiveness of Pop Mart. IP is the starting point of the commercial development of the art toy market. Incubation to create a number of high-quality IPs is the fundamental guarantee of commercial realization. Pop Mart hopes to continuously expand its consumer base by enriching its IP format, but in order to focus its resources, Pop Mart mainly promotes one IP per year. Based on IP, Pop Mart has formed an industrial chain that uses IP to realize (Fig. 9).

4.1 IP Resource Accumulation

Pop Mart has accumulated numerous IP resources and has the ability to create hot-sale IPs. As of June 30 of 2020, Pop Mart operated 93 IPs, including 12 self-owned IPs, 25 exclusive IPs and 56 non-exclusive IPs (National Business Daily, 2020).

(1) Self-owned IP

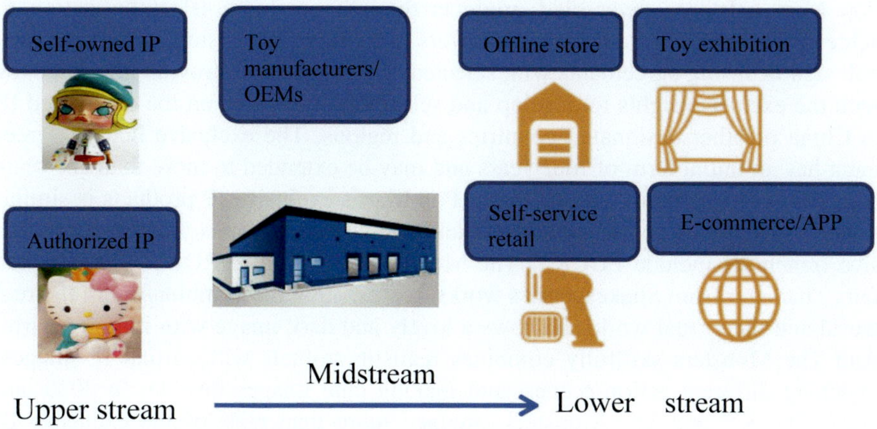

Fig. 9 The industry chain of Pop Mart IP realization is the guarantee of maximizing IP value. *Source* Company announcement, China Merchants Securities

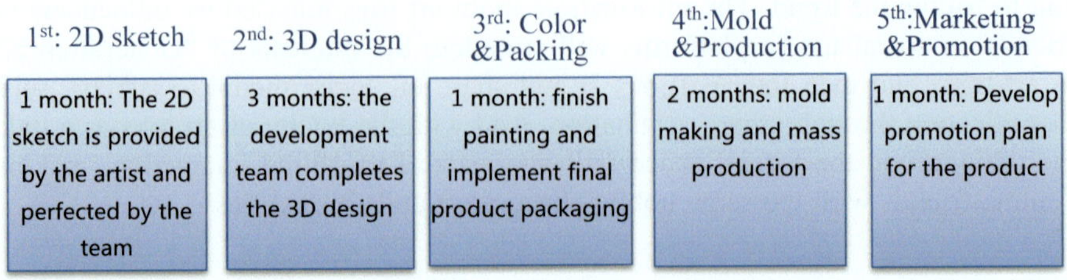

Fig. 10 Production flow chart of Pop Mart's self-owned IP products (about eight months) (China Merchants Securities, 2021)

Self-owned IP means that Pop Mart enjoys full intellectual property rights, including the right to develop and sell art toys, and license them for additional realization opportunities. Self-owned IP is designed and produced by Pop Mart's internal team. Its main self-owned IPs include: MOLLY, DIMOO, BOBO&COCO, and YUKI. Designer Kenny created the Molly series, which can be subdivided into 30 different sub-series, such as the constellation series, the propitious beast series combining traditional culture, and the steampunk series; the DIMOO series launched by Ayan wants to convey the concept of "symbiosis"; the BOBO&COCO series featured by warm and healing can make consumers feel deep love and energy; YUKI, created by artist Lang, is a little girl who is covered with thorns but has a kind and innocent heart. MOLLY and DIMOO series products are loved by consumers and have become best-sellers. In 2021, the revenue of MOLLY series products exceeded CNY700 million, among which that of the DIMOO exceeded CNY500 million (Fig. 10).

(2) Exclusive authorized IP

Pop Mart produces diversified products through obtaining IP authorization to achieve the purpose of attracting followers in multiple dimensions. The Company will sign licensing agreements with selected artists, who will provide the Company with the exclusive rights to develop and sell trend toys based on the contracted IP in China or other designated countries and regions. The exclusive license agreement has an initial term of four years and may be extended to more than six years (Lu, 2021). The production process of Pop Mart's exclusive IP products is similar to that of its self-owned IP, which also takes about eight months. Pop Mart's exclusive franchises include PUCKY, The Monsters, and SATYRRORY. PUCKY is a fairy character from Shakespeare's works, representing the combination of the real world and the virtual world. It shows a lovely and dark image with infinite charm. And The Monsters skillfully combines realistic animals with virtual IP images, matching different action scenes, and making cute images lovable. In 2020 and 2021, PUCKY and The Monsters obtained more than 60% of the exclusive IP revenue of Pop Mart (Fig. 11).

Fig. 11 PUCKY series products with exclusive IP

(3) Non-exclusive authorized IP

Pop Mart obtains non-exclusive IP mainly through the cooperation with mature IP providers. Through the signing of non-exclusive licensing agreements, it obtains the non-exclusive rights to develop and sell the trend toys based on the contracted IP in China or other designated countries and regions. Normally, Pop Mart, as the licensee in this type of cooperation, does not have the right to relicense IP. Its non-exclusive IP includes cartoon characters that launched with third parties, such as Mickey Mouse, Hello Kitty and Minions. In 2020, the revenue of Pop Mart's non-exclusive IP series products was CNY440 million, accounting for 17.7% of the company's total IP development revenue. In 2021, although its revenue rose to CNY600 million, the proportion decreased (Fig. 12).

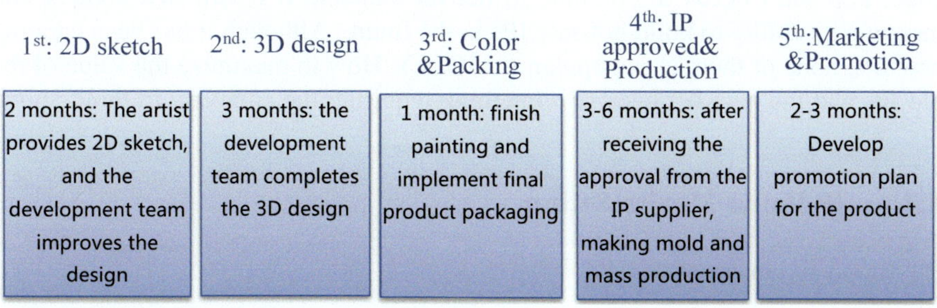

Fig. 12 Production flow chart of Pop Mart's non-exclusive IP products (about 11–15 months)

Table 2 Pop Mart's revenue in 2021

Product type	Revenue in 2021 (unit: CNY 1 thousand)	Revenue proportion (%)
Self-owned IPs	*2,586,827*	*57.6*
– MOLLY	705,098	15.7
– SKULLPANDA	595,256	13.3
– DIMOO	566,735	12.6
– Bunny	167,883	3.7
– Sweet Pea	161,526	3.6
– Other self-owned IPs	390,329	8.7
Exclusive IPs	*770,507*	*17.2*
– The Monsters	304,431	6.8
– PUCKY	182,245	4.1
– Other exclusive IPs	283,831	6.3
Non-exclusive IPs	*620,463*	*13.8*
External acquisition and consignment	442,886	9.9
Others	69,968	1.5
Total	4,490,651	100

Source Pop Mart Financial Report

Since launching its first "Molly Zodiac" series blind box in 2016, every year the IPs launched by Pop Mart has been successful. The company's revenue mainly comes from IP related industries. In 2021, the revenue of Pop Mart reached CNY4.491 billion, of which IP-related revenue accounted for 88.6% (Table 2). As the leading company in the art toy industry, Pop Mart has an excellent IP performance. In 2021, seven IPs' revenue exceeded CNY100 million, including 5 self-owned IPs and 2 exclusive IPs.

In addition to Pop Mart, IP Station, 52TOYS and TOP TOY are all competing for the market of the realization of art toy IP. In order to maintain its competitive edge, Pop Mart needs to continue to deliver valuable IPs with rich content and maintain its ability to build hot-sale IPs in the future. Although it has been creating new IPs, none of them is as popular as MOLLY. How to maximize the value of the old IPs and the new IPs became something requiring the company to think about.

4.2 IP Value Maximization

(1) Brand IP construction

Brand IP usually has the characteristics of high recognition, strong realizability, long realization cycle and self-contained traffic, and it can constantly derive new related products. Most of Pop Mart's products only have images but no stories. It is necessary to gradually complete the IP branding with the help of consumers' pursuit of IP products. At the same time, the IP matrix needs to be enriched to realize IP ecologicalization, further enhance the brand awareness, strengthen consumers' awareness of Pop Mart's brand concept of "creating trends and delivering beauty", and deepen the brand image.

(2) Sales model innovation

"Blind box" market lacks a threshold, and the dividends that Pop Mart wins in the art toy blind box track are seen by many other art toy brands and blind box players, and then it is followed suit. Therefore, a number of brands and IPs are trying to get a share of the blind box boom. The existing blind box images in the market have a high degree of homogenization, almost the materialization of the original IPs, which lacks diversified personalized marketing. Such an industry bubble has lowered the consumers' expectations towards and freshness of the blind box to a certain extent. At the same time, the high uncertainty of blind boxes makes the selection difficult for some customers. Drawing blind boxes is somewhat like gambling, and the act of buying blind boxes in bulk for getting the so-called hidden edition is not rational. The higher the price of the product, the more rational people tend to be when consuming it, which also causes the public to be reluctant to buy blind boxes with high price. When drawing a product they do not like, the loss is greater than that of low-value products, so that people are more cautious due to risk aversion. Some people think Pop Mart's blind box has "bubbles" and call it "Bubble Mart" (Tencent News, 2020). Therefore, the marketing model for blind boxes needs to be innovative, and when incorporating high-priced products into blind boxes, it is feasible to consider classifying the products and appropriately improving the cost performance of each product to reduce the risk that customers need to take and improve customer satisfaction.

(3) Enhancing the closed-loop advantages of the whole industry chain

In addition to its high-quality IP resources, Pop Mart is able to lead the development of the industry because of its complete online and offline retail terminals, community interaction integration platform, rapid iteration of diversified products and increasingly mature supply chain. Pop Mart divides the whole industry chain into three parts: upstream IP resources, midstream manufacturers, and downstream retail terminals, forming an integrated process. Based on its rich IP resources, Pop Mart has to continuously enrich its IP and product portfolio, explore diversified cooperation and innovation with companies in the industry chain to form better closed-loop advantages, extend the life cycle of corporate IP products and maintain competitive advantages.

5 Epilogue

Pop Mart, after all, does not have a long history of development, and it is important to keep plowing deeper in this field to develop greater brand awareness, a longer operating history and broader industry relationships. In addition, the popularity of IPs will significantly affect the sales and profitability of the company's products. To maintain a competitive advantage, the company must make full use of the advantages of IPs that have already gained market recognition and continuously launch new IPs that meet consumers' tastes to maximize the IP value of the new and old ones, otherwise the company's operating results will be adversely affected. Finally, the company can properly expand its business of overseas sales to meet a broader market.

References

CBN Data. (2020, August). *Insight report of consumer attitude of Generation Z*. https://www.cbndata.com/report/2381/detail?isReading=report&page=1.

China Merchants Securities. (2021, October). *Blind boxes are often found, but Pop Mart is not—On the competitive barriers of Pop Mart*. http://www.199it.com/archives/1279925.html.

Lu, C. (2021). *Research on the profitability of art toy enterprises—A case study of Pop Mart company* [Dissertation, Anhui University of Finance and Economics].

National Business Daily. (2020, December 1). *With the first-half revenue of more than CNY800 million, Pop Mart launched its IPO with an estimated value of USD7 billion*. https://view.inews.qq.com/a/20201201A0A9TZ00.

Sohu.com. (2021, October). *With 1.3 million views and GMV of CNY25 million, Pop Mart has opened a new "store" in the live broadcast room*. https://www.sohu.com/a/494410060_120948001.

Tencent News. (2020, May). *Market value shrunk CNY70 billion in three months. Does Pop Mart lose its patience?* https://new.qq.com/omn/20210519/20210519A0966U00.html.

Wang, Y. (2021). Changes and strengthening of brand positioning in Pop Mart. *Marketing Circles, 2021*(11), 139–141.

Zhang, Y., & Wang, X. (2021). Why Wang Ning? And why Pop Mart? *China Economic Review, 2021*(10), 80–84.

Looking at the Life Cycle of Koala, Where is the Next Breakthrough for Cross-Border E-commerce?

Ying Yan, Xiaofeng Shang, Yunxia Feng, and Li Zhang

1 Introduction

In recent years, China has introduced a number of new policies on e-commerce laws and cross-border e-commerce, which further regulated China's cross-border e-commerce market. At the same time, globalization and consumption upgrading have also driven China's cross-border e-commerce to scale up. Koala's sales exceeded CNY100 million in 229 s, exceeded the all-day sales of "Double Eleven" in 2017 in 78 min, and reached 4 times of the sales of the same day last year in 24 h. In the first half of 2019, Koala ranked first in the cross-border e-commerce market share for the seventh time with a market share of 27.7%. On September 6, 2019, Alibaba confirmed the acquisition of Koala for USD2 billion. Although cross-border e-commerce is still in the dividend period, problems such as commodity quality traceability and cross-border payment are still the difficulties that the industry needs to overcome urgently. As the former leader of cross-border e-commerce enterprises, Koala has experienced a life cycle of development, growth and decline with a "roller coaster" speed in a short period. It started at a high point, then reached the peak of the industry and finally came to the end of being acquired. Koala, the former giant of cross-border e-commerce industry, showed us how it has boomed and faded away from this industry. Since the self-operated mode of Koala failed to solve the predicament of fake goods in cross-border e-commerce, what should the e-commerce enterprises do to break through? It is a problem yet to be explored.

Y. Yan (✉) · X. Shang · Y. Feng · L. Zhang
School of Economics and Management, Southwest University of Science and Technology, Mianyang, China

J. Zhang et al. (eds.), *Innovation of Digital Economy*, Management for Professionals,
https://doi.org/10.1007/978-981-99-1741-9_18

2 Industry Background

China's cross-border e-commerce started from personal purchasing agent in 2005. Since Taobao founded its Worldwide store in 2007, many overseas goods merchants have gathered here, satisfying consumers' wish "to buy global fine products without leaving home". This C2C model makes overseas shopping more convenient. On March 7, 2015, the State Council officially approved the establishment of China (Hangzhou) Cross-border E-commerce Comprehensive Pilot Area, and a set of management systems and rules was gradually formed to promote the development of global cross-border e-commerce. With the substantial favorable policies introduced by relevant departments one after another, the enterprises will embrace more opportunities, and China's cross-border e-commerce market will enjoy broad prospects for development.

In 2015, NetEase Koala (Hangzhou) Technology Co., Ltd. was established in Hangzhou, Zhejiang Province. Its main business scope involves technology development, technical consultation, technical service, e-commerce platform technology, etc. Koala, an oversea product purchase platform, operated by it is a comprehensive e-commerce platform focusing on cross-border e-commerce business. By bulk direct purchase from the place of origin and overseas direct express, the platform provides users with overseas products covering maternal and infant products, cosmetics, household supplies, health care, food, digital domestic appliances, clothing, bags and so on. In 2019, Koala topped the cross-border e-commerce market for the seventh time, and was recognized by the industry as the biggest "dark horse" in the e-commerce industry.

Thanks to the large capital investment of NetEase, it took a very short time for NetEase to reach the leading position in the industry from its establishment. Ding Lei, the founder of NetEase, once aimed to reproduce the success of NetEase in the field of e-commerce within 3–5 years through Lifease and Koala. In order to ensure that the e-commerce transactions have a reliable commodity sources, Ding Lei built its own purchasing team. The CEO of Koala led the team to East Asia, Europe, America, Australia and other fine goods origins, set up self-operated direct purchasing channels, and obtained "overseas wholesale price" through long-term and stable purchasing with large investment.

3 Beginning of the Company

3.1 A Self-operated Mode

Benefited from the favorable policy, Netease entered the industry of cross-border e-commerce

At the beginning of 2015, Koala was released online for trail operation. In August 2014, as a new policy was announced in the cross-border e-commerce, this industry gained great momentum and boomed. But the market of oversea online shopping is complicated, and almost every cross-border e-commerce is challenged by the

No.1 problem of "fake goods". Given that Jumei founded by Chen Ou left halfway due to the endless fake goods, the CEO of NetEase made clear the direction of NetEase's self-operated mode when preparing for the Koala project. He said, "I don't reject operating a platform, but when everything on it is chaotic and the quality can't be controlled, I have to do it myself." Therefore, Ding built his own purchasing team, appointed Zhang Lei, an old employee of NetEase with experience in virtual e-commerce, as the CEO of Koala, and Zhang personally led a team to East Asia, Europe, America, Australia and other origins of fine goods in the world, and set up self-operated direct purchasing channels to ensure the effective control over the supply chain to the greatest extent. In March 2015, the first cross-border pilot area—China (Hangzhou) Cross-border E-commerce Comprehensive Pilot Area was established in China. Zhang Lei believed that "the key to win the battle of cross-border e-commerce is not to grab goods but to grab warehouses". Koala seized the opportunity and built a large number of bonded warehouses at a rapid speed, with the greatest number of self-operated bonded warehouses and self-operated overseas warehouses in China.

3.2 One-Stop Service

NetEase overtook on a bend using one-stop service
As the game kicked off in oversea online shopping of B2C cross-border e-commerce, the focus was mainly on overseas brands with high popularity among domestic consumers. However, the profit margin of these products was relatively low. Recognizing this, in 2015, Zhang Lei put forward the idea of "one-stop service", in which Koala would undertake services such as logistics, warehousing, customs clearance, operation and promotion, while its partners only need to be responsible for the production of products. The "nanny-style" mode reduced the burden on partners, and made it easier to gain the trust of overseas brands for cooperation and expand to the global market. However, as Koala was expanding globally, a new problem appeared, that is, how to build trust with "century-old brands" and get support. In order to solve this problem in time and achieve cooperation with overseas excellent brands, Koala has invested EUR3 billion, JPY500 billion and USD3 billion in local national brands and century-old brands, with the goal of standing out in the field of cross-border e-commerce.

4 Ride the Wave and Rise

Koala survived in the lightning battle
On April 8, 2016, the *New Policies on Cross-border Tax Reform in 2016* was implemented. The new tax reform policies have had a great impact on overseas online shopping. Some entrepreneurial teams with unstable foundations have declared bankruptcy. The tightening of capital and the uncertainty of policies made many small and medium-sized enterprises recognize the risk, and they withdrew orders

and returned goods in transit in order to reduce losses. At that time, Zhang Lei was also caught in a dilemma. Bearing the strategic investment of NetEase with expectation, she couldn't retreat and put the supply chain foundation built up over the past year under a reputational crisis; meanwhile, the unfavorable policies posted great risks for going forward. After careful consideration, Koala chose to go ahead. As long as the customer does not withdraw the booked orders, Koala would cover all the delay and transshipment costs of goods in the ports. This is the cooperative spirit of "win–win" that Lei Zhang pursues. Because of Koala's self-operated mode, the company reduced costs by purchasing in large quantities, optimizing logistics efficiency and independent pricing, which greatly reduced the impact of the new tax policies on commodity prices. With accurate decision-making and the advantages of supply chain and warehousing logistics accumulated in the early stage, Koala went upstream and survived the crisis.

4.1 Stabilize the Status

The fourth quarter of each year is a concentrated period of great promotion, and it is also an important opportunity to test the comprehensive strength of a platform and achieve win–win in sales volume and brand. From the "Super Foreign Goods Festival" on "Double Eleven" to the "Quality Foreign Goods Festival" on "Double Twelve", Koala has successively led or participated in three important promotions in one month. With each promotion applying differentiated competitive strategies and marketing methods, Koala displayed the highest strength and won the best reputation for performance.

According to the financial report data released by NetEase in the fourth quarter of 2016, the revenue of Koala's e-commerce and related businesses was gradually improving, and the overall net income of Koala's businesses has risen sharply to 38.2% year-on-year, making Koala a new engine for the growth of NetEase's business revenue.

4.2 All-Round Expansion

(1) Rapid growth in platform users

Koala promoted the GMV and the number of users of the platform through four levels: customer attraction, stimulation, retention and transformation. In terms of attracting new users, Ding Lei broadcast tea picking and started the e-commerce live broadcast; in terms of promotion, Koala launched activities such as giving coupons and group buying with CNY1; in terms of retaining old users, new communities were introduced to strengthen the communication and interaction between users and mobilize their enthusiasm; and in terms of business transformation, Koala participated in shopping festivals such as "618" and "Double Eleven" to stimulate users' desire to shop. Besides, Koala also continuously published subway ads and variety show ads to accumulate a reputation among users and build public awareness of the brand. From wining popularity to retaining it, Koala shifted from traffic mode to traffic pooling mode.

(2) Expanded cooperation with overseas brands

By April 2017, Koala has cooperated with more than 1,000 European brands, including OTTO, P+M, Rossmann and other European chain suppliers and local supermarkets. On September 6, 2017, Koala global factory stores have sprung up. They adopted the F2C mode, and the products were directly supplied by manufacturers, which was low-key and with high quality. At the beginning of 2018, Kaola further cooperated and upgraded with ten cosmetics, personal care and health care brands such as LG Group, JAYJUN, Amore Group and SNP from South Korea, aiming to accurately create high-quality products that meet Chinese users' needs.

(3) Coordinated cross-border logistics

In May 2016, Koala first tried to apply the "overnight delivery" of cross-border imported goods. Koala has cooperated with a well-known international logistics company in the industry, and with its strong distribution capability and network covering the whole country, Koala could deliver goods to users within 1–3 days after receiving orders.

In addition, Koala has strong logistic integration ability at home and abroad. In China, Koala has reached cooperation with domestic superior logistics and distribution companies; overseas, it has established more than ten overseas warehouses in European and American countries, Japan and South Korea, and made use of the global multimodal transport network of the shipping logistics giant Maersk to ensure the capacity of cross-border logistics.

5 Gridlock

In 2017, Koala launched its global factory stores, and introduced third-party merchants of the F2C mode, representing the first step from self-operation to "self-operation + platform". However, according to NetEase's annual financial report, the growth rate of total revenue of Koala was lowered to the least since 2014. In 2018, fake disputes were frequently heard in Koala. After China Consumers Association pointed out that the Estee Lauder products sold by Koala were fake, Koala denied and declared that the goods sold were genuine. But the merchant who issued fake identification results was Estee Lauder (China) Cosmetics Co., Limited. It ended up with nothing definite. Then came fake Canada Goose down clothing. After two disputes over fake goods, consumers began to question the reliability of Koala's good sources, leading to bad reputation.

In order to establish a supply chain advantage in overseas purchases to address the problem of counterfeit goods at the sources, in February 2019, Koala entered into negotiations with Amazon to acquire Amazon's China business. If the partnership had worked out, Koala could have shared the supply chain with Amazon's overseas shopping business in China, but the partnership failed because Amazon put a high price. NetEase's e-commerce business growth plummeted to 5% in the fourth quarter of 2018 alone, and the annual e-commerce business growth rate was 65%, only half of the last year's 116.7%.

6 A Matter of Life and Death

After the failure of negotiations between Koala and Amazon, there was constant news that NetEase would be acquired by Alibaba and Pinduoduo. Cross-border e-commerce business has always been the key layout of Alibaba's business lines, but the advantage of Tmall Global in cross-border e-commerce business lied in cosmetics, and the successful acquisition of Koala with maternal and infant products being its core competitiveness will enrich the layout of Alibaba's cross-border e-commerce business.

In September 2019, Ding Lei suddenly announced to the public that Koala had joined Alibaba. Eventually Alibaba Group wholly acquired NetEase's cross-border e-commerce platform Kaola with USD2 billion, and the brand will continue to operate independently under the leadership of Liu Peng, general manager of Tmall's import and export business group, while Zhang Lei, the former CEO of Koala, will serve as an advisor to Tmall's import and export business. Established with a "golden key", Koala eventually failed to bear Ding Lei's vision of "rebuilding a NetEase".

7 Conclusion

On January 9, 2015, Koala launched a public test; on March 29, 2016, it announced its official launch; on November 11, 2017, its sales were four times higher than that in 2016; in June 2018, it announced its entry into the integrated e-commerce market; and finally on September 6, 2019, Alibaba announced a strategic partnership with NetEase to wholly acquire NetEase's cross-border e-commerce platform Koala for USD2 billion. NetEase abandoned Koala not for that the cross-border e-commerce business does not have good prospects for development, but that the continued "war of spending money" has made it difficult for NetEase to cope with the financial pressure brought by business expansion. As NetEase CFO Yang Zhaoxuan said, "In terms of e-commerce business, balancing the growth rate and e-commerce profit model is the key move. Our business philosophy does not support the model of losses in exchange for rapid growth at all costs." Continued spending of money and slowing growth are the most direct reasons for NetEase to divest its e-commerce business, but the difficulty of testing the authenticity of cross-border goods has been a difficult point that Koala has not been able to overcome, but also the pain point of the entire cross-border e-commerce industry. Koala focused on an heavy-asset self-operated model, equipped with the bonded warehousing model, which puts extremely high requirements on logistics and storage capacity, thus increasing the supply chain cost pressure. Self-operated warehousing was once considered to be the core advantage of Koala, which can guarantee the controllability of the supply chain to the greatest extent, thus reducing the probability of counterfeit goods and improving the efficiency of procurement and distribution. But the successive incidents of counterfeit goods that have aroused consumer concern revealed that Koala's ability to control the supply chain was still very weak, and it has only solved the warehouse problem, and the source of goods was still a pain point.

The Innovative Development Road of Wenzhou E-commerce Park: The Practice of Xingdao E-commerce Industrial Park

Chenqing Su

1 Introduction

In 2013, to further gather and cultivate e-commerce enterprises, improve the development environment of e-commerce, promote the development and application of e-commerce, and boost the transformation and upgradation of traditional industries in Wenzhou, in accordance with the instructions and opinions of the State Council and the provincial government on accelerating the development of e-commerce, Wenzhou Municipal Government issued the *Implementation Opinions on Accelerating the Development of E-commerce (Trial)*, which clearly pointed out that various e-commerce public service platforms should be vigorously developed to support the establishment of the e-commerce industrial park. In addition, in order to materialize the *Implementation Opinions on Accelerating the Development of E-commerce (Trial)*, give full play to the guiding role of financial funds, further perfect the development environment of e-commerce, and accelerate the development of e-commerce in Wenzhou, the municipal government formulated the *Measures for Supporting the Development of E-commerce in Wenzhou*, which mentioned that the government would encourage and support the establishment of e-commerce industrial parks (bases and buildings), and provide public supporting services for the development of e-commerce.

In March 2020, to accelerate the high-quality development of commerce and trade, Wenzhou issued the *Implementation Opinions on Building a Commerce and Trade Center in Southeast Coastal Region*, and planned to transform Wenzhou into a regional consumption destination, a leading place for fashion consumption and a demonstration place for the integration of domestic and foreign trade by 2022, laying a solid foundation for the development of commerce and trade during the 14th

C. Su (✉)
School of Finance and Trade, Wenzhou Business College, Wenzhou, China

J. Zhang et al. (eds.), *Innovation of Digital Economy*, Management for Professionals,
https://doi.org/10.1007/978-981-99-1741-9_19

Five-Year Plan period, and promoting Wenzhou to be "an international fashion city and a reviving consumption city". The *Implementation Opinions on Building a Commerce and Trade Center in Southeast Coastal Region* also pointed out that Wenzhou should speed up the construction of e-commerce clusters, actively cultivate ecosystems for the industry, and introduce famous e-commerce enterprises in the industry to build regional headquarters; the supply chain around leading enterprises should be strengthened to promote the integrated development of the new economy and interdisciplinary industries; the government-led mode featured by enterprise operation and win–win cooperation should be further improved with upgraded supporting facilities to promote cooperation with major scientific research institutions, strengthen personnel training, and accelerate the building of a common community for industrial development.

Therefore, in the context of Wenzhou Municipal Government's constant acceleration of e-commerce clusters, the optimization of the competitive environment of e-commerce enterprises, and supporting of the creation of e-commerce industrial parks and other clusters, the Xingdao E-commerce Industrial Park was built.

2 Introduction to the Industrial Park

2.1 Brief Introduction

Xingdao E-Commerce Industrial Park (address: No. 59 Zhonghui Road, Louqiao Subdistrict, Ouhai District, Wenzhou City) is an integrated e-commerce industrial park comprising e-commerce supply chain, operation, art design, photography, training, logistics, live broadcast and other services. The industrial park is featured by self-contained supporting facilities, superior geographical position, covering an area of 120 μ, and a building area of 188,000 m^2. It is built with 2,070 stores, 230 apartments, configured with central air conditioning, and 85 sets of escalators, sightseeing elevators and freight elevators. Besides, it has a large parking lot, with business offices, warehousing and other ancillary facilities covering an area of 41,000 m^2, and a warehousing center with adequate ancillary facilities. The industrial park has perfect hardware conditions, as it can provide perfect basic hardware facilities for e-commerce merchants. The park includes not only office areas, negotiation areas, conference rooms, exhibition halls and other places, but also professional live broadcast rooms, photography bases, training bases and many other functional areas. In the second phase, shared live broadcast rooms, creative spaces, product selection centers and other areas will be built to provide entrepreneurial support for college students and e-commerce novices. At present, the park mainly focuses on the selling of children's shoes, led by the mode of "live broadcast + short video promotion". Taobao, Tiktok, Kwai, Pinduoduo and other live broadcast platforms and top MCN institutions were introduced, and professional operation teams and technical teams were used to provide one-stop solutions for live broadcast e-commerce, boosting the empowerment of the production and sales of children's shoes, children's clothing and glasses in Wenzhou, and assisting the digital economic development in Wenzhou.

2.2 Development Course

Xingdao E-commerce Industrial Park is a product of the new era of SinceTech, after its ups and downs, transformation and upgradation, and innovation development of the digital economy in a decade. Under the support of the preferential policies of the municipal and district governments, the restructuring of SinceTech has been underway. Since 2017, the industrial park has gradually embarked on its footwear industry, from the initial Shoe Market to the current e-commerce live broadcast industrial park. The specific development process is as follows.

In 2017, the Shoe Market was established, with hundreds of wholesale retailers of footwear products stationed, among which a few merchants were engaged in e-commerce, laying a sound foundation for the development of e-commerce live broadcast in the future.

On June 18, 2018, with the gradual increase in the number of e-commerce merchants for children's shoes, the development direction of e-commerce was gradually determined, and SinceTech Children's Shoes E-commerce Mall (now renamed as "Xingdao Children's Shoes E-commerce Mall") was established, planning to cultivate a group of high-quality shoes sellers to promote production through sales and try to boost the development of surrounding children's shoes manufacturers.

In 2019, large-scale live broadcast merchants stationed in the industrial park, forming an e-commerce framework featured by footwear live broadcast. In addition, the park gradually began to improve its e-commerce supporting services and provided services including express delivery, logistics, photography, and art design for e-commerce merchants.

In 2020, Xingdao E-commerce Industrial Park was established featured by e-commerce live broadcast with children's shoes as the mainstay, men's and women's shoes as the supplement and comprehensive development of various categories of goods. Five development priorities of the industrial park have been defined, namely, Xingdao Children's Shoes E-commerce Mall (focusing on investment attraction), E-commerce Product Selection Center (focusing on supply chain), E-commerce Training Center (focusing on live-streamer training), E-commerce Live Broadcast Center (focusing on live broadcast) and E-commerce Service Center (focusing on convenient service).

In 2021, over 300 e-commerce merchants were stationed in Xingdao E-commerce Industrial Park, achieving certain good results, boosting the development of the digital economy in Ouhai District and even Wenzhou City, and receiving more attention from the municipal and district governments.

2.3 Development Background

As we all know, with the focus of the global manufacturing industry shifting from Europe, America and South Korea to the Chinese mainland, the shoemaking industry also has become an important part of the Chinese manufacturing industry. After the development of footwear industrial clusters over the past 20 years, Guangzhou, Fujian (Jinjiang) and Wenzhou have become three shoe centers of producing children shoes, presenting a situation of tripartite confrontation in China. In Quanzhou, there are many superior brands of children shoes with high reputation across the country, such as Anta, Xtep and 361°. With the development of the shoes brands for adults, the children's shoes brands start another boom in Quanzhou. The brands of children's shoes in Guangzhou are at a medium level with high cost performance, such as MIFFY, Haiershi, Baby-Q, Dr. Kong and Morning. Compared with Guangdong and Fujian, children's shoes brands contend for markets with low price and large quantity. However, as the brand building lags behind Fujian and Guangzhou, there are many large children shoes enterprises, but the brands of Wenzhou in the same field still fall behind.

Nowadays, with the rapid development of e-commerce, children's shoes e-commerce in Guangdong and Fujian has gradually formed a cluster area, which promotes the development of children's shoes e-commerce. On the contrary, Wenzhou, as one of the three "shoe centers" of children's shoes production in China, has not yet formed a cluster area of children's shoes e-commerce. Louqiao of Ouhai District has a long history of producing children's shoes. Over the past few years, although the development of children's shoes e-commerce has been rapid, most of them were fighting their own battles. Besides, many manufacturers and merchants hesitate to move forward in the field of children's shoes e-commerce due to the lack of a fully-functional cluster area for children's shoes e-commerce, which cannot provide effective help for their growth. Therefore, Xingdao E-commerce Industrial Park not only can advance the development of traditional children's shoes manufacturing, but also can make famous children's shoes brands of Wenzhou.

2.4 Development Significance

The establishment of Xingdao E-commerce Industrial Park can provide all-round e-commerce services and corresponding subsidies for e-commerce enterprises in the park, which can not only provide a guarantee for e-commerce enterprises that have settled in SinceTech to continue to develop, but also attract more enterprises to SinceTech, which also can recast its development vitality. The significance of the Xingdao E-commerce Industrial Park is mainly reflected in the following three aspects:

First, for the government, the establishment of Xingdao E-commerce Industrial Park can not only drive the demand for children's shoes, but promote the production of children's shoes in Ouhai District as well, thus developing nationally renowned brands of children's shoes; in addition, the industrial park helps to give full play to the advantages of children's shoes production of Ouhai to make the nameplate of "children's shoes e-commerce" of Ounhai and even Wenzhou, and at the same time, it also can bring more tax for the government.

Second, for SinceTech, the building of Xingdao E-commerce Industrial Park not only helps relieve the problem of premise leasing, but also gains an opportunity to solve its debt restructuring, even making SinceTech a well-known e-commerce industrial park.

Third, for children's shoes e-commerce enterprises, the establishment of Xingdao E-commerce Industrial Park can not only reduce the operating costs and give support for their development, but also attract more enterprises planning to enter the children's shoes e-commerce industry to gain support and subsidies provided by the park.

3 Operation Plan of Industrial Park

3.1 Operation Mode

The operation of Xingdao E-commerce Industrial Park needs professional teams, but the current original management team of SinceTech is not suitable for this. Although a self-built operation team can solve professional problems, it costs too much. Therefore, in accordance with the mode of "government leading, enterprise operation and win–win cooperation" in the *Implementation Opinions on Building a Commerce and Trade Center in Southeast Coastal Region*, SinceTech carries out its operating activities by adopting the mode of "government leading, park supervising and enterprise implementing".

The specific operation mode is that under the leadership of Ouhai District Government and People's Court, the manager of SinceTech and the temporary management team supervise the third-party e-commerce service enterprises to carry out the daily operation affairs of the industrial park, and control the development direction of the industrial park. Xingdao E-commerce Industrial Park is responsible for supervising all business activities of third-party e-commerce service enterprises, and those enterprises are responsible for investment attraction and entry, assistance measures, subsidy rules, entrepreneurial services and daily operations of the industrial park.

The operation mode of Xingdao E-commerce Industrial Park conforms to the actual situations of SinceTech, which can not only relieve the financial pressure of the government, but help SinceTech to gain more rentals and popularity, and even cultivate large-scale e-commerce service enterprises of Wenzhou.

3.2 Functional Orientation

By combining with the current development of children's shoes industry in Ouhai District and the development background of SinceTech, Xingdao E-commerce Industrial Park has positioned its own functions as follows:

First, the cluster function of e-commerce enterprises. By providing a series of specialized supporting services such as ideal business office space, high-quality storage and express delivery, the park will introduce and support newly-established e-commerce enterprises with famous brands, thus gradually gathering online merchant and suppliers into this entrepreneurship center.

Second, the entrepreneurial function of e-commerce enterprises. Sharing the park's entrepreneurial service system to lower threshold for e-commerce enterprises to start businesses, achieve the rapid growth in the number of e-commerce enterprises, and become an incubator of branded e-commerce enterprises.

Third, the promotion function of children's footwear industry. Optimizing and improving the supporting services of children's footwear e-commerce industry chain, enhancing the comprehensive competitiveness of e-commerce enterprises in the national and even global network markets, and promoting the development of e-commerce enterprises towards building their own brands and large-scale operations.

Fourth, the driving function of e-commerce demonstration. Demonstrating e-tailing models and providing training for e-commerce business talent, to provide demonstration and support for traditional enterprises to enter the e-commerce field.

3.3 Service Scope

E-commerce enterprises are commonly faced with obstacles with financing, warehousing, sources of goods, human resources, management concepts, marketing means, logistics costs, and technical bottlenecks in their early and start-up process. In response to these problems that hinder the growth and development of e-commerce enterprises, Xingdao E-commerce Industrial Park will provide one-stop solutions for the e-commerce enterprises in the park.

(1) Infrastructure. The park can provide complete office facilities and practical warehouses, and those who meet the conditions can enjoy preferential policies such as rent reductions and exemptions.
(2) Financial services. The park encourages banks to work with businesses to provide professional financial services; it establishes a platform to match private capital with enterprises, and guide venture capital into enterprises and projects; and it actively assists enterprises in seeking various national, provincial and municipal support funds.
(3) Operation services. The park integrates the needs of enterprises in the park, realizes the sharing of high-quality resources in a group, and provides fast,

preferential and comprehensive professional services for e-commerce enterprises in the fields of online shop operation, logistics, computer maintenance, photography and artwork, live broadcast and supply chain.

(4) Human resources. Employment practice bases for university students will be established with a number of universities; and it will cooperate with major recruitment websites to unify recruitment and meet various talent needs.
(5) E-commerce training. The park will open public training classrooms and regularly invite e-commerce experts, operators experts and online marketing elites to give on-site lectures and provide free training on the basic knowledge of e-commerce, including: training for entrepreneurs on the basics of opening, operating, maintaining an e-commerce shop, and product developing, packaging, marketing, and logistics.
(6) Management consultancy. The park will provide professional consulting services such as strategic management consulting, corporate governance guidance, financial management guidance, human resources construction guidance, legal affairs consulting, and enterprise listing consulting through the university's corporate management research team.
(7) Living facilities. There is already a mature and convenient living service community in the park, with sufficient housing, low rent, good security environment and convenient transportation, suitable for young people to live and start their own businesses.
(8) Supportive policies. The park is led by the government and operated by an e-commerce service enterprises. The park will introduce and implement a number of preferential policies after its establishment and promises to continuously update its supporting policies according to the development needs of e-commerce enterprises in the park. In addition, more support and subsidies will be given to university students in starting their own businesses, including rent-free and free sources of goods.
(9) Other services. It also provides various services such as business registration, intellectual property handling, legal and financial services for enterprises entering the park.

3.4 Support Policy Overview

After the establishment of Xingdao E-commerce Industrial Park, a full range of supportive policies will be developed and implemented. As the policies cover a wide range of areas, only important policies are outlined below.

(1) Free training

Nowadays, e-commerce platforms are developing rapidly, and the focus of e-commerce operation is constantly moving, making many enterprises already engaged in children's footwear e-commerce and those planning to engage in children's footwear e-commerce face difficulties in operations. Therefore, after the founding of the park, free basic courses on e-commerce operations and practical courses of e-commerce operations will be carried out regularly to help e-commerce enterprises develop steadily. At the same time, the park will provide free training for new e-commerce start-ups and personnel on the basics of e-commerce shop opening, operation and maintenance, supply chain, packaging, marketing and logistics.

(2) Zero inventory supply chain

One of the important reasons limiting the profitability of children's footwear e-commerce enterprises is the inventory backlog, so in order to avoid more children's footwear e-commerce enterprises from being affected by this, the park will integrate the inventory and channels of the various e-commerce enterprises that have moved in, provide a quality supply chain for the enterprises in the park, and provide the basis for zero inventory operation for the new e-commerce enterprises that will move into the park in the future, eliminating the pressure of inventory.

(3) College students entrepreneurship

In response to the municipal government's support for college students' entrepreneurship, the park will be established at the same time to build another e-commerce business incubation base for college students, which will provide free office space, office equipment, training courses, computer maintenance, etc. for college students who enter the park to start businesses, support college students to survive the most difficult initial stage of starting their own businesses, and implement a cash subsidy policy for college students with excellent entrepreneurial performance.

3.5 Profit Model

First, the park's profit source is rental revenue of offices, warehouses, houses, etc.; second, the profit source of the cooperative enterprise is the revenue gained in providing operation, logistics, photography, artwork, live broadcast, training and other services for e-commerce enterprises in the park. In addition, the cooperative enterprise uses the profits from e-commerce services to provide support and subsidies for e-commerce enterprises in the park, and if the profits from the cooperative enterprise are not sufficient to support the funds required for subsidies, the cooperative enterprise is responsible for filling the shortfall. If the profit revenue of the cooperative enterprise exceeds the funds required for subsidies, the excess will be the profit revenue of the cooperative enterprise.

4 Dilemma of Development and Countermeasures

4.1 Fund Source of Subsidies

Development dilemma: Whether the park can successfully attract investment and entry depends on the implementation of the support subsidy policies. Therefore, the stability of the fund source of supporting subsidies has become an important basis for the development of the park.

Countermeasures: The funds needed to help subsidize the e-commerce enterprises in the park are provided by the cooperative enterprise, and the cooperative enterprise is self-sustaining, so its profit revenue is an important fund source for supporting subsidies. At the same time, it is necessary to avoid the problem of insufficient funds derived from the unprofitable situation of the cooperative enterprise, so there are two countermeasures to this problem. First, ensure that the cooperative enterprise is the only e-commerce service enterprise in the park, thus ensuring its relatively stable revenue from e-commerce services; second, the cooperative enterprise prepares the "special fund for supporting subsidies", which shall not be misapplied, and shall only be used for the implementation of the policies of supporting subsidies in case that the cooperative enterprise is not profitable.

4.2 Promotion Effect of Investment Attraction

Development dilemma: After the park is opened, the effect of investment promotion directly affects whether the park is able to attract children's footwear e-commerce enterprises to move in. Therefore, how to guarantee the promotion effect of investment in the park has become the first operation problem that the cooperative enterprise needs to solve.

Countermeasure: The promotion effect of the investment attraction can be improved by: (a) improving the park's supporting subsidies to help e-commerce entrepreneurship; (b) focusing on the park's unique cash subsidy policy; (c) mobilizing all e-commerce enterprises and staff in the park to use their personal self-media resources for whole promotion of investment attraction to reduce promotion costs and enhance promotion effects; (d) widening the promotion channels and scope as much as possible through funding by the cooperative enterprise and resource providing by the park; and (e) establishing an investment promotion department and employing professionals to carry out two-way promotion online and offline at the same time.

4.3 Long-Term Stable Development of the Park

Development dilemma: Whether the park can achieve long-term development and reach its intended goals depends on whether the cooperative enterprise can successfully carry out e-commerce services to achieve stable profits. Only if the cooperative enterprise achieves stable profits can it provide the stable funds needed for supporting subsidies, and then attract and retain e-commerce enterprises, thus achieving steady development in the long run. Therefore, how to improve the profitability of the cooperative enterprise's e-commerce services is one of the important issues that it needs to solve.

Countermeasure: The cooperative enterprise can improve the ability of e-commerce services by: (a) recruiting professional high-level practitioners to improve the quality of e-commerce services; (b) keeping up with the trend of e-commerce development and broadening the scope of e-commerce services on demand; (c) participation by the park to help it attract customers for e-commerce services; and (d) ensuring that the cost of all e-commerce services is lower than the average market level.

5 Conclusion

Xingdao E-commerce Industrial Park not only reflects the necessity in children's footwear industry and SinceTech's restructuring, but also can bring tax revenue to the government, opportunities to children's footwear industry, opportunities to SinceTech Group's restructuring, and assistance to the development of small and medium-sized e-commerce enterprises. Although Xingdao E-commerce Industrial Park came into being in the context of the "Internet+" era, and governments at all levels have given a lot of support, its innovation development path is still under exploration.

KZTON Enables Cross-Border E-commerce Export with Intellectual Property Services

Xiutian Zheng

As the first cross-border intellectual property services platform in China, KZTON was established in 2016 in the China (Hangzhou) Cross-border E-commerce Comprehensive Pilot Area, dedicated to providing one-stop cross-border business legal services such as international trademark registration, patent operation protection, global copyright registration, overseas company registration, brand packaging design, financial and tax planning, legal terminal litigation and new media information aggregation for the internationalization and globalization of Chinese manufacturing and enterprises (CifNews, 2019). The KZTON IP platform won the only "Legal Service Innovation Award" in the "EBox" innovation project of China (Hangzhou) Cross-border E-commerce Comprehensive Pilot Area in 2017, and also became the only recommended foreign-related IP service platform in the State Council's 2017 National Activity Week of "Widespread Entrepreneurship and Innovation" (Zhejiang News, 2017).

1 Established in Response to the Pain Points of Cross-Border Enterprise Exports

In the era of open development of the world economy, the use of domestic and international resources, the expansion of domestic and international markets, the implementation of internationalization and globalization of business are the only choices for many manufacturing enterprises to pursue growth and development. Under the international division of labor pattern, many manufacturing enterprises in China, which are located at the low end of global value chain, are facing with painful problems such as low value-added products, thin profits, and the lack of international brands, and are unable to achieve better development. With the

X. Zheng (✉)
Hangzhou Normal University Qianjiang College, Hangzhou, China

J. Zhang et al. (eds.), *Innovation of Digital Economy*, Management for Professionals,
https://doi.org/10.1007/978-981-99-1741-9_20

mutual integration of traditional foreign trade and the Internet, the cross-border e-commerce model is rapidly emerging, providing rare and favorable conditions for manufacturing enterprises to expand the global market and climb up to both ends of the global value chain. However, under this online trading model characterized by digitization and internationalization, problems such as low added value of products, especially intellectual property infringement, are the pain points faced by cross-border enterprises For example, in early 2015, the PayPal accounts used by more than 5,000 merchants in China were frozen by a temporary restraining order from a U.S. court due to the suspected sale of counterfeit products, involving an amount of up to USD50 million, and many merchants' PayPal accounts were eventually cleared due to the high cost of responding to lawsuits to defend their rights and low legal awareness. The cost of overseas lawsuits and the amount of compensation arising from cross-border e-commerce intellectual property issues are high and may cause significant harm to business development. The typical cases of infringement of intellectual property rights in 2021 announced by the General Administration of Customs involve the equal protection of intellectual property rights such as the exclusive rights to use trademarks and the exclusive rights to use the Olympic logo at home and abroad, covering consumer goods such as food, cosmetics, clothing, cigarettes and glasses, as well as key channels such as freight, cross-border e-commerce and postal delivery. The national customs increased enforcement of intellectual property protection, with 79,000 batches and 71.8 million pieces of suspected import and export infringing goods seized in 2021 (The Paper, 2022). In the context of China's enterprises going abroad, the importance of services such as branding and IP management has undoubtedly come to the fore. In August 2016, the cross-border intellectual property services platform—KZTON was born in the China (Hangzhou) Cross-border E-commerce Comprehensive Pilot Area.

2 Systematic Layout and Construction of Multi-disciplinary Knowledge Service System

In order to effectively cope with market competition and meet the requirements of cross-border e-commerce platforms in terms of product quality, more and more market players such as cross-border e-commerce enterprises need comprehensive IP services of multiple categories and high quality. Based on market demand, KZTON has built a multi-disciplinary knowledge service system including trademark service, patent service, copyright service, brand design service, foreign-related legal service and technology consulting service, which can provide foreign trade enterprises and cross-border merchants with a total of more than 500 business services in the field of intellectual property such as brand maintenance, trademark applications and global patents.

(1) **Trademark service**. Trademark is not only the essence of enterprise brand culture, but also an intangible asset of an enterprise, which can increase the total

assets of an enterprise and is the most direct embodiment of brand value. In the development of cross-border e-commerce business, registered trademark is the most effective means to prevent "following sale". KZTON integrates a team of senior experts with experience in trademark applications to provide free professional analysis services and timely filing services. It can quickly check likelihood of confusion for trademarks, strictly check the status of pending trademarks, develop high-quality and efficient trademark registration solutions, and inform the status of application processing in real time, and provide formal invoice and tracking consulting services.

(2) **Patent services**. As a kind of intangible assets, patent has great commercial value and is an important means to enhance the competitiveness of enterprises. The quality and quantity of patents are the necessary prerequisites for enterprises to declare the title of high-tech enterprises, innovation funds and other types of science and technology plans and projects. In cross-border e-commerce, patents have become a powerful business tool. With the core advantages of "confidentiality, professionalism, speed and regularity", KZTON provides patent services such as searching the novelty of products, patent registration, patent rejection reexamination, patent rights protection, patent invalidation, patent invalidation defense, patent entry item change, and patent opposition for enterprises.

(3) **Copyright services**. Registering copyright would benefit copyright owners in three ways: first, regular announcements of the registration agency would help promote products to the society; second, if copyright disputes occur, the *Works Registration Certificate* would be a powerful weapon to safeguard copyrights; third, copyright registration would be the premise for enterprises to apply for software products and enterprise evaluation and high-tech enterprise certification, so as to enjoy national tax incentives, subsidies and other policies. By providing copyright services such as copyright registration, copyright evaluation and software work registration, KZTON protects the original ownership and rights of enterprises and solves copyright disputes caused by copyright ownership.

(4) **Brand design service**. Brand design includes the naming of an enterprise or product, design of logos, graphic packaging, display, advertising and promotion, refinement of cultural concepts, or a specific process different from elements of other enterprises or products. KZTON can assist enterprises in establishing a complete brand strategy and visual tools, in order to create brand core concepts and culture, and provide services on the design of brand official website to e-commerce brand image.

(5) **Foreign-related legal services**. Legal services, just like other tangible commodities, can be accurately and effectively engraved and recorded by information technology, and the production, provision and transaction of legal services can be standardized, tangible and digitalized just like other commodities. KZTON carries out cooperation with a number of overseas local law firms and accounting firms to provide excellent Chinese enterprises with

high-quality cross-border legal services for foreign-related economic and trading issues, economic construction of free trade zones and the participation in the competition of international legal service market, thus escorting the internationalization of Chinese enterprises.

(6) **Consulting service on science and technology**. Technological resources are integrated for the empowerment of enterprises for innovation and upgradation. KZTON, possessing professional expertise in the intellectual property area, integrating relevant resources from government, industries and experts, provides considerate and comprehensive services for science and technology enterprises, establishing a scientific, rigorous and standardized consulting service process and a complete set of evaluation system for science and technology enterprises, to promote the transfer and transformation of scientific and technological achievements to enterprises and society, and maximize the value of technology.

Since its establishment, KZTON has continuously optimized and improved its service system on cross-border e-commerce knowledge, following an operation approach featured by "service standardization", "module e-commerce" and "business digitalization". By creating an e-commerce system of "Internet + IP", online business is rapidly promoted. Data accumulation, utilization, analysis and iteration enabled online access to service display, order acquisition, business processing, information feedback and file management, thus improving service efficiency, reducing transaction costs of enterprises and enhancing user experience. KZTON provides more than 2,000 times of overseas intellectual property services for Chinese enterprises every year, and has continuously served more than 10,000 small and medium-sized enterprises to establish new brands or related overseas services. Up to now, KZTON has launched over 80 IP right protection actions on Amazon and other e-commerce platforms for Chinese cross-border e-commerce brands, cracked down on unfair competition of over 120 overseas brands, and retrieved over USD 6 million for 200 enterprises in overseas business.

3 Multi-dimensional Empowerment for Chinese Manufacturing Going Abroad

By integrating various specialized service providers, KZTON provides foreign-related legal services for online business, and establishes a brand research institute, to continuously improve the ability for the empowerment of cross-border exporters for Chinese manufacturing with intellectual property rights to go abroad.

(1) **Multilateral linkage is realized to integrate various specialized service entities**. Brands of Chinese manufacturing going abroad involves various services and links such as overseas company registration, brand design, international trademark registration, patent operation protection, tax agency bookkeeping,

equity partnership agreement, and legal terminal litigation. Therefore, professional service talent and institutions should be accessible. To this end, based on the concept of open cooperation, KZTON integrates global service providers such as lawyers, accountants, designers, photographers and intellectual property agents, to form a service synergy in the creation, protection and utilization of various intellectual property rights. The company has established cooperative relations with more than 300 law firms and intellectual property agents in more than 100 countries around the world.

(2) **Model innovation is achieved to provide foreign-related legal services for online business**. In Hangzhou, a leading city of digital economy, the application of digital technology in various fields is at the forefront of China. By using Internet technology, KZTON have done a lot of things, such as creating a brand new mode of foreign-related online business legal service, integrating all kinds of professional service subjects around the world, connecting with the needs of enterprises through informatization, building an intelligent cross-border business legal service system, realizing trans-temporal and trans-regional service supply, which finally enables the majority of small and medium-sized enterprises to enjoy lower cost, higher efficiency and stronger professional business legal service. KZTON helps Chinese enterprises to build and protect their brands globally, and promote the orderly, standardized and high-quality development of cross-border e-commerce industry. In January 2022, *Cross-Border E-Commerce Terminology*, jointly launched by Hangzhou KZTON Intellectual Property Service Co., Ltd., Zhejiang GM Digital Technology Co., Ltd., Administration Office of Hangzhou Comprehensive Free Trade Park, and Zhejiang E-commerce Promotion Association, was released on the National Group Standard Information Platform.

(3) **Brand research is performed to create a management atmosphere for outrun brands**. KZTON Outrun Brand Institute was established in March 2018 by KZTON in conjunction with well-known think tanks, colleges and universities, consulting institutions and brand experts, mainly engaged in market applications such as brand internationalization theory research, brand value assessment, brand strategy management, brand communication and brand protection for Chinese enterprises. By publishing the "China Outbound Brand Value List", "Top 50 E-Commerce Outrun Brands" and other series of research reports, it focuses on the development of Chinese Internet outrun brands in overseas countries, shares the main trends of brand building and enhances the international influence of Chinese brands. On May 10, 2018, the first *Chinese Cross-border E-commerce Outrun Brand Development Report* was released at the "Chinese Cross-border E-commerce Export Brand Value Forum—Great Changes Cultivate Outrun Brands" hosted by KZTON, and the "Top 30 Recommended Chinese Cross-border E-commerce Outrun Brands List" was launched. The Institute provides a positive atmosphere for creating and managing outrun brands of Chinese manufacturing.

4 Epilogue

Innovation is the first driving force to lead the development. Intellectual property rights play an important role in stimulating innovation, building brands, regulating market order and expanding opening up to the outside world. In October 2021, the State Council issued the *National Intellectual Property Protection and Use Plan for the 14th Five-Year Plan Period*, which plans and deploys work for comprehensively strengthening intellectual property protection and efficiently promoting the use of intellectual property. According to Gao Jinjun, founder of KZTON, intellectual property rights will become the core asset of Chinese enterprises going abroad, and the internationalization and globalization of Chinese enterprises will inevitably lead to the fast development of international brands. Cross-border intellectual property services institution, represented by KZTON, should continue to play an important role in promoting the global competitiveness of Chinese manufacturing and high-quality development of the cross-border e-commerce industry.

References

Cifnews.com. (2019, May). *KZTON Outrun Brand Institute released the report of top 30 cross-border export e-commerce brands in china in 2019*. https://www.cifnews.com/article/44288.

The Paper. (2022, January). *Zhejiang E-commerce Standard Technology Committee promotes the release of Cross-Border E-Commerce Terminology in the National Group Standard Information Platform!* https://m.thepaper.cn/baijiahao_16234925.

Zhejiang News APP. (2017, September). *KZTON: A "good assistant" for the maintenance of intellectual property rights abroad*. https://zj.zjol.com.cn/news.html?id=758273&ismobilephone=1&t=1550961733143.

Stitch Fix DTC Business Model Innovation Path Based on Data Driven

Wenhua Li and Lu Sun

1 Introduction

Due to the new demand of the world, brand owners are also facing new requirements. The group of Generation Z (born in 1995–2010) has formed large-scale consumption power. They pursue personalized and unpopular consumption, as well as humanized shopping experience. The development of new consumption models has been promoted by the technology of e-commerce big data, endowing businesses with more choices to innovate distribution models, and establish close contacts with consumers through multiple channels. In that case, a business model, namely direct to consumer (DTC), has emerged. Data, "new consumption", "individuality and customization", etc. are the driving forces of DTC model innovation. The convenience of goods directly reaching the consumer end has been realized through big data technology, digital scene, and accurate channels. The rapid development of e-commerce and social networks has led to an unprecedented amount of fashion data and a move towards a data-driven model for decision-making in the clothing industry (Shi & Yang, 2020). Some data information, such as users' purchase preferences, types and sizes, has been recorded by online platform. Internet enterprises have accumulated many network behavior data of users in the daily operation process (Zhang, 2021). With the help of data algorithms on the platform, enterprises can analyze users' behavior and identify their needs and preferences. The penetration of data science in the process of fashion clothing development, operation management and marketing management can provide business decision-making direction for enterprises, keep up with market demand, grasp popular trends, innovate business models, promote clothing enterprises to

W. Li (✉) · L. Sun
Business School, Taizhou University, Taizhou, China

Alibaba Business School, Hangzhou Normal University, Hangzhou, China

J. Zhang et al. (eds.), *Innovation of Digital Economy*, Management for Professionals,
https://doi.org/10.1007/978-981-99-1741-9_21

implement differentiation strategies and open new markets, thus moving towards "Blue Ocean Strategy".

The case study of Stitch Fix business model is based on secondary data obtained from relevant research reports, academic papers, Internet literature, company websites, and speeches made by company leaders. Relevant theoretical models are used to clarify the logical structure of a large amount of data, to organize and elaborate, and to think about the theoretical analysis.[1]

2 Overview of DTC Model

DTC (Direct To Consumer) originated in the United States. It means that the brand directly interacts with consumers through its own official channels without passing through dealerships or intermediate platforms (The valuation is 3 billion! Clothing e-commerce stitch fix plays "Blind box marketing", 2020) to promote the purchase. DTC brand usually sells only online and focuses on a certain vertical category (Wikipedia). The initial originators of DTC brands were two postgraduate students from Stanford Graduate School of Business, who founded the fashion menswear brand BONOBOS in 2007. The dividing point of DTC brand development was in 2010, with the opening of fashion clothing brands Everlane and Stitch Fix. From 2007 to 2017, DTC brand in the United States developed rapidly and is now in a stable development period.

In terms of the choice of e-commerce channels, there have been a clear differentiation between domestic and foreign DTC brands. In the United States, for example, most of the foreign DTC brands are operated in the form of independent stations, while in China, third-party integrated e-commerce (Alibaba, JD.COM, etc.) is still the key position for online sales, and more and more attention is paid to the private traffic of social media for user operation and layout. There are not many independent brands e-commerce. The Chinese DTC brand has grown up with the development of social media in recent years and really emerged on a large scale after 2014, such as HFP, Nattitude, and Perfect Diary, which launched in November 2020. To some extent, Xiaomi is also a DTC brand born in the same period, and its measures to sell mobile phones through direct marketing platforms is completely consistent with the DTC peers in the United States. China's e-commerce platforms have a relatively large voice. Until around 2016, the emergence of social e-commerce platforms such as Tiktok revealed the trend of China's DTC brand, but the independent station model has not been well developed. Those who can establish direct contact with users and sell goods directly through all channels on

[1] This case was funded by the following projects: The Soft Science Program of Zhejiang Provincial Science and Technology Department(2023C35076); Regional Program of National Natural Science Foundation of China (71,962,013); Humanities and Social Sciences Research Project of Ministry of Education (19YJC630146); Taizhou Philosophy and Social Sciences Planning Major Project (22GHZ02); Hangzhou Philosophy and Social Sciences Planning (Z21JC100); Zhejiang Provincial Basic Public Benefit-oriented Research Plan Project (LY22G02005).

Tmall, Tiktok, Bilibili and Little Red Book. The DTC brands in China that are doing better include the beauty category of Florasis and Perfect Diary. On the whole, DTC model is not mature enough at present. DTC in China can be a marketing method of private domain operation. The core competence of Chinese DTC brand is marketing, and data insight is still lacking.

2.1 DTC Model and Its Characteristics

(1) **Essence of DTC model**

The essence of DTC model is a new business model in which branded goods are directly sold to consumers, and consumer demand can be delivered directly to the brand side (The valuation is 3 billion! Clothing e-commerce stitch fix plays "Blind box marketing", 2020). DTC's success path and key elements lie in the feedback and redesign of consumer demand and experience. The core of DTC brand is the operation of the customer base, not the traffic and sales-oriented operation. Those brands that grow up by operating customers are pure DTC. Key opinion leader (KOL) is used to collect demands and suggestions, and then complete product upgrading iteration or innovative R&D. Keep close to consumers and establish data introduction channels or data platforms, thus completing the creation of branded products, consumption experience and weekly management by using data. The purpose of DTC is to deeply interact in the private domain.

(2) **Type and characteristics of DTC model**

At present, DTC has three models. The first is the omni-channel direct retail mode, such as Uniqlo, which reaches target customers through online and offline multiple channels, and builds its own mobile mall, WeChat mini program, and Tmall flagship store to establish a global marketing channel to attract traffic to the brand's private domain for user activation (Uniqlo DTC mode omni channel retail, 2021). The second is the direct sales model, such as that of Amway, whose core is to enable distributors to establish direct contact with users. The third is the membership model, such as Stitch Fix, which enables users to establish strong links with brands through product mechanisms and play mechanisms. The essence of the first two is to "push" the brand to the user, which is not a pure DTC mode. Membership system is to "pull" consumers to the brand. The brand should become a manufacturer, commodity operator and customer spokesperson who can create trust with customers and create unique value for them, and customized according to their demands.

The DTC model is pure or not mainly depends on whether there are various data touchpoints set up in the complete user experience chain to contact and interact with customers, and whether the feedback obtained from these contacts is used to gain insight into user demands? Is there a value and emotional interaction with the customer? The brand must follow the users, create value for them and build their trust in the brand. The core of DTC lies in consumer demand and the relationship between brand and consumer. Digitalization is its means, and removing middlemen is just its appearance (What is DTC mode DTC brand success secret analysis, 2021). Many DTC brands are good at digital marketing, passing on brand information through social media, short videos, KOL/KOC and other channels, and quickly establishing brand/new product awareness.

2.2 Data Driving Force and Operation Process of DTC Model

The advantage of DTC model is that it emphasizes consumer centered interaction and pays attention to consumer behavior, lifestyle and experience, which requires the establishment of a series of data driven capabilities (DTC mode takes advantage of the wind to bring about rapid changes in new consumption & new brands, 2021). Only by mastering more accurate data, timely insight into consumers' shopping motivation and behavior, and timely response to changes and adjust business, can brands maintain sustainable competitiveness. The success of DTC brand is inseparable from service providers who understand business and have strong data technology capabilities. Data is the core element of DTC, and data technology is the driving force for the development of DTC model, which runs through the whole business model. Brands need to use big data and artificial intelligence technology to complete data collection, data building, data application, and service modeling capability to achieve DTC business. The advantage of DTC is that it drives channel demand in the reverse direction, avoids being priced out of the channel, improves the brand's controllability of product flow, masters end-customer data assets, establishes a data science system, improves the accuracy and efficiency of product development and marketing, and improves customer service efficiency by pulling end-customer demand, which in turn improves profit margins ("Why the perfect diary becomes popular" DTC mode practice behind analysis, 2020).

The DTC model requires brands to innovate opportunities around the four links of the value chain, including the R&D and manufacturing side (data side), the production and supply side, the marketing side and the service experience side (delivery side). The first is to involve users deeply in the development, increasing brand loyalty and word-of-mouth communication. The second is to combine user demand and product attributes through segmentation strategy to find the best integrating point for precise development according to user demand. The third is to graft the brand on the things that consumers themselves like, conduct precise correlation and flexibly implant the brand in the hearts of consumers. The fourth is to switch the frequency on the supply side of production to individualized production with low volume of high frequencies. The fifth is to consider from the perspective of the channel and the user, and the systematic design of marketing scenarios is used to stimulate consumer interest in consumption. The operation process of the data-centric direct-to-consumer DTC model is shown in Fig. 1.

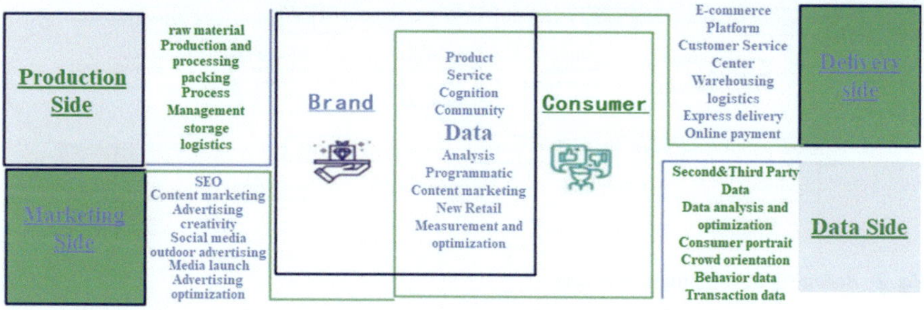

Fig. 1 DTC model operation driving force and process (from Baidu Encyclopedia)

3 Company Profile

(1) **Basic information**

Stitch Fix is an American DTC apparel retail brand founded in San Francisco's Silicon Valley that provides an e-commerce platform for clothing recommendation services and personalized styling with a combination of data-driven, machine-learning algorithms, and human-assisted judgment by design stylists (The valuation is 3 billion! Clothing e-commerce stitch fix plays "Blind box marketing", 2020), and its model fully demonstrates its data-driven characteristics. In more than 10 years of development, it has maintained its position as a leading enterprise for subscription e-commerce business, achieving positive cash flow in only 2 years. Unlike most e-commerce companies, Stitch Fix sells not only merchandise, but also its personal styling services done with the power of algorithms and data technology to help customers find the clothes they like. Stitch Fix offers two types of apparel brands, one designed in-house and one co-branded, and it has more than 1,000 co-branded brands in the United States.

(2) **Development history**

The founder, Katrina Lake, established Stitch Fix in 2011 after graduating from Harvard with the original intention of using technology to improve fashion retail and dedicating herself to providing women with a good match of clothes from various brands through algorithms, and received an angel investment of USD750,000 from Steve Anderson in the first round. Katrina Lake's entrepreneurial journey was by no means a smooth one, as she encountered rejection from more than 20 venture capital firms while searching for Series B funding, and was once unable to make payroll in 2012, before securing USD2 million in funding from Anderson. In early 2013, Stitch Fix received a USD12 million Series B investment from Benchmark Fund, ranked #1 on the New York Times Venture Capital list, for 100,000 sales. Successfully received USD25 million in Series C follow-on funding from Benchmark in 2014. Stitch Fix became profitable at the end of 2014, achieved full-year

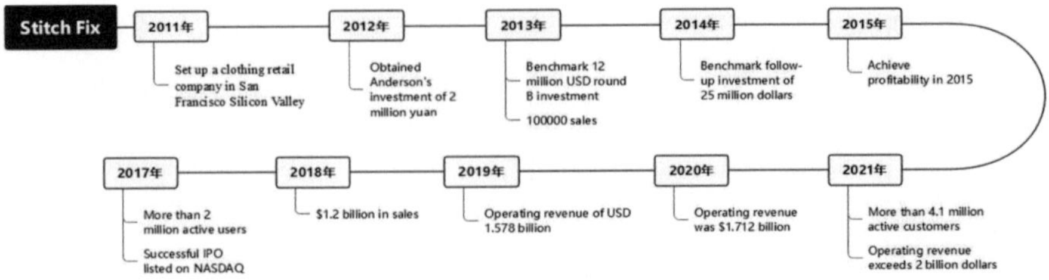

Fig. 2 Stitch fix development timeline

profitability in 2015, generated USD790 million in revenue in 2016, and had 2 million active users by November 2017, when Stitch Fix officially went public on NASDAQ to raise USD120 million. Since its IPO, the company has achieved revenue growth of more than 20% for seven consecutive quarters. Generated USD1.2 billion in sales in 2018 and reinvented the USD334 billion U.S. apparel industry with highly groundbreaking sales. Revenue for 2019 has reached USD1.58 billion and the number of active customers on the platform has grown to 3.2 million. Sales for the third quarter of 2019 increased USD408.9 million, or 29%. Operating income is USD 2.497 billion with increase by 5.81% on year-on-year basis. Stitch Fix reported net sales of USD536 million in the third quarter of fiscal 2021, up 44% year-over-year. Net revenue per active user was USD481, up 3% compared to the previous quarter. Stitch Fix reported its fiscal quarter after hours on December 7, 2021, with the company's revenue increasing to USD581 million (compared to expectations of USD571 million), up 19% from last year, beating Wall Street's expectations of USD571 million, and active users up 11% year-over-year to 4.18 million, with a growth history as shown in Fig. 2.

4 Stitch Fix's DTC Model and Composition

4.1 Elements of Platform Business Model

Harvard professors Johnson and Christensen constructed a model of the four elements of business models, namely, value proposition, profitability model, key resources, and key processes, with technological innovation as the core (Johnson, 2008). The four elements are interconnected and synergistic, and a significant change in any one of them will have an impact on the whole and the other elements. The case uses a four-factor model to analyze the Stitch Fix business model, and the framework diagram is shown in Fig. 3.

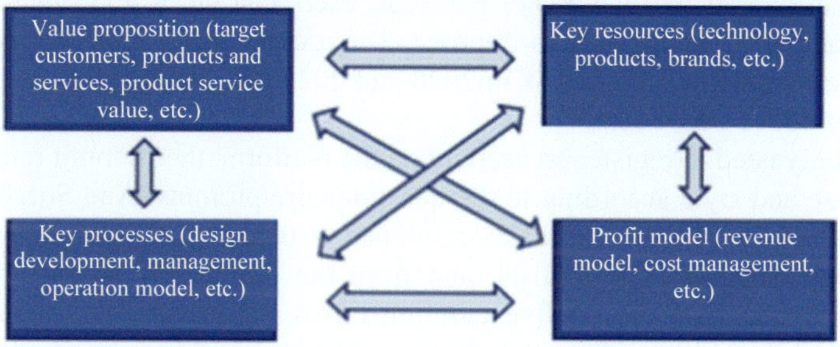

Fig. 3 Johnson and Christensen's four-factor model of business models

4.2 Customer Value Proposition

The components of Stitch Fix's customer value proposition include target customers, products and services, and product value.

(1) Target customers

When Stitch Fix was first established, the market was targeted at busy professional women for whom it provided a recommendation service. Consumers who don't have time to shop online, shop online with unsatisfactory results, or shop online for clothes that don't fit well are one of Stitch Fix's main target customers and are in immediate need. Private customizers who like personalized and unique clothing are two of its main target customers. As the platform continues to grow, Stitch Fix has expanded its business scope from initially providing clothing products and services only for working women to now covering multiple consumer groups of women, men, and children, and providing special services such as plus-size and maternity clothes (Dai, 2020). In terms of developing international markets, Stitch Fix has successfully developed its first international market by launching a clothing recommendation service in the United Kingdom for the first time in 2019 and opening a warehouse in Atlanta.

(2) Product and service

In addition to recommending personalized clothing products, Stitch Fix also offers a clothing "subscription" service to meet the needs of busy working people for personalized clothing. The unboxing experience of a consumer subscription to an e-commerce "box" is similar to the unboxing experience of a blind box, providing an emotional value through the customer's expectation of subscribing to a "box". In such a service model, consumers concede part of their independent choice of goods to algorithms and platform stylists to help them make shopping decisions, saving consumers the mental cost and time cost of purchase decisions and providing customers with convenience. Stitch Fix launched a paid subscription system, charging an annual fee of USD49 per year, users can get a good match of five products at any time, not only to improve user stickiness and increase the average value of user spending, Stitch Fix in 2020 and 2021 each active user generated net revenue of about USD500.

Users only need to register an account on the platform, then submit relevant data such as size and style according to the questionnaire prompts. And Stitch Fix's AI algorithm will learn from the data, combined with the matching suggestions of professional designers and stylists, and from the perspective of preference and professional matching, select five clothing boxes for users (The valuation is 3 billion! Clothing e-commerce stitch fix plays "Blind Box Marketing", 2020), from which customers can choose their favorite clothing, pay for it, and return and exchange free of charge. The AI algorithm will learn based on the user's selection results, continuously and iteratively optimize the algorithm model, and improve the accuracy of recommendation. Stitch Fix algorithm model knows customers' preferences, it will customize the style according to customers' taste, fitness and price range, and mail personalized products suitable for them, and give customers gift cards or gifts. In addition, Stitch Fix provides a direct purchase service "Shop Your Look" for purchasing members. Members can directly place orders for their matching clothes through the official platform, and they can shop immediately.

(3) Product and service value

By gaining a deeper understanding of the user, Stitch Fix dives deeper into specific product ranges and user groups, combining technology with the style of seasoned fashion experts. Through Elevate, designers are able to access Stitch Fix resources and learn data insights as well as artistic and scientific methods to inspire and drive change in apparel retail across the industry through resources, influence and innovation. Stitch Fix not only offers carefully curated programs to help customers save time, but also continues to develop the customer's personal style, offering a suitable size and type of style for each individual. It has 100 brands of Plus styles, helps more than 30 brand partners expand their sizing offerings, and offers all private label sizes and inclusive styles in sizes from small to plus size. The clothing products offered by Stitch Fix range in price from over USD20 to several hundred dollars, and the clothing recommendation service is priced at USD20, enabling consumers to enjoy personalized recommendations at a lower price (Dai, 2020). One of the founding philosophies of Stitch Fix is to make one-on-one personalized clothing recommendations available to most common consumers. Stitch Fix supports social justice. Starting from 2020, it will donate USD500,000 in five years to promote social justice, of which USD100,000 will be used to support black lives organizations, support the elimination of systematic racism and other injustices, and provide financial assistance and guidance to some black designers. In 2020, it launched Elevate, a grant, student subsidies and mentorship program designed to support the next wave of entrepreneurs of color.

4.3 Key Resources

Stitch fix's key resources consist of technical resources, team resources and brand resources.

(1) Technical resources

Stitch Fix is not only a clothing e-commerce platform, but also a data technology company, where technical resources are the most critical resources in its business model, running through every part of the model's components. Stitch Fix aims to bring personalized design to the masses on a large scale through the use of data and machine learning. The "Style Shuffle" function on the platform enables the collection of large amounts of data, and users' purchasing behavior data on the platform will be input into Stitch Fix's algorithm, which helping it better understand customer preferences based on different factors such as age or location. Stitch Fix collects data in three parts. The first is user information data, including user location, body type, age, social networking site information, consumption behavior and price affordability; the second is product information data, including brand, pricing, color, type, size, pattern and some design details; the third is the product feedback data, including the user's direct evaluation of the product, the record of returning and changing the product. As user's interaction increases, the site continues to expand the database and improve machine simulation capabilities. Stitch Fix is a great example of how online brands can leverage data and use it to continuously improve the online customer experience. In order to get a unique personalized experience and gift, customers are willing to provide personal information as well as product feedback and reviews. Due to Stitch Fix's high level of commitment to the service, 80% of customers leave feedback on returned products. Stitch Fix uses data analytics and consumer understanding to achieve higher inventory turnover, return on investment and lower return rates while meeting users' personalized needs. While data is at the core of Stitch Fix, its success is closely tied to the company's thousands of stylists, who make adjustments based on user profiles after the data model provides initial product matching suggestions.

(2) Algorithm and team resources

Stitch Fix's entire activities process is accomplished through three teams working together: the algorithm team, the engineer team, and the matchmaker team. Stitch Fix has a dedicated algorithm team to inform the design of its own apparel brands and has hired a chief arithmetic judge to oversee the data science team. Teams of algorithms and engineers process huge amounts of consumer data and product data to filter the most suitable clothing from the inventory through a series of algorithms, and teams of stylists make further selections based on the products selected by these two teams. In terms of partners, in addition to technical collaboration with Stanford University and the Stanford Industrial Alliance, Stitch Fix also works with hundreds of apparel brand parties all (Dai, 2020) to provide ample supplies. Work with thousands of stylists from across the U.S. who are trendsetters and fashion experts who understand the style and evolving needs of our clients. In short, Stitch Fix's success = user submission and feedback data + product data + continuously improved recommendation algorithms + personalized tuning by stylists = more satisfying user experience + higher repurchase rates + higher recommendation success rates.

(3) Brand resources

Stitch Fix has its own design and production brand, its DTC platform through data analysis, found that many users have some needs that are ignored by partner brands, to create their own original brand for some market product vacancies, and customize some new styles for specific customer groups, currently 20% of the platform is designed and produced by Stitch Fix itself, which is a unique service of Stitch Fix compared to other clothing e-commerce platforms. Stitch Fix has been able to increase sales by mining the database for potential information about users and catering to their preferences in detail. Stitch Fix selects different partnerships through resources and influence to ensure a sustainable and diverse brand. Stitch Fix partners with 1000 + brands to pre-order products from these brand owners at low prices. The website constantly provides product feedback suggestions from users to partner brands, bringing accurate design feedback to partner brands and fully understanding the changing consumer preferences. Brands that partner with Stitch Fix have access to the data it collects, and Stitch Fix provides each partner brand with its own "vendor portal" that gives them access to sales feedback. With Stitch Fix data, partner brands improve and develop their products based on feedback about fit, size, and design, increasing sales through Stitch Fix and other channels.

4.4 Key Activities' Processes and Models of Stitch Fix

The elements of Stitch Fix's key activities model are composed of customer data management mode, digital marketing management mode, the development and operation mode of permeating data science, and data based logistics management mode, as shown in Fig. 4. Stitch Fix data science (DS) permeates every module of activities processes. Stitch Fix is driven by data in terms of development, product selection, sales and inventory optimization. It combines data science with stylists, and always uses data technologies to create personalized styling services and product recommendation services with a unique experience for consumers.

(1) Customer data management mode
    ① Pre-sales customer management mode. Stitch Fix users are quizzed on their personal style. Stitch Fix users are asked to fill out a form that details size, style preference, clothing needs and price acceptability. They are asked to provide a total of 50 pieces of information, including weight,

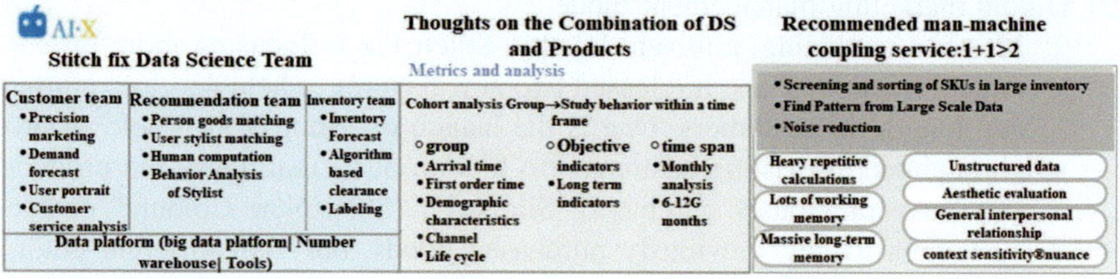

Fig. 4 Integration of stitch fix data science and key activities (Data from 51CTO ("What exactly did Stitch Fix, which uses algorithms to sell clothes & do right", 2019))

underwear size and links to their social networking sites. After filling in, a personal data file will be created for each user to precipitate the basic data, which will be used to record all data updates and changes of the user (The valuation is 3 billion! Clothing e-commerce stitch fix plays "Blind Box Marketing", 2020). Stitch Fix will produce a series of potential matching models based on the above information. Later, the company's stylists (mostly part-time) will select and match from more than 200 clothing brands that have cooperated with Stitch Fix to design "personal wear" for customers.

② In-sales customer data management mode. Besides personalized elements, Stitch Fix's appeal also lies in its convenience. Stitch Fix removes the customer's decision-making process, but still provides them with clothes and accessories that the customer would have chosen. Stitch Fix uses a subscription system to mail clothes to users regularly, and customers can also specify the mailing cycle time. After the registration is completed, the customer will receive a package regularly, including five sets of clothes decided and matched by the recommendation algorithm and real stylists, as well as a customer's opinion manual.

③ After-sales customer data management mode. Stitch Fix solicits customer feedback and accurately measures all dimensions of clothing, constantly collecting and accumulating customer feedback data to continuously refine its algorithmic model to better match customer interests and preferences. After receiving the product box, the customer will get the specific clothing matching method and reason carefully made by stylists for the individual. The customer will also fill in the feedback according to the price, style, upper body effect and other indicators of the clothing box. After that, the Stitch Fix platform collects customer feedback information in time, establishes a personal user-specific likes and dislikes database, predicts the type characteristics of customer concerns and preferences, and makes the recommended products more accurate, improves the repurchase rate, and reduces the user turnover rate. This can also lay the foundation for the subsequent production of more clothing types, expand the type of brand, enhance the ability to provide personalized style on a large scale, and reduce the cost of personalized services.

(2) Digital marketing management mode

① Member marketing, cultivate loyalty. Stitch Fix is focusing more on customer retention. Thus, it released two new features to help develop returned and long-term customers. One is the launch of "Shop Your Look", a program aimed at existing customers to find products that match the products they have previously purchased. Similarly, "Shop New Colours" enables customers to buy previously purchased goods, but with different colors, prints or patterns. The second is Stitch Fix's reinvention of the online shopping experience to foster customer loyalty through the "discovery element. "Therefore, customer awareness will translate into direct purchase motivation or loyalty to Stitch Fix's individual brands. Stitch Fix also uses the element of surprise brought by surprise boxes to entice customers to make repeat purchases and increase user stickiness.

② Emphasis on word-of-mouth marketing, play the value of KOC/KOL. KOC (Key Opinion Consumer) generally refers to friends and followers who can influence their consumption behavior. Compared with KOL (Key Opinion Leader), the former has the advantages of being more vertical and cheaper. Compared with the massive investment in data algorithms, Stitch Fix attaches importance to low-cost, accurate and effective marketing investment, and tends to KOC word-of-mouth marketing. Through the word-of-mouth effect of customers and mutual recommendation among friends or followers, it tries to avoid large-scale platform or offline publicity. Stitch Fix shares the "unpacking experience" with users on YouTube to obtain clicks and interactions from netizens. This advanced blind box improves the curiosity index of onlookers and increases the order volume (The valuation is 3 billion! Clothing e-commerce stitch fix plays "Blind box marketing", 2020). Stitch Fix directly links consumers through Facebook, Instagram, YouTube and other social media channels. Lake, the founder of Stitch Fix, is very active in interacting with customers on Facebook and actively carrying out social marketing. According to Yotpo's research, about 98% of respondents said that customer reputation and reviews on social platforms are important influencing factors for other consumers to buy DTC brands.

③ Carry out personalized marketing with the help of algorithms. Stitch Fix's success depends in large part on its data strengths and machine learning algorithms. With the help of algorithms, DTC mode gives full play to the personalized marketing of precise interaction. The algorithm will help the platform know whether a customer's life is busy or idle. Considering the current situation of customer expectations, the algorithm will bring customers unexpected clothing collocation recommendations and personalized marketing experiences in communication with customers. Due to the discount promotion, crazy advertising and platform clothing recommendations in the online and offline clothing industry, Stitch Fix also needs to solve three major problems: how to expand its customer base, maintain user stickiness, and improve the accuracy of data recommendations (The valuation is 3 billion! Clothing e-commerce Stitch Fix plays "Blind box marketing", 2020). Stitch Fix's next step will be to accelerate digital decision-making by using AI data algorithms to guide competitive business decisions.

(3) The development and operation mode of permeating data science

① Development and operation of a personalized recommendation system. Stitch Fix's personalized recommendation system begins to analyze, reason and actively recommend clothes to customers when users register and submit information about their height, weight and personal preferences. After continuous accumulation and inference learning, Stitch Fix stores a lot of customers' different kinds of basic information, style preference information and wearable attribute data of habit purchases, making decision-making results more accurate. In practice, the system will run different matching algorithms based on the data to produce an inventory ranking for a particular customer. Filtering steps are used to remove unattractive items that have previously been recommended to customers. For clothing that is accepted by customers, the algorithm also calculates how much they like it. The system also predicts the likelihood of recommending similar clothing to new customers based on the feedback or evaluation of the purchased clothing from different types of customers. The system also calculates the number of people who share the customer's preferences like the product. Stitch Fix's recommendation system personalizes innovations to its business model in addition to using classic coordination filtering algorithms. The recommendatory system will judge similar products based on the types of products the user has returned before, delete them synchronously, and then execute various algorithms. The artificial designers make a new round of product selection based on the products recommended by the machine algorithm. Therefore, the accuracy and novelty of the Stitch Fix recommendation system are relatively high.

② Iteration of personalized services through user data feedback. In order to accumulate more data on users' style preferences, Stitch Fix developed an IOS-based app "Style Shuffle", which allows users to open the app and receive an invitation to rate a set of outfit matching images every day. This program can train the model algorithm to improve the accuracy of recommendation, and also attract users to return to the Stitch Fix platform, increasing the users' open rate and repurchase rate (Under the Netflix algorithm, Stitch Fix in the clothing industry played the advanced blind box, & earned USD3 billion, 2020). The Stitch Fix backend algorithm makes preliminary recommendations based on multiple sources of information, such as season, customer's personal situation and clothes, which are then reviewed by stylists based on their own experience, and after accumulation, Stitch Fix has more than 50 types of users' personal information such as weight, underwear size and so on. The platform also stores information from partner brands, including 100–150 points of information on clothing, subdivided into color, sleeve length, garment length and other types of information. The Stitch Fix platform has a "mixed-effects model" machine algorithm that uses a trained neural network algorithm to generate vector images based on popular clothing images, customer feedback and purchase history, calculates the cosine similarity between the vector and the in-stock product vector, and then scores them according to various algorithms to produce a composite score ranking, and recommends the top-ranked clothing to stylists for redesign and optimization (Chen & Li, 2018).

③ New product development and service recommendation. In terms of new product development, Stitch Fix has developed a clothing attribute liking calculation model, which can determine the degree to which an attribute set is liked, and the system pushes the attribute set information to designers, who will review and refine and optimize the attribute set based on their experience, design a new generation of clothing styles, then produce them, and finally recommend them to customers, in a continuous cycle of improvement and innovation (Chen & Li, 2018). Stitch Fix's algorithm can match stylists with different types of styles to customers with similar styles based on the history of communication between customers and stylists, customer descriptions and potential style preferences, etc. The algorithm will calculate matching scores for different stylists and customers to match the best stylists for customers (Dai, 2020). A stylist may serve many similar customers to form their own customer base, design clothes for specific customer groups, and create their own brand for Stitch Fix.

④ Demand prediction and matching. Stitch Fix's robot tracks all customer touch points–every delivery, every feedback message, every incoming and outgoing email (Chen & Li, 2018). This data gives the Stitch Fix robot a basis for reasoning. The robot determines different needs based on different states of the customer, builds a state transformation matrix, and a Markov chain model to predict in advance the customer's possible future clothing needs.

(4) Data based logistics management mode

The Stitch Fix algorithm model is used not only in recommendation systems, but also in inventory and distribution management.

(1) Inventory management optimization

In inventory management, Stitch Fix relies on data analysis to flexibly manage inventory, avoid inventory backlogs, and solve the retailer's trouble–inventory problem. The Stitch Fix database records the fine behavioral data of each user, and the system can project the different states of users in different periods, timely predict user demand and update the inventory (Dai, 2020). From product logistics, product inventory to assigning stylists, the platform has a comprehensive data model to simulate scenarios and make reasonable choices. Stitch Fix shall maintain inventory levels before stocking to ensure that the recommendation system and the stylist team have enough stock to select clothes for customers when they need them. Stitch Fix builds a Markov model, which can predict customers' buying needs, restock stocks, arrange clothes and avoid backlogs based on their previous behavior data. Stitch Fix uses a system dynamics model to determine the timing of stocking, predict the amount of clothes ordered and to which warehouses the ordered clothes will be deployed, and determine which backlog of clothes will be disposed of at what time without affecting inventory levels or causing cost increases (Chen & Li, 2018).

(2) Warehousing and distribution optimization
In terms of warehousing and delivery, Stitch Fix has a "delivery warehouse selection model". After a customer places an order, the algorithm team will match the optimal delivery warehouse based on the receiving address and inventory, and the system will calculate each customer and generate a corresponding cost matrix to calculate the cost of shipping to the customer from each warehouse to ensure that the cost of each delivery is the lowest (Dai, 2020), and in terms of delivery, long-term cooperation has been reached with FedEx, UPS and other courier companies.

4.5 Summary Diagram of Stitch Fix's Key Activities' Processes

According to the four aforementioned modules, the key activities' processes diagram of Stitch Fix is summarized in Fig. 5, from which it can be seen that the data management and algorithm model are at the key center of the business process, starting from when users register as members, the data model starts to function to recommend products that meet customers' needs and preferences; the data algorithm model also acts on the inventory and delivery process; external marketing management and new External marketing management and new product development both input data information to the center, acting on model data optimization, and with the help of model algorithms acting on product development innovation and marketing innovation.

4.6 Profit Model

The components of Stitch Fix's profit model consist mainly of a revenue model and cost management.

(1) Revenue model

In terms of revenue model, Stitch Fix's main business income comes from two sources. For one thing, clothing sales business, more than half of the goods sold by the platform from other brand suppliers, through the purchase of clothing, shoes and hats and other goods from brand suppliers, and then recommended to customers through the DTC platform model operation, to earn the purchase and sale

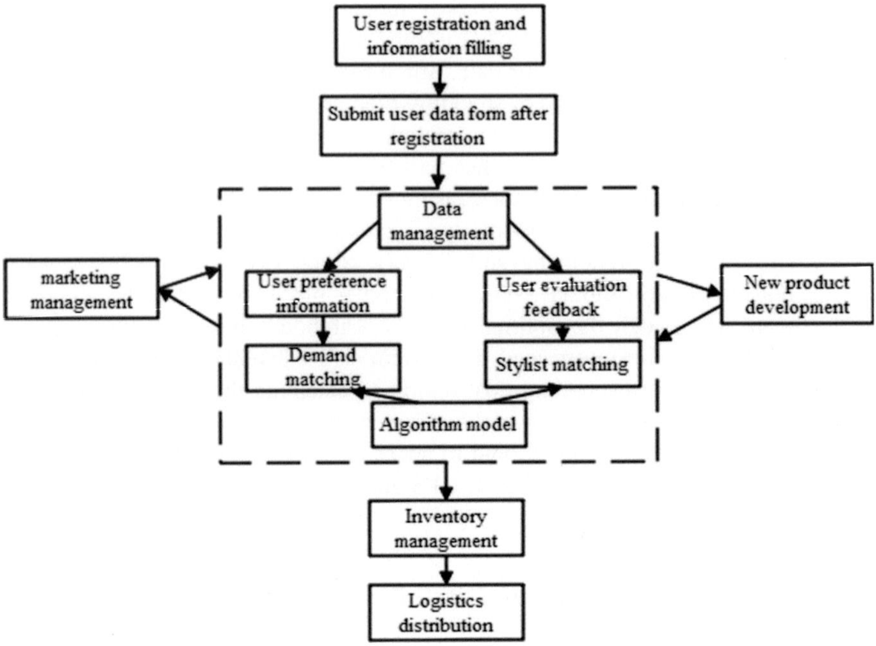

Fig. 5 Stitch fix's business process chart

price difference, and about twenty percent of the goods are Stitch Fix's own production and sales of clothing brands; And for another, Stitch Fix's revenue comes from the clothing recommendation service fee, and the platform provides personal matching service for each customer with clothing matching needs and charges a USD20 service recommendation fee (Dai, 2020). Through the DTC marketing model to attract traffic, the platform's click rate, attention rate, and user volume are increasing, customer demand is increasing, and revenue from clothing sales and clothing recommendation service is increasing.

(2) Cost management

Cost management, Stitch Fix cost mainly from the cost of its algorithm team, the algorithm team is also the core part of its business process, the initial construction costs are very high, but with the increase in platform awareness, the number of partner brands continue to increase, the number of platform goods and members greatly increased, the platform construction costs account for a smaller and smaller proportion. In addition, in order to control labor costs, Stitch Fix mostly employs relatively low cost part-time stylists. On the side supplier, Stitch Fix is able to use its own data to provide value to apparel designers, wholesalers and retailers. Traditionally, it has been difficult for designers, wholesalers and retailers to know why an inventory is selling poorly, but Stitch Fix is able to provide this information and use it to get a lower purchase price.

5 Analysis of Advantages and Disadvantages of Stitch Fix

5.1 Advantages

Innovative business model is the source of sustainable competitive advantage and an effective way for enterprises to adopt differentiation strategy to avoid homogeneous competition. Stitch Fix is one of the most successful independent platforms in the apparel category using data to bring unique experiences and innovative product services to customers, and is a successful representative of digital and model innovation in the garment industry. The main advantages of its business model are: Firstly, although Stitch Fix does not offer clothes exclusively, nor is it the cheapest and fastest logistics company, it faces competition from fast fashion and general retail department stores, but its recommendation system has higher prediction accuracy and a higher degree of personalization and novelty. The Stitch Fix advantages lie in its good understanding of consumers, knowing what is best for them. The values provided and the problems solved are how to find those things that are best for the customer. Secondly, Stitch Fix machine algorithm and data team has strong data collection and analysis capabilities. Through the continuous accumulation of user demand data, so that it has a richer user data than competitors, and by converting the many data into different styles and types of clothing, to ensure the diversity of products, it can quickly meet customer demand, to provide a guarantee for diversified sales model.

As an example of a brand that is constantly learning, Stitch Fix understands and anticipates the needs of its customers as well as better delivering value. With its core data technology, Stitch Fix is better able to adapt to consumer upgrades than traditional e-commerce retailers, adapting to new consumer needs for customization and better dynamic optimization to reconfigure its business model.

5.2 Problems with Stitch Fix

Stitch Fix DTC model operation based on data science and technology provide consumers with a private, exclusive, customized, and novel shopping experience, but its operating model also faces some challenges. On the one hand, its model is more complicated in attracting new customers to register and complete the personal clothing preference questionnaire filling procedure than the traditional e-commerce direct order model, making consumers more reluctant to take the time to register as members, which may cause the platform to lose the usage of new users and lose a large number of possible potential users. To change this, it may require more costly online and offline advertising campaigns. On the other hand, due to the core resource of Stitch Fix model is data, so the data algorithm and data technology team's judgment and prediction of consumer needs determine the accuracy of the products it develops or recommends. If the data acquisition is not rich and accurate enough and the algorithm optimization is not perfect, it will lead to the data team's budget and customer needs are not matched accurately enough, which will affect customer trust, affect the repurchase rate, and will cause the loss of old customers, and affect the sales volume and future development of the platform.

5.3 Problem Solving Strategies

In response to its growth dilemma, Stitch Fix has taken several steps to focus on pulling in new customers and increasing the value of old customers.

(1) Stitch Fix is mainly attracting in new customers by increasing its advertising efforts. In order to better guarantee the success of the IPO and to have more financial security afterwards, advertising expenditures increased almost three times in 2017 compared to 2016. In 2017, Stitch Fix also tried TV advertising for the first time, but it did not take a wide net approach for this, but relied on the product to do a natural conversion approach, using data analysis technology to accurately focus on prospective customers for placement, giving priority to the quality of users. In terms of advertising on Facebook, it has also launched advertisements in other countries to test the possibility of expanding its business in other countries, to do preliminary testing and user feedback, and to prepare for the next step of expanding into these markets.
(2) Enhance the value of old users mainly through the following ways. First, the introduction of direct buy method. Users can enjoy the direct buy mode in addition to the personalized recommendation mode, and can directly add the clothes they like, which is the company's attempt to break the scale bottleneck of the "recommendation + subscription" model with direct buy. For new users, the direct buy mode, before using the product, can better improve the first order rate, the USD49 annual subscription fee or USD20 styling fee creat a conversion barrier, while once the breakthrough of the user's first order, often leads to more purchases. Secondly, Stitch Fix has cooperated with more brands to increase SKUs, and currently it has obtained cooperation with 1000 + brands and also added more SKUs to enrich users' available choices, which have a certain effect on enhancing user value (Stitch Fix official website xxxx). Thirdly, keep optimizing the recommendation algorithm and increasing the number of stylists. Stitch Fix is as a subscription/membership model for verticals, and there will always be a certain ceiling of growth. Hence, Stitch Fix will most likely combine further category expansion and expansion into new areas.

6 Inspiration Brought by the Case

Stitch Fix proves the great future of data science and technology to transform and upgrade traditional industries. It uses data science and technology to transform and even subvert the traditional garment business model, and its data-driven DTC model has implications for the model innovation of the garment industry in China's digital scene. Stitch Fix platform focuses on business model innovation, and has created a unique digital business model in the industry, which is a reference for the innovation of clothing e-commerce model in China. Many domestic garment enterprises are still in the exploratory stage of DTC business model operation, and garment platforms can learn from Stitch Fix's data-driven DTC operation model. Under the background of big data, the business model of China's apparel e-commerce platform can improve the development and operation process, innovate products and services, improve customized service quality, and fully meet different types of individual needs through data and algorithm innovation. Although the third-party platforms of domestic major e-commerce giants, such as the brand SAINT ANGELO, which settled on "Tmall", have launched online customization services, JD.COM has successively launched personalized customization services of "JD·Made" and customized clothing services of free brands "JD Made". However, on the whole, there are some problems in the customization business of apparel e-commerce platforms in China. First, the cost of online customization is high. Generally, the actual customization is completed through online ordering and offline physical stores. Second, the types of customized products available for selection released on the e-commerce platform are not diverse enough to keep pace with the change of personalized demand. Third, most consumers' online clothing customization habits have not yet taken shape. The main reason is that the interactive communication between platform merchants and customers is not convenient enough, many clothing pictures are different from real objects, clothing details are not accurate enough, and personalized shopping guides need to be improved. China's apparel e-commerce platform can learn from Stitch Fix subscription system, directly communicate with consumers through DTC mode, obtain consumer demand preference information, continuously accumulate various data, design more different clothing styles, establish a personalized style library of clothing, so as to launch new products in time, and quickly recommend clothing to customers accurately through data algorithms, creating diversified new products and services for consumers. Cut off the price increase in the process of garment customization as much as possible, so that consumers can experience customized clothing services at a relatively low price. Optimize logistics links through big data, apply data algorithms to further optimize warehouse layout and management, reduce costs, and improve distribution efficiency.

References

Chen, Q., & Li, X. (2018). Stitch fix: Data driven clothing retail company. *Enterprise Management, 38*(7), 99–101.

Dai, Y. (2020). Comparative study on the business models of Chinese and American apparel e-commerce platforms based on big data. (Master's thesis). Jilin University.

DTC mode takes advantage of the wind to bring about rapid changes in new consumption and new brands. (2021). https://www.zgswcn.com/article/202104/202104071326131087.html

Johnson, M. W. (2008). Reinventing your business model. *Harvard Business Review, 86*(11), 50–59.

Shi, Y., & Yang, K. (2020). Analysis of fashion big data. *China Market, 26*(25), 188–189.

Stitch Fix official website. (n.d.). https://www.stitchfix.com/

The valuation is 3 billion! Clothing e-commerce stitch fix plays "Blind box marketing" (2020). http://www.woshipm.com/marketing/3707400.html

Under the Netflix algorithm, Stitch fix in the clothing industry played the advanced blind box, and earned USD3 billion? (2020). https://baijiahao.baidu.com/s?id=1663928240550138131

Uniqlo DTC mode omni channel retail. (2021). https://blog.csdn.net/upskill2018/article/details/117780197

What is DTC mode? DTC brand success secret analysis. (2021). https://zhuanlan.zhihu.com/p/374783119

"What exactly did stitch fix, which uses algorithms to sell clothes, do right?" (2019). https://www.sohu.com/a/343606840_463994

"Why the perfect diary becomes popular"? DTC mode practice behind analysis. (2020). https://www.opp2.com/200413.html

Zhang, X. (2021). Research on business model innovation of clothing customization on big data technology. *Textile Reports, 39*(6), 26–27.

Charity Blockchain: The Practice of the Public Trust by China's No. 1 Public Welfare Digital Platform

Junxin Yan, Minjun Teng, and Shiting Lin

1 Introduction

In recent years, with the increasing maturity of Internet technology and the increasing popularity of Internet concepts, China's public welfare undertakings are changing from traditional public welfare models to new ones. The Internet welfare model has gradually replaced the traditional charity model and become one of the main forms of social welfare. As President Wang of China Public Welfare Research Institute of Beijing Normal University said, "Internet plus public welfare is a revolution in public welfare (Wang, 2016)", this model will undoubtedly become a major trend in the future. Data show that in the past 10 years, the number of Internet users in China has increased from 500 million to 1 billion, and the Internet penetration rate has exceeded 70%. With more than 1 billion Internet users, China has become "the world's largest digital society". Under such a technological background, two seemingly unrelated fields, the Internet and public welfare, have created different sparks. However, this fierce collision brings not only a historic opportunity, but also an unprecedented severe test for public welfare. Since the Internet has the characteristics of low threshold and high efficiency of information dissemination, it undoubtedly increases the possibility of rapid dissemination and amplification of negative information. At first, the "Guo Meimei incident" in 2011 caused a huge uproar on the Internet, causing public doubts and unease about China's public welfare undertakings. Then the "Han Hong Charity Foundation incident" during the COVID-19 pandemic in early 2020 even made the crisis of confidence in public welfare reach its peak. So, how should Internet public welfare overcome the difficulties in the current era of rapid economic development? How should the "Internet plus public welfare" model with Chinese characteristics handle itself?

J. Yan (✉) · M. Teng · S. Lin
School of Economics and Management, Jiliang University, Hangzhou, China

J. Zhang et al. (eds.), *Innovation of Digital Economy*, Management for Professionals,
https://doi.org/10.1007/978-981-99-1741-9_22

2 Being Prepared: Public Trust is in Trouble

2.1 Struggling with Difficulties

Over the past 10 years, China's public welfare sector has developed rapidly and maintained a good momentum of development. While looking at the development process of public welfare in China, it does not show a smooth and upward trend, but has gone through ups and downs. Two of the most serious crises of confidence in our public interest occurred in 2011 and 2020.

On June 20, 2011, a girl named "Guo Meimei baby" who was certified as the "General Manager of the Red Cross Society" on Weibo attracted public attention. She showed off her "luxury life" on Weibo: driving the Maserati sports car, holding birthday parties in villas, and wearing expensive luxury goods. Posts like this have raised strong questions from the public: Is the property of the 20 year old general manager who owns the luxury car and bags related to the "Red Cross"? For a while, various statements related to Guo Meimei and the Red Cross Society were rapidly fermented on the Internet. Some said: "Guo Meimei's high profile allows us to think about the flow direction of China's public welfare capital (Zhihu, 2014)". Although Guo Meimei sent three microblogs to apologize after accepting the investigation, and explained that the title of "General Manager of the Red Cross Society of China" was invented by herself. In the face of public and theoretical doubts, the Red Cross Society did not remain silent, and responded three times in succession, but the effect was not ideal, because the Red Cross simply "explained", but did not release substantive evidence to support.

After the "Guo Meimei incident" went nowhere, public welfare once again became the target of public criticism when the the COVID-19 pandemic situation was most severe in 2020. Han Hong, a famous singer, who ran around for charity during the the COVID-19 pandemic, has been publicly questioned by a celebrity with millions of followers in a series of posts on social media. The core of his query was that Han Hong's public welfare expenditure two years ago was lower than the national requirements. At this moment, the so-called "scandal" of two years ago was brought out to comment and criticize the behavior of Han Hong and other caring people. Someone said: "Just do what you do best, singing can also be helpful, don't mess it up (Zhihu, 2020)!" Even in the end, Han Hong has been recognized by all walks of life and supported by netizens, but it has brought a heavy blow to our public welfare's social credibility.

After experiencing two crises of confidence, a platform called "Shuidichou" came into the public's view and became one of the most successful cases of Internet major illness fund raising platforms. "Shuidichou" can be described as a "timely rain". It provides a new idea and reference model for public trust to a certain extent by means of the acquaintance network between friends on Wechat and the trust between people. However, there are many loopholes in the actual operation of the Shuidichou platform. For example, the Deyun Agency practitioners "Wu Hechen crowdfunding" event, the promotion event, so that the social public opinion continues to ferment on the network, "Shuidichou" platform also fells into doubt. "The project itself is good. Shuidichou provides a good platform for public fundraising, and at the same time, it also transfers donations to families with serious diseases, which effectively solves the urgent need. However, it has to be admitted that there are all kinds of donation fraud news everywhere on the Internet. The main problem lies in the shameless fraudsters, which requires the platform to supervise more effectively to reduce the fault (Zhihu, 2019a)."

It can be seen that the trust system of the traditional public welfare model is not perfect, which arousing the general concern and worry of the public. All of these point to one thing in common: the need to have an in-depth understanding of the demands and concerns of the public, and to build a new public welfare model to solve the existing crisis of trust.

2.2 Identifying the Root Cause and Solving the Problem

Deconstructing the traditional public welfare model, does it really satisfy the demands of users? The traditional public model had been one of the most prevalent operating models before the emergence of Internet public welfare. However, under this model, China's charitable organizations are experiencing a credibility crisis, which has put a tremendous amount of social pressure on the sector as a whole and public welfare organizations specifically. The reason is that the public interest character of public charities determines that the public has the rights to know all kinds of information about public charity. However, in practice, it is impossible to guarantee its security, transparency and objectivity, particularly: Traditional public welfare has long been criticized both inside and outside of the public welfare community for its lack of crisis management capabilities, lack of knowledge regarding the precise flow of donations, lack of knowledge regarding specifics such as their use, and lack of evaluation and donor feedback.

In this context, the primary issue for public welfare is to repair social reputation and regain public trust and support. On the one hand, from the public's point of view, people need a public welfare digital platform with a high level of social trust, a database storing a large amount of information, with features such as true and open, full traceability, etc., to ensure the symmetry of public welfare information and coordinate the nodes of parties that do not trust each other, so as to solve the problem of consensus on mutual trust. How should such a digital platform be constructed?

On the other hand, such a platform must enable public participation and oversight, be able to swiftly adjust its business strategy in response to social pain points, offer open and systematic solutions to public welfare organizations and projects, and accomplish the objectives of complete donation disclosure, documentable processes, traceable information, reachable feedback, and multi-terminal participation. Only by providing these values can such a platform be sustained by the "engine of public trust".

"Charity Blockchain" came into being in respond to this demand. On September 5, 2019, "Charity Blockchain" was officially launched by Alibaba at the 95 Public

Welfare Week Forum, with the plan to build the future infrastructure of transparent public welfare and open it to public welfare organizations on the platform for free. On the day of release, the first landing project of the "Charity Blockchain" program-New Future High School Students was officially released. On December 17, 2019, the first automatic allocation of the Charity Blockchain plan was successful. "Charity Blockchain" goes deep into the field of charity, effectively escorts the destinations of donations, and allows those who should be helped to get due help, thus provide fresh blood to China's traditional public welfare undertakings. So how does it achieve full traceability of donations and practice trust?

3 Preparations: Model Innovation Draws the Blueprint

"The first automatic disbursement, successful!!!" A message with only some words and a screenshot of successful system payment were sent to the public welfare project group on Alibaba Charity Blockchain (Zhihu, 2019b). On that day, the first project of the "Charity Blockchain"—New Future High School Students finished the first automatic disbursement, realizing the first step in combining block-link technology with public welfare, and laying a solid foundation for building a perfect public welfare trust system. The "Charity Blockchain" based on ant blockchain has gradually achieved the whole traceability of donations. Since then, "Charity Blockchain" has devoted itself to the effective storage and display of the whole link information, maximizing the capital efficiency in the implementation of public welfare projects, further enhancing the transparency of public welfare and enhancing the public's confidence in participating in public welfare. For this, Hu Xiaoming, former CEO of Ant Group, once said: "Behind every donation is the trust of participants in the platform. It is our responsibility and mission to ensure openness and transparency and live up to every trust (Hu, 2019)."

3.1 Getting Rid of the Stale and Bringing Forth the Fresh

Blockchain is essentially a "decentralized" shared database, in which data or information is stored with important technical features such as "non-tampering", "openness and transparency" and "traceability". Blockchain enables people to collaborate without geographical restrictions and de-trust, allowing trust between people and trust between people and machines to become trust between machines (Xu, 2019). Therefore, blockchain technology, with the above characteristics, is a natural fit with the Internet plus Public Welfare model, which has a trust crisis, and is suitable for many realistic scenarios in Internet plus Public Welfare. The combination of the two is the only way for the sustainable and healthy development of China's public welfare undertakings in the future. In view of the current development of the Internet, the four major technical functions of blockchain, namely "decentralization", "unchangebility", "openness and transparency" and "traceability", have solved the four common pain points of the Internet plus Public Welfare project, including the cumbersome implementation process, the difficulty in distinguishing the authenticity of information, the difficulty in tracing the flow of funds and the difficulty in supervising the implementation of the process.

(1) Decentralization

The decentralization of public welfare digital platform means that third-party organizations are removed from the donation process and participants in the system are equal, thus upgrading the function of public welfare digital platform from intermediaries to information platforms. Donors and recipients can directly use the platforms to achieve digital "precise docking". By streamlining the step of donations and optimizing the donation and funding process, the loss and cost in the process are greatly reduced, and the public's doubts about the amount and destination of donations are largely eliminated.

(2) Unchangebility

Even without the participation of third-party organizations, the public still cannot have 100% trust in public information. The immutable nature of blockchain information specifically addresses people's concerns. Its unique construction which combine with scientific cryptographic algorithms can ensure the authenticity of information. Once the data is tampered with, the whole system will have a chain reaction, resulting in no progress to the next link. Therefore, after the integration of blockchain technology, the donation information on the platform is real and reliable, and cannot be changed at will, which provides great convenience for the supervision of public welfare undertakings.

(3) Openness and transparency

Now that the veracity of the information is assured, what exactly is available to the public? Based on the decentralization of blockchain, its information database is jointly maintained and built by each participant, each participant is a node of the system, and each node can view the complete information database. The application of blockchain technology has successfully broken the information barrier between participants and intermediaries in the traditional public welfare model, achieved the ultimate in information transparency, and achieved a major breakthrough in information symmetry and transparency.

(4) Traceability

Blockchain traceability combines blockchain technology with the traceability system to track public welfare funds throughout the process, synchronize donation information in real time, and completely present the flow of funds, which is convenient for all project participants to check the project progress at any time. The donor can see the money flow and the recipient, and the recipient knows the source of the money and the donor. The "Charity Blockchain" builds a "spiritual bridge" for the two sides who have never met, connecting the "this shore" and the "other shore", enabling the birth and continuation of the touch, and making people more willing to devote themselves to the charity cause. Therefore, the traceability of blockchain technology is of great significance not only for controlling the risks of public welfare projects, but also for gaining the support and trust of the public.

3.2 Keeping Detailed Records Step by Step

In recent years, the huge value of blockchain technology to public welfare has appeared, and more and more people in the public welfare field have begun to try to integrate them. With the vigorous development of philanthropy in China, the emerging Internet public welfare model of blockchain technology is increasingly abundant. However, due to the lack of strict supervision mechanism and complete audit process, some people always want to take advantage of this opportunity to make profits, which leads to frequent donation frauds, and seriously undermines the enthusiasm and confidence of the public. To ensure the sustainable development and the better practice of the public trust of public welfare chain, design a set of scientific and standardized project implementation process is particularly important. In that case, how many passes must a qualified donation go through before it reaches the beneficiary's account?

First of all, there are five types of participants in public welfare projects: Donors, fundraising platforms, public welfare organizations, service providers and beneficiaries, among which service providers can be subdivided into professional service providers, material or equipment providers and human service providers. Before any party can officially participate in the project, it has to go through a rigorous review: When registering as a user of the Platform, donors shall fill in their personal information in strict accordance with the regulations of the Platform; The fundraising platform shall have the qualification and ability to carry out fundraising activities, have the permission of relevant competent authorities, and timely submit donation records; The public welfare institution shall obtain the corresponding qualification certificate according to law, provide complete and comprehensive registration information of the institution and upload the certificate, and examine the qualification information of the partner in the process of project implementation; The service provider shall accept the identity verification of the public welfare institution, submit the identity information and qualification certificate to the public welfare chain certificate and timely update and change it. The service provider shall record the service record when accepting the entrustment of other parties to provide corresponding services; Beneficiaries should provide real and effective identity information to public welfare organizations and complete identity verification before receiving funding.

In the implementation process of the "Charity Blockchain" project, every participant has due responsibilities and obligations, and every link through the project should upload the true and complete execution record to the public welfare chain certificate. From the entry of the project to the end of the process, there are three steps: information confirmation, implementation and release, and service feedback. The implementation and release of the project are also carefully adjusted according to the three project categories: capital, materials and professional services. It is worth to mention that at the end of the process for any project, there is a step called "Stakeholder Feedback". While implementing the fund flow of public welfare projects, they also delivered love and hope.

In April 2020, a sum of money was donated to the "New Future High School Student Grant -2020 Spring Grant" project through charity baby; One month later, a middle school student in Anhui province had received the grants. At the same time, the platform sent feedback to the user who donated, along with a quote from the child: "Your love donation I have received, sincerely thank you for your help, generosity and selflessness. I will always refueling, thank you. I wish you a safe life (Anonymous 2020)", the child's sincere and simple thanks deeply touched the donor's heart. On May 27 of the same year, a child from Nanjing Child Care Center received the funding of the "Love You Freshmen" project through the platform of "Charity Blockchain". He thanked the donor on the platform and shared his current recovery status: "We're having a class with rehabilitation training and education combined! They said that I have made great progress in rehabilitation and language cognition and hope you can cheer for me (The web 2019)! ". Netizens have also posted thank-you notes, saying it's the best feedback they've ever received. "Let every penny of charity be seen and every sincere donation be responded to" is not only an ardent expectation for China's public welfare undertakings, but also an important step in promoting transparency and practicing trust in public welfare through "Charity Blockchain".

3.3 Many a Little Makes a Mickle

There is no competition for public welfare. "We should work together for public welfare" (Gao, 2020). On the day of the release of "Charity Blockchain", six Internet companies, including Alibaba, Sina Weibo, Tencent, Bytedance, Xiaomi and Easy Chip, discussed how to break the boundaries of Internet plus Public Welfare and promote the integration of Internet and public welfare. The secretary general Li Hong from One Foundation also participated in the launch ceremony of the "Charity Blockchain" at the Alibaba 95 Charity Week Forum. In March 2020, the product entered the public welfare commodity buyers' participation stage, allowing Taobao users to participate in public welfare undertakings while "spending money", and offer their own love for children in remote areas. In April of the same year, One Foundation's One Paradise public welfare program and Water Purification Program also completed the establishment of Charity Blockchain. Besides, it works with a number of charitable foundations, such as The China Foundation for Rural Development, Sina Yangfan Charity Foundation, China Charities Aid Foundation for Children, have established cooperative partnerships. Up to now, more than 84 public welfare projects have been launched, with a total donation amount of more than CNY800 million. Many of donations are only two cents (Taobao "public welfare commodity" project: each sale donation from merchants) The "Charity Blockchain" has truly made public welfare donations sustainable, formed an effective incentive mechanism for public welfare, and created a unique trickle-down effect, integrating public welfare into every transaction. To maximize the mobilization of consumers to participate in the enthusiasm of public welfare undertakings. Each donation is small, but over time, it can be powerful.

4 Forge Ahead: The Value is Clearly Visible

4.1 Keeping an Eye on the Situation to Break the Ice

If Internet public welfare is a chess game, trust mechanism is like a chess piece. Every step of trust mechanism determines the future development of Internet public welfare platform. As the top one public welfare digital platform on the Internet, "Charity Blockchain", every step of the "chess pieces" has undoubtedly been carefully considered and played an irreplaceable role. So, how did the "Charity Blockchain" set the "chess pieces"?

(1) Transparent, open and traceable systems

Yang YIN, the CEO of Fun in Funding once had such distress: "We say that our accounts are clear, that every account can be checked, but checking accounts is a matter for the audit department, and the keyboard man on the other side of the network says I can't see, how do you prove that your accounts are clear (Sun, 2020)? Yes, the traditional Internet public welfare platforms can hardly prove themselves. However, "Charity Blockchain" is supported by blockchain, a "black tech", which makes up for the defects of traditional Internet public welfare platforms that are difficult to prove their own "innocence". The "black" the technology shows "white" the information. "Charity Blockchain" will display the information of public welfare organizations, personnel management information, donation data, detailed amount, project information, etc., so that the public can query and supervise in real time. At the same time, donations for public welfare projects will be linked one by one, and the process will be documented step by step, so that information can be traced and feedback can be reached. The information asymmetry between charities, donors and beneficiaries will be eliminated, thus reducing disputes and improving trust issues.

(2) Credible participants

The identity authentication and audit are the key steps in the process of Internet public welfare Platform. How to avoid the situation that some users of traditional public welfare platforms falsify personal information to obtain donations, and those in real need can get help, is the key issue that Internet public welfare platforms need to focus on. If a counterfeiter is found on an old platform, he or she is likely to switch platforms and repeat the same trick. However, in the "Charity Blockchain" platform based on blockchain technology, if any fraud is found, the information will be added to the whole network blacklist, and the person will not be able to apply for assistance. This makes the counterfeiters face huge counterfeiting costs, crack down on the fraudulent behavior, and fundamentally reduce the possibility of fraud.

(3) Efficient Internet public welfare undertakings

The traditional Internet public welfare process is complicated, including the list of names, verification, funding, and the efficiency is low. If a "Charity Blockchain" platform is used, after necessary human research and review, the rest can be handed over to smart contracts. The smart contract can be executed automatically after the relevant conditions and requirements are set. The entire contract can be automated from collection to execution without human intervention In addition, the performance will automatically give feedback and be monitored by all participants, ensuring the efficiency and high credibility of each link.

4.2 Playing a Leading Role and Keeping Pace with the Times

With the development of Internet technology, the world has already presented an interactive social structure. How should Internet public welfare platforms shoulder their social responsibilities? "Charity Blockchain" has delivered a relatively perfect answer sheet at this stage. But in fact, the construction of Internet public welfare platforms has always been in progress. Sun Lijun, a partner of Charity Blockchain, said that many problems in public welfare projects have been exposed in the process of development. Many people do not want to engage in public welfare, which has caused great damage to the public trust. How much confidence do the public have in public welfare when their trust has been repeatedly betrayed? Strengthening trust and faith is an urgent problem today (Guo, 2020). He is well aware that the biggest advantage of Alibaba lies in its technology and platform, and he has always wanted to use the power of the Internet to drive the development of public welfare undertakings. "Charity Blockchain" will continue to deepen the blockchain in the field of public welfare and charity, effectively protect the whereabouts of charity funds, establish a relationship of trust through transparent operation, attract more users to participate in public welfare and charity, and enable the continuous development of social welfare undertakings.

Wang Ruihe, Secretary-General of Alibaba Foundation, said, "Trust is the life of public welfare, and technology should first serve this point. We hope that all public welfare organizations have such courage (Finance, 2020). "Alibaba is always on the way for public welfare. From the Green Initiative, Ant Forest, Code public welfare to Charity Blockchain, Alibaba is committed to cultivating samples of public welfare rooted in its business model, and relying on the synergy effect of the Internet, continuously expanding the social impact of public welfare projects. On September 5, 2020, Alibaba Foundation published the standard of public welfare chain group in the offline forum of the 95 Public Welfare Week, becoming an example in the industry. The efforts made by "Charity Blockchain" to make public welfare projects on the Internet more transparent are like a revolution in philanthropy It takes advantage of blockchain technology to innovate the Internet public welfare model, focuses on the transformation of public welfare platform functions, and aims to enhance social trust capital. It designs rules and incentive mechanisms, drawing a blueprint for the whole society to be open, transparent, shared. An increasing number of people will jointly engage in public welfare, and pursue more valuable goals: With the help of Internet technology, the construction of public welfare trust system will be further promoted.

5 Conclusion

From the official launch of Charity Blockchain in 2019 to the end of June 2020, over CNY3.5 billion donations have been made, benefiting more than 100,000 people. Until today, the cumulative number of public welfare donations has exceeded 17 billion, and the cumulative number of beneficiaries is even nearly 7 million. During this period, the project has also won the Gold Award in the 2020 China Charity Project Competition, can be said to hand in a satisfactory report card. Charity Blockchain hopes to "Respond to every love, evidence every wish", they always firmly believe that only extreme transparency can bring great trust.

However, we have only seen one side of Charity Blockchain, and the seemingly natural fit of blockchain + public welfare still faces many practical difficulties. Li Feng, head of blockchain of Du Xiaoman Finance, once proposed that "the high threshold of blockchain technology application, the strict requirements for the degree of regulation of public welfare institutions and the existence of cognitive bias of the public are the obstacles to the large-scale application of blockchain in the public welfare scene (Zhihu, 2018)." The so-called cognitive bias refers to the fact that the public often does not support public welfare organizations to charge "management fees", hoping that every donation will be handed over to the recipient intact, but it is inevitable that certain expenses are needed to maintain the operation of the organization, and public welfare actually has costs. The public's lack of understanding also makes many public welfare organizations reluctant to apply blockchain. Mr. Zeng from Ali has also questioned: "Because blockchain is a technological innovation, the trust problem is a human problem, and technological innovation is no way to solve the human problem. " Therefore, there is still a long way to go before the innovative model of Charity Blockchain can be implemented on a large scale. And what we need to do at this stage is to understand this technology rationally and actively explore the new model of blockchain + public welfare. The only way to bring more possibilities to the future of public welfare is to open our hearts to accept it, understand it and apply it.

6 Case Appendix

Appendix 1

See Table 1.

Table 1 Certificate information of public welfare chain

Information type	Information item
Donation information	Fundraising platform
	The registered account of the donor in the fundraising platform
	Name of public welfare institutions
	Public welfare project identification[a]
	Donation time
	Contents of donation
	Quantity and unit
	Donation voucher
Execution information	Name of public welfare institutions
	Public welfare project identification[a]
	Execution time
	Execution of activities
	Quantity and unit
	Execution voucher
Benefit information	Name of public welfare institutions
	Public welfare project identification[a]
	Beneficiary identification
	Beneficiary identity verification method
	Benefit time
	Beneficiary content
	Quantity and unit
	Beneficiary certificate
Implementation effect information	Name of public welfare institutions
	Public welfare project identification[a]
	Feedback time
	Feedback contents

[a]The name, ID, and other unique identification of the donation project. *Source* Made by the author according to the group standard of *Public Interest Chain Technology and Application Specification*

Appendix 2: Project Implementation Process (Material Category as an Example)

See Fig. 1.

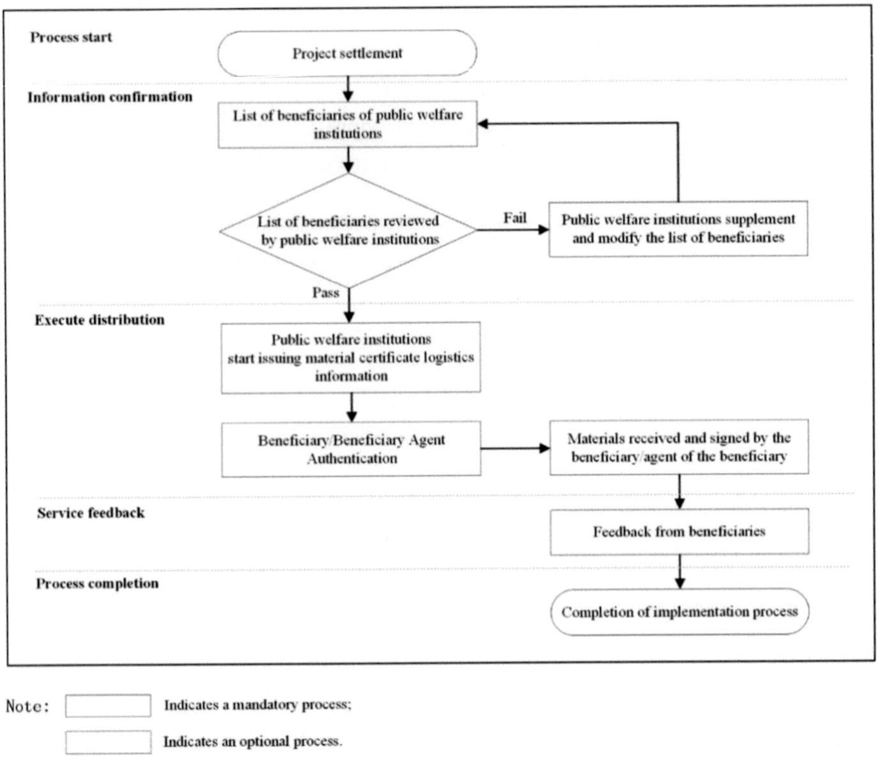

Fig. 1 Implementation process of material category. *Source* Made by the author according to the group standard of Public Interest Chain Technology and Application Specification

Appendix 3: Statistics of Charity Blockchain Projects

See Figs. 2 and 3.

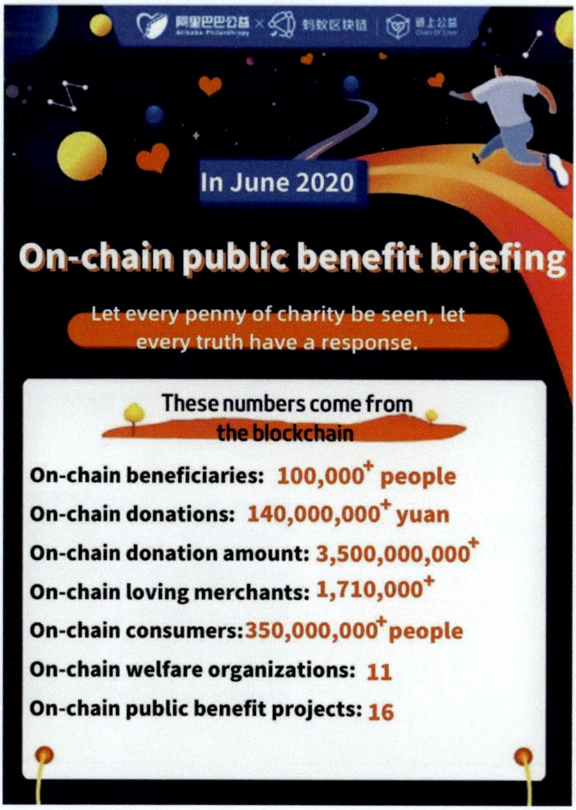

Fig. 2 Charity blockchain 2020 newsletter

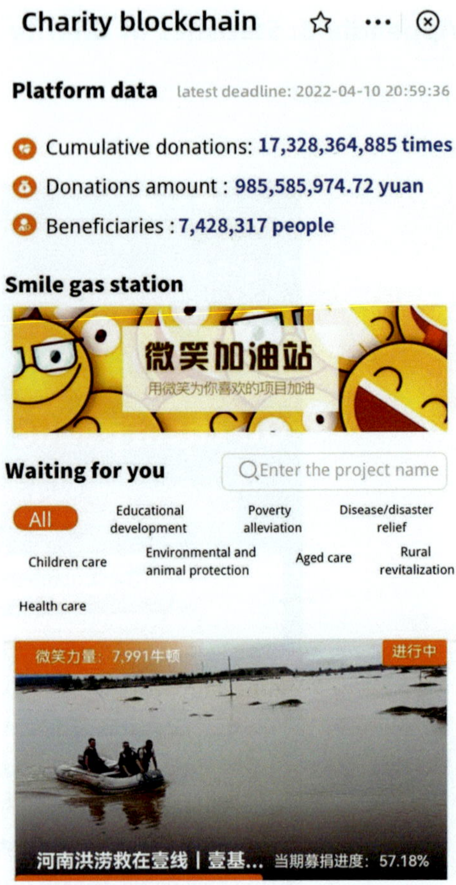

Fig. 3 Charity blockchain real-time donation data. *Source* Data released by official website.

Appendix 4: Platform Service Functions

In the operation of the “Charity Blockchain” platform, information related to the charity process, such as project plans, donation records, use of donations, as well as donation-related registration information are all recorded on the chain simultaneously. Due to the execution, service and information tracing functions of the blockchain public welfare platform itself, as well as the consensus mechanism of consistent data and openness of each node, the information will be able to be transparently and openly publicized to the public conditionally, which is convenient for the society to inquire and supervise at any time (Fig. 4).

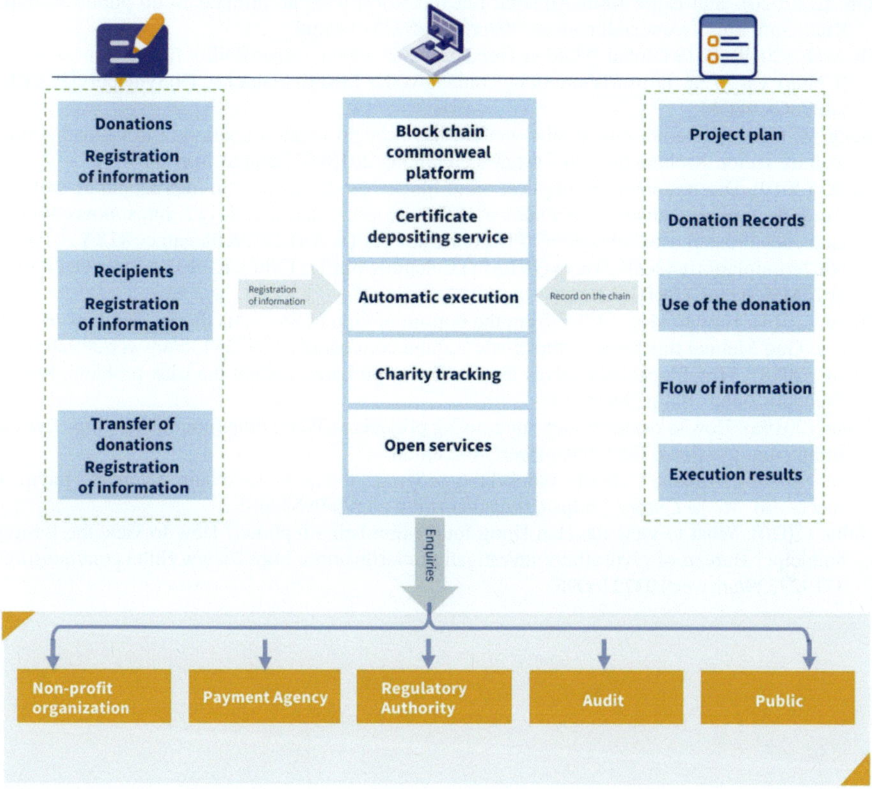

Fig. 4 Platform public welfare traceability flow chart. *Source* The author drew it according to the platform traceability process

References

Anonymous. (2020). Charity blockchain|They are all on the chain! It has also benefited more than 100,000 people. Alibaba public welfare—Phoenix news. https://ishare.ifeng.com/c/s/v002FFIK06vEGhYJz-_DoSvnUpeIvDLKRU-ydP7oQkzt8tJM__

Sina Finance. (2020). The red cross was criticized and netizens proposed charity blockchain to promote donation. https://finance.sina.com.cn/blockchain/coin/2020-02-11/doc-iimxyqvz1996009.shtml

Gao, X. (2020). Make public welfare on charity blockchain open and transparent—An interview with Wang Ruihe, Secretary-general of Ali foundation—a Chinese philanthropist. https://baijiahao.baidu.com/s?id=1679127557284549185

Guo, X. (2020). The public welfare is the first to be "Chained"! blockchain escort for public welfare—Xiaokang. https://www.sohu.com/a/367016607

Hu, X. (2019). Technology is the greatest public good of our time. China Economy Net, the National Economy. https://www.ce.cn/xwzx/gnsz/gdxw/201909/05/t20190905_33095296.shtml

Sun, L. (2020). Sun Lijun from Alibaba: Let the world have no difficult to do public welfare. Rmlt.com. http://www.rmlt.com.cn/2020/0905/592379.shtml

The web. (2019). 2019 Global "Golden Trends Award" annual responsibility fulfillment—Alibaba (China) Co., Ltd. https://ishare.ifeng.com/c/s/v002FFIK06vEGhYJz-_DoSvnUpeIvDLKRU-ydP7oQkzt8tJM__

Wang, Z. (2016). Internet plus public welfare has brought about a revolution in China's public welfare sector. Xinhua. http://www.news.cn/talking/20161027a/index.htm

Xu, R. (2019). Discussion on the application of blockchain technology in internet public welfare. *Journal of Xi'an University of Finance and Economics, 23*(6), 107–112. https://kns.cnki.net/kcms/detail/detail.aspx?dbcode=CJFD&dbname=CJFDLAST2019&filename=XIXY201906062&uniplatform=NZKPT&v=GVLMhTEbleumIz4mEOzTNbFjcK-uElKKPh9wOc7mmUyb7hMJ5AUbnE7Ba1GqLBMa

Zhihu. (2014). How to view CCTV from the bottom of Guo Meimei this matter, and how to evaluate Guo Meimei this person. https://www.zhihu.com/question/24725435/answer/28926343

Zhihu. (2018). Why blockchain solves the consensus problem, but not the trust problem. https://zhuanlan.zhihu.com/p/38915457

Zhihu. (2019a). How to evaluate such fundraising projects as Water drop fundraising. https://www.zhihu.com/question/67883755/answer/744240066

Zhihu. (2019b). Alibaba's charity blockchain program, the first blockchain automatic payment successful. *Micro Letters*—https://zhuanlan.zhihu.com/p/99593681

Zhihu. (2020). What to view the Han Hong foundation being reported? How to view the Beijing municipal Bureau of civil affairs investigation clarification. https://www.zhihu.com/question/371927729/answer/1037216096

Zall Smart Commerce: Intelligent Link Ecology Leads the Transformation Towards Industrial Internet

Pingfeng Liu, Han Gao, Jiaxian Huang, and Hongfu Yu

1 Introduction

B2B refers to the business model of information transmission and exchange, commodity trading and service activities between enterprises through the Internet. The B2B industry has experienced the development from B2B 1.0 to B2B 3.0 since its birth. According to the trading content and service level, its development process can be divided into three stages: information service, trade matching and ecological integration. In B2B 1.0, the application of Internet technology was just emerging, characterized with provision of supply and demand information for small and medium-sized enterprises at this stage. B2B platform solved the problems of information asymmetry and matching difficulty between trading parties while leaving most of the transaction process and activities to offline. In B2B 2.0, the platform gradually got interfered in the transaction process. Taking into consideration the demands of both trading parties, the platform acted as a transaction intermediary by providing traders with low-cost online matching service. Though the quality of services had been improved to a large extent, B2B platform only provided marketing services and commodity transactions which did not form a closed loop. Finance, warehousing, logistics and other businesses services were still separated from online platforms. Now, as domestic B2B platform services gradually become comprehensive and diverse, B2B has welcomed its 3.0 era and gradually realized the integration of information flow, fund flow and materials flow. B2B platform not only provides buyers with financing services, but also provides sellers with warehousing and logistics services, which fully realizes cost reduction and efficiency improvement. In addition, thanks to the application of cloud computing and big

P. Liu (✉) · H. Gao · J. Huang · H. Yu
School of Economics, Wuhan University of Technology, Wuhan, China

School of Entrepreneurship, Wuhan University of Technology, Wuhan, China

J. Zhang et al. (eds.), *Innovation of Digital Economy*, Management for Professionals,
https://doi.org/10.1007/978-981-99-1741-9_23

data technologies, B2B platform utilizes a tremendous amount of accumulated data to mine customer preferences so as to provide much more accurate and efficient services for both sides of the transaction.

During the evolution process of B2B, the development of one enterprise, Zall Samrt Commerce, can be said to be the epitome of the evolution of China's B2B field. Transforming from the initial traditional offline wholesale into online trading, Zall Smart Commerce finally formed an intelligent trading ecology integrating finance, warehousing, logistics and other service sectors. Since the initial B2B only got involved in the transaction process instead of integrating the whole supply chain channel, Zall Smart Commerce, as a pioneer in B2B 3.0, has successively launched platforms such as "Zall Buy", "Zall Delivery" and "Zall Finance" to provide the whole process services for the industrial chain. Those platforms have been utilized to empower the development of three main industries, namely agricultural products, steel and iron, chemical and plastics. Through the integration of digital technologies and industrial chain, data have been utilized to empower the innovation in services offered by the multi-category platforms. Through the sharing and exploitation of the resources of each platform, industries have been integrated to empower the business model innovation with open ecology. With the mission of "let transactions be smooth and simple, let elements flow without boundary", Zall Smart Commerce strives to build a more open and perfect Intelligent Link Ecology system.

2 Business Background

2.1 Enterprise Introduction

Zall Smart Commerce is an enterprise focusing on B2B intelligent transactions and services. It builds B2B trading platforms in agricultural products, chemicals, plastics, non-ferrous metals and other fields. Based on the trading scenarios and trading data of these platforms, Zall Smart Commerce provides users with financial, logistics, cross-border trade, supply chain management and other services. In 2021, with a total revenue of nearly CNY72.8 billion in 2020, Zall Smart Commerce ranked 155th in Fortune China 500, and was included in the "Annual Growth Power of Listed Companies TOP100", "Annual China Industrial Internet Listed Companies TOP10" and "Annual China Industrial Internet (Industry Digitization) TOP100".

2.2 Development History

Zall Smart Commerce initiated its business in industrial real estate. In 2007, Zall Amart Commerce turned its core business to commercial real estate for wholesalers and established Hankoubei International Commerce Exchange Center. Benefited from the geographical advantages of Hankou, Hankoubei International Commerce Exchange Center has gradually become the "first wholesale city in

China". In 2011, Zall was successfully listed and traded in the Hong Kong Stock Exchange, becoming the first Wuhan concept stock and the first wholesale market concept stock in Hong Kong main board market. In the same year, its founder Yan Zhi became the richest man in Hubei Province with a net worth of CNY7.6 billion. Impacted by the Internet wave and struggling traditional offline large-volume wholesale business in 2014, Zall began to realize the necessity of transformation towards industrial Internet. Therefore, it clearly put forward that it must promote the integration of industrial development and the Internet with a determined resolution, and took this decision as a guide to embark on the B2B transformation path from traditional offline wholesale to online-to-offline business model. Fully embracing the industrial Internet since 2015, Zall has acquired Shenzhen Sinoagri E-commerce and Huasuhui, and invested in Lightinthebox and Haishangxian. Moreover, it not only jointly established the Zall Steel with XBGF, but also established the Commodities Intelligence Center (CIC) with Singapore Exchange and other institutions, forming Zall's philosiphy of "linking world business with intelligence and creating value with services". In 2021, Zall Smart Commerce began to set up the International Trade Group to deal with import and export trade and services. It is composed of professional service brands including Singapore International Trade, Zall International Trade, Zall Foreign Trade and so on to provide one-stop comprehensive foreign trade and value-added services for import and export enterprises. The successful transformation of Zall Smart Commerce lies in the construction of Intelligent Link Ecology and its continuous exploration of industrial Internet. So how did Zall Smart Commerce transform itself into the industrial Internet by taking advantage of the development of Intelligent Link Ecology? Let's approach Zall and delve deeper into the Zall's land.

3 Intelligent Link Ecology 1.0 (Platform Empowerment Stage)

At the beginning of its establishment, Zall Smart Commerce built and operated Hankoubei International Commerce Exchange Center offline. After years of operation, Hankoubei has become the most influential commodity wholesale market in Central China. However, in the Internet age, with the emergence and development of the online market, the offline wholesalers are facing serious crises as follows. First, the number of wholesalers is increasing while the user retention rate is decreasing and the sales and profits are greatly squeezed by online platforms. Second, the information function of the offline wholesale market has been seriously weakened, which causes the offline market completely unable to compare with the online platforms in powerful information gathering and sharing function. Third, the disadvantages in logistics of the offline wholesale market is amplified. Compared with the one-stop logistics service of online platforms, the offline wholesale market often confronts repeated transportation and roundabout transportation problems, which leads to high logistics costs and slow response speed.

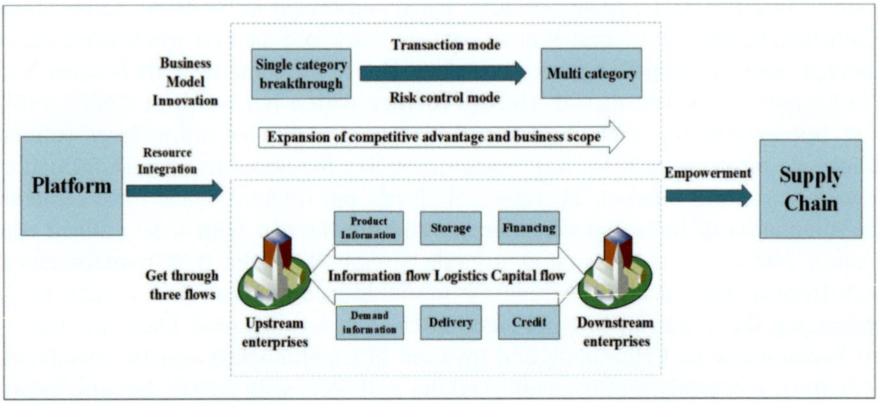

Fig. 1 Platform empowerment

Given this condition, in 2015, Zall Smart Commerce started to embrace the Internet and transform to the online platform, and launched successively three platforms, namely Zall Buy, Zall Delivery and Zall Finance. With the help of the company's years of operating experience in the offline wholesale market, it cooperated with Hankoubei to integrate transaction information, logistics information and financial service information onto the online platform, so as to move the offline wholesale market to the "cloud". This action improved the transaction satisfaction of both the supply and demand sides, and broke the barriers of online transaction and offline supply chain, and supported the whole supply chain with financial services, which resulted in cost reduction and efficiency improvement for the whole supply chain. The process of the platform empowerment phase of the Zall Smart Commerce is shown in Fig. 1.

3.1 Platform Empowerment—Integrating Resources to Get Through "Three Flows"

3.1.1 Zall Buy: Making Information More Transparent

The problem of opaque information in the traditional offline trading market seriously affects the profitability and capital turnover efficiency of upstream and downstream enterprises. As the Industrial Internet emerged later than the Consumer Internet, merchants are not able to select and purchase the raw materials or products they want as freely as they can with B2C online shopping, and the opacity of offline market information can bring losses to both buyers and sellers.

To this end, Zall Smart Commerce built a comprehensive trading service platform, Zall Buy, to get through the supply chain information flow and solve the negative problems caused by opaque information. Upstream suppliers display their products in stock, prices, storage locations, product specifications and other information through Zall Buy. Downstream buyers can purchase according to their needs based on the product information on the platform, which enables the buyers to compare different products before they find the ones that are highly compatible with their needs even if they do not physically visit the sites of suppliers. The establishment of Zall Buy has greatly enhanced the purchasing experience by enabling purchasers to save on purchasing costs while buying products faster and more easily to their satisfaction. In addition, suppliers can also use the product transaction information integrated on the platform to discover changes in demand for products from buyers and adjust production accordingly.

At the initial stage when the platform was just established, how to gather as a huge as possible amount of upstream and downstream customer resources and product information? After years of operation, Hankoubei has become the most influential commodity wholesale market in Central China. By moving the existing merchants in Hankoubei onto the e-commerce platform, many interrelated upstream and downstream enterprises can be brought in, bringing a large amount of product supply and demand information to the platform. At the same time, in order to help many merchants to register and publish their products on the Zall Buy platform, Zall Smart Commerce also recruited a group of university students with rich experience in using the Internet to guide merchants to use "Zall Buy". Thus the number of merchants moving onto the platform has soared sharply. In just eight months since its launch, Zall Buy has taken root in Wuhan, Guangzhou, Shenzhen, Kunming, Changsha, Zhengzhou, Yiwu and other cities, attracting nearly 40,000 merchants nationwide.

3.1.2 Zall Delivery: Making Logistics More Efficient

In response to the special needs of the toB industry in logistics, Zall Smart Commerce has built an independent logistics service platform and a complete logistics system to get through the supply chain logistics. Most of the products traded on Industrial Internet are bulk goods such as energy, basic raw materials and agricultural and sideline products, which have the characteristics of large amount in supply and demand, heavyweight, etc. At the same time, these goods are unevenly distributed geographically, causing problems such as long transportation distance, long cycle time and high cost. In response to problems of logistics information being difficult to obtain in real time and logistics costs being high in traditional trading scenarios, Zall Delivery integrated the existing logistics systems. Now merchants only need to submit transaction information in Zall Buy and then Zall Delivey will further provide one-stop logistics and warehousing services for them, using their own perfect logistics system and management experience, greatly reducing logistics costs and improving logistics efficiency.

3.1.3 Zall Finance: Making Fund More Stable

The stability of the fund flow is the key to ensuring the proper functioning of enterprises and stimulating market dynamics. Fund flows on the industrial internet are generally higher than on the consumer internet in terms of transaction volume, which means that a lot of financing is needed to keep the transaction chain running smoothly. Most of the companies in the upstream and downstream of the industrial internet, especially SMEs, might have problems in fund flow, which is the key to the limited B2B transactions. Downstream customers of B2B transactions need to pay upstream suppliers first to buy goods and wait to get funds back after the goods are sold. If the funds can't be collected back timely, the procurement of next batch of goods will be affected. Upstream suppliers of B2B transactions also often face problems with shortage in supply of raw materials and production equipment due to insufficient start-up fund. At this point, the industrial internet needs an intermediary to provide financing services for upstream and downstream users in order to maintain a stable fund flow.

In response to the problems of difficulty in financing and liquidity for enterprises, Zall Finance was created to get through the flow of funds throughout the supply chain. In cooperation with banks, insurance and other financial institutions, Zall Finance has launched a series of financial products to provide one-stop financial services for SMEs. In response to the difficulties in production and procurement financing, and capital turnover for upstream and downstream enterprises, Zall Finance provides them with financial leasing, production and procurement financing services. In response to the concerns of logistics enterprises about the damage of goods in the middle of transportation, Zall Finance provides them with logistics insurance services. Zall Finance has reduced the pressure on enterprises to run their fund flow and promoted productivity and transaction efficiency.

The platform empowerment stage is characterized by the integration of information resources and the smooth running of the "three flows" with the platform. Zall Smart Commerce believes that the focus of the process of "getting through the three flows" is to build a closed loop that connects all aspects of the supply chain. Taking advantage of the immediacy and extensiveness of information dissemination via Internet, that closed loop will enable a full and rapid flow of product information, demand information, transaction information, logistics information, financial services information. Zall Buy has changed Hankoubei merchants' years of habits of "sitting in shops and waiting for business". It has also solved the problem of asymmetric information on supply and demand, prices and products in the trading process. Zall Delivery has realized highly reliable freight transportation with standardized prices, on-time collection and delivery, and is known as the freight version of Didi Taxi. Zall Cloud Warehouse has built the standardized warehouses supported by Internet of Things and other information technologies, which solved the problems of high storage cost and overburden of goods turnover for the majority of merchants. Zall Finance actively expands and pools financial resources from large state-owned banks and local banks to solve the problems of difficulty and high cost in financing for enterprises of different scales along the supply chain. The online platform can empower each link of the supply chain and get through the flow of information, logistics and fund, so as to realize the cost reduction and efficiency improvement of the supply chain.

3.2 Business Model Innovation—Breakthrough in Single Category Extended to Advantages in Multiple and Full Categories

Explore market breakthroughs from a single category of products. Along with the establishment of the basic Internet ecosystem, it is clear that Zall Smart Commerce was faced with the challenges from many existing industrial Internet platforms. For example, Alibaba B2B is a big and comprehensive platform. Shanghai Steel Union has long been rooted in its specified industry and has occupied a large market share. In this situation, how should Zall Smart Commerce survive and grow in the fierce market competition? Zall Smart Commerce has adopted the differentiation strategy of breakthrough in single category. The differentiated competitive advantages of Zall Smart Commerce are mainly reflected in the two levels as follows. First, specialize in the differentiated vertical product application field to gain the huge competitive advantages in market segmentation. By applying the same product to different sectors and fields, different niche markets will be created. Selecting and concentrating on a certain niche industry sector can create cutting-edge leading advantages in the niche market. Zall steel, a subsidiary of Zall, digs deeply into the market of downstream infrastructure construction industry users and reaps more than 100 billion Renminbi in transaction volume in less than four years after its establishment. Second, focus on specified categories to obtain the head effect of the single category market. Zall Smart Commerce avoids the direct confrontations with other mature industrial Internet companies by focusing on specified categories and striving to gain greater competitive advantages and market dominance in the specified category market. Using the head effect of the closed loop of "high market share → high attention → high investment → high revenue → high growth", Zall Smart Commerce has continuously improved its influence and competitiveness in the industry. For example, Sinoagri E-commerce, a subsidiary of Zall Smart Commerce, focuses on B2B trading of bulk agricultural products such as white sugar and silk, and has become the leading enterprise in the field of white sugar and silk. The spot trading volume of white sugar on Sinoagri E-commerce platform accounts for 30% of the national total. More than 90% of users in the white sugar industry and more than 30% of users in the cocoon and silk industry nationwide have become business members of Sinoagri E-commerce platform.

The business model and successful experience of breakthroughs in single category market can be extended to all range within the Intelligent Link Ecology, allowing for the expansion of competitive advantages and business scope. Using the complete transaction model and risk control model built out in a single category, Zall Smart Commerce further expands the advantageous categories to other B2B business segments to achieve centralized control, thus accelerating the spread of business experience within the enterprise and generating spillover effects between industries.

4 Intelligent Link Ecology 2.0 (Data Empowerment Stage)

In the context of the big data era, data has become the fifth factor of production after land, labor, capital and technology. It is crucial for enterprises to leverage the dual empowering effects of data elements and digital technologies to achieve sustainable competitive advantage. The low-cost and highly efficient information dissemination on the Internet can significantly alleviate the information asymmetry in the original market, making the cost of customer transfer much lower and the competition in the industry much more intense. To win customers' favor, enterprises must reshape their customer strategies and take it as an edge tool to provide personalized and precise services to users.

After the first stage of data accumulation, Zall Smart Commerce has the foundation to transform the platform user data into user resources. At the same time, digital technology has become a key driver for the effective exploitation of user data resources and the improvement of supply chain service level. Therefore, it is imperative to use data elements and digital technologies to empower business innovation in enterprises. Since the previous stage of exploration demonstrates that the competitive advantage that can be established by providing B2B horizontal transaction services covering comprehensive categories of products is not obvious, Zall Smart Commerce decided to dig deeper into B2B vertical fields. Since 2015, Zall Smart Commerce has acquired Sinoagri E-commerce, Chemical and Plastic Exchange, established Zall Steel, and taken a stake in Sea Fresh, and built B2B platforms with significant influence in the fields of agriculture, steel, chemical and plastic, fisheries and other bulk commodities, expanding from a single category wholesale to covering multiple industry sectors. With the development of digital economy and the acceleration of process of digital industrialization and industrial digitalization, Zall Smart Commerce has upgraded its brand to build a service architecture system of "B2B transaction service + supply chain service + digital technologies cloud service" with the application of digital technologies such as big data, artificial intelligence and blockchain to help enterprises reduce costs and increase efficiency, further improve transaction efficiency, storage and logistics efficiency, capital efficiency and other synergistic capabilities. Zall Smart Commerce is committed to building a leading global digital trade platform. The process of the data empowerment phase of Zall Smart Commerce is shown in Fig. 2.

4.1 Data Empowerment—Digital Technologies Driving Value Creation to be Extended to Upstream and Downstream of the Industrial Chain

The potential for value creation inspired by the combination of digital technologies and the Intelligent Link Ecology is enormous. In order to further enhance its competitiveness, adapt to market demand and break the limitation of business scope, Zall Smart Commerce established the Zall Research Institute, which focuses on

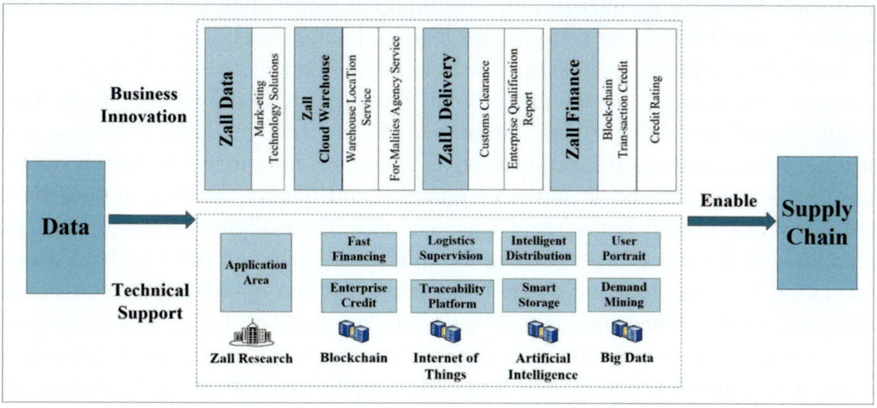

Fig. 2 Data empowerment

strengthening the application and innovation capabilities of blockchain, artificial intelligence, Internet of Things and big data in improving supply chain services, discovering the potential demand of users through deep mining of data from enterprises and platforms within the ecology, further innovating business and enhancing user stickiness based on the potential demand of users.

The driving force of digital technologies is fully reflected in the various vertical e-commerce platforms of Zall Smart Commerce. Based on its specialized operating experience in the industrial Internet field and driven by the application and innovation of digital technologies, the scope of Zall Smart Commerce's business began to extend to upstream and downstream of the industrial chain. Upstream extension is embedded within the production organization of upstream enterprises, helping them adjust their production strategies according to demand, improve the matching accuracy between production and demand, and reduce inventory pressure. At the same time, the Internet of Things and blockchain technology are utilized to bind production, logistics and warehousing information with products. Such data is carried to all links of downstream supply chain through online platform, so as to strengthen links between upstream and downstream, and to reduce the cost of product traceability and quality supervision. After applying digital technologies, Sinoagri E-commerce has adjusted its strategic positioning in the sugar sector from "B2B e-commerce of sugar industry" to "vertical e-commerce of sugar industrial chain", reconstructing the relationship among the upstream, midstream and downstream, and beginning to extend to both ends of the industry. Sinoagri E-commerce establishes an agricultural platform and a traceability platform at the upstream to improve production and help the processing firms build a supply chain system connecting farmers and cooperatives. It also uses relevant financial tools to help farmers, cooperatives and processing firms build a stable trading relationship. Besides, it has established a distribution platform for the downstream, invested in the "Good Partner" project, and built an intelligent procurement and distribution platform covering a number of cities for high net worth clients such as large food factories, professional chain stores and high-end restaurants.

In the data empowerment stage, the functions of data elements and digital technologies empowering the Intelligent Link Ecology are mainly reflected in: First of all, digital technologies have improved the internal production organization of enterprises, making the production of upstream enterprises accurately match the downstream demand in terms of quantity and quality, so as to reduce costs and inventory, and to better meet user demand. Then, digital technologies have strengthened the links of all parts in the industrial chain and have enabled timely adaptation to changes, reducing the connection cost and improving the connection efficiency of the industrial chain. Finally, the application of digital technologies, such as blockchain, in the field of supply chain finance has transformed business credit from enterprise credit into transaction credit and solved the financing difficulties faced by SMEs. Combined with data elements, the application of digital technologies has created exclusive solutions to different practical problems greatly improving the service level of enterprise supply chain and expanding the service scope.

4.2 Business Model Innovation—Digital Technologies Driving Business Innovation

Digital technologies extend deeply into the end activities of value creation making business innovation blossom everywhere in Intelligent Link Ecology. Where there is business, there is data. Where there is data, digital technologies can be exploited to mine the demand and empower business innovation. With the accumulated data management experience in long-term operation, Zall Cloud Warehouse leverages the power of digital technologies to portray shops and logistics warehouses. It also provides merchants with decision support in locations of shops and warehouses based on the market characteristics of specific regions. Zall International Trade provides customers with enterprise qualification reports by taking advantage of platform business and a lot of enterprise data resources, so that the cost for customers to obtain the business qualification of target enterprises is greatly reduced, and the probability of individuals or enterprises being cheated by adverse enterprises is greatly decreased. Together with Zhongbang Bank and other financial institutions, Zall Finance provides high value-added services such as qualification inspecting and credit rating of both parties by using the risk control system and the credit review and rating system owned by Zall Smart Commerce. It is clear that the acquisition and utilization of data will become one of the important drivers for Zall Smart Commerce to obtain sustainable competitiveness.

5 Intelligent Link Ecology 3.0 (Industrial Integration Empowerment Stage)

After the development of the former two stages, the industrial matrix of Zall Smart Commerce with the comprehensive transaction platform and supply chain services as its core has gradually taken shape. However, with the expansion of industry and business, Zall Smart Commerce is gradually unable to meet the increasing demands of enterprises on the platform for network interaction and interactivity. Therefore, it is urgent for Zall Smart Commerce to build an open ecosystem to promote transboundary cooperation and expedite the flow, aggregation and integration of resources among the members on the platform to create shared value. In order to further meet the needs of enterprise development and to expand its industrial competitive advantage, Zall Smart Commerce has gradually broken down the barriers among vertical industries and formed value co-creation paths through the interaction among and coupling of different modes such as mergers and acquisitions, inter-organizational coordination. It has also constructed a complementary and restructured resource pool to provide an essential elements basis for knowledge innovation and collaborative value creation. The above work leads to an open ecosystem and finally realizes value co-creation. The process of the industrial integration empowerment stage of the Zall Smart Commerce is shown in Fig. 3.

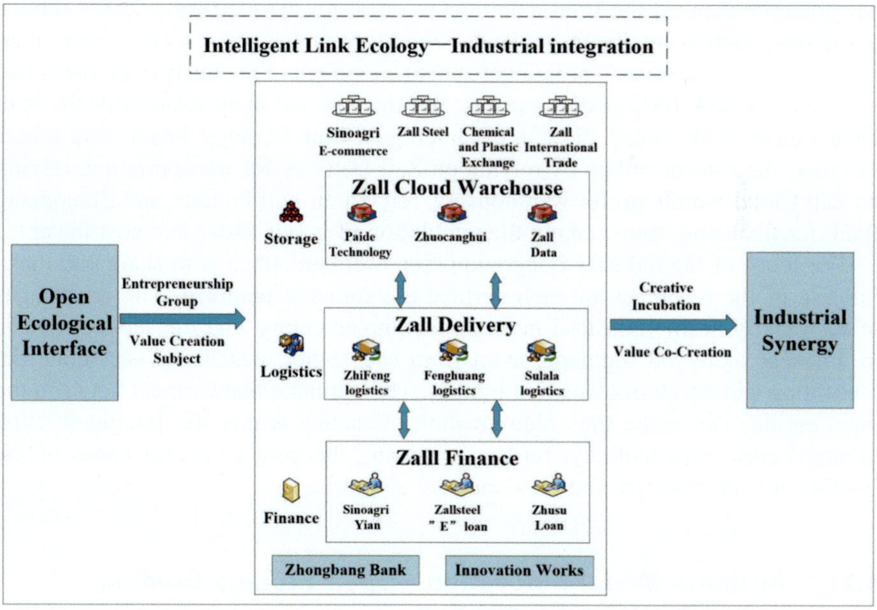

Fig. 3 Industrial integration empowerment

5.1 Industrial Integration Empowerment—Breaking Down Industrial Barriers and Promoting the Coordinated Development of Industries

Industrial integration empowers the commercial resources in the whole Intelligent Link Ecology to be integrated with one network and reached with one click. The synergy between supply chain financial services represented by Zhongbang Bank and e-commerce platforms of various industries in the intelligent ecosystem has achieved remarkable results. In order to better serve the ecosystem, Zhongbang Bank applies the Internet technology in designing specific financing products in correspondence with transaction entities, categories of transacted products, transaction modes and the position in industrial chain. Taking China Cotton Transaction Company as an example, because most of its trading clients are in other places and the traditional offline loan model is inefficient, Zhongbang Bank has specially developed an online financing product of cotton purchase E-loan to serve the financing needs of the clients of this company. This financing product can be accessed purely online which covers the whole process of financing operation from account opening and credit granting to make loan and repayment. Zhongbang Bank is committed to extending the advantages and experiences of cross-region, cross-industry and all-weather Internet finance to the development of the whole Intelligent Link Ecology. It has established the connections with platforms such as Chemical and Plastic Exchange, Zall Steel and Sinoagri E-commerce, which has greatly enhanced the transaction cohesion of all the platforms. Zall's service businesses, such as intelligent logistics, cloud warehousing and supply chain management, also demonstrate prominent synergetic effects. Previously, merchants had to separately look for logistics carriers, warehouses and bank loans after the bulk commodities were traded. Now in the Intelligent Link Ecology, buyers and sellers can meet their needs online by relying on Zall Delivery for transportation, relying on Zall Cloud Warehousefor warehousing, relying on Zall Finance and Zhongbang Bank for financing, thus making the circulation of goods faster and cost lower.

The focus of the industry integration empowerment stage is to share and make full use of the resources of each vertical e-commerce platform. The advantages of each entity in the industrial matrix are complementary, and the service models in different industrial segments learn from each other, which can accelerate the innovation and iteration of service models. The mutual empowerment between the main entities can make the value creation efficiency within the Intelligent Link Ecology grow exponentially, further enhancing the core competitiveness of the Intelligent Link Ecology and its associated enterprises.

5.2 Business Model Innovation—Open Ecology Guiding Industrial Value Co-creation

Create an open empowering network to aggregate the momentum of synergy among industries. The function of Intelligent Link Ecology 3.0 is no longer just a convergence of internal data and access to internal vertical industries, but more importantly as an open empowering network for all B2B industries. Any value creation entity within the Intelligent Link Ecology can realize the incubation of creativity from 0 to 1, can obtain one-stop services including plant and store selection, production and marketing strategy customization. It can realize a close-loop of logistics activities including product quality supervision, product logistics and warehousing and after-sale feedback. It can complete the financing process purely online, get extremely fast qualification review and loans. Intelligent Link Ecology 3.0 leverages its own empowerment network to provide all B2B businesses with the needed services and infrastructure. With a focus on enhancing the core competitiveness of the system, Intelligent Link Ecology 3.0 continues to attract value creation entities from various industrial sectors, thus further enlarging the scale and digging more deeply into industries to shape a new landscape of symbiosis, win-win and sharing among all the members of the ecology.

Build the nation's leading intelligent trading ecology and drive industrial value co-creation with creative incubation and service innovation. The Wuhan incubator, "Z Time—Innovation Workshop", jointly operated by Zall Venture Capital and Innovation Workshop of Zall Group, is dedicated to helping entrepreneurs in fields related to business intelligence obtain start-up funding support. Integrating internal resources of the Intelligent Link Ecology, Z Time—Innovation Workshop provides entrepreneurs with services in product design, R&D guidance, strategy development, operation coaching, technology platform and other start-up backup services. Zall Connected Technology, Zall Asset Management and Innovation Works, which are subsidiaries of Zall Smart Commerce, jointly initiated the establishment of Zall Innovation Smart Trading Industry Fund. The fund is focused on "building an intelligent business transaction ecosystem", with a focus on venture investment and equity investment in logistics and supply chain upgrading, intelligent transactions, Internet of Things and other related industries, helping Zall Smart Commerce build an intelligent transaction ecosystem with leading technologies and advanced business applications.

6 Outlook

From the start of the transformation in 2015 to the present, Zall Smart Commerce has always taken it as its mission to promote the economic development of Wuhan and even Hubei. In 2021, Zall's revenue reached 104.5 billion, ranking second in the revenue of private enterprises in Hubei Province. Zall Smart Commerce has driven the development of related enterprises with its Intelligent Link Ecology and become an important force in promoting economic innovation and development in Hubei Province. Zall Smart Commerce has become a leading digital trade platform in China. Zall research institute, affiliated with Zall Smart Commerce, has so far applied for 213 patents and been granted 42 patents, ranking 58th in the "2020 Global Enterprise Blockchain Invention Patent Ranking" and becoming the only enterprise in Hubei Province to enter the top 100 patent list. By continuously empowering the transaction scenarios of agriculture, steel, chemical and plastic industries and supply chain services such as logistics, warehousing and finance, Zall Smart Commerce has promoted the vigorous development of digital trade and digital economy in Hubei Province. In addition, Zall Smart Commerce also actively fulfilled its social responsibility during the COVID-19 epidemic. Relying on the industrial and supply chain service advantages of its platforms, it took the initiative to provide free consultation and support services on cargo transportation, customs declaration and customs clearance for medical supplies into Wuhan, and delivered medical supplies to the front line of epidemic prevention at the earliest time, which provided great help to the victory of the fight on epidemic in Hubei Province.

Intelligent mutual trust as the core to further release the value of industrial Internet is the development trend in the future. Although in the B2B 3.0 era, Zall Smart Commerce has built up an Intelligent Link Ecology covering the whole process of B2B transactions, there are still problems there. The cost of trust between the two sides of the transaction is not low enough. The efficiency of collaboration is not high enough. The intelligent level of enterprise production and product traceability is still to be improved. In order to solve these problems, Zall Smart Commerce will seize the opportunity of the new wave of technology and use the new trade platform to open up a new era of B2B4.0 with intelligent mutual trust as its core. What kind of an industrial Internet era will be? Yan Zhi, the founder of Zall Smart Commerce, introduced in his book *"B2B4.0: New Technology Applications to Detonate the Industrial Internet"* that "In the new B2B4.0 era, business flow, capital flow and information flow will be fully integrated; transactions will also be more real and secure with the support of underlying technologies such as blockchain, and the new credit system will be redefined; artificial intelligence will replace humans and assist in various aspects of transaction decisions; in the context of the Internet of everything and the maturity of big data technology, more clear and effective data will support the industrial system". Facing the existing challenges, Zall Smart Commerce still needs to reduce trust costs, improve transaction efficiency, and make resources and data more secure and fully interoperable. In the future, will Zall Smart Commerce be able to solve the existing challenges and become a pioneer in the B2B 4.0 era, truly realizing intelligent mutual trust? Let's look forward to it together.

FOMDAS FOODS: Digital Marketing Pioneer

Lan Shen

1 Development and Current Situation of the Company

1.1 Company Profile

Zhejiang Fomdas FOODS Co., Ltd. was established in August 1999 with a registered capital of CNY 65.85 million, focusing on the construction of the deep processing supply chain of agricultural products for more than 20 years. Belonging to Fomdas Holding Group, person and product", the company has driven 100,000 peasant households and nearly 300,000 farmers to achieve common prosperity with the value of "being a socially responsible and quality enterprise and person to produce better products". The company is mainly engaged in the processing, production and sales of canned food and orange by-products and related digital services, forming a whole industrial chain, supply chain and digital chain integrating the planting, acquisition, processing and sales of agricultural products.

1.2 Service Object

First, domestic and foreign customers, mainly those that products are mainly sold to more than 20 countries and regions such as the United States and Japan, and major large and medium-sized cities in China, with an annual export scale of about USD 50 million. Second is the raw material supplier in the upstream of the supply chain. Raw materials of agricultural products are purchased by the company for nearly CNY 100 million every year.

L. Shen (✉)
Shaoxing Vocational and Technical College, Shaoxing, China

J. Zhang et al. (eds.), *Innovation of Digital Economy*, Management for Professionals,
https://doi.org/10.1007/978-981-99-1741-9_24

1.3 Main Business Related to Digital Commerce

The company is mainly engaged in the processing, production and sales of canned oranges, canned yellow peaches, canned pears and orange by-products and related digital services, forming a whole industrial chain, supply chain and digital chain integrating the planting, acquisition, processing and sales of agricultural products.

Enterprise scale, industry status and number of employees: there are more than 200 employees in the company, and its products have passed BRC, ISO9001, ISO14000 and HACCP quality system certification. According to customs statistics, the company is now the largest producer and exporter of canned oranges in the world, accounting for 13% of the total export in China. At the same time, it is the first enterprise in China to adopt soft packaging of cans, the first enterprise in China to lead the research and development of orange automatic peeling and the first enterprise in China to lead the research and development of orange automatic splitting, participating in the drafting of national standards such as *Canned Orange*, *Canned Peach* and *Canned Pear*.

The enterprise is one of the first batch of key leading agricultural enterprises in China, the national technical center for citrus processing, one of the top ten canned enterprises in China, the small and medium-sized science and technology enterprises in Zhejiang Province, the second batch of provincial-level supply chain application and demonstration enterprises in Zhejiang Province, a key enterprise in supply chain innovation and application in Shaoxing City, and one of the top ten e-commerce enterprises in Xinchang County.

The company is an important reformer, participant and practitioner to promote the development of orange and other fruit industries, stabilize the industrial supply chain, increase farmers' income, promote the development of the fruit canning industry, overcome poverty, revitalize the countryside and achieve common prosperity.

1.4 Shareholding Structure and Business Relationship with Subsidiary (Parent) Company

The Company is a joint-stock enterprise, held by Fomdas Holding Group Co., Ltd., and its wholly-owned subsidiaries are Hubei Fomdas Food Co.,Ltd. and Zhejiang Haowang FOODS Co., Ltd.

1.5 Product Category

1.5.1 Food from Domestic Trade

See Fig. 1.

1.5.2 Food from Foreign Trade

See Fig. 2.

Fig. 1 Products for domestic market of Fomdas company

Fig. 2 Products for foreign trade

2 Present Situation of Company Digitalization

In daily operations, the company uses digital technologies such as cloud and big data to improve internal office capacity, enhance communication and sharing between departments, improve work efficiency and achieve energy conservation and green environmental protection.

Firstly, the company actively uses cloud service technology, and now has 2 PB cloud hosting for the enterprise, which is a cloud enterprise in Xinchang County. Secondly, a variety of information digital management systems are applied, including OA, HR, NC, ERP, intelligent weighing system of truck scale, video conference system, and data storage and backup system.

2.1 Introduction to Main Systems

(1) Office Automation System: based on the concept of workflow, modern information technology is adopted by office automation (OA) to collect, sort, process, store and use information widely, comprehensively and rapidly, so that internal personnel of the enterprise can share information conveniently and work together efficiently.
(2) ERP: the main function is to improve management efficiency, enhance the ability to refine management, improve work efficiency, solve the problem of information flow in the process of enterprise operation, and grasp inventory information, production status and sales situation in real time by checking upstream and downstream systems.
(3) Intelligent weighing system of truck scale: solve the shortcomings of traditional weighing methods, which are inefficient, error-prone, easy to cheat and labor-intensive, and highlight the advantages of scale intelligent weighing, such as safety, reliability and standard.
(4) Video conference system: provide high-definition, smooth and safe experience for multi-party conferences in enterprises, enhance conference experience and reduce communication costs.
(5) Data storage and backup system: guarantee data increment and information security.
(6) Human resource management system: from the long-term and overall perspective of the enterprise, formulate effective talent strategy, master the latest trends of employees, improve performance management and team execution.

In daily operation, OA, ERP and other systems are fully adopted by the company to achieve online approval and paperless office. Secondly, the systems have been fully integrated to reduce the waste of working hours. Digital technologies such as cloud and big data have been fully adopted by the company to save energy. Energy IOT has been mainly adopted to monitor water, electricity and gas, collect data, and effectively analyze the data required for production. Second, in the form of big data sharing and monitoring platform, a total of 15% change in energy consumption of office places and 10% change in energy consumption of other places has been achieved. The company has set up physical stores, counters and others in all supermarket systems through its sales subsidiaries, and the sales increased by 53% year on year in 2021.

2.2 The Company Operates Independently to Build a Digital Supply Chain

The company realizes the functions of basic goods quantity inquiry and automatic bookkeeping mainly through NC system. The company has contacted 65 upstream enterprises connected through digital supply chain, mainly including raw material suppliers, raw material base suppliers and packaging and other auxiliary material suppliers, and 2,000 downstream enterprises, mainly including downstream customers.

2.3 The Company Uses Big Data Technology or Cooperates with the Platform

Green environmental protection design is used for products and packaging. Intelligent packaging system is applied to the online sales of goods, which strengthens the scientific matching between express package and packing case. At present, the products using direct delivery packaging mainly include canned fruits.

3 Confronting Problems

3.1 Adjustment in the Proportion of Domestic and Foreign Sales Structure Due to the Impact of the COVID-19 Pandemic

Due to the outbreak of the COVID-19 pandemic in January 2020, the sales of agricultural products are facing a new round of "big test". According to relevant statistics, China's export volume has dropped by 15% in the first quarter due to the COVID-19 pandemic, and the impact on the export of important agricultural products is particularly obvious. However, the COVID-19 pandemic happened just in the peak season of the company's agricultural products during the Spring Festival, with sluggish consumption and blocked logistics circulation. On the whole, the proportion of domestic sales and export sales of the company has changed structurally, with the proportion of domestic sales increasing by 10% and domestic sales increasing from 30 to 40%. In this case, the company's export sales needs to be expanded through cross-border e-commerce platforms and other channels.

3.2 Digital Marketing Channels Need to Be Expanded

Although the company has set up a business in digital marketing, However, the channels involved at present are mainly domestic live broadcast platforms, Tiktok and Alibaba, while other platforms are less involved. However, the expansion of cross-border export platforms under the impact of the COVID-19 pandemic is still at the initial stage of exploration. Although Amazon is also involved, it is also difficult to expand the market due to the particularity of product storage and transportation.

3.3 Lack of Professional Digital Marketing Talent

At present, digital marketing is carried out by the company by means of internal staff transformation or part-time jobs. In the work, due to the lack of systematic digital marketing concept and professional talent in overall planning and layout of digital marketing products, marketing channels and services, the cost is high but the harvest is not necessarily high. In that case, it is necessary to train internally and introduce professional digital marketing talent from outside.

4 Digital Marketing Helps Enterprises Get Out of Difficulties

The company built and independently operated a digital supply chain, made use of big data technology or cooperated with the platform, and carried out the green design for products and packaging to actively cope with the impact of the pandemic. Intelligent packaging system is applied to the online sales of goods, which strengthens the scientific matching between express package and packing case. At present, the products using direct delivery packaging mainly include canned fruits. The specific performance is as follows:

4.1 Use New Media Marketing to Expand Sales

The company's team used tools such as social medium and mini programs to solve the problem of poor logistics during the pandemic with distributors covering all parts of the country as the main force, dealerships' business circle in cities as the delivery distance, and online ordering, offline delivery and offline distribution as the main forms. According to statistics, in the first quarter, more than 3 million consumers who were "at home" due to the pandemic successfully purchased the company's products and enjoyed the company's fresh fruit fishing products full of VC, ensuring that the company's products continue to activate the market. The chairman of the company appeared on the live broadcast channel, became the live-streamer, personally carried out live-streaming sales, tried his best to know, solved the confusion, distributed welfare to the company's followers in multiple dimensions and angles, and improved the viscosity and live effect. Meanwhile, the training company has its own live-streamers. In the first quarter, a total of three live-streamers were recruited. According to statistics, live broadcast has contributed nearly 20% of the company's sales since the outbreak. (Since the pandemic, there have been three live broadcasts a day, with an average of about 20,000 followers per round).

In 2020, through various e-commerce and social platforms, a total of 95 million people will be attracted and 25 million person-times monetized, including agricultural products and food; promoted the sales of rural products in poor areas to nearly CNY30 million, reflecting the company's values of social services, social contributions, taking root in agriculture, and being a high-quality enterprise; in 2021, 500 advertorials and short videos were released, with a click-through rate of 35 million; through Alibaba, Amazon and other cross-border e-commerce platforms, other business income was more than CNY50 million. Through the digital marketing model, the company has helped more than 20 enterprises achieve sales growth and enhance the brand value.

4.2 Expand the Market with "Cloud" as the Media

Affected by the pandemic situation, various product promotion conferences and exhibitions have been suspended indefinitely, resulting in the inability of some consumer terminals to obtain new products, new best-selling products and new celebrity-like products. The company seized the opportunity to recommend dealerships through dealerships, introduce the industry circles by industry circles, release product and investment promotion information on the company's own platform, third-party platform, and other cloud medium, carry out "cloud promotion", promote "cloud service", and distribute the company's new products and online celebrity products to new terminal markets to obtain higher product market rate and sales promotion, thus, the products can remain active in the market even though "home". According to statistics, in the first quarter, the company newly developed nearly 100 new terminal markets of RT-Mart South China market, Chongqing Yonghui Supermarket, Guizhou Heli Shopping, Zhongbai Warehouse Supermarket, Fulongtai, Mereo and other supermarket systems. Actively cooperated with third-party platforms such as "meicai.cn", focused on serving nearly ten million restaurants nationwide with avant-garde ideas, created a full range of worry-free catering materials procurement services, let the company's brand appear in the market with a new image, and improved new channels.

4.3 Actively Introduce Digital Marketing Operation Talents

The company introduced digital marketing talents through various recruitment websites, head-hunting companies, cooperative colleges and universities and other channels to provide technical support and guarantee services for itself to carry out systematic digital marketing services. First, gradually built customer relationship management (CRM), storage management system WMS, and initially built ET agricultural management intelligent brain, and the system that was capable of intelligent agricultural analysis, intelligent production management, output and quality prediction system; Second, constructed transparent supply chain; Third, promoted the construction of inventory logistics system; Fourth, quality traceability. The company promoted traceability of agricultural products through the two-dimensional code tag and other tracking and identification technology, constructed “one product, one code”, constructed agricultural product quality and safety traceability management information platform based on the product life cycle quality monitoring and traceability technology of big data to achieve link management; Five, promoted and applied the Internet of Things and the integrated Internet technologies of ERP, SCM and PLM production management systems to carry out digital transformation and networked management of the existing production equipment in the production workshop, built a digital collaborative manufacturing platform, established a complete digital manufacturing management collaboration platform from “order start—order coordination—order execution—order delivery”, and integrated planning management, quality management, process management, material management, personnel management, efficiency management and other modules and functional applications.

Xiaomi: How Do the World's Top Enterprises for Product Ecosystem Layout the Internet of Things?

Ziyi Zheng, Chuyan Li, and Yan Tu

1 Introduction

The Internet of Things (IoT), a concept coined by Ashton in 1999, is also called the third revolution in the information science and technology industry. Using information sensors and devices, Internet of Things can connect an item and the Internet, according to the provisions of the negotiation. Therefore, the items can through the network information transfer media achieve information exchange and communication, and then realize intelligent identification, positioning, tracing, supervision, and other functions. Since its development, the Internet of Things has been widely applied in industry. However, in life, it seemed that it was only a topic that technology lovers were keen to discuss.

When talking about Xiaomi, "a low price and high-grade configuration" and "hunger marketing" are its labels. As the leader of a product ecosystem enterprise, Xiaomi has developed rapidly in the complex and changeable business circle with its tenacious vitality. Xiaomi phone users have long been used to the convenience of "Mi AI", but the memory that other devices of Xiaomi began to integrated into daily life and form a web containing everything has already been blurred.

Technology such as the Internet of Things may be unfamiliar to people, but Lei Jun, the ambitious founder of Xiaomi, has gained great popularity. Since the day he founded the company, Lei Jun put forward the idea of "changing the Chinese manufacturing industry with Xiaomi", and found the inevitable trend of the development of platform enterprises to ecological enterprises. This was the ultimate goal of the development of Xiaomi Group, as well as the starting point for the

Z. Zheng (✉) · C. Li · Y. Tu
Central University of Finance and Economics, Beijing, China

J. Zhang et al. (eds.), *Innovation of Digital Economy*, Management for Professionals,
https://doi.org/10.1007/978-981-99-1741-9_25

continuous expansion of Xiaomi's product ecosystem and the activation of numerous industries. How did Xiaomi, the world's top product ecosystem enterprise, package a distant and vague concept and incorporate the goods into a whole step by step?

2 Start with "Born for Fancier"

2.1 "Born for Fancier"

Xiaomi Group was founded in April 2010, when Chinese manufacturing was still regarded as cheap knockoff replicas of major brands by the world. Lei Jun took his "triathlon"—"Internet + hardware + software"—created a community called "MIUI" quietly. In 2011, Xiaomi's first-generation mobile phone, the M1, became an instant hit with a crowd of fanciers. The top mobile phone configuration, low price and long-preheated hunger marketing strategy ignited the enthusiasm of consumers A new worldly reputed Chinese brand was growing vigorously.

Start-ups' concerns were soon echoed by Mr. Lei. Can such a small company, which was just getting started, sustain his ambition to revolutionize Chinese manufacturing and withstand the pressure to drive the industry? Lei Jun did not know, but he still firmly believed in his vision and thought the opportunity for future development was hidden in the product ecosystem development that arose at that time to go up. Therefore, in 2013, Xiaomi launched the product ecosystem connectivity plan and began to lay out the smart home; in 2017, Xiaomi's Internet of Things platform developed into the largest Internet of Things platform in the world; In 2019, Xiaomi among the world's Top 500, becoming the youngest company ever to make the list. Today, the legend of an Internet company continues (Fig. 1)...

Where should the story begin? Let's start with these "Xiaomi fanciers" who are "born for fancier" in the MIUI community.

3 Unstoppable Momentum: The Birth of Xiaomi Empire

3.1 MIUI Community: The Source of Follower Economy

In an age of consumer substitutes everywhere, who would pay for such a strange concept as a product ecosystem? Fortunately, with the creation of the MIUI community in the past, Xiaomi has a group of warm supporters as its solid backing. These "Mi followers" were willing to study Xiaomi's new technology, pay attention to its founder, buy its peripheral products, and feel its original aspiration and feelings. Because of this, they believed in Xiaomi's choice and were willing to use their own strength to leverage Xiaomi's voice volume.

This small community of only 100 people at the beginning, through its efficiency and reputation, expanded with a growth rate of almost 100% every week,

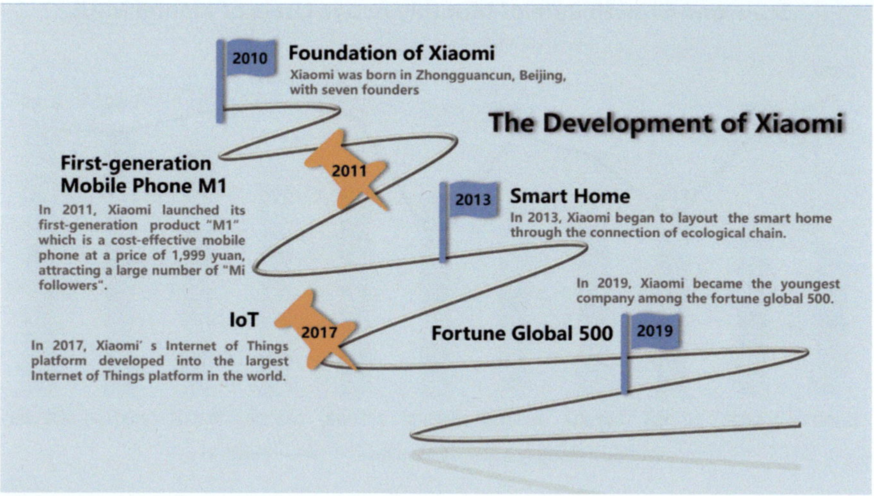

Fig. 1 The development of Xiaomi group (*Source* www.mi.com)

and developed into a follower community platform with tens of millions of loyal users. After the launch of the product ecosystem program, users used Xiaomi smartphones for an average of 4.5 h per day as of 2018, and more than 1.4 million users owned more than five Xiaomi connected products with non-smartphones and laptops. As can be seen from the data shown in Fig. 2, up to 2021, the monthly active users of Xiaomi MIUI still had a strong momentum of development and maintain a stable and high growth trend.

Through the MIUI community, Mi followers can provide advice directly to Xiaomi's engineers and developers. Engineers also can regularly participate in online discussions to understand the specific needs of users, which formed a two-way interaction. This business-as-friend relationship took a step further offline, too. The launch of an official offline campaign for "Mipop" further aroused the enthusiasm of Mi followers. At the event site, there were not only fan meetings, sports meetings, and other activities, but also Mi followers can have dinner with the management team and even participate in the organization and planning of the event.

As the guarantee of product sales of Xiaomi product ecosystem, the huge follower base determined the breadth of this ecological network was doomed not to end in a corner, but also the source of the productive power of Xiaomi, which continuously injected user vitality into product design. At the same time, the stickiness brought by follower interaction also greatly reduced the customer acquisition cost of Xiaomi and further improved the cost performance of the product. By listening to the voice of users, Xiaomi kept polishing and updating its own products to achieve the ultimate sense of simplicity and performance, forming a unique style of products.

At this point, Xiaomi laid out the cornerstone of the Internet of things.

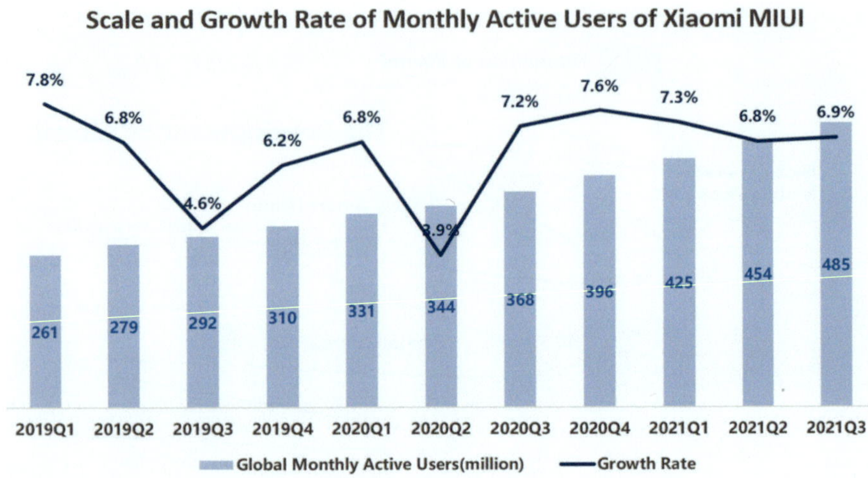

Fig. 2 Scale and growth rate of monthly active users of Xiaomi MIUI (*Source* Financial reports from www.mi.com)

3.2 From Connection to Intelligence

Back at the end of 2013, the prototype of the concept of a product ecosystem was initially shown, and Xiaomi's product ecosystem plan was also officially launched. The group began to gradually lay out the IoT hardware ecological model.

In order to take the first step into the Internet of Things, Xiaomi chose to focus on mobile phone peripheral products. On December 3, 2013, Xiaomi portable power source was released on the official website at a very low price of CNY69 with a simple appearance and advanced process, which suddenly set off a stormy sea in the portable power source market. Xiaomi portable power source has been a great success, and the Xiaomi router which released at the same time has also become a major weapon for Xiaomi to lay out the Internet of Things. And then more and more intelligent hardware products and peripheral products have been developed and listed through Xiaomi smart household App, creating the prototype of the network just like a spider spins. We call this stage as connection. At this stage, Xiaomi realized the simple and convenient control of its Bluetooth earphones, Bluetooth speakers, smart bracelets, set-top boxes, sweeping robots and humidifiers through the mobile phone pop-up. After these devices are connected to the mobile phone, the users only need to select the function on the mobile phone to control (Fig. 3).

As the pattern of this network becomes clear gradually, Xiaomi slowly began to realize that the mobile control equipment is only to facilitate people's control behaviors of the product and the control of the switch could also be realized with other tools. Once the "players" have run out of the freshness of terminal control, the ecological network they have painstakingly built will lose its attractiveness. Therefore, Xiaomi opened the door of intelligence, hoping to achieve the new

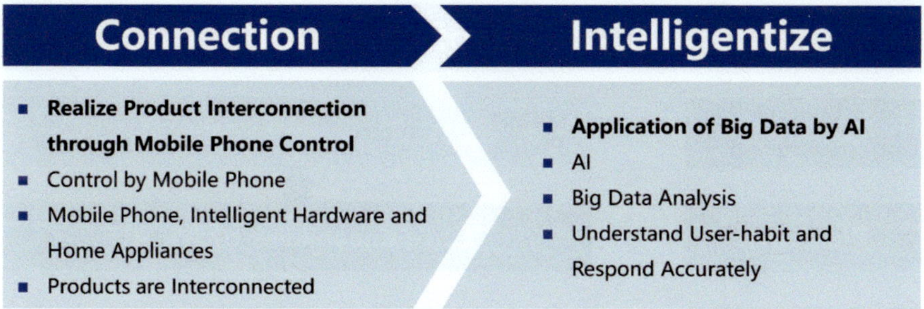

Fig. 3 An overview of Xiaomi's two stages in the field of the Internet of Things

goal of accurately responding to users' instructions through the prediction of big data, thus entering a new stage—the intelligent stage (Fig. 4).

In 2017, Mi AI, a new-generation artificial intelligence voice interaction engine, was released, which was installed in many Xiaomi product ecosystem devices such as Xiaomi mobile phones, Xiaomi speakers, and Xiaomi TVs. Since its first appearance, Mi AI's monthly active users have exceeded 100 million. It can control more than 100 models of intelligent hardware, covering applications in eight categories of scenarios such as life services, intelligent mobility, and smart wear, and can also collect user data and analyze users' habits through big data to achieve accurate response to instructions, which greatly improved the efficiency and user experience of Xiaomi products (Fig. 5).

From connection to intelligence, that is, from IoT to AIoT, from GUI to VUI, from individual to the whole, from interconnectivity to human-centered intelligent

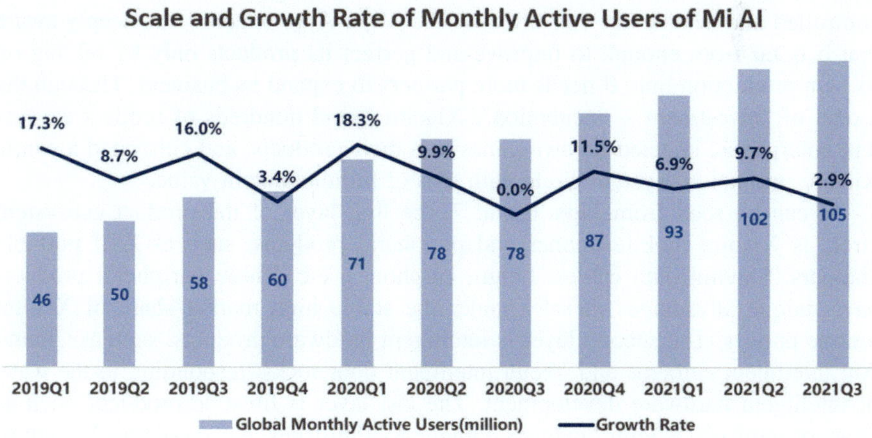

Fig. 4 The scale and growth rate of monthly active users of Mi AI (*Source* Financial reports from www.mi.com)

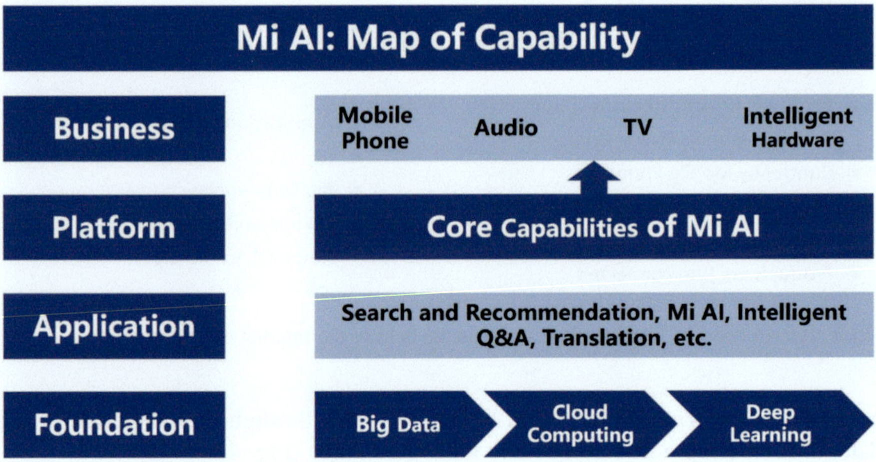

Fig. 5 The intelligent stage of Xiaomi

services, is the inevitable development trend of Xiaomi's product ecosystem and it is the two-stage path framework of Xiaomi's layout in the field of Internet of Things.

3.3 "Turning a Stone into a Gold"

After clarifying the development path, who should undertake the responsibility for production? Unlike other IoT companies, Xiaomi hopes that the products on the product ecosystem are diverse and affordable, requiring products to be uniformly controlled and seamlessly converted on the Mijia App. Xiaomi was deeply aware that it is far from enough to improve and perfect its products only by relying on its own production line. It needs more partners to expand its business. Through the model of "investment + incubation", Xiaomi found hundreds of product ecosystem enterprises, injected its own genes into their products, and cultivated a whole Xiaomi product ecosystem circle with tens of billions output value.

As can be seen from Figs. 6 and 7, the first layer of the product ecosystem circle is Xiaomi mobile phones and peripheral products, such as ZMI portable chargers, Shuomi data cables, Lanmi earphones, etc. These peripheral products have unique advantages in sales under the stable high market share of Xiaomi mobile phones. The second layer is intelligent hardware products, such as Clound Ant intelligent cameras and Yeeuu intelligent door locks, responding to the wave of intelligent hardware development. The last layer is lifestyle products, such as Ninebot segways, Runmi luggages, Qinghe toothbrushes, etc., assisting Xiaomi to locate users' preferences for living consumables more accurately.

By establishing this circle, Xiaomi can continuously expand its commercial territory, thus attracting more Mijia users, forming a virtuous cycle of "products

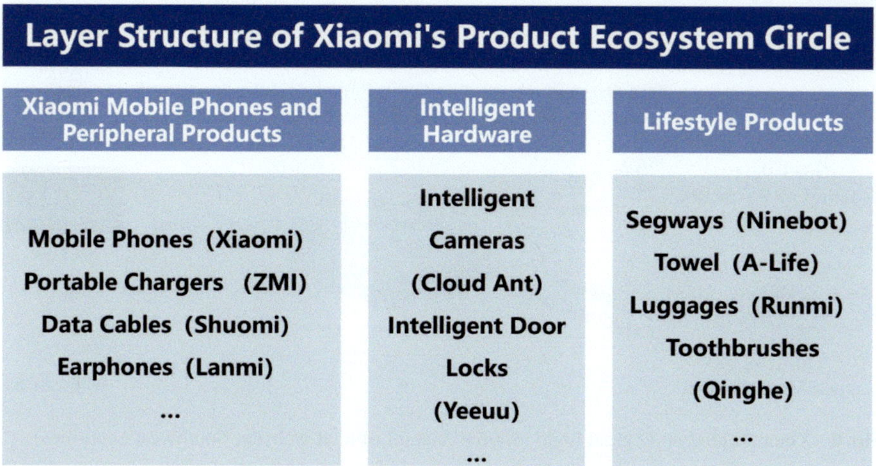

Fig. 6 Layer structure of Xiaomi's product ecosystem circle (*Source* www.mi.com)

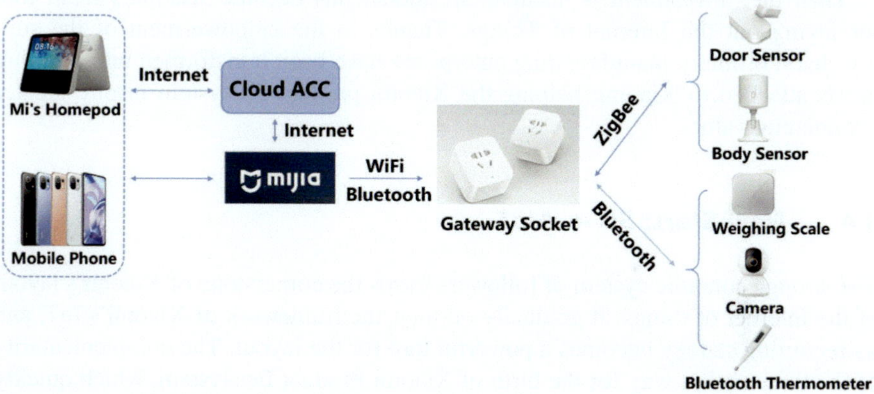

Fig. 7 The connection technology of Xiaomi smart home (*Source* Timehost Forensics)

attract users—users buy products —related products attract users", realizing the network externality effect of "the strong are stronger"; Product ecosystem enterprises, on the other hand, can focus on product research and development without worrying about various problems faced by other entrepreneurial teams, and achieve rapid growth without distraction.

The product ecosystem enterprises in the Xiaomi product ecosystem circle are not subsidiaries as the public understands, but partners of Xiaomi. In the process of cooperation, Xiaomi will assist product ecosystem enterprises in terms of brand, application, channel and financing, and support product ecosystem chain enterprises to incubate products. In this regard, Xiaomi proposed the strategy of

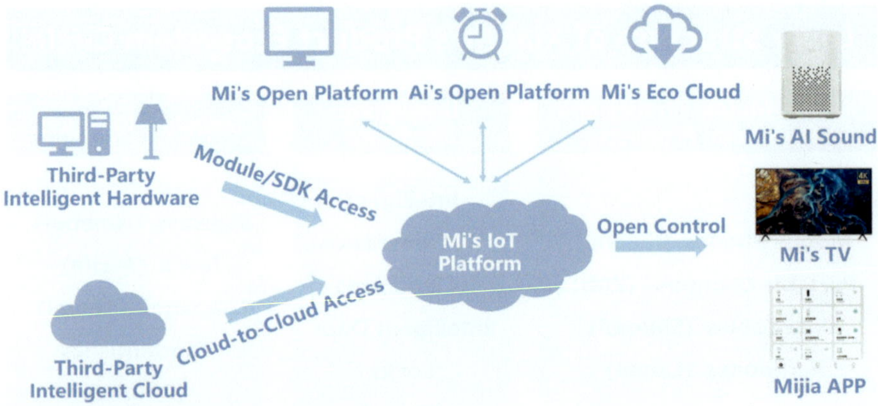

Fig. 8 Xiaomi cloud ecological logic (*Source* Xiaomi official website, Southwest Securities)

"investment without holding", which has also attracted a new batch of enterprises to enter the Xiaomi product ecosystem.

Then the "investment + incubation" model has become Xiaomi's main tool for laying out the Internet of Things. Thanks to the empowerment of the supply chain, ordinary manufacturing enterprises have been transformed into dazzling pearls attached to Xiaomi, helping the Xiaomi product ecosystem inspire greater commercial value.

3.4 New Start: 5G + AIoT

The strong economic system of followers forms the cornerstone of Xiaomi's layout of the Internet of things. It gradually outlines the framework of Xiaomi's IoT, and its recruiting stategy becomes a powerful tool for the layout. The complementarity of the three makes way for the birth of Xiaomi Product Ecosystem, which quickly pull out branches and leaves, burst out of vigorous vitality, and realize the basic layout of the Internet of things. However, against the backdrop of new challenges, it is doubtful whether Xiaomi could promote its Internet of Things, just as the poem "Horse flies in the warm spring wind so that I could see all flowers of Chang an in one day."

Going through the development of 1G, 2G, 3G and 4G, the mobile communication has entered the 5G era. As we can see, every leap of mobile communication considerably promotes the Industrial upgrading and economic and social development. Although the 4G network brought prosperity to the Internet, it faces the dilemma of skyrocketing demand for mobile data traffic. Today, with the rapid development of the Internet, new services and business continue to emerge. 5G can well meet the new needs of them, so it has been increasingly widely used. To be specific, as a new generation of mobile communication network, 5G could solve a wide variety of problems and apply to a wide range of scenarios. For example, it can provide users with extreme experiences such as augmented reality, virtual reality and ultra-high definition video during communication, and it can also solve the communication problems between not only people and things but also things and things. It meets the need of Internet of Things applications such as mobile health, Internet of vehicles, smart home, industrial control, and environmental monitoring. Generally speaking, 5G has become the key new infrastructure to promote the digital, networked and intelligent transformation of the economy and society. In this case, it is inevitable to penetrate into all fields of the economy and society.

Now, we would turn to the smart products, especially the smart phone industry. Shipments of 5G phones are growing even as overall smartphone sales decline. In 2021, 266 million 5G mobile phones were shipped in the domestic market, accounting for 75.9% of the overall shipments.

In addition, relying on favorable policies and the growth of the number of 5G base stations, the development of 5G industry is unstoppable. The application of 5G in intelligent products has become an inevitable trend in the development of smart products.

In order to meet the needs of the development of the era, in 2020, Xiaomi improved the dual-engine strategy of "mobile phone + AIoT", and took "5G + AIoT" as a new strategic starting point. It planned to invest at least CNY50 billion in the next five years to establish the next generation of super Internet, and to achieve full coverage of all products, all platforms, all intelligence and all scenes. The addition of 5G is not only the accelerant for the interaction behavior of Xiaomi's intelligent Product Ecosystem, but also the inward contraction of Xiaomi's circle, which makes peripheral productsbond more closely with its core product, Xiaomi mobile phone. The slogan of "Born for fancier" gradually developed into the vision of "Let everyone enjoy the fun of science and technology". Xiaomi started anew at the new intersection.

3.5 The Next is Xiaomi Eco-Empire

Reviewing the process of Xiaomi's Internet of Things layout, it can be found that the establishment of MIUI community, the improvement from connection to intellectualization, the specific construction of the ecological circle, and the implementation of 5G + AIoT strategy all play a pivotal role in the landing of Xiaomi's ecological empire. Now we talk about Xiaomi Product Ecosystem after the layout of its Internet of Things.

In terms of the composition of ecological products, there are some obscure consumer electronic products such as power bank, bracelet and sweeper. However, it is based on such obscure products that Xiaomi has gradually formed its ecological empire. There is a circuit called the "ant circuit", that is a situation where there is no oligopoly and huge demand is eaten by small players just like ants. Looking back to the product composition of Xiaomi's Product Ecosystem and the construction process of its ecological environment, it is obvious that entering the "ant track" is the first and relatively successful step of Xiaomi.

Although the current Product Ecosystem layout of Xiaomi is grand, at the beginning of its ecological chain construction, the idea of small rice is not complex. The Product Ecosystem defined by Lei Jun in the early stage has the following significance for Xiaomi: First is to maximize the traffic value. The release of Xiaomi mobile phone brings traffic to the brand itself, and the extension of the Product Ecosystem can realize the realization and maximization of the value of traffic. Second is to raise the Brand image. The Product Ecosystem provides suitable products for different groups based on the richness of products, enhances the in-depth communication between the brand and users, as well as the goodwill degree of the brand in the hearts of users. Third is to "duplicate" more Xiaomi through the Product Ecosystem. The aim is to make the group further improve earnings rely on the original "Xiaomi model". In such case, it is argued that Xiaomi Product Ecosystem is a social experiment of "Xiaomi model".

Therefore, in this socialization experiment, how does Xiaomi deal with the relationship between itself and cooperative Product Ecosystem enterprises? Many products in Xiaomi's Product Ecosystem are not directly manufactured by Xiaomi, but by enterprises that cooperate with Xiaomi. These Product Ecosystem enterprises themselves are independent from Xiaomi, so Xiaomi also faces problems such as quality control risk of in-production products in the process of constructing the Product Ecosystem. Besides, in the process of constructing the Product Ecosystem, Xiaomi will inevitably share the benefits with these enterprises. However, according to Xiaomi's "cost performance" strategy, the profits of the ecological chain enterprises will not be much. For these Product Ecosystem enterprises, the cooperation with Xiaomi is more about the traffic and brand effect brought by Xiaomi than profits. This cooperation mode makes Xiaomi's control over the Product Ecosystem enterprises weak, which also sows the seeds for Product Ecosystem enterprises to break away from Xiaomi and seek their own way after their strength is enhanced.

So has Xiaomi's ecological empire succeeded in the end? Select the "Ant Track", drive ecological enterprises, and turn the product into "Xiaomi model"... Under the support of these strategies, Xiaomi products quietly appear in every corner of consumers' homes, and Xiaomi's Product Ecosystem model has become the industry classic. After 5G + AIoT became Xiaomi's new strategy, Xiaomi's IoT revenue further increased. According to the report of the Future Think Tank, Xiaomi IoT's revenue increased from 8.69 billion yuan in 2015 to 55.91 billion yuan in the first three quarters of 2021, and its revenue share increased from 13% in 2015 to 25% in the first three quarters of 2021. With the continuous extension of Xiaomi's Product Ecosystem, it is expected that the contribution of IoT to income will further increase. On the other hand, the Xiaomi Product Ecosystem also drives the sales of Xiaomi mobile phone, the starting point and cornerstone of the Product Ecosystem. According to the latest report on the smartphone market released by Canalys, a research organization, on January 28, 2022, the market share of Xiaomi mobile phones in China in 2021 ranked third, with the shipment volume reaching 50.5 million units, a year-on-year increase of 27%. Therefore, we can be more optimistic to say that from these data, the Xiaomi ecosystem is indeed successful.

4 Internet of Everything: How to Realize Through Technology?

The successful development of the Internet of Things has created the second spring of Xiaomi's development. "Mijia" has become a brand that more and more consumers are talking about. The products of Xiaomi Mall with high cost performance and simple style continue to attract the "Mi followers" fascinated by them all over the world. Since then, everything in people's homes seems to be covered with "intelligent" color... Through Xiaomi's Product Ecosystem, users can control lights by voice, remotely control the whole house. The lights are off when people walk away, the windows are closed when it rains, and the electrical appliances are switched on and off automatically at regular intervals. However, what kind of technology does such an interconnection of everything need to rely on? Xiaomi's technical R&D department personnel showed their ingenuity, facing the tide of AI and 5G, and riding the wind and waves.

4.1 Connectivity Technology of Smart Home

The intelligent operation of Xiaomi's Product Ecosystem products cannot be separated from the Product Ecosystem, let alone the control center of the intelligent gateway. For some devices that do not support direct WiFi networking, gateways play a vital role, mainly including Bluetooth gateways and ZigBee gateways. The communication protocol between Xiaomi smart homes not only includes WiFi protocol, but also involves both gateways. Even with WiFi protocol, a multi protocol based device has been manufactured. The following describes the classification of Xiaomi smart homes with different communication protocols.

First, devices based on ZigBee gateways. Xiaomi uses ZigBee protocol on general sensor devices, such as door and window sensors, human body sensors, temperature and humidity sensors, etc. During operation, such devices connect to wireless routers by combining Xiaomi's ZigBee gateway to achieve mobile phone access to devices.

Second, devices based on Bluetooth gateway. For some devices that only need to collect data for one-way transmission, Bluetooth protocol is more widely used. Xiaomi Home mainly uses this gateway in Xiaomi cameras, Xiaomi weighing scales, Bluetooth thermometers and other data acquisition and transmission devices.

Third, devices based on WiFi protocol. The device connection mode based on WiFi protocol is mainly based on small household appliances, such as air purifiers and sweeping robots. The device and mobile phone terminal are connected to the

Table 1 Comparison of different communication protocol technologies

	WiFi	Bluetooth	ZigBee
Transmission rate	11–52Mbps	1–3 Mbps	10–250Kbps
Communication distance	20–200 m	20–200 m	2–20 m (Indoor)
Frequency band		2.4 GHz	
Security	Poor	Excellent	Good
Power dissipation	10–50 mA	20 mA	5 mA
Cost	High	Low	Low

(*Source* DIGTIMES)

same WiFi, and users can remotely control the device directly on the mobile phone App (Table 1).

4.2 Speech Recognition and Natural Language Processing Technology of Mi AI

As of March 2018, Mi AI of Xiaomi can control 118 models of intelligent hardware in the platform and support the interactive use of millions of intelligent devices in the scene. By collecting users' data and preferences, MI AI can have an intelligent conversation with users and complete the daily tasks assigned by users. MI AI is an integrated learning machine and analysis platform developed by Xiaomi according to special testing standards and certification systems, combining open source software and technology, and using the world's leading voice recognition technology and natural language processing technology. In terms of speech recognition, wake-up, echo cancellation, sound source location, recognition in noisy environments, different vocals, Chinese and English mixing are all difficult points to overcome. In terms of natural language understanding, knowledge base, question and answer pairs, grammar, vocabulary, equipment customization, AI training, etc. are the focus of technical breakthroughs Table 2.

4.3 Cloud Computing Technology of Product Ecosystem Operation

Figure 8 Xiaomi provides users with differentiated services through its powerful cloud computing functions. At the same time, in the business security operation of its Product Ecosystem, the partners signed with Xiaomi realize real-time data storage and data backup by connecting to Xiaomi's enterprise cloud. With the help of cloud computing technology, Xiaomi's IoT hardware can perform local edge AI computing, complete data processing behavior with high security, good

Table 2 Voice interaction analysis of Mi AI

The difficulties of voice analysis	
Front	Wake-**up,** Echo cancellation, Sound source Location recognition in
Recognition	Noisy Environments, Mixed Chinese and English, Different Vocals, Dialects
Composition	Nouns and Pronouns, Mixed Chinese and English
Natural language understanding	
Internal	Internal vertical domain, Grammar, Vocabulary, Knowledge base, Q&A Pairs
Device developer	Equipment customization
Skill developer	Open platform
User	AI training plan

(*Source* Wang Gang, Director of Mi AI Team of Xiaomi Group, China International Artificial Intelligence Conference)

scalability and large storage capacity in an efficient and flexible way, and achieve the goal of open control products. In addition, IoT hardware can also leverage the cloud for large-scale machine learning and global collaboration to optimize product configuration.

4.4 5G Communication Technology for Data Computing

5G communication technology has the characteristics of low latency and high density. In the future, Xiaomi will realize real-time cloud of CPU/GPU/AI by 5G + AIoT, so that data sinking to each terminal can get fast edge calculation, and achieve the effect of lightweight terminal, low power consumption and high response (Table 3).

For 5G Internet of Things applications, 5G mMTC is the main application scenario. Because 5G has a peak rate of 20Gbps and supports large-scale machine-based low-latency transmission, 5G can support the transmission of ultra-high-precision real-time video streams when applied to home devices such as

Table 3 NB-IoT Versus 5G

	NB-IOT	5G
Cost of network laying	Low	High
Cost of terminal	Low	High
Distance of coverage	Far	Close
Rate of spread	Low	High
Latency	High	Low
Number of connections	Low	High

(*Source* Founder Securities Research Institute)

surveillance cameras that rely on 5G low-latency capability, which greatly facilitates the real-time performance of the Xiaomi's Product Ecosystem. In the future, 5G will play a greater value in Xiaomi's IoT development through the complementary use of NB-IoT (narrowband Internet of Things) with lower power consumption and lower cost.

5 Epilogue

In recent years, depending on the Internet of Things, Xiaomi stands out with its ecological structure, which brings great convenience to consumers and also makes Xiaomi's products have more added value. According to the Q3 financial report of Xiaomi in 2021, the device connection number of the AIoT platform of Xiaomi is more than 200 million, the proportion of non-Xiaomi mobile phone users is more than half, and the business income of Xiaomi IoT and production of consumer products reaches 20.93 billion, which has become the second largest revenue source of Xiaomi.

Whether it is creating follower economy to form word-of-mouth marketing or creating Product Ecosystem products to form the ecosphere layer, Xiaomi undoubtedly has achieved great commercial success and leading position in the industry. From formulating the Product Ecosystem development plan to becoming the largest consumer-grade IoT platform in the world, to proposing a new strategic starting point of "5G + AIoT". As a leader of the IoT industry, Xiaomi bears not only the responsibility of the enterprise's own development, but also the expectation of people to drive the transformation of China's and even the global industry. However, the above is not the end point for Xiaomi to create the "Internet of Everything" ecological environment. Lei Jun formally proposed the concept of "Xiaomi idea" in his public speech on the 10th anniversary of Xiaomi, that is, to achieve the collaborative interaction of multiple devices. At Xiaomi's new product launch on December 28, 2021, Xiaomi further improved the MIUI system so that it is no longer a mobile-oriented operating system, but an operating system that spans multiple devices and connects multiple smart devices. Through the MIUI system, the products in the Xiaomi Product Ecosystem can not only achieve interconnection, but also achieve collaborative interaction, which greatly improves the efficiency of users. In addition, Xiaomi Automobile Co., Ltd. was formally established on September 1, 2021, and Lei Jun served as the legal representative, which means that Xiaomi will move from the light assets Internet mode into the heavy assets automotive industry. If Xiaomi automobiles come out in the future, it is very likely that Xiaomi will incorporate new energy vehicles into the built Internet of Things system, so that Xiaomi Product Ecosystem can be continuously expanded and iterated through further coverage of mobile travel scenarios.

Looking back on the development of Xiaomi, we have to admit that the strategy of Xiaomi from making mobile phone to establishing an all-encompassing and interconnected ecological Product Ecosystem is forward-looking. The classic label for Xiaomi used to be "cost performance", but it may no longer exist today and in the future when Xiaomi phones hit the high-end market. But at the same time, we also found that due to Xiaomi's ecological expansion over the years, "Product Ecosystem" has quietly become a new, competitive and discernible label for Xiaomi.

Of course, the development of Xiaomi is not smooth, Xiaomi also encountered various doubts and challenges in the process of its Product Ecosystem layout.

First of all, Xiaomi's Product Ecosystem layout may be suspected of excessive and blind expansion, and this blind expansion strategy may lead to Xiaomi's failure to achieve extreme concentration. As we all know, despite the wide range of products under the Xiaomi brand, the core selling point of Xiaomi is still mobile phones. In December 2021, Lei Jun withdrew from the legal person of Xiaomi Technology (Wuhan) Co., Ltd. and said that the company would concentrate on manufacturing cars. This act has caused considerable controversy in the industry and the consumer circle. Many people worry that Xiaomi may neglect the research and development of mobile phones and other products because it focuses on new industries, which will have a great impact on the development of Xiaomi.

Secondly, Xiaomi may have weak control over Product Ecosystem enterprises. Xiaomi's control over Product Ecosystem enterprises is mainly shown in two aspects: Control the quality of products produced by Product Ecosystem enterprises and control the Product Ecosystem enterprises themselves. The cooperation mode between Xiaomi and Product Ecosystem enterprises determines that Xiaomi cannot control the Product Ecosystem enterprises in a powerful way. From the perspective of Product Ecosystem enterprises, they are facing many other future development difficulties while growing rapidly, for example: Xiaomi's strategy of crushing other related enterprises through the supply chain is weak sustainability, the cost and profit constraints of Xiaomi's cost performance model on the Product Ecosystem enterprises, and the weakening of the Product Ecosystem enterprises' own brands due to cooperation. In order to promote their long-term development, some Product Ecosystem enterprises, such as Stone Technology, have even carried out the "Xiaomi elimination" campaign, jumping out of the ecological circle of Xiaomi and standing in the opposite side of Xiaomi ecological products.

Finally, although Xiaomi has built a relatively complete and powerful Product Ecosystem, injecting new momentum into economic development and increasing consumer welfare, there are also potential social problems in the actual operation process, such as users' information security problems, environmental problems, market competition disorder problems and so on, leading to potential crisis that users can still transfer to other brands' ecosystems easily and making it difficult to form a stable and effective customer precipitation mechanism.

Through the above analysis, we can easily find that the Product Ecosystem layout of Xiaomi has both opportunities and challenges. However, we believe that, relying on the strength of strong followers, with the persistence of faith and its own scientific and technological innovation and breakthrough, Xiaomi will continue to overcome difficulties and forge ahead.

Pimax: How to Subvert VR Industry and Break Through Record of Kickstarter Crowdfunding

Hanmi Lin, Guichao Jin, and Jianbo Weng

1 Introduction

At the end of 2017, Pimax launched an 8 K head mounted display on Kickstarter. The crowdfunding process of this Pimax head mounted display with binocular 8 K resolution and 200-degree field of view lasted for 45 days, and finally won more than USD4.23 million from nearly 6,000 users globally, which broke Oculus' crowdfunding record for five years, and won the "Guinness World Records in 2019", and became the highest VR crowdfunding project in the world. At the same time, it is also a crowdfunding project ranked 4th in all hardware categories and 24th in all categories on Kickstarter.

As we all know, crowdfunding provides a good financing channel for many enterprises, especially startups, to develop new products, and at the same time, it also allows companies to gain some early and loyal user support, making it a popular choice for many startups. So how did Pimax make great efforts on Kickstarter and achieve a great success that exceeded its expected crowdfunding target by 20 times?

2 Focus on Technical Performance Breakthroughs and Seize Differentiated Advantages in International Competition

2.1 End the Confusing History of VR Development

Metaverse seems to have become a fashion recently. Roblox completed the financing and listing and Facebook changed its name to allin. Along with the sharp rise

H. Lin (✉) · G. Jin · J. Weng
Hangzhou Normal University Qiangjiang College, Hangzhou, China

J. Zhang et al. (eds.), *Innovation of Digital Economy*, Management for Professionals,
https://doi.org/10.1007/978-981-99-1741-9_26

of related concept stocks, the metaverse has been defined as the "next generation Internet", which can be often described as a virtual space parallel to and independent from the real world. VR head mounted glasses, which can bring immersive 3D experience, will usher in a new round of development as the entrance of a metaverse. VR is an abbreviation of virtual reality. As early as 1930s, the writer Stanley G. Weinbaum first mentioned such VR glasses in his novel Pygmalion's Spectacles. Up to now, the VR industry has experienced three great changes snd confusing developments. The first phase is 1930s–1950s, from concept to reality, and in the mid-1950s, the tossed American photographer Morton Heilig invented the first VR device: Sensorama (patent filed in 1962). This device is considered by some to be the prototype of VR devices. The second stage is from 1990s to 2012, and the VR industry ushered in the first upsurge. Although the appearance is no different from the VR we see today, the display technology, 3D rendering technology and motion detection technology were immature. The viewing experience falls far short of the "usable" standard. The third stage is from 2012 to now, and the VR industry has ushered in a stage of continuous technological breakthrough. In 2012, Oculus Rift came out, which is a VR glasses device with crowdfunding of USD2.5 million on Kickstarter. It brought people's vision back to the VR field. In 2015, HTC vive was officially released on MWC2015. In 2016, Sony announced PSVR, and then a large number of manufacturers began to develop their own VR devices. The new year of VR officially began. In less than two years after that, VR industry did not seem to develop in a clearer direction, but became a bit "confusing". However, at the end of 2017, an 8 K head mounted display launched by Pimax on Kickstarter instantly revived the passion of many users who were disappointed with VR.

2.2 Create a Pimax Technology Focused on Technical Performance Breakthroughs

Weng Zhibin, the founder of Pimax, has experienced the invention and popularity of mobile phones in Dothink, BYD and other companies. The whole process from no-smart phone to smart phone with touch screen, that is the second generation computer system (the first generation is PC computer system), Later, he came into contact with Oculus's OEM project in Goer Tek Inc (Goer Acoustics VR Company Introduces a Company That Manufactures for Oculus and PSVR, 2016) (a company that manufactures the first generation VR products of Oculus and PSVR), which brought him great shock. He felt that VR was the bud of this third generation computer system, and it was likely to replace mobile phones one day in the future. He has a solid knowledge foundation and always wants to establish his own business. He thinks this is a very good opportunity. Therefore, in 2014, he decided to set up a research and development team composed of the first batch of technical engineers who are crazy about virtual reality technology in China. Most of the team members come from virtual reality, smart phones, wearable devices, Internet, games, medical and other professional fields, including Changjiang Scholars, research award winners of Google AR/VR College, etc., which laid a solid foundation for the establishment of Pimax Co., Ltd. in Shanghai in 2015 to focus on the breakthrough of VR technology performance.

With the Pimax into the VR market in the same period, there are about 200 to 300 companies doing hardware, but at this time most of the VR product performance is still immature, and the user experience is very bad. This makes Pimax, which is in the research and development stage, focus more on the two disadvantages of existing VR products-resolution and wide angle. After two years of hard work by the R&D team, Pimax successfully released the world's first 4KVR head mounted display in April 2016, and started mass production and delivery two months later.

2.3 Establish the Industry Position with Differentiated Competitive Advantages

At the conference in early October 2016, Michael Abrash, chief scientist of Oculus, predicted that 8 K, new interaction and AVR would appear within five years (Oculus predicts that 8K, new interaction and AVR will appear in 5 years 2016). However, in January 2017, Pimax had already completed 8 K demo, leading the industry level for at least 2 years. "Differentiated competitive advantages have strengthened our technology-oriented development ideas," said Weng Zhibin, founder of Pimax. The Pimax started mass production and delivery in October 2018. 8 K has become the most popular VR product for VR fancier all over the world, and users praise it as the only VR device in the world that can clearly see the dashboard of aircraft. At present, the resolution of VR products in the world is generally 4 K, and the Pimax reaches 8 K. The field angle of VR head mounted display in the world is generally 120°, and the Pimax extends to 200°. It has many global PCT invention patents, and the small pie 8 K is fully compatible with mainstream content platforms, such as Steam and Oculus Home. Pimax now owns 8 K, 5 K, Artisan and other series of high-performance PCVR head mounted display products, and has also developed black technology modules such as gesture recognition, eye tracking, smell module and smell module. Pimax's single breakthrough in several key parameters has owned many of stable and loyal geek users all over the world. Thus, Pimax can overtake big factories such as Facebook and HTC in VR field at key points.

3 Accumulate Experience Through JD.COM Crowdfunding and Cultivate Foreign Seed Customers Through Multiple Channels

3.1 JD.COM Crowdfunding Accumulates Experience

The first batch of thousands of equipment orders crowdfunded by JD.COM crowdfunding is the first step for Pimax to open up the market, which not only earned the first bucket of gold, but also accumulated some experience for it to launch overseas crowdfunding. The Pimax released the world's first VR device with a resolution of 4 K-Xiaopai 4 K, which landed in JD.COM for crowdfunding on April 14, 2016, and the price was 1,699 CNY, Fig. 1 shows a screenshot of crowdfunding in JD.COM (Zhang, 2017). The total amount crowdfunded is more than 3 million, far exceeding the expected target of 500,000, and good results have been achieved. After that, the goods were delivered on June 25th and ended on July 1st. After that, in July and August, "there was an accident from the giant", because "the whole company did customer service for more than a month without sufficient preparation for foreseeable industry changes". The main reason for the "accident" lies in the adaptation of products. On the one hand, NVIDIA introduced GTX 1080 to update the driver. At that time, the driver design of 4 K head mounted display did not consider this; On the other hand, Microsoft Windows 10 turned on the update, which caused users who used GTX 1080 graphics card to be unable to run the head mounted display, and the computer operating software could not support it normally. However, most users did not ask for a return immediately. Instead, they forced Pimax to constantly modify the bug. In one and a half months, the driver was changed from over 30 megabytes at the beginning to over 300 megabytes, and then it was compatible with NVIDIA's new driver and Windows 10 update again. The experience in crowdfunding 4 K products in JD.COM allowed Pimax learn a lot of experience to arrange crowdfunding release of 8 K products."

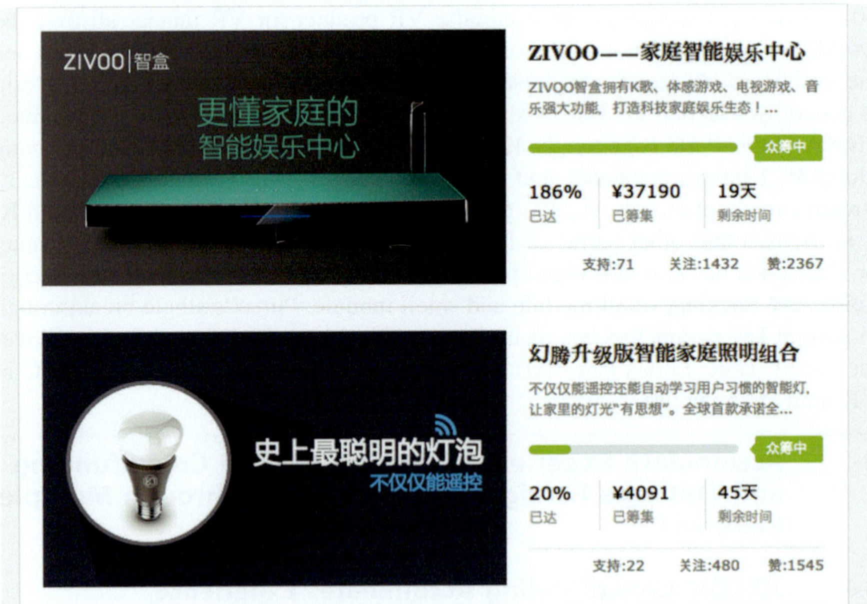

Fig. 1 JD.COM Crowdfunding

3.2 Cultivate Foreign Seed Customers Through Multiple Channels

At the beginning of 2017, Pimax unveiled 8 K products in the United States, but it didn't really start crowdfunding until September 14th. During this period, Pimax made a lot of preparations for overseas crowdfunding on the basis of absorbing JD.COM crowdfunding experience, mainly including crowdfunding platform selection and cultivate foreign seed customers through multiple channels For platform selection, Pimax mainly weighs Kickstarter and Indiegogo as the two crowdfunding platforms. "In comparison, the former is larger, but the threshold is also higher, the first platform requires to register foreign companies, the second platform is required to collect money by Visa. Therefore, we developed a strategy of going abroad before turning to domestic sales, first aim on target groups such as the United States, Europe, Japan, South Korea," said Weng Jianbo, Vice President of Pimax. After choosing the platform, Pimax started to cultivate seed customers in foreign target markets through overseas forums, third-party e-commerce platforms and social media, CES, independent stations and professional advertising agencies and other online and offline multi-channel layouts.

3.2.1 Register and Operate Overseas Forums

In September 2016, Pimax used Discourse technology, relying on cloud service, to build an overseas forum called OpenMR. For Pimax, the loyal users will not only be the guarantee of sales, but also the forward partner to provide feedback and refine the technology. The main purpose of building the overseas forum is to sink the customers accumulated in various channels, establish Pimax's own private traffic, strengthen communication with customers, and enhance customer stickiness. OpenMR mainly consists of sections for announcements, guide repository, Pimax hardware, Pimax software, other head mounted display, games and software, accessories, feedback, VR content, etc. Each section is managed by different moderators, who volunteer for forum services, they form a moderator committee, which regularly communicates with Pimax about some issues and recent news. Pimax has the right and obligation to monitor and regulate the forum, and also provide funds, products, gifts and other support to the moderator committee. If there is a problem that cannot be solved by the forum, the problem can be submitted to the Pimax Support Forum, Fig. 2 is the mechanism of running the Pimax Overseas Forum. In addition to daily communication, OpenMR plays a great role in handling the PR crisis of Pimax.

3.2.2 Rely on Third-Party E-commerce Platform and Social Media

In the same period of domestic sales, Pimax carried out the layout of the product abroad in September 2016, opening the first 4 K global sales on two third-party e-commerce platforms, Amazon (opened the U.S. station and European station) and Newegg. At the same time, Pimax contacted VR related opinion leaders on YouTube, sent the product to them, asked them to shoot real videos of product testing and post them on their channels. Later on, more and more celebrities in

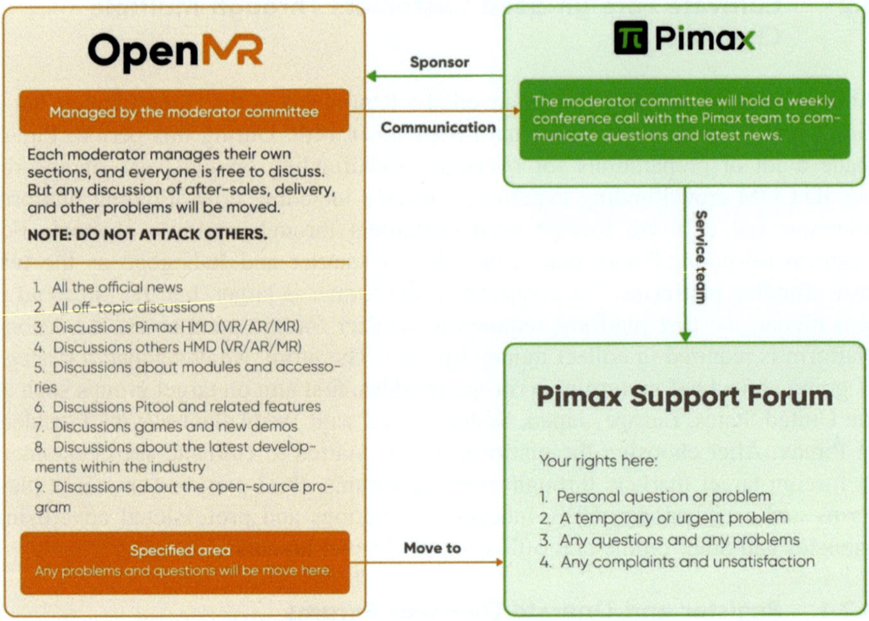

Fig. 2 Schematic diagram of the operation mechanism of Pimax Overseas Forum

Twitter and Instagram promote Pimax's products, thus creating a great impact among their followers.

3.2.3 Build a Standalone Site Based on Shopify

Like the forum, building a standalone site is also a way to create a private traffic pool for Pimax. Of course, for crowdfunding, it is especially important to set a clear crowdfunding goal, create a complete product introduction and an intuitive brand e-commerce website before starting crowdfunding for a product, as this is the only way to make the product more attractive and convincing. A standalone site not only helps to showcase the product, but also drives EDM email marketing. For the Shopify experience, Mr. Weng believes that it not only has the characteristics of building an e-commerce website with high efficiency, but also has the obvious advantages of good user experience, easy operation and intuitive data, "From the end of 2018, we started using Shopify branded e-commerce website to help us start 2C sales in the fastest and most friendly way to 2020 the first quarter we already have tens of thousands of users whose products need to be delivered." Mr. Weng added. Pimax's standalone site is divided into five modules: product, policy, explore, support and follow us. Under each module, there are a series of sub-functional modules, Fig. 3 shows the functional architecture of Pimax's standalone site schematic.

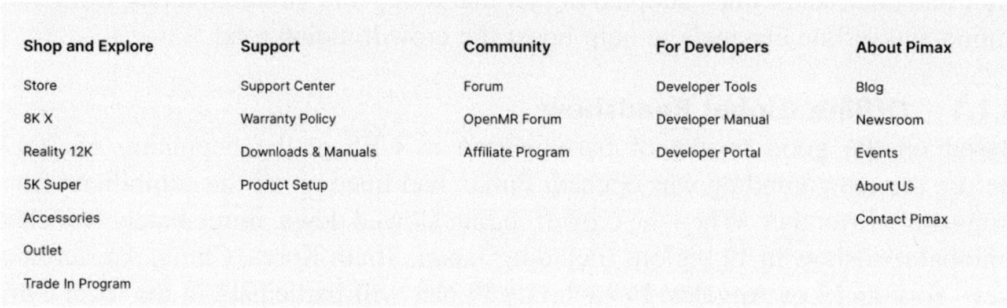

Fig. 3 Functional architecture of Pimax's standalone site schematic

3.2.4 Attend the Global Consumer Electronics Show in Las Vegas

In January 2017, Pimax participated in the Global Consumer Electronics Show (CES) in Las Vegas with a finished 4 K head mounted display and a demo of an 8 K head mounted display. "Although the station of Pimax was very small, it still managed to attract extensive attention from overseas media with the advantages of technology. Many well-known media immediately reported on Pimax's products at that time. The next day, Facebook, Qualcomm, and some big Google executives came to visit the booth, and the atmosphere at the scene gave Pimax's partners a boost of confidence." Mr. Weng said excitedly that the scene still seems to be vivid in his mind.

3.2.5 Cooperation with Professional Advertising Agency

In order to reach users more accurately and widely, Pimax cooperates with professional advertising agencies. Advertising agencies provide precise advertising to potential customers through some professional online and offline media. And the disadvantage of this type of advertising is that Pimax cannot receive feedback from consumers timely. However, it has been proven that finding the right professional advertising agency can bring unexpected results for enterprises. Mr. Weng said, "Before the crowdfunding officially started, Pimax only received 10,000 emails from customers, but at the beginning of the crowdfunding, once the media news was sent, the crowdfunding amount reached USD500,000 within a minute, so we felt that we underestimated the power of the media".

4 Crowdfunding Breaks Guinness World Record, Steady Progress in Delivery

4.1 Promotion of Online and Offline Crowdfunding

September 14, 2017 was the first day of Pimax crowdfunding launch, and it reached USD500,000 within a minute. It reached USD1 million in one hour, basically completing the set goal in one hour. The growth rate gradually slowed down after one hour, and Pimax adopted digital marketing and viral marketing from both online and offline channels to help boost the crowdfunding total.

4.1.1 Offline Global Roadshow

Based on the good results of participating in CES at the beginning of 2017. Before the crowdfunding was opened, Pimax had lined up all the exhibitions from August to November. When the crowdfunding slowed down, immediately launched a global roadshow in 12 regions including Japan, South Korea, China, Amsterdam, New York and Los Angeles. In each city Pimax will participate in the local exhibition being held and organize user experience activities, about 30,000 players around the world have participated in Pimax 8 K product testing. During the user experience, Pimax will also take the opportunity to carry out digital marketing, Mr. Weng said, "There were only 7,000 screens in stock, which could only support the delivery of 3,500 sets of devices, when our team limited the number of product reservations and also synchronized this information to the public." The roadshow + digital marketing approach proved to be very effective, with roadshows in almost every city bringing in nearly half a million dollars in bookings for crowdfunding. Attending the show also attracted a large wave of followers of Pimax, one of whom, Martin Lammi, later became the head of marketing for Pimax's European region.

4.1.2 Continued Promotion of Online Marketing

On the one hand, online marketing is carried out by way of extended targeting (i.e. viral marketing), mainly through existing customers mobilizing their relatives and friends around them. If the booking amount reaches a certain amount, Pimax promises to give certain heavyweight gifts, such as handheld recognition and eye tracking and other cutting-edge technology in the VR field, which is extremely attractive to users. "When we told the users that there was a limit to the number of products, all the models were sold out on the same day. Then, between October 25th and November 1st, users asked us to find a way to increase the number of pre-orders, so we borrowed more screens from our partners," said Mr. Weng with a smile. To ensure quality and quantity delivery, there was no further expansion, so the final amount of the crowdfunding stopped at November 1st.

On the other hand, another aspect of online marketing is to stay engaged with users on the crowdfunding page 24/7. Looking back now, Mr. Weng was excited, "Actually we were pretty crazy at that time, and we basically worked two shifts for 45 days straight, keeping 7*24 h and having to finish answering users' queries within an hour. It's easy to come across unexpected situations on the internet, such as encountering an incendiary user. We must explain things clearly in a sincere manner to keep the direction of public opinion in check." By explaining the problem in various ways such as text, drawing pictures and making videos, Pimax answered 7,000 questions in 45 days. The professionalism and sincerity solved some problems that could have led to a crisis many times, which laid a solid foundation for the crowdfunding to break the Guinness World Record.

4.2 Steady Progress on Delivery

4.2.1 Complete Product Research and Development and Production with Good Quality and Quantity

At the time of the crowdfunding, Pimax agreed with the customer to complete delivery in March 2018, but the actual delivery has been delayed until June 2019. This is mainly due to many unforeseen technical difficulties, such as the lack of a content ecosystem to support the 8 K head mounted display, and many other disturbing factors such as the questionable quality of raw materials and smelly packaging that have an impact on product delivery. Learning from the lessons of the repair of JD.COM Crowdfunding at the later stage, Pimax chose to complete the development and production of products according to the quality and quantity requirements, even they need to delay the delivery.

4.2.2 Keeping Information About the Delivery Process Transparent

The delayed deliveries not only directly affected user satisfaction, but also attracted the attention of the media. The press abroad carried reports on this, with Pimax being delayed from March to May in 2018, then to October and finally to June in 2019. Figure 4 shows a screenshot of a press report on the delayed delivery of the Piper. In the face of such a crisis, Pimax, as always, sought truth from facts and meticulously responded to the media queries, presenting the technical problems, production problems and product consistency problems encountered at each point in time, together with a detailed solution process and the corresponding time spent. For each extension, Pimax has sought the advice of users in the full process. It is this collision and communication with users again and again that makes Pimax get the first batch of loyal users. In the end, the media and the public understood the situation of Pimax. Figure 5 shows a screenshot of the response to a press query from Pimax.

At the same time, Pimax kept in constant communication with the intended customers through the overseas forum OpenMR, showing all the information about the development, production, packaging, delivery and logistic route of Pimax products. After knowing the relevant information, the users were less worried about the delayed delivery, and their trust in Pimax was enhanced during the interaction with Pimax. Therefore, the crisis was resolved through effective interaction.

Fig. 4 Screenshot of news media reports on the delayed delivery of Pimax (Pimax "8K" Headsets & Accessories Delayed Again, Now Estimated for Late 2019 & Early 2020, 2019)

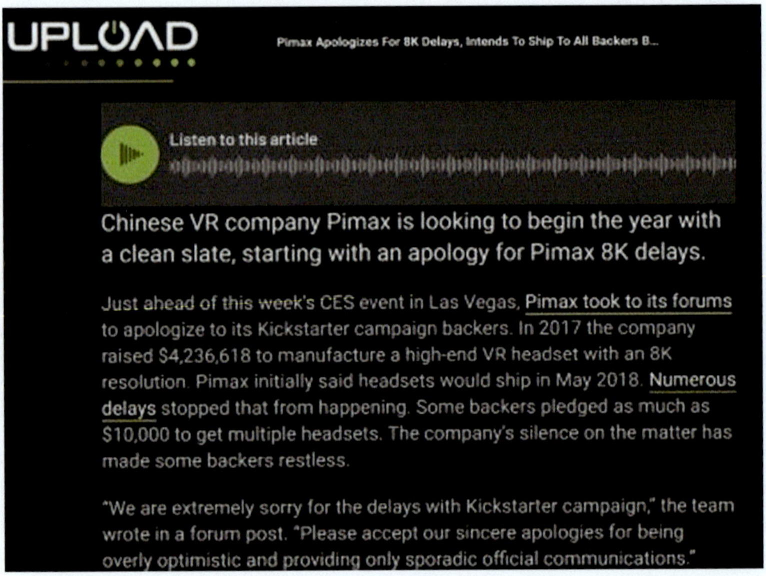

UPLOAD

Pimax Apologizes For 8K Delays, Intends To Ship To All Backers B...

Listen to this article

Chinese VR company Pimax is looking to begin the year with a clean slate, starting with an apology for Pimax 8K delays.

Just ahead of this week's CES event in Las Vegas, Pimax took to its forums to apologize to its Kickstarter campaign backers. In 2017 the company raised $4,236,618 to manufacture a high-end VR headset with an 8K resolution. Pimax initially said headsets would ship in May 2018. Numerous delays stopped that from happening. Some backers pledged as much as $10,000 to get multiple headsets. The company's silence on the matter has made some backers restless.

"We are extremely sorry for the delays with Kickstarter campaign," the team wrote in a forum post. "Please accept our sincere apologies for being overly optimistic and providing only sporadic official communications."

Fig. 5 Screenshot of Pimax's response to news media queries (Pimax Apologizes For 8K Delays, Intends To Ship To All Backers By Month's End, 2019)

4.2.3 Improving Delivery Quality Through Oversea Location

Oversea location is an important means to improve the delivery quality of cross-border e-commerce, Pimax has set up overseas warehouses in the US, UK, Germany, Canada, Japan, South Korea and Australia since 2018 to lay a solid foundation for improving the quality of product delivery, while the oversea location also undertakes the functions of returns and maintenance.

5 Epilogue

Through careful operations before and after the crowdfunding, Pimax has established a high-end brand image overseas, with hundreds of millions of media exposures per year and roughly 5,000 YouTube review videos alone.

During the period after 2019, Pimax continued to deepen its product development, successively launching Pimax Vision 8 K Plus, the upgraded product of Pimax Vision 8 K, and Pimax Vision 5 K Super and Pimax Artisan series, which are positioned at an affordable price. Pimax Vision 8 K X, the flagship product of Pimax, was launched in 2020. In October 2021, Pimax released the new Pimax 12 K Reality QLED product in the US, which raises the field of view to a horizontal 220° and achieves a screen resolution of 12 K while maintaining a high resolution and refresh rate. The realization of the 12 K head mounted display will promote the development of Pimax Technology five years ahead of the industry.

In combination with its leading hardware products, Pimax will develop towards a strong content ecology, so as to open up the market from top to bottom and cover mainstream users level by level, bringing the most ultimate VR experience to Chinese and overseas users.

References

Goer Acoustics VR Company Introduces a Company That Manufactures for Oculus and PSVR. (2016). Retrieved from http://www.paopaoche.net/article/105835.html.

Oculus predicts that 8K, new interaction and AVR will appear in 5 years. (2016). Retrieved from http://news.17173.com/content/11082016/114043491_1.shtml.

Pimax Apologizes For 8K Delays, Intends To Ship To All Backers By Month's End. (2019). Retrieved from https://uploadvr.com/pimax-apologizes-8k-delays/.

Pimax "8K" Headsets & Accessories Delayed Again, Now Estimated for Late 2019 & Early 2020. (2019). Retrieved from https://www.roadtovr.com/pimax-8kx-8kplus-launch-dates/.

Zhang, M. (2017, August 24). Xiaopai technology constructs a virtuous VR ecosphere. *Pudong Times*, p. 4.

Mixiaojiu Wine Industry: "In Virtue of the Opportunity, I Will Go up in the World"

Li Zhang and Jingwen Xiong

1 Introduction

A founding team led by a senior public relations director from different websites announced the official establishment of the brand of Mixiaojiu Wine Industry on the first day of March 2018. The team wanted to integrate the new concept of digitalization into the long-standing Chinese spirits. They intended to bring three screams to consumers by three new businesses.

The "three new businesses" includes new products, new social networking and new retail. The "three screams" is a product R&D concept proposed by Mixiaojiu Wine Industry on the basis of the user demand and experience. It is also a general principle to guide the R&D of Mixiaojiu. Its essence is to give consumers experience beyond their expectations in all aspects. The first one is to offer users specific experience beyond their inherent understanding of Chinese spirits when they get to know our products for the first time. The second one is that users are more satisfied with the product than the publicity. The third one is that users feel cost-effective after drinking our products.

On April 10, 2020, the products were sold in the live broadcast room of Luo Yonghao. It was the first time for him to try to sell Chinese spirits, facing all kinds of comments in the industry. Mixiaojiu Wine Industry gave a perfect answer—the sales exceeded 10 million in 90 min, exceeding the expectations of industry insiders. Since the COVID-19 pandemic, various scenes with drinking consumption have ushered in an ice age such as traditional family dinners. Under such background, Chinese spirits began to actively explore digital transformation and channel innovation. Mixiaojiu Wine Industry regards e-commerce as its main sales

L. Zhang (✉) · J. Xiong
Southwest University of Science and Technology, Mianyang, China

J. Zhang et al. (eds.), *Innovation of Digital Economy*, Management for Professionals,
https://doi.org/10.1007/978-981-99-1741-9_27

channel. It still maintains an upward trend and adheres to healthy and happy product services and missions even during the pandemic.

2 Source of the Flavor

In terms of the products, the original intention of Mixiaojiu Wine Industry is to brew natural raw materials. With the ecological beauty of nature, it takes all the grains, water and distiller's yeast from nature, without any artificial additives. In addition, the microorganisms in nature attracted by distiller's yeast are used in the fermentation.

The origin of the products is located in Yibin, Sichuan Province, which is known as the "Golden Triangle of Chinese spirits". Mixiaojiu Wine Industry directly seeks local distilleries with brewing capacity for production. That's because the ecological environment in this region is born to brew, which has produced the famous high-end Chinese spirits. The region also makes Mixiaojiu Wine Industry extraordinary! The company makes deep cooperation with two distilleries and hold the controlling share of them. It is the same reason that Xiaomi mobile phone is the product of Foxconn. Both of them use the model of Internet production, which hands over what it is good at to the best people. Mixiaojiu just integrates the capital, industrial chain, channels and brands. At present, the two distilleries controlled by the company have adhered to the traditional brewing method of Chinese spirits, which uses the grains to brew the spirits from the source of the supply chain. In addition to the national inspection, the products of Mixiaojiu have also been tested by the No. 1 testing agency in the world before being listed.

Mixiaojiu Wine Industry jointly invested CNY 300 million with Jiang'an County Government of Yibin to build a distillery there in 2019. The company selected a number of high-quality cellars and cultivated new fermentation pools by overall relocation, which formed its own local production capacity. The distillery built in Yibin is of complete digital demonstration. It can be seen from the design of assembly lines and the tracking of products. The reason for such a construction is that the company knows that the layout of the whole industrial chain is the best choice. The sales will depend on the ability of its own supply chain when the sales accumulate to a certain extent.

High quality grain is used for brewing. Besides, the grains are all from the three bases, which are famous for the grains for brewing in China. The nutritional components of these grains are more suitable for brewing after thousands of years of history and careful screening by craftsmen. The flavor of the spirits brewed with the grains is more attractive. The water for brewing of Mixiaojiu Wine Industry is respectively from the entrance of the Yangtze River, the Chishui River and the foot of the Xishan Mountains. These natural live water of high quality can make the taste of its products soft, delicate and elegant. Mixiaojiu Wine Industry uses the distiller's yeast that has never been brewed for all the time. The company has invested large manpower and energy to improve the variety and quantity of the microorganisms, which are beneficial for brewing in the cellar on the premise of safety and health. Therefore, the fermented grains can produce high-quality spirits with prominent flavor and special aromatic substances. The brewing technology in China includes 12,987 Kunsha technology, double bottom fermentation, mother tank moistening, low temperature cellaring, slow fire liquor flow, pinching the head and eliminating the tail, picking liquor with quantity and quality, mixing liquor with quality and storing in pottery jars. The products of Mixiaojiu Wine Industry are brewed according to the above peak brewing technology of different flavor types. As for this reason, the traditional culture of Chinese spirits can be inherited and carried forward in the new era.

3 A Recipe for the Flavor

The founder explained that "the reason why young people don't drink Chinese spirits is that there's no spirit that is suitable for them." Chinese people have the habit of drinking Chinese spirits. In the market of China, other drinks cannot be compared with the spirits. The founder said that he believed that young people would choose Chinese spirits if they were allowed to make a choice. Of course, the premise was that the spirits should not be old-fashioned with good quality and new ideas. "We can't make the conclusion that young people don't like Chinese spirits just because they don't drink spirits. That is putting the cart before the horse. Someone needs to make efforts to attract young people to love the Chinese spirits culture again." This is the essence.

With the increase of the income of residents, the consumers of high-end Chinese spirits turned to the middle class. The industry has witnessed a recovery in recent two years. At present, the market for spirits gathers to the leading enterprises, which also lays hidden troubles for the industry such as collective irrational price increases and large-scale sales. "The current growth of the whole industry and the profit of big brands comes from the price increase of high-end products. For ordinary families, high-end spirits such as Moutai and Wuliangye is always placed in the wine cabinet. The spirits that people need is the spirits of ordinary price." The founder believes that this proves that there is a huge market in the field of Chinese spirits of cost performance.

The Matthew effect of Chinese spirits industry is obvious at present. Small and medium-sized enterprises in various regions are facing the squeeze from the head enterprises in the high-end, secondary and high-end markets. There are various enterprises of Chinese spirits in the low-end market. The small spirits market represented by young players also became popular in recent years. There are also some first-line spirits enterprises. The fierce competition has led some enterprises to develop new product beyond the existing price positioning.

The "Internet digital gene" is the magic weapon for Mixiaojiu Wine Industry to break through. It is reported that the company is committed to redefining the beverage industry with new products, new social networking and new retail. It became the brand with the highest sales volume and sales volume of Xiaomi Youpin in the

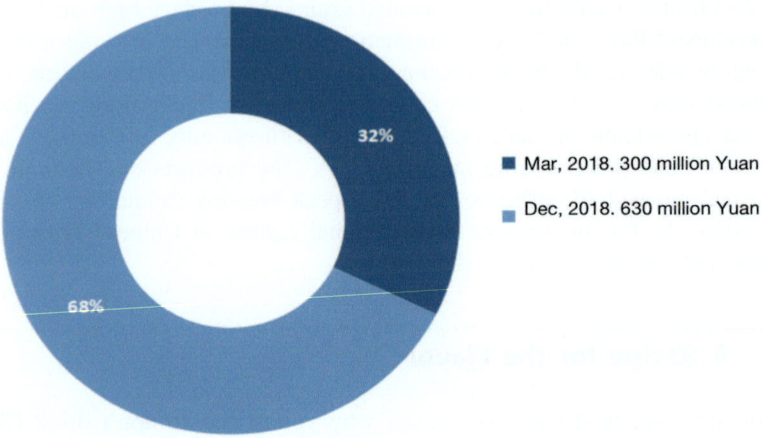

Fig. 1 First-year financing proportion

first year of its establishment. It also achieved a sales volume of over CNY50 million by e-commerce. Mixiaojiu completed two rounds of financing totaling CNY93 million in 2018, including CNY30 million angel rounds and CNY63 million Pre-A rounds. Investors include Zhen Fund, Zhongjin Huicai, Bojiang Capital and Wang Shuai, the partner of Ali. As a digital brand of Chinese spirits, Mixiaojiu has always used small products with low price as the main product to enter the young people market. However, it has begun to set foot in the field of high-end spirits with a price of CNY 1,000 in recent months. A number of innovative spirits enterprises represented by Mixiaojiu Wine Industry are seeking new competition points under the attack of dimension reduction of high-end first-line Chinese spirits brands. If they cannot get rid of the suppression of the leading companies, those weak Chinese spirits companies will confront an even harder time. In the highly competitive market, there are still some up-and-coming companies that have risen to the fore and become the bright spot in the industry to be noticed (Fig. 1).

Compared to the traditional product-centered Chinese spirits industry, Mixiaojiu Wine Industry is more concerned about customers and their consumption behavior and honest feedback, which is more helpful to its development. Also, Internet e-commerce is more efficient. So opening up both online channels and offline channels at the same time is definitely a long-term development. For model innovation, Mixiaojiu Wine Industry utilizes technical means on each product, so that can clearly know the various conditions of the market. For example, data obtained through technology in legal ways shows that people in Guangdong prefer Moutai-flavor liquor. Different regions have different consumption habits, making it convenient for enterprises to provide different service schemes.

Many people attribute Mixiaojiu Wine Industry's achievements to its high value and high cost performance, but this is clearly not the whole story. In fact, what is more enlightening for the Chinese spirits industry is perhaps the business model of Mixiaojiu Wine Industry based on "Internet thinking". Its founder said, "Our product line is constantly replenished with user demand. As long as the market has a pain point, we will consider to solve it." In fact, this is a typical Internet business model.

Generally, when Internet companies operating an App, they constantly adjust the interaction details of the product according to user behavior habits and preferences, or carry out marketing activities combined with market hotspots with positioning, in order to improve the scale of users and maintain user activity. It is also true for Mixiaojiu Wine Industry. The difference is, Internet products provide services, but Mixiaojiu Wine Industry provides Chinese spirits.

It is understood that, as of now, Mixiaojiu Wine Industry's wine product line has covered three types of flavor: Luzhou flavor, Maotai flavor and Fen flavor, with a total of more than 20 individual products. And the updates and iterations its products are much faster than those of other previous Chinese spiritscompanies. As a private Chinese spirits start-up, it achieved the best performance in the first year in 2018 with more than 50 million online omni-channel sales.

In recent years, Chengdu has been building a city of new economy, attracting a number of innovative companies to nest here, and Mixiaojiu Wine Industry is one of them. In the eyes of its founders, Mixiaojiu Wine Industry is a business with new economy characteristics. "The definition of a new economy enterprise does not mean that a new business concept can become a new economy enterprise. A real new economy means that it can create higher value for new consumer groups, which is a new economy." As a former executive of Xiaomi, the founder chose the startup base in Chengdu, Sichuan, which has a profound Chinese spirits culture. He believes that Chengdu, as a city of new economy, has a very strong business environment and more support for entrepreneurs. And in the next five years, at least in terms of startup environment, Chengdu will surpass the north, and become the first choice for entrepreneurs, and more head new economy companies will appear in the future.

4 Outline the Shape of the Fragrance of Wine

In the view of industry insiders, with the current liquor market competition and suppression from industry leaders, if small and medium-sized Chinese spirits brands to achieve a breakthrough, they should consider how to "empty" or even "give up" the brand, taking on a domineering rival. They should start from the product itself, polish the product in product design, wine body and other aspects, improve the experience of consumers, so that consumers can enjoy more actual added value. According to Mixiaojiu Wine Industry team, a wine product shall have good taste and reasonable price. But the reasonable price does not mean poor quality. Wine must have added value, but cannot too outrageous. Brands that choose added value should focus on added value, like Wuliangye and Maotai. While Mixiaojiu Wine Industry chooses Cost Performance, of course, and added value. Its product design, quality is not worse than other companies, but its prodcts only more than 100.

The wine is collected in authentic production areas, such as Maotai Town and Yibin. It selects distilleries with large reserves of old wine, chief brewers and large scale, and persuades a group of experienced drinkers to taste and buy; It offers affordable price, and the channel and advertising expenses are all invested in products. with the same quality of the liquor, other companies offer CNY400 or 500, while Mixiaojiu Wine Industry offers about CNY100; There are also many gifts: customers spend more than CNY300 to buy two bottles of wine, and it gives a set of high-grade ceramic wine sets with a cost of less than CNY100. If customers were not satisfied with the express delivery, the company paid for a bottle of wine first without asking about the right or wrong. If customers have suggestions on the products, the company should immediately adopt reasonable suggestions, cooperate with the supply chain within 24 h, and immediately change. In more than three years, the founder himself could not remember how many times Mixiaojiu Wine Industry was improved and iterated. But he understands that each improvement has better met people's desires and brought him one step closer to the ultimate. From the very beginning, the founder, who loves to drink, has been using the Internet's laws of product competition to operate Mixiaojiu Wine Industry: products shall have good quality, and not only satisfy users, but also surprise them.

Take the vast land of the Song Dynasty of the high-end line of products released by Mixiaojiu Wine Industry, the founder proposed to provide consumers with a set of products with the highest cost performance. Because it is a crowdfunding product, the sales pressure on it is not as strong as traditional sales. In addition, it uses Internet sale channels and eliminates a large number of intermediate links, thus the channel share can be returned directly to consumers. The company truly offer the lowest price to buyers, by the industry jokingly called the price butcher.

It is reported that "the vast land of the Song Dynasty" series is a tribute to a Chinese spirit in Song Dynasty. Its overall design uses the sky blue as the base color, and the bottle pattern incorporates elements of the Song Emperor Huizong's *Auspicious Crane* elements. Also, the bottle shape is integrated with the elements of Wang Ximeng's *A Panorama of Rivers and Mountains*, with metal kit as its completion design of ancient for the present expression. In addition, the craftsmanship part of "the vast land of the Song Dynasty" is made by Meijing Industrial Co., Ltd., a supplier of Swarovski, and the porcelain part is made of heirloom azure bone china, and the metal part is all made of gold-colored alloy kit. It is worth mentioning that the design of the matching wine set of "the vast land of the Song Dynasty" is inspired by the Songzhan (the small wine cup in Song Dynasty). Songzhan was originally a tea vessel, but it was filled with a high level of Chinese spirits now, so its capacity has to be reduced. In the end, the designer made a 30-degree angle cut on Songzhan. Finally, it presents the artistic effect of wine bottles, wine sets and other wine vessels, which are arranged in turn and echo each other. In terms of wine itself, Luzhou-flavor liquor has a five grain formula that has lasted for more than 600 years, while Maotai-flavor liquor is flavored with 10 year old base liquor and 30 year old and 15 year old liquor. The excellent Chinese spirit has also been recommended by three masters, including Chen Xingxi, a national liquor judge and former director of the Maotai Research Institute. This is the second time that the Mixiaojiu Wine Industry has joined hands with Xiaomi Youpin since it first launched its first liquor crowdfunding project, the "Single Grain Concept Series", last year, to announce a comprehensive layout of the high-end Chinese spirits industry. "We are trying to stir up the whole high-end Chinese spirits industry, penetrate the whole price system, so that consumers can rationalize their spirits consumption and afford to buy and drink." The founder emphasizes. "Our products represent the highest level of the industry in terms of bottle design, materials used and the body of the wine."

On 24 November 2019, Mixiaojiu Wine Industry was awarded the German Design Award 2020 for its "Single Grain Concept Series". Mixiaojiu Wine Industry's "Single Grain Concept Series" won the 2019 German IF design award, the first Chinese spirits product to actually be marketed on a large scale. At the 3rd China iBerry Awards Ceremony and Brand Marketing Summit, Mixiaojiu Wine Industry was awarded the "2018 Most Popular Brand - Emerging Brand Award" alongside other pioneering brands in the industry, such as 1919 and Pinduoduo. The 4th China Wine Industry Capital Forum and China Wine Industry Golden Bottle Award Ceremony 2019" was held in Chengdu, and Mixiaojiu's "Single Grain Series" was awarded "2019 China Wine Industry Star Product". On May 11, 2020, Mixiaojiu was named the most promising brand in China's spirits industry at the 2020 China Wine Industry Golden Bottle Awards. At the 2020 International Spirits (China) Grand Prix and International Wine (China) Grand Prix, the Gu Yuan Soju 42 degrees selected by Mixiaojiu Wine Industry won the Silver Medal at the ISGC International Spirits (China) Grand Prix.

The following design philosophy of Mixiaojiu Wine Industry: Taking the excellent Chinese traditional culture as the base and integrating it with the fashionable aesthetics of the times, the ancient liquor is given a contemporary charm, not only as Chinese spirits, but also as an excellent industrial artwork. With this design concept, Mixiaojiu's "Single Grain Series" has won the IF Design Award and the German Design Award within a year, the first of its kind in the highly competitive industrial design PK platform, spreading Chinese spirits culture and making the world applaud China!

5 Aroma of Wine

In 2019, Mixiaojiu's sales increased by 350% year-on-year during "Double 11", exceeding 140,000 bottles, with digital Chinese spirits exploding all over the internet. Then Mixiaojiu and Suning announced a strategic partnership, in which Suning will further open up its big data resources, new retail channels and logistics network to Mixiaojiu and help it launch more C2M customized products. Mixiaojiu Wine Industry and Luo Yonghao pulled off their live wine selling debut on Tiktok, with sales of the "Single Grain Series" exceeding CNY10 million in 90 min. Mixiaojiu Wine Industry and Kuanzhai Xiangzi co-branded Chinese spirits, which was presented at the Sichuan Non-Foreign Heritage Shopping Festival held in Kuanzhai Xiangzi, Chengdu. 2020 Wan Li Song Realm—Square Inch in Luo Yonghao's Double Eleven live broadcast, taking the number one spot in the entire wine category.

Mixiaojiu Wine Industry started out in Xiaomi Youpin, a subsidiary of Xiaomi. The first Chinese spirits "Microbrew Edition", developed and designed by Mixiaojiu Wine Industry, is officially launched at Xiaomi Youpin. Since then, Xiaomi Youpin has witnessed every step of Mixiaojiu Wine Industry's growth. Since Mixiaojiu Wine Industry is following the path of internet data-based development, it is also slowly developing itself in other e-commerce self-operated platform, with Tmall, JD.COM and Suning all involved. Most users are young people, and Mixiaojiu Wine Industry focuses on Tiktok, the huge traffic platform.

In the early and middle stages of development, the main difference between the Mixiaojiu Wine Industry and other enterprises in the industry lies in the channel, the e-commerce channel based on new retail. Take the user as the core, pay attention to whether the product is consumed and whether it is used. The basic means are able to pinpoint the place and time when the product is consumed. The user and the actual consumption behavior, everything revolve around these two points outwards.

By choosing to operate digitally, the company has clear access to user demand and is one of the more user-aware companies in the wine industry. Enable social marketing, the Chinese spirits industry belongs to the typical rich capital, but the means about marketing is very inefficient, the investment and return are not proportional to the industry. Mixiaojiu Wine Industry uses media resources and public relations resources, such as being the celebratory wine for Xiaomi's IPO, as a way to first gain a public awareness and brand recognition, using a small amount of resources to leverage a large project (Table 1).

The new product segment includes different versions of the various types of spirits we have seen. Mixiaojiu Wine Industry has made it the ultimate cost performance by matching the new design with a new body of wine, and all the products are built to revolve around the design of the new Chinese spirits. The logic is that the user, again, is the final product's landing point.

Mixiaojiu Wine Industry's new social presence now includes its own shopping mall, its own new media and community. In the new social segment, through a self-run community group with users, in addition to helping them with customer service issues, but also to help them answer more questions, even the founder himself works with them in this group every day. The construction of Mixiaojiu

Table 1 Concept sheet for three new businesses

New product	Designed and built around the user
New social	Make friends with users based on recognition of the product
New retail	Boutique e-commerce platform, leading e-commerce channel, first to enter Tiktok

Wine Industry is to channel these traffic to the Xiaomi Youpin Shopping Mall and absorb them. In fact, it has mastered the Internet users who need socializing and Chinese spirits.

In the whole new retail, Mixiaojiu Wine Industry plans to launch offline catering, offline eating, and O2O, which are small agents all over the country, equivalent to a flat product, just like Xiaomi's O2O stores. This part also has offline agent, which is also part of the New Retail. The part of self-operation includes Xiaomi, Tmall, JD.COM and other platforms.

Therefore, the current three business segments of the entire Mixiaojiu Wine Industry are new products, new social networking and new retail, which are also the central goal. The traffic and channels between them can support each other. As for why Mixiaojiu Wine Industry doesn't spend too much to get traffic now, it is actually that they first do a good job in new products, and second, they do a good job in new social networking. Through their own self-operation channels, such as Xiaomi, Tmall, JD.COM, and their own community operations, they can catch the traffic of the Internet.

6 Epilogue

The vision of Mixiaojiu Wine Industry is to be a good company with passion and righteousness. In March 2018, Mixiaojiu Wine Industry was officially established, with a financing of CNY30 million. In April, the first product was launched in Xiaomi Youpin and served as the designated wine for Xiaomi Corporation's listing celebration banquet. In September, the crowdfunding amount of "Rice Concept Series" exceeded CNY10 million, and in December, Mixiaojiu completed a round of financing of CNY63 million for Pre-A. In 2019, the first anniversary of the founding of Mixiaojiu Wine Industry, e-commerce omni-channel sales exceeded CNY50 million, and more than 300 tons of finished wine were sold, reaching the scale enterprise standard. In June, the strategic framework agreement was signed at the "2019 Chengdu Global Innovation and Entrepreneurship Fair". In August, the crowdfunding amount of the new product "Wan Li Song Jing" was more than CNY10 million. In April 2020, the debut of Tiktok Buying Wine exceeded CNY10 million in 90 min. In June, the sales of Mixiaojiu Wine Industry increased by 1400% year on year, far more than last year. Since its establishment, Mixiaojiu Wine Industry has been ranked Top1 in Xiaomi Youpin Chinese spirits sales volume and sales volume for 3 consecutive years. It has also won the honor of Annual Outstanding Service Award of Xiaomi, Annual cutting-edge brand of Tmall Wine, Leap and Progress Award of Tmall Wine and the brand with the most growth potential in China's wine industry. At present, Mixiaojiu Wine Industry has accumulated more than 2 million paying users throughout the network, covering more than 30,000 sales end users nationwide.

By 2035, we will be able to serve 1 billion users worldwide and provide happier and healthier products and services. Create 1 million jobs in the global wine industrial chain, and establish 10 million terminal scenarios to realize the comprehensive data of users, products and market. The mission of Mixiaojiu Wine Industry is to make sure that there is no bad wine in the world. Their values are customer first, employee second and shareholder third; Live a meaningful life and work happily and simply. Integrity, teamwork, embracing change and dedication. Keep in awe, and the next day will always be a new start.

Maybe there is some idealism, but you can run health and happiness through your career. Even if you have a slight setback and how to fear the bitterness of failure? What's more, the momentum of Mixiaojiu Wine Industry has been rising all the way, and the success or failure cannot be easily determined.

"Here Comes the Cat" Quietly Became Popular: Content Marketing in the New Media Era

Xusen Cheng, Bo Yang, and Kanliang Wang

1 Development and Current Situation of the Company

Founded in 2009, Sootoo Network focuses on building a sound operation system for the new media era, known as China's leading operator in the new media era. In August 2012, Sootoo Network seized the opportunity to take the lead in registering numerous WeChat Official Accounts. In October, the company achieved daily visits of 3 million, ranking first in China's Internet media industry at that time.

2 Confronting Problems

Although Sootoo successfully took the lead, the later operation of some official accounts did not receive good benefits. Moe Factory is one of the official accounts managed by Sootoo Network, whose early positioning was selected cute pet content, but lacked the main backbone, resulting in lukewarm page views for a long time.

Chen Lei, a post-90s young man who was facing unemployment due to Sootoo Network's strategic adjustment, tried to take over Moe Factory, but he did not expect that this would be the beginning of his entrepreneurship in Beijing and a big twist to change his life in the future.

At that time, in addition to Chen Lei, there was only one post-90s girl designated by Sootoo called Tian Xue, who was good at drawing cartoons. The team then only consisted of two inexperienced young people with limited resources.

X. Cheng (✉) · B. Yang
School of Information, Renmin University of China, Beijing, China

K. Wang
Renmin Business School, Renmin University of China, Beijing, China

J. Zhang et al. (eds.), *Innovation of Digital Economy*, Management for Professionals,
https://doi.org/10.1007/978-981-99-1741-9_28

After a thorough survey of the cute pet market at that time, it was found that there were only a few cute pet official accounts posting cat content. Therefore, Chen Lei changed the name of Moe Factory to Here comes the cat.

3 Solutions to Problems

Chen Lei believed that in the information-loaded Internet era, new media should continue to output user value. So, the team started to create the comic image of Here comes the cat, i.e., a wide range of content from emoji to four-panel comics, from wallpaper to long story. In addition, Chen Lei took relative measures such as content and community interaction to improve the user retention rate.

These measures gradually revived the official account, but soon it encountered new problems. The team applied for start-up funds from the company to develop comic products such as pillows and opened a Wechat Mall, but the sales volume was not satisfying. As the team did not witness remarkable results from its overall decisions and the number of followers did not see any growth, the group recruited a sales manager to explore the market. But after a month of inspection, the idea of putting printers and crane machines in shopping malls to attract followers did not come into reality. Chen Lei said that it was a failed attempt.

Chen Lei always worked day and night. Once he worked at 3:00 a.m., when he received a take-out food from a follower who placed the order after checking with the company staff for the address, and then he was even more determined in his love and belief in Here Comes the Cat.

Later, Chen Lei accidentally came into contact with Taobao Spreader and tried to change the official account into a Taobao Spreader, not only to facilitate the purchase of various cat lovers and account followers to buy IP products, but also to bring some revenue for the official account. In addition, game cooperation and commercial advertising have become the way to realize traffic. To avoid unfollowing due to the rise of other official accounts, Here Comes the Cat has been actively settled on Toutiao, Tiktok, and other platforms. Quality contents and followers with high viscosity boost the rapid growth of relevant accounts, but at the same time, competition becomes even more fierce.

At present, the number of active followers of Here Comes the Cat stands at over 500,000, and the account tries to explore a new business model based on its huge traffic. It also tries to take advantage of the e-commerce platform, and IP derivative business to receive revenue through the mall, game advertising, and other forms, taking the lead in the cute-pet consumption upgrading market.

Let us expect the future of Here Comes the Cat…

Questions from this case:

1. How did Here Comes the Cat find its market positioning? What was its idea?
2. What did Sootoo do to facilitate the birth of Here Comes the Cat?
3. How did Here Comes the Cat "expand its business or open up a new business after certain achievements?"
4. How to run an official account and what elements are important in the operation process?

SHEIN: How Does the Most Mysterious 10 Billion-Dollar Company in China Achieve Overseas Growth?

Yu Jin

1 Make a Breakthrough to Achieve Rapid Development

"What is SHEIN? We are not very familiar with it." When you talk about this company with Internet personage, most of them will give you such an answer (Li, 2020). Few dynamic reports about SHEIN can be seen no matter in China or overseas. Compared with other large factories, it has less popularity and influence. The most popular comment on SHEIN is that it is a mysterious company. It seems that such low popularity cannot match its large size. According to the data of Similar web, SHEIN currently ranks first in the world in terms of the number of visits to the websites marking fashion and clothing. In 2020, it benefited from the growth of the COVID-19 pandemic with a revenue of USD10 billion. Besides, its volume has been close to 1/2 of the parent company of ZARA (a clothing enterprise with the largest sales in the world). What is such a mysterious billion-dollar company like? What kind of wealth code does it have?

In October 2008, Xu Yangtian, an SEO search engine optimizer, founded Nanjing Dianwei Information Technology Co., Ltd., which was mainly engaged in cross-border wedding dress business. Then, the gross profit rate of wedding dress was second only to that of digital products. A wedding dress of CNY200 could be sold for USD200 overseas. As a middleman, SHEIN shipped the finished wedding dress from Huqiu to the United States for sale. It also made a lot of advertisements on Google and Facebook. With the traffic dividend from these two platforms and the price difference between the markets of China and America, the company soon accumulated enough original capital. The company launched a Spanish website in 2010 and a French website in early 2012. Xu Yangtian found a good business again. He gave up his wedding dress business and made every effort to cross-border

Y. Jin (✉)
School of Finance and Trade, Wenzhou Business College, Wenzhou, China

J. Zhang et al. (eds.), *Innovation of Digital Economy*, Management for Professionals,
https://doi.org/10.1007/978-981-99-1741-9_29

e-commerce of women's wear with a fixed domain SheInside.com. Meanwhile, he tried to make promotion on social networking sites with overseas online traffic. From 2013 to 2014, the company successively launched European sites including Russia, Germany and others. It also acquired ROMWE, a cross-border brand of women's wear and began to build its own supply chain system. In 2015, SheInside officially changed its name to SHEIN, focusing on fast fashion of women's wear. Its products gradually expanded to the full range of e-commerce including men's wear, children's wear, beauty, home, pets and others. It actively expanded sites in Australia, the Middle East, India and Arabia since then. The company established a designer team around brand operation with its own independent station channel to conduct cross-border sales of products worldwide. The business of SHEIN has covered 224 countries and regions by 2017. From 2017 to 2020, the revenue of the company continued to grow at a high speed. In 2020, the income of SHEIN was about USD 10 billion. Moreover, the revenue growth rate of this company exceeded 100% for eight consecutive years. SHEIN became the most popular e-commerce website for young people, second only to Amazon in the same year. The female youth team with high income loved SHEIN more than Amazon to some extent (Fig. 1).

According to the *Brandz Top 50 Chinese Global Brand Builders 2021* jointly released by Google and Kantar, SHEIN ranked 11th in the annual index of global brands in China, which was two places higher than that in 2020, catching up with cross-border e-commerce head sellers such as Tencent, Anker and Zaful. In the first half of 2021, SHEIN was downloaded about 75 million times on the iOS and Android platforms. The number surpassed that of Shopee and Wish (WISH. US), which made it the No. 2 brand in the global mobile fast fashion and second

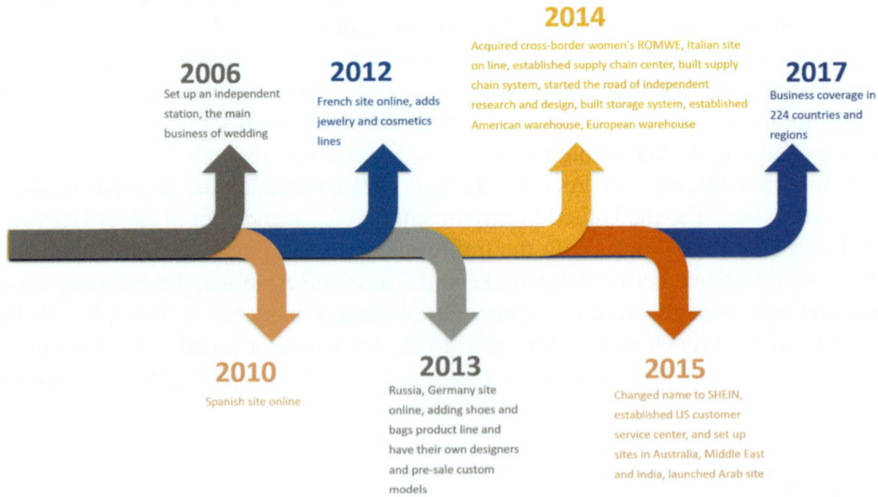

Fig. 1 Development chart of SHEIN

only to Amazon Shopping (78.8 million downloads) in the global shopping center application download list (Tables 1 and 2).

After continuous adjustment and personnel expansion, the company built an efficient and flat organizational framework. At present, the nine centers support the operation of the company, covering the operation, research and development, supply chain, product selection, digitization and others. The core departments

Table 1 Brandz top 50 Chinese global brand builders 2021

Ranking	2020 Ranking	Brand	Category	Brand Power Score
1	3	Alibaba	E-commerce	2064
2	4	ByteDance	Content-based App	2049
3	1	HUAWEI	Consumer Electronics	1993
4	5	Xiaomi	Consumer Electronics	1831
5	2	Lenovo	Consumer Electronics	1828
6	12	OPPO	Consumer Electronics	1299
7	7	Hisense	Home Appliances	1134
8	6	Haier	Home Appliances	1032
9	8	OnePlus	Consumer Electronics	1017
10	20	VIVO	Consumer Electronics	965
11	13	SHEIN	Online Fast Fashion	901
12	16	Tencent	Mobile Games	804
13	11	**ANKER**	Consumer Electronics	793

Source BrandZ Report 2021 Kantar Consulting

Table 2 SHEINAPP user downloads from 2019 to 2021

2019	2020	2021
1. Wish	1. Amazon Shopping	1. Amazon Shopping
2. Amazon Shopping	2. Wish	2. SHEIN
3. AliExpress	3. Shopee	3. Shopee
4. Shopee	4. SHEIN	4. Wish
5. Club Factory	5. Flipkart	5. Flipkart
6. PDD	6. AliExpress	6. AliExpress
7. Flipkart	7. Taobao	7. Alibaba. com
8. OLX	8. OLX	8. Taobao
9. SHEIN	9. PDD	9. Lazada
10. Lazada	10. Lazada	10. OLX

Source Author collated according to sensor tower

Table 3 Organizational structure of SHEIN

Departments	Main functions
Global operation center	To formulate and implement the overall marketing operation strategy of overseas markets, integrate global fashion resources, communicate with online celebrities and customers, search for needs, improve customer experience and formulate optimization plans
Product R&D center	To develop and maintain online mobile shopping malls, maintain the supply chain system and self-built systems of other companies and therefore improve the operational efficiency of SHEIN
Supply chain center	Be responsible for the whole industrial chain logistics system, including fabric management, sample clothing development, bulk production, quality control, logistics and distribution, warehousing management
Commodity center	Designer, buyer, investment promotion, price verification, quality control and photography team
Center for organizational development and empowerment	Corporate culture construction, personnel management and organizational efficiency improvement
Digital intelligent center	To develop SHEIN APP overseas, WEB, etc.
Financial center	5 international payment methods and 20 foreign currency conversion services

are product research and development center (system maintenance), supply chain center (production and manufacturing), commodity center (product design and development) and digital empowerment center (overseas APP and Web). The core management of the company has not changed a lot since its launch. They have been jointly running the company since 2012 (Table 3).

2 Achieve "Greater", "Faster", "Better" and "More Economical" Results to Create Core Competitiveness

SHEIN, a cross-border fast fashion company driven by Internet core, not only has a supply chain system, but also has marketing traffic. It has formed a real-time, flexible supply chain fully driven by big data and created a business secret of "Real time Fashion".

2.1 Extreme Fashion, Big Data Makes Popular Products

Compared with the new model of ZARA by designing products based on the feedback from the offline press conference, SHEIN moved design online. It used its self-built data system that could track global fashion trends in real time and got data from Google, Facebook, competitors and other ways to modularize design elements such as fabrics, colors, patterns, printing, embroidery, and patterns. The company saved the time of material selection for designers with B2B raw material procurement platform, upgraded the workshop distributed operation mode to the industrial assembly line, which greatly improved the work efficiency of designers and further reduced the dependence of brands on designers. Meanwhile, the pictures were carefully designed for the product. The pictures of products were taken by professional photographer team, which maximized the desire of purchase.

With a powerful design, professional buyer and version making team, SHEIN has realized the trend of fashion with the help of big data analysis and recombined the design elements. At present, the official website has about 3,000 new models every day, and 20,000 new models every week (about equal to the number of new models launched by ZARA in a year). Furthermore, the number is increasing. In terms of SKU, the SKU of women's wear of SHEIN is 170,000, far ahead of the level of the industry. In terms of the shelf life cycle, the cycle for average textile clothing company is six months, including design, version making, production and shelf. The preparation cycle for the first order of ZARA is two months, which focuses on fast fashion. The cycle for additional orders in the current quarter is three weeks, which can be as fast as two weeks. SHEIN compressed the first order cycle to three weeks, and the tracking cycle of the current quarter to one week.

2.2 Extreme Speed, Flexible Supply Chain Maximized the Desire of Purchase

(1) The supply chain capacity of "small order and quick return"

Why does SHEIN launch so fast? With the help of the constantly improved supply chain system of the company, the production mode of "small order and quick return" has been formed. The mode is that there were only 100 pieces of each product at the beginning, and then the product would be put on the market for testing. If consumers were satisfied with the product, the order volume would increase. It would return to order in large quantities. By adding orders subsequently, the cost of each piece could be greatly reduced. If there was little order volume, the product would be back to design to modify until it was turned to the popular one. SHEIN has realized the benign business model of adding new products, market testing, trial and error and iteration every day by the C2M mode that customers are directly connected to factories.

With the systematic and procedural product cycle management, the company can not only launch new models fast, but also deliver the products to consumers at the first time. In order to meet the market demand more quickly, SHEIN arranges its supply chain in the surrounding areas within 2 hours' drive from Guangzhou with more than 400 core OEM factories around, which has built a very efficient supply chain cluster. Most products are produced around Panyu headquarters in Guangzhou. The upstream and downstream factories in the industry are adjacent to each other. Therefore, orders can be received in time. In order to master the initiative and voice of the supply chain, SHEIN mainly signs contracts with small and medium-sized factories. The orders provided to large factories need to be determined one quarter to six months in advance, which has small flexibility. However, the orders provided to small and medium-sized factories can be relatively flexible, which is more suitable for the production mode of "small order and quick return". At the same time, SHEIN realized the rapid repeat order in small quantities and compress the cycle time to within 1 week with the advantage of lower labor cost, raw material cost and flexible output in China. Compared to large orders, the one-time cost of making plates in small orders is high and time-consuming, so why are small and medium-sized factories willing to take small orders? It turns out that SHEIN, which built its supply chain at an early time, provides additional subsidies to suppliers for making boards to ensure that factories do not lose money even when taking small orders; SHEIN never defaults on payments, and it even gives suppliers early settlements to make the billing period the shortest in the industry; In addition, SHEIN keeps inventory pressure to itself. No return is allowed unless there is a quality problem so as to reduce the pressure on suppliers. SHEIN even funds to assist factories in expanding their production capacity. Fast payback and no inventory pressure are important reasons why many suppliers are willing to follow SHEIN. Through continuous run-in in 7 years, SHEIN and its suppliers have formed a sound and solid relationship (Table 4).

Table 4 Freight subsidy policy for February 2020 in SHEIN

Incentive policy	Specific content
Provision of freight subsidy	For orders that meet the timeline and are completed in storage within the specified delivery time, we will subsidize CNY0.1/piece based on the number of orders in storage. In addition, in February 2020, we will subsidize freight for all inbound completed orders without any other requirements. Every delivery gets freight subsidy.
Supplier incentive system	The production department will assess and reward suppliers monthly, quarterly and annual assessment based on their performance in terms of timeliness, quality, capacity and cooperation. The annual reward money for a single supplier is up to CNY320,000.
10% increase in profit for the month	In February, 2020, for the first order and urgent order after receipt, an additional 10% of the original profit will be added.

Source SHEIN Cloud Factory, Kaiyuan Securities (Lv, 2021)

With the increased power of discourse to factories, SHEIN has put forward higher requirements for suppliers. For example, it introduced Japanese and Korean enterprise quality control standards, and formulated KPI content for suppliers, involving the timely rate of urgent picking and delivery, the timely rate of stock and delivery, the rate of inferior products, and the success rate of upgrading. At the same time, SHEIN grades suppliers through the digital scoring system of the supply chain. From high to low, the suppliers are divided into five levels: S, A, B, C and D. The purchase amount score accounts for 60%, the KPI score accounts for 40%, and the last 30% of the suppliers ranking at level D (below 60 points) will be eliminated. SHEIN has also cultivated a number of very strong supply chain factories in China through this system, such as FeiliuTech Cloud Factory, (won SHEIN 2021 Best Supplier), one of SHEIN's most important production suppliers. Although affected by the pandemic, it still delivered 100-300 high-quality small orders in 3-7 days on time for SHEIN. It is a truly technology-empowered factory (Fig. 2).

(2) Digital empowerment supply chain

Unified digital IT system to further enhance production efficiency. SHEIN has transformed every upstream supplier with a digital IT system in which the supplier can clearly see the details of each order, including SKU number, order volume, fabric and size. SHEIN also arranged special personnel to digitally collect and update information on the production process, including the production link, order completion ratio, fabric consumption and factory capacity saturation of each style. With this unified IT system, SHEIN can track each production link of each order in different factories in real time and visually, thus controlling and improving production efficiency. Secondly, SHEIN's management system can also be connected to the front end of the supply chain to get the measurement situation, and the data

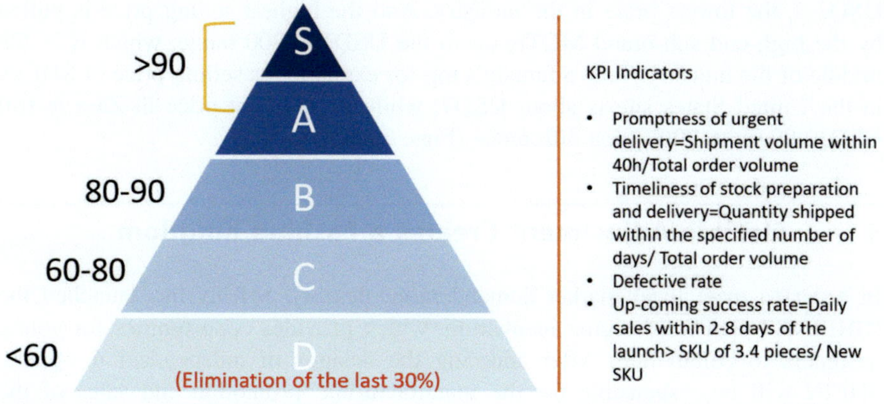

Fig. 2 Supplier classification elimination system. *Source* Based on SHEIN investment promotion and Kaiyuan securities Research Institute (Lv, 2019)

of browsing, clicking and order placing of App users will also be converted into the data of the supply chain management system. And this management system also provides timely feedback and additional orders to the back-end suppliers, so as to match the capacity gap with the market demand more accurately.

In terms of inventory management, SHEIN introduces four major functions of inventory barcode, covered inventory, inventory status, and external commodity inventory in its own inventory balance module of the goods giving system to improve inventory management efficiency, grasp inventory dynamics in real time, and dynamize and visualize its inventory management. Meanwhile, the inventory management system can also interoperate with the back-end production system, which can determine the inventory pressure to reasonably decide the replenishment amount and minimize the inventory cleaning pressure. In terms of logistics and distribution, SHEIN adopts data analysis to optimize logistics routes and design cost-optimal delivery solutions. SHEIN's customers are located in more than 200 countries and regions around the world, and each order and parcel may have different logistics and distribution delivery solutions. Therefore, SHEIN digitizes the logistics information online, and uses big data algorithm to determine the distribution route of each order, so as to drive the improvement of logistics distribution efficiency with data.

2.3 Extreme Cost Performance and Low Price Create "Addictive Consumption"

SHEIN has an absolute advantage over its peers in terms of pricing. With the downgrading of overseas middle class consumption, consumers' preference for low-priced goods is getting stronger and stronger. With the unparalleled low-price advantage, the visits of SHEIN's website and APP mobile witnessed a growth rate of over 40%, attracting many consumers and leading the industry in 2020. In terms of price range, SHEIN's lowest selling price for each product line is maintained at USD2-3, the lowest price in the industry. And the highest selling price is pulled by the high-end sub-brand MOTF, up to the USD100-200 range, which is in the middle of the industry. Take a female's top for example, its selling price of SHEIN in the United States site is about USD7, while its discount price in Zara is still USD12.99, with 70% price difference (Figs. 3 and 4).

3 Flexible Adjustment Creates a Fashion Kingdom

In order to meet local market demand more flexibly, SHEIN has launched the "SHEINX" plan for designer incubation, which provides opportunities for young designers to collaborate. After adopting the designs of independent designers, SHEIN will be responsible for the manufacturing, promotion and sales of the adopted designs, and the designers will receive a certain share of the profits while

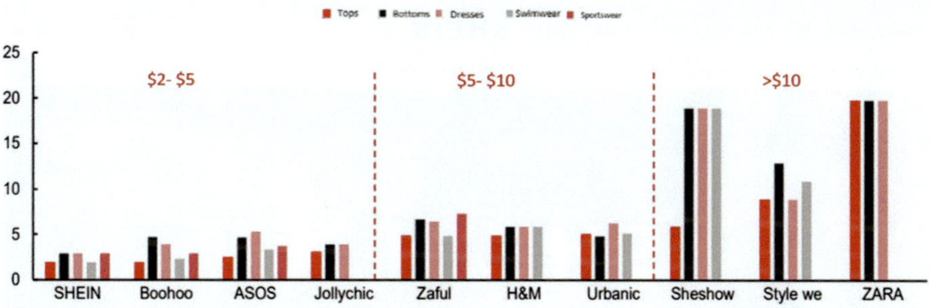

Fig. 3. Price range of each brand category. *Source* Official website of each company (as of June 2021), CITIC Securities Research Department (Feng et al., 2021)

Fig. 4 SHEIN product display and price

retaining ownership of the final designs. This will not only establish a good cooperation relationship with new designers in the early stage, provide designers with more resources and opportunities to show, but also attract more consumers and industry attention, so as to help the company further promote its brand and stabilize its leading position in the field of fast fashion clothing (Fig. 5).

In addition, for consumers from different regions, SHEINX provides customized products according to their consumption characteristics. SHEIN does business in 230 countries and regions around the world, and in order to meet the needs of consumers in different regions, SHEIN fully integrate local culture and consumer aesthetic style on the basis of massive SKUs. For example, in the U.S. stores, the products are sexy; in Saudi stores, the products tend to be conservative long dresses; in Japanese stores, the products tend to be youthful campus style; and in French stores, the products have more popular elements. In the process

Fig. 5 SHEINX plan's promotion on the home page

of development, SHEIN has gradually recruited local talents and teams to better adapt to cultural and policy changes in different markets.

4 Accurate Marketing and Establish Multi Traffic-Drainage Mode

The company complies with the trend of the Internet times and builds diversified marketing channels. Based on the traditional media advertising, such as Facebook and Google, it marched towards Instagram, Twitter and other social media traffic dissemination, and combine overseas KOL and stars for sales promotion of goods.

(1) Social media

At the beginning of its establishment, SHEIN has made layout on mainstream overseas social media platforms such as Facebook, YouTube, Pinterest and Instagram. On Instagram and Facebook, SHEIN adopts the operation strategy of "matrixing + localization", which uses a mother-account to divert traffic for sub-accounts in various regions to accelerate traffic precipitation. In terms of the number of followers, both Instagram and Facebook have more than 20 million followers on their mother-account, and the number of followers on their sub-accounts are in the million level, which has obvious diversion effects. In terms of the content displayed, SHEIN has opened sub-accounts in different languages according to different countries and regions to display differentiated content in terms of style, clothing fabric, and fashion trends to meet the diversified needs of different consumers for products.

(2) Content marketing

Use Hashtag tags, UGC, and PGCS for content marketing, focusing on user interaction to convey brand care. On Instagram, SHEIN is marketing content in a variety of ways. According to Instagram data, as of June 2021, the number of posts under the #shein hashtag has reached 3.05 million, and the remaining related hashtags such as #sheingals and #sheinofficial have hundreds of thousands of posts, and the number of posts is still growing rapidly with SHEIN's frequent content marketing. Since most users of SHEIN are young people, they are more willing to fully express their opinions, share their experience of clothing, and spread their feelings and feelings through social media. In addition, SHEIN also attaches great importance to the interaction with users. For example, SHEIN invited users to participate in the lucky draw by liking, commenting and sharing in a post on Instagram on June 13, 2021, which received 38,000 likes and 32,000 comments. Throughout 2019, SHEIN made 2,456 posts on Facebook and received 2.45 million post interactions, and 3,083 posts and 157 videos on Instagram, receiving 62.67 million interactions. The huge number of posts and interactions were able to bring the company closer to its customers, listen to user demand and convey the brand care to them (CITIC Construction Investment, 2021).

In order to increase user's activity, SHEIN encourages users to continue to produce content in the form of credits and cash, including daily logins, product reviews, user photos, collocations, etc., which further increases user addiction (Fig. 6).

(3) KOL Recommendation

In 2011, when the online long-form video emerged, SHEIN, as one of the earlier group of cross-border companies that used online celebrities to promotion

Fig. 6 The user is telling the process of SHEIN shopping addiction on YOUTUBE

goods, sent free samples to invite online celebrities to review and provide exclusive coupons to complete the sales conversion through online celebrity marketing. It also cooperates with the most influential online celebrities on a paid basis to enhance brand awareness and image. For example, in 2018, SHEIN is working with about 2,000 local influencers in order to open the Indian market and is in contact with potential partners almost every day. SHEIN has now added the affiliate marketing model (10%–18% of sales), which means that commission is used to attract users to make spontaneous purchases and publish reviews.

(4) Advertising

In 2012, SHEIN started to place a large number of low-cost ads to drive GMV by traffic. Currently, SHEIN mainly places measurement ads on Google, advertises on Facebook's Page Like, and publishes effect ads such as graphic posts in other social media to provide a power source for SHEIN's new pull. According to the data from SocialPeta, the video ad of pet wedding dresses placed by SHEIN on Facebook in April 2021 had an objective effect with a show value of 294,000 in one month. In terms of traffic sources, direct traffic accounts for 36.9%, mainly because the accumulation of brand awareness itself makes users remember the site and collection; 40.5% of search traffic, including natural search and paid search advertising; direct traffic and search traffic together accounted for 77.4% of the total traffic, which is the main traffic source of SHEIN. Other traffic sources are social traffic (10.9%, including free social media and paid social ads, mainly from Facebook, Instagram), display ads (6.3%, mostly from Google's image display ads), referral traffic (3.3%), and email marketing (2.2%).

5 Conclusion

Relying on the production mode of "small order and quick return", digital operation and flexible supply chain, SHEIN has achieved the scale effect of big data prediction of fashion trends, fast update and high repurchase rate, and at the same time, through the layout of multi-channel traffic entrance, deep cultivation of private traffic and other marketing strategies, SHEIN has quickly grown into a fast fashion giant for brand transform overseas, and also provided valuable strategic experience for Chinese enterprises to go abroad in cross-border e-commerce. However, in the future, SHEIN still needs to explore how to break the circle to achieve high-end, expand the diversified layout of categories, and develop different business fields.

References

CITIC Construction Investment. (2021). Special report on E-commerce industry: SHEIN, digital supply chain, diversified marketing means. Retrieved from https://www.vzkoo.com/read/9bd02500d7bd52046e258d6993922e15.html.

Feng, Z. G., Zheng, Y. M., Yang, Q. P., & Xv, X. F. (2021). Cross-border E-commerce apparel giant, riding the wind to accelerate growth. Retrieved from https://www.nisdata.com/report/3952.

Li, S. Y. (2020). Secret reveal: The rise of China's most mysterious billion-dollar company. Retrieved from https://baijiahao.baidu.com/s?ID=1674101440905110540&wfr=spider&for=pc.

Lv, M. (2021). Analysis of Shein mode under agile supply chain and digital operation. Retrieved from https://pdf.dfcfw.com/pdf/H3_AP202107271506397072_1.pdf.

Yimidida: The Road to Upgrade the Business Model of LTL Industry from "Block" to "Plane"

Chuanbo Zhu

1 Introduction

With the steady increase in the penetration rate of e-commerce consumption in China and the continuous upgrading of consumer demand for large cargo logistics, the fast freight has become the next main focus of logistics giants following the express industry. In recent years, e-commerce logistics and express delivery giants such as SF, JDL, YUNDA and ZTO Express have rushed into the less-than-truck-load (LTL) market. At present, the highway LTL industry is characterized by low concentration, and the top ten companies in the industry occupy less than 2% of the market share. The overall market presents the "weak, scattered and small" pattern, and the main participants are dedicated line companies. With the entry of express giants from China into the fast freight, as well as the forced transformation and acceleration of integration within the LTL industry, the overall market concentration will be improved continuously.

Currently, LTL industry is mostly of a pattern of regional network and dedicated line, except for the self-operation of Deppon Express and the national network established by ane with the franchise model. What are the opportunities for regional networks and dedicated lines? Is it possible to firstly form an industrial alliance through the cooperation and resource integration of different regional networks, and then rapidly grow bigger and stronger by upgrading business models and innovating operation models, and finally participate in a new round of industry competition? Actually, the enterprise mentioned in this case, Yimidida, participates in the market competition through the integration and reorganization of regional logistics enterprises, which provides some reference for existing enterprises and new entrants in the industry in the way of network construction. Different from the

C. Zhu (✉)
Alibaba Business School, Hangzhou Normal University, Hangzhou, China

J. Zhang et al. (eds.), *Innovation of Digital Economy*, Management for Professionals,
https://doi.org/10.1007/978-981-99-1741-9_30

self-operation and franchise model, the networking mode of Yimidida is regional alliances combined with the self-establishment, which builds a nationwide network by assembling different regional networks, and realizes the business model upgrade from "block" to "plane".

Yimidida quickly creates a national network through the industrial alliance networking. But, how to carry out the top-level mechanism design for the interest coordination and ensuring the stable operation of the new organization and network upgrade? The new network represents a new value proposition. How does Yimidida promote the innovation and upgrade of operation and management, so as to create new values for customers and users? What role does digitalization play in the operation and management innovation? How can enterprises gradually promote the digitalization? Yang Xingyun, CEO of Yimidida, and senior executives are in deep thinking…

2 Yimidida Creates Three Networks Through "Self-built Headquarters + Regional Alliances"

Yimidida, founded on June 9, 2015 and headquartered in Qingpu, Shanghai, is a comprehensive logistics enterprise determined to integrate logistics resources through the mode of "self-built headquarters + regional alliances", and build the fast freight business of national LTL network. According to the TOP10 list of 2021 LTL Cargo Volume of Tucmedia: the LTL cargo volume of Yimidida in 2021 is 9.5 million tons, second only to ane and SF Freight, as shown in Table 1.

The predecessor of Yimidida is several independent regional network logistics companies, such as Shaanxi Zhuohao (CEO Yang Xingyun's company). On March 11, 2015, six regional logistics companies (operating in the province), including Sichuan Jinqiao, Shandong Benteng, Hubei Dadao, JZL, Shanxi Sanmao and Shaanxi Zhuohao, established Yimidida with their own mature LTL network (B

Table 1 2021 Top 10 LTL freight enterprises

Rank	Enterprises	LTL cargo volume (ten thousand tons)
1	Ane	1025
2	SF Freight	1015
3	Yimidida	950
4	BEST Freight	840
5	Sanzhi Logistics	820
6	Dekun	656
7	ZTO Freight	652
8	Deppon Express	463
9	Yoka Logistics	455
10	Changtong Logistics	451

Source Tucmedia

network, referring to the network in the provincial area). On the basis of integrating several independent B-network logistics resources, Yimidida has built its own B network in East China, South China and other provinces, and different B networks have been connected and integrated, thus forming a nationwide LTL network (A network, referring to a network formed by connecting multiple B networks). Subsequently, leading enterprises in regional networks from five different provinces and autonomous regions also joined one after another, and the number of alliance enterprises of Yimidida increased from six to eleven. In 2019, Yang Xingyun took the initiative in the reform, and merged the outstanding representative enterprise in the field of large parcel express, UC Express (C network, referring to the national express network of large parcels) into Yimidida, and started the simultaneous operation of A, B and C networks, e.g. "national fast freight network + national express network + regional fast freight network", realizing the diversification of logistics products and the coverage of the whole weight ranges. Here is what president and CEO Yang Xingyun said in an internal open letter: "the coexistence of express network, fast freight network and regional network is the unique feature and advantage of Yimidida."

In the past six years since the establishment of the alliance, Yimidida has been granted the honors of "EqualOcean Top 10 Innovative Enterprises in the Logistics Industry of China in 2017", "Dark Horse of Entrepreneurship Top 50 Quasi-Unicorn Companies of China in 2018", and "Top 50 Quasi-Unicorn Companies of China's Internet Inverse Growth in 2018". CEO Yang Xingyun was granted "2018–2019 Top 10 Supply Chain Innovators" awarded by Shanghai Logistics and Supply Chain Entrepreneurs Association.

3 Background, Target Market and Orientation of LTL Industry

3.1 Background of LTL Industry

On the whole, the road freight accounts for the main part of the cargo transportation in China, and the proportion of it in the total freight volume has been maintained at more than 75%. As one of four major shipping methods (including road freight, railway freight, air freight and water freight), the road freight accounts for a higher proportion, and a part of the logistics industry. It should be pointed out that logistics enterprises operating from road freight carry out not only the single function of transportation, but also the combination of collection, turnover, transportation and delivery to achieve scale economy in some cases when the weight of goods is relatively light. Just like express logistics enterprises, distribution centers need to collect and sort parcels, transport on main and branch lines and deliver in the last kilometer to complete the whole process. The relevant data of Prospective Industry Research Institute shows that the road freight accounted for 77.81% of the freight market in the first 11 months of 2019.

According to the weight of parcels, the road freight market can be divided into three segments, such as 30 kg, 30 kg-3t and greater than 3t, corresponding to three markets of express delivery, LTL and carload respectively, as shown in Fig. 1. What needs to be explained is that the enterprise mentioned in this case is in the LTL express industry, a branch of the road freight industry under the LTL industry. The express is generally aimed at small items of enterprise customers, such as documents and e-commerce parcels. Thanks to the development of e-commerce, first-tier companies such as SF, JDL, STO Express, YTO Express, ZTO Express and YUNDA have emerged in the express delivery market. Less-than-truck-load (LTL) is divided into two market segments: LTL Express (also known as "small LTL waybill") and large LTL waybill according to weight of parcels (30–500 kg or 500–3,000 kg). The former has higher standardization and timeliness requirements, which is basically undertaken by network-based LTL companies; and the latter, generally directly targeting manufacturing enterprises, is undertaken by dedicated line companies. The carload mode refers to that the cargo weight is more than 3,000 kg. According to the *Research Report of China LTL Transportation* by Jinglue Consulting, the market size of LTL transportation in 2020 is close to CNY2 trillion, far exceeding the market size of express delivery of CNY300 billion. LTL is the logistics industry category of this case study.

Depending on the layout of transport routes, LTL enterprises are broadly divided into three categories: whole network, regional and dedicated line. Whole network enterprises, whose business process is similar to that of the express delivery, typically offer end-to-end services to customers through the layout of nationwide outlets and distribution centers, represented by Deppon Express, ane, TNT Hoau, SF Freight, ZTO Freight, etc. The process is generally as follows: outlets in the sending address→distribution centers within provinces (cities)→trunk transportation→distribution centers outside provinces (cities)→outlets in the arrival address→customers. Regional enterprises arrange outlets and distribution

Fig. 1 Market segmentation of the road freight

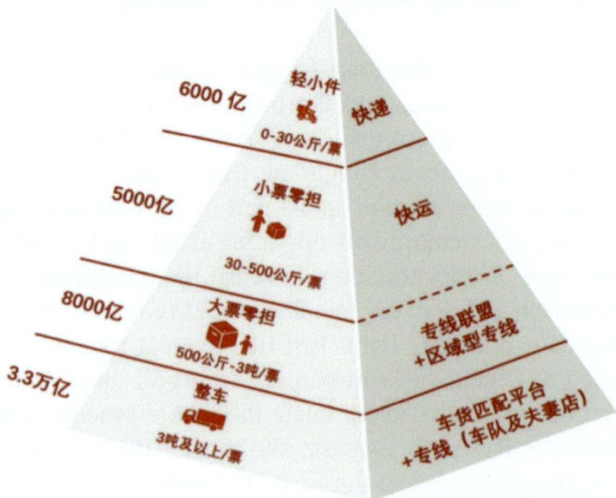

centers within a region (generally within the province) and generally offer freight services in the region, represented Guangdong MOCL, Shandong Benteng, JZL (Note: these three regional logistics companies have all already joined the headquarters of Yimidida), etc. Dedicated lines refer to the operation of a few special lines or large LTL waybills among several cities. According to the relevant data, dedicated line enterprises compose the largest enterprise group in the LTL industry, accounting for roughly 90%.

3.2 Target Market and Positioning

Through the alliance, self-building and mergers & acquisition, Yimidida has quickly built up A, B, C networks, corresponding to national LTL, provincial regional LTL and national large parcels and others covering the whole weight ranges. A network, i.e. national LTL network, serves fast freight businesses among provinces and regions, and its customer group is mainly enterprise-level customers, especially manufacturing industries. B network, i.e. local network within the regions of Yimidida alliance partners, is more centered on professional markets and channel customers, serving the fast freight businesses within provinces. C network, i.e. national express network of Yimidida, targets at e-commerce customers who have express delivery distribution demands of large parcels nationwide.

Growing from a regional network to a national network, Yimidida doesn't give up its business of the regional network (B network). While persisting the independent operation of Network B, it also relies on the intra-province direct access of B network to support A network. CEO Yang Xing believes that: "B network of Yimidida is a distinctive existence, which is built by regional leading companies in over ten years, and it is the core foundation of the current three-network operation." B network plays an essential role in optimizing the operation of A and C networks. The alliance members of B network, who have been working profoundly in provinces for many years, have completed the coverage in their respective provinces, counties and towns, and have relatively stable large customers in the fields of manufacturing, wholesale and retail in the professional markets of provinces.

Based on the features of these three networks, Yimidida has carried out the product segmentation. For example, due to its strong timeliness and excellent terminal advantages, B network concentrates on building the "overnight delivery" business within the province. C network is a large express delivery network directly targeting at C-terminal customers, and its core product is "330 Limited Time Delivery". A network meets the needs of manufacturing enterprises, and its core product is "Yimi Heavy Cargos", which provides full network coverage. Based on three networks, Yimidida develops a multi-category and diversified product strategy to offer customers more choices. At the same time, it also clarifies the key core products and provides differentiated services. The segmented products launched by Yimidida are shown in Table 2.

Table 2 Segmented products launched by Yimidida

	Weight coverage	Network coverage	Featured services
Yinuoda	Full coverage of weight above 70 kg	100% coverage of three major economic circles of Beijing-Tianjin-Hebei, Jiangsu-Zhejiang-Shanghai-Anhui and Fujian-Guangdong	Priority in terms of timeliness in receiving, transferring, transporting, dispatching and other links
Yimi small parcels	5–70 kg	Full network coverage, and 100% provincial and municipal coverage	100% door-to-door delivery, free of charge within 40 kg and a small amount of door-to-door service charge beyond 40 kg; priority in transiting and dispatching
Dida door-to-door service	70–150 kg	Coverage of remote counties and towns	As cheap as CNY16/order, special for customers in remote regions and providing door-to-door delivery services
Standard fast freight	150–500 kg	Coverage of remote counties and towns	High cost performance, matching with high-quality regional leading companies, and lower price than that in the industry
Yimi heavy cargos	Above 500 kg	Full network coverage	Price of approximately 50% off similar products in the same category; a bigger discount for higher weight ranges; full guarantee of benefits and low premium
330 limited time delivery	3–30 kg	Launch in 99 cities (including the first-tier cities such as Beijing, Shanghai, Guangzhou, Shenzhen and the second-tier cities such as Hangzhou, Chengdu, Chongqing and Xiamen)	Maximum full refund of freight cost out of the time limit

Source Official information and collation

4 Business Model Upgrade of Yimidida

What is the logic behind the rapid growth of Yimidida, which created the first echelon of LTL in just six years? What is the essence of the business model upgrade? What is the top-level mechanism design behind?

4.1 Business Model Upgrade of Yimidida from "Block" to "Plane" Through the Alliance

The business model upgrade is actually the upgrade of the role positioning in the industry. For example, the formation of the franchise business model of STO Express, YTO Express, ZTO Express and YUNDA has undergone an upgrade in role positioning from a single outlet (point) to the formation of logistic lines (line) and logistic network (plane). Behind the business model upgrade of STO Express, YTO Express, ZTO Express and YUNDA is the elevation of role status, from the traditional role to the platform party, dominant party and empowerment party, leading multiple participants to co-create by cooperation.

In accordance with the "point, line and plane" theory of Zeng Ming, former Chief of Staff of Alibaba Group, the network modes of logistics industry can be generally divided into three categories: "point→line→plane", "line→plane" and "block→plane". The network mode of STO Express, YTO Express, ZTO Express and YUNDA is "point→line→plane". From outlets to logistics lines and logistics network, the speed of forming a network is relatively slow. For example, STO Express, founded in 1993, was originated from the building of an outlet in Hangzhou. The founder, Nie Tengfei, picked up parcels from Hangzhou and delivered them to Shanghai (when he got the business, he rushed from Hangzhou to Shanghai by train on the same day); his wife, Chen Xiaoying, was accountable for calling phones and negotiating business; and co-founder, Zhan Jisheng, waited at Shanghai Railway Station to receive parcels and sent them to all places in the city. In 1997, STO Express built up outlets in Nanjing, Suzhou, Yiwu, Shaoxing, Beijing and others through self-building or franchise model. In 2010, the national network layout of STO Express was basically formulated, with outlets covering all major provinces, cities and county-level regions in China. It takes seven years for STO Express to develop from an outlet to a network basically covering the whole nation. Forming a network through franchise and replication of single outlets often needs a long time. If there are several established regional networks, a network covering the whole nation can be formed in a short time through the alliance.

In terms of the question of how to formulate a network quickly, Yimidida is a typical representative of "block→plane" type in the evolution to the role of "plane". CEO Yang Xingyun talked to several regional network leaders at the start in 2015: "as a regional network, although everyone is a leading company in its own region and province, the industrial alliance is an approach in a bid to achieve the expansion of the national network. We can combine our own networks to form a national network". Through the alliance, the commercial upgrade from "block" to "plane" can be realized, so as to expand the national businesses, which is the mode of Yimidida. Among them, the "block" refers to the regional networks in each place, and the "plane" refers to the national network. Yimidida acts the constructor of the "plane", integrating the scattered regional "blocks" into a national "plane" through "alliance + self-building". Before the alliance is established, each regional leading company has already gone through the whole process of "point→line→plane" as a "plane" in their own region. However, in the national network, each of them is a "block". Compared with the network modes of "point→line→plane" and "line→plane", the mode of "block→plane" enjoys the advantage of high starting speed, because enterprises can develop a national network relying on the regional network and direct-delivery dedicated lines among regions, instead of starting from "point" and "line".

Dekun has a typical mode of "line→plane" type, which was originally initiated by eight delicate-line enterprises, including ML Logistics, and they formed a loose alliance to jointly resist risks and share resources. Since then, with more and more regional dedicate-line companies joining the company with their "points", Dekun has integrated the equity of the initially loose logistics alliance, forming the current operation mode of forming "plane" with "lines" and accurately covering different regions.

In the process of Yimidida's business model upgrade, its role in the industry has been greatly improved. (1) It used to be a regional network, but now it runs a national network, making the network connectivity more extensive and deeper. Regional networks can operate independently to undertake regional orders and services, and at the same time, they can also undertake national orders and services with the interconnection of different networks. (2) The original networks are independent regional platforms, but now they are franchisees, becoming a part of the big platform community. Yimidida can dispatch regional orders (provincial orders) to an independent B network; and for national orders, multiple B networks can be connected to support whole network businesses. If B network is a small platform, A network is one part of such platform. A network can distribute regional orders to B network, and all B networks can form a joint force to undertake national orders.

4.2 Top-Level Mechanism Design, the Core of the Alliance Operation

The top-level mechanism design of the platform is the core priority in combining independent regional networks into an industrial community with the alliance co-creation. Yang Xingyun, CEO of Yimidida, said in an interview: "Before starting, we first entrusted lawyers and consulting agencies to draft a partner agreement, in order to clarify the relationship among member enterprises (partners) from the top-level design, so that each party can clearly know their rights and responsibilities and cope with different situations. Under the guarantee and constraint of rules and mechanisms, they create a strong relationship between the leading companies in each region and Yimidida in terms of equity, making their interests consistent all the time". The specific practice is to make all the regional leading companies become part of the self-operation system of Yimidida by means of one half of share exchange and one half of cash payment. Some of the former leaders in the alliance worked as executives in the company, while some resigned from their positions to just be shareholders.

That is to say, for the platform party and the headquarters, it is an important prerequisite to handle the interest relationship between the platform party and franchisees, if they want to maximize the initiative of each party. Taking ZTO Express as an example, in 2015, Chairman Lai Meisong mentioned that the company's business model exploration had gone through three stages of 1.0, 2.0 and 3.0. Stage 1.0 was the franchise mode of crowd innovation, crowdsourcing, crowdfunding and crowd support. However, in the cost settlement and business decision-making, the headquarters and online stores had quite different ideas. At this stage, the relationship between the platform and outlets was antagonistic and competitive, and their different demands would inevitably lead to conflicts. Stage 2.0: from 2010 to 2015, ZTO Express carried out a shareholding system reform, realizing the transformation of stakeholders from "many to one". CEO Lai Haisong gave up part of his equities and let franchise network be shareholders. Under the equity incentive mechanism, provincial and municipal franchisees had changed from bosses to professional managers. In stage 3.0, the benefit sharing could benefit all employees in the whole network, and dividends were shared according to different levels. Such measure successfully stimulated employees' enthusiasm and creativity. Nowadays, ZTO Express is in the stage of introducing the capital from outside parties, integrating resources, and sharing dividends according to different levels, i.e. the "Mass Entrepreneurship and Innovation 3.0" model.

4.3 Innovation of Alliance Networking of Yimidida

New value proposition based on the network upgrade

From independent regional networks to a unified national network, Yimidida puts forward a new value proposition as follows. Based on the alliance co-creation, Yimidida makes full use of the advantages of platform resources and digital technology to realize the empowerment of customers (channel customers, enterprise customers, etc.) and users (outlet leaders, terminal dispatchers, etc.).

Mr. Li, the IT technical director of Yimidida, mentioned in an interview that "customers pay for products directly and make direct contributions to company's profits. Users can obtain satisfaction effects and values depending on the resources of enterprises. As a logistics service platform of the alliance co-creation, the company aims to provide unique values to customers and users respectively." Before the alliance is established, the core customers of regional logistics leaders in B network are channel customers (for example, B-terminal merchants such as wholesalers and retailers in traditional professional markets). For customers in the channel industry, Yimidida's fast freight service in each province can exactly solve their problem of downstream distribution, for example, the goods delivery of specialized markets in provincial capitals to wholesalers and retailers in secondary cities and tertiary counties. For nationwide purchasing and supply (for example, delivering goods from upstream supply factories in A province to professional markets in B province), regional logistics companies have little to do. Hence, upstream supply chain and downstream distribution chain involved in the logistics link always cannot form a closed loop, need to be carried by national logistics companies and regional logistics companies respectively, it also adds to the communication and logistics costs of customers in the channel industry. After the alliance is established, Yimidida, instead of abandoning the channel industry customers in the regional B network, solved pain points and put forward a new value proposition by way of network upgrade, i.e. paying attention to the channel industry customers and promoting the full-chain and full-range circulation of goods in the context of new retail. As the new value proposition needs the support of network upgrade, Yimidida builds a national trunk, A network, and a large-parcel express, C network, one after another. A network guarantees the one-stop flow of materials and goods nationwide for enterprises, solving the pain point of "failure in the delivery". Large-parcel express, C network, mainly targets at the large-parcel e-commerce express business of enterprises and end consumers to build direct sales logistics to the terminal and solve the pain point of "failure of the full-chain closed loop".

Users can be satisfied and receive values dependent on enterprises' resources. Before the alliance is established, users of each regional logistics company are outlet billing clerks, drivers, etc. Even though regional logistics companies also have their own internal settlement, order management and other systems, the implementation of their vehicle routes, performance assessment and other decisions are still artificial. The values of the underlying data have not really been brought into play, therefore, at this stage, the user value has not been fully explored. After Yimidida is formed, the user group is enlarged from the original single regional B network users to A, B and C network users, specifically including the outlet leaders, terminal dispatchers, operators in distribution centers and personnel in dispatching command centers. Yimidida puts forward a new user value proposition, i.e. applying IT system to the empowerment of operators to achieve the quality and efficiency improvement and scientific performance assessment of whole business scenarios.

Network collaboration for new value creation

After the alliance is established, Yimidida needs to create new values for customers, users and industry.

The new values created by Yimidida for customers are mainly reflected in the breadth of service, the depth of service and the cost level. Firstly, in terms of the breadth level, it assists to realize the nationwide LTL. In the past, regional logistics companies could only provide customers with special line logistics services within the province. Secondly, in terms of the depth level, the integration of the three networks can provide full-chain and one-stop logistics services, including upstream raw material procurement, inter-provincial transport of goods, distribution of goods within the province and door-to-door e-commerce parcel services for consumers. In the past, regional logistics companies can only undertake the logistics business of the downstream distribution chain of professional market customers, while the upstream supply chain-related businesses (raw material procurement, goods processing and transportation, etc.), are carried out with the network fast freight + special lines due to its cross-regional nature. Thirdly, in terms of the cost level, the large-scale operation of three networks is characterized by effective logistics and transportation costs, and Yimidida's pricing for niche logistics products to customers is lower than those of peers.

The new value created by Yimidida for regional logistics companies is mainly at the level of business undertaking scope, scale cost reduction and development support. Firstly, in terms of broadening the business scope, after regional logistics companies joining the platform, they shift from a single provincial business to a diversified national business. Secondly, in terms of the scale cost reduction, the access to the whole network business of regional leading companies leads to cargo volume increase and cost reduction by sharing sites, equipment, human resources. Thirdly, in terms of supporting the development, unified brands and systems, finance, industry resources and others are provided by the platform for regional members. As for grassroots outlets, in comparison with the development method before the alliance, the new value is mainly reflected in the technology empowerment to enhance the operational efficiency of outlets. After Yimidida is established, it will speed up the information construction of the whole network, empower the grassroots outlets and their staff through Galaxy system, transform the rough management mode and improve the operation efficiency of outlets. For instance, via Yiwangtong, the grassroots outlet dispatchers can check their work progress and KPI for the month in real time; and via Yisubao, outlet leaders can check the total number of collections and deliveries for the month, as well as the completion of related indicators.

The new value created by Yimidida for the industry is mainly reflected in the network synergy effect. With the network expansion of Yimidida, the original "points" and "lines" in the region can be hosted and used nationwide, thereby enhancing the utilization of "points". Meanwhile, it can attract more "points" and "lines". For a network, the more "points" and "lines" that can be connected, the greater the value of the network will be stimulated.

Value transfer and delivery of collaborative parties

The platform party is required to collaborate with all parties, including headquarters, franchised regional logistics companies and outlets to do a good job in the design of the top-level mechanism, operation mechanism and incentive mechanism for better value deliver and transfer. Before the establishment of Yimidida, it sought external agencies for the top-level mechanism design and operational unification. Agreements such as entry mechanism, exit mechanism, equity distribution and voting firmly bind the interests of each regional logistics company together. In terms of the specific business operation, Yimidida seeks to unify product, brand, information system, management and settlement to have an overall image to the outside world. After standardizing the operation, the platform party/headquarters further dedicates to the empowerment and value delivery to terminal outlets. In the past, the benefit distribution mechanism between the regional headquarters and the outlets is a sharing system, with the regional headquarters paying labor compensation according to a fixed percentage of the income generated by outlets. In the early stage of business expansion, outlets are still able to get sufficient incentives. But later on, when the business is saturated, the incentive effect to outlets is not as good as before. After the establishment of Yimidida, it changed the share system to base price system, and in addition, it also provided outlets with preferences such as transit fee discounts and top-up rebates, giving outlets more freedom and profit space and effectively realizing the sinking of the network. At this stage, in order to help outlets adapt to the headquarters' strategic planning of integrating A, B and C network, the headquarters gives outlets the priority to choose to join in A, B and C network, and outlets can choose whether to join or not by combining their own situation.

Making the market bigger and acquiring value through altruistic thinking
The value acquisition logic of Yimidida is to make the market bigger through the alliance network model, empower all parties through altruistic thinking, and do a good job of distributing and controlling costs, so as to achieve mutual success with regional logistics companies and outlets. The company's sources of income include the order business incomes of clients and outlet franchise fees. Originally, orders came from regional businesses. But now, national business incomes have been increased to make the market bigger. In terms of distribution, the headquarters and outlets have a new mechanism, which has been discussed in the above. Costs mainly include base prices of receiving and dispatching outlets and hard costs of sites (referring to distribution centers, similar to the express delivery), trunk transport and personnel. The control of sites, trunk lines and labor costs is mainly reflected in the synergy of the three networks at headquarters, which has improved the operational efficiency of logistics elements by merging routes, thus achieving cost reduction.

5 Digital Operational and Management Innovation

Operational and management innovation is the guarantee of business model upgrade. In order to achieve the new position of upgrading from "block" to "plane", Yimidida also needs to upgrade its operation and management modes. For example, the digital empowerment can help realize the innovation of three-network operation and management.

5.1 Unification of Information Systems for the Digitalization of Network-Wide Operations

Construction of Galaxy system and the launch of microservice sector

At the beginning of its establishment, Yimidida set out to promote the unification of products and services, brands, settlement, management and information system. Among them, the unification of information system is the core, helping the whole network business to achieve digital operation and management.

Galaxy system, the underlying business platform independently developed by Yimidida, includes core business, intelligent mobile, electronic map, order management, customer management, vehicle and cargo matching, vehicle location management, business intelligence management, basic data management and other sub-systems, as shown in Fig. 2. Galaxy system makes it possible for the business connection and data sharing of different business unit phases and subsystems. In terms of the promotion of Galaxy system, Yimidida consulted its shareholders and adopted a compromise plan. The Galaxy system was first used in the incremental business in the national A network, and after the business development was on track, it gradually guided members to transfer their businesses to the regional B network, and achieved the network-wide information system replacement in June 2018. Based on the underlying architecture of the Galaxy system, the company developed a mobile microservice sector, including a mini program and official account for external customers and Yiwangtong, Yousubao and Yisubao for internal users, as shown in Fig. 3.

The official account and mini program are the tools through which Yimidida interacts with customers. Through the official account and mini program, customers can achieve the efficiency improvement with convenient functions such as online order placement, one-click order follow-up, and timeliness enquiry. The headquarters set up a direct channel to reach recipients and senders, solving the problem that only the end outlets could reach end users in the past.

Yiwangtong is a mobile app created by Yimidida Express Department for internal business process. Business personnel from all departments (such as grassroots dispatchers, customer services, drivers and management staff) can log into Yiwangtong by simply selecting their region and entering work numbers and passwords and check visual data statements, to-do tasks, performance appraisal, etc. As shown in Figs. 4, 5 and 6, these are the interfaces of the Yiwangtong for outlet leaders, drivers and customer service respectively. Yousubao is independently developed by

Fig. 2 Galaxy system of Yimidida. *Source* Official information

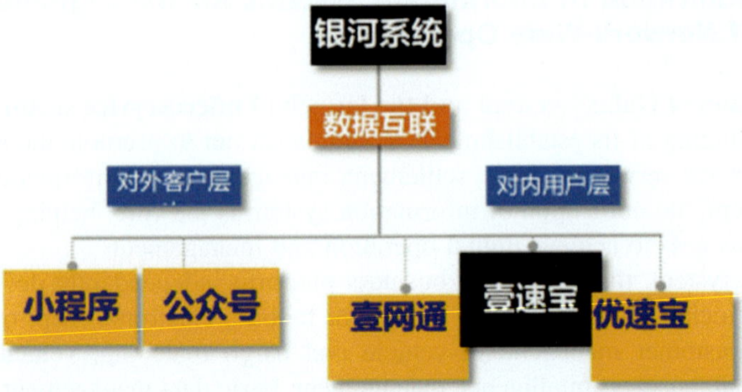

Fig. 3 Yimidida microservice module and underlying business support system. *Source* Official information and collation

Yousu Express Department under Yimidida, with the functional positioning similar to that of Yiwangtong.

The situation of different operation scenarios can all be displayed on Yiwangtong. For example, for the operators of distribution centers, their main business

Fig. 4 Interface of outlet leaders

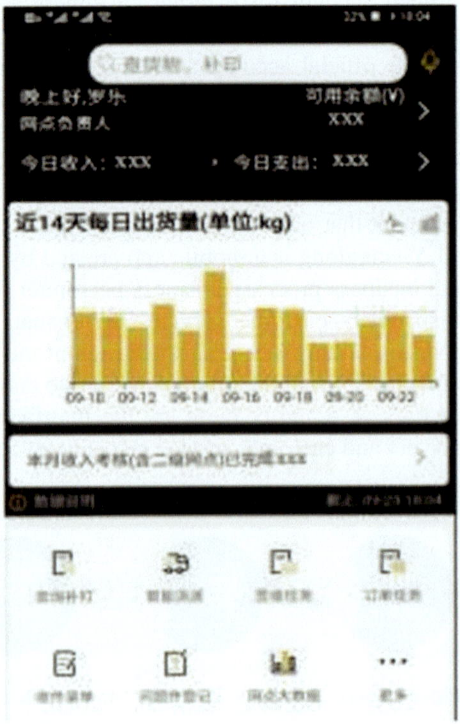

Fig. 5 Driver interface

scenarios are unloading and unpacking, systematic sorting, collecting and packaging, etc. Yiwangtong has customized functions for them, such as real-time monitoring of automatic sorting and overloading warning. The main business scenarios of grassroots dispatchers are dispatching particles, loading, scanning, etc. Yiwangtong has customized functions for them, such as order task, billing and printing, which are suitable for 9 mobile scenarios, as shown in Fig. 7.

Yisubao is designed for leaders. In terms of underlying data, Yisubao is interconnected with business operation apps (Yiwangtong and Yousubao), and every operation of staff in grassroots outlets will be recorded by IT system. The outlet leaders can monitor the outlet data under their management in real time through Yisubao, such as the number of parcels received, the punctuality rate of distributors or the total amount of goods circulating in outlets and other multidimensional data. Middle and senior leaders can check the real-time data under their jurisdiction. If there is an overloading situation in distribution centers of the jurisdiction, the system will send an alarm. Eight relevant indicators are set in the system, such as the number of vehicles, cargo volume and other key indicators. If three indicators are not up to the standards, an early warning will be sent, and leaders can timely dispatch vehicles to fill the personnel gap accordingly. Figure 8 shows the real-time early data warning platform of Yimidida.

Fig. 6 Customer service interface. *Source* Official information

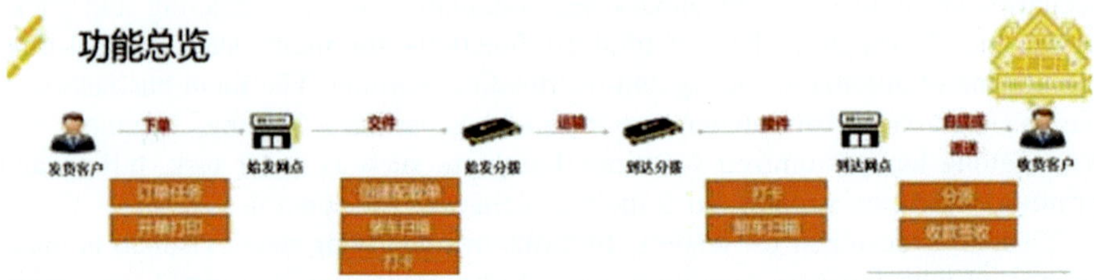

Fig. 7 Digitalization of the whole process of internal operations for Yiwangtong. *Source* Official information

5.2 Digital Empowerment and Three-Network Integration

The digitai goal is not only the process digitalization, but also the improvement of operational efficiency. In the meeting, CEO Yang made a request to Mr. Li, the head of IT department: "how does the digitalization change the situation that the three networks' separate operations, and realize the resource integration of three networks in the terminal outlets, distribution centers, loading delivery and other core logistics links to different degrees, as well as the refined cost management

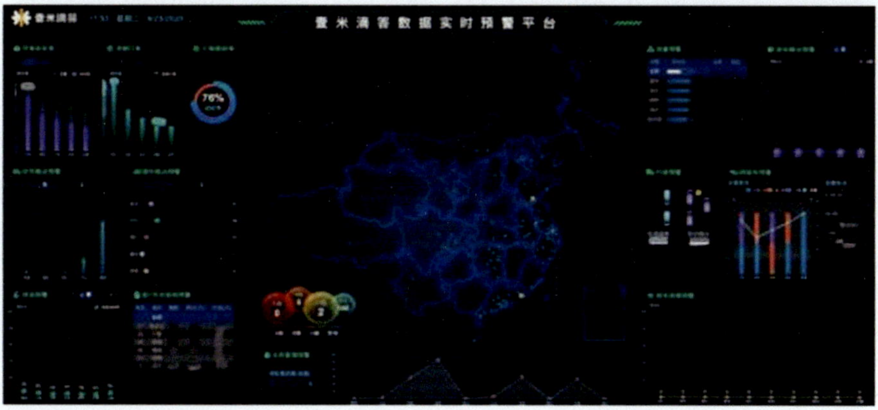

Fig. 8 Early data warning platform of Yimidida. *Source* Official information

and control". CEO Yang continued to say that, to realize the mutual circulation and transportation of goods in three networks, the essence is to improve the utilization efficiency of distribution centers, outlets and vehicles.

Mr. Li stood up and said that, to realize the integration of three networks and the improvement of the utilization efficiency of logistics elements such as vehicle lines, outlets and distribution centers, the digitalization and algorithms are the basis. It is necessary to make a good decision on business integration and distribution by taking into account such factors as cargo volume, distance, vehicle types and timeliness.

The heads of other departments also agreed with Mr. Li. Mr. Wang, who is in charge of network A operation, believes that: "the integration of three networks is related to technology, business and management". How to do well in empowering refined management by digitalization requires the framework thinking of three networks, and there are 3W and 1H to answer, namely WHY, WHAT, WHERE and HOW. WHY is to answer the question of why, because the integration can realize the control of single order costs and produce scale economy effects. WHAT is the answer of what to integrate and what to divide. For example, can different types of outlets (such as fast freight and express outlets) realize full weight range collection, and classify and operate in operation? WHERE is the answer of where to integrate and where to divide. For example, economically backward counties and districts have a small amount of daily collection and delivery, so they should try their best to integrate three networks. HOW is the answer of how to integrate and how to divide, which is mainly a technical issue. For 3W, our operation directors need to consider the framework of integration and the scheme of process reengineering of each business line. As for 1H, IT department should work together with others to make better technical solutions, so that the system can automatically make the decision of integration and division during operation.

Next, Mr. Li continued to air his opinions. He gave an example of operation. Assuming that there are goods sent from Shanghai to Gansu with fast freight (A network) and express (C network). The order management subsystem shows that there are 14 tons of goods on network A and 11 tons of goods on network C. The vehicle-cargo matching subsystem pre-arranges the scheme according to the real-time cargo volume and the year-on-year and month-on-month cargo volume. Therefore, two trucks of 9.6 m (net load of about 20 tons) are sent, of which the loading rate of network A truck is about 70%, and that of network C is only about 55%. When the loading rate is lower than the threshold, the system will trigger an early warning and send data such as the current cargo volume, loading rate and average cost of a single order to the headquarters dispatching center. The management personnel of the dispatching center will optimize the decision based on the above information. That is, after integrating A and C network in Shanghai distribution center, a 13 m truck (a net load of around 30 tons) will be sent, which can not only improve the loading rate but also reduce the fuel consumption on the basis of no filling up.

In the whole meeting, Mr. Li, Mr. Wang and Mr. Yang talked a lot. What's more, the managers and supervisors of other operation divisions all agreed with them. At last, they reached an agreement that all business management departments shall be required to cooperate in business, operation, management and technology, and they needed to appoint a department leader. Meanwhile, they also joked about Mr. Li the IT department that the employees of your department would have a "good life" in the future.

5.3 Improving the Management by Digitalization and Innovation of Performance Appraisal

The digitalization of performance appraisal is a trend in the field of human resource management. For grassroots employees, the number of parcels delivered and collected represents the working ability. For middle and high-level managers, the degree of business execution in the area in their charge is relevant to their management ability. Now, the IT system of Yimidida can make KPI and performance appraisal for grassroots employees and performance appraisal for district managers, which is based on the data of each outlet (such as the revenue situation and complaint rate). The managers are appraisees and appraisers of the grassroots outlets, and they also can appraise outlets in the light of the network operation data which are presented on the app.

6 Epilogue

When the express delivery giants enter into the field LTL, the competition in the field in China will be fiercer. Now, ane, SF Express, Deppon Express, ZTO and other giants are making efforts in the fast freight market. In competitive strategies, the price war is inevitable. However, using price for market is not a long-term solution at all. How to improve the comprehensive operational efficiency of the platform and create logistics products with cost performance by upgrading the operation is what to be considered by managers. At present, the platform of Yimidida belongs to the closed mode of alliance + self-building. In the logistics industry, Cainiao Network is an open digital logistics platform. In the future, will Yimidida disclose its accumulated digital capabilities in the LTL industry, and let more participants, such as huge dedicated line operators, come in to create value and build an open and collaborative LTL digital industry platform? If so, how to realize and when to start? And how does Yimidida arrange?

Lvwochuan Farm: How Does Traditional Agriculture Realize the Digital Transformation of the Whole Industrial Chain?

Jiarong Guo, Guohao Zhang, Yong Zhou, Zhili Lin, and Qianqiang Li

1 Introduction

Agriculture is not only the mainstay of the national economy, but also the backbone of meeting the people's needs for a better material life. However, the problems of "big but not strong" and "complete but not excellent" of Chinese traditional agriculture are still quite serious. From the realistic situation, the outstanding weaknesses of China's agriculture and rural areas are weak foundations and lagging development. The most obvious shortcomings of economic and social development and the weakest link in modernization have always lain in "agriculture, rural areas and farmers". Therefore, it is extremely urgent to promote the high-quality development of agriculture.

General Secretary Xi Jinping once pointed out: "the new normal should have new impetus, and the digital economy can make great achievements in this respect". As an important representative of the new economy, the digital economy is particularly important to the development of developing countries. Its characteristics of "reality, novelty and communication" enables itself to be deeply integrated with the national economy, help the digital development of the national economy and improve the developmental level of the national economy comprehensively. The agriculture is the main focus of both revitalizing the national economy and developing the digital economy. In the *Action Plan on Promoting Big Data Development* issued by the State Council recently, it requires to promote the sharing and opening of agriculture-related data resources in all regions, industries and fields, accelerate the research and development of key technologies of agricultural big data, and facilitate the data sharing of agricultural resource elements. In the *Action*

J. Guo (✉) · G. Zhang · Y. Zhou · Z. Lin · Q. Li
School of Business, Taizhou University, Taizhou, PR China

J. Zhang et al. (eds.), *Innovation of Digital Economy*, Management for Professionals,
https://doi.org/10.1007/978-981-99-1741-9_31

Plan for Promoting the Development of Agricultural E-commerce issued by the Ministry of Commerce and other two ministries, it is emphasized that new-generation information technologies such as mobile Internet, cloud computing, big data and Internet of Things (IoT) should be integrated into all fields and links of agricultural e-commerce to enhance the independent innovation capability effectively (Guo et al., 2019; Xue et al., 2021).

Therefore, under this background, this case group takes the digital transformation as the entry point and focuses on Taizhou Lvwochuan Farm. Through the digital economy, efforts are intensified to empower the high quality development of agriculture, and construct the whole digital industrial chain of agriculture centered on Lvwochuan's digital agriculture. It also explores the specific path of high quality development of Lvwochuan Farm to provide a beneficial reference for the high quality development of Chinese agriculture.

2 Development and Current Situation of the Company

Founded in October 2013, Taizhou Lvwochuan Agricultural Co., Ltd. is located in Lianhong Village, Beiyang Town, Huangyan District, Taizhou City and is adjacent to the famous foothills of Changtan Reservoir, covering an area of more than 300 mu. It boasts a picturesque scenery of green hills and clear waters, convenient transportation and unique natural environment. It is a modern high-tech agricultural enterprise integrating production and operation and several services such as fruit and vegetable planting, prevalent variety cultivation, freshwater aquaculture, agricultural sightseeing, agricultural technology training and promotion, and combination of agriculture and tourism.

Based on the high-tech agricultural planting, Lvwochuan introduced Dutch hydroponic vegetable technology and drip irrigation and soilless strawberry cultivation technology, and integrated automatic, intelligent, industrialized, three-dimensional and soilless culture technologies, among which the high-tech agricultural cultivation technology of vegetables and strawberries gets a good lead in China. Relying on the technologies of hydroponic vegetables and soilless strawberry cultivation, Lvwochuan has built an agricultural high-tech research and development center, a planting base promotion center and a modern agricultural training center. With Taizhou Lvwochuan Agricultural Demonstration Base as its center, Lvwochuan has carried out the project and technology cooperation nationwide.

2.1 Development Stage 1: Successful Transformation and Upgrading of the Enterprise

In 2013, the original state-owned enterprises started to transform into joint-stock enterprises to respond to the reform actively, and further realize the transformation from the planned economy to the market economy. As one of the typical examples of enterprise transformation and upgrading of Taizhou, Taizhou Feida Blister Factory successfully implemented the transformation of plastic, molding and other manufacturing industries into modern agricultural development, and registered and established Taizhou Lvwochuan Farm (Partnership Enterprise) on October 15, 2013.

In June 2014, Lvwochuan Farm reached an agreement with Lianhong Village, Beiyang Town on the transfer and use of collective land and officially started the development of modern high-tech planting industry and agricultural tourism industry. In October of the same year, the intelligent greenhouse project of hydroponic vegetable base in Taizhou Lvwochuan Farm was completed and put into production, and it also obtained a total of 4 patents, including "Seedling Raising Instruments for Large-scale Planting of Vegetable" and other utility models of China National Intellectual Property Administration.

In August 2015, the website of Taizhou Lvwochuan Farm was officially launched and put into the normal operation. In November of the same year, Lvwochuan products were put into trial operation in Taizhou, and Lvwochuan vegetable products were exhibited in the "Food Safety Exhibition of Zhejiang in 2015". Lvwochuan has obtained one utility model patent from China National Intellectual Property Administration.

2.2 Development Stage 2: The Marketing Mode of "Three-Line Integration"

On January 30, 2016, Taizhou Lvwochuan Agricultural Co., Ltd. was registered and established. In March of the same year, the marketing model of "three-line integration" of green agricultural products of Lvwochuan was put into operation officially. It mainly refers to three sales channels, i.e. the first-line direct ordering and distribution of the production base, the second-line retails of commission agents and the third-line Internet, sales hotline and ordering and distribution. Lvwochuan also passed the highest standard food safety certification in the world, i.e. "Kosher Certificate". The preparatory work for introducing the soilless strawberry cultivation technology of Korean "ENG" was also basically completed. The infrastructure construction of the second phase project was officially launched.

In 2017, Taizhou Lvwochuan Agricultural Co., Ltd. passed the Good Agricultural Practices (GAP) certification. In the same year, Taizhou Government issued a document to name a group of municipal leading agricultural enterprises, among which Lvwochuan Farm was listed. Lvwochuan Farm was then upgraded to one of the municipal leading agricultural enterprises.

2.3 Development Stage 3: Digital Transformation and Upgrading of the Whole Industrial Chain

Since 2018, Lvwochuan has obtained more than 30 related invention patents and utility model patents, including “vegetable cultivation and planting method”, “up-and-down suspended bed system” and other invention patents, as well as “a crop cultivation bed with adjustable soil temperature”, “hydroponic vegetable seedling fishing machine” and other utility model patents. In accordance with the business tenet of “to be a green eco-environmental protection industry and to make healthy, safe and nutritious products” and the business principle of “economic, social and ecological benefits”, Lvwochuan strives to build a well-known brand of green and pollution-free agricultural products, taking “based on the local, driving the whole province and radiating the whole country” as its development concept.

3 Digital Transformation Practice

3.1 Internet of Things: Superposition of Technologies and Connection of All Things

Lvwochuan vegetable factory and soilless strawberry garden are both intelligent greenhouses. With the intelligent and digital (Internet of Things) climate control system, sensors of air temperature, humidity, atmospheric pressure, light intensity, water level, wind direction, wind force, carbon dioxide concentration and insect condition in the greenhouse, wind direction and wind sensors outside the greenhouse, rainfall collectors, solar power supply system collectors and monitoring data collectors collect data and transmit to cloud computers for data analysis. According to the collected data, computers will make corresponding adjustments to the top skylights, sunshade nets, water curtains, circulating fans and negative pressure fans automatically, all links among which will run automatically step by step (He, 2021). The seasonal limit is broken and the most suitable growth environment can be provided for fruit and vegetables (Wang & Luo, 2020).

Lvwochuan intelligent and digital nutrient solution circulation control system, including the circulatory system, control system and online monitoring system, is composed of cultivation beds, nutrient solution pools, liquid supply pipelines and return pipelines. During the whole process, by carrying nutrient solution, cultivation beds provide some necessary nutrients and water, and a better root environment for the growth of crops. The nutrient solution provides the storage and supply function for the nutrient solution carried by cultivation beds. The solution is injected into nutrient solution pools through the control of electromagnetic valves with mother liquor tanks, acid base tanks and clear water tanks. Therefore, one cycle of the whole nutrient solution circulation system is completed. The water and fertilizer detection sensors collect data of cultivation elements in real time, and computer systems provide precise fertilization plans to meet the element requirements of vegetable growth.

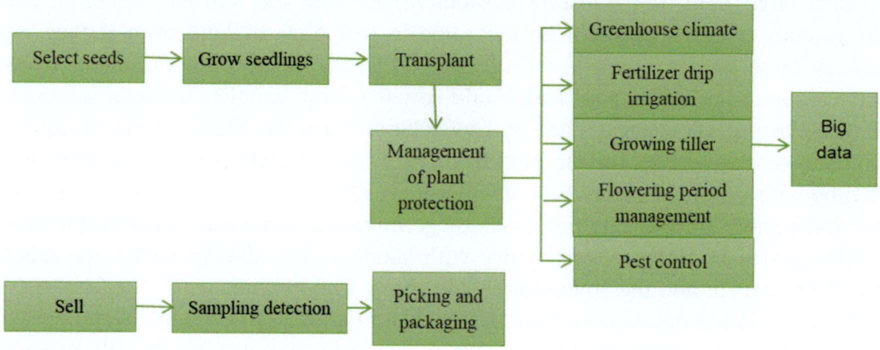

Fig. 1 Big data decision-making process

3.2 Big Data: Precise Data Control for Decision-Making

With the development of rural e-commerce, upstream and downstream agricultural sales, agricultural production, agricultural product circulation data, as well as agricultural data related to land transfer, meteorology, soil, hydrology, etc., have been accumulated and collected in a large scale (Sun, 2021). All these big data will be the "brain" of agricultural decision-making.

Lvwochuan Farm applies big data in the product production to sales for the agricultural decision-making. It takes only abot 40–45 days from fruit and vegetable planting to sales, and only 3–5 workers are required from planting to packing selenium-rich vegetables, greatly saving the decision-making time and labor. Lvwochuan Farm has changed the dependence of traditional agricultural on the season, land, climate and other factors, and achieved a new model of four-season cycle of multiple cropping, "all-weather" operation, factory-scale production, automated assembly line operation, leading the modern agriculture to high yield, high efficiency, high technology development goals (Fig. 1).

3.3 Digital Intelligence: Intellectualization on Numbers, and Turing Intellectualization into Power

In the era of digital economy, two most important key elements are "numbers" and "intelligence". Digital intelligence, as its name implies, is the combination of "digitalization" and "intelligence". The "number" means digitalization, the whole-domain, whole-scene, whole-chain digitalization from the consumer side to the supply side. "Intelligence" means intellectualization, making intelligent decisions based on digital closed loops, and realizing the accurate response, real-time optimization and intelligent decision-making to changes in market demands (Li, 2009).

In a large field, the moisture content of the soil, the nutrient situation, and the growth of crops may not be the same in two plots of land even if they are two or three meters apart. For thousands of years in the past, farmers did not differentiate such differences and would sow the same varieties at equal intervals. Today, the precision agriculture of Lvwochuan Farm has changed this tradition. The substances needed for the growth of fruit and vegetables can be replenished in time with the cloud computing whether it is hilly areas or highlands and whether the soil is poor or not. The processes of germination, sprouting and transplanting seedlings can be done automatically with seeders. The sowing speed can reach 100,000 seeds/h, and the sowing area can reach 15,000 mu/h.

In the seedling cultivation stage, Lvwochuan Farm applies flexible water spraying and automatic fans to ensure a certain level of humidity while still keeping the constant temperature below 26 °C. After seedlings are cultivated in the greenhouse for 10 days, they are automatically sent to cleaning machines for cleaning and disinfection through the pipes above the greenhouse, and then sent to the planting area with seedling transplanting machines. When seedlings are ripe, the umbrella-type gear-shaped machine equipment automatically removes vegetables to production lines for manual harvesting and packaging. The whole process, except for packaging, is all automated, requiring only 3–5 workers.

The digital operation of Lvwochuan Farm can achieve continuous daily sowing (up to 100,000 seeds/h), transplanting (up to 10,000 plants/h) and harvesting, realizing the factory production and increasing the multiple cropping rate by 4 times compared to the traditional method (3 times/mu/year with traditional mode, and 12 times/mu/year in this project), with an annual yield of 25 tons per mu. Under the same conditions, it can save 40% of land, 50% of water resources and 90% of labor costs compared to traditional methods.

3.4 Traceablity Codes: Full Supervision and Product Traceability

With the support of independent intellectual property technology, each product in the system is given a special QR code similar to an ID card, "Z-code" and can be written to data for multiple times. By simply scanning codes with relevant applications on phones, comsumers can understand the "origins and destinations" of goods, and enterprises can also accurately grasp destinations, thus constituting a whole-chain supervision system covering the production, logistics, warehousing, consumption and other aspects. With the spread of smartphones and plane terminals, it will be possible to provide mobile phone client services containing cloud system analysis to farmers, thereby improving the farm management efficiency and agricultural cultivation effectiveness. The food traceability can be achieved with technologies that record the production processes of agricultural products.

Lvwochuan Farm adheres to the implementation of the certificate of conformity system for edible agricultural products in all its operated projects. The certificate of conformity for edible agricultural products should include at least the names and weights of products, information on producers and operators of edible agricultural products (name, address and contact information), methods to ensure compliance, seals or signatures of producers and operators of edible agricultural products, date of issuance, etc. The purpose is to achieve the main responsibility traceability. A certificate of compliance with the traceability QR code is affixed to the outer packagings of agricultural products, and the traceability information of the whole process of production, processing, logistics, storage and sales can be obtained by scanning the code.

4 Digital Transformation: How to Achieve?

4.1 Relevant Theoretical Basis

1. Industrial Chain Theory
   The industrial chain is an industrial entity formed by certain intrinsically related industries, and it is an industrial structure that achieves overall positive development by satisfying special needs with certain services as the core, or by carrying out certain commodity production activities and bringing corresponding services (Zhang, 2016). Many related products or services are applied in the industrial chain to explore the needs for corresponding products. From the supply of raw materials to the sales in the market, a series of components such as sequential relationship, horizontal extension, and orderly economic behavior are covered. In essence, it is used to mark structures of enterprise groups with internal connections, and in fact, it is a macro concept with a two-dimensional character, i.e. both structural and value attributes. The industrial chain also involves large-scale upstream and downstream relationships and value exchange activities, with the former delivering products and services to the latter, and the latter in turn bringing feedback to the former.
   The whole agricultural industrial chain refers to the whole process of "agricultural production – processing and logistics – sales management of agricultural products", and the whole chain is under the management and control of the core management body. The key factors affecting the value-added of the whole industrial chain can be analyzed through the value demands of the core body, so as to promote the solution of problems such as the connection of industrial chains and the lack of diversified sales channels. Compared with traditional industrial chains, the whole industrial chain is characterized by smoother linkage, more complete linkage connotation, and more attention to the management and overall efficiency (Fig. 2).
2. Empowerment Theory
   Empowerment theory was first put forward by American scholar, Solomon in *Black Empowerment: Social Work in Oppressed Communities*. There is no fully unified definition of empowerment theory, and researchers in different fields have proposed many definitions based on their backgrounds and differences (Zhang et al., 2021). For example, Malcolm argues that the purpose of empowerment is to help the disempowered gain the right to make decisions and act

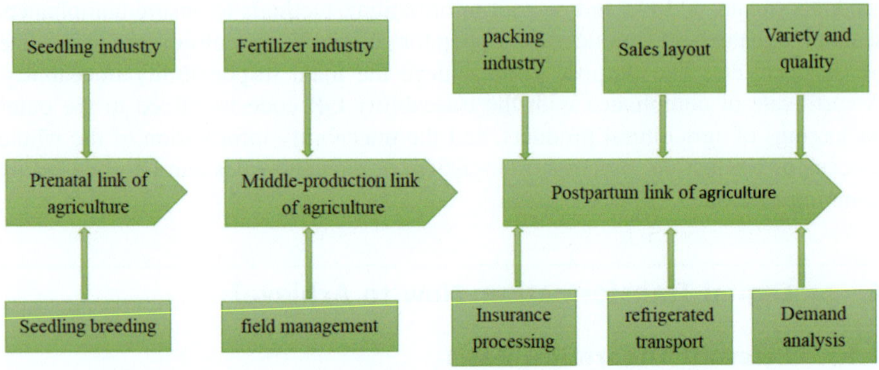

Fig. 2 Diagram of the whole agricultural industrial chain

on their own lives, thereby improving their life quality. Swift and Levin see empowerment as a state of mind, and a process of power redistribution. Zimmerman believes that the empowerment involves individuals, organizations, and communities, and aims to increase the social participation of the empowered and to improve their sense of self-efficacy and control.

With the development of digital technology, more and more scholars have started to focus on the digital empowerment research, but due to different research contexts and focuses, no consensus has been reached on the definition of digital empowerment. Hermansson emphasizes that the digital empowerment is about empowering people to cope with or solve problems through technologies such as big data and mobile internet, thus moving from "unempowered" to "empowered". Lenka pointed out that three abilities are included in the digital empowerment, i.e. analysis ability (the ability to obtain valuable information by analyzing big data), intelligence ability (the ability to solve problems independently in the production process) and connectivity ability (the ability to connect and control all processes of enterprise organizations). In the *World Development Report 2016: Digital Dividends*, it is pointed out that the digital technology is rapidly promoted in most parts of the world, and the extensive development benefit generated by applying these technologies is the digital empowerment. Sun Xinbo defined the digital empowerment as the process of realizing values through the scene transformation and skill upgrading of the digital technology.

4.2 Digital Transformation Empowerment Before the Production

Effective connection of supply and demand under the information construction: such a "planting cycle" of "earning money in one year, losing money in one year, and breaking even in another year" can be described as a heartbreak for farmers. In order to find a way out of the "planting cycle", Lvwochuan Farm started to upgrade its digital information infrastructure. Firstly, the establishment of efficient ecological planting mode has solved the problem of low anti-risk ability of traditional agriculture. Secondly, the digital technology can be used to build an information platform to cover the supply chain, solving the problems of impeding access to information in the production and operation.

Establishing an intelligent, unmanned and digital factory and an agricultural and rural digital resource system: the development of digital agriculture puts forward higher requirements for infrastructures, which requires to further strengthen the rural infrastructure construction. In terms of planting facilities, the numerical control equipment is adopted in intelligent hydroponic vegetable gardens and intelligent soilless strawberry gardens of Lvwochuan Farm, where intelligent robots and machines and equipment complete the progress from sowing, seedling planting and maturity to packaging. It is more efficient, and reduces the dependence of traditional agriculture on labor.

4.3 Digital Transformation Empowerment During the Production

Comprehensive analysis with big data to help the agricultural decision-making: under the guidance of big data, the precision agriculture of Lvwochuan Farm has changed the dependence of traditional agricultural on the season, land, climate and other factors, and achieved a new model of four-season cycle of multiple cropping, and "all-weather" operation, leading the modern agriculture to high yield, high efficiency, high technology development goals.

Improving the production efficiency in an all-round way with the digitalization of production and operating decisions: Lvwochuan Farm adopts the artificial intelligence to summarize and analyze the data, which greatly excavates the potential meaning behind big data, so as to understand the growth of crops more accurately and provide the planting guidance for farmers. In terms of planting, the artificial intelligence helps Lvwochuan to increase its yield and plant with scientific methods according to the fertility of soil. The water and fertilizer monitoring sensors of Lvwochuan use the big data collected by the Internet of Things to automatically analyze and allocate different nutrient elements needed in growing. The water and nutrient solution are automatically added quantitatively at fixed points. To a great extent, it improves the production efficiency and value of the planting process with total production increasing, production cost reducing and efficiency improving.

Reducing agricultural production costs with the large-scale production: with the digital operation, Lvwochuan Farm has realized the large-scale production. Compared with traditional planting methods, it has greatly improved the multiple cropping rate, saved a lot of land and water resources and labor costs. In addition, after the harvest of strawberries, Lvwochuan Farm will plant other fruit and vegetables, such as cherry tomatoes, cucumbers, melons and watermelons. It makes full use of land in time and space.

Improving the agricultural production efficiency by the operation of digital intelligence. In vegetable factories of Lvwochuan, there are digital and intelligent air shower purification system, intelligent germination acceleration system, intelligent sowing, transplanting and seedling system, intelligent nutrient solution circulation control system and intelligent harvesting system. In soilless strawberry gardens, there are numerical control and liftable cultivation beds, nutrient solution circulation system, precision fertilization system, etc. The operation of the digital intelligence system can not only improve the quality, but also greatly alleviate the dependence on labor. Intelligent agricultural machineries greatly enhance the operation quality, and a germination rate of 95% can be reached. Through the intelligent equipment, Lvwochuan Farm can monitor the accuracy of the equipment and each system in real time, so as to improve the agricultural production efficiency.

4.4 Digital Transformation Empowerment After the Production

Product traceability for the improvement of the safety traceability of agricultural products: there is a safe traceability system for Lvwochuan agricultural products. With advanced agricultural Internet of Things, anti-counterfeiting and other technologies, agricultural products are managed under the system of "identity cards", so as to realize the traceability of the key quality and safety aspects, such as production environment, agricultural inputs, agricultural production process, quality testing, production and processing. By scanning QR codes, consumers can get all traceability information from production to sales of agricultural products. The use of traceability codes can not only make consumers associate Lvwochuan agricultural products with green, safety and health, but also increase the customer loyalty. Therefore, enterprises can build high-end agricultural product brands, and governments can supervise the safety in the whole process.

Making the sales model diversified and shortening the transaction process: Lvwochuan applies the digital thinking to create a diversified sales model to change the sales end. In the aspect of sales channels, Lvwochuan is committed to building a rural e-commerce ecosystem. The online direct marketing channel is composed of the independent e-commerce platform "You, Me and Village" (WeChat official account and mini program) and other third-party cooperation platforms, while the offline direct marketing channel is established by Lvwochuan Youxian. They can enrich the channels of sales end, and greatly shorten the intermediate trading process by direct marketing mode, thereby reducing the cost of agricultural management and circulation of agricultural products. In the sales model, Lvwochuan Farm changed the traditional planting model of "products coming before customers". The customized selling was shifted to a new model of "customers coming before product", and established an integration process of production, packaging, sale and logistics. This can not only meet the quality and personalized demands of consumers, but also greatly improve the circulation efficiency, thus reducing the distance between the production and sales end, and more convenient for the transfer of product values at the production end.

Making intelligent logistics to save costs and provide optimized experiences: Lvwochuan Farm empowers digitalization to logistics. Before the distribution, big data technology and artificial intelligence technology are applied to build and improve the e-commerce information system of agricultural products. Through the integration of agricultural products, platform data, consumer data and other information, the system realizes the digitalization of agricultural product information and platform networking. With the big data, types of consumer order, turnover and browsing time are integrated to predict consumer preference behaviors in each region and at each time point, and then accurately predict the demands of consumers. Based on these information, the recent market price of products and the demands can be predicted to control the product quantity in advance better, reduce the inventory and save the storage costs. According to demand differences of agricultural products in different seasons and regions, the storage quantity of agricultural products can be reasonably allocated to achieve the purpose of high efficiency and saving.

5 Epilogue

Lvwochuan Farm, as a developing innovative enterprise, urgently needs to seek a transformation and upgrading path about the digitalization of the whole industrial chain, in order to make people eat healthily and maintain its own competitive advantages in the industry. Because traditional agricultural production methods are no longer desirable, Lvwochuan Farm is painstakingly exploring the path of digital transformation and upgrading of the whole industrial chain, using advanced technical support and insisting on the digital empowerment to create future farms, thus enabling Lvwochuan to play a benchmarking role on the path of digital agricultural construction.

However, Lvwochuan Farm also faces challenges in the transformation process. Firstly, the lack of capital can greatly restrict the updating of production technology and the expansion of the scale of agricultural enterprises. Lvwochuan also faces the same problem of "difficult financing" for the majority of agricultural enterprises. Secondly, the shortage of land is also a major problem faced by Lvwochuan. Finally, as the priorities of development of the society vary from different times, agricultural policies may change continuously, which can speed up the development of the industry, or slow it down due to other risk factors. Therefore, it seems that Lvwochuan Farm still has a long way to go on the road of digital intelligence.

References

Guo, S. B., Wei, Y. B. & Wei, Y. J. (2019). Reflections and suggestions on the development of intelligent agriculture in China. *China Journal of Commerce, 4.*

He, H. X. (2021). Research on the pain points and paths of intelligent agriculture development in china in the internet age. *Agricultural Economy, 06.*

Li, W. W. (2009). *Research on the realization of the function of agricultural industrial chain and the evaluation of the function of pork industry chain in Hunan Province.* Unpublished doctorial dissertation, Hunan Agricultural University, Changsha.

Sun, Y. (2021). Exploration of the application of internet of things in the facility agriculture in the development of intelligent agriculture. *Modernizing Agriculture, 03.*

Wang, Y. H. & Luo, X. W. (2020). Intelligent agriculture, the future development direction of Chinese agriculture. *Agricultural Machinery, 07.*

Xue, J. T., Sun, Y. T. & Lyu, H. (2021). 5G and the development of intelligent agriculture in China. *Northern Economy and Trade, 05.*

Zhang, L. B. (2016). *Research on the development of agricultural industrial chain: An example of Heyetang Village, Changyangpu Town, Shaoyang County, Hunan Province.* Unpublished Master's Thesis, South China Agricultural University, Guangzhou.

Zhang, G. S., Du, P. F. & Chen, M. M. (2021). Digital empowerment and enterprise technology innovation – empirical evidence from chinese manufacturing sector. *The Economy Today.*

The Value Chain Construction of Cross-Border E-Commerce Platform "AliExpress"

Zhan Li and Hao Zheng

1 The Rise of Cross-Border Retail as a Business Model

Since the first year of e-commerce in China, the Internet has motivated the birth and development of e-commerce with its characteristics of breaking spatial boundaries. Cross-border e-commerce, as a new trade link and business form, develops rapidly in the Internet wave. The *China Cross-border E-commerce Development Report 2020* jointly released by CBEC.100EC.CN shows that the scale of China's cross-border e-commerce market reached CNY12.5 trillion in 2020, with a year-on-year growth of 19.04%; Besides, China's cross-border e-commerce transaction volume accounted for 38.86% of the total value of China's import and export of goods in 2020, showing a year-on-year growth trend compared with 29%, 29.5% and 33.29% from 2017 to 2019. B2C cross-border e-commerce is also known as cross-border e-commerce in a narrow sense, which is different from B2B cross-border e-commerce. It is represented by goods trading between exporters and overseas final consumers through cross-border online e-commerce platforms or enterprise official websites, so it is also known as cross-border retail. The data in the above report show that B2C cross-border e-commerce, that is, cross-border retail trade, accounted for 22.7% in 2020, compared with 14.8%, 16.8% and 19.5% from 2017 to 2019, showing great development potential, as shown in Fig. 1 (Forecast & Analysis of Market Size & Development Trend of China's Cross-border E-commerce Industry in, 2022; Zhang, 2020). Furthermore, according to the development mode analysis and investment risk research report of China's e-commerce industry from 2020 to 2026, the B2C business of China's cross-border e-commerce has shown an increasing trend year by year from 2010 to 2019, as shown in Fig. 2 (Analysis of China's E-commerce Industry Development Model &

Z. Li (✉) · H. Zheng
Alibaba Business School, Hangzhou Normal University, Hangzhou, China

J. Zhang et al. (eds.), *Innovation of Digital Economy*, Management for Professionals,
https://doi.org/10.1007/978-981-99-1741-9_32

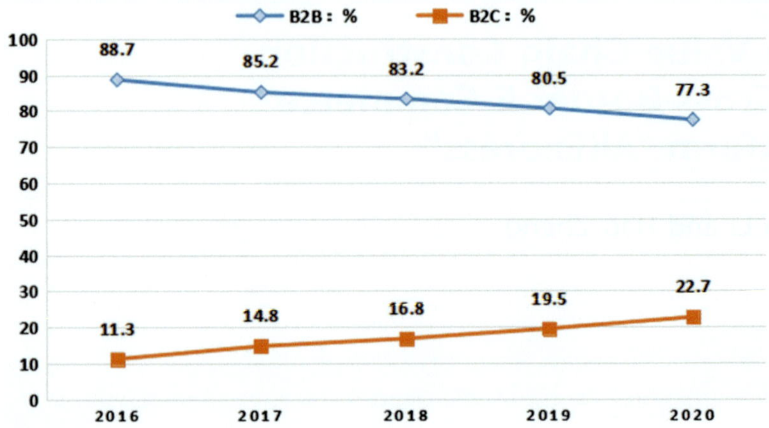

Fig. 1 Transaction scale of china's cross-border e-commerce 2016–2020 (*Source* CBEC.100EC.CN, AskCI)

Investment Risk Research Report 2020; Xue et al., 2016). With the development of cross-border e-commerce and the upgrading of cross-border consumption, cross-border retail for the global market has become an important part of China's foreign trade. Cross-border retail, which meets the needs of global consumers for more abundant, fragmented and personalized goods, has become a strategic pattern for Chinese traditional industries to participate in the global market division of labor and promote the transformation and upgrading of traditional industries; it facilitates the China's innovation advantages in shaping an open economy, and the international competitiveness of "Chinese manufacturing" and "China Service". Cross-border retail plays a pivotal role in China's traditional industries to develop the international market.

2 Development of the Cross-Border E-Commerce Platform "AliExpress"

Considering different operation modes, B2C cross-border e-commerce mainly includes two modes: Open platform and self-operated platform (Fang & Hang, 2015). The former provides export enterprises with shared resources such as network, payment, security and management, and help them carry out business activities efficiently and at low cost. The latter not only opens the data of buyers and sellers, but also publicizes stores, goods, deals, warehousing, logistics, evaluation, promotion and other businesses. This model is represented by B2C cross-border e-commerce platforms such as AliExpress, Amazon, eBay and Wish. They usually have massive platform traffic, sound payment channels and good credit system. B2C cross-border e-commerce platform integrates fragmented

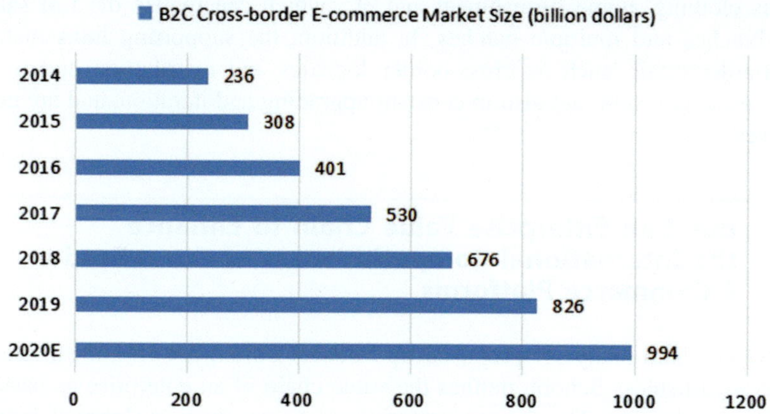

Fig. 2 Scale of B2C cross-border e-commerce market 2014–2020 (*Source* Smart Research Consulting)

industrial channels and personalized mass-decentralized needs, becoming an effective network medium to break the status of traditional industries. It makes money by providing an interactive mechanism for multiple groups on the platform, while satisfying the needs of those groups. On the contrary, the self-operated platform means that the enterprise has its own cross-border e-commerce platform, which carries out unified production, display, promotion and trading of the products, and delivers the products to the consumers through efficient logistics. This mode is represented by LightInTheBox, Globalegrow E-Commerce and Milanoo. In recent years, cross-border e-commerce has shown positive characteristics, such as the continuous increase of business entities, rapid expansion of sales scale, continuous improvement of industrial chain, obvious multi-platform trend, regional agglomeration, and smooth implementation of pilot projects.

To sum up, in the field of cross-border e-commerce, the pattern of third-party cross-border e-commerce platforms represented by AliExpress, eBay, Amazon, Wish and DHgate.com has initially taken shape. Some Taobao merchants and traditional foreign trade enterprises that have transformed to engage in cross-border business have become important business entities of cross-border e-commerce platforms. Aliexpress, a B2C cross-border e-commerce platform founded by Alibaba Group, has grown rapidly by virtue of its low threshold and wide coverage. By providing self-established logistics, online payment, customer service, on-site search, promotion, etc. to the settled merchants, it offers merchants information display and transaction services of enterprises, products and services. In this process, "AliExpress" charges enterprise annual fees according to product categories and promotion fees according to paid listings. The platform gains revenue from sales and services, and cross-border consumers get the products they need; in this way, the same side and even multilateral network effects under the platform mode are realized. Up to now, AliExpress has developed into a mainstream cross-border e-commerce platform in the world. Its products cover dozens of categories such as clothing, home furnishment and 3C, which can realize the fast sales in small batches and multiple batches. In addition, the supporting links matching cross-border retail, such as cross-border logistics and distribution and international online payment, are also in constant upgrading and iteration, and are getting improved.

3 Build an Enterprise Value Chain to Enhance the International Competitiveness of Cross-Border E-Commerce Platforms

The "value chain analysis" proposed by Michael Porter, a well-known strategist at Harvard Business School, defines the value chain of an enterprise as basic and supporting activities. The former centering on value creation (internal logistics, production and operation, external logistics, marketing and sales, service, etc.) serves as the core function of building the value chain, while the latter (infrastructure, human resource management, technology development, procurement) is the main means to undertake the building of value chain (Co & Ltd., 2015; Fu, 2020). Thanks to the cross-border retail business model, the transaction process between buyers and sellers is greatly reduced, accompanied by significantly reduced cost, steadily increased enterprise profit, and maximal value added to both the front-end suppliers and the terminal consumers. Furthermore, Mr. Stan Shih, the founder of Acer Group, a leading technology company in China, came up with the famed Smiling Curve theory in 1992 as a strategy to "re-create Acer". In the industrial chain, the added value is more reflected in the two ends of the curve, namely product development and after-sales service; The manufacturing in the middle of the curve has the lowest added value. The rise of the cross-border retail model provides hard-won development opportunities for AliExpress to innovate its business mode and open up emerging markets. By investing more resources in high value-added R&D, design, service, marketing and other business links, AliExpress has gained effective value addition in key links of the value chain (Porter, 2014), enhancing its international competitiveness. From the perspective of value chain, this paper focuses on the four basic activities of AliExpress, namely production and operation, external logistics, marketing and sales, and service, and on the supporting activity of technology development, and then systematically defines and analyzes the value chain of "AliExpress". The building of value chain of AliExpress is analyzed from the aspects of partnership, cross-border logistics, customer service, marketing and cross-border payment (Fig. 3).

3.1 Partnership

For sake of smooth progress of "Production and Operation", AliExpress has established a close partnership with platform merchants, suppliers, service providers and external enterprises, facilitating the platform production and operation in

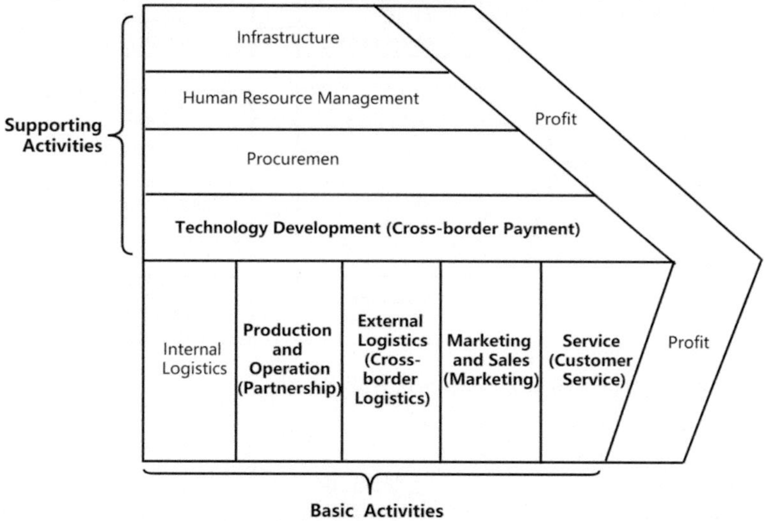

Fig. 3 The value chain construction of cross-border e-commerce platform "AliExpress"

the aspects of business growth, product selection and business expansion. It is specifically demonstrated as follows: First, partnership between platforms and merchants. For the merchants, AliExpress has established "AliExpress University" (now renamed as "Global AliExpress Training Center") since its initiation to help them solve the problems and difficulties in business links. As a learning community to carry out cross-border e-commerce rules training and experience sharing, Global AliExpress Training Center provides merchants with business operation knowledge, and seeks to establish long-term and close partnership with sellers through active interaction in this process. In addition, the functions of AliExpress official website and merchants' backstage, such as "New Merchant Assistance", "Super Private Class" and "Tools Library", also assist sellers to further understand the play rules of cross-border e-commerce and help merchants achieve rapid growth. Second, supplier partnership. For sake of efficiency and convenience of communication between merchants on the platform and upstream suppliers, AliExpress cooperates with 1688 platform and makes use of its powerful supplier resources to support store selection, ensuring the quality of goods and the stability of supply links. Third, ERP service provider partnership. By establishing partnerships with numerous third-party ERP cross-border authorized service providers, such as Dianxiaomi, Superboss and wxwERP, AliExpress further helps merchants connect their services in distribution and store management, so that they engage in cross-border business with higher quality and efficiency. Fourth, strategic partnership. Strategic cooperation focuses on some cooperation programs including cross-border technology and user implementation. For example, AliExpress signed a strategic cooperation agreement with Hisense in May 2020 to jointly

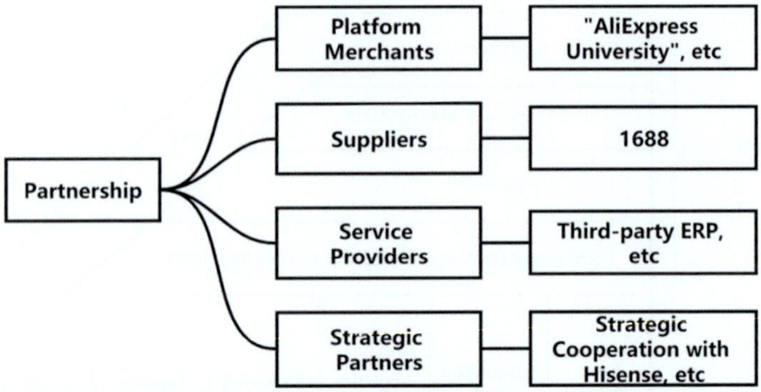

Fig. 4 Building of production and operation of AliExpress

Fig. 5 ERP service providers of AliExpress (*Source* AliExpress)

explore the overseas online retail market. By taking advantage of Hisense's business advantages in 14 industrial parks, 18 R&D centers and covering more than 160 countries, AliExpress further expanded its business territory. The cooperation between Hisense and AliExpress has already built in Russia, France and Spain (Figs. 4 and 5).

3.2 Cross-Border Logistics

Against the backdrop of cross-border retail mode, the platform must face the problems in transportation timeliness and safety and cost control. It is very important to provide the proper logistics route schemes according to the user demand and product characteristics. By optimizing several key links in cross-border logistics,

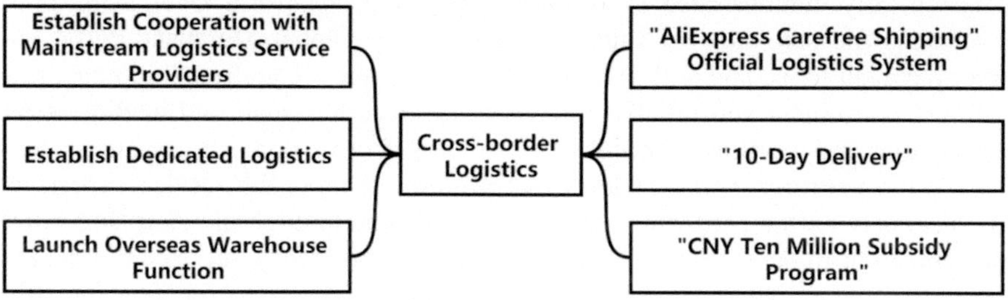

Fig. 6 Building of external logistics of AliExpress

AliExpress improves its "External Logistics" to ensure efficient delivery of products. AliExpress now has established cooperative relations with all mainstream logistics service providers in the world, including EMS International, FedEx, TNT, DHL, UPS, etc., and also supports dedicated logistics in different countries and regions, like special Line-YW (Ye, 2018). In February 2015, AliExpress platform officially launched the function of oversea location. At present, the platform can set the delivery authority of oversea location service in 22 countries. The introduction of oversea location significantly improves the efficiency of cross-border logistics transportation and makes the logistics more secure and timely. In addition, AliExpress has creatively launched the official logistics system of "AliExpress Carefree Shipping" in conjunction with Cainiao to provide merchants with one-stop logistics solutions including collection, distribution, logistics tracking and after-sales compensation (AliExpress University, 2016), and offer merchants multiple choices based on different regions, timeliness and product attributes. By virtue of the full link logistics service system above and new business segments such as the "10-day Delivery" and "CNY Ten Million Subsidy Program", AliExpress has greatly improved the overall quality and service level of logistics while selecting more efficient and guaranteed logistics routes for goods, and accelerated the layout of AliExpress overseas logistics network (Fig. 6).

3.3 Customer Service

Customer service, as a key element for a cross-border e-commerce platform to establish good customer relations, improve customer satisfaction, build a good platform image and optimize business results, is an important link to attract user retention and re-purchase (Alexander & Yves, 2010). In order to improve the quality of "Service", AliExpress takes consumers as the core and starts from the three levels of platform, merchants and consumers to ensure the smooth trading link of the platform and facilitate the purchase of goods by consumers; encourage merchants to improve the overall quality of stores and optimize consumers' shopping experience; introduce key indicators for merchant evaluation, enhance communication with consumers, and build a multi-directional consumer service system. It is specifically demonstrated as follows: First, at the platform level, AliExpress guarantees the safe flow of funds through Alipay Global Merchant Portal and other payment tools, and with the support of "AliExpress Carefree Shipping", providing a convenient and reliable full set of services for small and medium-sized transactions and meeting the needs of consumers in cross-border transactions. Second, at the platform merchant level, AliExpress monitors the service experience of consumers on the platform merchants in real time through the store star rating mechanism from the three aspects of "description consistency, service attitude, and logistics service", which in turn encourages the merchants to improve the store rating by providing products consistent with images and texts, customer service services that respond in a timely manner, and fast and efficient logistics services, and constructs a good path for improving service quality. Third, regarding overseas consumers, to develop the relationship with overseas consumers, AliExpress has strengthened two-way communication with consumers, and introduced a number of key indicators for merchant evaluation (Li et al., 2019), such as praise rate, dispute rate, rate of not selling after a deal, adjudication initiation rate, and seller liability adjudication rate. These indicators are based on overseas consumers, conveying the most authentic consumer feedback to the merchants. AliExpress has also established an online review and additional review system for consumers. Consumers communicate with each other through scoring, rating and additional review to provide reference for potential consumer groups with similar needs. AliExpress has also won a good user reputation among users through the above links of high-quality customer service (Fig. 7).

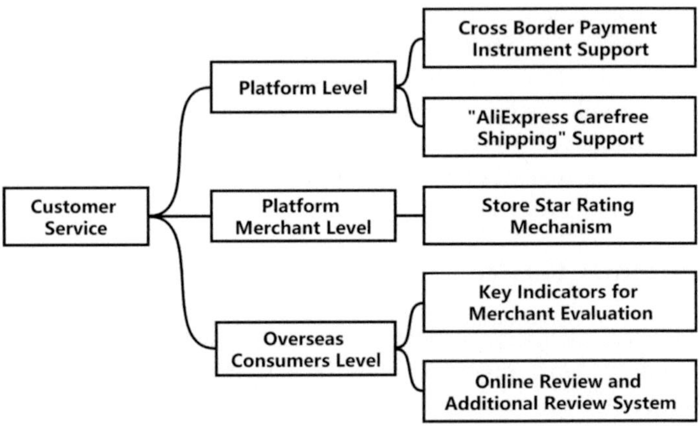

Fig. 7 Building of service of AliExpress

3.4 Marketing

In the context of economic globalization, cross-border e-commerce, as an extension of e-commerce, is different from the traditional online consumer market, and its "Target Market" is also unique. For example, AliExpress aims at the market of Russia, and its revenue of Russian market also occupies the first place all the year round. In addition, the public data of the State Post Office of the People's Republic of China in 2022 show that, the total turnover of AliExpress in Russia amounts to SUR306 billion in 2021, with a year-on-year growth of 46%, which is still in a rapid growth period; Followed by mature and emerging markets represented by the United States, Spain, France and Brazil. Due to the popularity of online shopping concepts and habits, and the strong per capita purchasing power of these countries, the cross-border retail market enjoys considerable sales scale and profit margins. For sake of sales results in important target markets, AliExpress assisted the development of cross-border business in target markets through a series of strategies such as technical support and improved infrastructure construction. Take the Russian market as an example. In addition to establishing many oversea locations and dedicated logistics in cooperation with this country, AliExpress also carries out the new project AEPLUS to further satisfy the two major demands of Russian buyers for faster logistics and easy sales return (Retail, 2021). In addition, AliExpress also cooperates with Russia Post to add tens of thousands of delivery lockers and pickup locations to further improve the logistics efficiency and expand its market coverage and influence in Russia. In the meanwhile, AliExpress started to allow merchants from Russia, Türkiye, Italy and Spain to settle in 2019, gradually opening the pace of overseas investment (Fig. 8).

Centering on the marketing of cross-border e-commerce platform, it mainly covers internal marketing and external marketing. To optimize the "Sales" flow of

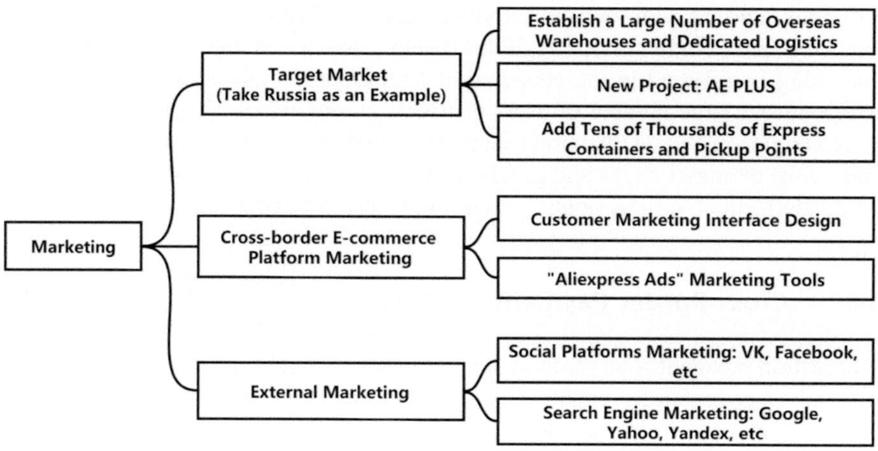

Fig. 8 Building of marketing and sales of AliExpress

the platform, AliExpress makes efforts from both the internal and external aspects of the platform, assists the platform merchants to improve product transformation through internal marketing tools, and improves the external traffic of the platform and expands sales channels with the help of external social platforms and search engine tools. First, regarding the marketing via e-commerce platforms, AliExpress has set up a special customer marketing interface for the merchants' backstage. On this interface, merchants can select a customer group from multiple aspects, such as add-to-cart, add-to-favorites and followers, communicate with specific groups by virtue of buyer conversation, email marketing, targeted coupon issuance, etc., to guide overseas consumers to browse and further purchase products, and provide support for increasing store exposure and sales volume. Besides, AliExpress also improves the search order and exposure of products by providing merchants with AliExpress Ads that charges per click, so as to help merchants better promote their products. Second, the external marketing is reflected in social platforms and search engines. For the former, the marketing cooperation between AliExpress and VKontakte (VK for short), the largest social platform in Russia, is the most representative one. As of 2019, VK has a total of more than 250 million users, basically covering the entire Eastern European Internet users, and is the main traffic entry of cross-border e-commerce into Russia. It creates a separate mini program for AliExpress in the application so that users can browse and place orders on AliExpress directly. What's more, the two parties also jointly build a sharing column to guide the users of AliExpress and VK to share the orders they have placed on AliExpress or the good goods they have found in the column. These measures have brought numerous new users to AliExpress, promoted the interaction between AliExpress and young Russian users, and spurred the cooperation progress in social e-commerce of AliExpress. Another example is AliExpress's sales promotions on the day of Cyber Monday in the United States, during which AliExpress attracted many new users and traffic, and saw obvious publicity results, which greatly improved the sales of goods by advertising at international social platforms and forums such as Facebook, and carrying out the activities such as "Red-envelope Wars on Christmas Day" and "Red-envelope Fight on Beach" launched in the site. Search engine marketing is reflected in the cooperation with Google, Yahoo and Yandex, all of which have a large number of users overseas, among which Yandex is the largest search engine in Russia by market share. By working with these companies, AliExpress aims to attract clicks and purchases from overseas consumers by placing ads on its platform at various points in the user's search engine use.

3.5 Cross-Border Payment

Transaction payment is an inseparable part of cross-border retail. For sake of basic demand of cross-border payment, AliExpress has taken the business strategy of coexisting payment methods, including Bank Transfer, Western Union and local Qiwi, Web Money, DOKU, MercadoPago, Sofort, etc. Thus, the unimpeded transaction payment is fully guaranteed (Deng, 2019). However, diversified payment methods are not a competitive part of their value chain, compared with other cross-border e-commerce platforms. In order to further enhance the competition and difference in the transaction payment technology, AliExpress has developed and applied the mature Alipay system into the cross-border transaction payment, and named it Escrow. Escrow, an independent international payment system of AliExpress, is an indispensable payment tool for online trading. By completing payment on Alipay system with a large customer base, ESCROW not only guarantees the mutual trust of buyers and sellers, but also reduces the incidence of disputes and the withdrawal rate of international small trade. Unlike PayPal, which is widely used by many cross-border e-commerce platforms at home and abroad, Escrow is the pioneer of AliExpress in payment business, and also an important measure to unify collection methods and integrate payment channels. In the meanwhile, in order to encourage consumers to pay with Escrow, akin to Alipay Global Merchant Portal, on the platform, AliExpress charges merchants a lower service charge to encourage them to advocate consumers to use it. Furthermore, to further improve the payment of the cross-border e-commerce platform, Ant Financial acquired WorldFirst, a cross-border payment company of British on February 14, 2019 (Ant Financial acquired WorldFirst, 2019). WorldFirst operated international remittance, foreign exchange option trading, collection and settlement at international e-commerce platforms, etc. Its payment business covered 71 online sales platforms worldwide, with an annual trading volume of more than 10 billion pounds. This acquisition will further pave the way for AliExpress's payment globalization plan.

To sum up, based on the business model of cross-border retail, AliExpress focuses on the building of basic activities of the value chain, supplemented by technical optimization at the level of supporting activities. Building a diversified partnership helps the platform advance its "Production and Operation"; multi-route solutions for cross-border logistics realize the efficiency and security of "External Logistics"; omni-channel marketing tools connect "Marketing and Sales"; "Service" outcomes are further improved based on multi-dimensional customer service construction; "Technology Development" is strengthened through the development and introduction of cross-border payment technologies. In this way, AliExpress strategically builds the enterprise value chain in a systematical and continuous manner, so as to effectively build and enhance its core competitiveness.

Case Appendix

Appendix 1 Alibaba-AliExpress Cross-border Supply Chain

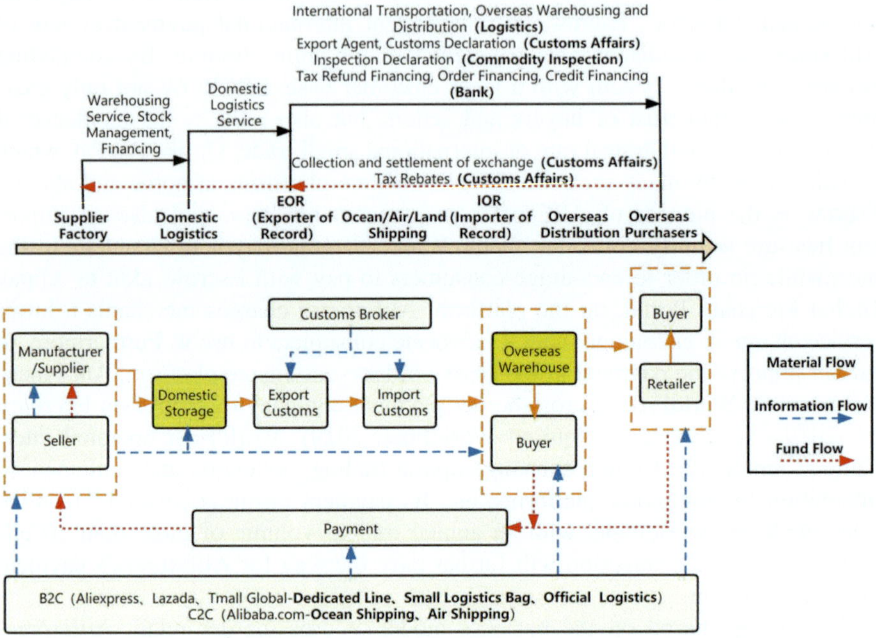

(*Source* sorted by the authors of the case)

Appendix 2 Four Kinds of Logistics Services Provided by Cross-border E-commerce Platform "AliExpress" Carefree Logistics

Logistics name	Logistics type	Delivery scope	Delivery limitation
AliExpress saver shipping	Saver shipping	Reachable areas of post offices in Russia, Spain, Ukraine, Belarus and Chile	Any electrified goods and cosmetics are not allowed in Belarus, Ukraine and Chile; articles containing batteries (batteries need to be built in), instead of pure batteries, are accepted in Russia

Logistics name	Logistics type	Delivery scope	Delivery limitation
AliExpress Standard Shipping	Standard shipping	254 countries and regions around the world	Supporting batteries and pure batteries are not accepted; Any electrified goods and cosmetics are not allowed south Africa; any electrified goods are not accepted in the Dominican Republic
AliExpress PickUp	Standard shipping	Nearly 800 delivery lockers in 66 States and 183 cities in Russia	Ordinary goods, instead of electrified, pure batteries and cosmetics, are accepted
AliExpress Premium Shipping	Rapid	176 countries and regions around the world	Ordinary goods, instead of electrified, pure batteries and cosmetics, are accepted

(*Source* AliExpress)

Appendix 3 Business Layout of AliExpress in Target Market Countries (Taking Women's Wear Industry as an Example)

High GMV high growth rate

Country&Region	Payment amount ratio	Rising index	Delivery time
Russian Federation	22.46%	1,237	21
France	6.27%	1,182	12
United Kingdom	4.25%	1,175	13
Republic of Korea	3.50%	1,336	7
Spain	3.20%	1,255	12
Germany	2.09%	1,215	14
Switzerland	1.39%	1,173	14
Italy	1.23%	1,210	16
Kuwait	1.12%	1,238	25
Poland	1.11%	1,204	14

High GMV low growth rate

Country&Region	Payment amount ratio	Rising index	Delivery time
Peru	0.39%	1,071	23
Belgium	0.70%	1,115	13
Chile	1.14%	995	16
Netherlands	1.53%	1,144	14
Australia	1.82%	972	14
Saudi Arabia	1.67%	1,145	13
Mexico	2.10%	1,140	15
Japan	2.35%	1,166	9
Canada	2.63%	1,077	16
Brazil	3.90%	1,045	17

Low GMV high growth rate

Country&Region	Payment amount ratio	Rising index	Delivery time
Belarus	0.38%	1,312	23
Ireland	0.34%	1,307	25
Lithuania	0.33%	1,268	23
Latvia	0.31%	1,341	20
Slovakia (Slovak Republic)	0.29%	1,281	14
Kazakhstan	0.29%	1,215	33
Estonia	0.21%	1,293	21
Turkey	0.23%	1,174	12
Romania	0.21%	1,221	20
Bulgaria	0.19%	1,286	20

Low GMV low growth rate

Country&Region	Payment amount ratio	Rising index	Delivery time
Hong Kong	0.10%	1,108	13
Finland	0.11%	1,108	21
Denmark	0.14%	1,104	22
Croatia	0.15%	1,148	16
Indonesia	0.18%	1,055	20
Thailand	0.21%	1,047	11
Colombia	0.22%	993	21
Singapore	0.27%	1,095	12
Sweden	0.27%	1,098	21
Austria	0.27%	1,162	15

(*Source* AliExpress – Business Advisor. Statistical period: January 15, 2022 - April 14, 2022)

Appendix 4 Promotions of AliExpress

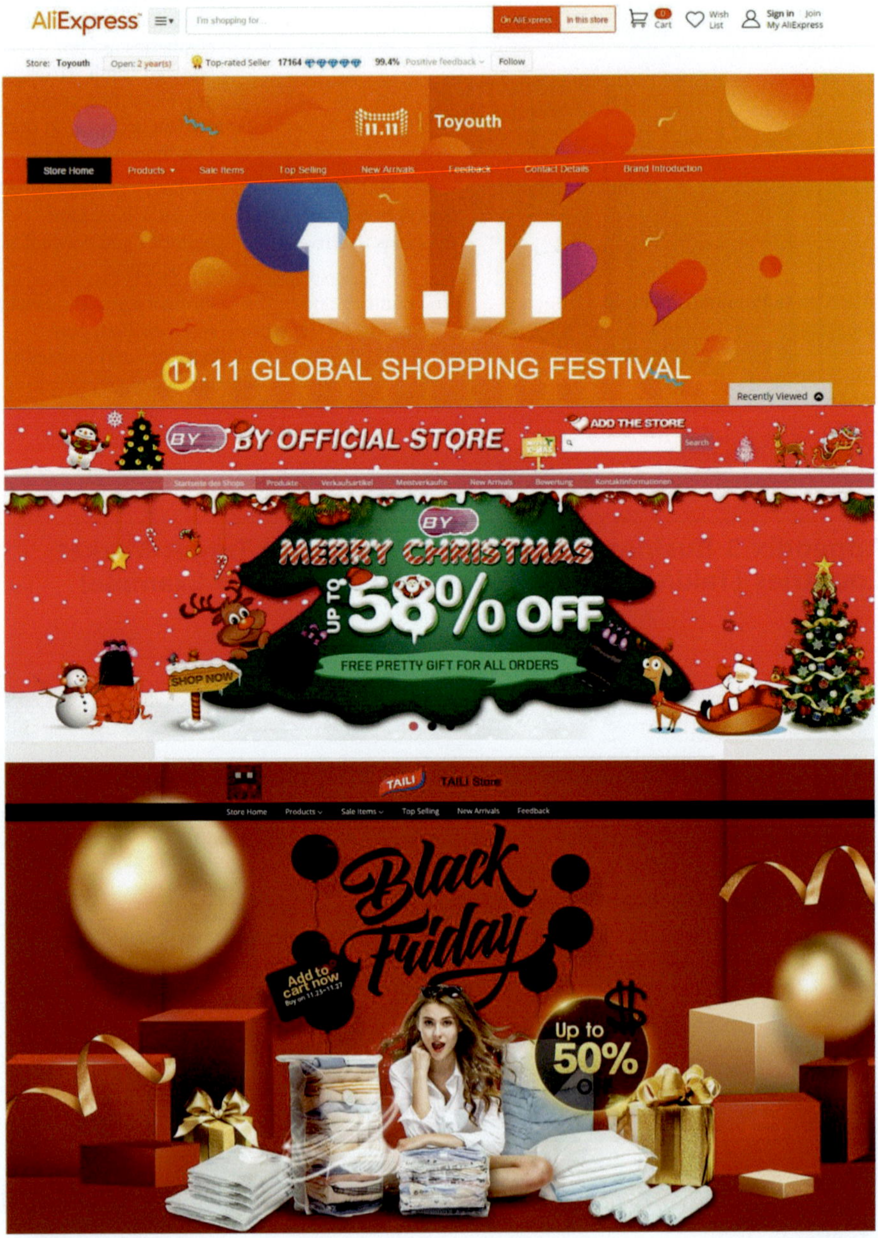

(*Source* AliExpress)

References

Alexander, O., & Yves, P. (2010). *Business Model Generation: A Handbook for Visionaries, Game Changers, and Challengers*. John Wiley & Sons.

AliExpress University. (2016). *Cross-border e-commerce logistics: Alibaba AliExpress*. Publishing House of Electronics Industry.

Analysis of China's E-commerce Industry Development Model and Investment Risk Research Report from 2020 to 2026. (2020). Retrieved from http://www.chyxx.com/industry/202002/831924.html.

Ant Financial acquired WorldFirst. (2019). Retrieved from http://www.cngold.com.cn/dealer/jysxw/20190220f12103n5641357915.html.

Beijing Xinhuaxin Business Risk Management Co., Ltd. (2015). Beijing: China Renmin University Press.

Deng, Y. (2019). Comparative Study on Business Models of B2C Cross-border E-commerce Platform between Amazon and Alibaba. Unpubished doctorial dissertation, Lanzhou University of Finance and Economics, Lanzhou.

Fang, C., & Hang, Y. Y. (2015). Discussion on the Operation Mode of China's Cross-border E-commerce Platform. *Times Finance, 32*, 13–14.

Forecast and Analysis of Market Size and Development Trend of China's Cross-border E-commerce Industry in 2022. (January 16, 2022). Retrieved from https://www.askci.com/news/chanye/20220106/1116201715930_3.shtml.

Fu, X. (2020). *Enterprise Value Chain Management*. Zhejiang Gongshang University Press.

Li, J., Cui, Y. W., & Wang, T. (2019). *Operation and Management of Cross-border E-commerce AliExpress*. Posts & Telecom Press.

Porter, M. E. (2014). *Competitive Strategy*. CITIC Press.

Online Retail. (2021). Aliexpress Russia's GMV comes to 209.6 bln rubles in 2020. Interfax: Russia & CIS IT & Telecom Weekly.

Xue, Y., Ouyang, C., Wang, H. J. & Jiang, Z. W. (2016). China's Cross-border E-commerce Development Report 2016. AliResearch & Alibaba Cross-border E-commerce Research Center.

Ye, Z. H. (2018). Analysis of the Impact of B2C Cross-border E-commerce Platform on China's Foreign Trade-Taking Alibaba AliExpress as an Example. *Knowledge Economy, 02*, 77–78.

Zhang, Z. P. (May 2020) China Cross-Border E-Commerce Development Report.

Quality-Oriented and E-commerce-Empowered: Entrepreneurial Practice of Wangxianji Hairy Crab

Chunfeng Jiao and Jiawei Li

1 Introduction

It's a good time to enjoy crabs in autumns. In golden autumn, Wangxianji Ecological Farm, located in Lingtang Hui Township, Gaoyou City, Yangzhou, saw crabs spitting foam out of the water as cages were pulled up one by one. After being bundled, boxed, placed in ice packs and packed, they will be sent to thousands of families. Gaoyou Lake, as the sixth largest fresh water lake in China, is the source of water diversion from south to north and the primary water source protection area. Its water quality has reached the second class surface water standards, surrounding the lake pollution-free industry and abundant water resources. Wangxianji Farm, which is only more than 2,000 m away from Gaoyou Lake, is a modern agricultural enterprise mainly engaged in the breeding of Chinese mitten crabs, the deep processing and sales of primary products, and the promotion and application of technologies. It is the largest aquaculture base in Gaoyou City at present, jointly established by 53 farmers. Wangxianji has a planned area of 5,000 mu, and has devised 3,000 mu for production, among which the farm has a breeding area of 2,000 mu for adult crabs and 500 mu for coin-sized crab seeds. It is the largest breeding base for hairy crabs along the Gaoyou Lake. In addition, 2,000 mu of area is provided for freshwater aquaculture and grain cultivation areas, including co-occurrence areas for rice, fishes and ducks, vegetable growing areas and so on. The company has built its complete industrial chain from breeding of crab seeds and adult crabs to deep processing of adult crabs, product services and technical support. By virtue of professional breeding and brand sales, Wangxianji has exploited its markets in crab breeding and sales. In the meanwhile, Wangxianji

C. Jiao (✉) · J. Li
Yangzhou University, Yangzhou, China

J. Zhang et al. (eds.), *Innovation of Digital Economy*, Management for Professionals,
https://doi.org/10.1007/978-981-99-1741-9_33

hired the fishermen and the surrounding labor force, and passed on the farming experience to them, so that more people could find jobs and become rich.

Undoubtedly, the founder Wang Jun and Wangxianji are successful paragons. At the same time, we are encouraged to think about how to combine traditional and modern elements to play a new way of eating against the backdrop of Internet plus, and how to integrate online and offline more reasonably.

2 Wangxianji was Built Along the Beautiful Gaoyou Lake

2.1 Speed and Passion in the Community of Food

Wangxianji is located at the Gaoyou Lake. Originated from the former Wangji Fish Store, Wangxianji takes the old name of "Wangji", plus the word "xian (fresh)", to follow the ancestral motto, with truth, sincerity, faith, and reality as the foundation of the business, inherit and carry forward the essence of the century-old shop culture.

"Xian" of its name means fresh. Wang Jun's grandparents grew up along Gaoyou Lake for four generations. In the past, they used to fish with nets. To keep the fish fresh, they have to carry a load to take the fish to Yangzhou fair at night, arrive before 6 a.m. and sell them. They had to run 60 km almost every day and then build up their strong bodies. Mr. Wang keeps a calligraphy work in his home, unframed and dark with a hint of age, that over the past seven or eight years, Mr. Wang said, he has often taken out and reflected on, encouraging himself with these words. This calligraphy work was written by Mr. Li Qiushui, a painting and calligraphy artist in China, known as one of the "new Eight Eccentric Artists in Yangzhou" in his octogenarian. He specially gave the work showing the words "Business is Craft" to junior Wang Jun, meaning that Mr. Wang is doing fresh business, but also a craft. Mr. Li encouraged him to be serious and do business with a down-to-earth approach.

Business is Craft? It seems to be different from the traditional idea towards the traditional craft. In a traditional sense, a craftsman is a person who makes a living with his hands, which means stubborn, slow, small amount and hard work. Wang Jun, however, likens himself to a craftsman, which also makes sense to some extent. He said, "my ancestors started to rely on "fresh goods business" as early as the late Qing Dynasty and the early Republic of China." So far, it has been passed to me for the fourth generation. "Fresh Goods Business" has long become a skill for me to settle down. The so-called "Fresh Goods Business" is an old saying that, fishermen catched fish with nets, and sold fresh fish to vendors at the docks; to keep the goods fresh, vendors needed to rush to the market to sell. No matter in windy or rainy days, or in clear days, these vendors had to collect or sell fish days and night in cold or summer-heat days, so as to support the family. It was hard work. Inheriting their ancestors' pursuit of fresh ingredients, Wangxianji has always placed the taste of customers in an extremely important position. Now it is using modern scientific means to provide customers with fresh goods.

2.2 Difficulty in Starting a Business

It has been more than 10 years since Wangxianji started raising crabs in 2010. Now here is crowded. However, what else could one expect this is the aquaculturist who lost nearly 10 million yuan in successive years. Ten years ago, Wang Jun and his wife decided to raise crabs. They chose a low-lying land of 3,000 mu in Lingtang Hui Township and invested CNY10 million. However, they had just changed from "selling" to "raising" crabs. They lacked preparation for such problems as how to select the crab seeds, how to feed the crabs, and how to deal with the sick crabs. Moreover, they did not often go to the site at the beginning, and their lack of experience combined with the lack of control management made their farm soon exposed problems. In the first year, each crab raised by others was three to four taels, while Wangxianji's crab was only two taels, resulting in a loss of CNY six million. In next year, their crabs became sick, making them a loss of nearly CNY three million. Two consecutive years of losses gave them profound lessons that basic skills are necessary to keep a good crab.

2.3 Learn Lessons and Rally

Facing the bitter lesson, Wang Jun moved his family to the beach and built a shack that served as both a dormitory and an office. From then on, they spent most of the year at the Wangxianji Aquatic Farm in Lingtang. Only during the sales season did the wife Zhang Yuluan return to Yangzhou. Every time Mr. Wang returned to Yangzhou, he was always in a hurry. He made up his mind to study hard and raise good crabs. Good crab seeds are critical to good adult crabs. Due to ragged quality of crab seeds from others, the couple decided to culture their own seeds. Wang Jun specially built a crab nursery in Qidong, using fresh water with a salt content of 0.15% to simulate the natural environment. At the same time, he sought advice from experts on purification and rejuvenation technology, and finally bred the first batch of 10 million high-quality crab seedlings, which met his own needs.

To make crabs grow fat and fast, live food is required. Therefore, Wang Jun hired men to catch snails every day and feed crabs on minced snails. Mr. Wang believes baits are the key to tasty crabs. Hairy crabs are omnivorous creatures that feed on fish and shrimp, corn, squash, snails and aquatic plants. In order to raise high-quality hairy crabs, Mr. Wang is very willing to pay for the baits, insisting on buying a large number of sea fish from Shandong Zhonghai Fishery as fodders, so that the hairy crabs that feed on sea fish all year round are not only big, healthy and plump, but also tasty. Zhang Yuluan said that although the cost of breeding has increased, good hairy crabs will attract visionary buyers. In the fourth year, they finally got what they wanted. In the autumn and winter of that year, the average weight of crabs coming out of the pond was more than four taels and the largest reached eight taels. Many customers came in droves. Despite the success of their unremitting efforts, Mr. Wang did not relax. Since then, he has personally supervised the process from selecting and transporting the crab seeds to his seaside breeding center, to sending coin-sized crab seeds to the crab pond, until the crabs grow into hairy crabs and are placed in the storage room.

3 Adhere to High Quality and Good Reputation

3.1 Good Crabs are Inseparable from Good Water and Seedlings

What Wangxianji culture is the Chinese mitten crab, commonly known as hairy crab. With its unique shape, delicious flesh and rich nutrition, this kind of crab is an aquatic treasure and has always been favored by the Chinese people. For thousands of years, the Chinese mitten crab has been praised in the articles. The ancients have a saying that "if you don't climb on the Mount Lu, you won't live up to your eyes, and if you don't eat crab, you won't live up to your stomach". During the Double Ninth Festival when Chinese mitten crabs are full of fresh roe, it is a good time to admire the beauty of chrysanthemum and eat crabs. Chinese mitten crabs are not only a delicacy but also a tonic. According to analysis and determination, 100 g of crab meat contains up to 5,900 IUs of vitamin A, heat up to 582 kJ. Crab can be referred to as the King of Aquatic Products since its fat, carbohydrate, and riboflavin contents are much higher than many other special aquatic products. Hairy crab also has medicinal value. Its pharmacological function has been described in details in historical drug monographs such as *Bencao Fengyuan* (a book related to Materia Medica) and *Supplement to Medica.* According to traditional Chinese medicine, crab meat can clear heat, remove stasis, cure wound, regulate pulse, nourish Yin, etc. Crab carapace can also clear heat, detoxify, and eliminate stasis and qi stagnation. Modern medicine believes that the rich vitamin A in the Chinese mitten crab is an indispensable nutrient in the human body. It can promote growth, delay aging, maintain the health of epithelial tissues, enhance the human body's resistance to infectious diseases, and prevent the occurrence of night blindness.

Good adult crabs must be from good crab seedlings. Wangxianji's crab seedlings are produced and raised by itself. At the beginning of the business, Mr. Wang spent a lot of effort to breed high-quality crab seedlings. To ensure the purity, the parents were all selected for his farm use. Every year, every mu of pond will be disinfected by 150 kg of lime in Wangxianji farm before putting the crab seedlings into the pond. Both lime and labor costs are expensive, but it keeps the pond away from pollution and drugs, and can produce better crabs. In the breeding of adult crabs, Wangxianji makes full use of safe and green biotechnological means to ensure the safe and healthy growth of crabs and the whole process is controllable. Since 2016, Wangxianji Hairy Crab have been certified as "Green Food" every year.

The favorable growing environment of crabs is directly related to the size of the crabs. Every external factor like sufficient growing space, baits full of nutrition, dense water plants avoiding natural enemies, or good water quality in the living area, is indispensable for the growth and development of the crabs. According to the average level of the population, the standard body size of the Chinese mitten crab needs to be more than 200 g for males and 150 g for females. 800 crab seedlings are stocked in one mu of pond, which is Wangxianji's data based on years of breeding experience. Mr. Wang said the higher the density of breeding, the higher the incidence of crabs. However, low density will affect economic benefits, so 800 is just an ideal data.

The high standard of shrimps and crabs is not the only goal. Wangxianji has also made great efforts in the breeding environment. Everyone who has been to the farm knows that there is not only a crab pond here, but also gorgeous flowers, a technology corridor, fishing areas, small gardens, lotus ponds and villas. Instead of overgrown weeds and polluted water, Wangxianji tries to limit the use of pesticides and treat the sewage from their farms, making the farm as environmentally friendly as possible.

In order to win higher credibility from the public, Wangxianji always takes high standards in the breeding to avoid environmental pollution. It occupies some breeding area to provide a space for the equipment for water recycle, water treatment and water quality monitoring, specially grows water plants and snails, and builds a treatment area for aquaculture water. What's more, it requires higher quality of treated aquaculture water than that of exogenous water. As a result, Wang's aquaculture water is not usually discharged but recycled. There were a lot of growing weeds near the pond in the past. Mr. Wang insisted that the workers cut the grass by hand instead of using herbicides. It took time and effort, but he still sticks to environmentally friendly principles. Now Wangxianji is no longer in the era of artificial weeding. Now it uses film to prevent the growth of weeds, which is both environmentally friendly, beautiful and saves time and effort. Although a lot of money may be invested in the early laying, a set of equipment can be used for ten years, which is affordable.

Wangxianji hairy crabs go through a triple-selection process: Quality, appearance and net weight. Each crab is automatically weighed and manually sorted to ensure that the net weight of the naked crab (excluding straw rope) is the criterion. The crabs in every order are caught and delivered on the same day to ensure them fresh as possible.

3.2 Unique Crabs as Gifts in Golden Autumns

In addition to high-quality crabs, a proper form of goods is also required for a good gift. In order to adapt to the fast and convenient trend of modern society, Wangxianji crab gifts are mostly sent in the form of crab gift cards. Customers may specify the delivery time and method according to their own requirements during the crab season every year. Once the customer activates the crab gift card, he/she will have the priority for delivery. The farm will deliver the goods before all other supply requirements according to the demand of the customer, with the purpose of giving priority to time and service. The crab card issued by Wangxianji will never expire. If you miss the crab season of the current year, you can use it in next crab season. The crab gift card is usually designed in "pairs", that is, a set of cards contains both cards to buy male and female crabs. The pick-up time of the female crab card by default is not the same with that of the male carb card, but depending on the best time of "females in September and males in October". Such design not only gives consideration to the best taste of the crab, but also expresses the blessing of "good things come in pairs". With the gift cards, crabs can be bought separately or combined. It is recommended to use the female crab card, also known as "Zhegui card", from September, because the female crabs are most mature when osmanthus flowers are in full bloom. It is the most attractive time when the female crabs are full of fresh roe. And because autumn semester starts in Septembers, "Zhegui" also wishes the students to get merit in entrance exams. The male crab card is also known as the "card of good fortune", and the recommended delivery time is generally in October. The male crabs are fat and tasty before and after the Double Ninth Festival when golden chrysanthemum is in full bloom. At that time, male crabs are full of delicious roe. The crab gift on the occasion of the Double Ninth Festival takes the name of "Ruyi (good fortune)" to express the blessing, happiness and well-being to the families.

In addition, as one member of the fresh food industry, Wangxianji must solve the problem of "preservation". In the past, "freshness depending on speed" in the past; now with the broader scope of business, Wangxianji has an increasing number of orders, and the speed is no longer the sole key factor for keeping fresh. With more than 30 years of aquatic experience, Wangxianji has become an expert in the field of aquatic transportation and preservation. Regarding Wangxianji gifts, each qualified crab is individually packaged in a customized box, to avoid the damage caused to the crab due to collision, extrusion, temperature rise and other reasons during transportation. The customized ice pack keeps the container in a low temperature for a long time, so that the crab lies dormant, waiting to be awakened when the box is unpacked. The thickened foam inner box not only ensures that the cold air is fully sealed, but also provides double protection of anti-collision and anti-pressure for the crabs. In addition, the label on the outer box clearly indicates the number, weight, producer, producing time, storage method and time of the crabs in the box, and other important traceable information. It can be clear at a time without opening the box, so as to avoid unnecessary damage caused by the interruption of the dormancy of the crabs caused by opening the box for inspection and other reasons. Wangxianji crab gifts are delivered in an order system. According to the orders and the recent logistics efficiency, they are distributed in the principle of customer convenience. The crabs caught from the lake farm, will be delivered as far as possible to the shortest transit time to the customers.

3.3 Adhere to the Integrity and Quality, and Establish the Concept of Quality

With the development of social economy, the change of living habits, and the gradual younger consumer group, consumers begins to focus on the added value of products, such as appearance, cultural attributes and portability. Wang Jun was originally as an aquaculture broker, to help customers choose crabs. Customers believed that he was an expert who can pick up fat and delicious crabs. On his busiest days, he had to hire four people to select crabs for his customers. Later, Mr. Wang reflected that modern consumers have no ability to distinguish the quality of products and need the help of professionals. Moreover, they attach more importance to the added value of products, and service is undoubtedly a good way to increase the added value. So Wang opened a specialty store, selling high-quality crabs and offering certain professional services, such as how to cook or keep them. Facts have proved that Wang has made the right decision. Now his store is well-recognized and popular.

High-quality crabs are the basic business of Wangxianji. In order to get the favor of consumers, Wangxianji also seeks to enhance the value of the brand in different aspects. The couple has been trying to make Gaoyouhu hairy crabs more close to the public. After the First Frost Solar Term in 2017, the wife Zhang Yuluan had the fat pigs raised on the farm killed and used the good suet to boil the lard. She also split the meat of the hairy crabs and cooked the crab butter paste according to the ancient recipe in the *Menu of Sui Garden*. Once the food was introduced, it was warmly received. While exploring the cultural connotation, the couple also guided the fashion of hairy crabs. They tried to introduce successful designs that borrowed the simple and elegant design styles of fresh ingredients from other goods in season and incorporated them into the packaging of hairy crabs, forming Wangxianji's unique style.

Thanks to the efforts of Wangxianji's team, many repeat customers order hairy crabs in advance before the crabs go on sale, and regular customers also introduce new customers every year. Some customers who accept the quality of the crabs will buy them back in the manner of group buying as employees' welfare. An interactive business will always be rewarded with consumer feedback, and that feedback is what keeps people like Wang going. Wang said that one of his customers, a painter, would buy Wangxianji crabs every year. After eating, he would give them his vivid crab painting in return.

4 By Virtue of the Internet Celebrity Economy and Empowered by E-commerce

If the husband Wang specializes in raising crabs, the wife Zhang Yuluan is adept at selling them. Wangxianji's sales team is managed by Zhang Yuluan, the "Sister Biandan". Offline stores are mainly distributed in Yangzhou, with sales outlets all over the country. Every year, the couple will participate in some promotion events in Hong Kong, Macao and overseas areas, in order to introduce the Gaoyou crabs to the world, and allow the foreign countries to learn about Gaoyou crab industry and Wangxianji products. In the past, crabs were exported as fresh goods, and in the future, they may be highly processed before export. River crabs are usually sold around the Mid-Autumn Festival, and it will be heart-warming if the overseas Chinese can taste them during this reunion festival. A deal requires flexible thinking that always complies with consumer demand. In 2020, to provide a delicacy for "foodies", Wangxianji extended the crab season by one more season, introducing "June hairy crab" during the Great Heat solar term. Although the crabs in June are not well-developed until they moult their shells again, the largest "June hairy crabs" can reach 3.5 taels due to the good quality of Wangxianji hairy crabs. In recent years, Wangxianji also introduced Crab Fried Roe in its offline restaurants. Only by pursuing development through multiple channels can one ensure the vitality.

In order to expand sales channels, Zhang opened the first e-commerce channel for agricultural products in Gaoyou, selling crabs online and offline. She led Wangxianji into the Tmall, JD.COM, weidian (micro store) and other powerful e-commerce platforms, building a sound e-commerce operating system for fresh goods. "Your Crab Expert" is labelled on the top left corner of the cover of every product of Wangxianji in the flagship store of Tmall, conveying the specialty and warm-hearted service commitment. Relying on word of mouth to win in community marketing is the pride of Wangxianji sales team. Upholding the faith of "integrity and quality impress customers", Zhang Yuluan has gotten touch with more than 50,000 customers in her WeChat account. Their products are in short supply in the market. Today, "Wangxianji" e-commerce has built its teams in planning, marketing and design, and retains enormous influence in the operation of new media platforms such as Weibo and WeChat. "… Try to be worthy of love. The rest is fate. We are trying to raise crabs well. Aren't you going to start our relationship?" Wangxianji's official Weibo once wrote. Now in the era of live streaming, Wangxianji also seizes the opportunity to build a live room and promote its products to the consumers all over the country. In October 2017, Zhang Yuluan became popular after appearing on the show "Day Day Up" as the "Sister Biandan". She has been active on online platforms as the "new farmer" Internet celebrity. On July 15, 2020, Sister Biandan made her debut in live streaming with the theme of "Fresh Gaoyou Crabs", which was watched and supported by more than one million netizens. Although Wangxianji is thriving thanks to e-commerce, Wang Jun remains perfectly calm. E-commerce can help expand channels and increase demand, but Wangxianji's actual orders still depend on the production volume. A blind increase in the number of crab seedlings due to increasing demand will degrade the quality of crabs, and cause disastrous consequences.

5 Stay True to the Original Aspiration and Drive Common Prosperity

Talking about the dream in his mind, Wang Jun is full of emotions: It can be said that we put all into the crab breeding, but when we come to this place, there may be decades to come, we always have to leave something behind. The property is not to be taken away, but the "wealth" left can benefit more people!

There are also many native fishermen and livestock farmers in Lingtang, often facing unpredictable risks and suffering for a whole year with little success. In order to help villagers cope with the risks, the successful couple, with the support of the local government, united 52 members and organized Gaoyou Lakeshine Aquatic Products Cooperation Association, introducing modern management and brand operation mechanism. Wang holds regular training for all farmers in Gaoyou Lake area to share breeding experience and technology with the aim of driving farmers to grow rich. Over the years, the average annual direct economic income of each household has increased by about CNY 50,000, and more than 100 local workers have been employed. Among them, the young people are involved in e-commerce operations, while the older ones are engaged in farming and other labor. Thanks to the labor during the slack season, each person has the annual income increased by about CNY30,000, and many farmers' average annual income is increased by nearly CNY100,000 through technological improvement. Wang built a green crab chain for Gaoyou, which is "integration of propagation, breeding and promotion, and one-stop production and sale". It is in line with the requirements of high-quality development. Unexpectedly, when hairy crabs sold well, Wang transferred his trademark of Gaoyouhu Hairy Crabs, which he had worked so hard to create, to the government for free. In fact, however, Wang invested more than CNY 500,000 of advertising expenses for the trademark every year, up to CNY 3 million in total. In his opinions, this trademark will be great if it is reserved by the Gaoyou people. Practice has proved that Wang Jun is forward-looking. Through the unremitting efforts of the market players and the government, this trademark has become one of the China Well-known Trademarks and won the sign of China Protected Geographical Indication Product in 2018. Gaoyou is a strong city of aquatic products in Jiangsu Province, the couple's hard work makes them become the men in the news. Wang Jun now is the vice president of Gaoyou Lake Hairy Crab Association, and Zhang Yuluan is the vice president of Gaoyou New Social Class People Association. Now, they are active in technical training occasions, sometimes in the nursing homes, in charity initiatives of Hui Township, or in promotions spreading Gaoyou crab culture in Tiktok… They are more and more busy. The solid footprints behind them reflect the beautiful and affluent Gaoyou Lake. The Gaoyou Lake Hairy Crab brand created by the couple in 15 years has been well-recognized and trusted by more and more consumers.

Kylin Plan: Building a Cross-Border E-Commerce Service Ecology, Empowering the Transformation of Chinese Manufacturing to Go Abroad

Guichao Jin and Hanmi Lin

1 Introduction

"In the past 3 years since the launch of Kylin Plan, more than 40 Kylin Pavilions have been implemented, realizing the full coverage of 11 prefecture-level cities in Zhejiang Province, covering more than 500 industrial belts, 4,000+ cross-border enterprises incubated, and launching 100 million USD's worth of accelerator… It will expand the entire industrial landscape along the Beijing–Hangzhou Grand Canal, along the Yangtze River and into Southeast Asia. In December 2021, Han Jie, COO of Zhejiang GM Digital Technology Co., Ltd., released these data at a sharing meeting held by this company (hereinafter referred to as GM Digital).

The audience were incredulous and curious about the company's experience. Staring at the audience, Mr. Han's thoughts went back to 2018…

2 Kylin Plan was Born

2.1 Setbacks Encountered by the Cross-Border Distribution Mode

In 2018, cross-border e-commerce, with its rapid growth, encountered setbacks in its development. Some cross-border merchants who started their business based on the rough distribution model began to face problems of capital chain rupture. The market traffic dividend and the advantages of China's supply chain made the goods distribution mode of cross-border e-commerce boom in the early stage. After the

G. Jin (✉) · H. Lin
Hangzhou Normal University Qianjiang College, Hangzhou, China
e-mail: jinguichao@hznu.edu.cn

J. Zhang et al. (eds.), *Innovation of Digital Economy*, Management for Professionals,
https://doi.org/10.1007/978-981-99-1741-9_34

dividend period of the increment era, merchants who failed to keep pace with the development of the times have encountered problems one after another.

Globalegrow E-Commerce, once one of the industry's proud storefronts, has since gone into decline. As a major cross-border enterprise, sustained inventory overhang and internal and external management problems for many years led to its continuous losses, and it finally fell into financial mire. Early cross-border e-commerce star enterprises such as Globalegrow E-Commerce and ValueLink have collapsed.

That lesson taught a group of new entrants looking for a quick buck that cross-border e-commerce is not all it seems. Mr. Han said, "The core problem is supply, and the merchants who blindly distribute its goods don't have the capacity to supply. The distribution model will eventually decline. China's cross-border e-commerce has shifted from 'traffic is king' to 'supply is king'. "Han Jie has also changed from an observer of cross-border e-commerce industry to an industry participant.

2.2 Industrial Clusters Resort to Cross-Border E-Commerce

In 2018, when the distribution crisis was revealed, the People of Government of Zhejiang Province put forward the "No. 1 Project" of digital economy to accelerate the building of a modern economic system with digital economy as the core and new economy as the driver.

As early as April 2016, seven departments including Department of Commerce of Zhejiang Province issued the *Guiding Opinions of the People's Government of Zhejiang Province on Promoting the Development of Cross border E-Commerce in Industrial Clusters*, which set up the first 25 pilots for cross-border e-commerce development in industrial clusters to promote the rapid development of cross-border e-commerce in industrial clusters.

Zhejiang Province has always been a developed private economy, industrial clusters cover most of the traditional industries, and some clusters have played a decisive role in the development of regional economy. Most districts and counties in Zhejiang Province are rich in industrial resources and have obvious advantages in supply chain. For example, Yiwu is the largest distribution center of petty commodities in China; Hangzhou is famous for women's wear, Haining for leather, Pujiang for crystal, Zhili, Huzhou for children's wear, and Yongkang for hardware.

With the introduction of the guiding opinions, industrial clusters in the province have resorted to cross-border e-commerce on the transformation and upgrading of foreign trade.

2.3 The Kylin Plan was Released, Together with the First Kylin Pavilion

In 2018, GM Digital, Han Jie released the "Kylin Plan" in Hangzhou, which is committed to better and faster promoting the development of digital trade and industrial transformation.

After that, many service companies similar to the GM Digital were established successively, which constitutes the strategic layout of the "No.1 project" of the digital economy in Zhejiang Province. It is also a trend of cross-border merchants in Eastern China to take the advantages of manufacturing and digital marketing as the starting point and follow the development trend of cross-border e-commerce which focuses on product research and development.

In Han Jie's view, there are two forces driving the birth of the Kylin Plan. First, at the market level, cross-border e-commerce, a new commercial form, is still exploring how to optimize all links of the chain. Compared with the mature and sound traditional international trade ecosystem, cross-border e-commerce still lacks a suitable service ecosystem. Second, at the policy level, governments at all levels in Zhejiang Province have been trying to promote the development of cross-border e-commerce industry. Generally speaking, the measures are scattered and not systematic, and the frequent flow of leading cadres affects the continuity and coherence of policies to a certain extent, which makes it difficult to achieve the expected results.

Just two weeks after the launch of the Kylin Plan, the first Kylin Pavilion – Pingyang Kylin Pavilion was completed, which means the project has taken a solid first step.

Pingyang, Wenzhou has become the first Kylin Pavilion in China, which depends on the rich industrial resources and active cross-border e-commerce activities in Pingyang County. Pingyang County has won the titles of "Pet Town", "The Capital of Leather in China", "The Capital of Plastic Knitting in China", "A Business Gift Production Base in China", etc. In recent years, by virtue of booming industries such as leather products, pet supplies, and furniture, enough conditions are created for Pingyang County to develop its cross-border e-commerce business.

3 A Basic Service Ecology Provides Operation Conditions and Talents for Manufacturers

3.1 Operation Conditions: Build an Incubation System for Operation

Traditional manufacturers operate well and have good goods, but they don't know how to open cross-border channels and online stores. Therefore, Kylin Plan launches a series of services for global store initiations by cooperating with more than 40 cross-border e-commerce all-platform channels such as Amazon, eBay,

Wish, AliExpress, Shopee, Lazada, etc., providing manufacturers with convenient and quick global one-click shop initiation service.

Most manufacturers are experienced in OEM mode and have a strong ability in product research and development. However, they are ill-informed on the market and first-line consumer experience due to disconnection with the foreign terminal retail market for a long time. In response to these problems, the Kylin Plan has established an incubation system for operation. By integrating experienced first-line project operators, senior project managers and experts in cross-border e-commerce, and courses on third-party cross-border e-commerce platforms such as Amazon, eBay, Wish, AliExpress and Shopee, enterprises are helped to play cross-border e-commerce.

Luo Hongbo is a student of the "Kylin Pavilion Amazon Cross-border E-commerce Advanced Course". With the help of the team of Shangyu Kylin Pavilion, he began to run cross-border e-commerce. Every day, he received dozens to hundreds of orders from the United States, Russia and other countries, and saw explosive growth in the sales performance of his company.

Zhou Quan, the person in charge of Shangyu Kylin Pavilion said, the Pavilion has successively contacted and visited more than 1,000 local enterprises in Shangyu, held more than 200 online and offline training and salon activities, with more than 3,000 participants. The three incubation courses and three advanced courses have guided and helped the enterprises in Shangyu to open more than 100 cross-border platform accounts, and incubated nearly 100 enterprises. More than 30 of these incubated enterprises have achieved an annual sales of cross-border e-commerce exceeding US $100,000, including 10 enterprises with cross-border e-commerce sales exceeding US $1 million and one with sales exceeding US $10 million.

3.2 Talents: A Talent-Corbelled System

With the continuous progress of the Kylin Plan, the Kylin Pavilion has expanded from Pingyang to Shangyu, Pujiang, Rui'an, Zhenhai, Qiantang, Sanmen, Yongjia, Jiangshan, Nantaihu, Dongyang and other places in 2019. The number of Kylin Pavilions has exceeded 10. The persons in charge of Kylin Pavilions all expressed that local enterprises were motivated to transform into cross-border e-commerce, but they soon encountered a thorny problem. There was an extreme shortage of cross-border e-commerce operators. Alibaba International estimated in 2021 that the gap of cross-border e-commerce professionals in China exceeded 6 million. There is a large demand for cross-border e-commerce talents, and this problem has become the bottleneck of the rapid development of cross-border e-commerce industry.

However, cross-border e-commerce has high requirements on the comprehensive ability of operation personnel, including skilled foreign language ability and cross-cultural communication ability, professional knowledge of the company's products, as well as the skills and experience of e-commerce operation.

How to solve the problem of talent supply is the new challenge for the Kylin Plan. To this end, GM Digital specially established Hangzhou Hongyu Education Technology Co., LTD., to train talents for the whole industrial chain of cross-border e-commerce. Colleges and universities are the cradle for talent training. Therefore, the Kylin Plan cooperates with colleges and universities at the beginning of the release. For example, it, together with Hangzhou Normal University Qianjiang College, has set up a practice week of "Cross-border E-commerce Brands Going Abroad", a practice week of "Talents in Business Management and in Qianjiang", and a cross-border e-commerce talent class of "eBay Youth" to jointly incubate cross-border e-commerce innovation and entrepreneurship teams. What's more, it established "Kylin Talent Class" with Zhejiang Technical Institute of Economics to explore a way for universities and enterprises in the training of application-oriented talents for cross-border e-commerce. In 2020, the Kylin Plan built the "Kylin Plan &LianLian Global Cross-border E-commerce Practice", together with LianLian Global, 20+ universities, 10+ cross-border e-commerce enterprises, 3 provincial-level training agencies, and 20+ training instructors, for the purpose of talent training. The cooperations with colleges and universities alleviates the problem of talent supply in Kylin Pavilion to a certain extent.

4 Professional Service Capacity Drives Manufacturers to Go Global and Develop More Normative

4.1 Focus on the Building of Brands Going Global

A new transformation is impending in China's manufacturing industry from low-end manufacturing to high-end manufacturing, from Chinese products to Chinese brands, from OEM to ODM and then to OBM. Cross-border e-commerce market has once again set off a wave of Chinese brands going overseas.

How to make good use of big data, do statistical screening, customer portrait description, in-depth analysis of high-value customers, and finally achieve stable and sound development of cross-border e-commerce enterprises will be a key step for the brand to go overseas.

In 2020, GM Digital strategically acquired Hangzhou Fenglan Information Technology Co., LTD., and established the global Digital Marketing Innovation Center in December of the same year. The marketing center has well combined Google's huge digital marketing advantages with the quality services of "Kylin Plan", and it is furnished with an experienced digital marketing team, of which more than 80% of the team members have studied abroad. In addition, relying on the advantages of big data and intelligent marketing, it provides cross-border e-commerce enterprises with customized mainstream advertising media delivery, SEO optimization, social media marketing operation, independent site construction, overseas crowdfunding, overseas brand building and communication, and other full-link overseas digital marketing services.

Han Jie believes that, the methodology is not complicated for building different marketing channels, and the details of the implementation are still the key to determine the effectiveness. When it comes to content marketing, for example, putting 5,000 articles on Little Red Book is a familiar strategy. If this strategy is widely adopted, the difference lies in the control of details and content. If the details are crafted, the brand will be a success if 5,000 high-quality articles instead of cliches are posted.

4.2 The Building of Compliance System

In April 2021, Amazon, the world's largest cross-border e-commerce platform, continued to crack down on violations in an unprecedented way. A large number of illegal stores and accounts of many leading star enterprises were closed, and their brands are banned from selling. Mpow, a brand of Patoson, one of the Amazon's top sellers, was blocked. A trend of blocking has swept across cross-border merchants in China. A large number of Amazon merchants have been shut down from their stores. The most severe "store closure" in the history of Amazon affected more than 50,000 Chinese merchants, and the industry loss was estimated to exceed CNY100 billion. Many Chinese merchants suffered from a heavy loss.

What's more, in this wave of compliance, both cross-border e-commerce platforms and governments of different countries and regions around the world have intensified their compliance supervision on cross-border e-commerce. Compliance operation has become a key word that cross-border e-commerce cannot avoid since 2021.

Han Jie, who witnessed the setbacks in the cross-border industry, said that these setbacks in recent years were predictable in fact, and it became inevitable for products and brands based on compliance to go abroad.

In the short run, compliance is bound to increase costs, but in the long run it will lead to bargaining. Enterprises can maintain a long-term stable existence and obtain certain profits on the premise of compliant operation. On the contrary, once they fail to comply with the regulations, the merchants may suffer irreparable consequences in the increasingly standardized cross-border e-commerce conditions. Therefore, compliance is imperative.

Therefore, the "Kylin Plan" begins to include the compliance system into the cross-border ecological system, including VAT tax compliance, product compliance, logistics compliance, data compliance, etc.

In order to meet the needs of the cross-border e-commerce market and solve the difficulties and pain points of the compliance export of the enterprises on Amazon, GM Digital Kylin Cloud successfully applied for the export process of Amazon FBA under the "9810" supervision pattern on May 14.

Mr. Wang, one of Amazon merchants, had exported his goods in the way of Delivered Duty Paid (DDP) before cooperating with Kylin Cross-border Comprehensive Services, and the monthly flow of his personal cards is up to millions of yuan. With the growing business scale, Mr. Wang wanted to upgrade the whole set of cross-border e-commerce export processes. The team of Kylin Cross-border Comprehensive Services started to sort out the whole process links of export customs declaration, foreign exchange collection and settlement, tax refund, etc., and provided him with comprehensive financial and tax compliance guidance. The compliance problem that puzzled Mr. Wang for a long time has finally been properly solved.

5 Expanded Kylin Plan and Territory

5.1 Expanded Kylin Plan: A $100 Million Accelerator Launched

The "Kylin Plan" divides cross-border e-commerce merchants into three levels, namely, junior, growing and leading merchants, providing different services for them. Junior merchants are provided with one-stop basic service solutions, including global store initiation, operation services, talent support, etc.; growing merchants are furnished with professional vertical domain solutions, such as compliance services, brand building and omni-channel marketing; leading merchants are offered personalized customization solutions, including a $100 million accelerator, etc., as shown in Fig. 1.

In March 2021, the Kylin Plan launched its "$100 million accelerator" project. This project is at the top of the Kylin Plan, which aims to accelerate the growth of Chinese-made brands going abroad. By integrating the top service resources in the whole link of the industry, the project fully empowers and optimizes enterprises on the core development factors of digital trade business, such as brand building, sales growth, team training, capital planning and supply chain integration, so as to rapidly realize the sales development and capital appreciation of enterprises, and help the Chinese Manufacturing accelerate to become a global brand, and enable manufacturers to reach the top of the value chain.

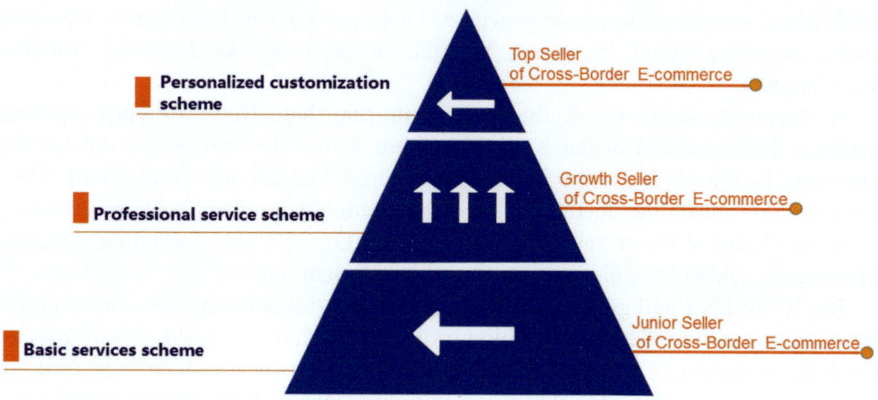

Fig. 1 Service levels of the Kylin plan

For Chinese brands going abroad, Han Jie has been full of expectations. He said, in order to enable Chinese Manufacturing to be well-known and give it more capabilities, we will not only charge processing fees for labeling, but also gain profits from retail, distribution and distribution, which will eventually contribute to the development of the domestic economy, including China's global influence. This is our original intention.

Pan Lingjie, CEO of Zhejiang Fengchi Mechanical Co., LTD., a beneficiary of the $100 million accelerator project, said, "Relying on cross-border e-commerce, we can break the dependence on traditional channels and open the link between Chinese manufacturing and consumer terminals, so that Chinese products can be delivered directly to overseas consumers, instead of having to communicate with offline agents to sell products as before. That's a big help for manufacturers like us".

"Under the guidance of the $100 million accelerator team, we launched a brand new brand to enter the field of cross-border e-commerce, and benefited from transforming traditional manufacturers into brands going abroad". Pan Lingjie said with a smile.

Of course, it is not easy for Chinese brands to go abroad. The path is long and difficult, but it must be taken.

5.2 Expanding Kylin Territory: Develop Across the County

With the successful implementation of the first batch of Kylin Pavilions such as Pingyang and Zhenhai, the Kylin Plan has been taking stage and the territory of the Kylin Pavilions has been continuously expanded. In 2019, 10 Kylin Pavilions were launched in Shangyu, Pujiang, Ruian, Zhenhai, Qiantang, Sanmen, Yongjia, Jiangshan, Nantaihu and Dongyang. In 2020, 16 Kylin Pavilions, including Beilun, Tiantai, Longwan, Wucheng, Puyuan, Ouhai, Longyou, Lanxi, Nanxun, Linhai, Haishu, Cangnan, Zhoushan, Jiashan, Yueqing and Quzhou, have been established successively. By December 2021, nearly 40 Kylin Pavilions in Zhejiang have been established, covering the whole province. There are 8 Kylin Pavilions in Wenzhou alone, including Ruian, Pingyang, Yongjia, Ouhai, Longwan, Lucheng, Yueqing and Cangnan.

In December 2020, the Kylin Pavilion in Tangshan, Hebei Province opened, marking the expansion of the Kylin Plan from within the province to outside the province. In March 2021, the Kylin Plan entered Yunnan and jointly built "Digital Lijiang". Next, the Kylin Plan will be gradually implemented in provinces along the Yangtze River and Beijing-Hangzhou Grand Canal, including Sichuan, Chongqing, Hubei, Anhui, Jiangsu, Shandong, Fujian, etc.

The Kylin Plan will go deep into the local industrial belts and serve local enterprises by expanding the Kylin Pavilion project. The plan is to build 100–150 Kylin Pavilions nationwide, and expand to overseas markets such as Southeast Asia, in order to commit to the "Belt and Road Initiative" digital new infrastructure.

6 Epilogue

There is never a smooth career in the world, only perseverance. During the continuous progress of the Kylin Plan, the team has experienced some moments when the project completed by the team overnight was rejected and faced some doubts, but the team did not give up. According to incomplete statistics, from January to the end of September 2021, GM Digital members of Kylin Pavilions from all over China visited 11,825 enterprises in total, promoted service enterprises inside and outside the province to carry out business in more than 30 cross-border e-commerce platforms, successively helped to set up more than 3,100 cross-border e-commerce stores, and helped enterprises to apply for more than 500 overseas trademarks. Besides, they organized 126 incubation activities of cross-border e-commerce training, 1,317 incubation enterprises, with an incubation sales of CNY1.71 billion in total, and held more than 600 activities.

Han Jie and his team always believe that a new era of Chinese brands going abroad has arrived, and it is no longer just a dream for Chinese companies going to the top of the value chain of international trade, and the wonderful stories of Chinese brands going abroad will continue to be staged here.

GOFANS E-commerce: Make the Down Lighter, Make the Supply Chain Softer

Jianshan Sun, Yezheng Liu, and Yuanchun Jiang

1 Introduction

Founded in 2004, the "GOFANS Down Clothing" brand is located in Hefei, Anhui Province, and it is committed to providing high-quality fashionable down clothing for urban fashion customers. In 2010, while building a more powerful brand, the company pointed its eyes to e-commerce and won at the turning point. GaoFan set apart some employees to work at e-commerce. As a result, it sold CNY1 million's worth of goods, radically overturning the company's understanding of e-commerce. After a lot of hard work, GOFANS quickly jumped to the women's down clothing category of Tmall in just three years (its Tmall homepage is shown in Fig. 1). Today, GOFANS has transformed from a traditional clothing enterprise into an Internet brand with e-commerce as its core channel, and has established a market position. How can a clothing brand rising in Anhui quickly become a renowned e-commerce "Tao Brand"? Wu Kunming, the founder, believes that success benefits from nothing but focus: We have not made any other products but down clothing since we started our business in 1994. To sum up our entrepreneurship journey in a word, it is: 20 years of attention on the fashion clothing industry. As the e-commerce and the consumer demand evolve, the era when it was possible to create a Tao Brand only through a few popular products is no longer the case, and the former brilliant Tao Brand's living space has also been compressed. GOFANS faced difficulties in new conditions therefrom. How to make its Internet brand stand firm? How to go against the trend in competitive conditions? How to remain the control ability of its down products? Facing grave COVID-19 pandemic, how to maintain a sustainable development system for endogenous

J. Sun (✉) · Y. Liu · Y. Jiang
School of Management, Hefei University of Technology, Hefei, China

J. Zhang et al. (eds.), *Innovation of Digital Economy*, Management for Professionals,
https://doi.org/10.1007/978-981-99-1741-9_35

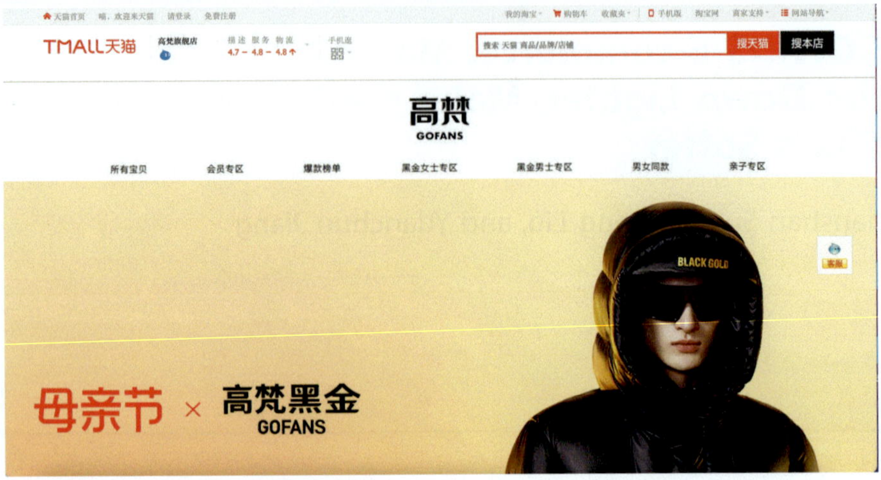

Fig. 1 GOFANS Flagship Stores in Tmall

power and a defensive core competitiveness system? GOFANS is left with more management problems under the new circumstances.

2 History of GOFANS E-commerce

Speaking of GOFANS, we have to mention its brand founder Wu Kunming. Born in Nan'an, Fujian Province in 1974, Wu was born with a business gene and has been in the fashion clothing industry for more than 20 years. As early as 1996 when most of his peers were still struggling with employment or entrepreneurship, Wu, aged 22, was already the general agent of the famous Chinese trademark KIPONE in Anhui Province. In 2004, after careful planning, Wu decided to create his own brand. The "GOFANS" brand came into being. It is a fashionable and luxury down clothing brand for Chinese elegant women, developed by Wu, together with Aoersbin, a well-known down clothing brand in British. In 2005, the company further positioned itself as an ODM of high-end women's wear brands. In 2006, GOFANS down clothing made its debut at Beijing International Exhibition Center. In 2010, after years of development and down-to-earth efforts, the company further expanded its scale, with more than 700 physical stores and more than 30 ODMs. However, at this time, the domestic clothing industry is in a low ebb. Due to overcapacity, consumption upgrading, the impact of foreign well-known brands, and the influence of channel changes under the Internet environment, clothing enterprises no longer have the development trend of wanton expansion and easily doubling their net profits. Under the dual pressure at home and abroad, garment enterprises have to take transformation measures.

Wu also began to think about his own way of transformation. In 2010, GOFANS set apart some employees to work at e-commerce. As a result, it sold CNY1 million's worth of goods, radically overturning the company's understanding of e-commerce. After tasting the benefits of e-commerce, GOFANS began to devote more energy to the e-commerce market. However, GOFANS sold its down clothing via e-commerce in traditional ideas, but did not make a good estimate of market demand. When 3,000 down jackets were found to place an order, as high as 50,000 down jackets were produced but only 1/5 of them were finally sold, resulting in a loss of more than CNY7 million. This setback made Wu think again about the production management mode of down clothing in the e-commerce environment: E-commerce is a new market, and a new competitive environment has emerged. Traditional clothing business ideas no longer apply to e-commerce sales. Business concepts must be changed and the enterprise operation had to be re-examined under the environment.

There's no making without breaking. GOFANS resolutely abandoned the traditional offline business mode and tried its best to enter the online market. Finally, it ushered in a magnificent turn in 2012, seeing the transition from traditional "production-driven promotion" to "sales-driven promotion". On the day of the Singles' Day, the sales volume of down clothing reached nearly CNY10 million, ranking first in Anhui Province. In 2013, GOFANS started to establish Anhui Guigu E-commerce Company and set up its e-commerce team. The participation of Li Wei, another senior executive of the company, also improved the confidence and ability of e-commerce operation. Li Wei graduated from the University of Science and Technology of China, used to work at Analysys International as the consulting director and the general manager of e-commerce operation center. He is adept at strategic and marketing planning, data mining and data analysis, and e-commerce multi-platform operation and management. Since then, GOFANS has carried out a series of e-commerce innovation practices, and improved product development, network marketing and innovation capabilities with the help of network big data analysis. In the mid-year promotion event of Tmall on June 26, 2013, the sales volume of GOFANS flagship store surpassed those of Bosideng and ERAL, ranking first in the down category in China, and was surprised to be called the "dark horse" in the industry. In Tmall Women's Wear Hot Sales Ranking List, GOFANS ranked top 10 in the women's clothing category for three consecutive months from November and December 2014 to January 2015; in the same period, GOFANS also won first place in the sales of women's down clothing per store on the JD.COM. In 2014, the annual online sales reached CNY200 million, ranking third among the national down clothing brands, second only to Bosideng and ERAL. In 2015, GOFANS kept rapidly growing and created outstanding sales performance. On the day of Singles' Day, the sales volume of Tmall amounted to CNY 41.06 million, ranking first in women's down clothing on the Internet and second in down clothing on the Internet. GOFANS also began to expand its business from women's wear to men's wear and children's wear, trying to become the first brand of sales in the Internet down clothing.

The rapid growth of business and the expansion of categories also prompted GOFANS to plan a more flexible supply chain. The participation of Zhao Chuanshu, another senior executive of the company, has improved the ability of GOFANS flexible supply chain. Zhao Chuanshu, a supply chain expert, joined the GOFANS team in April 2015. He serves as the supply chain director of GOFANS Group, in charge of the supply chain management center. Mr. Zhao used to be the head of Greater China Supply Chain Center of McKinsey & Company. He has worked in one of Global Fortune 500 for more than ten years and served Maersk Group, Volkswagen and Odense Steel Shipyard in Denmark. He experts in the operation of procurement management, production management and flexible supply chain management. In 2016, GOFANS saw its annual sales of CNY420 million, and online sales of more than CNY80 million on the day of Singles' Day. In the nominee finalist of the first batch of "CCTV China Brand" released by CCTV in 2017, GOFANS stood out and was listed in the "clothing, footwear and hats" category of Chinese brands, creating a legendary road for national clothing brands with strength, innovation and ingenuity. In the meanwhile, live-streaming e-commerce, a new form of e-commerce, has also begun to develop. GOFANS has also taken advantage of this favorable situation to create a new record of sales, and constantly update and build the new flexible supply chain that adapts to the rapid development.

3 Make the Down Lighter

3.1 Dual Pressure at Home and Abroad

Driven by the Internet boom, many new shopping sites have sprung up, which has hit the traditional garment industry a lot. Many consumers tend to choose clothes from physical stores and then buy them online at a lower price and discounts, making physical stores harder to run. Bosideng, the largest down clothing manufacturer in China, closed 3,436 down jacket retail outlets in six consecutive months from March 31 to September 30, 2014; while in 2013, it had closed 1,357 outlets. According to the latest retail operation data of the first quarter of fiscal year 2014 released by Belle International, the largest shoe manufacturer and retailer in China, its retail outlets have decreased by 167 in mainland of China, while the sales of its footwear business decreased by 7.8% year on year.

In recent years, China's garment industry has been beset by high inventory for a long time. In addition to the continuous development of clothing e-commerce, traditional clothing enterprises have also launched their e-commerce channels. E-commerce is a general trend for clothing categories. Traditional garment enterprises are faced with more problems in developing e-commerce, such as destocking, competitions between O2O and independent brands, between online and offline franchisees, and between self-own platforms and outsourcing third-party platforms. Many traditional clothing entity brands have launched their e-commerce business at this stage. The self-own official mall requires a professional O&M team and a high labor cost. Instead of instant results, it takes a long time and a lot of advertising to gain popularity. Therefore, many enterprises, especially small and medium-sized enterprises with low reputation, often use third-party platforms to develop their e-commerce channels. After years of development, the third-party platforms have built a sound shopping process and a good credit system. Their standard mall templates help enterprises build online stores as soon as possible, attracting intensive customers and large traffic for platforms, facilitating enterprises to quickly distribute their products.

In the overall downturn of the clothing retail industry, cost performance has become a yard stick for consumers to buy clothes. In less than ten years, many large and small clothing brands have developed relying on Taobao platform. However, with the popularity of online shopping, e-commerce transaction volume has also increased all the way and is constantly eroding the sales share of physical stores. In this regard, more and more merchants began to build and expand their online channels, which further intensified the competition in the e-commerce market. Also, they need to spend more money in acquiring online traffic. The continuous downturn of the physical retail industry has made the traditional clothing retailers feel more stressed. The increasingly fierce offline and online competition has also made clothing Tao brands based on the e-commerce platform start to think about how to go next.

GOFANS has had to make changes in the face of external pressures such as the transformation of channel formats, the loss of the consumer market by online channels, the overall downturn of the garment industry, the huge change in market consumption demand, the transformation of the homogeneous brand market into a precision fragmented market, as well as internal pressures like excess inventory, declining profitability and high operating costs.

3.2 Layout in Light Assets

Facing the dual pressure above, GOFANS is bound to take measures in transformation. As the saying goes, there's no making without breaking. GOFANS resolutely abandoned the traditional offline business mode and tried its best to enter the online market. Since 2012, GOFANS has successively cancelled its offline physical stores. By 2017, it has closed all offline stores, but made every effort to online stores and built light assets. At the end of 2018, GOFANS established its brand operation department. In the whole year of 2019, it spent more than CNY 4 million in brand building, including the building of a brand operation team and innovation of product design. In its online sales system, GOFANS has built a unified price system, using its flagship store as an icon to expand its brand influence. Among the sales of GOFANS in 2019, the proportion of distributors accounted for about 60% of the total sales, playing a decisive role in the growth of GOFANS performance. In 2020, GOFANS continued to support distributors, strengthen the operation and management of brands, and build light assets. Compared with the offline stores in the past, the model of light assets has enabled GOFANS to have stronger profitability, faster speed and more sustainable growth. Through the effective integration of the industrial supply chain, GOFANS develops faster, and is capable of keenly catching changes in market demand and making a response quickly, obtaining valuable time opportunities in the market.

3.3 The Model of E-commerce and Live Streaming

The traffic dividend period of traditional e-commerce has passed. As a new and increasingly important model that directly connects users and commodity sales, live streaming + e-commerce has provided the next opportunity for online retail. Live streaming service will also be one of the key points of GOFANS in the next stage. In Wu Kunming's opinion, one generation does what one generation does. The post-80s generation performs well in traditional e-commerce. It is a chance for the post-90s generation to strut their stuff in live e-commerce. In 2016, GOFANS tried Taobao live streaming for the first time. Since 2019, it has started to cooperate with universities in Hefei to select students for live streaming and selling goods in their studios. Moreover, excellent live-streamers are signed for cooperation, with fixed salaries and commissions. To keep up with the pace of talent, information, resources, work habits and entrepreneurial climate, GOFANS entered the Hangzhou market. In 2020, GOFANS officially built its live-streaming branch in Hangzhou. It recruited a team dominated by the post-90s generation, in charge of live-streaming business such as live-streamer connection, products selection and backend operation. In the month when the company was founded, it saw more than CNY 15 million's worth of goods by holding a special live streaming of the brand with Kwai live-streamer Super Dan. In 2020, the total GMV of GOFANS Live streaming on Taobao, Kwai, Tiktok, Mogujie, etc., exceeded CNY 1 billion, of which the total amount of Super Dan special session on Kwai exceeded 100 million; the sales of down clothing on Tiktok during Good Things Festival ranked first; the sales of GOFANS Taobao store via its live streaming accounted for more than 30%, and that during Singles' Day and Double 12 promotions ranked the top in the industry.

After a holistic practice, GOFANS has also found an effective way to manage its live streaming. That is, the CEO leads its team to select products for consumers to help the live-streamers better understand their needs, and stay the same on the bestsellers and discounts in each live streaming. When cooperating with the livestream superhosts, GOFANS also provides a special service team and postpones large-scale promotion activities on other platforms to fully cooperate in customer service, warehousing and logistics. When some businesses were still struggling to promote on Taobao, Tiktok or Kwai, GOFANS has decided to cooperate with all of them. In Taobao full of e-commerce merchants, GOFANS focuses on its own business live streaming and appropriate discounts to attract customers; In the Kwai with strong community atmosphere, GOFANS cooperates sales stars to carry out special brand activities; In Tiktok, featured with prominent media and content attributes, GOFANS accurately locates followers through advertising to obtain a better input–output ratio.

The booming e-commerce live streaming requires a higher demand for the response speed of GOFANS supply chain. The order management and turnover between different platforms, and the management and standardization of different suppliers have become new challenges GOFANS needs to face.

3.4 Brand Upgrade

The slogan of "GOFANS, A Sign of Comfort" comes out. GOFANSn advocates that comfort is the core demand of life, and it is intended to build a more comfortable and relaxed lifestyle by providing proper clothing products. Based on the brand concept of "functionalism", GOFANS put forward the "1 + 1 DOUBLE DESIGN" mode in the clothing industry, advocating the design philosophy of "two designers for one garment". The garment designer starts from the physical property to meet the fashion demand, while the life designer commences with the human nature to meet the comfort demand. In this way, both comfort and fashion demands are available. This Double Design mode provides customers with comfortable and fashionable high-quality garments and meets their demand for quality life.

The company no longer focuses on one bestseller, but adds technological elements to show higher brand premium and additional value. Together with universities and governments, GOFANS has made the whole process traceability specification for dress-goods to improve the quality. Utilizing "big data, cloud computing, intelligence", GOFANS has innovated the clothes manufacturing modes. The data-driven mode in the whole process and the deep integration of traditional production lines and information technology make the mass production of multiple varieties, small batches, and personalized customization available.

In addition to well-known brand agencies and material suppliers, GOFANS has also built the relationship with renowned individuals and Ips to enhance consumers' recognition of GOFANS quality. GOFANS has successively cooperated with celebrities and launched the same style of clothes that Charmaine Sheh Sze Man, Jiang Mengjie, Jian Renzi and Uncle Tong Dao have, and also co-branded with "Doraemon" IP, all of which have achieved good results both in terms of brand awareness and sales. In addition to cooperations with IPs to raise awareness, control of product quality is also more important. In terms of supplier management and supply standardization, what measures has GOFANS taken?

4 GOFANS E-commerce's Flexible Supply Chain Management

To realize the light assets strategy and make down "lighter", GOFANS must establish a supporting supply chain system. To transition from traditional "production-driven promotion" to "sales-driven promotion", GOFANS starts to devise a more flexible supply chain to make the supply chain more flexible, including supplier management, shell fabrics and auxiliaries procurement, quality management, production and manufacturing, sales logistics and information construction. Through years of efforts, GOFANS has established its flexible supply chain system of "multiple styles, small batches and multiple batches", which is characterized by many styles & small quantity, quick-response orders, agility and flexibility, and constantly improves the comprehensive control capability of the supply chain of quality, delivery date, order quantity, and adjustment and optimization.

4.1 Demand-Driven Flexible Order System

In traditional supply chain management, the "bullwhip effect" caused by inaccurate ordering information often leads to excessive overstock of product inventory, which weakens the liquidity of enterprises. Utilizing the e-commerce platform, information technology provides a high quality mode for information fast transmission and sharing. With the continuous optimization of the global technological environment, supply chain management will see an open, shared and integrated big data platform with information technology as the carrier. With big data collection, analysis and application as the core and corporate IT as the support, GOFANS has enhanced the accuracy and timeliness of supply chain management. It makes use of the feedback data from front-end sales personnel to forecast sales and dynamically adjust its order quantity. Usually, 5–6 times of data analysis a day and adding orders in real time according to user demands help GOFANS adjust its production process in time. GOFANS sold its first batch of 200 online styles on trial at first, and collected data to see the number of views, collections, evaluations, etc., while making promotion tests on various social media. In March and April, it further optimized these products, and picked up and put 30% of them into production. In August and September, it replenished and placed additional orders in time for the bestsellers that have been sold 200, so as to ensure agile, real-time and dynamic ordering. By the means of small amount and multiple batches of orders, GOFANS creates a myth of a 7-day supply cycle in the down clothing industry. GOFANS, keeps its delivery term at "7 days", which is the same as ZARA, an international fast fashion brand. GOFANS has reached international leadership by being able to improve its time to 7 days while maintaining the same quality. Other traditional down brands and emerging Tao brands have been depressed due to inventory, but GOFANS sees a high growth of 100% in sales performance, while its inventory rate is 5% at most. GOFANS digitalizes its full operation from product planning to sales, reorders and bestsellers recommend and synchronizes information in real time. The integration of quick response and flexible supply chain allows it to shorten its delivery term to 7 days, and keep a sell-through rate of more than 95% for a long time. GOFANS always runs well.

In the flexible supply industry chain, the collaborative procurement, manufacturing and logistics of upstream and downstream enterprises, as well as the specialized division of labor and collaboration, have shortened the time to market and the production cycle of new products to a certain extent. To solve the inventory problem and reduce the cost of transaction, production and operation, production and inventory on demand is the most effective solution.

4.2 Strict Supplier Management

Supply chain quality management is based on supplier management. There are certain uncertainties on suppliers, including whether they can supply goods on time as required and ensure the quality qualification rate and transportation safety; flexibly adjust the capacity of spare parts as per the manufacturers' product development plan; provide superior after-sales service to the manufacturers in good financial condition. All these will, to a certain extent, hit the overall operation of the downstream manufacturers of the supply chain, thereby affecting the efficiency and benefits of cooperation between enterprises in the supply chain and reducing the performance of the entire supply chain.

GOFANS has gone through three stages in supplier management. In the first stage, it mainly developed suppliers to meet basic sales needs and gradually built a supplier team; In the second stage, it set up its own supplier team and began to change the supplier's concept. Utilizing the advantages of Internet brands, it produced on demand and drove the supply chain to return orders as soon as possible; in the third stage, it took the strategy of "product above all", and paid more attention to product quality, and thereby established its scientific supplier management system. Its supplier management system consists of strict supplier access process, efficient supplier assessment system and win–win supplier training system. Flexible strict management is conducted in supplier selection, assessment, cooperation mode, etc. In terms of supplier access, the supplier list is established by evaluating the credit rating, production capacity and operation status of the manufacturers. The suppliers that pass the review must guarantee 50% of the production capacity provided to GOFANS, and at the same time have 30–40% flexibility. For supplier assessment, GOFANS decides the payment and order allocation for the next batch according to the delivery of the suppliers. The excellent suppliers, for example, will be rewarded for the next batch of orders. In regard to cooperation mode, GOFANS manages the entire supply process, builds its supplier training system and distributes proper proportion of production lines to achieve a win–win purpose.

4.3 Standardize Supply Chain

To better manage suppliers, strengthen collaboration and cooperation with them, and improve inventory management and shipment response speed, GOFANS starts to standardize its supply chain. Usually, a down jacket is composed of fabrics, accessories and down, and is produced by multiple factories. There is a big difference between fabrics and accessories, and the details of some ingredients will be stricter. By splitting the supply chain, GOFANS further subdivided its orders, paid more attention to the fabrics and reduced the use of auxiliaries. In this way, it standardized its production. On the basis of higher efficiency, faster speed and better quality, it obtained shorter capital turnover cycle, less inventory and less risk. In the meanwhile, GOFANS further upgraded its basic style of down jackets and launched the world's first down jacket with visible light filler. It attaches importance to product quality and makes the jackets that become the first ones that meet the Japanese down standard after spot checks in China.

4.4 Coordination Between Sales and Supply

To optimize the supply chain system, GOFANS strengthens the coordination between sales and supply by means of the strategy of "sales-driven promotion". Traditionally, the production plan of the supply chain management lacks accurate prediction of market demand, ignores consumers' need and in the mode of "production-driven sales", which is out of touch with the market. On the e-commerce platform, the key enterprises of the supply chain such as sellers and manufacturers can collect market demand information in a timely and comprehensive manner to achieve the goal of demand-driven production. Supply chain enterprises can also release new product on this platform, tap and stimulate the demand of potential consumers, and timely adjust product design and production plans. GOFANS first sold its products in small batches, and produced according to the sales volume; what's more, it took proper measures to manage its suppliers. In this way, an effective communication system between front and rear ends. Meanwhile, GOFANS determined the capacity of the factory to produce hot goods, and set the pre-sale quantity according to the maximum capacity of the factory, thus establishing a scientific capacity reservation system. In addition, GOFANS also made use of big data to understand the age, living habits and consumption habits of different customer groups, as well as their regions to develop different types of products and provide different groups with differentiated products. When organizing production, it used proper fabrics and auxiliaries according to the order task to ensure the fulfillment of the orders. This full digital and refined operation mode maximizes the advantages of the Internet, builds a competitive advantage of "more styles, faster updates, and high cost performance"; it also solves the most troublesome inventory problem in the clothing industry, and provides customers with more commodities at high cost performance.

4.5 Logistics and Distribution System

Delivery management under traditional supply chain management is often the last link that affects the overall efficiency of supply chain enterprises. Uncertain transportation information, poor timeliness and high rate of cargo damage are the direct reasons for the decline of customer satisfaction. In the e-commerce environment, distribution speed is a problem that consumers are very concerned about. In order to support the rapid response to distribution efficiency and ensure customers receive goods quickly and in good condition, GOFANS has brought about the building of a warehousing and logistics system through the development of industries. GOFANS has established an industrial belt in Anhui, which can effectively ensure that goods can be delivered within 4 h in Hefei and within one day in the rest of Anhui. Next it will replicate this model to other regions across the country, including Northeastern China and Southwestern China. GOFANS cooperates with third-party logistics enterprises such as SF Express, STO Express, YTO Express, ZTO Express and YUNDA to distribute its goods. It usually packs the goods ordered by consumers in the warehouse center, and then delivers them to the logistics enterprises for distribution. Individual goods are often distributed by the logistics enterprises designated by the consumers, or by an effective logistics agency selected through the big data of Cainiao in different regions. Meanwhile, the upstream enterprises of the supply chain are able to release the logistics transportation information in time, providing convenience for downstream enterprises and consumers in query and tracking; in addition, they can adjust the delivery batch or delivery time in time when the market sales change, increasing the flexibility of the enterprise's delivery quantity and time, and reducing the risk of the enterprise's material reserves.

5 Conclusion

In addition to the founder's unique experience and entrepreneurial mind, every successful enterprise is also inseparable from the internal genes inherited and integrated in the process of incubation and growth. GOFANS, as a young firm, does not stop the path of upgrading and transforming its supply chain. It puts the competitiveness of the entire supply chain as the core to explore a supply chain innovation mode.

In the context of the COVID-19 pandemic in this year, GOFANS further invests more money to build its brand operation team, innovate product design, and expand its brand influence. What's more, GOFANS followes the industry trend to develop the "e-commerce + live streaming" model, further build light assets, and make down "lighter".

Besides, GOFANS is managing to look for suppliers in the raw material origin and transferring the supply chain to Jiangsu, Zhejiang and Shanghai regions, so as to ensure product quality and target the high-end market. It also attaches much attention to brand operation and design, shows its brands at GOFANS Tmall flagship stores and GOFANS children's garments flagship stores to build an iconic brand; it provides support for distributors and further optimizes the supply chain, making the chain "softer".

JACK: How a Manufacturing Enterprise Transforms Digitally?

Jiahui Ye, Jiaorong Zhao, Kecheng Chen, Junping Wang, and Chengbin Wang

1 Introduction

The outline of the National "14th Five-Year Plan" specifies the requirements of "accelerating digital development and creating new advantages of digital economy". With the flourish of digital technologies such as artificial intelligence, big data, cloud computing and the Internet of Things, the research and exploration of digital transformation of manufacturing enterprises has become a hot spot in the academic circles at home and abroad.

Digitalization creates value. Digitalization creates value in new ways and realizes organizational change, which can help enterprises take advantage of the value of interactive digital technology based on modularization and IT support (Liu et al., 2021). As the best means to further expand the advantages of production and operation in the new era, digital transformation requires enterprises to be able to manage the ever-changing network of partners and accurately grasp new market opportunities. The Internet of Things (IoT) technology enables companies to establish long-term relationships with customers. To realize the digital transformation, the entire organization needs to greatly change its routine and capabilities (Liu et al., 2020). The company should evolve from empowerment to enabling, and explore the path and method of digital empowerment through the key links of demand forecasting, product design, pricing and inventory management, supply chain management, etc., improve the operating efficiency of enterprises, focuses on demand creation, business design, and value creation, and reconstruct the supply chain and ecosystem to create higher business value (Chen et al. 2020; Chen et al., 2020; Osterwalder et al., 2014).

J. Ye (✉) · J. Zhao · K. Chen · J. Wang · C. Wang
Business School, Taizhou University, Taizhou, China

J. Zhang et al. (eds.), *Innovation of Digital Economy*, Management for Professionals,
https://doi.org/10.1007/978-981-99-1741-9_36

Digitalization implies risks. Even so, not all enterprises exploring digital transformation hold the opportunities of the times and stand out. Digital investment and performance are characterized by "U" and have certain risks (Ali et al., 2020). One company's cognitive awareness may prevent its digital process (Cenamor et al., 2019). Different backgrounds produce distinct results, and some companies are difficult to benefit from digitalization. A cognitive map is required to help a company find the path of digital innovation development by establishing "innovation mechanism—innovation output—innovation results" (Eller et al., 2020).

The competition in the sewing machine industry is very cruel in China. There are nearly 500 similar enterprises in the country, who are beset by homogeneous competitions and price wars. Therefore how to blaze a new trail, and carve out a differentiated path becomes a problem that JACK has to face. As a traditional manufacturer, JACK has provided cloud computing products and services such as intelligent production control and process control optimization for middle and downstream garment makers in recent years by building an intelligent garment manufacturing Internet platform, thus greatly improving the automation of garment factories, and solving many technical problems encountered by garment enterprises in the garment sewing process. How did JACK break out of the tight encirclement and goes well under severe market conditions?

2 Bottleneck of Digitalization

2.1 Information Island—There is Data but Usage

Due to the large differences in data definitions and data usage among departments, as well as the large number of business links in the manufacturer, and the fact that most of the data are distributed in different systems, the inconsistency of the chain port leads to the failure of data interoperability between departments, and the lack of business function interaction leads to the disconnection of enterprise logistics, capital flow and information flow. In data processing, business users need to spend a lot of time and energy to classify, integrate and analyze data from different systems, which makes data processing unable to meet daily business needs, and information synchronization is extremely poor. In the face of the increasingly competitive market, enterprises have growing demand for fast data processing, and higher requirements for precision. Lagging construction of information departments, and difficulty of business departments in independent development of business systems lead to poor data interchange due to the urgent need for business. In the long run, the data flow and information flow that enterprises spend large costs and a long time are silent in the jumbled system, and cannot generate positive feedback.

JACK also faced severe "**information island**" in its early stage of digital transformation. All data are sealed in systems. JACK has invested a lot of money in digital construction to launch ERP, HR, MES and other management systems. In normal applications, however, ERP is only used for finance and inventory, and the data between the two departments are not connected. Meanwhile, MES is not integrated with ERP, and OA system can only be used for day-to-day administration. As a result, employees need to download an APP to handle one business. In this way, a piece of information is scattered in different departments, and permission is required to query some information among them, which leads to low efficiency. These "information islands" greatly affect the digital transformation. To make data valuable, JACK must get rid of the barriers between different software systems and flow the information between departments, so as to allow data to spread in the entire enterprise.

2.2 Output Limitation—Know How to Use but not Well

How to maximize the value of a powerful and convenient digital tool in practice? In fact, manufacturers are generally short of personnel with strong digital capabilities. Most of them expect to improve their staff members' digital capabilities through internal training, so as to facilitate the overall digital transformation. However, it is difficult to achieve this in practice. The benefits brought by digitalization are superficial, and are hard to make the digital transformation in a "virtuous circle". If employees are expected to empower the enterprises through short-term training, it not only needs to combine the actual business of employees with data development to provide them convenience, but also offer them more welfare, give the team more voice, and stimulate the innovation of employees and teams.

3 Digital Road: From Traditional Manufacturing to Digital Intelligent Manufacturing

Founded in 1995, JACK focuses on the manufacturing and R&D of intelligent hanging, intelligent cutting equipment, intelligent sewing machines, motors and control systems. Since its initiation, JACK has regarded technology R&D as the core driving force for its development. In recent years, it has actively built digital transformation of core business. In 2018, its sales turnover and sales volume exceeded that of JUKI, becoming the largest sewing manufacturer in the world. JACK's industrial Internet platform for intelligent sewing industry that has been laid out since 2018, was selected into the *List of Innovative and Pilot Application Cases of Industrial Internet Platform in 2021* by the Ministry of Industry and Information Technology, which successfully enabled JACK to move from a traditional manufacturer to a digital intelligent manufacturer.

3.1 Four Precisions

In the practical application of digital technology, JACK has studied and summarized a new business model of "four precisions". This model, from R&D to marketing and then to production and service, has grasped all the elements and links in the business process from the customer level through the closed-loop digital business application that meets the actual needs.

I. **Precision marketing creates sales opportunities**. Following the market-oriented and customer-centric principles, JACK, together with Jack, Bruce, Brinkmann, MAICA and VBM, provides end users with a comprehensive set of intelligent garment manufacturing solutions.
II. **Precise delivery leads to precise prediction**. For precise delivery, JACK has targeted the leading enterprises in the medium and high-end market, and explored the key customers by establishing the LTC system consisting of a key customer center, intelligent complete solutions and fast service delivery.
III. **Precise service upgrades consumer experience**. To further improve the company's service quality, JACK has established a 400 service hotline and a non-working time telephone for technical consultation, and built an end-to-end quality feedback system to ensure that internal and external problems can be quickly solved. For customer experience, JACK has launched the service software of "one-click order, easy warranty" on the Jack Quick Repair Platform, and also released training courseware and videos related to service stewards to help customers learn online and solve problems. In the overseas market, it has set up a number of overseas offices, localizing people, spare parts and spare machines, and responding to and solving service problems more quickly.
IV. **Precise R&D creates bestsellers**. From product development to ideas management,

JACK has built a large R&D platform to constantly create differentiated technologies, and improve weak core technologies of intelligent complete solutions. Gradually, IT department put the cutting machine order tracking system into practice through the further integration with R&D, production, marketing, etc.; the production management system WMS project of the four major manufacturing plants was successfully launched; the project management system of R&D system was placed in service; The DMS system fully opens up the business process from R&D to production and marketing, gradually builds the large digital intelligence, simplify the business process, and help promote the business efficiently (Fig. 1).

3.2 Internet of Everything

The industrial Internet platform for clothing intelligent manufacturing created by JACK aims to achieve the two-way empowerment of intelligent complete solutions and clothing order operation, innovate the marketing modes, optimize channel management, and thus become an Internet ecological platform for the clothing intelligent manufacturing industry. JACK introduces new media of live streaming and e-commerce platforms to increase brand communication and brand reputation; optimizes channel management, improves channel sales breadth and channel sales

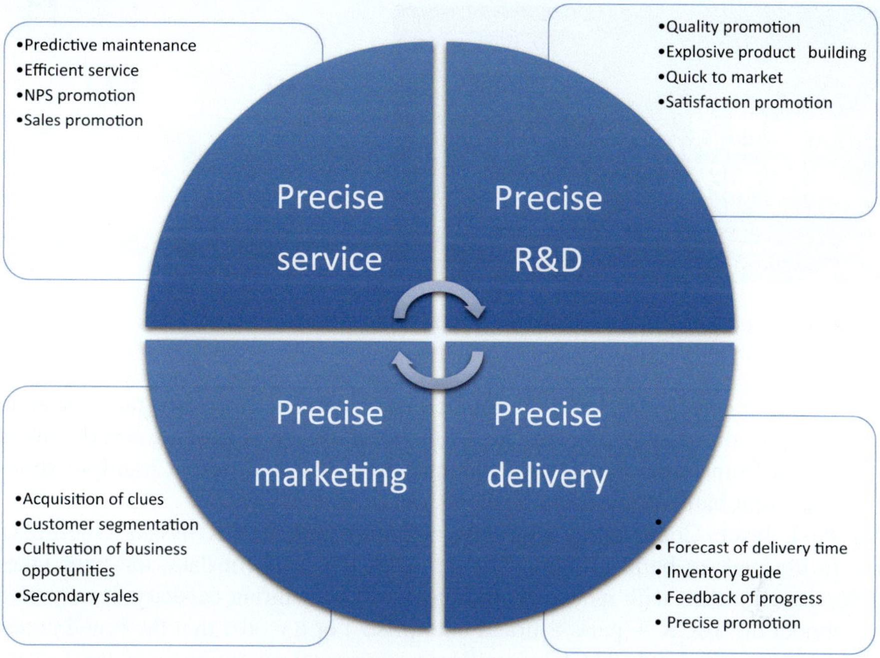

Fig. 1 Schematic diagram of "Four precisions"

ability, and constantly develops intelligent manufacturing complete product solutions for automation equipment and sewing equipment among medium and large customers.

This platform is designed for continuous integration of a series of businesses including R&D design, supply and demand of shell fabrics and auxiliaries, order receiving center, order issuing center, data service, goods distribution, application market and financial service. At service level, it mainly focuses on digital services—digital garment factories and industry platforms; At platform level, cloud platform is centered on issues such as equipment Internet of Things, data development, application development and industrial security (Fig. 2).

With the high-end industrial Internet platform, how can we use technology to make profits in business? To give full play to the role of the platform and dig the strong potential of digital technology from the actual data, JACK has devised three landing modes for the intelligent garment manufacturing industry Internet platform.

(1) **Enterprise level**: drive the transformation and upgrading of garment manufacturers and train proper professional capabilities through orders and free intelligent devices. Specifically, the production efficiency and quick return capability are improved through equipment upgrading, technical transformation, financial services, etc. In the meanwhile, the platform is used to further

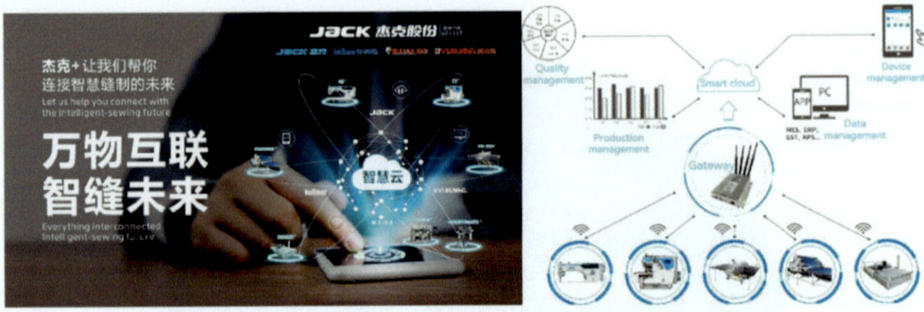

Fig. 2 Poster of "Smart cloud" platform of JACK

empower enterprises, build digital factories, and effectively integrate manufacturing resources with the big data of the platform, so as to share and distribute orders from brand names to different enterprises and present multiple styles and small batches of orders.

(2) **Park level**: Cooperating with the industrial park, JACK assists enterprises in the park to build a digital factory; with the platform data, the park takes external orders with its overall intelligent manufacturing capacity. It may be a model of "JACK + park + brand enterprise"; or a model that the brand enterprise buys and puts JACK's intelligent equipment on the basis of the factory building, builds a shared cutting room to share resources, and improve the utilization efficiency of equipment and resources; or a model that the park leases the whole plant and equipment to small and medium-sized garment factories.

3) **Region level**: cooperate with local governments of garment clusters to improve the overall level of the clusters and achieve unified management. In addition to teaming up with the local government where the industrial cluster is located to support the creation and promotion of digital model enterprises, JACK works with enterprises to build shared smart cutting rooms to reduce the investment threshold of enterprises in the park, and improve the quality of products; build a three-dimensional industrial cluster through digital production factories, and connecting with design and sales practices; implement flexible matching and sharing, and finally realize collaborative manufacturing and supply by gathering consumers, workers, suppliers, producers, service providers in the industrial cluster.

4 Methodology of Digital Transformation

Against the backdrop of global industrial transformation, manufacturers are eager to carry out digital transformation, improve their technological competitiveness, seize the high ground of market in the future, ease the pressure of rising labor costs, improve production efficiency and corporate income, and expect to bring vitality into development via digitalization. The digital transformation of China's manufacturing industry, however, is still facing difficulties from the shortage of core technologies and high-end talents. How to speed up the transformation and upgrading of manufacturing industry at high quality and high level, and change the unfavorable situation of being under the control of others have become a major concern that the majority of manufacturers need to consider. **How to promote the digital transformation and upgrading of manufacturers?** JACK answered with actions.

First, digitally empower small and medium-sized enterprises (SMEs). Intelligent manufacturing will be a must for the transformation of traditional manufacturers in the future (Hanelt et al. 2021). With a new round of technological revolution sweeping again, finding intelligent manufacturing solutions with strong practicality and taking into account the needs of traditional enterprises in all production links has become a major demand of SMEs(). With years of successful digital experience, JACK, based on its own advantages, provided complete sets of digital solutions for downstream small and medium-sized garment manufacturers as the bellwether in the industry, and partially showed its digital resources to help SMEs transform and reduce transformation costs.

Second, train a new model of intelligent manufacturing. JACK pays attention to cultivating a new platform based design model, and has built a "digital factory" based on its own business needs. Focusing on the main processes of R&D, process, manufacturing, testing across the whole life cycle of sewing equipment, the digital factory makes use of virtual design tools to form parametric parts, assemblies and engineering drawings as soon as possible to achieve modular and parametric design, which is used for the development and design of the same series of new products, greatly reducing design waste. The production mode dominated by intelligent automation makes the visual progress, quality statistics, process tracing available in the production process, improving the production efficiency while reducing the management cost, and realizing the flexible perception, intelligent management and control, and interconnection of the whole link of the production workshop (Kohtamäki, et al. 2020; Kohtamäki et al. 2019).

Third, accelerate the building of an industrial Internet platform. The industrial Internet platform requires high requirements for data collection, processing and calculation (Paiola & Gebauer, 2020). A competitive industrial Internet platform will bring strong vitality into enterprises. Regarding the hardware, the clothing industry interconnection platform built by JACK uses its own digital technology to provide cloud computing products and services for middle and downstream clothing enterprises, such as intelligent production control, optimized process control, network collaborative manufacturing, product remote diagnosis, process and energy consumption management, personalized customization, equipment predictive maintenance, and product lifecycle management, which greatly improves the automation of clothing factories and solves many technical problems encountered by garment enterprises in the process of garment sewing.

Fourth, strengthen the R&D of key technologies. Aiming at strategic fields with large potential, such as big data and cloud computing, JACK has established

Table 1 Jack's digital projects and partners in recent five years

No	Time	Event	Partners
1	2017/08	Digital overall planning	E-works technology Consulting firm
2	2018/06	PLM project	SIPM
3	2018/06	JACK- Huawei IPD consulting project	Huawei
4	2018/08	Group office project	SEEYON.com
5	2018/11	SRM project	Hoteam sofeware
6	2018/12	BPC comprehensive pre-management project	HAND
7	2019/03	HCM HR project	HAND
8	2019/04	JACK made a debut of sewing machines with IoT technology	Huawei
9	2019/08	M8 international trade sales project	FUMASOFT
10	2021/05	JACK started SCADA project	HITopIM

a special information team with professional software companies to jointly overcome key technologies and improve the independent supply capacity (Nambisan et al. 2017). In this way, a new business form of cross-border cooperation of "traditional enterprise + digital enterprise" has been built, which provides new ideas for manufacturers on how to deal with the weakness of core technology (Table 1).

5 Epilogue

JACK has become the industry leader in the digital transformation. Considering only the sewing machinery businesses, the proportion of the company's revenue scale has increased from 13% in 2011 to about 30% in 2020 in the global leading enterprises. After ten years of growth, JACK's income scale has stepped into the first echelon in the world. In 2020, its income scale has been significantly ahead of the global leader JUKI. In 2020, with its digital platform, JACK has built its large-scale production capacity of 1.2 million intelligent industrial sewing machines, 2,500 automatic sewing units and 850 sets of intelligent garment manufacturing solutions. The average sales price of industrial sewing machines has increased by 17.42% in the past three years. The expansion of pre- and post-sewing equipment not only helps JACK open up more market space, but also enables it to provide complete sets of solutions, which can meet the needs of high-end customers for intelligent and flexible production.

On the other hand, JACK also heads for troubles. The rise of bulky goods in 2021 caused a slight decline in the gross profit margin of JACK. The annual report of 2021 shows that the overall gross profit margin of the company is—4.2−22.5% year on year, and the net profit margin is 2.6−7.8% year on year. In the second quarter, the gross profit margin is –0.7 to 22.1% month on month, and the net profit margin is −0.5−7.5% month on month. The manufacturing industry has been facing the test of **high labor costs, low operating efficiency** and other issues for a long time in China.

To adapt to the changing market and the competitive pressure from peers, traditional manufacturers have to take digital transformation into account. Under the support of the Internet of Things, JACK will further promote new high value-added products, use digital technology to solve the high labor costs and other business difficulties, and digitally transform itself in the round. Only in this way can JACK increase its technological competitiveness and maintain its leading position in the industry.

References

Ali, O., Ally, M., Dwivedi, C. Y. (2020). The state of play of blockchain technology in the financial services sector: a systematic literature review. *International Journal of Information Management, 54*, 102199

Cenamor, J., Parida, V., & Wincent, J. (2019). How entrepreneurial SMEs compete through digital platforms: The roles of digital platform capability, network capability and ambidexterity. *Journal of Business Research, 100*, 196–206.

Chen, D., Wang, L., Chen, A. (2020). Digitalization and strategic management theory: review, challenges and prospects. *Management World,* (05), 220–236+20. https://doi.org/10.19744/j.cnki.11-1235/f.2020.0080.

Chen, J., Huang, S., Liu, Y. (2020). Operations management in the digitization era: from empowering to enabling. *Management World, 36* (02), 117–128+222. https://doi.org/10.19744/j.cnki.11-1235/f.2020.0025.

Eller, R., Alford, P., Kallmünzer, A., & Peters, M. (2020). Antecedents, consequences, and challenges of small and medium-sized enterprise digitalization. *Journal of Business Research, 112*, 119–127.

Hanelt, A., Bohnsack, R., Marz, D., & Antunes, C. (2021). A systematic review of the literature on digital transformation: Insights and implications for strategy and organizational change. *Journal of Management Studies, 58*(5), 1159–1197.

Kohtamäki, M., Parida, V., Oghazi, P., Gebauer, H., & Baines, T. (2019). Digital servitization business models in ecosystems: A theory of the firm. *Journal of Business Research, 104*, 380–392.

Kohtamäki, M., Parida, V., Patel, P. C., & Gebauer, H. (2020). The relationship between digitalization and servitization: The role of servitization in capturing the financial potential of digitalization. *Technological Forecasting and Social Change, 151*, 119804.

Liu, Y., Dong, J., Wei, J. (2020). digital innovation management: theoretical framework and future research. *Management World*, (07), 198–217+219. https://doi.org/10.19744/j.cnki.11-1235/f.2020.0111.

Liu, S., Yan, J., Zhang, S., Lin, H. (2021). Can digital transformation of enterprise management improve input output efficiency. *Management World,* (05), 170–190+13. https://doi.org/10.19744/j.cnki.11-1235/f.2021.0072.

Nambisan, S., Lyytinen, K., Majchrzak, A., & Song, M. (2017). Digital Innovation Management: Reinventing innovation management research in a digital world. *MIS quarterly, 41*(1).

Osterwalder, A., Pigneur, Y., Bernarda, G., Smith, A., & Papadakos, T. (2014). *Value proposition design: How to create products and services customers want*. Wiley.

Paiola, M., & Gebauer, H. (2020). Internet of things technologies, digital servitization and business model innovation in BtoB manufacturing firms. *Industrial Marketing Management, 89*, 245–264.

Joint Efforts for Mutual Development, Collaborative Innovation for Future—National Undergraduate E-commerce "Innovation, Creativity and Entrepreneurship" Competition

Qi Li, Shuai Liu, and Cuihua Zhu

1 Introduction

"China catches my heart. No one can break us apart. No matter where I travel, you are what I'm singing for. I'm singing of your high mountains, singing of your land and rocks…" With the loud singing of the whole audience, the final of the 12th National Undergraduate E-commerce "Innovation, Creativity and Entrepreneurship" Challenge (hereinafter referred to as the ICE Competition) was successfully concluded at Hubei University of Economics on July 24, 2022.

It is a national academic competition for college students, which is hosted by the Nationwide E-commerce Teaching Steering Committee of Schools and Universities of the Ministry of Education delegated by the Ministry of Education since 2009. This competition attracted 133,729 teams from more than 1,000 universities nationwide. 320 teams finally reached the final after the school competitions and the provincial competitions of 31 provinces, municipalities, autonomous regions, and the Macao Special Administrative Region. The successful holding of the 12th ICE Competition reflects the vigor of digital innovation in modern China, which will have greater value and far-reaching influence.

Q. Li (✉) · S. Liu · C. Zhu
Xi'an Jiaotong University, Xi'an, China

J. Zhang et al. (eds.), *Innovation of Digital Economy*, Management for Professionals,
https://doi.org/10.1007/978-981-99-1741-9_37

2 Guided by Government Policies, and Well Prepared for Competition

2.1 College Students Need Higher Abilities of Innovation and Entrepreneurship in the New Century

The concept of "innovation and entrepreneurship" was originally scattered in China's educational policies. In response to the prediction of the World Higher Education Conference on the future development trend and direction of world higher education, the *Decision of the CPC Central Committee and State Council on Deepening Educational Reform and Promoting Quality Education in All All-round Way* in 1999 clearly pointed out that "higher education should attach importance to cultivating college students' abilities in innovation, practice, and entrepreneurship", and quality-oriented education is adopted "focusing on cultivating students' innovative spirit and practical ability".

In the twenty-first century, college graduates are showing a large scale of growth every year in China. In 2000, the total number of college graduates nationwide was 1.07 million, and in 2008, it was 5.5 million. With the increasing enrollment of colleges and universities year by year, the number of college graduates is increasing. In addition to the impact of the international financial crisis, college students have less and less chance to find new job demands. By 2008, the initial employment rate of college graduates had dropped from 90% to about 65%. As stated clearly in the report of the 17th National Congress of the Communist Party of China, we should implement the development strategy of job enlargement and promote entrepreneurship to drive employment. In recent years, the government has built green channels and issued relevant policies to support college students entrepreneurship. A trend of youth entrepreneurship prevails in China.

2.2 ICE Competition is Intended for Quality-Oriented Education of College Students

The ICE Competition was born at the right moment. The first ICE Competition has been launched under the guidance of the Department of Higher Education, the Ministry of Education, the Department of Innovation and High-Tech Development of NDRC, the Information Promotion Department of the Ministry of Industry and Information Technology, the Information Department of the Ministry of Commerce, Department of High-tech Development and Industrialization of the Ministry of Science and Technology, the Youth League's Central Student Affairs Department, etc., and it been actively supported and responded by local governments and enterprises and institutions. This competition has played a positive exemplary role for colleges and universities to implement the *Opinions of the Ministry of Education and the Ministry of Finance on the Implementation of the Undergraduate Teaching Quality and Teaching Reform Project in Colleges and Universities* (JGH [2007] No. 1), carry out innovative education and practical teaching reform, and strengthen the links between industry, education, and research. The first to the ninth sessions from 2009 to 2019 was hosted by the Nationwide E-commerce Teaching Steering Committee of Schools and Universities of the Ministry of Education. See Fig. 1 for the organizational chart of the ICE Competition from 2009 to 2019.

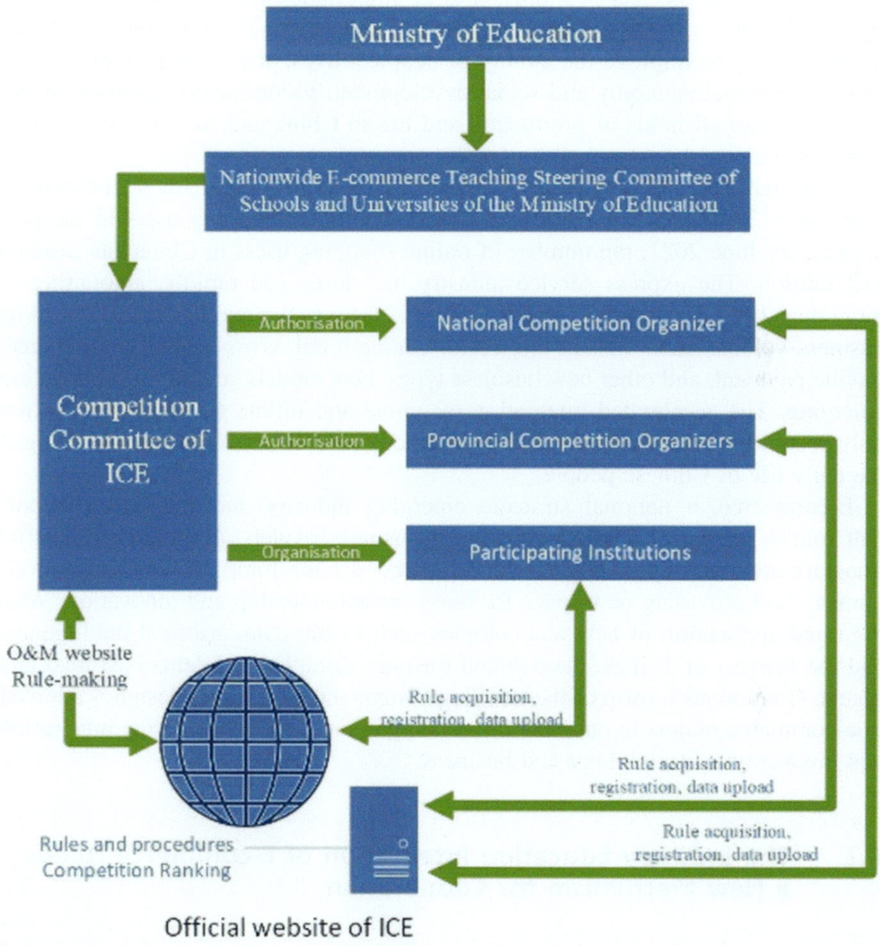

Fig. 1 Organizational Chart of ICE Competition (2009–2019)

3 E-commerce Industry Development Boosts the Integration of Industry and Education

3.1 Booming E-commerce in China

E-commerce is a business activity that sells goods or provides services through the Internet and other information networks. As an important part of the digital economy and the real economy, it is an important engine to promote, digital industrialization, drive industry digitalization, and promote digital governance, an important way to improve the quality of people's lives, and an important force to promote national economy and social development. E-commerce has been deeply integrated into all fields of production and life in China and has played a pivotal role in the digital transformation of economic society.

China has become the world's largest online retail market for 9 consecutive years since 2013 and saw explosive growth in online shopping users in the past decade. By June 2021, the number of online shopping users in China has reached 812 million. The express service industry has developed rapidly, amounting to more than 100 billion parcels in 2021, nearly 20 times the number in 2012, and its business volume ranks first in the world. Online retail, cross-border e-commerce, mobile payment, and other new business types, new models, and new scenarios are emerging. The accelerated integration of online and offline consumption has not only become an important driver of economic growth but also profoundly changed the daily life of Chinese people.

E-commerce, a national strategic emerging industry, has played an important role in leading the transformation of business models, optimizing industrial transformation and upgrading, becoming a new driving force for economic development, and providing new space for mass entrepreneurship and innovation. With the rapid application of new technologies such as big data, artificial intelligence, and the Internet of Things, the demand for inter-disciplinary talents is crucial and urgent. Continuous reform of the teaching system and curriculum design is adopted in e-commerce majors to cultivate outstanding talents who can lead the integration and innovation of technology and business.

3.2 The Industry-Education Integration of E-commerce Needs a New Mechanism for Cooperation

It is urgent to develop new mechanisms and systems and integrate all resources of China's e-commerce ecology to better promote the i innovation development of the integration of industry and education in the field of e-commerce in China, deepen the integration of industry and education in e-commerce, promote the organic connection between the education chain, talent chain, industry chain and innovation chain, as well as the structural reform on the supply side of human resources, comprehensively improve the quality of education, expand employment and entrepreneurship, promote economic transformation and upgrading, cultivate new drivers of economic development, and enhance the training of e-commerce professionals in colleges and universities, employment and entrepreneurship under the new situation, promote college teachers to better integrate with practice, test theory and innovate theory in practice, and the development of enterprise e-commerce, carry out talent training, project planning, achievements transformation, technology R&D and other activities, realize the deep integration and innovation of enterprises, industries and universities, and achieve win–win cooperation between both sides and multiple parties.

3.3 The Building of IEEAC-NIEA

For the innovation and reform of e-commerce education and industry, and the high-quality development of e-commerce education and industry, the IEEAC-NIEA was established in December 2019 based on voluntariness, equality, mutual benefit, and cooperation. It is an open, non-governmental and non-profit organization formed by colleges, enterprises, scientific research, and service agencies related to e-commerce industry-education integration innovation. Based on the principle of joint construction and sharing, the IEEAC-NIEA gathers the advantages of its members, promotes high-quality education and industrial resource sharing, the deep integration of e-commerce industry and education, as well as education reform and industrial innovation and development, and strives to improve the quality and innovation of talent training. The first IEEAC-NIEA conference attracted 32 members, including 9 enterprises and 23 universities.

To provide better service for the participating universities and students, the 10th ICE Competition in 2020 was sponsored by IEEAC-NIEA. The Alliance will not only boost the further development of the competition, but also further promote the training and use of innovative e-commerce talents, e-commerce training in enterprises, and the transformation of innovative projects.

4 Continuous Growth After 12 Sessions of ICE Competition

The final of the 12th National Undergraduate E-commerce "Innovation, Creativity and Entrepreneurship" Competition was started at 08:30 a.m. on July 24, 2022, and the 16 teams determined in the group competition attended the final competition. The competition was broadcast live online, with more than 60,000 viewers. After years of development, the number of participating teams has been growing from more than 1,500 in the first session to more than 130,000 in the twelfth session; The participating projects have growing subjects from the initial campus e-commerce to the "agriculture, rural areas, and farmers" e-commerce, industrial e-commerce, service e-commerce, cross-border e-commerce, as well as innovative applications in AI, 5G, blockchain, etc. The 12th competition added cross-border e-commerce practice. The increasing number of new products, new services, new formats, and new models are coming out, experts and professors from colleges

Table 1 Basic situation of previous ICE Competition events

Sponsor	Session	Year	Organizer of National Finals	Number of registered teams
2006–2010 Nationwide E-commerce Teaching Steering Committee of Schools and Universities of the Ministry of Education (First)	The first	2009	Zhejiang University	1,500+
	The second	2010	Xi'an Jiaotong University	3,800+
	The third	2011	Southwestern University of Finance and Economics	4,900+
2013–2017 Nationwide E-commerce Teaching Steering Committee of Schools and Universities of the Ministry of Education (Second)	The fourth	2014	Central China Normal University	6,300+
	The fifth	2015	Chengdu University of Technology	14,000+
	The sixth	2016	Xi'an Jiaotong University	16,000+
	The seventh	2017	Xi'an Jiaotong University	20,000+
2018–2020 Nationwide E-commerce Teaching Steering Committee of Schools and Universities of the Ministry of Education (Third)	The eighth	2018	Taiyuan University of Technology	40,000+
	The ninth	2019	Xi'an Jiaotong University	60,000+
IEEAC-NIEA	The tenth	2020	Henan University of Science and Technology	65,000+
	The eleventh	2021	Yunnan Technology and Business University	100,000+
	The twelveth	2022	Hubei University of Economics	130,000+

and universities are attending, research achievements begin to be transformed, and more and more young students are going out of campus and into industries, becoming an important support for innovation-driven development (see Table 1).

5 Favorable Development for Cross-Border E-commerce, and Building Competition for Innovation, Creativity, and Entrepreneurship

In recent years, China has paid more attention to cross-border e-commerce and provided more support in policies. Since Hangzhou was approved to build the first comprehensive pilot area for cross-border e-commerce in China in 2015, China, relying on the construction of the comprehensive pilot area, has accumulated a lot of experience in institutional innovation, management innovation, and service innovation of cross-border e-commerce, formed many mature practices that can be used for reference at home and abroad, and made outstanding contributions to the high-speed and high-quality development of cross-border e-commerce. China (Hangzhou) Cross-border E-commerce Comprehensive Pilot Area is the first cross-border electronic commerce comprehensive pilot area approved by the State Council on March 7, 2015. Its establishment has been included in the centennial memorabilia of the founding of the Communist Party of China (CPC). Since its initiation, China's (Hangzhou) Cross-border E-commerce Comprehensive Pilot Area has always been committed to solving development problems, innovating management systems, and exploring development models of cross-border e-commerce. It has carried out innovation in the institution, management, and service around the top-level design of "six systems and two platforms". The innovation practice achievements have been replicated and promoted to other 104 comprehensive pilot areas nationwide. "Hangzhou experience" of cross-border e-commerce has become an important reference and construction model for other regions.

For the rapid development of cross-border e-commerce, the organizing committee of ICE Competition, together with the Leading Group Office of China (Hangzhou) Cross-border E-commerce Comprehensive Pilot Area, held the ICE Competition "Cross-border E-commerce Competition" from December 2021 to July 2022. The competition was open to college students and international students in domestic universities. With an open, inclusive, and win–win purpose, it was driven by innovation, creativity, and entrepreneurship. Domestic and foreign students work together with all sectors to achieve high-quality construction of "the Belt and Road Initiative" and promote the construction of a community with a shared future for mankind. It can be divided into four categories: Alibaba International, eBay, Live, and Independent, and three stages: theoretical, practical, and comprehensive. The competition was launched in 31 provincial and municipal universities, with nearly 10,000 registered teams from 689 universities.

6 Talent Training Support Excites the Development of High-Quality E-commerce

6.1 Outstanding Results Made in Talent Training of E-commerce in China

The development of e-commerce industry is inseparable from the huge support of e-commerce talents. In recent years, e-commerce talents are trained at relevant levels in China. The talent training modes, such as undergraduate education, vocational education, and social training, have blossomed, providing a large number of e-commerce talents of different levels. At present, there are 634 e-commerce programs in 600 undergraduate universities nationwide; among vocational colleges nationwide, there are 1,476 e-commerce programs, 126 online marketing programs, 74 mobile commerce programs, 98 business data analysis programs, 321 cross-border e-commerce programs, 30 rural e-commerce programs. In 2020, the number of e-commerce-related employees in China reached 60.15 million, contributing to the rapid development of China's e-commerce industry.

The E-commerce program is a new cross-discipline with strong practicality. The development of China's economy and society has also put forward an urgent demand for the cultivation of innovative e-commerce talents. The ICE Competition aims to further cultivate college students' innovation and entrepreneurship, such as network interaction, team cooperation, project organization, and development, and encourage students to integrate theory with practice, apply knowledge to practice and learn in practice and grow in practice. It provides a broad space for talent.

6.2 ICE Competition Promotes the Innovation of Industry-University-Research Cooperation

Adhering to the tenet of "innovation, creativity, and entrepreneurship", the ICE Competition is committed to cultivating college students' innovation awareness, creative thinking, and entrepreneurial ability, building a platform for college teachers and students to combine professional knowledge with social practice, and providing a space for free creation and independent operation. In this competition, the resources of industries and enterprises of e-commerce were fully mobilized, and member enterprises were organized to participate in the whole process of the competition in various forms together with associations. The role of industry associations as a bridge was given full play to promote the innovation of the industry-university-research cooperation mechanism.

Based on foresight, practicality, popularity, and guidance, the competition is committed to creating good conditions and environment for e-commerce training and practice, exploring a group of high-quality colleges and universities for e-commerce major construction, and training a group of key teachers with strong practical ability. In addition, it aims to build a group of practical training bases combining industry, teaching, and research, innovate an interactive mechanism for cooperation between colleges and enterprises, and make progress in the construction of an e-commerce major in colleges and universities.

7 Conclusion

Driven by the coordination of government, industry, university, and research, ICE Competition is about to start a new journey. In the report of the 19th National Congress of the CPC, General Secretary Xi Jinping proposed the strategic measure of "accelerating the construction of an innovative country", and stated that innovation is the first driving force for development. Innovation and entrepreneurship talents, as the core elements of building an innovative country, play an irreplaceable role in improving the ability of independent innovation. The importance of innovation and entrepreneurship talents has become a global consensus. The 13th ICE Competition will fully summarize the organizational experience of the previous 12 sessions, explore and establish a long-term mechanism for the national college students' e-commerce competition under the guidance of the Department of Higher Education of the Ministry of Education, strive to make the competition an important way to cultivate and seek talents, effectively stimulate young students' rich imagination and creativity, and build the competition into a brand event in China's higher education.

MIX
Papier aus verantwortungsvollen Quellen
Paper from responsible sources
FSC® C105338

FSC
www.fsc.org

If you have any concerns about our products,
you can contact us on
ProductSafety@springernature.com

In case Publisher is established outside the EU,
the EU authorized representative is:
Springer Nature Customer Service Center GmbH
Europaplatz 3, 69115 Heidelberg, Germany

Printed by Libri Plureos GmbH
in Hamburg, Germany